Professional Microsoft® SQL Ser¦ Reporting Services

(Continues)

Part VI: Reporting Services Integration and Custom Programming

Professional

Microsoft® SQL Server® 2008
Reporting Services

Professional

Microsoft® SQL Server® 2008 Reporting Services

Paul Turley, Thiago Silva, Bryan C. Smith, and Ken Withee
(Hitachi Consulting)

WILEY

Wiley Publishing, Inc.

Professional Microsoft® SQL Server® 2008 Reporting Services

Published by
Wiley Publishing, Inc.
10475 Crosspoint Boulevard
Indianapolis, IN 46256
www.wiley.com

Published simultaneously in Canada

ISBN: 978-0-470-24201-8

10 9 8 7 6 5 4 3 2 1

Library of Congress Cataloging-in-Publication Data

Professional Microsoft SQL server 2008 reporting services / Paul Turley ... [et al.].
    p.   cm.
Includes index.
ISBN 978-0-470-24201-8 (paper/website)
    1. SQL server.   2. Database management.   I. Turley, Paul.
QA76.9.D3P7663   2009
005.75'85—dc22
                                          2009042930

This is dedicated to the memory of my Mom, who always believed in me. To my family: my wife, Sherri, for her unwavering love and support; my wonderful daughters and son for their understanding and patience; and to my Dad, Mark, for always being there.

—Paul Turley

I dedicate this book to the women in my life: my lovely wife, Michelle, who has patiently put up with me and supported me in this venture; my beautiful daughter, Gabriella, whose sunshine smiles have lit up my every day; and, finally, I dedicate this to my mother, Lucia, who has encouraged me and given me words of wisdom my entire life.

—Thiago Silva

I dedicate this book to my family, immediate and extended, for their support and encouragement throughout the development of this book.

—Bryan C. Smith

I dedicate this book to my wife, Rosemarie, and thank her for giving up nearly every weekend outing during the summer of 2008 while I was writing this book. Rosemarie has been my strength in this world, and her presence in my life has taken me further than I ever dreamed was possible. I love you!

—Ken Withee

About the Authors

Paul Turley (Vancouver, WA) is a Manager of Specialized Services for Hitachi Consulting Education Services. Paul manages the Business Intelligence training team and teaches classes for companies throughout the world on Microsoft SQL Server technologies. He works with companies to design architecture for and build BI and reporting solutions. He has been developing business database solutions since 1991 for companies like Microsoft, Disney, Nike, and Hewlett-Packard. He has been a Microsoft Certified Trainer since 1996 and holds several industry certifications, including MCTS and MCITP for BI, MCSD, MCDBA, MSF Practitioner, and IT Project+.

Paul has authored and coauthored several books and courses on database, business intelligence, and application development technologies. He is the lead courseware developer for the Hitachi Consulting courses: "SQL Server 2008 Business Intelligence Solutions" and "SQL Server 2008 Reporting Services Solutions." His books include *Professional SQL Server 2005 Reporting Services, Professional SQL Server Reporting Services (SQL Server 2000), Beginning Transact-SQL with SQL Server 2000 and 2005, Beginning SQL Server 2005 Administration, Beginning Access 2002 VBA, Data Warehousing with SQL Server 2000 Analysis Services*, and *Professional Access 2000 Programming* — all from Wrox. He is also a contributing author to *SQL Server 2005 Integration Services Step by Step* from Microsoft Press.

Thiago Silva (Dallas, TX) is a Manager of Specialized Services for Hitachi Consulting. Thiago has also been designing and developing custom .NET, business intelligence, and Reporting Services solutions since the early days of .NET and SQL Server 2000. He is a part of the Microsoft Strategic Alliance leadership group within Hitachi Consulting, where he helps create, manage, and deliver internal training materials and intellectual capital around the Microsoft technology stack. He also teaches the SQL Server Reporting Services course offered by Hitachi Consulting.

Thiago has been a featured guest on the talk show podcast *.NET Rocks* and is an active member of the .NET development community, frequently writing on his blog Silvaware, at `http://silvaware .blogspot.com`. Thiago holds a Bachelor of Business Administration degree in Management Information Systems from Texas A&M University, and a MCAD.NET technical certification.

Bryan C. Smith (Irving, TX) is a Manager of Specialized Services for Hitachi Consulting. Bryan has been developing and administering database solutions since 1997 for clients in a variety of industries. These days, he focuses on helping clients build Business Intelligence solutions using the Microsoft SQL Server product suite. Bryan holds MCITP, MCTS, MCDBA, A+, Network+, and Server+ certifications, and serves as an instructor for Hitachi Consulting's SQL Server Analysis Services course.

Ken Withee (Seattle, WA) is a Senior Consultant with Hitachi Consulting. He earned a Master of Science degree in Computer Science studying under Dr. Edward Lank at San Francisco State University. Their work has been published in the LNCS journals and was the focus of a presentation at the IASTED conference in Phoenix. Their work has also been presented at various other Human Computer Interaction conferences throughout the world.

Ken has more than 7 years of professional computer and management experience working with a vast range of technologies.

Ken is a Microsoft Certified Technology Specialist and is certified with Microsoft Office SharePoint Server 2007 and SQL Server 2005, and has passed the certification exam for .NET 2.0.

Ken currently lives with his wife Rosemarie in Seattle, WA.

Credits

Acquisitions Editor
Katie Mohr

Development Editor
John Sleeva

Technical Editor
David Dillon

Production Editor
Christine O'Connor

Copy Editor
Cate Caffrey

Editorial Manager
Mary Beth Wakefield

Production Manager
Tim Tate

Vice President and Executive Group Publisher
Richard Swadley

Vice President and Executive Publisher
Joseph B. Wikert

Project Coordinator, Cover
Lynsey Stanford

Proofreader
Publication Services, Inc.

Indexer
Johnna VanHoose Dinse

Acknowledgments

I acknowledge Thierry D'Hers, Brian Welcker, Jason Carlson, Chris Hays, Sean Boon, Lukasz Pawlowski, and all the other members of the Reporting Services product team who have been so accessible and supportive of this effort.

Thanks to Lance Baldwin for his guidance; to Drew Naukam for his leadership; and to Stephanie Gulick, Chris Leiter, D.J. Norton, and the rest of the Microsoft National team at Hitachi Consulting for their support and many contributions. Thanks to Reed Jacobson for his contributions and to everyone at Hitachi Consulting for being a world-class organization, co-workers, and friends.

Thanks to Katie Mohr and John Sleeva at Wrox for their patience, support, and encouragement.

Finally, thanks to the dedication of my coauthors: Thiago Silva for his hard work and resourcefulness, Bryan C. Smith for his help and advice, and Ken Withee for stepping up to try something new. You're all true professionals.

—*Paul Turley*

I acknowledge:

Thierry D'Hers, Robert Bruckner, Lukasz Pawlowski, Chris Hays, Chris Baldwin, and Brian Welcker, at Microsoft, for their guidance and technical assistance during the authoring of the book;

Lead author Paul Turley for giving me the opportunity to be a part of this project, as well as my coauthors Bryan C. Smith and Ken Withee for assisting with ideas and insightful discussions throughout the entire writing process.

John Sleeva and Katie Mohr at Wrox for their flexibility and guidance during the development of the book.

My colleagues at Hitachi Consulting, who have helped me sharpen my skills and become a better consultant and developer.

My family in Brazil, who have provided encouragement during the writing of this book.

And, finally, God, who gives me strength each day and lifts me up when I've fallen down.

—*Thiago Silva*

I acknowledge:

John Sleeva and Katie Mohr at Wrox for their guidance on the book.

Carolyn Chau, Chris Baldwin, John Sirmon, and Matthew Hofacker at Microsoft for their response to technical questions.

Acknowledgments

Coauthors Paul Turley, Ken Withee, and Thiago Silva for their ideas, suggestions, and assistance in designing and authoring the book.

Haruka, Akimori Charles, and Harumi Katheryn for their patience and support throughout the last year.

—Bryan C. Smith

I acknowledge my mother, Maggie Blair, who has taught me persistence and compassion and who gave me the best upbringing I could ever have hoped for; and my father, Ken Withee, who offered to autograph copies for a price since he has the same name. Dad also taught me that commonsense will take you very far in this world. Thanks, also, to my sister, Kate Henneinke, who is working her way through college and who, I am confident, will achieve all of her goals. I am confident, as her older brother, that she is a stronger person because of all the karate moves I pounded her with growing up. I also acknowledge my grandma, Tiny Withee, who recently turned 95 and is as strong as ever; and in memory of my grandpa, Del Withee, who taught me there is never a problem so difficult that it cannot be solved with the right amount of thought and effort. Thanks also to my parents-in-law, Alfonso and Lourdes Supetran, and family, for all their support and practicality. They have truly made me a global thinker and taught me how to be a successful businessman. I only hope that Rosemarie and I can have a fraction of the success they have had in their lifetimes.

Thanks to Dr. Edward Lank, who got me started down the publishing path back in graduate school.

I also acknowledge the Microsoft SSRS team (especially Thierry D'Hers), who have always taken the time to answer questions and clarifications, and my fearless Microsoft National team at Hitachi Consulting, including our leader Drew Naukam and my career advisor Dave Cooper.

Thanks to Katie Mohr and John Sleeva at Wrox for their patience and support.

Thanks to my coauthors: Paul Turley, who gave me the chance to be a part of this book; Bryan C. Smith, for the long weekend chats as we nailed down technology; and Thiago Silva, for always going the extra step to help through all aspects of the book. It has been a great experience, and I truly enjoy working with all of you at Hitachi Consulting.

—Ken Withee

Contents

Part I: Getting Started

Contents

Contents

Contents

Contents

Contents

Part III: Business Intelligence Reporting

Chapter 9: Reporting with Analysis Services   309

Chapter 10: Report Solution Patterns and Recipes   345

Contents

Contents

Foreword by Jason Carlson

Many people have asked me, "How can you be so passionate about reporting when it is so mundane?" To me, the most exciting thing about reporting is that it is so very common. Like basic transportation, everybody uses it in some way or another. A report is a piece of art meant to convey a message; but unlike traditional art, that message changes based on the data driving it. The potential to help, and be used by, millions of people and companies is one of the reasons I started writing software and eventually joined Microsoft. No other company can reach out to so many people by making great products accessible.

Reporting is a very broad topic, covering areas ranging from packing lists and telephone bills to ad hoc analysis and Excel spreadsheets. When designing Microsoft SQL Server Reporting Services, I started with a simple definition for it: an information delivery platform. Although this definition is also very broad, it did allow us to focus on our design while leaving us significant room to expand in later versions. This book will help you understand the power of Reporting Services and to fully utilize its capabilities.

Information is not just data; it is data that has been transformed into something meaningful. This transformation is important. Any tool can read and display data; what people really need for doing their jobs is well-thought-out, correct, and pertinent information. There are many tools that let anyone with access to data build "views" or "reports." However, often these users are unfamiliar with all of the nuances of the data storage and this can produce inaccurate results or inadvertently affect the performance of the data engine. Reporting Services acts as the official source so that there is only one version of the truth that everyone uses.

In the future, Microsoft plans to take this even further by integrating with Information Rights Management so that not only will the information come from a single source, but it will also be certified, can expire, and can be access-controlled even after it is delivered to the end-user. The data does not always exist in one database or even come from a database. For those of us who have spent careers working with corporate data, this is a painful truth. Very few reports (or sets of reports that give you sufficient insight) come from a single source. Building some type of data mart or data warehouse is the best solution, but it is not always possible because of timing, policy, or budgetary constraints. Reports must be able to retrieve data from any source and combine them in a single report.

What good is information if you do not have it when you need it? Delivering information is more than just processing it and making it available; it is providing information when you need it, in any format, and on any device you have. The common case today is the ubiquitous online access via HTML in a browser. This is perfect when you have a computer and connectivity to the server. However, as we all know, nothing is perfect. We need the reports when we are on a plane, in a car, with the customer, at the game, on the production floor, and so on. This may include on your pager, telephone, fax machine, laptop, paper, and other devices. We also need different capabilities: interactivity, pixel-perfect printing, integration into applications like MS Excel for "what if" scenarios and additional analysis, universal access via PDF, and the like. A single format and a single delivery channel are not enough, but how do you know which ones you will need? Reporting Services insulates you from these choices. All reports can be distributed in any channel or rendered in any format. Report design is independent of how it will be consumed. It is the responsibility of the system to provide the report as accurately as possible, given the constraints of the specific format or channel requested.

Building a platform is very different from building a solution. In fact, the goals are in many cases completely opposed. A platform is successful if the developers and administrators have complete access to all aspects of the product. They need to be able to optimize, extend, restrict, embed, and replace parts of the product to meet their needs. This means that all of the APIs are available and documented, all formats are open and described, and every component is configurable or replaceable. While there are always restrictions due to the many trade-offs in software design, this was the goal when building Reporting Services. Very much like Windows, SQL Server, or Visual Studio, Reporting Services is designed to enable developers to build on a solid foundation and mold it to meet their business needs in significantly less time and with more functionality, but without losing the flexibility and power of building it themselves.

Looking into the future, there's an endless list of features and scenarios that Microsoft will add to make the platform more powerful with little or no additional in-house development required. I have mentioned some, and there are many that haven't even been considered yet.

We look forward to hearing from all our customers about what is important to them and how we can make designing, building, and operating their information delivery systems easier, faster, and (I hope) more fun.

—Jason Carlson
Product Unit Manager
SQL Server Reporting Services
Microsoft

Jason Carlson is the Product Unit Manager for SQL Server Reporting Services. He joined Microsoft in 1996 as a Program Manager for Visual Source Safe and Repository. In 1997, the Repository team joined SQL Server, and Jason became the development manager for SQL Server Meta Data Services. In 2001 he built a team and started work on V1 of Reporting Services. Before joining Microsoft, Jason owned and operated an independent software development company. This company provided consulting and vertical software solutions for healthcare and telecommunications.

Foreword by Thierry D'hers

Six months ago, a major change happened in the SQL Server Reporting Services team. Brian Welcker, who had been a key figure of the team since its inception, decided to change course in his career. Brian Welcker is one of the reasons Reporting Services is where it is today. When Tom Casey (General Manager for SQL Server Business Intelligence Unit) and Jason Carlson (Reporting Service Product Unit Manager) approached me 6 months ago to offer me Brian's position, I was honored, excited, and scared at the same time. How does one step into Brian's shoes? But at the same time, how do you pass on such a great opportunity to work on one of the coolest and most successful products at Microsoft?

You see, SSRS is not just a reporting product; it is a platform, with pieces shipping in many different Microsoft products — from Microsoft Office SharePoint to Microsoft Visual Studio to the Microsoft Business Division suite of business-line applications. In less than 6 years, Microsoft Reporting Services has grown from a small incubation reporting server to a full product suite, with information worker client tools, DBA management and configuration tools, a scalable enterprise-ready server, developer controls, and Office add-ins. It is now a mature product that stands its ground very well against the competition.

With SQL Server 2008, Reporting Services is now in its third version — but it is not just the third version of the same code. We reached a point where the Reporting Services team realized that in order to break new ground in terms of usability, performance, and scale, some core pieces of the product had to be re-architected and rebuilt. We also decided to remove a major dependency on IIS, which required even more re-design. As a result, not only the server, but most of the tools also had to be majorly revamped and redesigned. The result is a brand new product that you will discover in this very detailed and thoroughly written book.

You might ask, "Why join a product group that is now mature and well built? Some could think not much else can be done." Really? That is never the case in software development. Reporting is an area in full swing and is evolving rapidly. The needs and expectations of users are changing, as is the role of traditional IT and its relationship with its user base. Report Builder and our SharePoint integration are a first step toward empowering more information workers to take an active role in authoring and collaborating with reports. There are so many things we can do, and so many ideas we have, to make information workers more efficient and more proficient with reports, while providing the right management and provisioning tools for IT to ensure data quality availability and consistency. The future is bright; the future is exciting; the future will be fast paced with a lot of momentum. I fully believe we are on the edge of entering the Reporting 2.0 phase . . . but that will be the topic of a future book.

For now, I leave you in the hands of Paul Turley and his team from Hitachi Consulting. Hitachi has been a very close partner to Microsoft for years and, most importantly, has always kept close ties with the Reporting Services R&D team. Since I joined the team, I don't think a week has gone by that I haven't interacted with Paul, Thiago, Bryan, and Ken. It has been a real pleasure and blessing to have them work on the product while it is still in development. As they were writing chapters of the book, they were testing every single feature, trying every API, playing with the tools, building samples.

Not only did this allow us to have interesting conversations and gather very useful early feedback on our design, but as a result, Paul's team is almost a virtual extension of our test team. They know the product very intimately and have developed a level of expertise that is pretty unique in the industry at this time. So, I hope you enjoy reading this book as much as I have, and just as much as the rest of the Reporting Services R&D team have enjoyed helping Paul and his team write it.

—Thierry D'hers
Group Program Manager
SQL Server Reporting Services Microsoft

Thierry D'hers is the Group Program Manager for the SQL Server Reporting Services team. His group oversees the requirement gathering, features definition and design, as well as evangelization of the product. Prior to this position, Thierry occupied various roles on the SQL Server Analysis Services team and the Microsoft PerformancePoint team. Thierry has more than 18 years of experience in the BI software industry, and has been at the source of many products at Microsoft, and prior to that, with Hyperion Solutions. When he is not building teams and designing BI software, Thierry enjoys skiing, mountain climbing, and playing the guitar.

Introduction

The book in your hands has been written and improved over the past 6 years and is now in its third edition. As consultants, solution architects, and instructors, we spend our time at companies and in front of many people who need serious solutions to meet business problems. We've been using SQL Server Reporting Services to build reporting, business intelligence, and decision-support solutions for large and small companies. The authors work for Hitachi Consulting, a leading business intelligence, information technology, and business services solution provider. Since the earliest release of Reporting Services for SQL Server 2000, we have developed and deployed many reporting solutions in dozens of corporate environments, including the world's largest software company; the largest airplane manufacturer; the largest meat and poultry distributor; the leading cosmetics company; savings and investment banks; the largest investment and insurance company; the world's most recognizable sportswear company; and the largest theme park, film, and entertainment company — to mention a few.

We've helped business users understand their reporting needs and then designed reporting solutions for many types of organizations. Reports were integrated into web sites and portals, intranet sites, and desktop applications. We've trained hundreds of users, developers, and administrators, and have presented at conferences. With this experience, we've learned a lot about how not to design reports and how to build reporting solutions more efficiently. This book is based on this foundation of expertise.

Who This Book Is For

There are several other books about Reporting Services. Some are for beginners and others for serious developers and advanced report designers. Leonard Nimoy's character Mr. Spock once said, "The needs of the many outweigh the needs of the few." While this generally may be a true statement, we've made it a point to address the needs of the many without sacrificing the needs of the few. We wanted to write a book that would meet the needs of the broad audience of report designers, developers, administrators, and business professionals, without sacrificing any content. To meet this objective, we've divided this book into six sections — "mini-books," if you will. Depending on your needs, you may spend more of your time focusing on the material in one of these sections and using the others for reference. This book is written for the novice report designer and the expert interested in learning to use advanced functionality. For the application developer, we will cover programming in reports and custom applications that integrate reports. You will also learn about report server administration and security issues.

A common practice among development groups at Microsoft is to profile their target users and to even give these personas names and profiles. As we've come to know more about the types of folks who use Reporting Services in various ways, we thought it might be interesting to do something similar. The following are descriptions of three fictitious people who are characteristic of the more common Reporting Services users we have worked with. See if you can identify with any of these descriptions.

Report Designer

Mary works in the financial group for a company that provides consumer services. She is a computer-savvy worker who possesses a wide range of office skills. She has worked in this group for several years and could easily do her boss's job. She understands her company's business processes, financial reporting practices, invoicing, and billing systems. She's not a computer genius, but she knows her way around word processing, spreadsheets, e-mail, and simple database reporting. Mary started using Microsoft Access a few years ago and used the wizards to create some simple reports from data exported from the HR and customer billing systems. After a while, she learned how to write queries and build Access reports without the wizards, with custom formatting, groups, and summaries. Two years ago, she learned to use Crystal Reports to report on the data in the company's data warehouse. She has designed several reports with charts and pivots to analyze sales trends and profitability.

Mary's focus is on out-of-the-box reporting, getting reports designed and deployed as easily as possible, using the tools readily available within the product. She may design standard server-based reports that users will access from a central report server via the corporate intranet. She may also want to create her own ad hoc, client-side reports from data models created by an administrator or more advanced designer.

The following sections of the book will be of most interest to Mary:

❑   Part I: Getting Started

❑   Part II: Report Design

❑   Part IV: Enabling End-User Reporting with Report Builder 1.0

Application Developer

Joe has been writing database applications for several years. In 2004 he began using Microsoft .NET programming tools and landed a programming position in the company's Information Technology group. Joe has designed many of the company's web sites and portals using the Visual Basic .NET and C# programming languages. Most of the reports Joe has created were written from scratch as custom web pages. He has worked a little with a few specialized reporting applications. He wants to add reporting capabilities to some of the company's custom business applications.

As far as Joe is concerned, writing simple reports is for others to do. His focus will likely be to add filtering, custom formatting, and conditional logic using program code and query script. He will also design his reports so that they fit right into applications as an integrated part of a solution. He may also want to create customized management utilities to automate report server maintenance routines.

Joe understands that Reporting Services offers many flexible options for integrating reports into different application interfaces. He may want to build reports into a custom Windows desktop application, web application, SharePoint Portal, or mobile device application.

Joe will be most interested in these sections:

❑   Part II: Report Design

❑   Part III: Business Intelligence Reporting

❑   Part VI: Reporting Services Integration and Custom Programming

Systems Engineer

Bob is our Network Engineer and Database Administrator. He is more concerned with the security and stability of the corporate servers than with the aesthetics and features of each report. He will want to make sure that our report managers, designers, developers, and users are organized into roles and that the report server is appropriately secured. Bob will install and configure options on the report server. He will schedule maintenance tasks, optimize the database and queries, and provide ongoing maintenance and disaster recovery.

Bob will find these sections most useful:

❑ Part I: Getting Started

❑ Part V: Administering Reporting Services

Business Leader

As a business owner, corporate executive, or project manager, you may be the consumer of a reporting solution or the director of the development effort. Perhaps you have enlisted the services of a business intelligence consulting firm to architect a decision-support system to help you run your business. You need to be informed about your options and understand the capabilities of the products and technologies used to create your solution. This book will help you to understand these features and the choices necessary to put them into practice. The implementers of this solution will look to you for business requirements and feature choices. Chapters 1 and 2 are a good place to start. Part III, Business Intelligence Reporting, may be of particular interest. The first section of Chapter 10 discusses how to define and manage reporting business requirements and specifications. This will serve as a communication forum between you and your report designers.

What This Book Covers

This book is divided into six sections:

Part I: Getting Started

Part II: Report Design

Part III: Business Intelligence Reporting

Part IV: Enabling End-User Reporting with Report Builder 1.0

Part V: Administering Reporting Services

Part VI: Reporting Services Integration and Custom Programming

Part I: Getting Started

Chapters 1–4 provide an introduction to the capabilities and features of Reporting Services. You'll learn about its extensible architecture, which makes it a very powerful and flexible addition to nearly all existing business systems. This section builds a foundation of understanding upon which you will learn to design, deploy, manage, and, perhaps, customize business intelligence and reporting solutions.

Chapter 1, "Introducing Reporting Services," gets you started with a high-level view of the uses and applications for reporting solutions. Reporting Services can be used to easily deploy reports to a central report server for use with the Report Manager web interface; or be integrated into a business portal using Microsoft Office SharePoint Services. Reports can also be integrated into a simple application or a fully customized business application. You'll learn about report user profiles and report application and solution types. The new report design tools for SQL Server 2008 will be introduced. These include the new Business Intelligence Development Studio 2008 Report Designer and the new Report Builder 2.0.

Chapter 2, "Business Intelligence Solutions," explores reporting tool options. You will learn about the Reporting Services scalable architecture and how a reporting solution can be used in businesses of all sizes with relative ease. You will see how to plan for reporting in a small business, department and business enterprise. Information-worker users can perform ad hoc and self-service reporting using report models, the Report Builder 1.0, and the new Report Builder 2.0. This chapter discusses the components of a complete BI solution that enables Reporting Services to work with a variety of data sources, including operational data stores, a data warehouse, data marts, and OLAP cubes.

Chapter 3, "Installation," details the process by which Reporting Services is installed in your development environment and introduces concepts critical to planning your enterprise deployment.

Chapter 4, "Reporting Services Architecture," will help you understand the core services and technologies used by Reporting Services. This chapter addresses server and solution design. By learning how the product works and how the components interact, you will be better prepared to design and maintain a scalable solution.

Part II: Report Design

Designing reports can be as simple as running a wizard, or it can be a highly complex development process to define advanced features. In Chapters 5–8, you'll learn about how reports actually process and render data and then how to use parameters and expressions to define creative report solutions.

Chapter 5, "Basic Report Design," starts with the fundamentals and teaches you to create basic reports using simple design tools. You'll learn the essentials about what you need to get started building basic reports using the Report Wizard and common Report Designer features. You'll be introduced to the fundamental building blocks of report design: report items and report layout properties. This chapter introduces the two report design tools used to create standard reports: Report Builder 2.0, for users who want a simple, straightforward tool for designing simple reports; and the Business Intelligence Development Studio, to manage report projects and to design reports in the Microsoft Visual Studio development environment.

Chapter 6, "Report Layout and Formatting," addresses different report design layouts and the components used to assemble a report. This chapter will introduce the report body, headers, footers, and page-formatting properties. You will learn about the capabilities of each report item and the data range components that are used to organize and present data.

After you explore the basics, you'll learn about grouping data, lists, and data regions; using tables and the matrix reports; defining drill-through reports; and using charts. You'll also learn to write expressions and custom code to extend formatting and apply business logic, and to design reports for mobile devices.

Chapter 7, "Designing Data Access," reveals that reports are based on a data source and that Reporting Services may be used to present data from many different data sources. You'll learn to define stand-alone and shared data sources, queries, and datasets and to use parameters to filter data at the database and at the Report Server. You'll learn to use new parameter features introduced in the latest version of the product.

This chapter is a primer on T-SQL queries and stored procedures. You'll also learn to build reports using Analysis Services and the MDX Query Builder. Query examples are provided for Oracle PL/SQL, Sybase, and Access SQL dialects.

Chapter 8, "Advanced Report Design," helps you take design elements to the next level and learn to creatively use data groups and combinations of report items. Calculations and conditional formatting may be added by using simple programming code. Whether you are an application developer or a report designer, this chapter contains important information to help you design reports to meet your users' requirements and raise the bar with compelling report features.

Part III: Business Intelligence Reporting

Chapter 9, "Reporting with Analysis Services," specifically addresses the design techniques and unique best practices for reporting on OLAP cube data. You will learn to create MDX queries with parameters, calculations, and aggregations.

Chapter 10, "Report Solution Patterns and Recipes," takes you into the real world of business problems and reporting solutions. You'll start by learning how to document business requirements and to manage successful report projects.

This chapter presents report design from a different view — not the nuts and bolts but the overall pattern of design. We have assembled an extensive list of models and instructions to show you how to build several detailed report solutions to address a variety of specific business problems. This chapter serves as a practical guide to designing reports and building reporting solutions in the real world. It contains several examples of advanced report designs as recipes to solve specific business problems. You will apply the techniques you've learned in the previous three chapters to implement specific functionality.

Part IV: Enabling End-User Reporting with Report Builder 1.0

Report Builder 1.0 technology puts simple report design into the hands of everyday users without requiring complex design tools. Chapters 11 and 12 introduce the Report Builder 1.0 platform and the tools used to define data sources and semantic metadata models. Using the elements you deploy, your users can create simple reports without installing software or learning the intricacies of report design.

Chapter 11, "Report Models," shows you that a report model is the key component behind performing ad hoc, end-user queries. A model provides the means to navigate through either a SQL Server database or an Analysis Services database. This chapter will teach you to build a Reporting Services report model using sample data.

Chapter 12, "Report Builder 1.0," covers Report Builder 1.0, a platform for defining ad hoc reports using prepared data structures. You'll learn to use the Report Builder 1.0 application with a familiar Microsoft Office interface for building reports. Using predefined report layouts, users can fulfill various reporting needs with ease. You'll learn to easily format, to sort and filter data, and to perform calculations. Finally, you'll learn how to manage and administer models and reports.

Part V: Administering Reporting Services

Report server administration has an important job: to keep data secure and available to the right users. Server-side reports can be configured and secured to optimize performance and to provide the right information to the appropriate user communities. Chapters 13 and 14 teach you how to use all of the tools necessary to configure and manage your Report Server.

Chapter 13, "Content Management," teaches you how to use management tools and Reporting Services features to publish reports and manage execution and delivery. You'll learn to create automated scripts and custom solutions to manage all the Report Server content. You'll revisit the stages of report execution from an administrator's point of view and learn how to optimize them. You'll also learn how to automate report delivery and server management.

Chapter 14, "Report Server Administration," is a comprehensive administrator's guide. You'll explore the related considerations for reporting requirements and deployment scenarios for Reporting Services. You'll learn about the configuration tools and utilities, backup and restore procedures, and monitoring a Reporting Services instance for issues and optimal performance.

Part VI: Reporting Services Integration and Custom Programming

Practically all the built-in functionality in Reporting Services can be automated and performed through custom program code. This includes report rendering and the core services of the reporting environment: data access, rendering formats, security, and delivery.

Chapter 15, "Integrating Reports into Custom Applications," shows you that Reporting Services is a flexible reporting tool that can be easily incorporated in different applications. In this chapter, you'll learn to use URLs to access reports from document and web page links, use the Reporting Services Web service to programmatically render reports, and use the ReportViewer controls to embed reports into custom Windows Forms and ASP.NET Web Forms applications. You'll learn to display reports in web portals using SharePoint web parts and other techniques. You can use programmatic rendering, URL, or the ReportViewer controls to create custom report viewers and parameter interfaces. Examples are provided in C# and VB.NET.

Chapter 16, "Integrating Reports with SharePoint," shows you how to integrate Reporting Services with the SharePoint technologies. SharePoint has quickly become widely adopted by many business organizations and, as such, sits at the center of the information workers world. Integrating reports into this world is a natural fit, and Microsoft has made it a priority to provide a tight and seamless integration between these two products. This chapter walks you through the types of integration available and how reports can be created, hosted, surfaced, secured, and managed in the SharePoint environment.

Chapter 17, "Extending Reporting Services," is written for serious application developers using object-oriented programming techniques, with examples in C# and VB.NET. You will learn how to create custom libraries and extensions to add functionality to the reports and Report Server features. These extensions may be used to access unique data sources, to render reports to specific formats, to authenticate users, and to deliver reports outside of the default methods provided with the product.

Appendixes

The appendixes at the end of this book include a comprehensive Reporting Services object programming reference, T-SQL syntax, commands and functions, and MDX language functions and reference.

What You Need to Use This Book

To use SQL Server Reporting Services and to run the samples presented in this book, you will need:

❑ SQL Server 2008, any edition. An evaluation version of SQL Server and Reporting Services may be downloaded from Microsoft at www.microsoft.com/sql.

❑ The sample databases, AdventureWorks2008 and AdventureWorksDW2008, may be downloaded from www.codeplex.com. In addition to the relational database sample, Chapter 9 uses the Adventure Works DW 2008 sample Analysis Services database.

❑ Windows Server 2003 SP2, Windows Server 2008, Windows Vista, or Windows XP Professional SP2

❑ Pentium III class PC with a 1 GHz processor or better (2.0 GHz recommended) and at least 1 GB of RAM

Note that for Chapter 16, SharePoint has its own requirements. In particular, SharePoint requires a server operating system (OS) such as Windows Server 2003 SP2 or Windows Server 2008. Although IIS is no longer required by Reporting Services, it is still required by SharePoint. Refer to the Microsoft SharePoint site for additional and specific recommendations around SharePoint requirements.

The complete source code for the samples is available for download from our web site at www.wrox.com. For programming examples, there are versions available in both Visual Basic .NET and C#.

Conventions

To help you get the most from the text and keep track of what's happening, we've used several conventions throughout the book.

> **Boxes like this one hold important, not-to-be forgotten information that is directly relevant to the surrounding text.**

Notes, tips, hints, tricks, and asides to the current discussion are offset and placed in italics like this.

As for styles in the text:

- ❏ We highlight new terms and important words when we introduce them.
- ❏ We show keyboard strokes like this: Ctrl+A.
- ❏ We show filenames, URLs, and code within the text like so: `persistence.properties`.
- ❏ We present code in two different ways:

```
We use a monofont type with no highlighting for most code examples.
We use gray highlighting to emphasize code that's particularly important in the
present context.
```

Source Code

As you work through the examples in this book, you may choose to either type in all the code manually or use the source code files that accompany the book. All of the source code used in this book is available for download at www.wrox.com. Once at the site, simply locate the book's title (either by using the Search box or by using one of the title lists) and click the Download Code link on the book's Detail page to obtain all the source code for the book.

Because many books have similar titles, you may find it easiest to search by ISBN; this book's ISBN is 978-0-470-24201-8.

Once you download the code, just decompress it with your favorite compression tool. Alternatively, you can go to the main Wrox code download page at `www.wrox.com/dynamic/books/download.aspx` to see the code available for this book and all other Wrox books.

Errata

We make every effort to ensure that there are no errors in the text or in the code. However, no one is perfect, and mistakes do occur. If you find an error in one of our books, like a spelling mistake or faulty piece of code, we would be very grateful for your feedback. By sending in errata, you may save another reader hours of frustration, and at the same time you will be helping us provide even higher-quality information.

To find the errata page for this book, go to `www.wrox.com`, and locate the title using the Search box or one of the title lists. Then on the book Details page, click on the Book Errata link. On this page you can view all errata that have been submitted for this book and posted by Wrox editors. A complete book list including links to each book's errata is also available at `www.wrox.com/misc-pages/booklist.shtml`.

If you don't spot "your" error on the Book Errata page, go to `www.wrox.com/contact/techsupport.shtml`, and complete the form there to send us the error you have found. We'll check the information and, if appropriate, post a message to the book's Errata page and fix the problem in subsequent editions of the book.

p2p.wrox.com

For author and peer discussion, join the P2P forums at p2p.wrox.com. The forums are a web-based system for you to post messages relating to Wrox books and related technologies and interact with other readers and technology users. The forums offer a subscription feature to e-mail you topics of interest of your choosing when new posts are made to the forums. Wrox authors, editors, other industry experts, and your fellow readers are present on these forums.

At http://p2p.wrox.com, you will find several different forums that will help you not only as you read this book, but also as you develop your own applications. To join the forums, just follow these steps:

1. Go to p2p.wrox.com and click the Register link.
2. Read the terms of use and click Agree.
3. Complete the required information to join as well as any optional information you wish to provide and click Submit.
4. You will receive an e-mail with information describing how to verify your account and complete the joining process.

   You can read messages in the forums without joining P2P, but in order to post your own messages, you must join.

Once you join, you can post new messages and respond to messages that other users post. You can read messages at any time on the web. If you would like to have new messages from a particular forum e-mailed to you, click the "Subscribe to this Forum" icon by the forum name in the forum listing.

For more information about how to use the Wrox P2P, be sure to read the P2P FAQs for answers to questions about how the forum software works as well as many common questions specific to P2P and Wrox books. To read the FAQs, click the FAQ link on any P2P page.

Part I
Getting Started

1

Introducing
Reporting Services

What a long, strange trip it's been. . . . SQL Server Reporting Services is all grown up now. This product has matured quite a lot over the past five years or so since enjoying a favorable start in the industry. This is our third edition of this book, about a product in its third version. We've seen it grow from what was essentially a free download for SQL Server 2000, to a substantial but relatively untested component of SQL Server 2005, to a serious force in the industry — and a very capable, enterprise-ready reporting tool.

Since we started writing about Reporting Services for the first edition of this book in 2003, there is much more to say about this product and the rest of the integrated Microsoft SQL Server Business Intelligence platform. There are stories to tell about IT projects, training classes, and consulting engagements. Along the way, we've learned quite a lot from other members of the IT community about the many creative ways to use Reporting Services. We'll tell some of those stories and discuss our experience with the past three generations of this product. But for now, let's focus our attention on the fundamental applications and capabilities. In other words, *What can you do with Reporting Services? Who should use it, and for what purpose?*

The topics introduced in this short chapter are explored in greater detail in the next chapter and throughout this book. The purpose of this chapter is to provide a high-level introduction only to the concepts and capabilities of this powerful reporting tool and the data analysis platform of Microsoft SQL Server 2008. This chapter introduces common reporting scenarios, beginning with the most basic and then moving to the more advanced. In subsequent chapters, you will explore these capabilities in depth and learn to use them in your own reporting solutions.

The Reporting Services Revolution

It was during my morning commute that my life and career took a different path because of this product. In 2003, my daily trek to downtown Seattle was by passenger ferry with a group of fellow co-commuters. I had been working on a side project that had a substantial reporting element. It was a web application with a lot of database work that I was developing on my laptop during every spare minute I could muster. I was trying to use the version of Crystal Reports included with Microsoft Visual Studio, and according to some of the documentation, it should have been possible to integrate Crystal into an ASP.NET web site. Whether or not it was possible, it certainly wasn't easy. After weeks of frustration, a friend on the boat, who worked as a data warehouse architect for the Walt Disney company, handed me a CD-R with a beta 1 copy of SQL Server Reporting Services. By the next day, I had working reports deployed to my web site. I was hooked.

In 2003 and 2004, we wrote the first edition of *Professional SQL Server Reporting Services*. At that time, I knew that Reporting Services was going to be a big deal, and I also knew that writing a book on something as substantial as this new product wasn't going to be a walk in the park. In the coming years, my employer, Hitachi Consulting, took on many reporting projects. We had several people with deep business intelligence and report design experience. Companies, large and small, migrated their business reporting to Reporting Services. They recognized its elegant architecture, which made it adaptable and capable of meeting a range of needs from out-of-the-box reporting solutions to tightly integrated application design. It was an overnight sensation. Reporting Services became a staple product for us, and many large companies wanted to convert their reports from other, less scalable and more expensive products. In 2005 and 2006, we wrote the second edition of this book for SQL Server 2005 — this time, with a few more years of substantial project experience and having learned many of the best practices for report design and solution deployment.

Not Your Father's Reporting Tool

Since 2003, when users were first able to work with Reporting Services, the way you use this product has changed substantially. Rather than just a simple tool used to create tabular reports, it has become a foundation upon which you can construct complete report, scorecard, and dashboard solutions for business users and consulting customers. This is not your father's reporting tool. Today, it does everything from simple, ad hoc data reporting to delivering enterprise-ready, integrated reporting into business portals and custom applications. Now, in the third release for SQL Server 2008, the report design environment is dramatically improved, with a fine-tuned product architecture and the addition of several feature improvements. Reporting Services not only comes with a proven track record, but also is ready to meet the needs of serious IT developers and business information workers who just need a simple tool without a lot of complex, technical sophistication.

We authors have learned a lot about this product with each project and continue to find creative ways to stretch its capabilities. For the first edition of this book, we worked primarily with the beta-release product. The second edition was based on our experience with Reporting Services for SQL Server 2000 and SQL Server 2005. Over the past five years, we've had many conversations with members of the Reporting Services product team at Microsoft as we put the product through its paces to learn what Reporting Services could and couldn't do well. We've also done a lot of consulting work for Microsoft, designing integrated reports for several Microsoft products that are currently on the market today. Over the years, we've presented sessions at industry conferences and written books, white papers, and knowledge-base articles. As with most Microsoft products, we found that there are about 18 different ways to implement each feature. Since then, we have deployed Reporting Services in many corporate environments and trained thousands to use it. We've talked to business users to understand their reporting needs and then designed reporting solutions for many types of organizations. We've integrated reports into web sites and portals, intranet sites, and desktop applications. We've designed reports for savings and investment banks, financial services, support centers, software companies, sales and customer management system vendors, sportswear companies, theme park and entertainment companies, manufacturing, construction, supply chain, retail, wholesale, and medical, government, and telecom organizations. Having the luxury to invest so much energy into the use of one tool, we've learned how to do a few things really well, but I think we've also learned to keep an open mind toward using creative new methods to solve problems. We've learned a lot about how not to design some reports and how to build reporting solutions more efficiently — and which of those 18 feature options makes the most sense. This book is based on this foundation of experience.

Who Uses Reporting Services?

Probably one of the most significant lessons of the past five years of teaching training courses on Reporting Services is how diverse the demographics of the audiences are. The roles and backgrounds of those who design and implement reporting solutions are diverse. As an application developer, I was accustomed to teaching programmers and other technology professionals whose life quest is to make the world a better place by writing program code and software. However, I quickly learned that there wasn't a stereotypical report designer. Some are very business-focused and aren't necessarily in love with technology and program code. Many are simply charged with managing or facilitating a line of business. They need tools to get information quickly and don't want to reinvent the wheel or work with cumbersome tools. The figures in the following table aren't substantiated by any kind of survey or study but are merely this author's objective observation of those who attend Reporting Services training classes:

Approximate Percentage	Role	Description
15%	Business Managers	Those who working seriously with Reporting Services, having attended classes or engaged in consulting services. They are mainly interested in the bigger picture: how reports can address their analytical needs and help them make informed decisions. They have little interest in the implementation details or the technology used to make it work. They direct people who can do the detail work.
15%	System Administrators	Consists of server system builders, hardware professionals, and database administrators. In smaller organizations, they often share with the software developer and are typically concerned with the setup and ongoing maintenance of servers and the infrastructure to keep reporting solutions available and working. They typically spend their time and energy managing security and optimizing the system for efficiency.
20%	Software Developers	To achieve advanced reporting features, software developers write complex queries and custom programming code to process business rules and give reports conditional formatting and behavior. Developers typically feel right at home with the report design environment because it's very similar to familiar programming tools.
50%	Business Information Workers	The people in this role have strong computer user skills, but they don't spend their time writing code and using tools like Visual Studio, Enterprise Manager, or SQL Server Management Studio. They need to design reports to run their businesses.

Wait a minute! This is a book about creating reports to display information in meaningful and interesting ways. I can't just display this information in a boring list, so I've created a simple report and put it into a chart (an exploded, semitransparent doughnut chart, to be specific), shown in Figure 1-1.

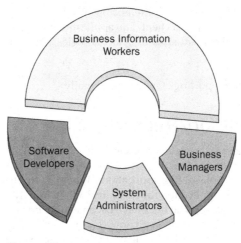

Figure 1-1

As a software developer, coming to the realization that the largest group of reporting professionals is not the software developer or other technical expert was a wake-up call. As I taught Reporting Services 2000 classes for Microsoft, I often spent a large portion of the classroom time just teaching students to use the Visual Studio user interface. It was new to them and unlike any other application they were accustomed to. Report designers who have been using other tools such as Crystal Reports, for example, will typically be a little intimidated by the Reporting Services design tools because they may be unfamiliar and may seem to be more "raw" and developer-centric than what they're used to using. In order to take advantage of advanced report capabilities, these individuals must either acquire some simple programming skills or work with software developers to add custom code and expressions to their reports.

Today, Reporting Services in SQL Server 2008 meets the needs of information workers and technology professionals with two different design tools. The stand-alone report designer is simple, focused, and familiar — with a user interface similar to Microsoft Office applications. A more advanced report design experience is available to application developers and other technical professionals, integrated into the Visual Studio solution design environment shell. This tool is optimized for adding custom expressions, complex features, and program code.

Application and Reporting Technology

The definition of reporting is changing. Like so many components of the computer/information industry, the lines between one thing and another have become very fuzzy. This applies to so many concepts in our industry. For example, many traditional desktop applications now run in a web browser. Are these client or server applications? These days it's hard to draw a line and categorize a business solution. Not long ago, if an application opened in a web browser, it was considered to be a server-side application — all the processing occurred on a web server. Likewise, if an application ran from a shortcut on your computer, it was a client-side application, where all the files and processing occurred on your own computer. Have you attended an Internet-hosted meeting or seminar? If so, you probably navigated to a site in your web browser, entered a meeting number, and, magically, you were looking at PowerPoint slides and a demonstration running on the presenter's desktop computer. Although you may have started from a web page and the conferencing application may have been started from your web browser, it was actually running in a client-side application, which you allowed to be installed on your computer, using advanced content-streaming technologies, allowing you to interact with the server-hosted conference.

What does this have to do with reporting? Quite a lot, actually.

Blurring the Application/Reporting Line

With Reporting Services, you can integrate reports into applications in such a way that users may not be able to tell the difference between the two. With a little bit of programming code, reporting features can be extended to look and act a whole lot like applications. Where do applications stop and reports begin? When do reports start replacing application functionality? What, exactly, is the difference between a report, a dashboard, and a scorecard? The lines have become quite blurred. Your task is to decide which tool best meets the need. Many intranet sites run on web portals, rather than custom-programmed web sites, and Reporting Services naturally plays well in practically any web portal environment — and now it has native integration with Microsoft Office SharePoint Services.

The exciting news is that you now have a tool that can do some incredible things. As my favorite superhero's uncle said, "With great power comes great responsibility." If you are a simple report designer with simple needs, the good news for you is that using Reporting Services to design simple reports is . . . well, simple. If you are a software developer and you intend to use this powerful framework to explore the vast reaches of this impressive technology, welcome to the wonderful world of creative, custom reporting.

Information, Now!

Imagine that you are sitting in a presentation meeting at the corporate office of a key customer. You are a senior sales representative for a company that sells high-volume data backup systems, and the solution they decide on will be implemented in several regional data centers around the world. Your team has been preparing for this meeting for months. Your success depends on your ability to demonstrate your competence to the customer and your clear understanding of their needs. Your team has done its homework, and you know that the customer has a history of scanning printed medical records and storing them as image files. Based on this information, you are certain that a particular product will adequately provide the file backup facilities for their moderate volume of image files. You have made it a point to familiarize yourself with the capabilities of the system that appears to be the best fit.

During your customer's opening presentation, they tell you that they have recently made a huge investment in full-motion video-imaging equipment. Now they need a backup system that can handle large file capacities. They are prepared to make an investment that is substantially larger than what you had anticipated for a capable backup solution. Your company began to offer a large-scale solution just a couple of weeks ago, but you aren't very familiar with its capabilities. You've spent so much time preparing to sell the smaller system that you haven't had time to learn more about this new product. Your associate is doing introductions, and it will be your turn in about 15 minutes.

Discreetly, you open your Pocket PC Phone and access the World Wide Web. You log in to your company's secure report server, select the product catalog report, choose the product category, and then drill down to the new product. The report has a drill-through option that lets you quickly view a detailed specification report for the new, high-volume backup system. After noting the pertinent specifications, you save this report to a PDF file and then choose the customer sales inquiry history report. Looking up this customer, you learn that someone named Julie from this very company made an inquiry about two months ago regarding video media backups.

Looking around the room, you find a name card with Julie's name on it. You explore the details of this call, and you find that she had asked if you offer a solution comparable to a very expensive product from a competitor. Checking the competition's web site, you discover that the competing product Julie had mentioned uses older technology, has a smaller capacity than the new system, and costs considerably more. You save a report with all the pertinent specifications to your memory card, hand the card to the administrative assistant sitting next to you, and ask that he make printed copies of the PDF file it contains.

Your colleague finishes her presentation and then introduces you. Taking another quick glance at the new product specs, you begin your introduction (see Figure 1-2).

Figure 1-2

You explain that one of your team's greatest strengths is your real experience and understanding of how business can change direction from day to day. In order to be responsive and competitive, it's necessary to adapt to these changes. You show the brochure for the midscale product and explain that this product would be an excellent solution for a company that just scans documents. But for digital video, a more capable solution is required. You share the product specification and qualify the product to meet your customer's needs. During your presentation, the administrative assistant returns with the printed specification report. Not missing a beat, you distribute copies to everyone and conclude your presentation. You make brief eye contact with your colleague, who raises an eyebrow just before your customer's chief decision-maker, Julie, aggressively shakes your hand and thanks you profusely for your time and the extra effort you made to understand their needs. After the big sale is closed, the promotion, the new company car, and corner office . . . you get the idea.

Solution Types

One of the things I've learned in the business consulting field is that giving people a lot of choices doesn't necessarily solve their problems. An impressive aspect of Reporting Services is that there are so many different ways to implement it into a business environment. The fact that reports could be integrated into a custom desktop application, web application, static web site, or a document or through low-level programming code may appeal to programmers because of the many choices and flexibility. However, to a business user or leader, too many choices may just be confusing and overwhelming. At the end of the day, someone must decide how reports will be used in the business environment and set a standard for most report designers to follow. Experience has shown that the majority of new Reporting Services implementations will use the de facto Web-based Report Manager interface. In more sophisticated enterprise business intranet environments, SharePoint portal integration is becoming a common choice. Most of the other options are specialized and may be used to meet specific business needs but are less common. For completeness, these options are all covered.

Reporting solutions come in a variety of sizes and shapes. These range from the standard Report Manager Web interface to a completely customized application with integrated reporting features. The types of software solutions that might incorporate reporting include:

❑   Out-of-the-box, server-based reporting features, using reports created by report designers and deployed to a central web server

❑   Client-side ad hoc reports created by users on demand with the Report Builder tool using predefined data models

❑   Reports integrated into web applications using URL links to open in a web browser window

❑   Reports integrated into SharePoint Portal server applications using SharePoint web parts

❑   Custom-built application features that render reports using programming code. Reports can be displayed within a desktop or web application interface or saved to a file.

Out-of-the-Box Reports

What does Reporting Services provide if you just want to use its simplest features right out-of-the-box? Quite a lot, actually.

Since the product was released for SQL Server 2000, Reporting Services required the Microsoft development environment to design and deploy reports to a central web server. Compared with other report design tools on the market, this presented a challenge. Prior to the release of SQL Server 2005, the development environment was available only as a separate product called *Microsoft Visual Studio*. This was a tool for serious application developers to create custom software. It still is, but as of SQL Server 2005, the development environment, called the *Business Intelligence Development Studio* (or *BIDS*), installs with the SQL Server client tools and has been tailored to manage SQL Server databases, write queries, and design reports. Using this powerful tool has likely been the most significant challenge for the new report designer.

In the 2008 product, a simplified report design tool makes the process even easier than before. The stand-alone report designer serves only one purpose — keeping the interface simple and uncomplicated and the process of report design as straightforward as possible. Experienced report designers who learned to use the previous toolset will still have access to the Visual Studio/BIDS designer, which may be installed with the SQL Server client tools.

Once you learn the basics of the development environment, designing reports and managing projects are actually quite easy. Both report design tools include a simple Report Wizard that can lead you through designing common reports. Tabular, grouped, cross-tab, and chart reports are relatively easy to build just by following the Wizard prompts and setting a few properties.

After a new report has been designed and tested, it can be deployed to a central report server, where it will be available to all users through a simple web browser application called the *Report Manager*.

Beyond Wizard-built reports, many aspects of more complex reports may be managed by creating simple programming expressions. An expression builder guides the designer through the simple use of functions and logical expressions that may be used to modify colors, visibility, and formatting aspects and to perform calculations. Because the expressions in Reporting Services are based on Visual Basic .NET, the power of conditional expressions is virtually limitless.

Server-Based Reports

It's important to understand the difference between SQL Server Reporting Services and a desktop reporting tool like Microsoft Access. Reporting Services isn't an application that you would typically install on any desktop computer but, rather, is designed for business use. It requires Microsoft SQL Server, a serious business-class relational database management tool. For this and other reasons, Reporting Services runs on a file server instead of a desktop computer. Therefore, you can scale this powerful tool for use by thousands of users and report on very large sets of data stored in a variety of database platforms. But just because Reporting Services is a business-sized product, this doesn't mean that reports have to be complicated or difficult to design.

Report users need to be connected to a network, or perhaps the Internet, with connectivity to the report server. When a report is selected for viewing from a folder in the Report Manager, it is displayed as a web page in the user's web browser. Optionally, the same report can be displayed in a number of different formats including Word, Excel, Adobe PDF, or as a PNG, JPEG, GIF, or TIFF image. Reports may be saved to files in these and other formats for offline viewing. Reports may also be scheduled for automatic delivery by the report server by e-mail or may be saved to files. These features are standard and require only simple configuration settings and minor user interaction.

User-Designed and Ad hoc Reports

With the stand-alone Report Builder report design tool, less-technical users can create standard reports to be deployed beside enterprise reports developed by the IT staff. This bridges the gap to some degree for the capable information worker. Standard reports are designed for users ahead of time and deployed to the server for users to select and display, print, or save to a file. This may be useful for standard reporting needs shared by most report users. However, savvy users cannot modify the design or these reports without access to the design and development tools.

Ad hoc reporting for Reporting Services is in a state of transition. Report Builder was introduced with SQL Server 2005 Reporting Services and remains a viable tool for non-programmers to create their own reports. It will eventually be replaced by a new tool called *Report Builder 2.0*, which is being introduced with the 2008 version of the product. Although the name is similar, the tool is very different. You can be the judge, but for now, two options are available for creating simple reports with an easy-to-use design tool.

Ad hoc reporting is an alternative to creating predesigned, server-side reports. The Report Builder design tool allows users to build their own reports on the fly, using prepared queries and data models. Using this option, the IT staff or system administrator prepares a variety of common data models to simplify and expose the underlying data sources in a concise form. This allows users to construct ad hoc reports using simple drag-and-drop techniques. These reports may be used once and discarded, or saved for others to use or to be built on in later sessions.

The actual design work is performed using a client-side builder tool delivered on demand in the user's web browser. The user experience is quite simple. As far as the user is concerned, a new report is created using a simple web page selection, and Report Builder opens in a browser window without specifically installing a software package ahead of time. These reports are stored on the server in the same folder space as other reports. The Report Manager web interface is used to access and maintain standard Reporting Services reports as well as Report Builder reports and their associated data models.

The advantages of Report Builder reports are that they give users the ability to design and customize their own reports without involving a report designer or developer. Report styles and features include standard report layouts like columnar, hierarchical, pivot/matrix, and charts but can only include one of these data range elements, unlike standard reports that can include as many as you like. Report Builder reports cannot contain or use custom code. Data-formatting options are more restrictive, and the data models must be prepared ahead of time. Models may be created to mirror the details of source data tables or may be simplified. This allows the data model designer to hide sensitive data and to simplify complex data sources with alias columns, aggregations, and calculated data members.

Report Design Tools

When Reporting Services was released for use with SQL Server 2000, only one design tool could be used to create reports. Since that time, third-party vendors began creating design tools designed specifically for users with different needs. High-end report developers require different tools to create corporate reporting solutions from those required by information workers to design personal and departmental reports. Information Technology architects, database designers, and application developers who create large-scale business intelligence solutions need a design environment that allows members of formal teams to share and manage various files and reports. They need to write and debug program code and shared components.

Information workers may not need to use such sophisticated tools and will benefit from a simple design environment with familiar features and options. A simplified, stand-alone report designer will assist users to create departmental and personal reports that need to be deployed to a central server, shared with other users, and available for future enhancements.

An ad hoc design tool should be simple and lightweight and should require little or no installed software on the user's computer. It should allow IT professionals to expose a simplified and secure view of corporate data sources that ad hoc report designers use to simply select predefined data elements and organize them in common report presentations.

Report Builder 2.0

Report Builder 2.0 is an addition to the report design suite for the information worker to create fully capable, server-hosted reports. It's a serious tool with a moderate learning curve. Unlike its predecessors Visual Studio or the Business Intelligence Development Studio, it doesn't expose some advanced capabilities that may be unnecessary for someone designing typical departmental or personal reports. In Chapter 5, you learn to use to use the Microsoft Office-like user interface to design data sources, queries, and report layouts to meet a variety of business needs.

Report Builder 2.0 is a stand-alone application that may be installed on the desktop of any user from the SQL Server 2008 installation media, or it may simply be launched from the central Report Manager Web interface. Using this tool to design reports, a user will need permission to read data sources and will also need permission to deploy reports to the report server using this tool.

Business Intelligence Development Studio

The Business Intelligence Development Studio tool (BIDS) is the most capable and sophisticated report design tool that may be installed from the SQL Server 2008 installation media. BIDS is the **more** traditional tool that report designers have been using with SQL Server 2005. It requires some project management knowledge and has a steeper learning curve than those of the stand-alone Report Builder 2.0 or ad hoc Report Builder designers.

BIDS is very similar to all the editions of Visual Studio and allows report projects to be integrated with other database and business intelligence projects to form a comprehensive data analytic or BI solution.

Designing Reports

To recap, SQL Server 2008 Reporting Services currently has three different tools for designing reports: The first option is the new Report Builder 2.0 report designer, which is optimized for non-technical users and has a simplified interface, similar to Microsoft Office products. The purpose of this tool is to make report design as easy as possible and accessible to users who just need to design simple reports but don't need to develop applications or structure business database solutions. The second option is the integrated Report Designer, created with the information technology professional in mind. It is an add-in for the Microsoft Development Environment or Visual Studio. In Reporting Services for SQL Server 2000, report design was performed exclusively using Visual Studio, which had to be purchased separately. In SQL Server 2005 and 2008, a lighter edition of the development environment is installed with the SQL Server client tools, called the *Business Intelligence Development Studio* (or *BIDS*). Now reports may be designed and created using either Visual Studio or BIDS, both of which are implementations of the development environment. The third option is the older Report Builder tool, which, although easy to use, creates less capable reports based on a different technology standard.

Confused? You shouldn't be. You can design reports using the Report Builder 2.0 report designer, which is for non-technical folks who just want to design reports. The more technical tool comes in two flavors depending on whether you have installed any edition of Microsoft Visual Studio on your computer. If you only have the client tools for SQL Server 2008 installed, you will use BIDS. If you have Visual Studio installed, you can use either Visual Studio or BIDS. Here's a little secret. . . . BIDS is actually just a shortcut to Visual Studio. If you have Visual Studio installed, they both take you to the same place (shhh . . . don't tell Microsoft that we figured this out). Regardless of the tool you use, your design experience will be nearly the same, and throughout this book you are provided examples for each option.

Building standard, server-side reports in the designer can be as simple as 1, 2, 3: First, you create a data connection to the data source and dataset (or query) for the report. The second step is to design the report layout using simple drag-and-drop tools. Formatting attributes are set by changing properties in the Properties sheet or Dialogs. The report may be previewed and debugged within the designer. The third and final step is to deploy the report to the report server. This may be done using a menu action or a button. The stand-alone Report Builder 2.0 report designer, shown in Figure 1-3, supports this three-step paradigm with corresponding features and designer views.

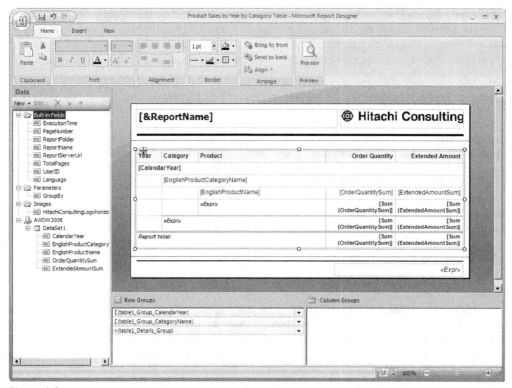

Figure 1-3

The report design tools are covered in Part II. You'll learn about the basics beginning in Chapter 5, "Basic Report Design," and about advanced techniques in Chapter 8, "Advanced Report Design." In Part III, Chapter 9, "Reporting with Analysis Service," and Chapter 10, "Report Solutions Patterns and Recipes," will take you beyond the features and discuss several common business scenarios. In these chapters, you will learn techniques for designing the best reporting and data analysis solutions to meet some common and unique challenges.

End-user and ad hoc reporting is covered in Part IV. These are different from Reporting Services' standard server-side reports. Because this feature is intended to give users the power to create and modify their own reports, it does not require Visual Studio, Business Intelligence Development Studio, or the new stand-alone Report Builder 2.0 designer to be installed on their computers. First, a data model is prepared to support the reports users may build. These data models are stored on the report server with shared data sources and reports. The data model serves two important purposes. First, it provides a simplified view to hide the complexity of relational or hierarchal data. Second, it allows the data model designer to control access to sensitive or irrelevant data stored in the database. When a user wants to build a report from the Report Manager, the Report Builder design components are downloaded and activated in the user's web browser. This design environment shares common features and characteristics with the Report Designer but is simpler to use and specifically designed for creating these client-side reports. Report Builder reports are automatically laid out and formatted for ease of use. Finished reports may be stored on the server for reuse.

Part IV, including Chapter 11, "Report Models," and Chapter 12, "Report Builder 1.0," thoroughly covers client-side reporting concepts, data model preparation, and the Report Builder ad hoc design environment.

Simple Application Integration

There are a few options available for integrating reports into business solutions. Using reports from an external application isn't hard to do, but choosing the right technique depends on the type of application and the desired behavior of the report interface. Even with all these options, you may still have a few different implementation choices. There are now several different methods for rendering reports in a custom implementation, which include:

❑   A standard web request using a Uniform Resource Locator (URL)

❑   A report embedded into a Windows or web application using an IFrame or Browser control

❑   A programmatic web request using the Simple Object Application Protocol (SOAP)

❑   The ReportViewer control integrated into Visual Studio for custom Windows Forms or Web Forms applications

❑   The ReportViewer web part for SharePoint Portal Server or Microsoft Office SharePoint Services

The first option is much easier but may be used in a variety of ways. In its simplest form, a hyperlink is used to open the report in the web browser. The user uses a standard toolbar to provide parameters for filtering and other report options.

Launching Reports from an Application

Hyperlinks and application shortcuts can easily be added to documents and custom applications. Using this simple technique, report links can be added to Windows Forms, documents, and web pages.

Much of the standard report viewing environment may be controlled using parameters passed to the report server in the URL. By incorporating these commands into a hyperlink, reports may be displayed with or without toolbar options and features. You can change the zoom factor and modify the rendering format. For example, clicking a link for one report may open it as a web page in HTML, and another link for a different report may open it in Excel or the Adobe Reader.

Reports may be designed to prompt users for parameter values used to filter data and to modify the report format and output. These parameters may also be incorporated into a URL string. This way, one hyperlink will display a report with one set of data, and another hyperlink will display the same report with different data. Parameters can even be used to change display attributes such as font sizes and colors, and to hide and show content.

User Interaction and Dynamic Reporting

There are many opportunities to use report features that provide a rich user experience. In the past, many reports were nothing more than a list of values with totals. Now reports can be a starting point that can guide users to the information they need to make decisions. Report elements such as text labels, column headers, and chart points can be used to navigate to different report sections and to new reports. Since navigation links may be data-driven and dynamically created based on program logic, report links (see Figure 1-4) may also be used to navigate into business applications. Imagine using your reports to launch programs and to navigate to document libraries and online content!

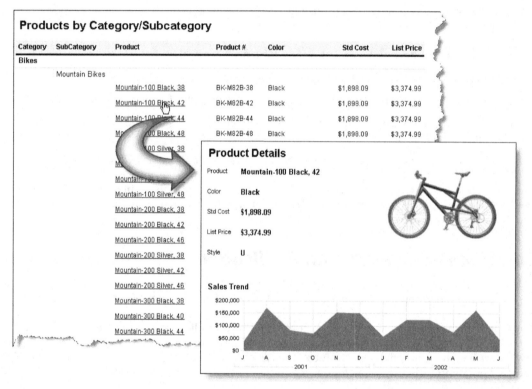

Figure 1-4

Dynamic reporting means that the content and layout of a report can change as the user selects parameter values or clicks different items. Summary headers (shown in Figure 1-5) may be used to expand and collapse detail sections, giving users the ability to drill down to more specific information.

Products by Category/Subcategory

Category	SubCategory	Product	Product #	Color	Std Cost	List Price
⊞ Accessories						
⊞ Bikes						
⊟ Clothing						
	⊞ Bib-Shorts					
	⊞ Caps					
	⊟ Gloves					
		Full-Finger Gloves, L	GL-F110-L	Black	$15.67	$37.99
		Full-Finger Gloves, M	GL-F110-M	Black	$15.67	$37.99
		Full-Finger Gloves, S	GL-F110-S	Black	$15.67	$37.99
		Half-Finger Gloves, L	GL-H102-L	Black	$9.16	$24.49
		Half-Finger Gloves, M	GL-H102-M	Black	$9.16	$24.49
		Half-Finger Gloves, S	GL-H102-S	Black	$9.16	$24.49
	⊞ Jerseys					
	⊞ Shorts					
	⊞ Socks					
	⊞ Tights					
	⊞ Vests					
⊞ Components						

Figure 1-5

Intranet and Internet Report Access

One of the marvelous things about the SQL Server Reporting Services architecture is that it is based on modern Internet technologies, namely, XML Web services and the .NET Framework. The report server, running under Windows Server Internet Information Services, is essentially a complete web portal. At its core, Reporting Services exposes all its features and capabilities as a web service. This means that there are virtually no practical limits to how the features of reports and the report server may be expanded to meet specific needs.

At the simplest level, this means that reports may be accessed by privileged users who are connected through a corporate intranet or through the World Wide Web. Reports may be made available through the out-of-the-box Report Manager web page interface or may be built into custom applications, as you will see in subsequent chapters.

Seamless Application Integration

How and why you would build reporting into a custom business application is a big question. Although there are some common (and rather simple) techniques, there isn't just one way to incorporate reports into a business environment. Whether you want your users to simply link to a report in a standard browser-based report viewer or to have report content seamlessly melded into a custom application user interface, there are a handful of methods to get there. Whatever the chosen technique, users need not even realize that they are using Reporting Services to view their content. In fact, they may not even realize that they are viewing a report. From the users' perspective, their experience is simply a convenient and smooth flow of information as they navigate from one simple interface to another, without ever leaving your business solution.

Part V will help you explore opportunities for integrating Reporting Services reports into applications and business solutions. Chapter 12 will show you different techniques for including reporting features in Windows and web applications. You will learn how to program the Reporting Services web service to gain control over the report-rendering process and to manage reports through custom applications.

Web Application Integration

It's impossible to know for sure, but by some estimates, as many as 90 percent of all desktop business applications have been replaced by browser-based applications, most in the past five years. The power of the Web and Internet technologies has drastically changed the way we use our computers. For this reason, web applications have come a long way in just the past few years. Once stodgy, static web pages, many "web sites" have been replaced with interactive information portals and dynamic application interfaces that provide feedback and tactile response to user interaction.

The page paradigm has turned once-standard gray window dialogs into artistic-yet-efficient, fashionably color-coordinated data input and management screens. One of the reasons that Reporting Services integrates so easily with modern web applications is that it natively supports HyperText Markup Language (HTML), the standard markup language used to create web pages.

Techniques may be used to incorporate reports into a web application in a variety of ways, for example:

- ❏ Hyperlinking to navigate the web browser window to a report

- ❏ Hyperlinking to open reports in a separate web browser window, with control over report display and browser features

- ❏ Embedding reports into a page using a frame, IFrame, or ReportViewer web control

- ❏ Programmatically feeding report content to an Active Server Page (ASP or ASPX) using server-side custom code

- ❏ Programmatically writing reports to files available for downloading from a web site

- ❏ Using a web part to embed reports into a SharePoint Web portal

- ❏ Fully integrating the report server in SharePoint Integration mode

The fact is that there are a lot of creative ways to integrate reports into a web application. These techniques range from very simple, requiring little more than a little HTML script, to very complex, custom methods. And if it's not enough to be able to embed reports into custom web pages, it's also possible to use custom program code to embed additional content into reports. Imagine the possibilities . . . actually, you don't have to imagine anything. Just keep reading!

Portal Integration

As web technologies and products have matured, a new breed of web applications has evolved. Most web sites consist of several HTML page files, which contain mainly text content. Portal frameworks like Microsoft Office SharePoint Services, IBM Websphere, Plumtree, and DotNetNuke have replaced many large, complex web sites. A portal server takes much of the programming out of web-site construction by providing a framework and the building blocks to assemble an intricate web site from modules. Most of the content is managed in a database rather than in physical web pages.

Now your corporate reporting solution can be completely integrated into the enterprise intranet portal. Chapter 16 covers report server integration with SharePoint. Rather than managing reports, security, and configuration settings on a separate report server and then using a SharePoint portal to just display the reports, SharePoint integrated mode allows all your reports and report administration to be managed completely within SharePoint. If you choose to manage the report server separately from your SharePoint portal, you can still use ShapePoint web parts to navigate folders and reports and to view reports hosted on the report server running in Reporting Services Native mode.

SharePoint integrated mode is supported in Microsoft Office SharePoint. A Reporting Services report can integrate with practically any portal site in some of the same ways that it integrates standard web pages — by using IFrames and hyperlinks. SharePoint integration is particularly easy for non-developers because it involves the use of simple menu options rather than writing script or program code. Adding the report viewer web part to a portal site page is as easy as dragging and dropping it into a page zone and then setting some simple properties. Microsoft offers a simple portal framework with limited features with Windows Server, called *Windows SharePoint Services* (*WSS*). The full-featured, corporate-scale edition — SharePoint Portal Server — is a separate product that adds features and advanced scalability to the WSS foundation.

Windows Application Integration

Reports may be viewed in custom Windows desktop applications using one of two techniques. The ReportViewer control or embedded web browser may be used to view server-based reports in a form. These reports are still managed on the report server and maintain all the security settings and configuration options defined by an administrator. Queries and data access are still performed on the server. The other option is to embed these reports directly into the client-side application. The Windows Forms ReportViewer controls can act as a lightweight report-rendering engine. This means that reports built into a custom application can run independently from the report server. Figure 1-6 shows a report rendered on a Windows Form using the ReportViewer control.

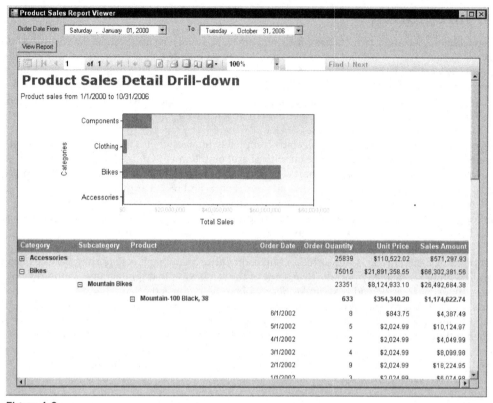

Figure 1-6

Managing and Customizing the Report Server

Reports may be delivered in a variety of ways (not just when a user navigates to a report in real time). Reports may be automatically rendered to the server cache so that they open very quickly and don't burden data sources. They may be delivered via e-mail and to file shares on a regular schedule. Using data-driven subscriptions, reports may be "broadcast" to a large audience during off-hours. Each user may receive a copy of the report rendered in a different format or with data filtered differently. You will learn to plan for, manage, and configure these features.

Chapter 14 guides you through report server administration. You learn how to optimize, back up, and recover the ReportServer database, web service, and Windows service. You also learn to use the management utilities, configuration files, and logs to customize the server environment and to prevent and diagnose problems.

Chapter 17 covers programmatic extensions to the Report Server. You learn to write custom data source, rendering, delivery, and security extensions. That chapter shows you how to build new features on top of the Reporting Services architecture. As a report designer or business manager, you learn how these powerful capabilities enable you to address specialized requirements and to direct application developers to develop custom extensions. As a system administrator, you learn to enable custom extensions and define appropriate security allowances to enable custom extensions to run on your report server. As a custom extension developer, you learn how to use the Reporting Services object model to extend the features of reports and your server, to solve business problems and enable advanced capabilities.

Summary

Different people use Reporting Services in different ways. Our goal in this book is to address the needs of the broad community of power users, report designers, solution architects, system administrators, and business managers. For some, the material contained in sections of this book will help them build and deploy reporting solutions to meet their needs. For others, it may open their eyes to powerful capabilities beyond their skill set and how to work beside other professionals as educated members of a project team.

As a non-programmer report designer using Reporting Services, you are likely to learn to write some custom expressions and program functions to meet specific reporting needs. Perhaps this is as far as you will need to take Reporting Services. For the vast majority, this is enough to design, build, and deploy reports with capabilities far greater than any other reporting tools you may have used in the past. If you are a serious programmer, then your needs are probably a little different from those of the casual report designer. For the custom business solution developer, there are very few boundaries set by limitations of this product. With some creativity and the techniques you will learn in the chapters ahead, you can take reporting further than you have before and provide your users with real business intelligence rather than just the ability to print out data.

Reporting Services takes data accessibility to the next level. Microsoft is making good on its promise of making information available "any time, any place, and on any device." Reports may be designed using specific rendering formats and page sizes to support mobile devices, the browser window, Office documents, and — oh yes — the printed page.

2

Business Intelligence Solutions

This chapter is less about Reporting Services and more about reporting and analyzing data in general. By understanding the state of data analytics in the industry and characteristics of reporting requirements, you will have a better understanding of how Reporting Services fits into the bigger picture. A Business Intelligence (BI) solution is the foundation upon which a capable business reporting platform can be constructed. Depending on your needs and your business environment, this may simply entail designing a new database. Constructing a full-scale BI solution may also encompass investing in and learning to use new database tools and technologies.

Somewhere between 1999 and 2005, the industry began to go through an important transition. Prior to this period, businesses ran reports to keep track of simple things like sales totals, invoices, inventory, and production runs. As an industry, we had reached a point where we were quite proficient at gathering and storing data. Most businesses have gigabytes and terabytes of data to report on. What we (as an industry) were less proficient in was transforming that data back into useful and actionable information. Business has changed in recent years. Today, we compete on a global scale. Business must be efficient, competitive, and adaptable. Large corporations merge, acquire, outsource, downsize, and realign their strategies more often than ever before. Today's business leaders must be adaptable and prepared to react to industry trends and opportunities in order to thrive.

As a result of this demanding environment, yesterday's static reporting applications are giving way to BI solutions. True, BI is more than the ability to "go get" data. It involves mechanisms that put high-level intelligence in front of leaders in the form of ad hoc report tools, dashboards, and scorecards. It proactively alerts users when important events occur and when thresholds are exceeded. A dynamic BI solution integrates with business forecasting and planning processes so that leaders can investigate the cause and effect of activities and their related metrics.

Reporting Tool Options

One of the greatest challenges with all the reporting and data analysis tools on the market is knowing which product or application to use to solve a problem. On a daily basis, I see e-mail messages pass through my inbox from some of our 1,500-some IT consultants asking for advice about what product or development platform would best meet a client's data analytics needs. Just within the Microsoft product line, we have tools like Excel, Excel Services, SharePoint, PerformancePoint, ProClarity, Access, and Reporting Services. We also have the capability to develop custom desktop or web applications from the ground up. And what about the packaged BI reporting solutions from companies like Business Objects, Hyperion, Panorama, and Cognos? There are so many choices on the market. Some are very expensive but offer a lot of functionality right out-of-the box. Others require custom programming, configuration, and design effort before delivering results. Some require users to be savvy and educated, and others require less training investment but give less flexibility.

In Reporting Services, there are actually three different report design tools. Two of these report designers are used to create the same type of standard reports. One is designed for simplicity and ease-of-use, while the other is centered on more advanced capabilities and project management. Yet another option applies a different type of reporting technology and a much simpler and somewhat less capable design tool. Ad hoc reporting places report design into the hands of information workers rather than only IT professionals and application developers.

Scalable Architecture

Simple report design tools like Microsoft Access and Excel are easy to use for analyzing data and creating reports for an individual or a small group of users, but in all cases they will not serve a large audience or provide adequate analysis over complex or large volumes of data. A scalable solution must be hosted on a central server and based on technologies that allow information to be shared and protected.

Aside from the ability to create advanced report features and to present data in unique ways, Reporting Services is designed from the ground up as a highly scalable, hosted service. Hosted reports are delivered through standard Internet technologies and highly capable application programming interfaces.

Rather than requiring every user to install proprietary software to view reports, a revolutionary approach allows reports to be rendered and delivered in standard formats such as HTML, Excel, and PDF. Reports may also be delivered on-demand through a web interface or may be scheduled for automated delivery by e-mail or file share.

Reporting Services architecture and all of the related components are presented in Chapter 4.

Corporate Reporting

Designing and delivering reports to the masses requires a scalable, server-hosted reporting environment. Rather than bringing data from source databases to the desktop for processing, Reporting Services processes queries and then renders reports on the report server. Because Reporting Services uses Windows Services, shared server-based components, and HTTP web services, all of the processing occurs in an efficient and secure environment. Standard data source connection providers for SQL Server and other enterprise-class databases allow for connection pooling, which further promotes efficient use of server resources. In simple terms, this means that many users can run reports at the same time while consuming minimal server resources.

A corporate BI reporting and data analysis solution typically involves the integration of data from multiple sources into a data mart or data warehouse. Complex analysis solutions often require OLAP data structures like those created with Microsoft Analysis Services. Reporting Services reports may use data from all of these sources using Transact-SQL language queries for SQL Server relational data sources or MDX queries for OLAP cubes hosted by Analysis Services.

The Reporting Services report server exposes its functionality in the same way that a standard ASP.NET web site is hosted for internal users or externally to Internet users yet is fully securable. This way, reports may be accessed from anywhere within or outside of the corporate firewall and are still available only to selected users.

Reports deployed to the server are available to users through a standard web-site application called *Report Manager*. This web site is installed with Reporting Services and requires very little administrative effort to maintain. Reports are deployed to folders that are also managed and secured through the Report Manager Web interface. Reports can also be exposed in custom-developed web applications using practically any set of web technologies or development tools.

Reporting Services offers integration with Microsoft Office SharePoint Services, which is used to build and manage corporate portal sites without having to develop custom web sites. Using SharePoint, reports may simply be viewed within standard portal site pages through an easy-to-use Report Viewer web part, or the entire report server may be integrated with SharePoint to be managed as a single service. With the latter option, reports are deployed to SharePoint report libraries with integrated SharePoint security.

Department and Personal Reporting

Managing a fully scaled corporate BI solution can be complex and expensive. Fortunately, all of the components of a working solution can be scaled down to a single server if necessary. Small and mid-scale reporting solutions may use a single, multipurpose database serving as an operational data store and a reporting data structure. As the solution matures, the eventual separation of these databases is almost inevitable. A small-scale data mart, populated from operational databases at regular intervals, will provide a simpler data source for reporting that doesn't compete with users and applications for system resources.

Simple reports are easy to design and to deploy for short-term use. With a little planning and discipline, reports can be designed to meet future requirements. Properly designed reports can have advanced features added to meet simple needs now but more sophisticated needs in the future.

Individual users can create their own reports using Report Builder 2.0. Each user can have his or her personal report folder.

Ad hoc and Self-Service Reporting

Ad hoc reporting technologies allow users to create reports on-the-fly using a simple reporting tool. This employs simple drag-and-drop techniques to visualize data rather than having to learn how to write queries and to design and deploy reports. Ad hoc reporting is simple and convenient, and with most tools, there is typically a trade-off between the rich reporting experience you would expect from custom-designed reports and a simple ad hoc report.

BI Solution Components

Most businesses will progress through a series of reporting and data analytics stages as they grow and as business data matures. Depending on the size and type of the business and the dependency on certain technologies, the landscape will be different, but these patterns are common and somewhat predictable. A small business will typically invest in a database system and then add others to automate certain processes. Eventually they will recognize the need to report on this data and to integrate multiple systems.

At first, a simple reporting application may use data from a data source or two, but eventually reports may be based on multiple data sources. Sustainable BI solutions are designed around consistent and reliable data sources engineered specifically for reporting. Data is transformed from multiple sources into a central repository using data transformation packages and then may be processed into an OLAP cube. Reports may use a relational data mart, data warehouse, or a cube. A variety of reports can be created to support business leaders and the decisions they need to make about important business processes. These decision-support reports may take on the form of charts, detail summaries, dynamic drill-down and drill-through reports, dashboards, and business scorecards.

Report Data Sources

Operational data stores are often the most complex and largest databases. Some packaged products have databases with hundreds or even thousands of tables. I recently presented at an industry conference on this topic and asked the audience how many tables they had in their largest databases. One attendee said that their customer relationship management system, purchased from a well-known vendor, contained about 8,000 tables.

As the dependence on databases and on data-driven computer systems increases, most organizations will cross thresholds in three areas:

❑ The complexity of each database will grow to accommodate more complex processes.

❑ The volume of the data will increase.

❑ The number of different databases will increase to handle different business data management needs.

A *relational database* promotes a highly complex, normalized design in which tables and fields are constrained by relational constraints and rules to govern and protect the consistency of data records as they are added, modified, and deleted from various tables. All of these rules require processing overhead on the server that can slow down queries and make it very cumbersome to obtain comprehensive information from several tables at a time. The rules of normal form — a customary set of rules that govern the design of standard database systems — encourage efficiency in data storage and reduce duplicate values, but also promote a very complex environment for reporting applications.

Aside from sheer complexity, it's not uncommon for even mid-sized companies to store terabytes of data. After all, database systems are relatively easy to design and maintain, and storage space is fairly inexpensive when compared with equally capable systems just a few years ago. There may be great value in tracking orders, shipments, calls, cases, and customers, but all of this adds up over time. Recording all of this activity means that you simply have a lot of data on-hand for reporting. Putting data into a database is the easy part. Getting intelligent, useful information back out — there's the challenge! Finally, different systems are used to manage the same types of data in different ways. For example, a customer relationship management system tracks sales leads and potential customers for a marketing organization differently than an order management system does to support the sales team. In each of these two systems, you may track something called a "customer," but in these systems, the definition may vary. Perhaps a "customer" may represent a consumer, contact, or company in one system, and a lead, vendor, or reseller in another system. Larger companies may have similar records duplicated across other systems like enterprise resource planning, human resources management, benefits, vendor management, accounting, and payables and receivables systems.

At some point, most businesses will arrive at the conclusion that to obtain valuable reporting metrics from all of these operational data sources, they will have to be consolidated into a central, simplified data store specifically designed to support business reporting requirements. Although there may be different disciplines of thought, generally a *data mart or data warehouse system* is a central data store used to simplify and standardize the data extracted from these complex and specialized data sources. It typically makes use of the same relational database technologies used to house the operational data stores, but does so in a protected, Read Only environment to keep reporting simple and straightforward.

Many businesses need to do more than just list transactional records on reports and add up the totals. Simple data aggregation can be performed with large sets of data from a data warehouse, but deep analysis requires special data storage technology and a more capable mathematical and statistical reporting engine. On-Line Analytical Processing (OLAP) systems, like Microsoft SQL Server Analysis Services, provide a simple platform to manage and report on complex, multidimensional, hierarchal data structures called *cubes*. Designing OLAP databases is a specialized discipline that opens the door to high-level analytics using simple, user-enabling ad hoc reporting and data-browsing tools. Microsoft Office Excel may be used to browse cubes using pivot tables and charts. In addition to ad hoc reporting and cube browsing, standard Reporting Services reports may be used to report on cube data using a special query language called *Multi-Dimensional Expressions (MDX)*. See Figure 2-1 for a representation of what Report Data Services can do with OLAP cubes and MDX queries.

Report Data Sources

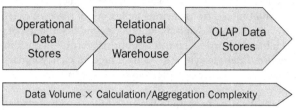

Figure 2-1

Designing reports for SQL Server 2008 Analysis Services, OLAP technologies, and key performance indicators (KPIs) are discussed in Chapter 9.

The BI Data Process

To manage the flow of data through a functional BI data process requires an investment in technologies and in process and IT project mythology. The ideal solution takes planning, vision, and leadership. Some trial-and-error is almost inevitable in any project of this magnitude, but with careful planning and some experienced guidance, success is achievable. There are patterns of success that seasoned professionals have learned to recognize and apply to BI solution projects of different scale.

The process begins with a thorough understanding of the business analytic and reporting requirements. It's not imperative to understand the need for every report, but you must know what business entities and measures will be required. Data attributes are translated into reporting facts and dimensions. Dimensions encompass the descriptive attributes organized into hierarchies. Facts are the measure values that can be aggregated for reporting. BI professionals typically work from a standard checklist of requirements that includes the following:

❑ **Granularity requirements of each dimension or the level of detail necessary for reporting** — Aggregated data may be summarized at various roll-up levels across each dimension to support high-level summaries with drill-down to lower-level detail.

❑ **Frequency of data updates and reporting cycles** — Some scenarios may require near-real-time data visibility, while data refresh intervals often need to align with standard business reporting and data reconciliation cycles.

❑ **Auditing and historical reporting requirements for changing data** — When existing data in the source systems changes, how should these changes be reflected in reports, and how should related discrepancies be resolved?

❑ **Report performance requirements** — How responsive must reports be to user requests? This may depend on whether users will run reports interactively or whether reports will run unattended and be delivered using automated batches.

❑ **Report visualization requirements** — How do users prefer to view the report data? A variety of graphical reporting tools may be used for analysis including charts, KPI dashboards, and scorecards. However, many users prefer to export data to spreadsheets or view it in list or printed form.

These requirements will drive the data warehouse design and then the OLAP cubes that are based on the warehouse tables. The bridge between operational data sources and the data warehouse or data mart is an ETL package. SQL Server Integration Services may be used to Extract, Transform, and Load data from the data sources to the data warehouse. An ETL package typically cleanses and standardizes records as it loads them into a consistent structure. Once verified and isolated from all other applications, the data warehouse becomes a "single version of the truth" and validated source for business reporting (see Figure 2-2 for a graphical representation of this process).

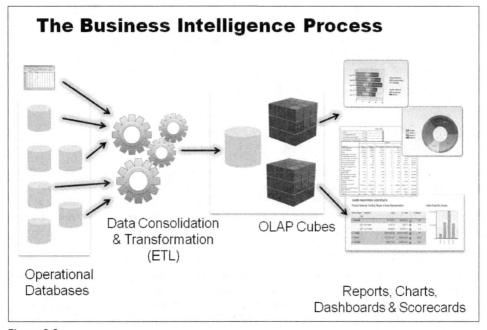

Figure 2-2

The BI Maturity Continuum

One BI and reporting solution doesn't fit all businesses. In fact, many small and mid-sized businesses don't require the complexity and sophistication of an end-to-end BI solution to meet their reporting requirements. Figure 2-3 demonstrates this concept by comparing small-, medium-, and large-scale business reporting needs. With relatively simple reporting requirements and with low data volumes and complexity, reporting directly from an operational data store is sufficient.

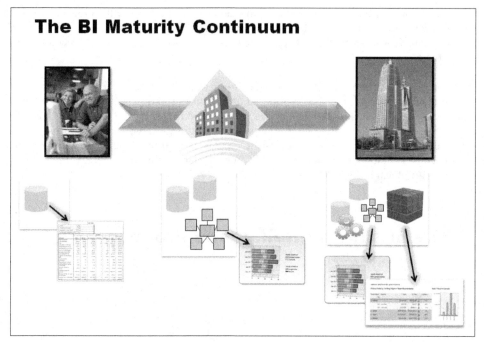

Figure 2-3

As the requirements grow, so does the need for more complex data. In a mid-sized business with moderate data reporting needs and a few data sources, a small data mart or warehouse may serve as a complete BI reporting solution. However, in a larger, sophisticated business environment, a comprehensive ETL solution, data warehouse, and OLAP database may be used to feed the appetite for deeper reporting and analysis.

OLAP cubes are also much easier for users to explore and browse using ad hoc reporting tools. This is because the data is organized into dimensional hierarchies and measure groups that most business users already understand. The cost of this investment will often be recovered very quickly as information workers and business-savvy users are empowered to browse cubes and design simple reports without a lot of hand-holding and development support from the IT staff.

Report Types

Once reports were little more than transaction records printed on paper, called ledgers, journals, and lists. As the need for more useful information arose, so did the sophistication of reporting. Today, reports serve as more than just a method to dump records to the printed page. Users need to gain insight and education about their business. Dynamic reports allow users to interact and investigate trends in their business environments, rather than just view static lists. The diagram shown in Figure 2-4 demonstrates the progression of simple, static reporting — commonplace in many businesses — to sophisticated reporting styles that provide true business insight.

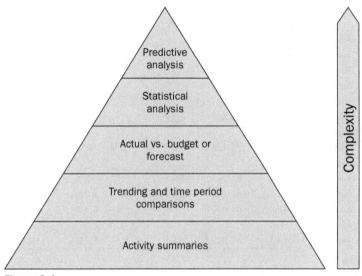

Figure 2-4

At the bottom of the pyramid, you can see that most consumers use reports for little more than summarizing volumes of data on common business activities. As the sophistication of the business users increases (as you move up the pyramid), so does the complexity of the data and the reporting medium. You'll also note that the general trend is from a historical perspective to the future. The top of the diagram shows less-common predictive analysis and forecast reporting. Essentially, the more accurate and reliable data you have about the past and present, with appropriate reporting models, you can use this to forecast and predict trends and future activities.

Take a look at some examples that match up to the categories in Figure 2-4. The first example, shown in Figure 2-5, is a simple, columnar report of product information. This report is grouped and organized by product category, subcategory, and then product.

Cat/SubCat/Product	Product #	Color	Std Cost	List Price
Accessories				
Bike Racks				
Hitch Rack - 4-Bike	RA-H123		$44.88	$120.00
Bike Stands				
All-Purpose Bike Stand	ST-1401		$59.47	$159.00
Bottles and Cages				
Mountain Bottle Cage	BC-M005		$3.74	$9.99
Road Bottle Cage	BC-R205		$3.36	$8.99
Water Bottle - 30 oz.	WB-H098		$1.87	$4.99
Cleaners				
Bike Wash - Dissolver	CL-9009		$2.97	$7.95
Fenders				
Fender Set - Mountain	FE-6654		$8.22	$21.98
Helmets				
Sport-100 Helmet, Black	HL-U509	Black	$13.09	$34.99
Sport-100 Helmet, Blue	HL-U509-B	Blue	$13.09	$34.99
Sport-100 Helmet, Red	HL-U509-R	Red	$13.09	$34.99
Hydration Packs				
Hydration Pack - 70 oz.	HY-1023-70	Silver	$20.57	$54.99

Figure 2-5

The second example, shown in Figure 2-6, is a variation on the first. Rather than requiring the user to scan several pages to find what they are looking for, this report has product categories collapsed into interactive drill-down regions. The user can click to expand a category and then expand a subcategory to show more detail. Aggregated totals can be added to a drill-down report to show numeric summaries.

Products by Category/Subcategory

Category	SubCategory	Product	Product #	Color	Std Cost	List Price
⊞ Accessories						
⊞ Bikes						
⊟ Clothing						
	⊞ Bib-Shorts					
	⊞ Caps					
	⊟ Gloves					
		Full-Finger Gloves, L	GL-F110-L	Black	$15.67	$37.99
		Full-Finger Gloves, M	GL-F110-M	Black	$15.67	$37.99
		Full-Finger Gloves, S	GL-F110-S	Black	$15.67	$37.99
		Half-Finger Gloves, L	GL-H102-L	Black	$9.16	$24.49
		Half-Finger Gloves, M	GL-H102-M	Black	$9.16	$24.49
		Half-Finger Gloves, S	GL-H102-S	Black	$9.16	$24.49
	⊞ Jerseys					
	⊞ Shorts					
	⊞ Socks					
	⊞ Tights					
	⊞ Vests					
⊞ Components						

Figure 2-6

Charting may be used to visualize trends and numeric comparisons. The report in Figure 2-7 combines textboxes to display product details with a chart to show a 2-year sales trend. Rather than requiring the user to digest a table of numbers, the area chart makes it much easier to follow the trend line and gain an understanding with less effort. The image on this report also shows the product using visual information stored in the product table.

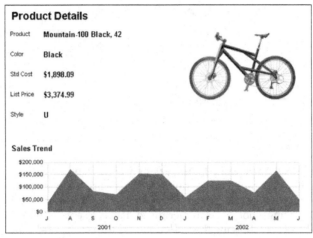

Figure 2-7

By combining two reports, users can navigate from a summary table to a detail report using data-driven hyperlinks. This drill-through report, shown in Figure 2-8, allows the user to click the report name on the table report and then see the product detail and sales trend for the selected product.

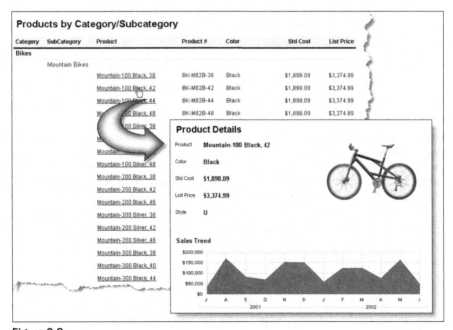

Figure 2-8

A variety of visualizations are possible with charts and gauges (see Figure 2-9). These provide visual insight and summaries using graphical paradigms, familiar to most users and appropriate for a variety of common business scenarios.

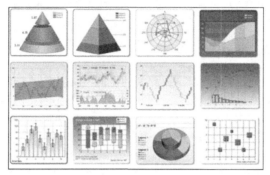

Figure 2-9

The balanced scorecard, shown in Figure 2-10, is created by combining several common report items. Report design elements, like data range tables, pivot matrices, and lists, may be used as containers for repeated icons, gauges, and charts. Interactive features allow the context of the report to change when a user interacts with it by clicking a hotspot or hyperlinked data element. In this example, clicking a row for a sales region displays a chart showing the sales trend for the selected region.

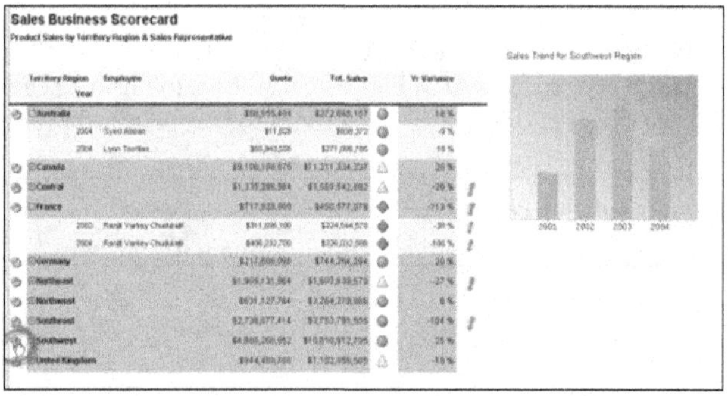

Figure 2-10

Beyond the built-in capabilities of Reporting Services, additional features may be added with custom programming or third-party components. The report in Figure 2-11 displays a map generated by a custom rendering extension using a standard Web-based mapping service. Reporting functionality may be extended to gain access to unique data sources, to render reports in customized formats or delivery methods, and to override the default security authentication mechanisms for report users.

Figure 2-11

Data Complexity and Report Performance

System performance is often one of the most significant drivers for a proper BI solution. As the reporting needs for an organization become more sophisticated and the complexity and volume of the data increase, the cost is usually measured first in performance. Queries take longer to run and will compete for resources on the report and database servers. In this case, IT professionals typically react by recognizing the value and need for a simplified database. Whether this is to be a truly enterprise-ready data warehouse, a departmental data mart, or a simple "reporting structure," the basic concepts are usually the same — simplify the database design to focus on reporting requirements.

As mentioned above, some performance and advanced analytical requirements may also drive the maturity of the solution to include OLAP cubes. This doesn't necessarily mean that all of the reports designed against other data sources must be updated. There are a variety of reports that may work just fine with an operational data source or relational data warehouse. But other more sophisticated reports will require specialized data sources (like OLAP cubes) to perform well.

Figure 2-12 demonstrates that as the data source efficiency improves as you move from the left to right side of this model, so does the ability to produce more capable reports. This is because the report designer has more time on his hands to invest in the report design. Because fewer debugging and testing cycles are required for report design, you can spend more time developing more useful reports.

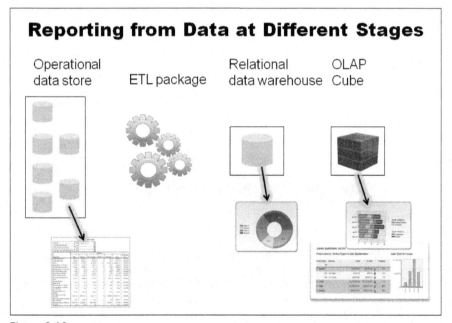

Figure 2-12

I recall a consulting assignment where I developed reports with complex financial formulas using the original database structure as the report data source. The TSQL queries were very complex and difficult to debug. The client was thrilled when one of the more complicated reports was taking only 45 minutes to run instead of the 90 minutes it took before we "optimized" the query. After transforming the same data into a simplified data mart structure, it took less than 3 minutes to run the same report. With an OLAP cube in Analysis Services, the same report ran in just a few seconds. Needless to say, the "acceptable" 45-minute report rendering time was no longer acceptable after the users found out that they could run the same report in a few seconds!

This example is not an exaggeration. As Figure 2-13 illustrates, as the database complexity, volume, and query complexity increase, the query execution time increases exponentially in many cases. At a certain point, a threshold is crossed at which point, query and report execution performance becomes unacceptable. At some point, resource demands will be so extreme that complex reports simply cannot execute, regardless of the performance. All technologies have their limits, and a relational database is not the right solution for certain business analytics.

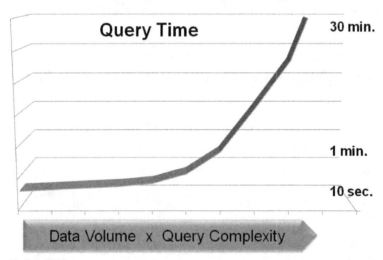

Figure 2-13

One important consideration in this equation is that the cost of a data warehouse design or an OLAP database can be very low when compared with poor report performance and unnecessarily long report development cycles. SQL Server Analysis Services is an impressive and compelling technology with tremendous value for even small and mid-sized businesses. If you have not explored this option and you need to do reporting beyond the basics, we urge you to take a serious look at this impressive toolset so that you can appreciate its value. To reinforce this point, take a look at the following diagrams that demonstrate a realistic comparison between a common relational data source and reporting from an OLAP cube. Figure 2-14 illustrates the result of a report developed against a complex relational data structure. In this case, a complicated T-SQL query that joins 30 or so tables together returns about 500,000 rows of data in about 20 minutes. Because this query took so long to write, test, and debug, the report designer had little time left to develop a useful report.

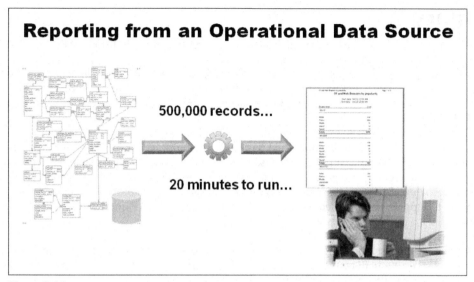

Figure 2-14

The next diagram (Figure 2-15) uses an OLAP cube. Because of the drastically more efficient data structure, paired with preprocessed hierarchies and data aggregation, a query based on a much larger volume of data runs in just a fraction of the time. Because the query was so much easier to create and less time is invested in the query design, the report designer was able to invest more time and effort into investigating report requirements and developed a KPI dashboard with interactive features.

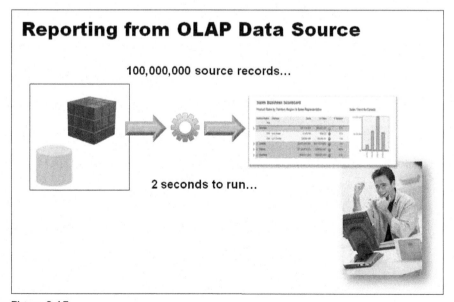

Figure 2-15

Summary

Business Intelligence raises the bar beyond basic reporting. A BI solution will enable business leaders to use the right technologies to be proactive and to make informed decisions about their business. Sophisticated reporting and analytics allow information workers and leaders to look beyond the history of their business data. By using the past and present, you can spot trends and patterns. Reliable business analytics can be used to forecast future trends and to plan for improved business processes and to make informed decisions.

A data warehouse or data mart is a simplified data structure built using relational database technology, designed specifically for reporting. Reports based on these data sources are easier to design and may perform better than reports designed using transactional, operational data stores. OLAP databases, like SQL Server Analysis Services, use specialized, multidimensional data storage and aggregation technology to support sophisticated data analytics and reporting. OLAP queries are typically very fast, enabling ad hoc reporting and advanced report visualizations.

A BI solution is the foundation upon which solid business reporting rests. Understanding these core concepts and investing in BI before report design will often reduce costs and enable you to create an enduring reporting platform for your business users and leaders.

3

Reporting Services Installation

To gain familiarity with Reporting Services, developers and administrators often perform a basic installation to a personal computer or development server. Although the basic installation glosses over many of the choices critical in an enterprise deployment, it provides an environment in which features and the installation process itself can be explored. Such an environment is ideal for performing the exercises and tutorials found in Books Online and within this book.

In this chapter, you will be guided through a basic installation of SQL Server 2008 Reporting Services. Then you will review some important considerations for an enterprise deployment.

The Basic Installation

To understand the installation of Reporting Services, it is important to have some knowledge of its components. At its core, *Reporting Services* is a Windows service that relies on a pair of databases hosted by an instance of the SQL Server Database Engine. Interaction with the Reporting Services Windows service is provided through applications such as Report Manager, hosted by Reporting Services, and other applications such as the Business Intelligence Development Studio, installed on client systems. These applications, the Windows service, and the Reporting Services databases are explored in greater detail in Chapter 4.

With the basic installation, server- and client-side components are installed on a single system. The Reporting Services databases are also installed to a local instance of the SQL Server Database Engine. With no dependencies on other systems, the basic installation is often referred to as a *stand-alone installation*.

The basic installation typically makes use of the Developer or Enterprise Evaluation editions of the SQL Server software. Both editions provide access to the full range of Reporting Services features. With the Enterprise Evaluation edition, the software is free but restricted to 180 days of use. With the Developer edition, the software is provided at a significantly reduced cost but is restricted to use in non-production environments only. These editions are obtainable through the Microsoft site, subscription services, or software vendors.

In addition to providing access to the full suite of Reporting Services features at a reduced or no cost, both editions support a wider range of operating systems than other production-ready versions of SQL Server. The operating systems supported include Windows Server 2003 and 2008 but also various editions of Windows Vista and XP.

Additional system requirements include 512 MB of RAM and either a 1.0 GHz (32-bit and IA64 64-bit) or 1.4 GHz (x64 64-bit) processor. As directed below, the basic installation will also require at least 2 GB of free hard drive space plus additional space for the system updates and SQL Server samples.

Installing Reporting Services

Before performing the Reporting Services installation, it's a good idea to be certain your system is up-to-date with the latest service packs. You will also need to be a member of the local Administrators group on the system on which you intend to perform the installation or be prepared to run the set-up application using the credentials of an account that is.

To start the installation, access the installation media for SQL Server 2008 Enterprise Evaluation or Developer Edition. This may be a DVD or installation files accessible on a local drive or file share. It is important that the media be accessed from the system on which you intend to install the Reporting Services software. Start the set-up application by launching SETUP.EXE, located at the root of the installation media.

The very first thing the set-up application will do is check your system for the Microsoft .NET Framework 3.5 and the Windows Installer 4.5. If these are not present, the set-up application will initiate their installation.

The installation of the Windows Installer (presented as a hotfix) is quite fast, but the .NET Framework can take significantly longer than the minute or two indicated by the set-up dialog. The steps for the installation of these components are not shown here but are very typical of Microsoft software installations. If either the .NET Framework or Windows Installer is installed by the set-up application, your system may require a reboot. Upon restart, you will need to re-launch the SQL Server 2008 set-up application.

The set-up application will bring up the SQL Server Installation Center, as shown in Figure 3-1. The Installation Center is divided into several pages, each providing access to documentation and tools supporting various aspects of the installation process.

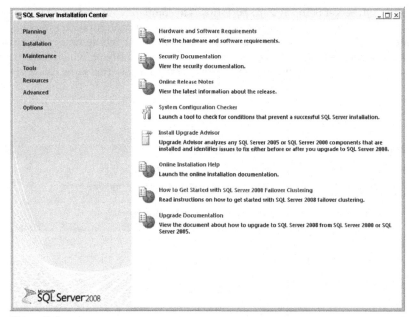

Figure 3-1

For the purposes of the basic installation, proceed to the Installation page by clicking the appropriate link on the left-hand side of the Installation Center form. On the Installation page, shown in Figure 3-2, select the "New SQL Server stand-alone installation or add features to an existing installation" option. This will launch the SQL Server Setup Wizard.

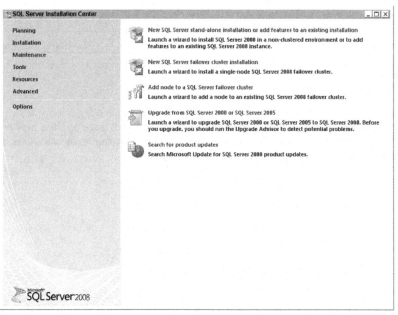

Figure 3-2

The first step the SQL Server Setup Wizard performs is to compare your system against a set of "setup support" rules. These rules determine whether the system configuration prerequisites for installation are met. Upon completion of the analysis, the Wizard shows summary information. If there are violations, you will be presented with the list of rules identifying which ones require attention. If there are no violations, you can click the Show Details button to see this same list, as shown in Figure 3-3.

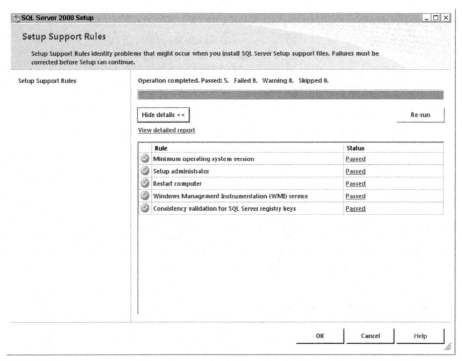

Figure 3-3

Clicking the "View detailed report" link on the Setup Support Rules page opens a new window with a detailed report containing recommendations for addressing any warnings or violations, as illustrated in Figure 3-4. After reviewing this report, you can close this window.

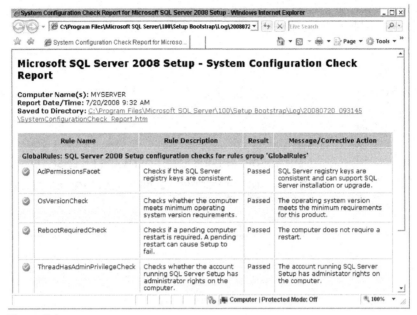

Figure 3-4

On the Setup Support Rules page of the SQL Server Setup Wizard, click the OK button to take you to the Product Key page, as shown in Figure 3-5. You can select one of the free editions of SQL Server or enter a product key for one of the other editions. Select the Enterprise Evaluation edition or enter the product key of the Developer edition to proceed.

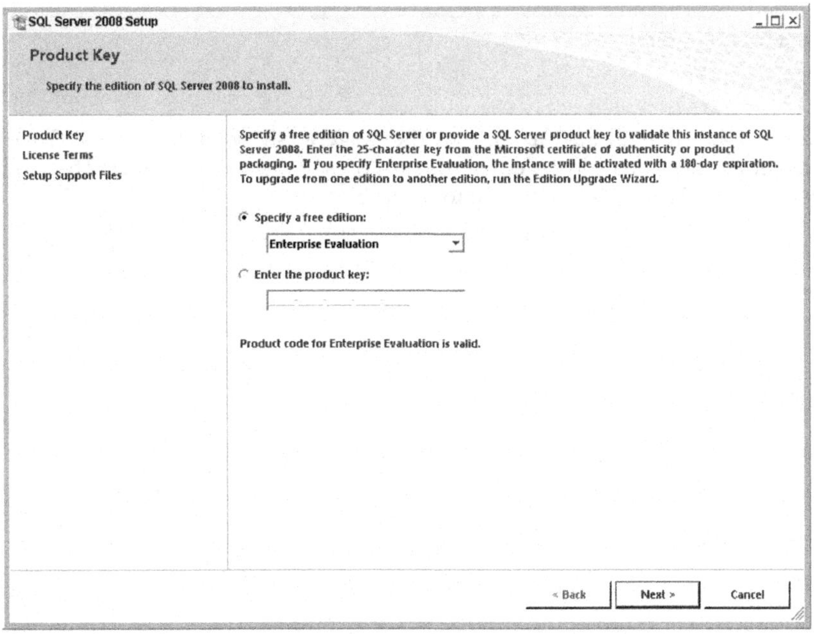

Figure 3-5

Click the Next button to proceed to the License Terms page, as shown in Figure 3-6. Carefully read the terms of the Product License. To continue with the installation, check the box labeled "I accept the license terms."

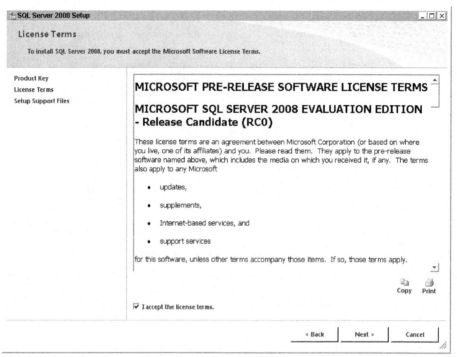

Figure 3-6

Click the Next button to enter the Setup Support Files page, as shown in Figure 3-7. This page informs you that some set-up files will be installed for the purposes of the set-up process. There is not much to do on this page except click the Install button to proceed.

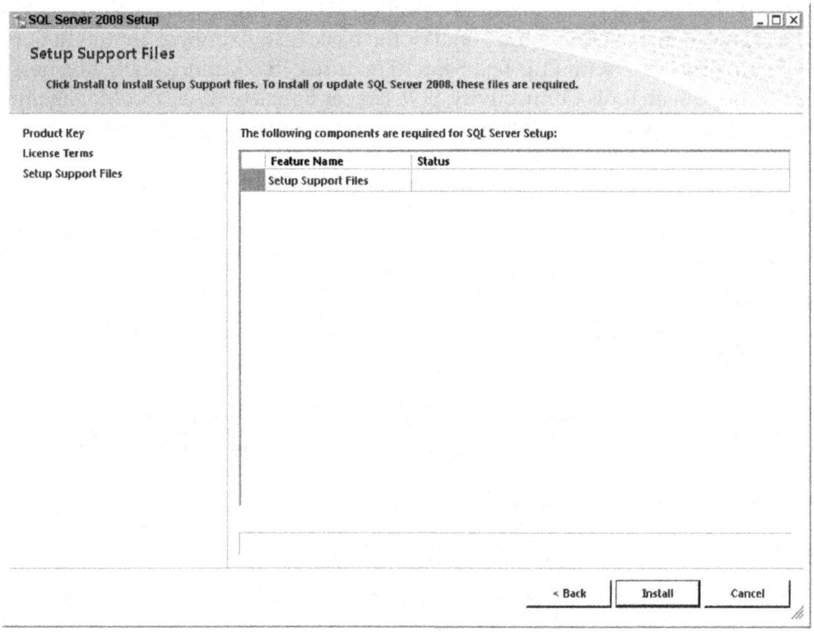

Figure 3-7

Once the support files are installed, the Wizard proceeds to another Setup Support Rules page, as shown in Figure 3-8, to confirm the system configuration against a different set of rules. As before, the "View detailed report" link can be used to obtain additional information. You should review all warnings and address all violations before proceeding.

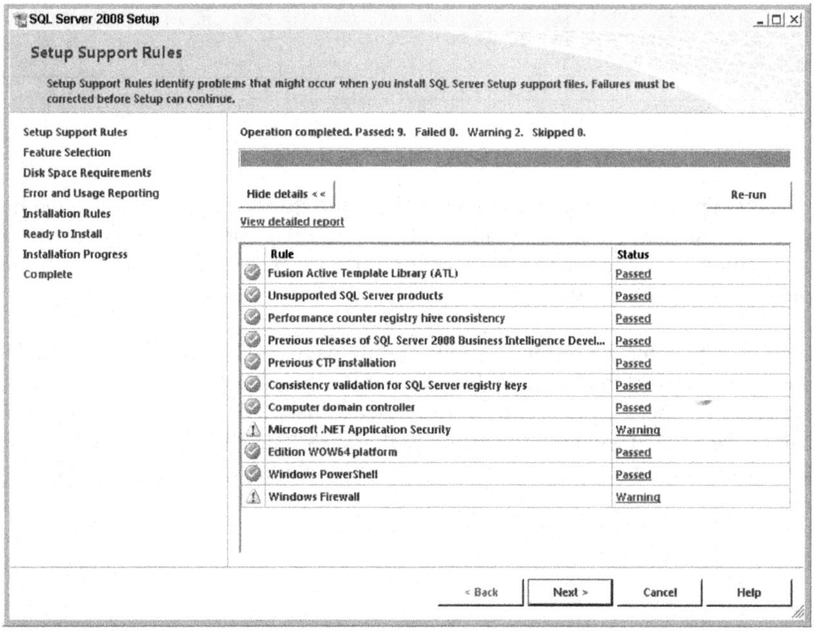

Figure 3-8

Click the Next button to proceed to the Feature Selection page, within which you select the SQL Server products and features to install (see Figure 3-9). For the basic installation, select the Reporting Services and Database Engine Services (with Full Text Search) features. In addition, select Business Intelligence Development Studio, Client Tools Connectivity, SQL Server Books Online, and Management Tools, both Complete and Basic. If you want to install other components, such as Analysis Services, you can select these as well.

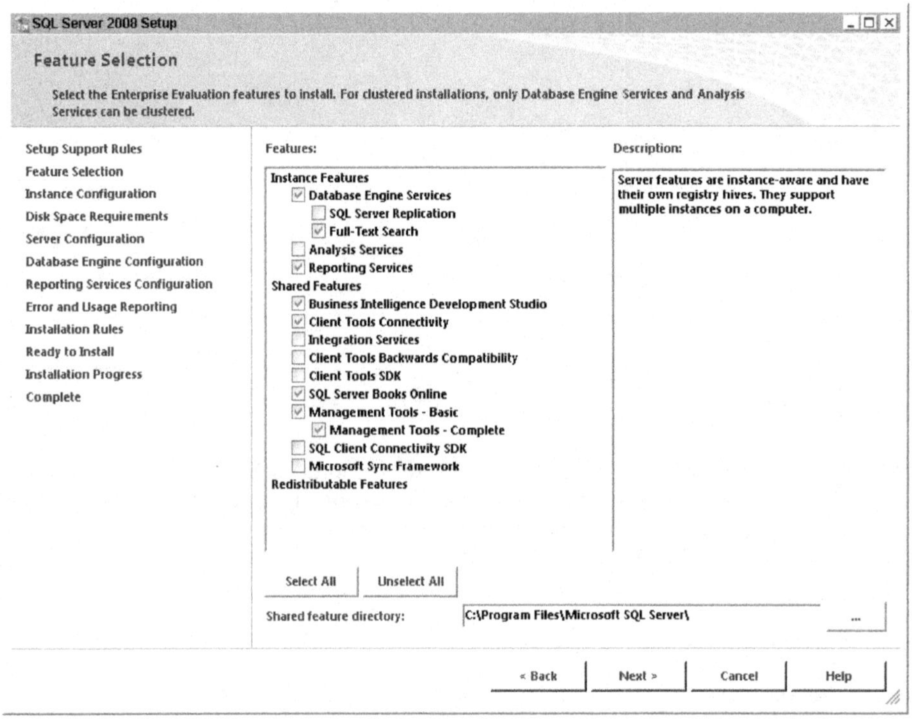

Figure 3-9

The Feature Selection page also provides you with the ability to modify the path to which shared components will be installed. For the basic installation, this will typically be left to the default location. If you have a compelling reason to change this location, click the button next to the displayed path, and select an appropriate alternate location.

Click the Next button to enter the Instance Configuration page, as shown in Figure 3-10. Here you will identify the instance name for the Database Engine and Reporting Services instances selected on the previous page. A list of other SQL Server instances already installed on the system is provided in the bottom half of the page. If a default instance has not already installed, you can choose to perform this installation to a default instance; otherwise, you will need to provide an appropriate instance name.

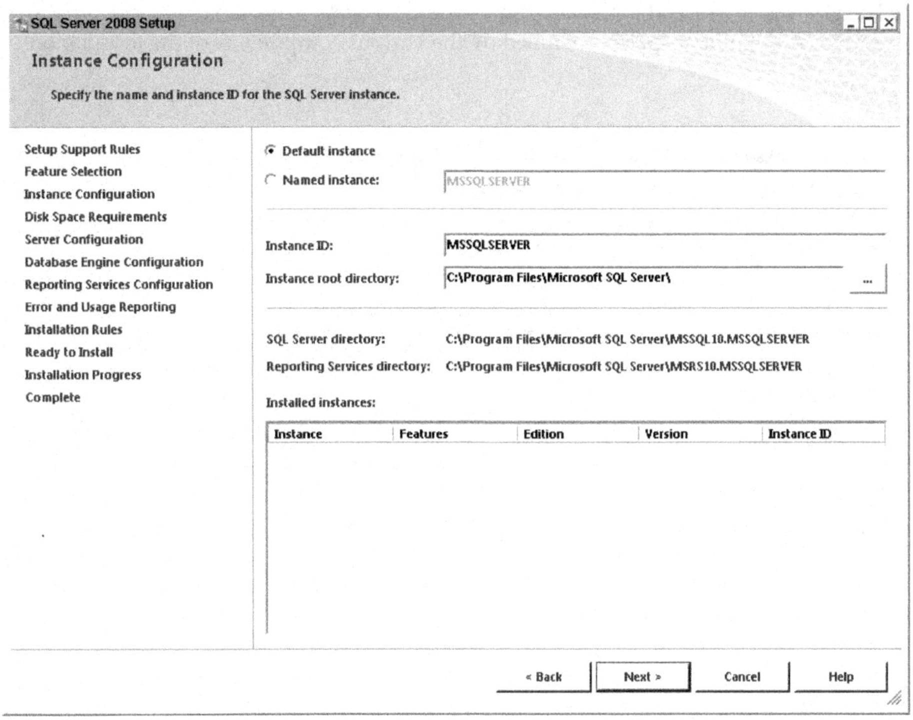

Figure 3-10

When naming an instance, it's important to keep in mind that the name is not case-sensitive and must be unique on the system. The name must also be no greater than 16 characters in length and may include letters, numbers, underscores (_), and the dollar sign ($). The first character must be a letter, and the instance name must not be one of the 174 set-up reserved words listed in Books Online. In addition, it is recommended that the instance name not be one of the 235 ODBC reserved words, also listed in Books Online.

The Instance Configuration page also allows you to alter the path to which the instance-specific components will be installed. As before, this will typically be left to the default location. If you have a compelling reason to change this location, click the button at the end of the path, and select an appropriate alternate location.

The Instance Configuration page also allows you to enter an installation ID other than the instance name. The instance ID is used to identify installation directories and registry keys for the SQL Server instance. In general, you should not alter the instance ID without a compelling reason to do so.

Click the Next button to proceed to the Disk Space Requirements page, as shown in Figure 3-11. Here you can review the amount of space consumed by the various components of the installation.

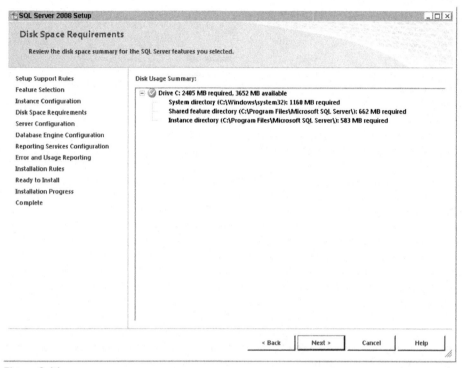

Figure 3-11

Click Next to enter the Server Configuration page. This page contains two tabs — Service Accounts and Collation — with the Service Accounts tab being the default.

On the Service Accounts tab, illustrated in Figure 3-12, select the service account to be used for each service to be installed. For the basic installation, it is generally recommended that you use the local service or network service account for the Database Engine and Reporting Services Windows services. As described in Chapter 14, you can change the service account after the installation.

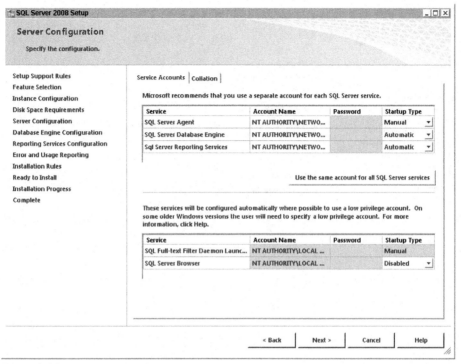

Figure 3-12

On the Collation tab, illustrated in Figure 3-13, you can alter the collation to be used for the Database Engine instance. The default selection is determined by the locale configured with the local operating system. As with other options, it is generally recommended that you not alter the collation unless you have a compelling reason to do so.

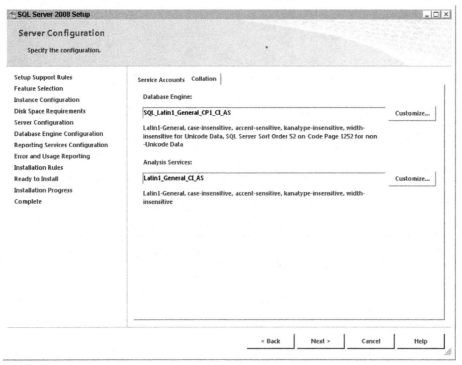

Figure 3-13

Click the Next button to proceed to the Database Engine Configuration page. This page allows you to configure the instance of the SQL Server Database Engine you are installing with Reporting Services. It is divided into three tabs: Account Provisioning, Data Directories, and FILESTREAM.

On the Account Provisioning tab, shown in Figure 3-14, press the Add Current User button so that you will be set up as an administrator of the Database Engine instance. Leave all other options on this tab as they are, unless you have a compelling reason to change them.

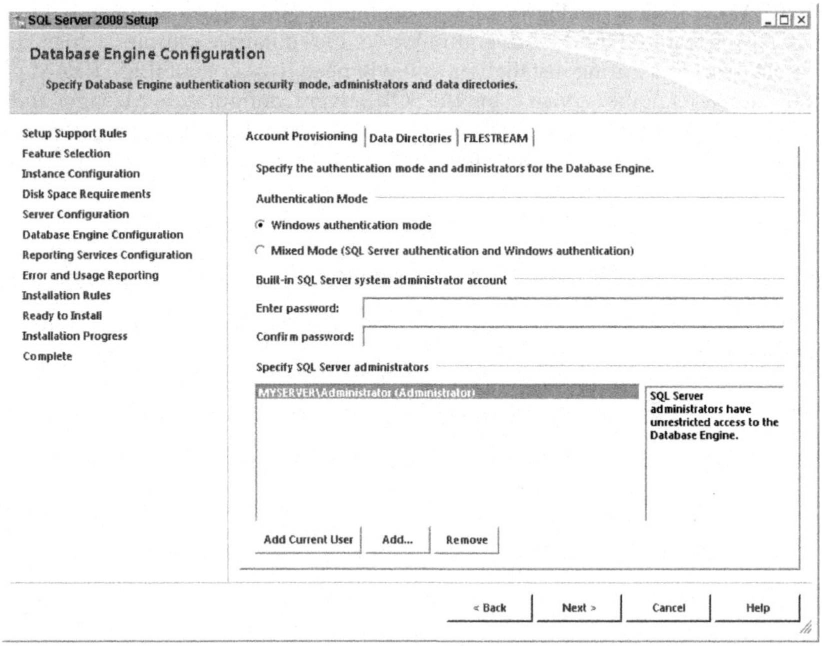

Figure 3-14

On the Data Directories tab, shown in Figure 3-15, you can alter various paths used by the Database Engine instance. Again, unless you have a compelling reason to make changes, leave the settings as is.

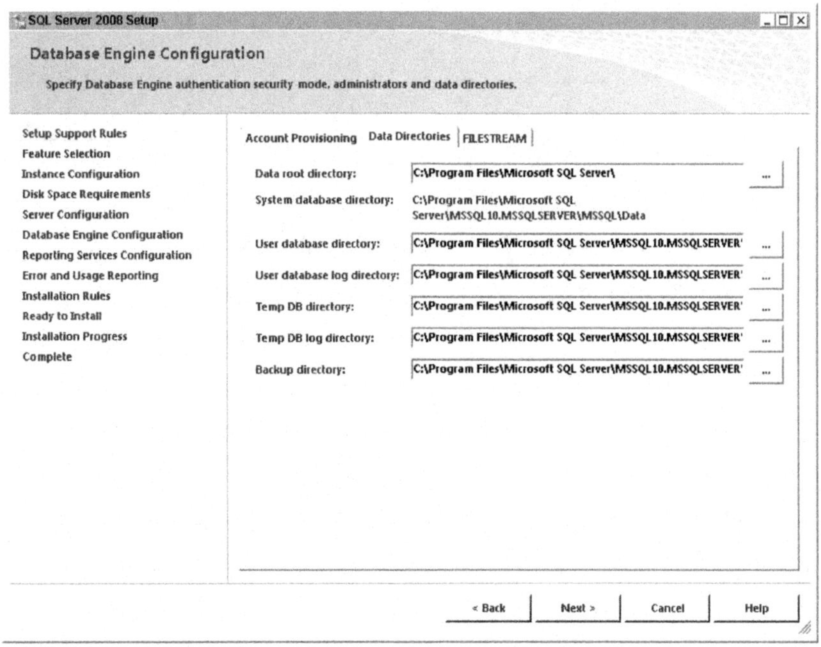

Figure 3-15

On the FILESTREAM tab, shown in Figure 3-16, select the "Enable FILESTREAM for Transact-SQL access" option. This is required for the Adventure Works 2008 database samples, which you will install later. If you forget to set this during installation, you will need to alter the FILESTREAM properties of the SQL Server Database Engine service using the SQL Server Configuration Manager and update the configuration option "filestream access level" with an appropriate value using sp_configure. Additional details of these steps for configuring the database engine can be found in Books Online.

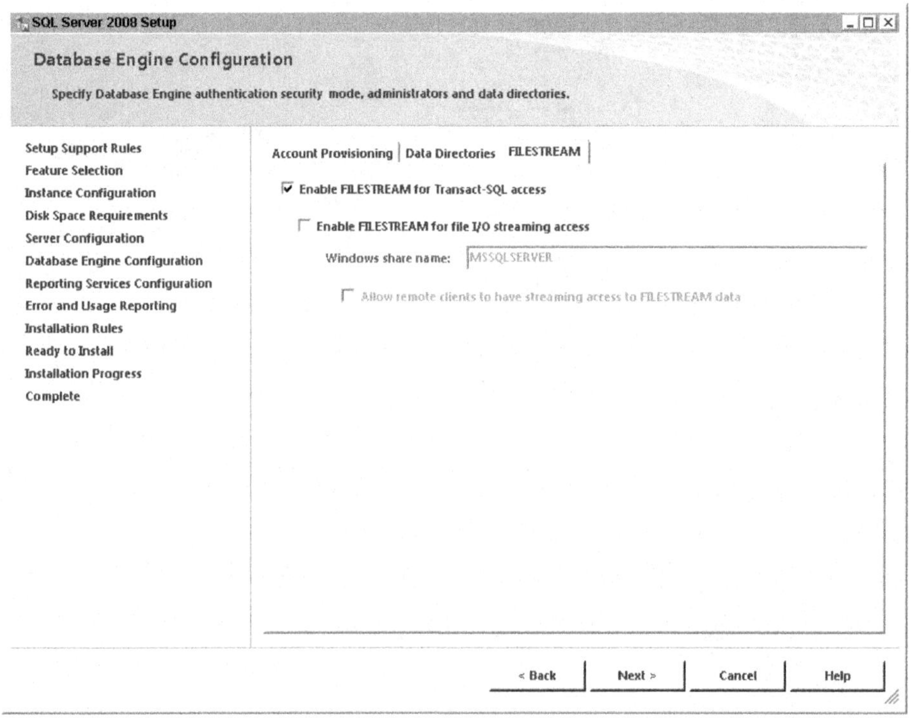

Figure 3-16

Click the Next button to enter the Reporting Services Configuration page (see Figure 3-17). On this page, you can select from one of three Reporting Services installation options. The various options are discussed in the second half of this chapter. For most basic installations, you will want to select the "Install the native mode default configuration" option. The remainder of these instructions assumes that you have selected this option.

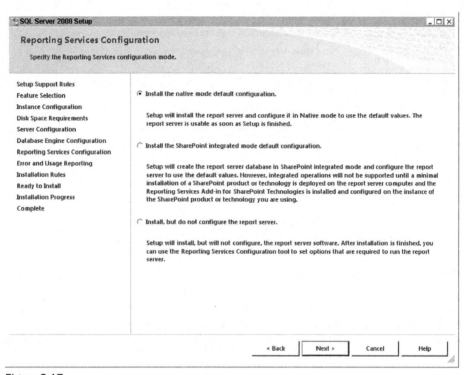

Figure 3-17

Click the Next button to proceed to the Error and Usage Reporting page, as shown in Figure 3-18. Select whichever options align with your willingness to participate in this program. Although you are encouraged to participate, the options you select will not affect the installation.

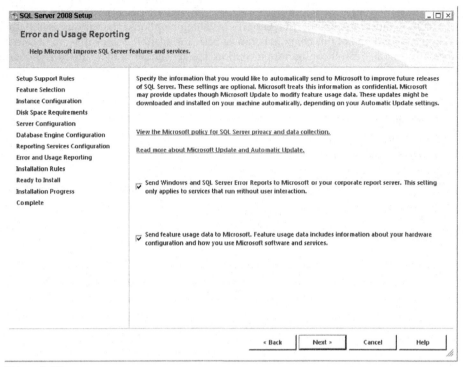

Figure 3-18

Click the Next button to enter the Installation Rules page (see Figure 3-19). These rules check that everything is in order to proceed with the installation given the options you have selected. As before, the "View detailed report" link opens a separate report.

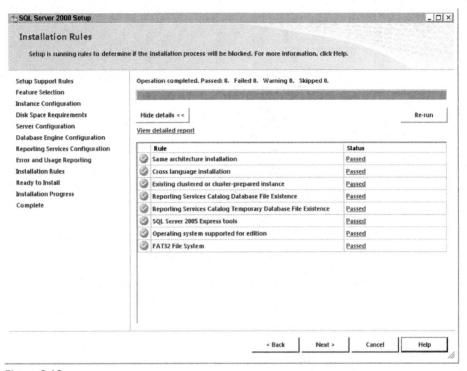

Figure 3-19

Click the Next button to enter the Ready to Install page, as shown in Figure 3-20. Carefully review the options you have selected. If you will be repeating this installation on other systems, consider copying the path of the INI file listed at the bottom of the page. The INI file can be used for future command-line installations, as described in the latter half of this chapter.

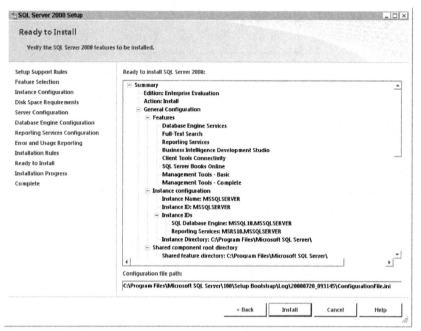

Figure 3-20

Click the Install button to start the software installation. The installation processes can take quite a bit of time to complete. During this time, you are presented with an Installation Progress page. Upon completion, a summary of the installation process is presented, as shown in Figure 3-21.

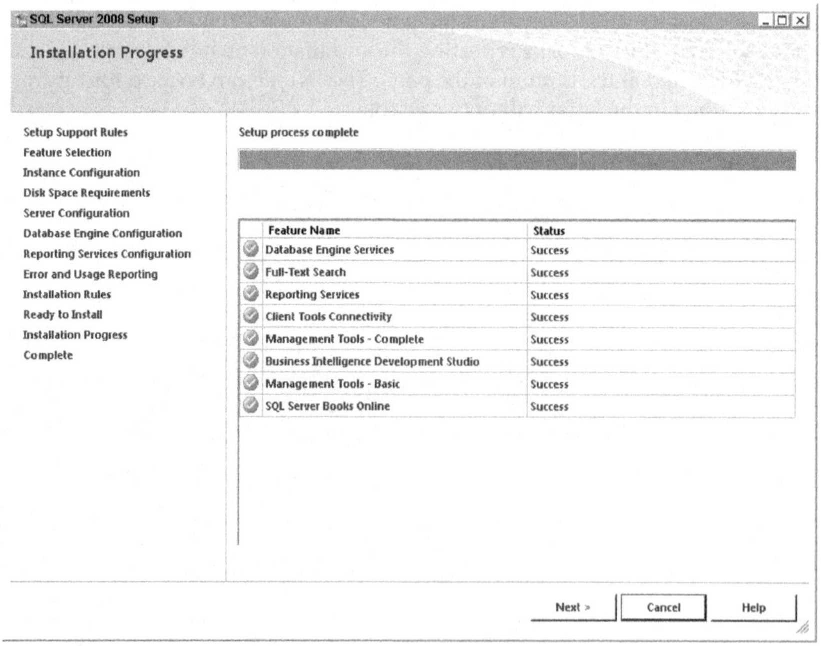

Figure 3-21

Click the Next button to proceed to the final page of the SQL Server Setup Wizard, as shown in Figure 3-22. Here you can review a summary log from the installation and notes on the components installed. Click the Close button to complete the Wizard and return to the Installation Center.

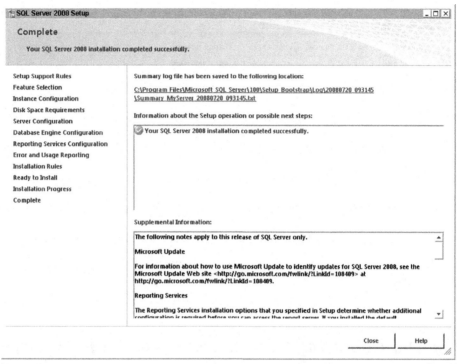

Figure 3-22

You can now close the Installation Center or use the "Search for product updates" option on the Installation Center's Installation page to look for any SQL Server hotfixes or service packs.

With the installation completed, your final step should be to verify the installation. Open Internet Explorer, and enter one of the following URLs:

❑   If you installed a default instance, enter `http://localhost/reports`.

❑   If you installed a named instance, enter `http://localhost/reports_instancename`, with the appropriate substitution.

The URL may take a little while to completely resolve upon this first use but should return a screen like the one in Figure 3-23 that indicates the service is working properly. If you do not see the two tabs and the options bar below them, as shown in the figure, try launching Internet Explorer as Administrator.

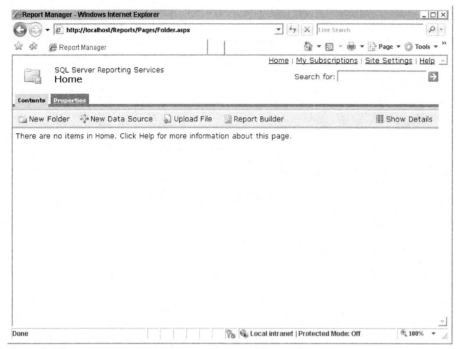

Figure 3-23

Installing the Reporting Services Samples and SQL Server Sample Databases

With the Reporting Services software installed, it's now time to install the Reporting Services samples and SQL Server sample databases. These are used throughout this book and in various tutorials available through Books Online.

The Reporting Services samples consist of various applications, extensions, models, reports, and scripts. These samples can assist you in learning about various aspects of Reporting Services or, in some cases, serve as starting points for production applications.

The SQL Server sample databases primarily consist of two databases containing data related to a fictional bicycle manufacturer, Adventure Works Cycles. The OLTP sample database contains structures typical of a transactional system, whereas the DW sample database contains structures typical of an analytical system. Together, these will assist you in gaining familiarity with both operational and analytical reporting.

The Reporting Services samples and SQL Server sample databases are available on the CodePlex web site at www.CodePlex.com/SqlServerSamples. For each sample database and the Reporting Services samples, you will need to download an installation file appropriate to your hardware platform. These files are identified in the table below.

CPU	MSI	Sample
32-bit	SQL2008.Reporting_Services.Samples.x86.msi	Reporting Services Samples
	SQL2008.AdventureWorks_OLTP_DB_v2008.x86.msi	AdventureWorks2008 Sample Database
	SQL2008.AdventureWorks_DW_BI_v2008.x86.msi	AdventureWorks2008DW Sample Database
x64 64-bit	SQL2008.Reporting_Services.Samples.x64.msi	Reporting Services Samples
	SQL2008.AdventureWorks_OLTP_DB_v2008.x64.msi	AdventureWorks2008 Sample Database
	SQL2008.AdventureWorks_DW_BI_v2008.x64.msi	AdventureWorks2008DW Sample Database
IA64 64-bit	SQL2008.Reporting_Services.Samples.ia64.msi	Reporting Services Samples
	SQL2008.AdventureWorks_OLTP_DB_v2008. ia64.msi	AdventureWorks2008 Sample Database
	SQL2008.AdventureWorks_DW_BI_v2008. ia64.msi	AdventureWorks2008DW Sample Database

Before starting the sample installations, verify that the SQL Server Database Engine and Reporting Services are running. Then, launch each downloaded MSI and follow the instructions provided to install the samples.

The move of the samples from the installation media to the CodePlex site makes the precise steps through which they are obtained and installed highly subject to change. For this reason, we are unable to provide detailed instructions. Please refer to information on the CodePlex web site for the most up-to-date installation instructions for these files.

The Enterprise Deployment

As stated at the start of this chapter, the basic installation side-steps many of the considerations important to an enterprise deployment of Reporting Services. This is done to avoid being overwhelmed so early in the game, but when it's time to start planning how Reporting Services will be installed, configured, and distributed within your enterprise environment, the following topics need to be carefully considered:

❑   SQL Server editions

❑   Named instances

- ❏ Topology
- ❏ Modes
- ❏ Installation options
- ❏ Command-line installation

SQL Server Editions

SQL Server 2008 comes in nine editions, the following seven of which include Reporting Services:

- ❏ Enterprise
- ❏ Standard
- ❏ Developer
- ❏ Enterprise Evaluation
- ❏ Workgroup
- ❏ Web
- ❏ Express with Advanced Services

The Enterprise and Standard editions are the only editions supported in a production environment. The Enterprise edition provides access to the full set of features available with Reporting Services and runs on 32-bit, x64 64-bit, and IA64 64-bit platforms. The Standard edition provides access to a reduced feature set and does not support the IA64 64-bit platform. It costs less than the Enterprise edition and may be more appropriate for smaller installations.

The Developer and Enterprise Evaluation editions provide access to the same features available through the Enterprise edition. The Developer edition is very inexpensive and is intended for development and testing environments only. The Enterprise Evaluation edition is free but expires after 180 days. These two editions support 32-bit, x64 64-bit, and IA64 64-bit architectures and a wider range of operating systems than either the Enterprise or Standard edition.

Workgroup and Web editions support a reduced feature set, even more so than Standard edition, and reduced capacity as may be appropriate for small-scale or web-based deployments, respectively. Both editions support 32-bit and x64 64-bit platforms and have low licensing costs appropriate for their intended uses.

Finally, the Express with Advanced Services edition is a highly restricted edition of SQL Server with limited support for Reporting Services. This edition is freely available, but its limitations make it unlikely to be used for anything other than highly specialized needs. The Express with Advanced Services edition is available on 32-bit and x64-bit platforms.

For precise system requirements and features available through each of these editions, please consult SQL Server Books Online. A limited comparison of core feature and hardware differences relevant to Reporting Services is provided in the following table. For the operating systems supported, please refer to the details within Books Online.

Feature	Enterprise[a]	Standard	Workgroup	Web	Express Advanced
Reporting Services Windows service	Yes	Yes	Yes	Yes	Yes
SharePoint Integrated mode	Yes	Yes			
Scale-Out topologies	Yes				
Role-based security	Yes	Yes	Yes, limited	Yes, limited	Yes, limited
Custom security extensions	Yes	Yes	Yes	Yes	
Export to Word, Excel, PDF, and Images	Yes	Yes	Yes	Yes	Yes
Remote and non-relational data sources	Yes	Yes			
Data source, Delivery, and Rendering extensibility	Yes	Yes			
Report delivery	Yes	Yes			
Report history, scheduling, subscription, and caching	Yes	Yes			
Data-driven subscriptions	Yes				
BIDS Report Designer	Yes	Yes	Yes	Yes	Yes
Report Manager	Yes	Yes	Yes	Yes	Yes
Report Builder 1.0	Yes	Yes	Yes		
Infinite click-through	Yes				
Server memory (minimum)	512 MB	512 MB	512 MB	512 MB	256 MB (32-bit) 512 MB (64-bit)
Server memory (recommended)	2+ GB	2+ GB	2+ GB	2+ GB	1+ GB
Server memory (max)	Unlimited	Unlimited	4 GB	4 GB	4 GB

(Continued)

Feature	Enterprise[a]	Standard	Workgroup	Web	Express Advanced
Supported CPU architectures	32-bit 64 64-bit IA64 64-bit	32-bit x64 64-bit	32-bit x64 64-bit	32-bit x64 64-bit	32-bit x64 64-bit
CPU speed (minimum)	1.0 GHz (32-bit and IA64 64-bit) 1.4 GHz (x64 64-bit)	1.0 GHz (32-bit) 1.4 GHz (x64 64-bit)	1.0 GHz (32-bit) 1.4 GHz (x64 64-bit)	1.0 GHz (32-bit) 1.4 GHz (x64 64-bit)	1.0 GHz (32-bit) 1.4 GHz (x64 64-bit)
CPU speed (recommended)	2.0+ GHz	2.0+ GHz	2.0+ GHz	2.0+ GHz	2.0+ GHz

[a]Applies to Enterprise, Enterprise Evaluation, and Developer editions.

Named Instances

On a single server, more than one instance of Reporting Services can be installed. Each instance runs independently of the others and may be of a different version and/or edition. Each has its own Windows service, its own code base, and its own pair of Reporting Services databases with which it interacts. These databases may be housed on separate SQL Server Database Engine instances or on a shared instance, so long as each database is assigned a unique name.

To distinguish between the Reporting Services instances on a server, each is assigned a name, unique on that system. This is referred to as the *instance name*, and an instance with a name assigned to it is known as a *named instance*.

In addition to named instances, one instance on a given server may be assigned no instance name. This is referred to as the *default instance*. When only one instance is installed to a server, it is often a default instance.

Multiple instances on a single server, whether all named or a combination of named and a default instance, can be very practical for supporting the migration of a Reporting Services instance from SQL Server 2000 or 2005 to SQL Server 2008 when server hardware is limited. Multiple instances can also be a convenient way to minimize the licensing requirements associated with a deployment. That said, historically it has been recommended that a single Reporting Services instance, whether named or default, should be deployed to a production server for the optimal allocation of resources and overall stability.

Topology

Topology refers to how Reporting Services components are distributed among servers while presenting users with unified access to the service's features. The emphasis is on the Reporting Services Windows service and the Reporting Services databases, as opposed to the client tools. Reporting Services provides support for two generalized topologies: standard and scale-outs.

In a standard topology, the Reporting Services Windows service is installed on a system. It interacts with a pair of Reporting Services databases hosted locally or remotely and dedicated for use by this one instance of Reporting Services. The basic installation performed at the start of this chapter is an example of a standard topology.

With a scale-out topology, multiple instances of the Reporting Services Windows service are installed across various servers. These instances share a pair of Reporting Services databases. By sharing these databases, each server, referred to as a *node*, hosting the Reporting Services Windows service has access to the same content and security configuration as the other nodes within the scale-out topology. If load-balancing hardware or software is available on the network, some or all of the nodes in the topology can be presented to end-users as a single resource but with greater and more flexible capacity than available through a standard deployment. Other nodes within the scale-out topology can be configured to be dedicated to scheduled processing, removing this burden from other nodes in the environment.

As you are deciding between a standard and scale-out topology, it is very important to note that scale-outs are only supported with the Enterprise edition of the product. Setup of the scale-out will also require additional configuration following the standard installation.

Finally, if you are considering a scale-out topology in pursuit of higher availability, you may wish to consider implementing the Reporting Services databases on a failover cluster. It's important to keep in mind that while the SQL Server Database Engine supports failover-clustering and Reporting Services can interact with databases hosted on a cluster, the Reporting Services Windows service itself does not have any clustering capabilities.

Modes

Reporting Services runs in one of two modes: Native or SharePoint Integrated. In the Native mode, Reporting Services manages its content using its own internal, or "native," functionality. This is the traditional mode under which Reporting Services instances have been run.

Reporting Services deployments using Enterprise, Developer, Enterprise Evaluation, or Standard editions are capable of running in the SharePoint Integrated mode. In this mode, content management is handled through SharePoint. Native content management interfaces, such as Report Manager, are no longer accessible. A detailed discussion of the SharePoint Integrated mode is provided in Chapter 16.

The SharePoint Integrated mode is a very appealing option for many organizations that want to leverage SharePoint as their enterprise content-management solution; however, there are some limitations, such as the lack of support for linked reports in this mode.

For those organizations that want to run Reporting Services in Native mode but still want to display Reporting Services content through SharePoint, the Reporting Services 2.0 web parts provide an alternative to SharePoint Integrated mode. A detailed discussion of these web parts is provided in Chapter 16.

Installation Options

During installation, you are presented with three Reporting Services configuration options. You can install Reporting Services in Native mode using a default configuration, in SharePoint Integrated mode also using a default configuration, or in a minimally configured mode, referred to as a *files only* installation.

The Native and SharePoint Integrated mode with default configuration options are only available if you are installing Reporting Services and the Database Engine as part of the same installation process. These installation options leave Reporting Services in an operational state following the completion of the set-up process, although not all Reporting Services features (e.g., the unattended execution account and e-mail delivery) are configured upon completion. If you are installing Reporting Services using the SharePoint Integrated mode with default configuration options, additional steps must be performed for integration to be completed, as outlined in Chapter 16.

For enterprise deployments, the files-only installation is the option most frequently used. With the files-only option, the server components are installed but not configured. Following installation, you are required to use the Reporting Services Configuration tool to configure the Reporting Services databases and URLs for the Reporting Services Web service and Report Manager before the service can be made operational. These steps are discussed in Chapter 14.

Command-Line Installation

For large-scale enterprise deployments, command-line installations using script files, as opposed to the interface-driven installation performed at the beginning of this chapter, are encouraged. By making use of a common script file across installations in your organization, greater consistency between installations can be achieved.

To execute the command-line installation, launch the SETUP.EXE application from the command line using the /CONFIGURATIONFILE parameter. The /CONFIGURATIONFILE parameter requires the path of the script file containing the installation instructions. This file can be created using a text editor and information in Books Online or through an interactive setup, as mentioned in the first section of this chapter. If you create the file through an interactive setup, you will need to review its parameter settings and make appropriate modifications.

The following demonstrates the call to SETUP.EXE for a command-line installation:

```
SETUP.EXE /CONFIGURATIONFILE=c:\temp\configuration.ini
```

And the following are the contents of the INI file instructing SETUP to install a default instance of Reporting Services using a files-only configuration:

```
[SQLSERVER2008]
QUIET=True
ACTION=Install
FEATURES=RS
INSTANCENAME=MSSQLSERVER
RSINSTALLMODE=FilesOnlyMode
RSSVCACCOUNT="NT AUTHORITY\NETWORK SERVICE"
RSSVCSTARTUPTYPE=MANUAL
```

Summary

The purpose of this chapter was to help you get a basic installation of Reporting Services up and running so that you can explore the product as you progress through this book. While highly useful, this installation ignored many of the issues considered during an enterprise deployment. To assist you in planning your enterprise deployment, a brief introduction to each of these issues was provided.

Reporting Services Architecture

In this chapter, you will explore how features in Reporting Services are implemented and exposed. This information is foundational for both administrators and developers. Subsequent chapters in this book build off concepts explored here.

You will start with a look at the reporting life cycle. This provides you the context within which Reporting Services is employed. You will then explore the various applications and utilities associated with Reporting Services.

Following this, you will dig a little deeper into Reporting Services itself by examining the architecture of the Reporting Services Windows service, its components and supporting databases. By the end of the chapter, you will have a solid understanding of how all these pieces come together to deliver Reporting Services' functionality.

This chapter covers:

- ❑ The reporting life cycle
- ❑ Reporting Services tools
- ❑ Reporting Services Windows service
- ❑ Reporting Services processors and extensions
- ❑ Reporting Services application databases

The Reporting Life Cycle

The reporting life cycle is often described as a process consisting of three sequential phases. A report is first designed and developed in the authoring phase, made accessible to end-users in the management phase, and then placed in the hands of end-users in the delivery phase. These three phases are illustrated in Figure 4-1 and discussed in the following sections.

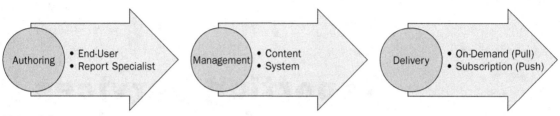

Figure 4-1

Authoring

The *authoring phase* of the reporting life cycle starts with the gathering of requirements through formal and informal processes. These requirements then drive the design of queries that provide data for the report. Data is integrated with charts, tables, matrices, or other presentation elements to form the basic report. Formatting and layout adjustments are then applied to produce a draft report that is validated for accuracy and consistency with the requirements before being published to a centralized management system in preparation for end-user consumption.

Report authoring is handled by two general classes of workers:

❑ **End-User Authors** — End-user authors develop reports as a secondary part of their job. These folks typically belong to the non-IT part of an organization and tend to require less technical, more user-friendly report authoring tools. These tools present data in a manner that is easy to interpret and incorporate into the report design and make report layout and formatting a relatively simple task.

❑ **Reporting Specialists** — Reporting specialists, on the other hand, are focused on report development as a primary part of their job. These folks often reside within the IT department. Reporting specialists demand precise control over query and report design. Their authoring tools tend to be more technical, providing access to the complete array of features available through the reporting system.

Of course, not every report author falls neatly into one of these two buckets. The end-user author and the reporting specialist represent two ends of a spectrum, with many authors leaning toward one end or the other. A variety of report development tools are needed to address the full range of needs along this spectrum.

Management

In the *management phase* of the reporting life cycle, published reports are organized, secured, and configured for end-user access. Resources employed by multiple reports and specialized features, such as subscription delivery and caching, are configured. These activities are collectively referred to as *content management* and are often handled to some degree by both authors and administrators.

The report management system itself requires configuration and ongoing maintenance to ensure its continued operation. System management activities are often the exclusive domain of administrators.

Delivery

Once deployed and configured, a report is ready for end-user consumption, in the *delivery phase* of the reporting life cycle. End-users may view reports on demand or may request that reports be delivered to them on a predefined schedule. These are referred to as the *pull* and *push* methods of report delivery, respectively. The key to successful report delivery is flexibility.

Reporting Services Tools

Reporting Services supports the full reporting life cycle. This support is provided through a collection of tools that come with Reporting Services, as identified in the following table:

Authoring	Management	Delivery
Report Designer	Report Manager	Report Manager
Report Builder 1.0	SharePoint reports library	HTML Viewer
Report Builder 2.0	Reporting Services Configuration Manager	SharePoint libraries and web parts
Third-party authoring tools	SQL Server management applications	Report Viewer controls
	Command-line utilities	Reporting Services Web service
		Subscriptions

Report Designer

Report Designer exposes the full range of available report-development features, providing report specialists with precise control over their reports. The application is accessible through the Business Intelligence Development Studio (BIDS), which is a collection of specialized designers available through Visual Studio. BIDS is installed with SQL Server and integrates with existing installations of Visual Studio. If Visual Studio has not been previously installed, SQL Server setup installs a Visual Studio shell from which BIDS will be run.

Report Designer is divided into two tabs: Design and Preview. Each of these tabs provides access to interfaces supporting query development, report layout and formatting, and validation. Wizards and dialogs accessible through Report Designer provide support for the development of highly customized, sophisticated reports. In the chapters that follow, you will gain deep exposure to these features.

Report Builder 1.0

Report Builder 1.0 enables end-users to author their own reports. The application allows tables, matrices, and even charts to be assembled with simple drag-and-drop functionality. Data access is supported through report models, which shield less technical users from the technical challenges of query development.

Although highly approachable, Report Builder 1.0 provides access to a surprisingly rich array of features, including the ability to implement formulas, parameters, and filters. Chapter 11 provides detailed coverage of report models, and Chapter 12 addresses Report Builder 1.0.

Report Builder 2.0

The Report Builder 1.0 application is poised for a makeover. The Reporting Services product team has been actively working on a new version, currently referred to as *Report Builder 2.0*, that sports more of a Microsoft Office look and feel.

As of the time of this writing, Report Builder 2.0 is only available as a stand-alone, release candidate application. It is currently expected that the product will be officially released as a stand-alone application in an SQL Server 2008 Feature Pack and will displace the original Report Builder application at a later date, possibly within the SQL Server 2008 product life cycle.

Third-Party Authoring Tools

Reporting Services reports are recorded as XML documents. The particular flavor of XML used by Reporting Services is known as *Report Definition Language (RDL)*. Report authoring tools provide graphical interfaces for report development, shielding authors from the gory details of assembling the underlying RDL document.

As an open standard, third parties have developed their own report authoring tools generating RDL documents that are consumable with Reporting Services. A list of third parties providing such tools is available from the Microsoft web site at `www.microsoft.com/sql/technologies/reporting/partners.mspx`.

Report Manager

Report Manager is primarily a content-management tool, providing access to reports and other items through an intuitive, folder-based navigational structure. Because it is securable and easy to navigate, Report Manager often serves double duty as a report delivery application. Use of Report Manager is covered in detail in Chapter 13.

It is important to note that Report Manager is available only with Reporting Services instances running in Native mode. For instances running in SharePoint Integrated mode, content management and report display functionality are provided through SharePoint. For more information on the Reporting Service modes, refer to Chapter 3.

SharePoint Libraries and Web Parts

For Reporting Services instances running in SharePoint Integrated mode, reports and other Reporting Services items are presented as part of standard SharePoint libraries and managed as SharePoint content. The Report Viewer 3.0 web part, installed during the setup of SharePoint integration, allows reports from instances in this mode to be presented through SharePoint.

Access to Reporting Services content through SharePoint is not the exclusive domain of instances running in SharePoint Integrated mode. Native-mode instances can also present content using the Reporting Services SharePoint 2.0 web parts. These consist of the Report Explorer 2.0 and Report Viewer 2.0 web parts, which allow Report Manager and rendered reports from Native-mode instances to be displayed within a SharePoint site.

Books Online provides a detailed comparison of SharePoint Integrated mode and Native-mode integration with the 2.0 web parts to assist you in determining the best option for your environment. Chapter 16 provides more details on this topic as well, including instructions for installing the 2.0 web parts and configuring an instance for SharePoint Integrated mode.

Reporting Services Configuration Manager

Access to system-critical settings is provided through the Reporting Services Configuration Manager. In addition, the tool provides support for certain administrative tasks, such as creating the Reporting Services application database and backing up and restoring encryption keys. These tasks and the use of the Reporting Services Configuration Manager to perform them are covered in Chapter 14.

SQL Server Management Applications

Because Reporting Services is a member of the SQL Server product suite, support for it can be found through the standard SQL Server management applications. SQL Server Management Studio allows you to perform various administrative tasks including the management of shared schedules and roles. Configuration of the Reporting Services Windows service is supported through the SQL Server Configuration Manager, although some of this functionality is redundant with the Reporting Services Configuration Manager. The use of SQL Server Management Studio for various management tasks is addressed in Chapters 13 and 14.

Command-Line Utilities

To assist with the automation of management tasks, Reporting Services comes with a series of command-line utilities. Each utility along with a brief description and its default location is listed in the following table:

Utility	Description	Default Location
Rs.exe	Executes VB.NET scripts, automating administrative tasks. This tool may be used with Reporting Services installations not running in SharePoint Integrated mode.	\<drive>:\Program Files\ Microsoft SQL Server\100\ Tools\Binn\rs.exe
Rsconfig.exe	Modifies connection information for the Report Services database and sets the default execution account used by Reporting Services to connect to data sources when no credentials are provided.	\<drive>:\Program Files\ Microsoft SQL Server\100\ Tools\Binn\rsconfig.exe
Rskeymgmt.exe	Manages the encryption keys used by Reporting Services. It is also used to join a Reporting Services installation with another Reporting Services installation to form a "scale-out" deployment.	\<drive>:\Program Files\ Microsoft SQL Server\100\ Tools\Binn\rskeymgmt.exe

HTML Viewer

Web browsers, such as Microsoft Internet Explorer, are the most popular tools for viewing Reporting Services reports. In most cases, when a report is rendered to HTML, Reporting Services adds JavaScript to provide several interactive features. These features include a toolbar, document maps, fixed table headers, and table sorting. Collectively, these script-based features are referred to as the *HTML Viewer*.

To ensure compatibility with the HTML Viewer, it is recommended that you use the latest version of Internet Explorer. Currently, Microsoft guarantees full HTML Viewer functionality in Internet Explorer versions 6.0 and 7.0 with up-to-date service packs and scripting enabled.

Other web browsers can be used to view Reporting Services reports rendered to HTML, but many of the HTML Viewer features will not be available. Refer to Books Online for more details on which features are supported by which browsers if you plan on distributing reports to users employing browsers other than current versions of Internet Explorer.

Report Viewer Control

The *Report Viewer control* allows Reporting Services reports to be displayed within custom applications. The Report Viewer control is actually two controls — one for use in web applications and the other for Windows Forms applications. Each supports the same functionality.

The Report Viewer control should not be confused with the Report Viewer 3.0 web part and the Report Viewer 2.0 web part used to support the display of Reporting Services content within SharePoint.

The Report Viewer control runs in one of two modes. In the default Remote Processing mode, reports are rendered by a Reporting Services instance and displayed through the control. This is the preferred mode as the full feature set of Reporting Services is available and the processing power of the Reporting Services server can be employed.

In situations in which a Reporting Services server is not available or retrieving data directly through the client system is required, the Report Viewer control can be run in the Local Processing mode. In this mode, the application retrieves data and couples it with the report definition to produce a rendered report on the host system without the support of a Reporting Services server. Not all Reporting Services features are available when the control is executed in Local Processing mode.

Integration of reports with custom applications through the Report Viewer control is covered in detail in Chapter 15.

Reporting Services Web Service

To support specialized application integration needs, Reporting Services offers a web service through which reports can be both managed and delivered. As described in the following table, the web service has several endpoints that provide access to various programmatic classes:

Endpoint	Description
ReportExecution2005	Provides programmatic access to Reporting Services report processing and rendering functionality. Available in both Native and SharePoint Integrated modes, although different URLs are used.
ReportService2005	Provides programmatic access to Reporting Services report management functionality. Available in Native mode only.
ReportService2006	Provides programmatic access to Reporting Services report management functionality. Available in SharePoint Integrated mode only.
ReportService Authentication	Provides support for user authentication when Reporting Services runs in SharePoint Integrated mode and SharePoint is configured for forms authentication.
ReportService	Provides access to the web services classes originally implemented with Reporting Services 2000. This endpoint is available for backward compatibility only and should not be used for new applications.

The use of the Reporting Services Web service is addressed in Chapter 15, and complete documentation of each endpoint is provided through Books Online.

A special feature of the Reporting Services Web service is referred to as *URL access*. Through URL access, a rendered report is retrieved through a relatively simple call to a URL. Parameters and rendering options are supplied in the URL's query string to affect the resulting report. URL access is also addressed in Chapter 15.

Subscriptions

Subscriptions allow you to put reports into the hands of your users based on a predefined schedule or following an event, such as the update of data. Reporting Services has support for two types of subscriptions:

❑ **Standard** — Through *standard subscriptions*, a report is rendered in a specific format with predefined parameter values and delivered to a single, pre-set location. This type of subscription meets the needs of many report consumers, allowing them sufficient freedom in determining how, when, and where they will view reports.

❑ **Data-Driven** — Data-driven subscriptions support even more flexibility and are better suited for managing delivery of reports to a large number of users with varying needs. These subscriptions are established with a reference to a custom relational table holding a record for each report recipient. Each record in the table may specify rendering and delivery options as well as report parameter values. Through data-driven subscriptions, a single subscription can be tailored to the specific needs of many individual consumers.

By default, subscription delivery is limited to e-mail transmittal or file share drop-off. Additional delivery options are supported through the integration of custom delivery extensions. Custom extensions are addressed in Chapter 17.

Reporting Services Windows Service

In the previous section of this chapter, we looked at the applications through which authors, administrators, and end-users interact with Reporting Services. In this section, we'll look at the basic architecture of the Reporting Services Windows service itself.

Reporting Services runs as a Windows service on a host system. Interaction with the service takes place through HTTP and WMI interfaces. The HTTP interfaces provide access to Reporting Services' core report management and delivery functionality, while the WMI interface provides direct access to service management functionality. External configuration files and application databases support the service. A visual representation of these interfaces and features is provided in Figure 4-2.

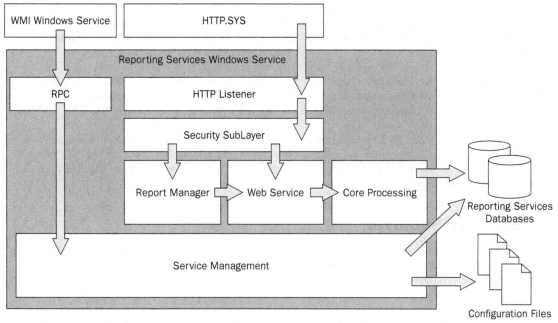

Figure 4-2

The following sections explore each of these aspects of the Reporting Services Windows service:

- ❑ HTTP.SYS and the HTTP Listener
- ❑ The security sublayer
- ❑ Report Manager and the web service
- ❑ Core processing
- ❑ Service management
- ❑ Configuration files
- ❑ WMI and the RPC interface

HTTP.SYS and the HTTP Listener

When an HTTP request is sent to the Reporting Services server, the request is first received by the server operating system through the HTTP.SYS driver. HTTP.SYS is responsible for managing a connection with the requestor and routing HTTP communications to the appropriate application on the server.

URL reservations recorded in the Registry by Reporting Services provide the instructions HTTP.SYS requires to route communications to Reporting Services. The HTTP Listener feature of the Reporting Services Windows service receives the rerouted requests from HTTP.SYS and engages either the Report Manager or the web service application that it hosts.

Why is this important? Well, it's important for various reasons, but the biggest is that Reporting Services no longer uses Internet Information Server (IIS), Microsoft's web server. This greatly simplifies the installation and management requirements for this application and is expected to translate into greater stability for Reporting Services.

Although Reporting Services has no dependency on or interaction with IIS, you can still run IIS on the Reporting Services server if you have some other need for it. So long as URL reservations recorded by the two do not conflict, both Reporting Services and IIS can even communicate over the same TCP ports.

The one exception is that IIS 5.1 and Reporting Services cannot share TCP ports on 32-bit Windows XP. If you have this configuration, you will need to alter the URL reservations to use different TCP port numbers. You can alter the Reporting Services reservations using the Reporting Services Configuration Manager, as described in Chapter 14.

The Security Sublayer

As requests are received, the HTTP Listener hands them over to the Reporting Services security sublayer. The sublayer has responsibility for determining the requestor's identity and then determining if the user has the required rights for the request to be fulfilled. These steps are referred to as *authentication* and *authorization*.

The Reporting Services security sublayer is implemented through a component referred to as a *security extension*. The extension handles the mechanics of authentication and authorization and exposes a standard set of interfaces for Reporting Services to call. Various security extensions can be used with Reporting Services, but Reporting Services deployment can be configured to make use of only one at a given time.

Reporting Services comes preconfigured with the Windows-integrated security extension. This extension authenticates users based on their Windows credentials. Four mechanisms for exchanging credentials, referred to as *authentication types*, are supported by this extension. These are the following:

❑ **Kerberos** — Kerberos is the preferred mechanism for authentication if the feature is supported within the domain. Kerberos is highly secure, and if delegation and impersonation are enabled, Kerberos can be used to allow Reporting Services to impersonate the end-user when querying an external data source.

❑ **NTLM** — NTLM employs a challenge-response mechanism to authenticate end-users. This is a secure but limited method of authentication in that impersonation and delegation are not supported.

❑ **Negotiate** — The Negotiate authentication type is the default authentication type of the Windows Integrated Security extension. With this authentication type, Kerberos is used if available. Otherwise, NTLM is used.

❑ **Basic** — Basic authentication is the least secure of the authentication types. With Basic authentication, user credentials are passed between the client and Reporting Services in plaintext. If you are using Basic authentication, you should consider implementing a Secure Socket Layer (SSL) certificate to encrypt your HTTP communications.

The default Windows Integrated Security extension is not ideal for all situations. Delivering reports over the Internet or integrating Reporting Services functionality with applications employing custom security mechanisms are two common scenarios within which Windows Integrated authentication may not be an option. In these and other scenarios, custom security extensions may be developed and employed by Reporting Services. Custom extensions are addressed in Chapter 17.

Regardless of whether the default or a custom security extension is used, once identity is established, the user's rights to perform a requested action must be verified. (Closer to the actual sequence of events, the user is authenticated, and the request is passed directly or indirectly to the web service, which then calls back to the security extension for authorization.) Like many other Microsoft products, authorization in Reporting Services is based on role assignments. As roles are created, the rights to perform system- and item-level tasks are assigned to a role. Users are then made members of a role, providing the linkage required to determine whether a user is authorized to perform a requested task.

Report Manager and the Web Service

All requests sent via HTTP are targeted to the Report Manager or web service applications. The functionality of these applications is outlined in the previous section of this chapter.

What's important in the context of this discussion is to understand that both ASP.NET applications — the Report Manager and the Reporting Services web service — are hosted from within the Reporting Services Windows service (with no dependencies on IIS, as discussed above). Both operate in their own application domains. This allows the Windows service to manage these as independent applications (despite Report Manager's functional dependency on the web service). The benefit of this is that problems within an application domain can be isolated. The Windows service can respond by starting a new instance of the application domain while dissolving the problem instance of the application domain.

Core Processing

Reporting Services' core processing features — scheduling, subscription management, delivery, and report processing — are performed by a collection of components hosted within the Windows service. Although not based on ASP.NET, these components are managed as a third application domain within the Windows service. In the "Reporting Services Processors and Extensions" section below in this chapter, you will explore these components in more detail.

Service Management

There is a lot going on within Reporting Services. To ensure that resources are available and the service is working properly, a collection of internal service management features is implemented. Although not truly a single entity, these can be thought of collectively as a service management sublayer.

One critical feature of the sublayer is application domain management. As mentioned above, Report Manager, the web service, and core processing features are hosted within the Reporting Services Windows service as three separate application domains. Occasionally, problems within these will arise. The service management sublayer's application domain management feature takes responsibility for monitoring for these problems and recycling the affected application domains. This helps to ensure the overall stability of the Reporting Services Windows service.

Another critical feature of this sublayer is memory management. Report processing can be memory-intensive. The Reporting Services team has invested quite a bit of time and energy into improving memory utilization in the 2008 release. Reporting Services is now significantly more responsive to memory pressure. Much of this is achieved through dynamic memory allocation and the use of disk caching in memory-constrained situations. (Changes to Reporting Services models for data retrieval and integration are a big part of the story as well.) The Reporting Services memory management model is outlined in Chapter 14.

Configuration Files

Reporting Services' internal and external features are controlled by collections of parameters recorded in configuration files. *Configuration files* are XML documents that follow a prescribed structure containing information governing the behavior of various components of the Reporting Services Windows service. The most critical of these configuration files are identified in the following table:

Configuration File	Description	Default Location
ReportingServicesService.exe.config	Contains settings affecting tracing and logging by the Reporting Services Windows service	*<drive>*:\Program Files\ Microsoft SQL Server\ MSRS10.*<instancename>*\ Reporting Services \ ReportServer \Bin
RSReportServer.config	Contains settings affecting numerous aspects of Reporting Services. This is the primary configuration file for Reporting Services functionality.	*<drive>*:\Program Files\ Microsoft SQL Server\ MSRS10.*<instancename>*\ Reporting Services \ ReportServer
RSSrvPolicy.config	Contains settings regulating code access security policies for the Reporting Services extensions.	*<drive>*:\Program Files\ Microsoft SQL Server\ MSRS10.*<instancename>*\ Reporting Services \ ReportServer
RSMgrPolicy.config	Contains settings regulating code access security policies for Report Manager.	*<drive>*:\Program Files\ Microsoft SQL Server\ MSRS10.*<instancename>*\ Reporting Services \ ReportManager

WMI and the RPC Interface

Microsoft's Windows Management Instrumentation (WMI) technology provides a mechanism for the consistent management of devices and applications running on Windows platforms. The Reporting Services Windows service exposes itself to WMI by registering two classes with the local WMI Windows service. These classes expose properties and methods that the WMI service makes available to administrative applications.

The first of the two classes registered by Reporting Services, MSReportServer_Instance, provides basic information about the Reporting Services installation, including edition, version, and mode.

The second class, MSReportServer_ConfigurationSetting, provides access to many of the settings in the RSReportServer.config configuration file and exposes a host of methods supporting critical administrative tasks. Administrative interfaces such as the Reporting Services Configuration tool leverage this provider for their functionality.

Developers can also take advantage of these and other WMI interfaces. The chief difficulty is making sense of the namespace organization within WMI. The WMI Code Creator utility, available from the Microsoft web site, is an excellent tool for exploring the WMI namespaces and the properties and methods exposed through each.

A Remote Procedure Call (RPC) interface provided by the Reporting Services service acts as a bridge between the WMI and Reporting Services Windows services. Through this bridge, calls against the registered classes received by the WMI service are relayed to Reporting Services.

Reporting Services Processors and Extensions

In the previous section of this chapter, you looked inside the Reporting Services Windows service. The service's core processing features were introduced as an application domain whose functionality is provided through a collection of components. You will now explore those components to gain a deeper understanding of just how Reporting Services delivers its primary functionality and where that functionality can be extended.

Before jumping into the specific components, you should be aware of the difference between extensions and processors. *Processors* are the coordinators and facilitators in Reporting Services' component architecture. They are responsible for calling the extensions as needed and providing mechanisms for data exchange between them (see Figure 4-3). Although configuration settings may alter their behavior, the processors cannot be extended through custom code.

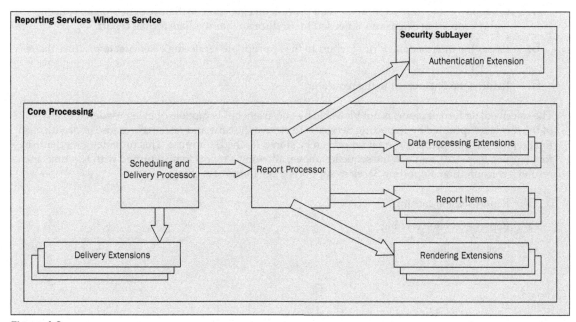

Figure 4-3

Extensions are components registered with Reporting Services to provide specific functionality. They expose standardized interfaces, which provide the mechanism by which Reporting Services engages them.

With these concepts in mind, let's now take a look at the following:

- ❏ The Report Processor
- ❏ Data processing extensions
- ❏ Report items
- ❏ Rendering extensions
- ❏ The Scheduling and Delivery Processor
- ❏ Delivery extensions

The security extension was discussed in the previous section of this chapter, *The Security Sublayer*.

The Report Processor

The Report Processor combines data and layout instructions to produce a report. Following the arrival of a request for a report, the processor

1. Calls the security extension to authorize the request.
2. Retrieves the report definition from the Reporting Services database.
3. Communicates data retrieval instructions in the report definition to the data processing extensions.
4. Combines data returned from the data processing extensions with layout instructions, using report processing extensions if needed to produce an intermediate format report.
5. Passes the intermediate format report to the appropriate rendering extension to produce the final report.
6. Returns the final report to the requestor.

The intermediate format report is not viewable by end-users but is capable of being rendered to any of the formats supported by Reporting Services. To reduce the time and resource expense of producing a final report, the intermediate format report can be stored (cached) for reuse. This provides a mechanism for skipping Steps 2, 3, and 4 in the sequence above, allowing a report to be returned with less time and resource consumption. Reporting Services supports three forms of caching:

- ❏ Report session caching
- ❏ Report execution caching
- ❏ Snapshots

Report Session Caching

When an end-user connects to Reporting Services, a session is established. Requests from an end-user are made within the context of a specific session until that session expires.

During a session, users will often request that the same report be rendered multiple times, possibly in differing formats. Reporting Services anticipates this by storing the intermediate format report in its Session cache. The cached copy is recorded with Session identifiers so that when an end-user repeats a request for a report as part of his or her session, the cached copy can be leveraged. This feature of Reporting Services, known as *report session caching*, is always enabled.

Report Execution Caching

Why tie cached reports to a session? Why not make them available to all users requesting the same report? The reason has to do with security.

Reports are populated by data retrieved from external data sources. Connections to those data sources are established using credentials. The credentials used depend on the configuration of the report or the shared data source used by the report.

If data is retrieved using the requestor's credentials, the report may contain data only appropriate for that specific user. The intermediate report contains this data so that if it is cached and made available to another requestor, that user may be exposed to data that he or she otherwise should not see.

For this reason, only reports that do not use the requestor's credentials to retrieve data from external data sources can be configured for report execution caching. With report execution caching, the intermediate report generated from a report request is cached for some period of time and used to render reports for other users until the cached copy expires.

Snapshots

With both report session and report execution caching, the end-user requests a report, and the Report Processor checks for a cached copy. If none exists, the Report Processor must assemble the intermediate format report, store it in a cache for subsequent requests, and then render the requested final report. While later requests may take advantage of the cached copy, the first request does not have this option. This can lead to an inconsistent end-user experience.

To address this, snapshots are scheduled to populate the cache in advance of an end-user request. Snapshots are recorded in the same intermediate format and have the same security requirements as report execution caching.

Data Processing Extensions

As mentioned above, the Report Processor reads data retrieval instructions from the report definition but hands over the work of establishing connections and retrieving data from external sources to the data processing extensions. These extensions expose a data reader interface back to the Report Processor, allowing data to flow through them to the Report Processor and into the intermediate report.

Multiple data source extensions can be in use on the Report Server and even employed from within a single report. Reporting Services includes several data extensions, providing support for the following data sources:

- ❑ Microsoft SQL Server
- ❑ Microsoft SQL Server Analysis Services
- ❑ OLE DB data sources
- ❑ ODBC data sources
- ❑ Oracle
- ❑ XML data sources
- ❑ SAP NetWeaver BI
- ❑ Hyperion Essbase
- ❑ Teradata

It's important to note that the SAP NetWeaver BI, Hyperion Essbase, and Teradata extensions require the separate installation of client components or .NET data providers. If you need to make use of these data processing extensions, refer to Books Online for details of how to make these fully operational.

If access to other data sources is required, you can implement a custom data processing extension and register it with Reporting Services. This topic is addressed in Chapter 17.

Alternatively, you may be able to use a standard .NET or OLE DB data provider to obtain the data access you require. As mentioned at the start of this topic, data processing extensions expose a standard data reader interface. This interface is based on .NET specifications, which are themselves not that far removed from interfaces exposed by some OLE DB providers. As a result, many .NET and OLE DB data providers can be registered and used by Reporting Services in place of a formal data processing extension. Books Online provides details on the registration of data providers for use with Reporting Services.

Report Items

The Report Processor is capable of generating tables, matrices, charts, and various other report items. These standard report items meet the needs of most report authors. Still, there are times when other report items are required. In these situations, additional report items can be registered with Reporting Services.

Typically, these report items are purchased from third-party vendors. Dundas is one such vendor whose products are very popular with report developers. Custom report items can be developed as well.

Report items, whether purchased or custom, consist of both design and runtime components that must be registered with the Report Designer and Reporting Services, respectively. Both expose standard interfaces allowing the Report Designer or the Report Processor to interact with them appropriately.

Rendering Extensions

Once the intermediate format report has been generated (or retrieved from cache) by the Report Processor, it is delivered to a rendering extension for translation to the end-user requested format. Reporting Services comes standard with seven rendering extensions, as described in the following table, each supporting one or more report formats. Custom rendering extensions are also supported, although Microsoft does not encourage their development.

Rendering Extension	Formats Supported
HTML	HTML 4.0 (default) MHTML
CSV	Excel-Optimized CSV (default) CSV-Compliant CSV
XML	XML
Image	TIFF (default) BMP EMF GIF JPEG PNG WMF
PDF	PDF 1.3
Excel	Excel 97
Word	Word 97

Parameters affecting how each rendering extension generates the final report are known as *device information settings*. Default settings for each rendering extension can be set in the rsreportserver.config file. These can be overridden as part of a specific request to deliver the report in the precise format required.

It is important to note that the Report Processor does not simply hand over the intermediate format report to a rendering extension. Instead, the processor engages the rendering extension, which, in return, accesses the intermediate report through the Rendering Object Model (ROM) exposed by the Report Processor.

The ROM has undergone some significant changes with the release of Reporting Services 2008. Custom rendering extensions developed for the 2005 or 2000 versions of Reporting Services will not work with this release. Although the changes are inconvenient for some, there are also many benefits. The most significant of these is improved consistency between online and print versions of a report and reduced memory consumption during rendering.

The HTML Rendering Extension

HTML is highly accessible and a generally good format for interactive reports. For these reasons, HTML 4.0 is the default rendering format for Reporting Services reports.

The downside to HTML is that web pages have never been very good for printing. The HTML Viewer, a JavaScript-based application embedded in most HTML-rendered reports discussed toward the start of this chapter, provides client-side printing that overcomes some of the challenges experienced when printing from a web browser. (Client-side printing is accessed through the HTML Viewer toolbar.)

The HTML rendering extension can be instructed to return MIME-HTML (MHTML) as an alternative to the HTML 4.0 default. With MHTML, images, style sheets, and other referenced items are embedded in the HTML document. This allows a report to be delivered without dependencies on external resources. This can be very useful in certain scenarios such as the e-mail delivery of a report to a user. (Not all e-mail products support MHTML, so check with your user community before selecting this format for e-mail delivery.)

The CSV-Rendering Extension

The *comma-separated values (CSV)-rendering extension* renders the data portion of a report to a comma-delimited flat-file format accessible by spreadsheets and other applications. With the 2008 release of Reporting Services, this extension has been improved to keep formatting elements out of the resulting data file.

The 2008 CSV-rendering extension operates in two modes. In the default, Excel-optimized mode, each data region of the report is rendered as a separate block of comma-delimited values. In CSV-compliant mode, the extension produces a single, uniform block of data accessible to a wider range of applications.

The XML-Rendering Extension

XML is another format commonly used for rendering reports. The *XML-rendering extension* incorporates both data and layout information in the XML it generates.

One of the most powerful features of the XML-rendering extension is its ability to accept an XSLT document. XSLT documents provide instructions for converting XML to other text-based formats. These formats may include HTML, CSV, XML, or a custom file format. The Reporting Services team recommends attempting to leverage the XML-rendering format with XSLT for specialized rendering needs before attempting to implement a custom rendering extension.

The Image-Rendering Extension

Through the *Image-rendering extension*, reports are published to one of seven image formats, the default of which is Tagged Image File Format (TIFF). TIFF is a widely used format for storing document images. Many facsimile (fax) programs use TIFF as their transfer standard, and many organizations make use of it for document archives.

The PDF-Rendering Extension

Reporting Services comes with a rendering extension for Adobe's Portable Document Format (PDF). The PDF format is one of the most popular for document sharing over the Internet. It produces clean, easy-to-read documents with exceptional printing capabilities. In addition, PDF documents are not easily altered.

Although not as interactive as an HTML report with the HTML Viewer, PDFs do support document maps. This functionality enables the creation of a table-of-contents-like feature, which is invaluable with large reports. Adobe Acrobat Reader 6.0 or higher is required for viewing the PDF documents produced by Reporting Services. This application is available for free download from the Adobe web site.

The Excel-Rendering Extension

Rendering reports to Excel is another option supported by Reporting Services. Rendering to Excel is highly useful if additional analysis is to be performed on the data by the end-user.

Not all report elements translate to Excel. While many features not available in prior versions of the Excel-rendering extension (such as nested data regions and subreports) are supported in this release, other features continue to render poorly or not at all. It is a good idea to review your reports rendered to this format prior to publication to end-users if Excel rendering is a critical requirement. Reporting Services Books Online provides details of how each report feature is handled when rendered to Excel.

The Word-Rendering Extension

The *Word-rendering extension* is new for Reporting Services 2008. The extension renders reports in Microsoft Word 97 format with many of the same features and limitations as rendering in PDF. Unlike PDF, the Word format allows reports to be more easily edited by the end-user following rendering.

The Scheduling and Delivery Processor

The Scheduling and Delivery Processor's primary function is to send requests for subscribed reports to the Report Processor, accept the returned report, and engage the delivery extensions for subscription delivery. The processor also handles the generation of snapshots.

The processor works by periodically reviewing the contents of tables within one of the Reporting Services application databases. These tables are populated through on-demand events, programmatic execution of the Reporting Services Web service's FireEvent method, or through schedules configured through Reporting Services. Schedules themselves are jobs created by Reporting Services but executed by the SQL Server SQL Agent Windows service. Reporting Services handles the details of setting up and configuring these jobs when you create a schedule, but the use of schedules creates a dependency on this additional Windows service.

Delivery Extensions

The delivery extensions are called by the Scheduling and Delivery Processor to send reports to subscribers. Reporting Services comes with delivery extensions for e-mail and file share delivery. If running in SharePoint Integrated mode, Reporting Services also supports the SharePoint delivery extension for delivery of content to a SharePoint site.

As with other extensions discussed in this chapter, custom delivery extensions can also be assembled and registered for use by Reporting Services. Books Online provides sample code for a custom delivery extension, sending reports directly to a printer.

Reporting Services Application Databases

Throughout this chapter, there have been repeated references to the Reporting Services application databases. These databases store report definitions, snapshots, cache, security information, and much more. Although it is strongly recommended that you not directly access these databases, it is important to understand their basic structure and role within the Reporting Services architecture. These two databases are:

❑ ReportServer

❑ ReportServerTempDB

When run in SharePoint Integrated mode, Reporting Services stores content and settings in the SharePoint content and configuration databases. These databases are the domain of the SharePoint application and therefore are not discussed here. As with the Reporting Services databases, it is recommended that you not directly access those databases.

ReportServer

The *ReportServer database* is the main store for data in Reporting Services. It contains all report definitions, report models, data sources, schedules, security information, and snapshots. Because of this, it is critical that the database be backed up regularly. Backup and recovery to the application databases are discussed in Chapter 14.

The following table lists some of the tables and their related functions:

Functional Area	Table Name	Description
Resources	Catalog	Contains report definitions, folder locations, and data source information.
	DataSource	Contains individual data source information.
Security	Users	Contains user name and security ID (SID) information for authorized users.
	Policies	Contains a listing of references to different security policies.
	PolicyUserRole	Contains an association of users/groups, roles, and policies.

Functional Area	Table Name	Description
	Roles	Contains a list of defined roles and the tasks the roles can perform.
Snapshots	SnapshotData	Contains information used to run an individual snapshot, including query parameters and snapshot dependencies.
	ChunkData	Stores the report snapshots.
	History	Stores a reference between stored snapshots and the date they were captured.
Scheduling	Schedule	Contains information for different report execution and subscription delivery schedules.
	ReportSchedule	Contains an association between a given report, its execution schedule, and the action to take.
	Subscriptions	Contains a listing of individual subscriptions, including the owner, parameters, and delivery extension.
	Notifications	Contains subscription notification information such as date processed, last run time, and delivery extension.
	Event	Contains temporary storage location for event notifications.
	ActiveSubscriptions	Contains subscription success/failure information.
	RunningJobs	Contains the currently executing scheduled processes.
Administration	ConfigurationInfo	Contains Reporting Services configuration information, which should be administered through prescribed interfaces and not by directly editing this table's data.
	Keys	Contains a listing of public and private keys for data encryption.
	ExecutionLogStorage	Contains a listing of reports that have been executed and critical metadata about the event.
Report Models	ModelDrill	Contains information used when implementing Report Builder infinite drill-down feature.
	ModelItemPolicy	Contains an association between a given report item, model, and policy.
	ModelPerspective	Contains an association between a given report model and its perspectives.

ReportServerTempDB

The ReportServerTempDB stores temporary Reporting Services information. This includes both session and cache data.

Reporting Services will not function properly without the ReportServerTempDB database. Still, there is no need to back up the database, as all data within it is temporary. If the database is lost, you can simply rebuild it. The rebuilding of this database is covered in Chapter 14.

The following table lists some of the tables and their related functions:

Table Name	Description
ChunkData	Stores report definition and data for session cached reports and cached instances.
ExecutionCache	Stores execution information including time-out for cached instances.
PersistedStream	Stores session level rendered output for an individual user.
SessionData	Persists individual user session level information, including report paths and time-outs for given session information.
SessionLock	Temporary storage to handle locking of session data.
SnapshotData	Stores temporary snapshot.

Summary

The purpose of this chapter was to give you a tour of the Reporting Services architecture. Through this chapter, you have explored the following:

❑ The reporting life cycle as a three-phased process through which reports are authored by end-users and reporting specialists, managed as part of a centralized reporting system, and ultimately delivered to end-users through various means

❑ The numerous applications provided by Reporting Services in support of the reporting life cycle. These include but are by no means limited to Report Builder, Report Designer, Report Manager, the Reporting Services Configuration tool, HTML Viewer, the Reporting Services Web service, and subscriptions.

❑ The structure of the Windows service as well as the components (processors, extensions, and databases) used by the service to provide its functionality

The knowledge you have obtained in this chapter as well as the three preceding chapters will provide a solid foundation for your detailed exploration of topics in the chapters that follow.

Part II
Report Design

5

Basic Report Design

If you are new to Reporting Services, you'll get started in this chapter with some basic report design concepts. If you have had prior experience with earlier versions of Reporting Services, you may be able to skip ahead after we introduce a few things that have recently changed. In order to meet the needs of those readers who are new to the product and also those who have done report design with SQL Server 2000 or 2005, we have organized this section on report design to make it easy for you to learn what you need without having to read each of these chapters from start to finish. Using this approach, you also shouldn't have to learn about all the low-level details if you simply want to know the basic steps. But you also shouldn't have to read through an elementary introduction of the topic if you are ready to take on advanced report design.

Part II, "Report Design," consists of the following four chapters:

❑ Chapter 5 introduces the report design environment and then teaches you the essentials of the report design elements. The theme of this chapter is *what* you can do, rather than *how* to do it. You'll learn the fundamental components and building blocks: data sources, datasets, report body, report items, data ranges, and page layout properties. You'll see how to use the Report Wizard to get started with common report design features. In this chapter, you will learn to use both the new Report Builder 2.0 designer and the integrated development report designer in Business Intelligence Development Studio (BIDS).

❑ In Chapter 6, you will see *how* different types of reports are created using these report items and design elements. Once you understand the core components and how to put all the pieces together, you will learn design patterns for common report styles used in creating real-world report solutions.

❑ Chapter 7 is about data access — designing data sources and datasets. You will learn techniques for writing efficient queries to filter data and apply business logic. You will use parameters to prompt users for input and filter and change the report output based on user selections and values passed to the report. You also learn to use expressions to modify report properties and to dynamically change the way data is displayed based on parameterized input or field values.

❑ In Chapter 8, you will learn to take reporting to the next level by combining the skills learned in these previous chapters with techniques learned from many report projects. You will learn to apply design patterns to solve business problems in creative ways. You'll see how to combine different report items and data ranges with data groups, parameters, variables, and expressions to create "super reports" that have advanced and dynamic functionality. In this chapter, we will demonstrate several actual reports based on real business problems encountered over the years in report solution consulting.

The four chapters in this section will progressively explore more functionality. It is the nature of this technology that different report design elements will be introduced and then covered at more advanced levels. To help you better understand our approach, refer to the following table of report design elements and the degree to which each will be covered.

Design Element	Chapter 5 Basic Report Design	Chapter 6 Report Layout and Formatting	Chapter 7 Designing Data Access	Chapter 8 Advanced Report Design	Chapter 10 Report Solution Patterns and Recipes
Textbox	Introduction	Example		Detail	Detail
Table	Example	Exercise		Detail	Detail
Matrix	Example	Exercise	Example	Detail	Detail
List				Introduction	Detail
Chart	Example	Exercise		Detail	Detail
Gauge	Introduction	Example		Detail	Detail
Composite reports		Introduction		Exercise	
Row and column groups	Introduction			Detail	Detail
Parameters and filtering			Introduction and exercise	Detail	Detail

Report Design 101

You're going to learn how to design reports using the simplest of all methods. If you are new to report design and Visual Studio, you will find the Report Wizard to be a convenient way to design simple reports. If you are an experienced report designer or application developer, or if you need to learn to design complex, custom reports, you're likely to use the Report Wizard a few times and then leave it behind.

Let's take a look at the big picture of designing reports in SQL Server Reporting Services. We will examine most of the important features of Reporting Services just to get an idea of what you can do with the product. We'll also point you to later chapters to get more information and to learn about the details. We will be using Visual Studio to design and create reports. You may use any edition of Visual Studio 2003 or later.

Before you read on, you need to get your bearings and get a sense of this chapter's direction. In any technical book, it's necessary to get every reader to a basic level of understanding before moving on to advanced material. Different readers may have varying levels of expertise or experience with Visual Studio, so let's start with the basics. Don't worry — whether you've never seen Visual Studio before or you are a tenured Visual Studio developer, we're going to cover the right material at the right depth at the right time. If you have used Visual Studio for application development, please be patient as you read through the next section. If you have never written a line of code in your life or if you are new to Visual Studio, you're in luck.

This chapter covers the following topics:

- ❑ Using the Report Wizard
- ❑ Importing reports
- ❑ Planning for extensibility
- ❑ Report items and data regions
- ❑ Formatting considerations
- ❑ Pagination and printing considerations

Report Designers

One of the most significant changes in the SQL Server 2008 reporting arsenal is the introduction of a new report design tool — and a major overhaul of the old one. That's right; there are now two different report design tools that you can use to create the same type of reports. Before we get into the longer version of the story about these two different design tools, I'd like to introduce them at a very high level. Chances are, as a report designer, your needs fall into one of two general categories:

If you work in a small business unit and you just need to design a simple report, you aren't concerned about managing the reports that have been created by other report designers. You will likely find the Report Builder 2.0 tool the easiest and best choice. This is for new report designers who don't necessarily want to contend with a lot of technical sophistication and features they won't need to use.

If you work in the IT group for your company and need to coordinate your report design efforts with others, you may need a more capable tool. If you are familiar with project-based development tools, work within a formal IT project methodology, and require version control, development, testing, and deployment management, you will likely benefit from the Report Designer integrated with BIDS or Visual Studio 2008.

To understand how this came to be, here's a quick Reporting Services history lesson. In 2003, I taught the first beta delivery of the Reporting Services course we had written for Microsoft at a training center near

Boston. The product was a few months from official release, but many people in the industry were anxiously awaiting Microsoft's first enterprise-ready reporting tool and wanted to learn to design reports. I had been teaching Microsoft development technologies for years and was accustomed to teaching classes for programmers and database professionals. On Monday morning, I had a room full of report designers who were versed in using a competing report product. After I introduced the Reporting Services architecture, I asked everyone to open Visual Studio and to create a new project. They just looked at me, not understanding what I had asked them to do. I learned a valuable lesson that day. Like the SQL Server product development teams at Microsoft, I was reminded that not everyone on the planet who may need to design reports was a seasoned IT professional. That morning in Boston, it occurred to me that these weren't programmers, and most of them had never used Visual Studio before.

As the release of SQL Server 2005 neared, which was to include the second edition of Reporting Services, the product team added a tool designed specifically to enable nontechnical users to design their own reports. This tool was called *Report Builder*, based on a newly acquired, third-party reporting technology. Although the report design experience was somewhat similar to the programmers' tool, the resulting report didn't have the same capabilities as the standard reports designed using Visual Studio. When the product shipped with SQL Server 2005, an edition of Visual Studio, called *Business Intelligence Development Studio (BIDS)*, installed with the SQL Server client tools. Users could design their own reports using the Report Builder technology, which was accessible from the central Report Manager web site. Once users and IT managers learned about the limitations of Report Builder, when compared to the more powerful features in standard Reporting Services, many chose to put the majority of their effort into developing standard Reporting Services reports rather than using the Report Builder technology.

The Report Builder experience taught us that users wanted a simple report design tool, but they also wanted the option to leverage the more capable Reporting Services features, prompting an overhaul of the Report Designer for creating standard reports. The result is a sleeker, easier-to-use report designer that now comes in two flavors: a stand-alone application for dedicated report designer/power users and an integrated version that runs in the Microsoft Visual Studio environment.

Report Builder 2.0

Let's clear up any confusion about the name of this tool. If you are a SQL Server 2005 Reporting Services user and are familiar with the old Report Builder, this isn't the same thing. If you haven't used the 2005 Report Builder, well, don't worry about it.

Report Builder 2.0 Availability

As of this printing, the Report Builder 2.0 report design tool is just wrapping up development and is available for download from www.codeplex.com. This tool will also be included with later service releases of SQL Server 2008.

Report Builder 2.0 is a fully capable, stand-alone report designer used to create standard Reporting Services reports. It's simpler, though, and designed with the information worker in mind. Unlike Visual Studio, it isn't used to manage projects or IT solutions. It doesn't have integrated version control or multiple deployment configurations. It's simply a report designer with all the features necessary to design simple and advanced reports.

After installing Report Builder 2.0, you can start it by choosing Start ➪ All Programs ➪ SQL Server 2008 Report Builder> ➪ Report Builder 2.0.

Rather than managing reports in a project, as you would with Visual Studio or BIDS, a single report is opened from any location, just like a Word or Excel document (see Figure 5-1.).

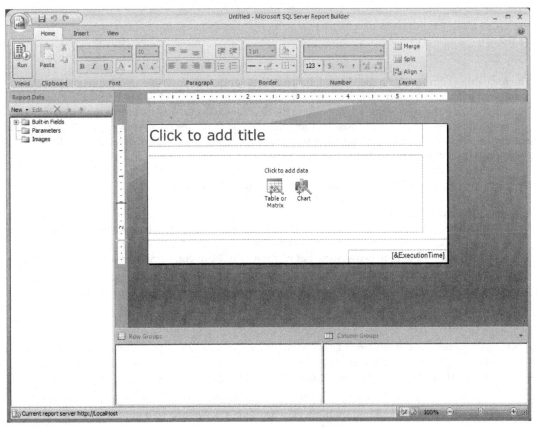

Figure 5-1

Office Tabs and Ribbons

The Report Builder 2.0 Designer sports a look much like the Office 2007 applications. Large icon buttons are arranged on ribbons that may be accessed using tabs that are arranged along the top of the interface. Tabs and ribbons are part of the Microsoft Office Fluent user interface and replace the dropdown menus found in earlier Microsoft applications. When a tab is selected, the corresponding ribbon displays icon buttons and commands related to different activities. Commands are organized into logical groups that are enabled only when the appropriate object is selected or when you are in the appropriate designer mode.

Home Tab

The Home tab, as shown in Figure 5-2, is the starting point in the Report Designer and contains common layout and formatting features for designing reports.

Figure 5-2

The formatting commands on the Home tab ribbon will work with multiple selected items. To select multiple items, draw a marquee box entirely around a group of items while holding the left mouse button, or click individual items while holding the Shift or Ctrl key. Note that most report item properties may also be set using a custom Properties dialog that appears after right-clicking on an item, but this option doesn't work with multiple selected items. Using the Properties window or Ribbon commands does work with multiple selected items.

On the Home tab, you will find the following groups and commands:

❑ **Clipboard** — This group contains common Windows Clipboard features including Copy, Cut, and Paste. The Clipboard is an essential tool in report design and is used often for duplicating captions and expressions. You can use the Clipboard with objects such as report items and images, in addition to text values that you might want to cut, copy, or paste using the Windows Clipboard.

❑ **Font** — The items in this group correspond to the font-related properties for textboxes. Using the command buttons on the ribbon is typically much faster than setting all the individual properties for each object in the Properties window.

❑ **Alignment** — The Alignment commands allow you to easily format multiple report items by aligning the edges or centers of all items selected. When this option is used with a group of items, all items are aligned with the first selected item.

❑ **Border** — The Border commands allow you to quickly set the border style, weight, and color for the top, left, right, and bottom borders of any object. Using the ribbon commands to set an outside border for an item actually sets all these individual properties. Keep in mind that nearly all items have border properties and may contain child items that also have borders. For example, setting the borders for a table does not set the borders for all the cells within the table. If you need to fine-tune borders, you may find it useful to set the borders for the entire table, rows, columns, or a range of cells and then adjust the borders for individual cells afterward.

❑ **Arrange** — Commands in this group are used to change the layered order of report items and are used for placing items in front of or behind other items. This feature is useful for managing items in the design environment. Except in rare cases, it is not advisable to stack report items unless an item is contained within another report item or data range. For example, two textboxes or images shouldn't share the same screen space, but a textbox or an image may be placed into the cell of a table or into a rectangle item. Some report renderers will move stacked items to make reports compatible with different viewers and browsers.

❑   **Preview** — Toggles between the Report preview and Design view of the report.

Insert Tab

The Insert tab and corresponding ribbon contain report design components that you can place on the report body to visualize data or format the report layout (see Figure 5-3). Items in the Data Regions, Report Items, and Subreports groups are added to the top-left corner of the report body when the ribbon button is clicked. Note that this behavior differs from the Visual Studio report design Toolbox items. In the other report designer, items are dragged or drawn onto the report body.

Figure 5-3

These items are organized into the following groups:

❑   **Data Regions** — The data regions consume data from a dataset and visualize it into rows, columns, chart items, and gauges. Data regions are actually report items, but they are different from standard report items because they consume whole sets of data rather than just individual values.

To add a data region to the report in Design view, click the ribbon button for the appropriate data region. The data region is added to the top-left corner of the report body. Click once on the item to show the repositioning handle, and then use the mouse to drag and drop the data region to the right place on the report.

❑   **Report Items** — Report items may be visual elements used to enhance the report layout, such as lines and rectangles. Some report items are designed to display or visualize a specific value or aggregated value from a dataset, such as a textbox or image.

Report items are added to the report body in the same manner as data regions. Often, you will want to place a report item into a data region or other report item so that it becomes a container.

❑   **Subreports** — This group contains only one item — a subreport. This is a special report item that allows you to place an existing report within this report body. If a subreport is placed directly on the report body, it will be rendered once, at that location, within the report. If it is placed within a data region, a separate instance of the subreport will be rendered for each row or column of the data region. Subreports can be filtered based on a field value to define master/detail relationships between datasets based on separate data sources.

❑   **Header & Footer** — This group is used to enable or disable page headers and page footers for the report. Unlike the other items in the Insert table, headers and footers are not "added" to the report body but are designated sections of the report.

View Tab

The View tab and ribbon, as shown in Figure 5-4, includes the Report Views group. You can view the report design in one of two different modes. This group on the View tab enables you to view the report in Design mode or to preview the report as it would appear if it were deployed to the report server. You can toggle the view mode by using the Preview group/button on the Home tab and ribbon.

The View tab also contains a group to show or hide utility panes and rulers. The Data pane, displayed on the left side of the Report Designer, is used to manage built-in fields, parameters, images, data sources, datasets, and data-set fields. This pane replaces the Data tab in earlier versions of the Report Designer that contained some of these options.

Figure 5-4

The grouping pane is displayed at the bottom of the Report Designer and shows the row and column groups associated with the currently selected data range object. You can drag fields into the row and column list boxes to create data groups. Each group is displayed with a set of tools to enable adding, editing, and deleting a group. The dropdown button displayed on each group item enables a dropdown menu with additional group management options.

The Properties pane is used to browse and change nearly all the properties for the currently selected design object. This is the traditional method used to manage property values. Although it duplicates some property settings that may be set using more convenient methods, it provides a consistent interface for managing all properties without the need to use different methods to access them.

Run Tab

When a report is previewed, the Run tab and ribbon are displayed with several feature groups and corresponding icons.

❏   The Views group includes the Design button, which is used to return to the report designer.

❏   The Zoom group and button are used to change the magnification of the report preview.

❏   The Navigation group includes several buttons. The First, Previous, Next, and Last buttons provide a convenient way to navigate through the report pages, and the page textbox allows you to navigate to a specific page. The Refresh button will force a requery of all data sources and rerender the report. The Stop button suspends report execution and stops the queries and the report from running. The Back button navigates to a previous report when using a drill-through report action.

❏   The Print group contains client-side printer controls.

❏   The Export button allows a report to be rendered into selected formats and to be exported to a separate file.

❑   The Options button allows you to hide and show optional toolbars in the report preview interface, including a document map (if the previewed report contains document map settings) and the parameters selection pane.

❑   The Find group includes a search textbox and corresponding button used to find a string of text within the body of the rendered report.

Figure 5-5 shows a report in preview mode. While the report is previewed and the Run tab options are visible, a smaller pane is displayed between the ribbon and the report with a link to change user credentials and the View Report button. Click this button after making parameter selections to execute the report with these selections.

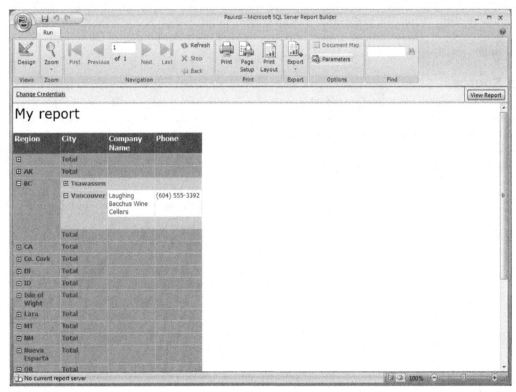

Figure 5-5

When the Run tab is displayed, you can switch back to design view using the Design button in the Views group. This will replace the Run tab and ribbons with the Home, Insert, and View tabs that are visible while in design mode. You can also always toggle between report design and preview using the smaller icons in the status bar, to the left of the zoom slider control.

Viewing and Setting Properties

You can set properties for different objects in the Designer using three different methods. The first and most convenient method is to use the Home tab on the Ribbon. For simple report items, like a textbox, just click the report item, and then use the Ribbon commands to make changes. You can also choose multiple objects of the same type. This is easy to do with the properties font size, color, background color, and so on.

Another method is to use the Properties pane to display all the properties for a selected object or group of objects. With more than one object selected, those properties with common values are displayed and can be set as a group.

The final method is to right-click on the object and then use the object-specific Properties dialog. This window typically displays specific properties and has an interface designed specifically to manage the selected object. This technique cannot, however, be used to change properties for multiple objects at one time.

Data Sources

A new addition to the Report Builder 2.0 interface is the ability to use shared data sources that have been deployed to the report server. Figure 5-6 shows the data source selection dialog in the New Table or Matrix wizard. When using the report or report item wizard or when creating a dataset, you can select a deployed data source, browse to a data source file in the local file system, or create a new data source, using corresponding buttons in this interface.

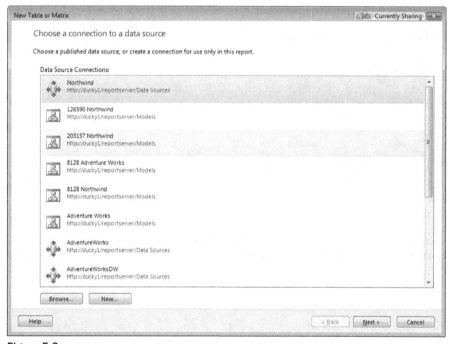

Figure 5-6

Keep in mind that when prompted for a data source file location, you may use a traditional file path or report server URL. If you are using SharePoint integrated mode, you may also have the option to provide the URL for data sources located in a SharePoint data connection library.

Server Reports

The new Report Builder 2.0 is a true ad-hoc reporting tool that allows users to create reports directly on the server without using the local file system. This capability is not enabled in a new Reporting Services installation by default. To enable server reports, a script file is provided that will enable this capability and set up folders on the report server for server-based report design for users running Report Builder 2.0. The following command should be executed on the command line, substituting your report server name for the hostname in this example:

```
rs.exe -i SetDefaultFolders.rs -s http://hostname/reportserver
```

With server reports enabled on the report server, any standard reports to which the user has access can be opened directly in Report Builder 2.0 using the standard Open dialog. To open a report on the server, local, or network file system, click the "orb" start button in the top-left corner and choose Open from the menu. You can navigate to a folder using the most recent items or other folder shortcuts on the Open Report dialog window.

Report Design with Report Builder 2.0

Many of the report design features in Report Builder 2.0 are the same or very similar to the BIDS report designer, but it's a more sleek and uncomplicated interface. To create a new report, you can either use the Report Wizard or manually build a data region and a dataset to supply its data. The basic theme in Report Builder 2.0 is simplicity. To this end, designer and wizard dialogs will automatically open when a required object (such as a data source, dataset, or report data region) must be defined. Although I do a lot of report design in Visual Studio projects, I often prefer to start designing new reports with Report Builder 2.0 because it's so much more convenient.

Figure 5-7 shows a basic report in the designer. In this example, the matrix data region was added to the report body from the ribbon on the Insert tab. After defining a dataset, fields are dragged from the Report Data pane on the left side of the designer directly into cells of the data region or to the Row Groups or Column Groups lists below the report design surface.

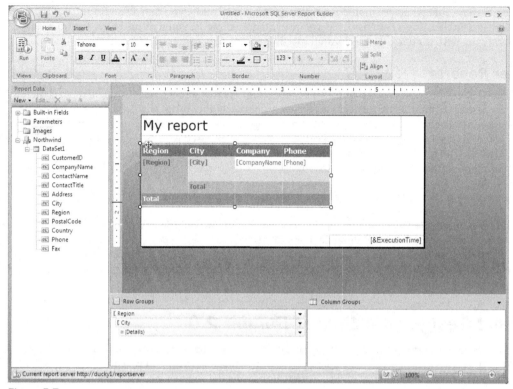

Figure 5-7

You'll learn more about specific report design techniques in the chapters that follow. Whether using the BIDS report designer or Report Builder 2.0, the process is much the same.

Data Region Wizards

A new addition to Report Builder 2.0 is a set of data region-specific design wizards. Back in Figure 5-2, you can see that when a new report is opened (or you simply open Report Builder 2.0), two icons are displayed in the center of the new report design surface. Click either of these to launch the appropriate design wizard that will lead you through the process of adding a data source and dataset query and organizing data fields and groups in a table, matrix, or chart. Figure 5-8 shows the New Table or Matrix dialog. After defining a query, fields are simply dragged into row or column groups, or into the data area of a table or matrix report. Again, you will learn to design all these report types in the chapters that follow.

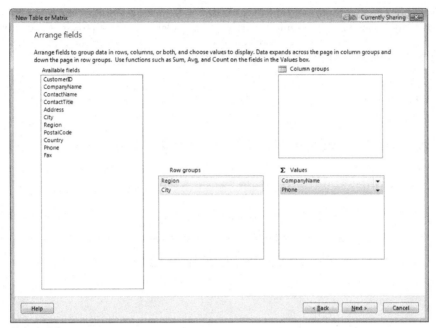

Figure 5-8

Another convenient, new feature is shown in Figure 5-9 on the report wizard page titled Choose the Layout. After you add field groups, a preview of the report using actual data is displayed in the following wizard page. I'm impressed with this behavior because this is an actual preview of the report, with all the features chosen in the report wizard up to this point in the design process.

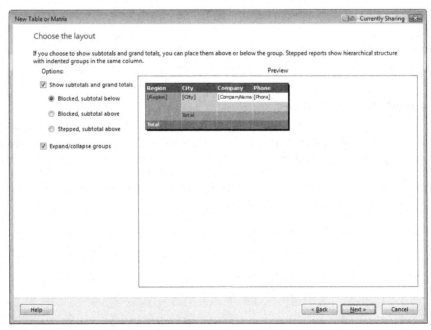

Figure 5-9

Note the selections on this page, which include the option to include subtotals and totals. You can alter the way totals are arranged and presented — in blocked headers rows (with totals above or below) or in-line with group summaries. You can also include drill-down report functionality, in which group details can be dynamically expanded or collapsed by the user.

Figure 5-10 shows the report wizard page titled Choose a Style. These styles are based on templates that affect default fonts, borders, and colors on the report.

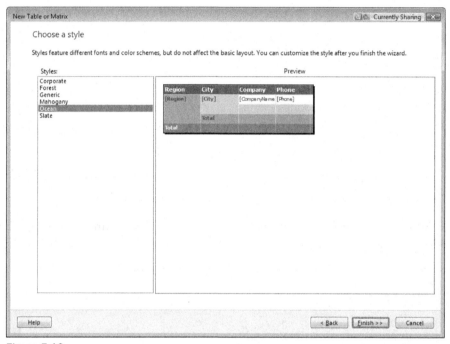

Figure 5-10

Formatting and Sample Values

Numeric formatting can be applied very easily using the ribbon. This is another convenient design feature and a significant improvement over previous versions of the report designer. Not only can you apply a variety of predefined format options to a field on the report, but you can also preview the format at design time. Figure 5-11 shows the Sample Values preview feature. Select the field value textbox in the designer. A format can be applied using the Number group on the Home tab ribbon. Choose Sample Values from the numbers drop-down list to view a representative formatted numerical value in the textbox.

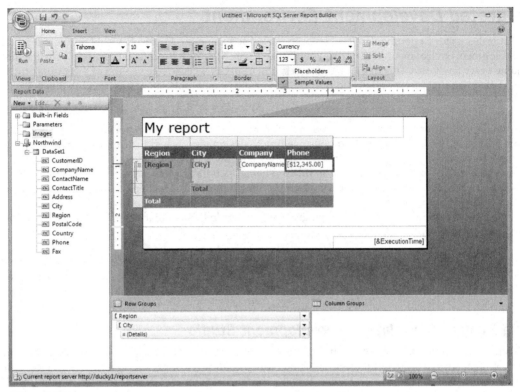

Figure 5-11

Report Builder 2.0 brings reporting to the business user. It enables information workers to design reports without using tools that were created for application developers. The Report Builder tool introduced in Reporting Services for SQL Server 2005 (now called Report Builder 1.0) made simple report design possible for less-sophisticated users, but it doesn't expose the powerful capabilities of the Reporting Services architecture. The older tool, Report Builder 1.0, is still fully integrated with SQL Server 2008 Reporting Services and is available to use if you need to support the older Report Builder-style reports. You can learn more about this tool in Chapter 12.

Report Builder 2.0 is a simple, easy-to-use report design tool that creates standard Reporting Services reports with all the features and capabilities of those created with more complex design tools. This tool effectively bridges the gap between ad-hoc, self-service reporting and enterprise reports that are typically designed and supported by information technology professionals.

Integrated Development Environment

Report design for Reporting Services has been performed using the Microsoft Visual Studio integrated development environment (IDE). This wouldn't be a true Microsoft product if they didn't change the name every few years. This tradition continues, and a special, license-free version of the Visual Studio .NET IDE was first incorporated into the SQL Server 2005 client tools called Business Intelligence Development Studio, commonly referred to as *BIDS*.

When Reporting Services was introduced in 2004 for SQL Server 2000, the report designer was integrated into Microsoft Visual Studio 2003. Anyone needing to design reports had to acquire a separate copy and license for Visual Studio. In the SQL Server 2005 version, the relatively unchanged Report Designer could be used in Visual Studio 2005 or in BIDS. Whether you had a retail version of Visual Studio or you used BIDS, the report design experience was pretty much the same. The Report Designer has once again been updated to work with the current version of Visual Studio or BIDS. However, the recent overhaul of the Report Designer components has changed a few things in this familiar environment, with several notable improvements.

You should find it relatively easy to switch between the stand-alone Report Builder 2.0 designer and the BIDS designer, as many of the components are the same. Some of the utility windows and menus are unique to BIDS and work differently from the ribbon commands in the stand-alone designer.

Using Business Intelligence Development Studio

Business Intelligence Development Studio, or BIDS, is an edition of Microsoft Visual Studio 2008 with project templates to create solutions that include Integration Services packages, Analysis Services cubes and databases, and, of course, Reporting Services reports. With the SQL Server 2008 client tools installed, you can open BIDS by choosing Start ➪ All Programs ➪ Microsoft SQL Server 2008 ➪ SQL Server Business Intelligence Development Studio.

If you have installed any edition of Microsoft Visual Studio 2008, that application will open when you launch BIDS. You will note in Figure 5-12 that I have Visual Studio Team System 2008 installed, which shows up in the Start Page header. If you are not using Visual Studio, you will see the Business Intelligence Development Studio edition. The only significant different between these editions will be the list of available project types and languages.

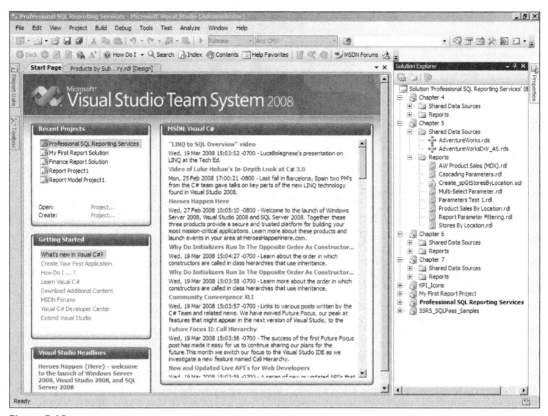

Figure 5-12

When the development environment is opened, a start page is displayed with the Visual Studio 2008 logo. The first order of business is to open an existing project or create a new one. To create a project, you can either use the File menu or the left-most button on the toolbar. When you use either of these options to create a new project, the New Project dialog is displayed (see Figure 5-13).

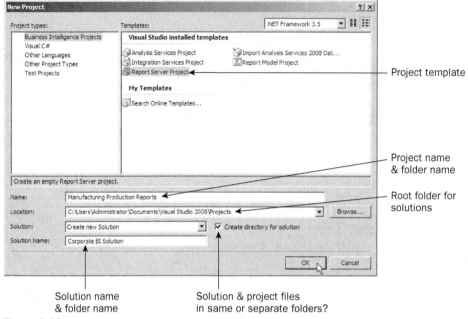

Figure 5-13

The Reporting Services installation adds a project type category to the Microsoft Integrated Development Environment called *Business Intelligence Projects*, which you see in this dialog under the "Project types" pane. Select this item to display the installed project templates in the pane on the right.

Choosing Report Server Project enables the Report Designer for the new project. Pay attention to the properties at the bottom of the New Project dialog, and enter an appropriate project name and solution name before you click the OK button. It's important to take your time with these settings because this will result in creating several folders and files. It's easier to name these correctly the first time than to go back and reorganize an existing project. By default, new solution and project folders are stored under the path in the Location field. Note that the default path is under the user-profile-specific My Documents folder. In this case, C:\Users\Administrator\Documents translates to the Documents user folder when the Administrator is logged in to this Windows Server 2008 system. If another user were logged into this computer, the Documents folder would represent a different path. Where you store your projects is up to you, but you should have a plan. Personally, I like to create a Projects folder on my C: drive and keep all the projects organized in subfolders for clients, classes, and other events. I also make it a point to name the solution and the project differently, especially if my solution will include multiple projects.

Designer Utility Windows

The Visual Studio interface, as shown in Figure 5-14, includes several utility windows that can be docked to the inside edges of the main application window or set to float independently. Each of these utility windows can be shown, hidden, or set to auto-hide when the mouse pointer is placed over an icon. This gives you access to features while maximizing report design screen real estate by moving these windows out of the way when not in use.

Solution
explorer

Report data

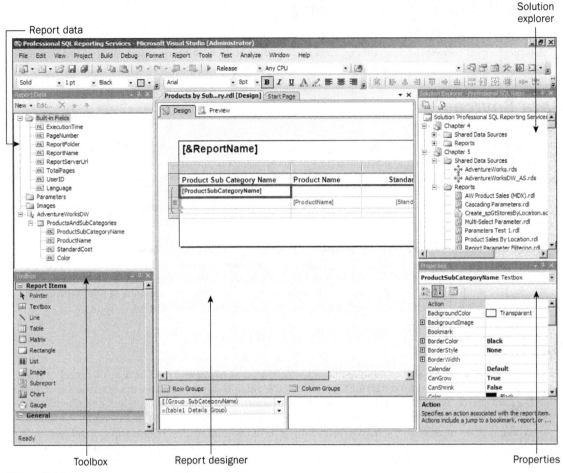

Toolbox

Report designer

Properties

Figure 5-14

The "dockable" utility windows used for report design include:

❑ **Report Data** — Tree view shows built-in fields, parameters, data sources, datasets, and fields that can be dragged into the Report Designer to assemble report design elements.

❑ **Toolbox** — Lists report items available to be added to the report design surface.

❑ **Solution Explorer** — Used to manage all projects and project files. For a report project, contains shared data sources and reports.

❑ **Properties** — Shows all the properties for the object currently selected in the Report Designer.

The tabbed Report Designer windows are located in the center. Unlike Report Builder 2.0, you can have multiple report designers open at the same time. Each has a tab that allows you to switch between them.

Report Design Elements

Reporting Services uses a modular approach, making the report design process logical and flexible. A typical report consists of data sources, datasets, a report body with headers and footers, and various report items and data regions bound to fields in a dataset — that are placed in the report body.

Data Sources

A *data source* stores connection information used to access databases or other resources that return data to a report. A data source can be either embedded into a report definition or stored as a separate file and shared among multiple reports. Shared data sources are easier to maintain in formal business environments where you have several reports using multiple database servers. If the location or name of a server changes, it will be much more convenient to modify one data source than to open and modify each report. On the other hand, it does require a little more coordination among report designers and administrative personnel.

A data source references a data provider installed on the report designer's computer and on the report server. Data providers enable connectivity to database products and may include .NET native providers, OLE DB providers, and ODBC drivers. SQL Server 2008 installs several data providers for Microsoft and third-party products that will allow reports to retrieve data from different versions of SQL Server, SQL Server Analysis Services, Microsoft Access, Oracle, XML data, and other third-party sources.

Datasets

A *dataset* is typically a query or database object reference used to retrieve a set of records for reporting. The query language used for a dataset is specific to the data provider or processing extension specified in the data source. A dataset must have only one data source. But a data source, whether embedded or shared, can serve any number of datasets. Because the query command text is processed by the data provider, queries must be in the native query language of the data source. For example, a dataset for SQL Server uses the T-SQL query language. When using an Oracle data source, the query is written in Oracle P/L SQL. For SQL Server Analysis Services, queries are written using the MDX query language.

> *Appendixes B, C, and D provide detailed information about specific T-SQL and MDX query language commands.*

Reports

There is a specific hierarchy of objects used to manage all the items and properties within a report. Keep in mind that a report definition is stored in an XML file and all the objects accessed in the Properties window relate to nested XML element tags in the XML structure of a Report Definition Language (RDL) file. The Report object contains properties related to the report itself but not the data regions on the report. These data regions are contained within the report body. Report properties are defined within these categories.

Page Setup

These properties consist of the page scale units, page orientation, height, width, and margins. The Report object also contains the following advanced properties used for adding custom internal or externally referenced programming code, which can be used to extend a report's capabilities:

❑ **Code** — Custom Visual Basic functions may be written and stored in the report and then called from expressions on any of the properties for this report.

❑ **References** — Like custom functions stored in the Code element, external code libraries may be referenced and also used in property expressions. The advantage of this approach is that a single code library may be used by multiple reports.

❑ **Variables** — Custom variables may be defined and used within the report to enable dynamic and advanced functionality. These variables are typically set and used within expressions or custom code functions in the report.

Body

The Body object contains just a few properties and serves as a container for all the data ranges and report items within the report. In the Designer, the report body really is a blank canvas on which you place report items and data ranges. This is a unique approach when comparing Reporting Services with most other reporting products. This is a very flexible approach to report design that encourages free-form report formatting and unconstrained layout. Rather than being constrained to placing items at specific rows or columns, you have the freedom to place items anywhere within the report body. Later, you'll see how the List data region extends this pattern by repeating a free-form region for each record.

Headers and Footers

As a result of the free-form approach, there is no need to designate a specific area to be the report header or footer. Essentially, the *report header* is all the space at the top of the report body before the first data range. Likewise, the space between the last data range and the end of the report body is the *report footer*.

This is because of the way a report is rendered. Like the carriage of a typewriter (or inkjet printer, for those of you who might have no idea what a typewriter is), the report is rendered from the top-left-hand corner, from left to right, and then down the page until it reaches the bottom-right corner of the report body. Any singe report items, like textboxes and images, are rendered once. Data ranges, like tables and matrices, cause rows and columns to be repeated, making the report body grow. It's really quite an elegant approach — and the area of the report body above and below these data ranges is the report header and footer, respectively.

A report, however, does have a specific area defined for the page header and page footer. In the Designer, these areas are enabled using the Header & Footer group on the Home ribbon or the Report menu in the BIDS designer.

Report Definition Language

One very compelling aspect of this product is that the definition of each report is managed in a standard, text-based file format called *Report Definition Language* (RDL). An *RDL file* is an XML document with a standard definition for markup tags that define all the properties for a report. All objects added to a report in the Report Designer and the related property settings result in entries made to the RDL content for that report. This simple approach makes it easy for independent software vendors and custom solution developers to generate a report definition from a variety of sources and tools. It also makes it easy for report designers and developers to open the report definition in a text editor to make changes outside of the Report Designer. Contrast this with the proprietary binary formats used in other popular reporting products.

As an example, the following is a small snippet of RDL file content describing a textbox report item:

```
<Textbox Name="textbox1">
  <Style>
    <PaddingLeft>2pt</PaddingLeft>
    <PaddingBottom>2pt</PaddingBottom>
    <PaddingTop>2pt</PaddingTop>
    <PaddingRight>2pt</PaddingRight>
  </Style>
  <Top>0.25in</Top>
  <rd:DefaultName>textbox1</rd:DefaultName>
  <Height>0.25in</Height>
  <Width>1in</Width>
  <CanGrow>true</CanGrow>
  <Value />
  <Left>0.375in</Left>
</Textbox>
```

The textbox described by this XML element has default padding properties of 2 points all around. It's located a quarter-inch from the top of the report body and .375 inches from the left edge. It's a quarter-inch tall and one inch wide.

Report Migration and Integration

There are now several applications and products that have the ability to create report definitions for Reporting Services. The extensible RDL allows reports to be created, converted, or modified by custom tools. For example, I've worked with products from Panorama and Cizer that provide custom report designer front-ends within their own web browser–based business intelligence reporting applications. These products put report design capabilities in front of corporate business users without installing complex desktop report authoring software.

Because RDL is simply an XML grammar, building reports can be performed programmatically with relative ease. Because of the complexities of parsing and deciphering proprietary report formats, converting existing reports from other products is more complicated. To date, there are no universal report conversion utilities on the market. Report conversion is a common request from businesses that have already invested in older, expensive reporting products and want to migrate to Reporting Services. Hitachi Consulting offers report migration as a service rather than a product for this reason. If this is an option that you or your company are considering, report migration may be more cost-effective than starting from scratch.

A point to consider is that the fundamental approach for designing reports most effectively may be quite different using different products. A "converted" report, like the one you design in another tool, may not run as efficiently or give you the flexibility to use Reporting Services to its full capability.

Report Design Elements in Detail

Report design elements — or items than can be added to the report body in the Designer — consist of data regions and report items. Technically, a *data region* is a type of report item, but we differentiate between data regions, which consume a whole dataset, and report items, which may consume a single row and field value.

Data Regions

Data regions are discussed and demonstrated in Chapter 8, "Advanced Report Design." In brief, *data regions* are used to render and display the results of an entire dataset query. The *tablix*, which can be designed to behave as a table, matrix, or list, renders rows and columns containing constituent report items. A table, for example, contains a textbox in each cell, used to display a specific row and column value.

Charts don't grow and shrink with the data but translate rows and columns into graphical form. A chart's data region can be configured to render several different standard chart presentations as row, column, line, area, pie, and radial charts, just to name a few.

Textboxes

The textbox item can be used to display data from a dataset, calculations, or expressions, or static data, much like a label control in a Windows Forms project. When you drag fields from the Fields list onto the Report Designer, data-bound textbox items are created. Common expressions can refer to a field in the report.

Figure 5-15 shows a textbox used as a label and another textbox bound to the LastName field of the report data source.

Figure 5-15

Right-click on the textbox, and select Properties from the pop-up menu to display the Text Box Properties dialog, as shown in Figure 5-16.

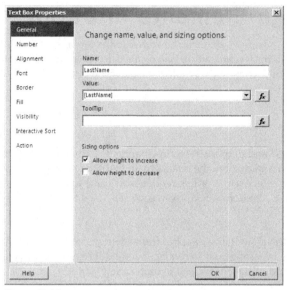

Figure 5-16

You can also view and set properties by using the standard Properties pane located to the right of the Designer. This window may be pinned down or will auto-hide by default. As in Figure 5-17, this window contains quite a bit more detail than the custom Properties window. However, the property information is not as conveniently organized. As a general rule, use the right-click Properties dialog to get to the most common properties, and use the Property pane when you need to set other properties.

Figure 5-17

Lines

Lines can be drawn in any direction and can be set to a variety of styles and colors. The properties for a line are simple and can be set using the Properties window or Designer toolbar.

It's the job of each format-rendering extension on the Report Server to use the appropriate technique to build each report element output. Because each extension creates a different output format, elements as simple as lines are output in different ways. For example, the Excel renderer will use cell borders. Some clever techniques are used to render lines in HTML. Depending on the need, lines may be rendered as table borders, as a DIV tag filled using a JavaScript function, or even using Virtual Reality Modeling Language (VRML) commands.

Rectangles

A rectangle item can have many different uses. A rectangle is simply used to visually separate a region of the report. It can be used to visually contain other items. If items such as textboxes, grids, and so on are placed into a rectangle, all these items can be moved together by simply moving the rectangle. A rectangle may also be used as a data container for data items and can be related to and repeated with a parent container.

Images

Images can be embedded into a report, linked to an external file or URL location, or obtained from a data source. Images can be of the BMP, GIF, JPEG, JPE, PNG, or X-PNG type. Adding an image in the Designer is pretty straightforward. A critical factor is that images are sized and cropped prior to being added to a report. You can resize the image in the Report Designer, but this will not result in a smaller file size. Use a graphics editing tool like the Office Picture Library, the free Paint.NET, Adobe PhotoShop, or Adobe Fireworks to resize or crop the image, and then save it to a new file. You can scale and fit an image to fit the image item container, but it's advisable to use image files that are already the correct size. This conserves disk space, improves performance, and prevents image distortion.

Dropping an image item from the Insert ribbon or Toolbox onto the report will launch the Image Properties dialog (see Figure 5-18). Select the method you want to use; the image can be from a table in the database or a file and may be linked or embedded into the report. Getting external image files to render correctly can be a bit tricky at times owing to file access permissions on the server. If in doubt, it may be easiest to either store the image in the database or embed it into the report definition.

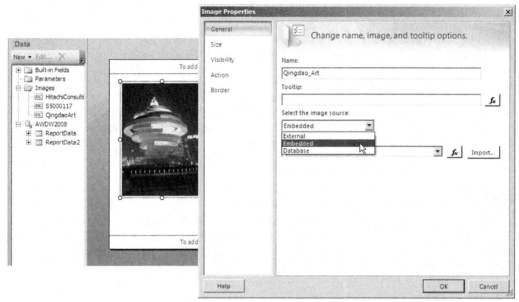

Figure 5-18

Embedded images are encoded as text and stored in the report definition file. Although this increases the size of the report definition file, it can simplify the deployment and configuration. Selecting the Database option will allow you to extract an image stored in an Image or Binary type column within a database, exposed through your dataset. The External option allows you to use a URL to reference an existing file either on the Report Server or elsewhere. If your picture data is stored in the database and the Database option is selected, the Database Field page is displayed in the Wizard. This gives you the option to derive an image file type from the image.

Generally, the JPEG format is most conservative, and PNG graphics are higher quality and more flexible. The GIF and JPEG formats are the most widely used on the Internet and are supported by all web browsers. The GIF or PNG formats support transparency If you need an image to appear non-rectangular (such as an icon and indicator graphic), set backgrounds to white over a white report area, or place the transparent image inside a rectangle item.

Subreports

A *subreport* is a container for another report embedded into a parent report. The subreport can contain practically any other report with its own, independent data source. It can optionally have its data linked to a key or value in the main report, often referred to as a *master/detail report*. Subreports are an important element in complex report designs. Figure 5-19 shows a simple report containing a master record and related detail records in the subreport.

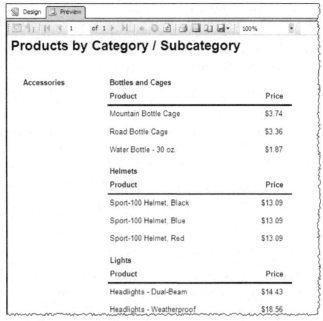

Figure 5-19

The design details of the subreport are not visible in the Designer. The report shown in Figure 5-20 is designed separately and then inserted into the main report as a subreport item.

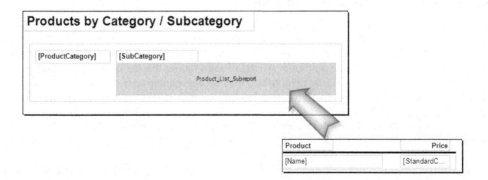

Figure 5-20

Be cautious about using subreports with large results. This report item is appropriate for embedding unrelated content within a report that is bound to a different data source or for detail rows related to few master records. Although this may be a useful technique for consolidating reusable report content, it can be very inefficient when compared with some other techniques. For example, if you create a complex query to return all related data in a single result set, a single table item may be used in place of the subreport and may prove to be more efficient. Significant improvements have been made in the 2008 product for subreport support. In addition to the inherent performance issues, rendering subreports to different formats has been problematic in the past. For example, a report containing a subreport wouldn't render correctly to an Excel workbook. Most of these types of issues have been resolved in the current product, but if you test the limits of report design and rendering, you will likely find the boundary with subreports first. As a rule, use subreports when necessary, and test them thoroughly when you need to render reports to different formats.

The Tablix

In earlier versions of Reporting Services, there were three different data range items that could be used to group data across rows or columns. The list, table, and matrix had some similar characteristics and capabilities but were three distinctly different objects, each with its own design goals, capabilities, and limitations. Shortly after the release of SQL Server 2005 Reporting Services, the product team began an effort to combine all these capabilities to create a super data-region item to replace the former list, table, and matrix items. Now, the *tablix* serves this purpose — and, yes, as the name suggests, it's a "table/matrix."

Combinations of properties will cause an instance of the tablix to behave and exhibit the characteristics of a list, a table, or a matrix. The advantage of this design is that you are no longer bound by the limitations of any one of these objects. For example, the characteristic of a table is that it has static columns that are typically bound to individual fields in the dataset. You will often define dynamic row groups that expand with each distinct field value according to the row group definition. But, if you decide, after the original design, to add a dynamic column group, this is now a possibility without having to start over with a different data range item.

During report design, you will drag a table, matrix, or list onto the report body, which creates a tablix with present row and columns with these pre-set property values.

Static and Dynamic Columns and Rows

An additional concept introduced with the tablix is that of static and dynamic columns and rows. A *static column or row* is a band of cells with an associated field expression. Take a row group, for example; for records in the dataset, as long as the group expression's field value remains the same, this causes only one instance of the row group to be rendered. All detail rows below this grouping may either be displayed as lower-level detail rows, or field values may be aggregated at the group level. Previous versions of the matrix have always treated columns in this way. Now, in the Tablix, a column may be inserted at any position and designated to behave as a static column (without grouping) or as a dynamic (or grouped) column. By taking this approach, the Tablix has more flexibility than the previous table, list, or matrix data regions.

When the row group spits out a new distinct value, a new row for the group will be rendered, perhaps with lower-detail rows under it or with values to be rolled up and aggregated for inclusion in the row.

By far, the majority of report designers will not concern themselves with adding dynamic columns to change the natural order of things and contend with the delicate balance of a happily working table or matrix, which is why each of these fine, preconfigured items — the table, matrix, and list — stands alone in both Designers. As far as we are concerned, a table is a table, and a matrix is a matrix.

On the off chance that you are brave enough to contend with the natural order of things and rewire a table so that it behaves somewhat like a list or a matrix, this could get interesting. The practical use for these concepts will make more sense as we apply them to an understandable business case.

Row Groups in a Table

A table has a static list of columns — one for each field — and rows are either grouped on a field value or simply output one per row from the dataset. Any number of row groups may be added to a single row, and a row can have no row groups, one, or any number of row groups. This provides a tremendous amount of flexibility to table design. Compared with Reporting Services in SQL Server 2000 and 2005, the model has changed, but the same design patterns are reproducible, with even more options.

The example report shown in Figure 5-21 has row headers with simplified field labels. Five columns are used to return values for the Year, Category, Product, Order Quantity, and Extended Amount fields, respectively. Note that in the Designer, three row groups are defined by dragging fields into the Row Groups pane in the lower-left-hand corner of the Designer window.

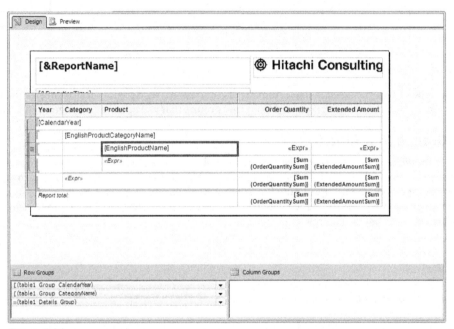

Figure 5-21

Figure 5-22 shows the first page of this report in Preview mode. Note that the 2001 year header precedes the Accessories category, and then three products are listed before a subtotal row for this category.

Year	Category	Product	Order Quantity	Extended Amount
2001				
	Accessories			
		Sport-100 Helmet, Black	331	$6,681.73
		Sport-100 Helmet, Blue	353	$7,118.43
		Sport-100 Helmet, Red	319	$6,439.49
		Accessories total:	*1,003*	*$20,239.66*
	Bikes			
		Mountain-100 Black, 38	312	$630,178.13
		Mountain-100 Black, 42	297	$600,613.22
		Mountain-100 Black, 44	315	$636,320.61
		Mountain-100 Black, 48	273	$552,823.36
		Mountain-100 Silver, 38	289	$589,558.27
		Mountain-100 Silver, 42	263	$535,566.42
		Mountain-100 Silver, 44	268	$545,086.40

Product Sales by Year by Category Table   ◎ **Hitachi Consulting**

Figure 5-22

When this type of report is used, a fixed number of columns are rendered. In this example, the five columns are fixed, but rows are generated from row groups that can span many pages in the final report.

Column Groups in a Matrix

A *matrix* is simply a table with dynamically grouped columns — so that each distinct group value outputs a new column. The example shown in Figure 5-23 uses the same query to output groups of data in the same order. Note the groups defined in the Row Groups and Column Groups panes at the bottom of the Designer window. The difference between this and the previous report is that the CalendarYear group is on columns rather than rows.

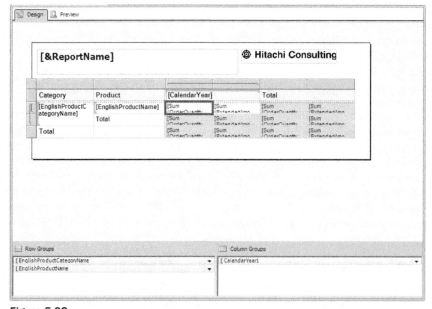

Figure 5-23

When this report is previewed, column headers are generated for each year, and then rows are generated for the category and product field values. Figure 5-24 shows the first page of this report.

Product Sales by Year by Category Matrix				⊕ Hitachi Consulting		
Category	Product		2001		2002	
Accessories	Sport-100 Helmet, Black	331	$6,682	1,279	$25,189	1,967
	Sport-100 Helmet, Blue	363	$7,118	1,365	$26,822	2,035
	Sport-100 Helmet, Red	319	$6,439	1,186	$23,298	1,810
	Cable Lock			676	$10,105	410
	Minipump			701	$8,363	429
	Bike Wash - Dissolver					1,461
	Hitch Rack - 4-Bike					1,721
	Hydration Pack - 70 oz.					1,291
	Patch Kit/8 Patches					458
	Water Bottle - 30 oz.					1,554
	Total	1,003	$20,240	5,207	$93,797	13,136
Bikes	Mountain-100 Black, 38	312	$630,178	321	$566,526	
	Mountain-100 Black, 42	297	$600,613	292	$520,423	
	Mountain-100 Black, 44	315	$636,321	303	$545,061	
	Mountain-100 Black, 48	273	$552,823	286	$507,092	

Figure 5-24

Chart Essentials

In 2007, Microsoft acquired the latest generation of charting gauge components from Dundas Data Visualization, Inc., the company that originally developed the charting components that were integrated into Reporting Services for SQL Server 2000. The result is that in SQL Server 2008, several new chart types were added, along with many new charting features and capabilities. This is a very capable and easy-to-use charting solution with a variety of available chart types.

Data Aggregation

Numeric data values are always aggregated, usually using the SUM() function, along axis groups. This grouping and aggregation is functionally similar to a matrix, with aggregated values representing the intersection points of distinct group values. The difference is that a chart plots or visualizes the values rather than displaying the number in a cell.

Series Groups

The *series group* is the axis associated with the chart's legend, if you choose to include it. In a column chart, for example, series values are displayed in the legend and/or column clusters.

Category Groups

Category groups are the labeled group values that are usually represented with a single column, point, or bar. In a column chart, categories are plotted along the X-axis with labels typically along the bottom of the chart.

Chart Type Categories

There are now many different types of charts available. Following are most of the categories and all the essential charts used in basic report design. Some of the advanced charts are showcased in later chapters to demonstrate more advanced features.

Column Charts

Probably the most common and most recognizable chart type is the column chart. The example in Figure 5-25 shows sales data for a given year, grouped by quarter and the sales territory country. The total sales amount is plotted on the category or Y-axis (columns) of the chart.

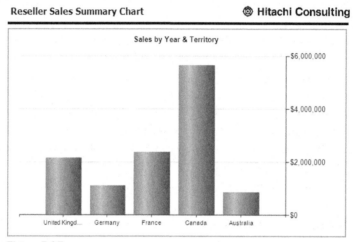

Figure 5-25

Adding a group to the series axis can cause the column chart to show a cluster of columns side by side. The columns are color-coded with a color key shown in the legend. Figure 5-26 shows a category group based on the CalendarYear field with a cluster of two columns. Column clusters may be displayed in a flattened, two-dimensional view like this or arranged along the Z-axis when three-dimensional (3D) visualizations are enabled. Figure 5-27 shows the same chart in 3D mode.

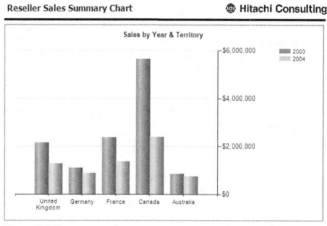

Figure 5-26

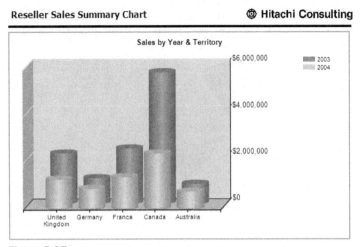

Figure 5-27

One of the powerful features of the chart item is the ability to group data within each axis. Figure 5-28 shows a simple column chart with two field groups on the X-axis, representing related categories. In this example, columns are grouped by calendar year and then by the sales territory country.

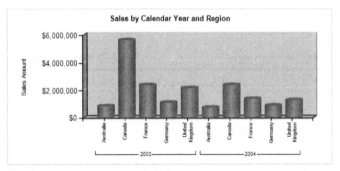

Figure 5-28

A number of these features — including multiple axes, clustering, and nested groups — can be combined to create some interesting and compelling chart visualizations.

Some charts require only one axis group. For example, the pie chart shown in Figure 5-29 uses only a series group, based on the SalesTerritoryRegion field. Pie charts put proportional values into perspective. This type of chart comes in two pastry types: pie and doughnut. Values are presented visually as a percentage of the total for all values in a series. Pie and doughnut chart views may be either *simple* or *exploded*. The exploded presentation may help to visually separate values, especially the smaller slices. These types of charts can be useful for placing values into comparative perspective.

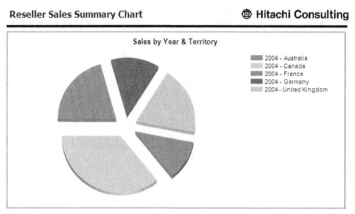

Figure 5-29

All the chart types discussed so far existed in the SQL Server 2000 and 2005 versions of Reporting Services. Following are just a few of the newer chart types introduced in the 2008 product.

Polar and Radar Charts

Figure 5-30 shows one of these new charts. This is a radar chart, one of the new and polar chart types in the new product. This is an interesting visualization that combines elements of a line chart with a pie chart-like format.

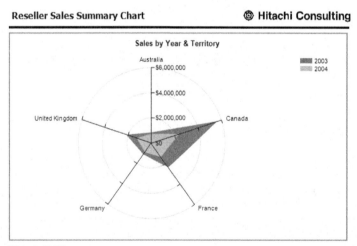

Figure 5-30

Shape Charts

Some special-purpose charts are commonly used to visualize data for certain vertical applications. For example, the funnel chart, shown in Figure 5-31, is commonly used as an illustration of customer sales leads "flowing down" through the funnel in customer relationship management (CRM) solutions, to help manage a sales opportunity pipeline.

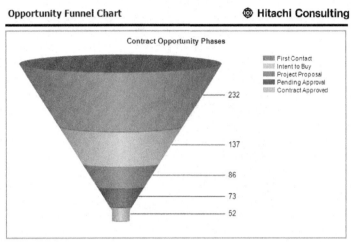

Figure 5-31

Figure 5-32 shows another unique shape-type chart that expresses data values in a pyramid. This is commonly used for organizational ranking and progression.

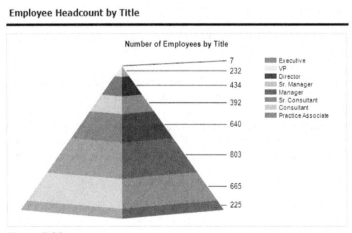

Figure 5-32

Bar Charts

Bar charts and column charts are pretty much the same in functionality. You can tilt your head to the side to get the same view as the other. Figure 5-33 shows the same data from the previous column chart, in a bar chart. When this chart type is chosen, category group values are visualized with values plotted on the Y-axis and the value scale along the X-axis — a 90-degree rotation of the same column chart.

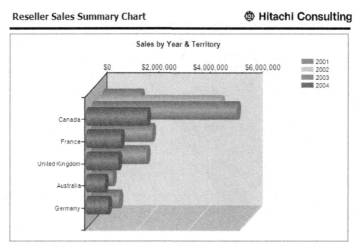

Figure 5-33

In addition to the standard, single-bar view, the stacked view provides a consolidated look at a series of values by using fewer bars or columns. Each bar is like a mini pie chart, where each value in the bar's range is in proportion to the others. A series of related values is stacked in the column to show the aggregate sum of values and their proportional values. A variation, the 100 percent stacked bar or chart, displays each bar with the same height or length as others, regardless of the total values. This type of chart is useful for comparing values within the bar's range but not for comparing the aggregates represented by each bar.

There are many chart variations and special chart types that are not pictured here. Some of the more advanced chart implementations are covered in Chapters 8 and 10.

In addition to the standard report items that ship with the product, application developers and third-party companies can create custom report items (CRI) that can be installed and used in the Designer. You are likely to see more CRI suites for Reporting Services that will add even more capabilities to your reports.

Gauges

Humans have been measuring things for a long time, and we use a lot of different ways to keep track of things like air and water pressure, speed, torque, and temperature. Whether using a ruler, meter stick, progress bar, or the dashboard of a car, we are all accustomed to using a variety of standard gauges. In the right situations, gauges are an ideal visualization for business data using a familiar display metaphor. Many users will immediately identify with important information displayed using a variety of linear and radial gauge indicators that apply context and importance to measurements, status indicators, and business metrics. The new gauge report items introduced in Reporting Services 2008 enable you to control virtually every aspect of gauges, including background colors and shading, borders, scales, pointers, and markers. Practically any characteristic you've seen in a physical gauge or meter is possible. You can even reproduce the tachometer and speedometer in a Mercedes S550, the pressure value on a fire extinguisher, or the Sick Bay vital sign monitors in the Star Ship Enterprise.

Although there are many properties, most are fairly easy to work with and to discover with just a little bit of guidance. Figure 5-34 shows the chart types dialog, which provides a thumbnail preview of all the available gauge types.

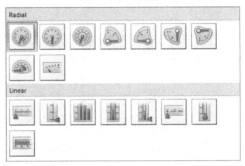

Figure 5-34

When I started working with the Dundas Gauges product a few years ago, before it was integrated into Reporting Services as a standard feature, I spent several hours configuring the interface to get each one just right, simply because this tool gave me so much control. I warn you that this cool new report capability can lead to late night obsessive report design if you have a propensity toward design perfection.

Like the new chart data range, a single gauge can contain several gauge areas. This essentially lets you create an entire dashboard with one gauge item. Each gauge area has its own scales, pointers, ranges, and markers.

Scales

The *scale* is the set of markers and reference numbers around the dial of a radial gauge or along the range of a linear gauge. Any number of scales can be added to a single gauge.

Pointers and Markers

In a radial gauge, pointers are typically needles and arrows or small "tick" marks that can extend from the center of the gauge and point to a scale, or simply indicate certain points on a scale. Several pre-set pointers and markers are available in different shapes. Each can be resized and, like every other element, can be set with solid or gradient shading.

Ranges

Ranges typically are used to provide some sort of context and are typically displayed on or near the scale, behind pointers and markers. A range can be used to indicate that a value is within acceptable or exceptional boundaries. Ranges can be color-coded, tapered, or shaded with solid or gradient fills.

Radial Gauges

Radial gauges can be circular or partially circular, with one or more pointers extending from a central fulcrum. The simplest form of gauge, shown in Figure 5-35, has a single scale and pointer. The maximum scale value in this example is set with an expression to indicate the total number of sales units for a calendar year. The pointer value gets its value from an expression to show the total units in a quarter, thus showing the proportion of the quarter units to the year.

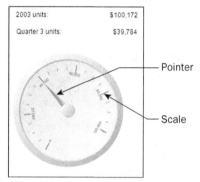

Figure 5-35

Figure 5-36 shows an example of the same gauge with a second pointer added. The larger arrow pointer indicates units sold for the quarter, and the smaller pointer shows units for the month on the same scale as the previous example.

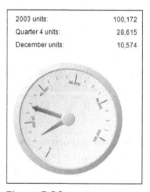

Figure 5-36

Linear Gauges

Linear gauges can be arranged vertically or horizontally in a variety of formats. Markers are typically used in the place of radial pointers but behave in much the same way. The example in Figure 5-37 shows a linear gauge with a single marker. This gauge has three color-coded ranges, which are used to indicate threshold values along the scale.

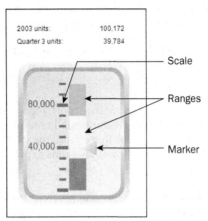

Figure 5-37

Gauges become very useful when they are used to compare a group of related values side by side. For example, Figure 5-38 shows a composite report designed by embedding a single gauge into a tablix with repeating columns.

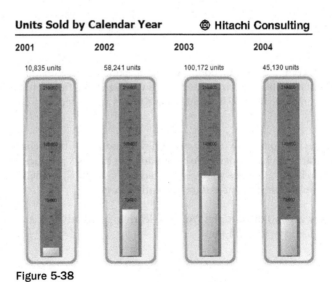

Figure 5-38

Summary

In this chapter, you learned about the essentials of report design and were introduced to the report building blocks. You were introduced to the report design tools, which include Report Builder 2.0, for information workers to create their own ad hoc and server-hosted reports. For the corporate information technology staff, you also learned how advanced report design capabilities continue to be part of the Microsoft integrated development environment, through Business Intelligence Development Studio and Visual Studio. These tools allow application developers and solution teams to share report source code and manage reports as part of a business intelligence project or corporate solution.

You saw how the Report Wizard is used to create a simple report. Like the other report design tools, this defines a report as an RDL file. The visual report design tools provide a graphical user environment to manage the objects and properties in an RDL file.

You learned that the building blocks of a report are the report, report body, data regions, and report items. This modular object approach provides greater flexibility to report design and management. Report items such as a textbox contain properties that control the value and formatting of report data and content. Nearly all properties can be set using expressions to provide dynamic behavior and formatting.

The tablix is the new replacement for the data regions in previous Reporting Services versions. This one object provides greater flexibility and capabilities than the old table, matrix, and list. The Report Designer offers these three objects as predefined instances of the tablix data region, used to present entire sets of data returned from dataset queries.

A table is used to present grouped rows of columnar data — where columns correspond to query fields, and rows are rendered from the records returned from a data table or query. These values may be grouped, with separate headers, footers, and subtotals. The matrix is a pivot table and, like a table, renders grouped rows with headers and summaries. But a matrix also groups values into columns, which may also be summarized. A list is a simple data region that repeats a section of the report based on a row grouping. It is typically used to repeat other data regions or report items presented in a free-form layout.

Subreports allow you to combine the functionality of an existing report into another report. This makes it easy to combine prebuilt reports into composite reports with reusable functionality. Using a list or other data region, a subreport may be used to integrate data sources and to federate data into repeating groups and sections.

The new charting engine includes many new capabilities including multiple chart areas — used to create composite charts. Several new chart types have been added in the 2008 product, making this a much more powerful tool than before. Gauges were also added to the toolbox, enabling compelling new visualizations and options to present linear data in creative ways.

The chapters that follow expand these topics. You will learn to build advanced reporting solutions using the elements discussed in this chapter.

6

Report Layout and Formatting

You have numerous options for presenting information in a report. One of the most important factors in report design is to understand these options and to provide an appropriate report layout to meet the needs of your users and their business requirements.

This chapter will introduce the features of report layout and formatting in the following areas. For most of these features, I will provide brief instructions to implement that feature and show some examples:

❑   Basic report layout types, including the table, matrix, list, and chart reports

❑   Page layout options for tabular, matrix, list, chart, dashboard, and composite reports

❑   Report navigation features

❑   Formatting properties for visually enhancing various reports

❑   Pagination control

Over the years in some industries, we have been presenting data the same way for a long time. I think this is the case for a variety of reasons. The primary reason is that many of us started out using restrictive tools that only provided limited options. Another reason is that the business community has become accustomed to doing things the same way for a long time, even if there might be a better way. I've become a firm believer in getting the requirements at the beginning of a project. This way, we know up front what kind of reports we are designing, and what a report should and shouldn't do. This chapter is about report design options and the elements you will use in later report design.

I like to shake things up sometimes, and I think change can be a healthy thing in business. But we also need to maintain some consistency. For some of your users, the reports you create will be their lifeline to important business information. The manner in which you present data may affect business decisions and the way people go about doing their jobs. When I start a report project or a new set of reports, I try to carefully consider these factors and take the time to show users and business leaders a selection of report layout options and then discuss the pros and cons of each option, to decide which are most appropriate and valuable to the people who will be using them.

Your challenge as a report designer is to find the best way to present information to business users so that it's logical, makes sense, and is appealing and readable. The right format for your business users may be different for someone in a different industry, culture, or discipline.

I learned an important lesson a few years ago when I was asked to design a set of reports for a large, commercial airplane manufacturer. The users were all structural and aerospace engineers, and they had been using the same, static, mono-spaced, spreadsheet-like reports for ages. I decided to add some flair to the new reports with charts and graphics. I made them colorful and attractive. I made a point to use different font sizes and weights. I added background shading and borders. Proud of the updated design, I created a standard report template with the company colors and logo in the report header, as I had for other clients in the past. When the users saw the first report, they immediately shot them down and complained about the "fluff" and "pretty pictures." In their rigid, engineering world, data is a serious matter and shouldn't be dressed up and decorated. At the request of our project sponsor, I took out the graphics and embellishments and changed all the text to one size of Courier New. They were elated with the design.

Report Layout Types

Report layout can be boiled down to a few, simple design patterns. These simple styles also can be combined with others to form composite reports and more advanced layout to visualize data. This section offers a quick review of the report layout types, followed by some examples.

Tabular Reports

Tabular reports have been around for thousands of years. Well, they may not have been reports in the modern sense, but when you think about it, some common reports are really little more than "lists of stuff" organized into rows and columns. Ever since early merchants began trading seashells or precious gems for beaver pelts or goat cheese, someone was recording the transaction in some kind of list, be it on papyrus, stone tablets, or a tablet PC.

Ever since VisiCalc, the predecessor to Lotus 123 and Microsoft Excel, was released in 1981, the tabular spreadsheet format has become the way many computer users are accustomed to viewing business data. For decades, the only printed reports available from mainframe and midrange computer systems were green-bar reports printed on pin-fed, fan-folded "greenbar" paper in classic spreadsheet style.

In Reporting Services for SQL Server 2000 and 2005, Tabular reports were defined using the Table data range item. In addition to the repeating detail rows, data can be grouped on various fields, and each group can have headers, footers, breaks, and subtotals. Tabular reports have a finite number of columns, typically representing the fields in a database table.

Matrix Reports

Tabular reports can be fine for logging detailed transactions and lists, but business reporting is often about summarizing information for analysis and to provide context to all the numbers and listed items. This is often best done by rolling up the details along groups and hierarchies and then viewing the aggregate totals, rather than the details. A matrix, cross-tab, or pivot report aggregates data along the X-axis and Y-axis of a grid to form a summarized table. The most unique characteristic of a matrix is that columns are not static but are based on grouped values. Both rows and column groups may be multilevel hierarchies, and there may be an infinite number of grouped members on rows and columns.

A matrix is most useful for viewing aggregated values along two different dimensional hierarchies, such as time and geography. For example, a product sales summary report might show aggregated sales with years and months on the columns axis and then the customers' countries and regions along the rows axis. At the intersection of each member along each axis, a cell displays the summarized product sales for that time and geography. For example, a single cell might represent the total sales for April of 2008 in Berlin, Germany.

List Reports

A List report consists of a single, rectangular detail area that repeats for every record or group value in the underlying dataset. If you think about it, a list is a simplified table of sorts, but it has no headers with only one column and only one detail row. The main purpose of the list data region is to contain other related data regions and report items, and to repeat them for a group of values. A chart, table, matrix, and any combination of textboxes or images can be repeated as a group for every record or distinct group value returned by a query.

Because the table, list, and matrix had similar characteristics, all three have been combined into one designer object in the 2008 product, called the *tablix*. The capabilities and unique behaviors of each of these three reporting paradigms are made possible by enabling different group types and properties.

Chart Reports

Behold, the mighty chart — no longer an exception, but very much the rule for expressing aggregated data values for comparison and trending. Column and line charts have become a natural medium to visualize a series of data in a meaningful and intuitive way. We've grown accustomed to seeing charts on the stock page of the newspaper, and on the home page of our news portal site, showing gas prices and housing market data. And, of course, we expect to see charts in the executive board room, used to explain the latest widget sales trends.

The nice thing about charts is that they provide visual context for a lot of different kinds of data. When used appropriately, the right chart types can tell a complex and important story with very little explanation required. Your challenge is to choose the right type of charts to visualize data in the most meaningful way for your users. In addition to the typical set of column, bar, line, point, and pie charts, you have a huge array of specialized chart types at your disposal.

Gauge Reports and Dashboards

The term *dashboard reports* gets tossed around loosely these days, often without much qualification. Although different people may not be able to clearly define exactly what a Dashboard report is or is not, I think the essential concept is quite clear. Think of the dashboard in your car. Its purpose is not to provide deep and detailed analysis of your car's performance. If it did, there would be more road accidents because of distracted drivers. No, the purpose of a dashboard is to provide a quick, at-a-glance status of important metrics. All you really need to know is if your speed is in an acceptable range, whether the engine is revving too little or too much, if the oil and water are too hot or too cold, and whether you have enough gas to get to the office for that meeting in 10 minutes (or if you're going to have to make your presentation to the CEO by phone with your hand cautiously cupped over your cell phone at the filling station).

Dashboard reports are the same — important information available at a glance. Everyone knows how to read a simple gauge, so why not use the same gauge visualizations as those we're accustomed to using in the car or on the machines on the production floor? Actually, there are several tangible gauge-type metaphors that are very appropriate in business, and the great thing about using these components is that when a business user sees a thermometer, VU meter, dial, or partially full cylinder, they immediately understand its meaning.

Composite Reports

The layout types discussed above are more than a set of finite report design options. These report items and data range objects can be used as building blocks to assemble more complex and compelling report solutions.

Once you have the basics down, you can combine the report design and layout elements to create more advanced and compelling reports. Different report items and data ranges can be embedded into a data range to repeat the data visualization within the scope of a group row or column. We'll explore techniques used to combine report items in Chapters 8 and 10.

Page Layout

Let's discuss some important information you need to understand before you move on. These examples were created on a computer configured with US/English regional settings. As a result, all of the scaling units are set to inches. If your computer is configured for another culture or regional setting, your environment may use metric units.

It's also important to understand how a report fits onto a page. The report content fits onto a design element called the *body*. The report defines the page for printing and displaying purposes with associated margins. The relationship between these two design elements will be discussed shortly.

Different scaling units — such as inches, points, pixels, and metric scale units — can be used for the report, body, and margins and control size measurements. The Designer will automatically use either inches ("in") or centimeters ("cm"), depending on the current locale setting in Windows. The following examples use inches, with the default "US letter 8.5in × 11in" page size. If you are using metric units or a different page size, it should be a simple matter to make the appropriate adjustments. For example, if you are designing reports for A4 paper, the report width and height would be set to "21.0cm" and "29.7cm," respectively.

By default, the Report Designer is only 5 inches wide, and the grid containing the fields partially fills this space. You need to make some adjustments to use the available space.

You should be able to use all of the available space to fill your target page size. Apply the following formula to calculate the report page width:

```
Report Width = Body Width + Left Margin + Right Margin
```

You can set the report size by either resizing the report body in the Designer with the mouse or by setting the Height and Width values in the Properties window. Although it usually makes sense to match the report size to the paper size for printed reports, the report width can be set as wide as 160 inches.

If you are using Report Builder 2.0, you will need to enable the Property pane from the View ribbon. If you are using Business Intelligence Development Studio (BIDS), the Properties window should be visible by default. If not, select it from the View menu.

Click on the report background, and view the Properties window (either right-click and choose Properties, or just click the Properties tab on the right side of the Designer). Verify that *Body* is displayed in the dropdown list at the top of the Properties window. Now, click the small plus sign next to Size to expand this item and set the properties, as shown in Figure 6-1.

Figure 6-1

To set the report margins, click outside the report body. You should see the Report displayed in the Properties window. Expand the Margins item. Change the Left, Right, Top, and Bottom margins, as shown in Figure 6-2.

Figure 6-2

Here's a quick review: The report body contains the actual report content. This area must fit within the area defined for a page of the report.

Using the Properties window, set the report dimensions to be 8.5 inches wide by 11.0 inches tall, with the left and right margins set to 0.25 inches each. This leaves 8.0 inches of available width for the report body. To use all this horizontal space for report data, set the body to be 8.0 inches wide.

Designing Tabular Reports

We're all familiar with the Tabular report style because it resembles a paper ledger. Tabular reports have been around for many years and are still the mainstay for many business units because of their simplicity. Tabular, or table-like, reports have a fixed number of columns that typically correspond to static fields in the underlying data source — like a spreadsheet or grid.

Beyond a simple list of records, Tabular reports can be grouped with headers, footers, and subtotals for each band of grouped records. Grouping is performed on one or more column values, with group values either repeated on each row, appearing only once in the grouped field column, or appearing only in the group header. Aggregated values for numeric columns may be displayed in the group header or footer. Aggregation is performed using one of several aggregate functions, such as SUM or AVG. Some aggregations can be used with non-numeric columns, such as COUNT or COUNTDISTINCT.

Chapter 7 covers the details of data access. Just to get you started, I'll step quickly through the process of creating a simple data-set query using one of the sample databases provided for SQL Server 2008. Whether you choose to use Business Intelligence Development Studio or Report Builder 2.0, the process is the same, and there are only subtle differences in the tool interface. If you are unfamiliar with these tools, I recommend that you use the new Report Builder 2.0 to follow along. If you have been using Reporting Services in earlier versions of SQL Server, you may use the BIDS Designer instead.

Place a table on the report body. Using Report Builder 2.0, select the Insert tab, and then click Table on the ribbon (see Figure 6-3). In Business Intelligence Development Studio, a table is added from the toolbox.

Figure 6-3

You will need to repeat the following steps for creating a data source and dataset in the report design examples for a matrix and chart that follow. I'll step through them here but will not repeat these steps for each example.

Since the new report didn't previously contain a dataset and data source, a dialog opens to define these objects. Using the Data Source Properties window, enter a name for the new data source (see Figure 6-4). I'm calling this data source *AWDW2008*, which is an abbreviated form of the database name: AdventureWorksDW2008, the sample data warehouse database available for SQL Server 2008. Enter the data source name, and then click the Edit button to create the data source connection string.

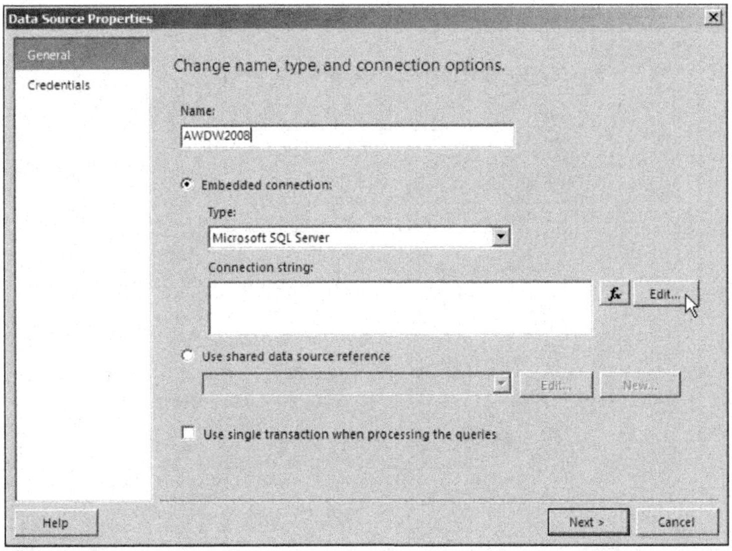

Figure 6-4

The Connection Properties dialog, shown in Figure 6-5, is used to build a connection string. Leave the default Data Source set to Microsoft SQL Server (SqlClient).

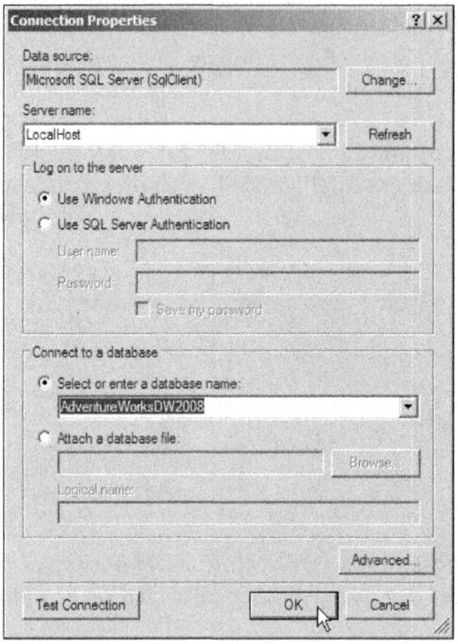

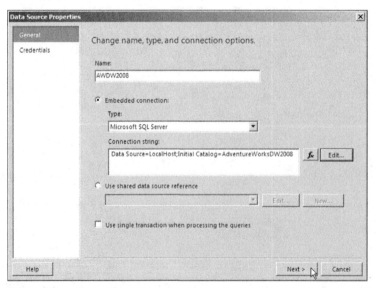

Figure 6-5

For the Server Name property, type **localhost** or the name of your database server. In the section titled "Connect to a database," click the dropdown list button, and select the AdventureWorksDW2008 database. Click OK to accept these settings and close this dialog.

You should notice that the "Connection string" property has been set in the Data Source Properties dialog, as shown in Figure 6-6. Click Next to accept this and move forward.

Figure 6-6

Chapter 7 will cover query design in detail. Our present task is to focus on report design, so for this and the following report examples, I'll just provide a query string for you to type in the Query Designer window.

Type the following T-SQL script into the Query Designer, as shown in Figure 6-7. Note that carriage returns, tabs and leading spaces aren't critical:

```
SELECT CalendarYear, SalesTerritoryRegion, SalesAmount
FROM
        FactResellerSales AS F INNER JOIN DimDate AS D
        ON F.OrderDateKey = D.DateKey
        INNER JOIN DimSalesTerritory AS ST
        ON F.SalesTerritoryKey = ST.SalesTerritoryKey
ORDER BY CalendarYear, SalesTerritoryRegion
```

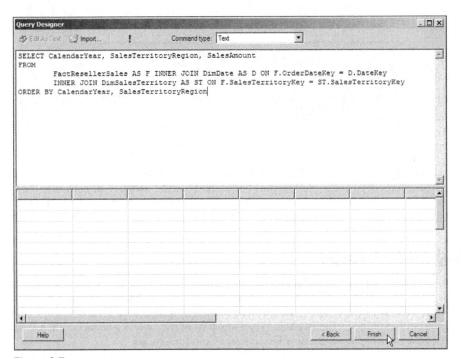

Figure 6-7

You can test the query by using the Run button (the red exclamation mark icon). If you typed the query script correctly, results are displayed in the grid below; otherwise, an error will be reported. Click Finish to complete the process and save the new dataset.

Remember that the Data Source Properties dialog popped up when you added a table to the report. Now that you've finished adding the dataset, you'll see that the table has been placed in the top-left corner of the report body. You can move the table by clicking and dragging the repositioning handle, as shown in Figure 6-8. Objects in the Designer will automatically snap to align with other objects on the report body.

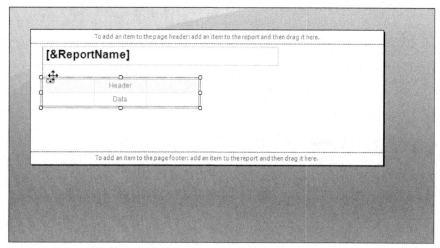

Figure 6-8

If you are designing the report in BIDS, either drag the table item from the toolbar or click once and draw the table wherever you like on the report body. Fields can be dropped directly into the table cells from the data window, or a list of fields is provided when you click in a table cell. If you need to group on any field values, hold off on dragging these fields into the table.

Defining Table Groups

Groups are used throughout Reporting Services and are useful in many ways. A significant change has been made from the 2000 and 2005 versions of Reporting Services in the way that groups are created and managed. The SQL Server 2008 report design environment now uses field drop zones to define groups located at the bottom of the Designer pane. When any part of the table is selected in the Designer, separate list boxes are displayed for Row Groups and Column Groups.

In earlier product versions, each table group was used to define a separate group header row or footer row. Although this pattern is still possible, multiple groups can now be defined on the same row with separate headers that don't take up additional row space.

In this example, you'll be grouping the rows of this table on the CalendarYear and then the SalesTerritoryRegion fields. Note that, by default, a DetailsGroup item is displayed in the Row Groups list. This is a placeholder for fields to include at the detail level of this table. To add the CalendarYear field as a group at a level above the details row, drag and drop this field from the Data window to above the DetailsGroup item in the Row Groups list, as shown in Figure 6-9.

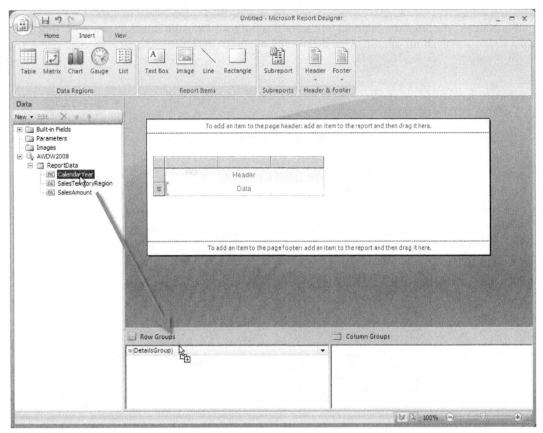

Figure 6-9

A new group is created for the CalendarYear field that appears above the DetailsGroup item in the Row Groups list.

To add the second group, drag the SalesTerritoryRegion field from the Data window to the Row Groups list, just below the CalendarYear and above the DetailsGroup, as shown in Figure 6-10.

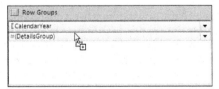

Figure 6-10

Measure values typically appear on each detail row and are then summarized in header or footer rows. In this example, the SalesAmount field will serve this purpose. Drag the SalesAmount field from the Data window to the third column in the details row, as shown in Figure 6-11.

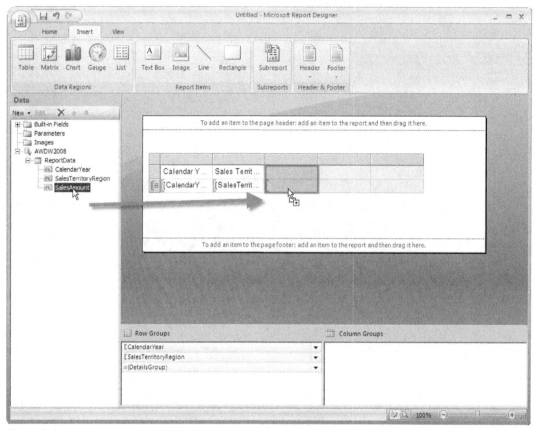

Figure 6-11

Group Expressions and Options

By dragging and dropping fields into the Row Groups list, you automatically add group definitions to the tablix. If you have used the table data region in prior versions of Reporting Services, you'll recall that this required a few more steps. If you need to modify a group or define specific properties, you can do so using the Tablix Group Properties dialog. To do this, in the Designer, select any part of the table to enable the Row Groups list. Clicking the down arrow on any row group will enable the menu. From this menu, select Edit Group to display the Tablix Group Properties dialog, as shown in Figure 6-12. (I've edited the CalendarYear in the dialog.)

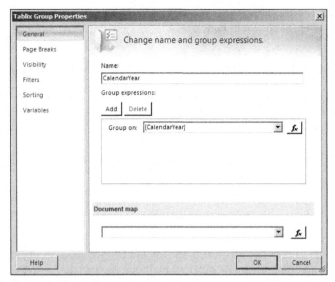

Figure 6-12

These properties are covered in later chapters that explore more advanced design patterns. Keep in mind that this is where a lot of the magic happens. The following steps are used to dress up the report. Start with the font weight and background color of the table header. Select the table header by clicking the row selection handle for the header row (see Figure 6-13). Any property buttons enabled in the ribbon or items in the properties window will be applied to all cells in the selected row as you apply formatting to the table values in the following steps.

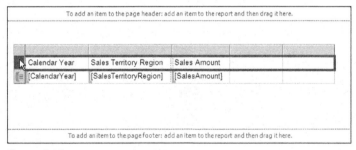

Figure 6-13

Formatting Table Values

Values in a table are formatted using the properties of constituent report items. Since each cell contains a textbox, property settings are applied to each textbox, including the background color, foreground color, font style, size, weight, and number formatting. On the Home ribbon, click the Bold icon to set the header text to be bold. Use the background fill bucket icon to show a color palette, and then choose a tan background for the header, as shown in Figure 6-14.

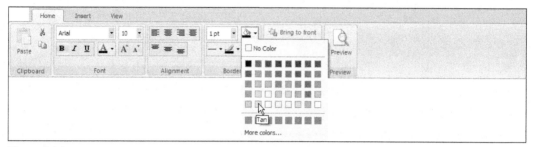

Figure 6-14

The SalesAmount field is a currency type value and should be formatted appropriately. Text formatting is set for each textbox, and there are a few different methods you can use to do this, including using the Properties pane window to set the Format property and the right-click menu in the following step. Right-click on the SalesAmount textbox, and then choose Textbox Properties, as shown in Figure 6-15.

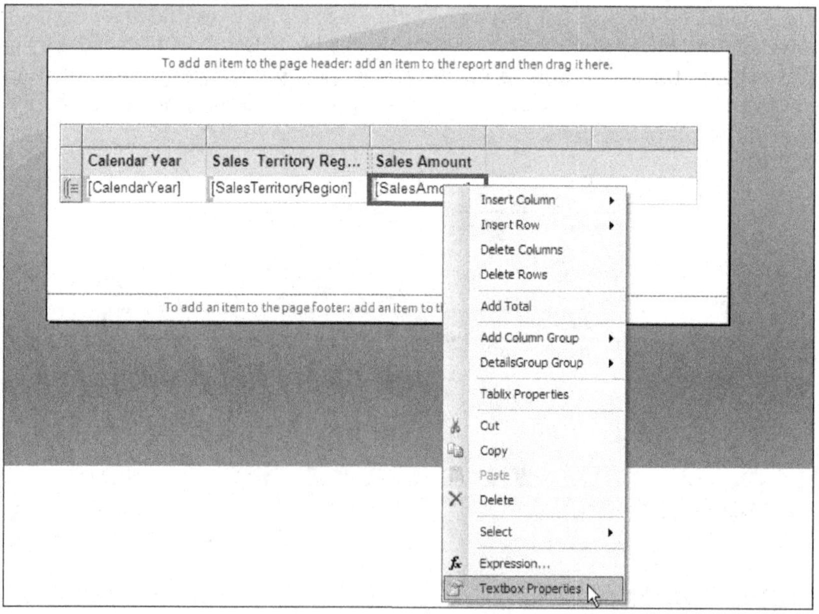

Figure 6-15

The Text Box Properties dialog, shown in Figure 6-16, contains a list of property categories on the left side. Selecting Number displays several numeric formatting options. Select Currency, and then check the box indicating that you want to include a thousands separator. Click OK to apply these settings and return to the Designer.

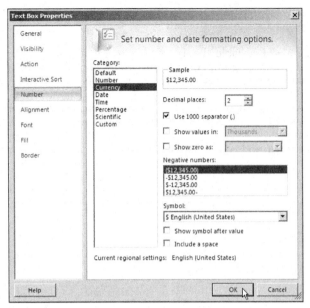

Figure 6-16

You'll recall that when the table was added to the report body, it contained three blank columns. Adding the two groups created two new columns, and dragging the SalesAmount field occupied one of the empty columns. You are left with two empty columns that need to be deleted. The best way to do this is to drag the mouse across both of the blank column headers and then right-click to show the menu shown in Figure 6-17. Choose Delete Columns to remove the columns from the table.

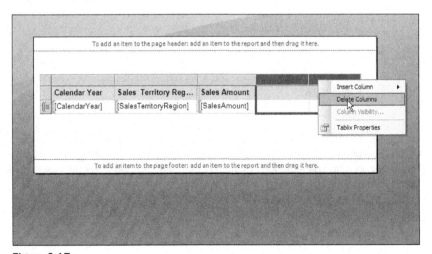

Figure 6-17

Now pause to take a look at the report so far. Using the Preview button on the Home ribbon, the report is rendered and displayed.

The report shows a detail record for every row returned by the query. With this level of detail, the report has over 1,300 pages! Switch back to design view.

By grouping the detail rows of the table, the size of the report will be reduced by summarizing the Sales Amount for each record within the group. In the Row Groups pane located on the bottom, left side of the report designer. Click the down arrow next to the (Details) group and choose Group Properties . . .

In the Group Properties dialog, use the Add button to add a group expression and select the SalesTerritoryRegion field. Click the OK button to accept the change.

Now preview the report again and you will see that the report is significantly shorter, as shown in Figure 6-18.

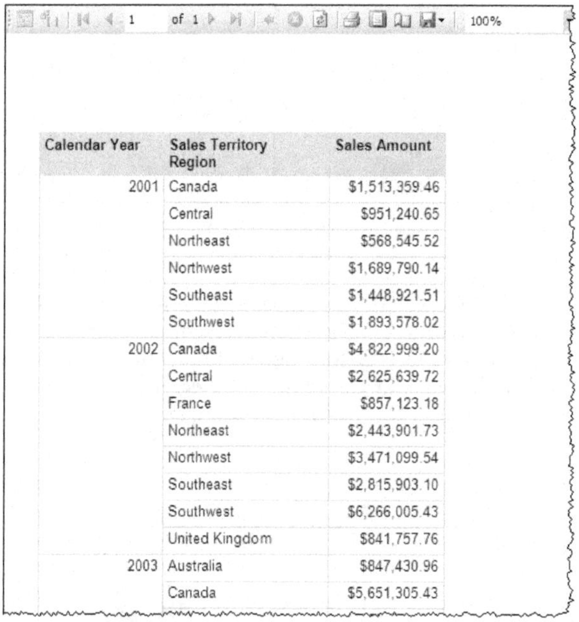

Calendar Year	Sales Territory Region	Sales Amount
2001	Canada	$1,513,359.46
	Central	$951,240.65
	Northeast	$568,545.52
	Northwest	$1,689,790.14
	Southeast	$1,448,921.51
	Southwest	$1,893,578.02
2002	Canada	$4,822,999.20
	Central	$2,625,639.72
	France	$857,123.18
	Northeast	$2,443,901.73
	Northwest	$3,471,099.54
	Southeast	$2,815,903.10
	Southwest	$6,266,005.43
	United Kingdom	$841,757.76
2003	Australia	$847,430.96
	Canada	$5,651,305.43

Figure 6-18

Switch back to Design view. Two different design methods may be used to add totals to the end of a group break with the same result. These include adding an explicit row to the group and choosing the Add Totals menu option. The first technique is more convenient, but the latter provides a little more flexibility.

Right-click on the CalendarYear textbox, and choose Insert Row ⇨ Inside Group - Below (see Figure 6-19).

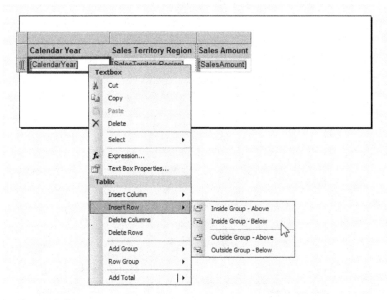

Figure 6-19

The new row is added below the group values. Hover the mouse over the new cell below the SalesAmount field, and then click on the field list icon. This displays a list of fields like you see in Figure 6-20. Select the SalesAmount field to set the value of this cell to that field.

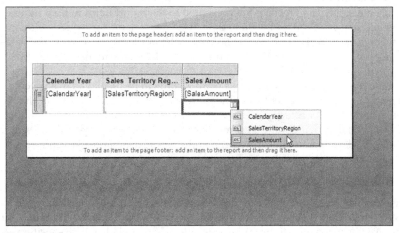

Figure 6-20

If you've worked with earlier versions of Reporting Services, the end result is the same as before, even though the design experience is a little different. Simply selecting a field for this cell applies the SUM function to this field in the footer row of the group.

Optionally, you can apply formatting to the field value, as shown in Figure 6-21. As you see, I have changed the number format of the textbox. I've also changed the font size and weight.

To view the report in Report Builder 2.0, click the Preview button on the Home or Preview ribbon. To view the report in BIDS, click the Preview tab.

Calendar Year	Sales Territory Region	Sales Amount
2001	Canada	$1,513,359.46
	Central	$951,240.65
	Northeast	$568,545.52
	Northwest	$1,689,790.14
	Southeast	$1,448,921.51
	Southwest	$1,893,578.02
		$8,065,435.31
2002	Canada	$4,822,999.20
	Central	$2,625,639.72
	France	$857,123.18
	Northeast	$2,443,901.73
	Northwest	$3,471,099.54
	Southeast	$2,815,903.10
	Southwest	$6,266,005.43
	United Kingdom	$841,757.76
		$24,144,429.65

Figure 6-21

Sorting Options

You have a few different options for sorting the data displayed in a table. The best method to choose depends on your needs and any interactive features you may want to support. When the report is executed, after making a connection to the data source, the first thing that happens is that queries are executed by the data source, and records are presented to the report items in their natural order or the order specified in the query. A dataset is more than just a fancy name for a query. It's actually an object managed by the report execution engine that holds a cache of the report data. As the data-set records flow to a data region, it can group and reorder the records before the report is rendered.

In short, you have three options: If you always want records to be displayed in a specific order, you should use a query or database object to sort them. In case you use a data provider that doesn't allow sorting or you need to reorder records after a query runs, you also have the option to reorder records in the report. If you need to provide some dynamic data reordering using a parameter selection or some other creative report design, you can sort records in the report using more advanced methods. These options are covered thoroughly in Chapter 7.

Sorting in the Query

It's important to realize that the SQL Server database engine, like many other relational database products, doesn't guarantee that records will be returned from the database tables in a particular order unless you specify this in a query. To be on the safe side, it's a good idea to be specific and use an `ORDER BY` clause in your T-SQL queries when records should always appear in a specific order. The query feeding data to this report table includes an `ORDER BY` clause that will always return records sorted by the CalendarYear and then the SalesTerritoryRegion field values:

```
SELECT
  DimDate.CalendarYear, DimSalesTerritory.SalesTerritoryRegion,
  SUM(FactResellerSales.SalesAmount) AS SalesAmount
FROM FactResellerSales INNER JOIN DimDate
    ON FactResellerSales.OrderDateKey = DimDate.DateKey
  INNER JOIN DimSalesTerritory
```

```
      ON FactResellerSales.SalesTerritoryKey =
          DimSalesTerritory.SalesTerritoryKey
  GROUP BY DimDate.CalendarYear, DimSalesTerritory.Sales Territory Region
  ORDER BY DimDate.CalendarYear, DimSalesTerritory.SalesTerritoryRegion
```

To optimize report performance, if you intend to use dynamic features in the report to reorder these records, it might be best to leave off the ORDER BY clause so that your report isn't working against the database engine. Another option would be to parameterize the query to dynamically change the ORDER BY clause, letting the database engine do the reordering rather than the reporting engine. You'll see an example of this technique in Chapter 7. To keep things simple, I will typically specify a natural ORDER BY in a query and then use other sorting features to apply exceptional rules, unless I have good reason to do otherwise.

Sorting in a Group

Part of the tablix's job is to apply groups and sorting options. Any group can be sorted in any order using any combination of data fields and expressions. For example, to set the sort order for the CalendarYear group to show more recent years first, click the down arrow on the first group listed in the Row Groups list when the table is selected in the Designer, and then select Edit Group from the dropdown menu, as shown in Figure 6-22.

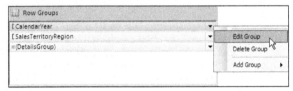

Figure 6-22

The Tablix Group Properties dialog, shown in Figure 6-23, is displayed with a list of pages on the left side. Select Sorting, and then click on the Add button to add a new sorting expression.

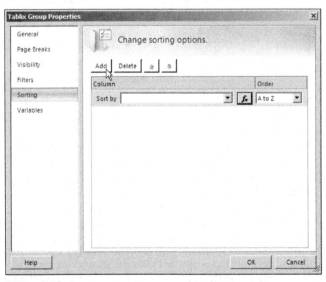

Figure 6-23

Complex expressions and combinations of fields may be used for sorting and grouping. This simple example shows a typical sorting expression based on one of the fields displayed in the report. Simply select CalendarYear from the "Sort by" field list in the column labeled Column, and then specify descending

147

order (Z to A) from the dropdown list in the Order column (see Figure 6-24). In a more complex report, you might add multiple sorting definitions based on different column/field values or other expressions.

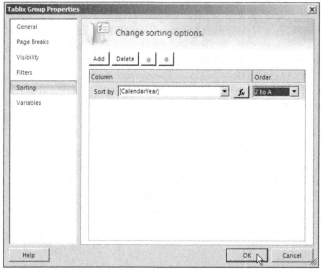

Figure 6-24

Use the Preview button to eyeball the report. The results are shown in Figure 6-25. Note that the CalendarYear values are now displayed, from highest to lowest, in the first table column.

Calendar Year	Sales Territory Region	Sales Amount
2004	Australia	$746,904.41
	Canada	$2,390,261.51
	Central	$1,323,536.38
	France	$1,376,610.72
	Germany	$885,121.35
	Northeast	$1,056,456.93
	Northwest	$2,633,651.25
	Southeast	$1,173,311.72
	Southwest	$3,175,103.09
	United Kingdom	$1,277,105.23
		$1,277,105.23
2003	Australia	$847,430.96
	Canada	$5,651,305.43

Figure 6-25

Interactive Sort

The Interactive Sort feature was added to the table in the 2005 product version and now works much the same way in the tablix. Interactive sorting is applied after the groups are processed, so the entire report doesn't need to be re-rendered each time a user clicks the column header to reorder column values. This is actually a feature of a textbox located in a header. To add interactive sorting for the SalesRegionTerritory field, right-click on the cell for this column header, and choose Textbox Properties. The resulting Text Box Properties dialog is shown in Figure 6-26.

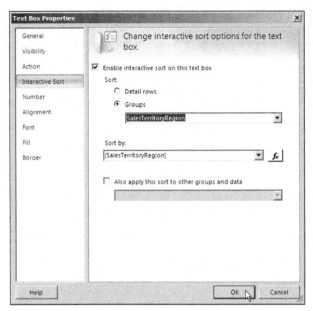

Figure 6-26

On the Interactive Sort page of this dialog, choose the group name and Sort by field. In this case, the group name is the same as the field name because the group was created by dragging the field into the Row Groups list. By specifying this group, rows within this group will be sorted within their parent group. In other words, when a user clicks on the column header textbox, the SalesTerritoryRegion rows will be resorted in either ascending or descending order, while the CalendarYear heading values will remain the same. Figure 6-27 shows a preview of the report. Before resorting the column, a pair of up and down arrows is displayed. Hovering over these arrows changes the mouse pointer to indicate that each is a hyperlink.

Calendar Year	Sales Territory Region	Sales Amount
2004	Australia	$746,904.41
	Canada	$2,390,261.51
	Central	$1,323,536.38
	France	$1,376,610.72
	Germany	$885,121.35
	Northeast	$1,056,456.93
	Northwest	$2,633,651.25
	Southeast	$1,173,311.72
	Southwest	$3,175,103.09
	United Kingdom	$1,277,105.23
		$1,277,105.23
2003	Australia	$847,430.96
	Canada	$5,651,305.43

Figure 6-27

Click the up button to sort in descending order or the down arrow to sort in ascending order. After sorting, the arrows pair changes to a single up or down arrow to indicate a toggled state for the sort order. Click the up arrow to sort the regions in descending order, as shown in Figure 6-28.

Calendar Year	Sales Territory Region	Sales Amount
2004	United Kingdom	$1,277,105.23
	Southwest	$3,175,103.09
	Southeast	$1,173,311.72
	Northwest	$2,633,651.25
	Northeast	$1,056,456.93
	Germany	$885,121.35
	France	$1,376,610.72
	Central	$1,323,536.38
	Canada	$2,390,261.51
	Australia	$746,904.41
		$746,904.41
2003	United Kingdom	$2,160,145.83
	Southwest	$7,131,772.25

Figure 6-28

Adding Headers and Footers

By combining the table, list, and matrix reports from previous product versions into the tablix data region, the grouping paradigm has changed slightly in SQL Server 2008 Reporting Services, enabling a more flexible reporting interface. In previous versions, inserting a group into a table would add two additional rows by default: one header row and one footer row. This same pattern is still possible, but the tablix now works differently out-of-the-box. The default behavior for a group is more akin to the old matrix data region. When a group is added, a non-repeating header is automatically added to the same row rather than a separate header row. This new design pattern looks a little different from the old method that required more vertical table space for header rows.

To apply the former method, you can create a group and then add a row within the group, either above or below. Figure 6-29 is an example of a table with separate group header and footer rows.

Year	Category	Product	Order Quantity	Extended Amount
[CalendarYear]				
	[EnglishProductCategoryName]			
		[EnglishProductName]	«Expr»	«Expr»
		«Expr»	[Sum (OrderQuantity Sum)]	[Sum (ExtendedAmount Sum)]
	«Expr»		[Sum (OrderQuantity Sum)]	[Sum (ExtendedAmount Sum)]
Report total			[Sum (OrderQuantity Sum)]	[Sum (ExtendedAmount Sum)]

Figure 6-29

Adding Page Breaks

By default, page breaks are added when repeated data fills the available space for a page. You can add page breaks explicitly before or after a tablix region. You can also add page breaks before or after a group value changes. To force a break for the entire table, display the Tablix Properties dialog, and use the "Page break options" section on the General page, as shown in Figure 6-30.

Figure 6-30

You've seen that this dialog is opened when editing a group from the Row Groups or Column Groups pane in the Report Designer window. The Tablix Properties dialog is also opened when you select a table, list, or matrix and then right-click on the top-left gray selection handle and choose Tablix Properties.

You can also control page breaks at the group level. This is a common reporting requirement to break before or after a group header or subtotals displayed in a footer row. Show the Tablix Group Properties dialog, and then use the Page Breaks page to set the page break options for the group (see Figure 6-31). It's often a good idea to repeat header information at the top of each printed page. This is done using the Repeat header rows on each page option in the Tablix Properties dialog (refer to Figure 6-30).

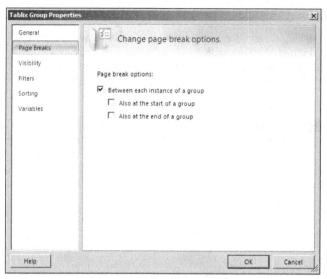

Figure 6-31

Creating Drill-Down Reports and Dynamic Visibility

A dynamic reporting experience is created by hiding and showing report elements. Various techniques may be used to show and hide fields, groups, rows, columns, and entire data regions using conditional expressions and toggle items. All report items and group definitions have a Visibility property that can be set either permanently or conditionally.

A common use for the Visibility property is to create drill-down reports, where table or matrix group headers are used to toggle, or expand and collapse, details. Typically, a plus [+] or minus [–] icon is displayed next to the toggle item row or column header. Figure 6-32 shows a drill-down report with toggle items set for the group header rows of a table.

Reseller Sales by Year and Territory

Calendar Year	Sales Territory Region	Sales Amount
2001	Canada	$1,513,359.46
	Central	$951,240.65
	Northeast	$568,545.52
	Northwest	$1,689,790.14
	Southeast	$1,448,921.51
	Southwest	$1,893,578.02
⊞ 2002		$4,822,999.20
⊞ 2003		$847,430.96
⊞ 2004		$746,904.41

Figure 6-32

Creating a drill-down report is a simple matter of hiding a group and setting its ToggleItem property to refer to a report item, usually a textbox, in a higher-level group. In our example report, records are grouped by Calendar Year and then Sales Territory Region. The properties for the latter group are set using the group pane in the lower part of the Design window, as shown in Figure 6-33.

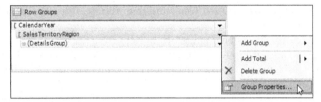

Figure 6-33

In the Visibility page of the Group Properties dialog, set the display options to Hide the group contents, check the box labeled "Display can be toggled by this report item," and then select the textbox bound to the CalendarYear field, as shown in Figure 6-34. Note that this textbox may not always have the same name as the field to which it is bound. Click OK to save these property changes.

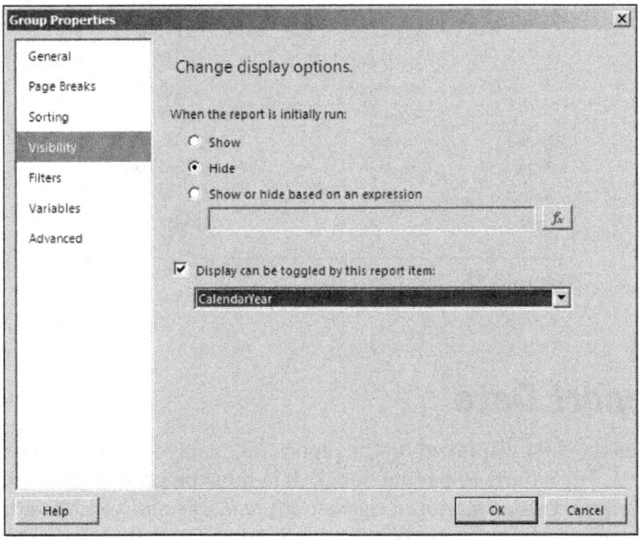

Figure 6-34

Dynamic visibility can also be used to hide and show areas of a report based on parameters or field threshold values. With a little creativity and some basic programming skills, some very interesting things are possible.

Adding Totals and Subtotals

Even the simplest table or list reports will typically have summary totals. A grand total is typically placed at the bottom of the report body or at the end or beginning of a data range. Group totals or subtotals (totals applied to any intermediate group) can also appear before or after a range of group values. To add totals to a group, use the group pane at the bottom of the Report Designer. Click on the dropdown button for the group, select Add Total, and then choose either Before or After.

Note that the grouping feature has been changed from Reporting Services in SQL Server 2000 and 2005. It is no longer necessary to add group header or group footer rows to a table. The table report item is now based on the new tablix, which is easier to design and offers greater flexibility.

Figure 6-35 shows the previous drill-down table report with totals added to the CalendarYear and SalesTerritoryRegion groups.

Reseller Sales by Year and Territory

Calendar Year	Sales Territory Region	Sales Amount
⊟ 2001	Canada	$1,513,359.46
	Central	$951,240.65
	Northeast	$568,545.52
	Northwest	$1,689,790.14
	Southeast	$1,448,921.51
	Southwest	$1,893,578.02
	Total	$8,065,435.31
⊞ 2002	Total	$24,144,429.65
⊞ 2003	Total	$32,202,669.43
⊞ 2004	Total	$16,038,062.60
Total		$80,450,596.98

Figure 6-35

Formatting Report Data

Nearly as important as the data displayed on the report are the layout and the visual elements that make the data readable. For reports to be functional, data must be presented in a format that makes sense to the user and conforms to a standard that is both readable and visually appealing. Reports may be static in design, or certain elements can be set to dynamically adapt to user requests. Report elements can be designed to change or to appear only under specific conditions.

All formatting features are based on property settings. Static formatting involves the use of several properties, such as background color to apply shading, the font, font size, weight, style, foreground color, and borders.

In Report Builder 2.0, formatting properties are applied to selected items using the Format ribbon. In Business Intelligence Development Studio, formatting can be applied using the Report Format toolbar.

Background colors, font sizes, weights, and borders are added using either the formatting options on the Report Builder 2.0 Home ribbon or the Report Formatting toolbar in BIDS. The ribbon and toolbar buttons are used to set properties that can also be changed using the Properties window. Figure 6-36 shows the same report with these properties changed on the group footer rows for the SalesTerritoryRegion and CalendarYear groups. This makes the report easier to read and helps the user to visually separate each group section with the corresponding details and totals.

Reseller Sales by Year and Territory

Calendar Year	Sales Territory Region	Sales Amount
⊞ 2001	Total	$8,065,435.31
⊟ 2002	Canada	$4,822,999.20
	Central	$2,625,639.72
	France	$857,123.18
	Northeast	$2,443,901.73
	Northwest	$3,471,099.54
	Southeast	$2,815,903.10
	Southwest	$6,266,005.43
	United Kingdom	$841,757.76
	Total	$24,144,429.65
⊞ 2003	Total	$32,202,669.43
⊞ 2004	Total	$16,038,062.60
Total		$80,450,596.98

Figure 6-36

Introduction to Dynamic Formatting

You've seen how a report can be formatted using simple features and properties. Totals can be added to groups; sections can be made to expand or collapse using drill-down toggle items; values can be formatted; and areas of the report can be dressed up using borders, shading, font sizes, weights, and colors.

Expressions are the heart and soul of dynamic reports. You can design simple reports without special coding, but if you want to take your reports to the next level, you'll need to learn some simple programming. Chapters 8 and 10 demonstrate how to use expressions to incorporate more advanced report design techniques. Here, I'd just like to give you a taste of the kinds of things you can do.

As the reports grow and evolve in a business, often different reports are just variations of other reports. You can define unique behaviors, such as dynamic sorting, filtering, or visual subsets of report data, by using a single report to include all the features, and then use expressions to modify the report's behavior and to enable or disable certain features.

Chapter 8 demonstrates a table report designed for use by two different groups of users. A parameter is used to indicate whether the report should display retail or wholesale sales information. Using this dynamic formatting technique, you can create one report to meet the reporting requirements for multiple users.

Designing Multicolumn Reports

Tabular reports can be designed to display continuous data in snaking columns. To create a multicolumn report, add a table to the report body that occupies a fraction of the report width, allowing for column margin spacing. The Columns and ColumnSpacing properties are set for the Report object in the Properties window. For example, a report with two columns should contain a table that is less than one-half of the report width plus the ColumnSpacing. Use the following formula to calculate the width of a multicolumn report:

```
Report Width = (Body Width x # Columns) + (ColumnSpacing x # Margins between
columns) + Left Margin + Right Margin
```

Designing Matrix Reports

Matrix reports allow you to visualize data in a pivot or crosstab table, with groups defined on rows and on columns. Values displayed in the intersecting cells between the row and column group headers are aggregated. Like a table report, totals can be added along with formatting and styling such as headers, footers, and drill-down report features.

With the table and matrix overhaul made since the 2005 product, designing table and matrix reports is now very similar. Since both of these report styles use the tablix report item under the covers, the option to design a table, matrix, or list report simply applies a set of templated properties to a tablix object. Regardless of what the designer does behind the scenes, you still select one of these specific report items to place on the report body. The only significant difference between a table and a matrix is that the columns of a matrix are dynamically generated from grouped values.

To demonstrate the design of a matrix, let's begin by creating a brand new report. If you are using Report Builder 2.0, click the Start button "pearl" in the top-left corner and then choose New. If you are using BIDS, right-click on the Reports folder in Solution Manager, select Add ⇨ New Item, and then select Report from the Add New Item dialog. Name this report **Reseller Sales by Quarter and Region**.

From the Insert ribbon (in Report Builder 2.0) or the Insert toolbar (in BIDS), add a matrix to the report body. In Report Builder 2.0, the matrix is added by clicking the Matrix icon in the ribbon. In BIDS, you drag and drop the Matrix from the toolbox.

You need a dataset with a few more fields than the previous example. Follow the steps to design a tabular report, and then use the following query instead of using the Query Designer. You will learn more about query design and data access in Chapter 7. For now, this query will serve to provide a set of data for the following sample reports. Remember that you can see the finished reports in the Chapter 6 sample project provided on the Wrox download website for this book. If you would like to create the following reports yourself and you'd like to save yourself some typing, I recommend that you copy and paste the query text from the Reseller Sales by Quarter and Region report in the sample project. Otherwise, type the following text directly into the Query Designer:

```
SELECT
  CalendarYear, CalendarQuarter, EnglishMonthName, SalesTerritoryCountry,
  SalesTerritoryRegion, SUM(FactResellerSales.SalesAmount) AS SalesAmount,
  SUM(FactResellerSales.OrderQuantity) AS OrderQuantity
FROM
  FactResellerSales INNER JOIN DimDate
    ON FactResellerSales.OrderDateKey = DimDate.DateKey
  INNER JOIN DimSalesTerritory
    ON FactResellerSales.SalesTerritoryKey = DimSalesTerritory.SalesTerritoryKey
GROUP BY
  CalendarYear, CalendarQuarter, MonthNumberOfYear, EnglishMonthName,
  SalesTerritoryCountry, SalesTerritoryRegion
ORDER BY
  CalendarYear, CalendarQuarter, MonthNumberOfYear, EnglishMonthName,
  SalesTerritoryCountry, SalesTerritoryRegion
```

Drag the CalendarYear field from the data-set Field list on the left to the Column Groups pane in the lower right area of the designer. Drag the CalendarQuarter field to the Column Groups pane, and drop it under the CalendarYear field. This is demonstrated in Figure 6-37.

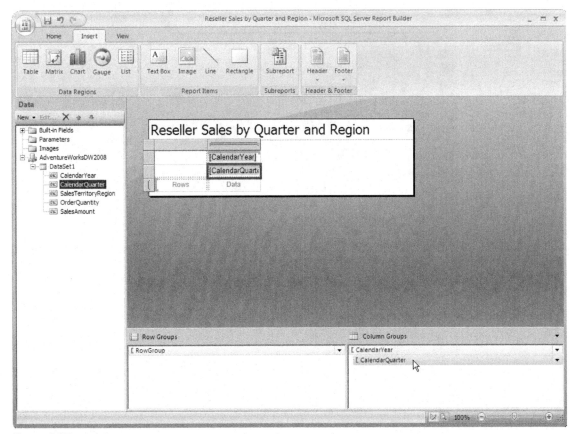

Figure 6-37

Drag and drop the SalesTerritoryRegion field to the Row Groups pane, under the Report Designer on the left side.

Drag the OrderQuantity to the cell labeled Data in the matrix. Drag the SalesAmount field to the right side of the new OrderQuantity cell. Before you release the mouse button, make sure that the bold "I-beam" marker indicates that the field will be dropped to the immediate right of the existing cell. This should appear as it does in Figure 6-38. Release the mouse button to drop the SalesAmount field at this location.

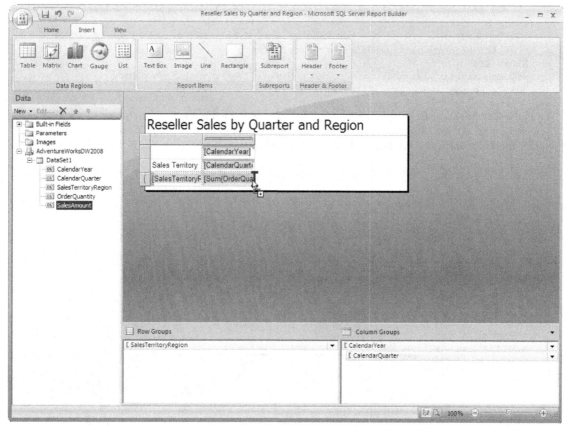

Figure 6-38

At this point, the report is functional but should be formatted to be more readable.

Left-justify the CalendarYear and CalendarQuarter fields by dragging across and selecting both cells, and then click the left text alignment button on the Home ribbon, as shown in Figure 6-39. Select the same cells again, set the text to bold, and set the background color to a light shade of gray using the Paint Bucket icon. Do the same for the SalesTerritoryRegion field in the detail row.

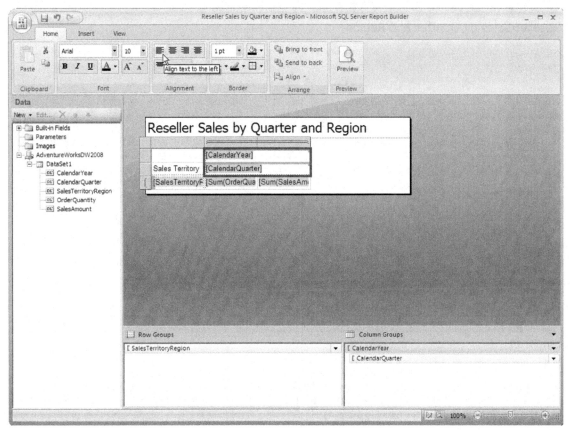

Figure 6-39

Before adding the totals, test the report to see what you've done so far. Use the Preview option from the Home ribbon to view the report. Figure 6-40 shows the results. For each unique combination of sales region and quarter, the order quantity and sales amount values are aggregated and displayed in an intersecting cell.

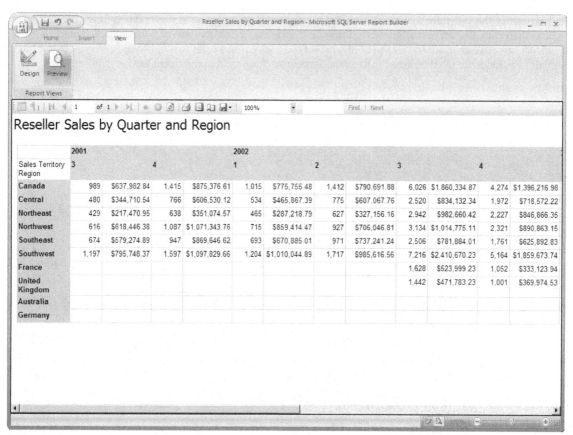

Figure 6-40

Adding totals is a simple matter. First, switch back to Design view. In the grouping pane, below the Designer window, click the dropdown arrow for the SalesTerritoryRegion group. From the dropdown list, select Add Total ⇨ After (see Figure 6-41).

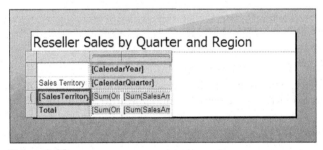

Figure 6-41

This action adds a new row after the detail row, within the SalesTerritoryRegion group. As shown in Figure 6-42, a textbox, labeled *Total*, has the same font, size, weight, and background color as the row group header label. The new cells under the OrderQuantity and SalesAmount column headings also take on the formatting of the detain cells by default.

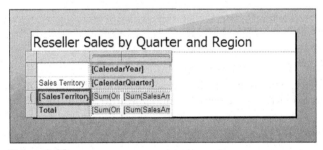

Figure 6-42

Select these two cells in the last row, and set the font weight to bold using the Home ribbon format options. Finally, preview the report again to see the new footer with the totals (see Figure 6-43).

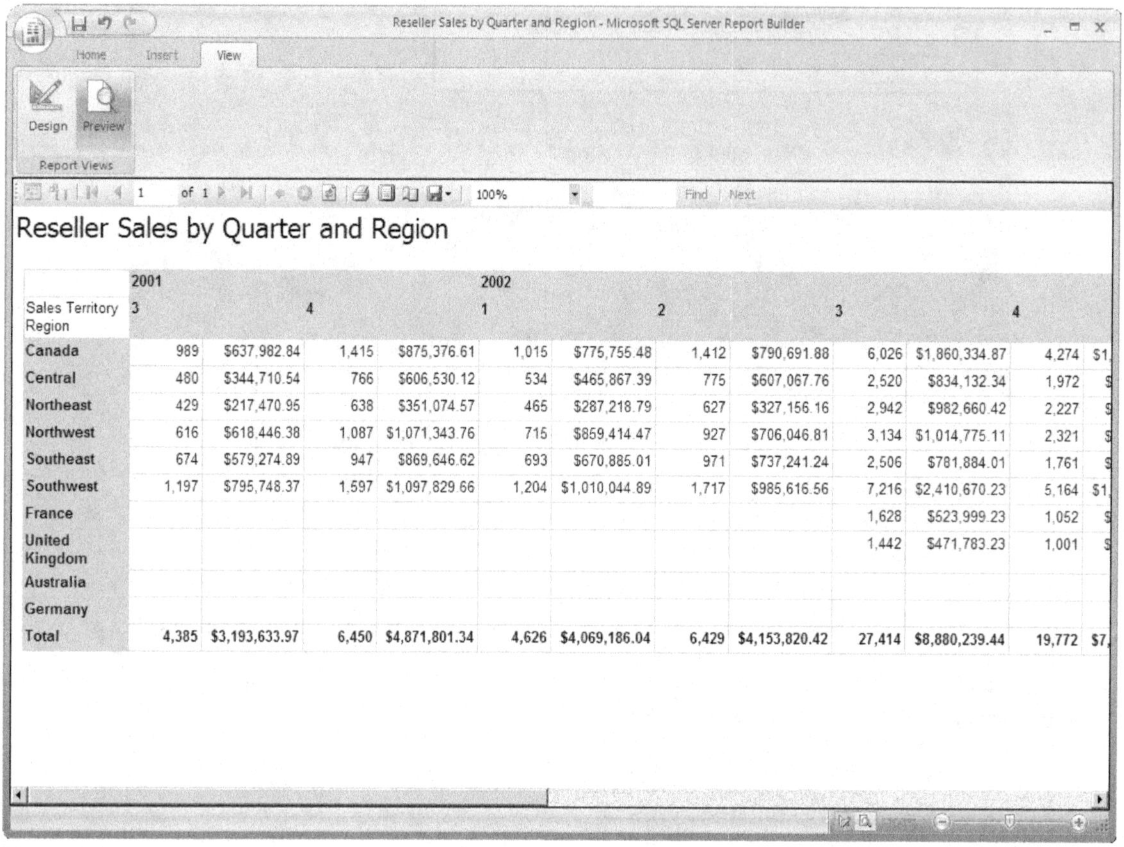

Sales Territory Region	2001 3		4		2002 1		2		3		4	
Canada	989	$637,982.84	1,415	$875,376.61	1,015	$775,755.48	1,412	$790,691.88	6,026	$1,860,334.87	4,274	$1,
Central	480	$344,710.54	766	$606,530.12	534	$465,867.39	775	$607,067.76	2,520	$834,132.34	1,972	$
Northeast	429	$217,470.95	638	$351,074.57	465	$287,218.79	627	$327,156.16	2,942	$982,660.42	2,227	$
Northwest	616	$618,446.38	1,087	$1,071,343.76	715	$859,414.47	927	$706,046.81	3,134	$1,014,775.11	2,321	$
Southeast	674	$579,274.89	947	$869,646.62	693	$670,885.01	971	$737,241.24	2,506	$781,884.01	1,761	$
Southwest	1,197	$795,748.37	1,597	$1,097,829.66	1,204	$1,010,044.89	1,717	$985,616.56	7,216	$2,410,670.23	5,164	$1,
France									1,628	$523,999.23	1,052	$
United Kingdom									1,442	$471,783.23	1,001	$
Australia												
Germany												
Total	**4,385**	**$3,193,633.97**	**6,450**	**$4,871,801.34**	**4,626**	**$4,069,186.04**	**6,429**	**$4,153,820.42**	**27,414**	**$8,880,239.44**	**19,772**	**$7,**

Figure 6-43

There is much more that can be done in a table or matrix report. Chapter 8 will take over where we left off and show you how to create more compelling and powerful reports by building on the basics you've learned so far.

Designing Chart Reports

Charts are a simple and effective way to visualize aggregated measure values grouped along one or more axes. The charting capabilities of Reporting Services have been expanded significantly in SQL Server 2008. If you have worked with Reporting Services in SQL Server 2000 or 2005, you will notice some differences in the design environment. The same types of charts can be created, but several new types and capabilities have been added. Designing a chart is a lot like creating a matrix report in that you can group field values on one or two axes and then the measure fields are aggregated along these groups. Groups and data point aggregations are defined by simply dragging fields into drop zones within the Designer.

We will use the same dataset as in the matrix report example. The easiest way to do this is to open the Matrix sample report and then use the Save As option to create a duplicate copy of the report.

Delete the matrix from the report body, and then insert a chart from the Insert ribbon or toolbox. The Select Chart Type dialog opens, as shown in Figure 6-44, to show all of the chart-type selections. Select the "3-D Clustered Cylinder" chart, and click OK.

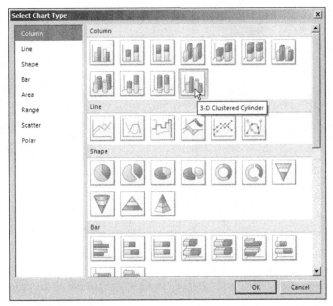

Figure 6-44

Reposition the chart and resize it so that it occupies most of the Design window. Click once in the center of the chart to show the field drop zones, as displayed in Figure 6-45. These zones are labeled "Drop data fields here," "Drop series fields here," and "Drop category fields here," respectively.

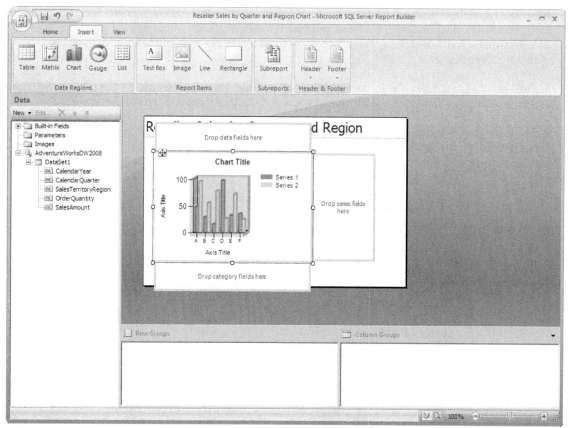

Figure 6-45

Defining the data series, series group, and category groups is as simple as dropping the appropriate fields into these zones.

From the data-set tree in the Data window, drag and drop the OrderQuantity field into the data field zone above the chart. Drop the SalesTerritoryRegion field to the right in the series zone, and drop the CalendarYear field into the category, below the chart. Your designer should look like Figure 6-46.

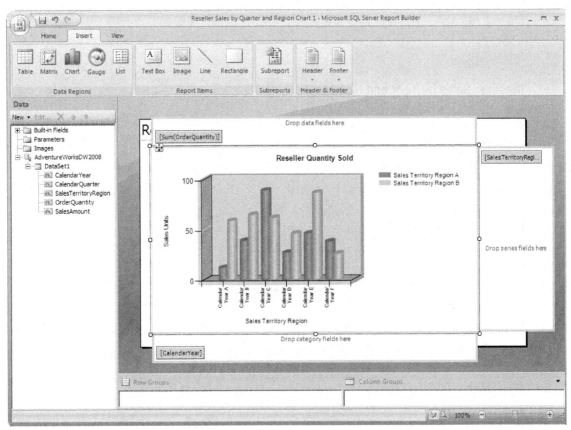

Figure 6-46

Preview the report to see the rendered chart, as shown in Figure 6-47. Note that the title and axis labels have default values.

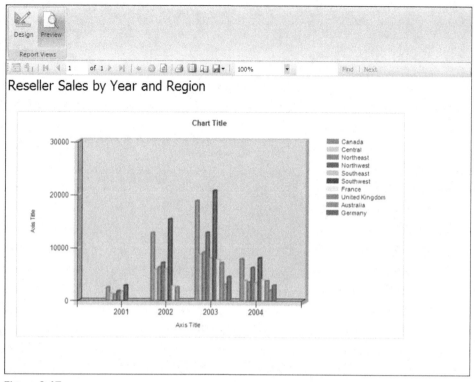

Figure 6-47

Changing the chart title and axis labels is simple. Switch back to Design view, and then click on the Chart Title text. Replace the Chart Title text with **Reseller Quantity Sold**. Do the same to change the X-axis text to **Sales Territory Region** and the Y-axis to **Sales Units**. Figure 6-48 shows a preview of the report with these changes.

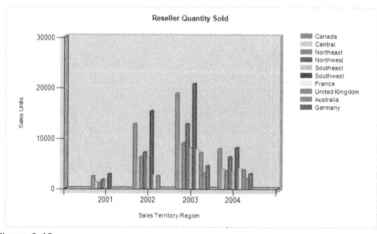

Figure 6-48

Changing chart types is easy as long as the chart type is suitable for the dataset and fields you have used.

Choosing Chart Types

There's some philosophy and perhaps a little tradition behind chart-type selection. Given all the choices, there are certainly some creative and interesting ways to express a trend or business metric graphically using a chart. The most important consideration is to choose a visualization that meets the need and adds business value to the report. In brief, linear bar and column charts are good for visualizing quantitative data points along two different axes. When time is measured on one axis and the data values progress to show a trend, a line chart may be the best choice. To express portions and ratios, a pie or stacked chart is often suitable. Most other chart types are either special in purpose or adaptations of these basic chart types.

Switch back to Design view, right-click over the chart, and then choose Change Chart Type. When the Select Chart Type dialog opens, change the column chart to a pie chart by selecting the 3-D Exploded Pie (see Figure 6-49), and then click OK.

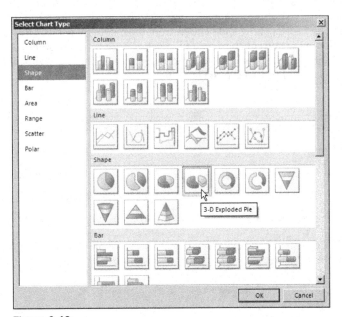

Figure 6-49

Pie charts are typically used only to display one group axis. Strange things happen when grouping on both category and series fields in a pie chart. Select the CalendarYear field in the category field drop zone, and press the Delete key to remove it. This leaves only the SalesTerritoryRegion field on the series axis, as you can see in Figure 6-50.

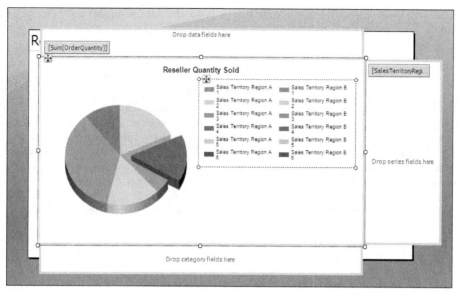

Figure 6-50

We're almost done with this chart, but first let's display data point labels over each pie slice.

Right-click on a slice, and select Show Data Labels from the menu. By default, this displays black text labels over every color in the current chart area fill palette. Since there are some dark colors in the palette, however, this may not be ideal. To set a contrasting label fill color, right-click on a data point label, and select Series Label Properties (see Figure 6-51).

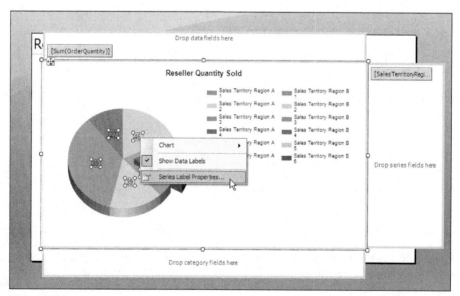

Figure 6-51

In the Series Label Properties dialog, change the number format and the fill color as you see in Figures 6-52 and 6-53.

Figure 6-52

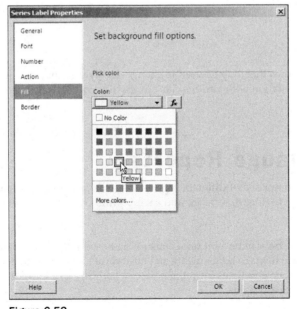

Figure 6-53

Finally, preview the report to see the data point label with contrasting background colors. The report is shown in Figure 6-54.

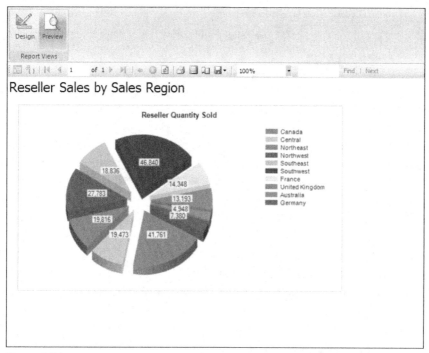

Figure 6-54

There are several properties that may be used to change the style, layout, and format of the chart and values. A little experimentation with various chart properties will reveal some very creative ways to visualize data.

Designing Gauge Reports

A Dashboard report is comprised of different report items that provide quick status information at a glance. A recent addition to Report Services, and a simple and compelling new visualization tool, is the Gauge report item.

Gauges are simple to use but can be a bit time-consuming to set up because there are so many properties and so much opportunity to make adjustments and customize a gauge. Figure 6-55 is an example of a Radial gauge, where the scale radiates from the pointer axis. You can control the sweep angle to create a quarter-angle gauge, for example.

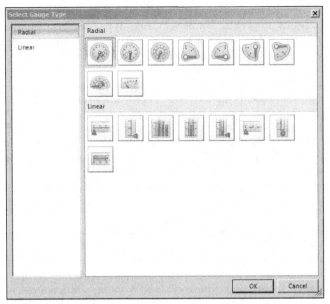

Figure 6-55

The scale and pointers both have minimum and maximum value properties that can be set to either fixed or variable values using expressions and field values. A gauge can have multiple pointers using a common scale or multiple scales. Figure 6-56 shows the same gauge with two pointers having different characteristics.

Figure 6-56

Although there are two distinct types of gauges (radial and linear), there are several varieties made possible by adjusting various properties. The Select Gauge Type dialog is displayed when you add a gauge to a report. Making any of the selections shown in Figure 6-57 will add a new radial or linear gauge with properties based on one of these templates.

Although gauge design is quite simple, Gauge reports typically require the use of some design techniques we'll cover in subsequent chapters. Several practical examples of Gauge reports are provided in Chapters 8, 9, and 10. The following is one example of a simple Gauge report. Figure 6-56 shows an example of a completed dashboard that includes four radial gauges. Each gauge displays a monthly total for a different metric, including the reseller sales, freight charges, sales quantity, and the total Internet sales. You can view this working report in the Chapter 6 sample project. Each gauge consists of a scale and a pointer. The pointer is set to a field expression that shows the current value for a selected month and year. The scale for that gauge shows the highest monthly value for the selected year and then divides the range into thirds, displaying the first, second, and third range value for comparison.

Figure 6-57 shows the first gauge in the dashboard, with callouts to show the values for three significant properties (which are set using field expressions). You can see that the pointer represents the sum of the SalesAmount field value; the scale maximum value is the Max, or highest monthly value, for the year; and the scale interval is one-third of this range so that it doesn't become crowded with several very large numbers. You'll learn more about using expressions and working with parameterized and grouped data-set queries in the chapters that follow, all of which are used to feed data to a simple gauge item like this one.

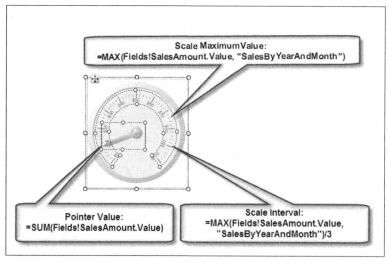

Figure 6-57

Converting Reports from Other Formats and Products

Because each report is defined in a single Report Definition Language (RDL) XML file, a report can be generated from a custom application or report migration utility. Microsoft has made a point to document the RDL specification and encourages third-party vendors to build report-generation tools. We have worked with several consulting clients, using internally developed tools at Hitachi Consulting to assist the conversion of Crystal Reports files to RDL-based reports. With more than 5 years of report migration experience on many projects, we've learned how these reporting products differ. Our report migration tool suite has gone through several version cycles as features and capabilities have been added. Certain report design elements can be converted straight across, while others require redesign because of the architectural similarities and differences between the two products.

Compared to some other report tools, a key difference is that Reporting Services uses a modular approach for report design and data rendering. Rather than the report binding to a query and defining groups, headers, footers, and detail rows, all this functionality is provided by the individual data range report items. And since a single report can contain any number of distinct datasets and data ranges, this changes the way report design is approached. In the end, report conversion tools are helpful to reduce redundant report redesign, but we have found that no tool can effectively replace experience and expertise with differing report platforms.

Students and clients ask me the same question all the time: "Which is a better reporting tool, Reporting Services or XYZ Reports?" That's a very subjective question. I think Reporting Services is the most flexible reporting solution available, but is every feature superior to its competitors? To answer yes across the board would be a bit naive. Every tool is different.

When migrating reports from another reporting tool, break down the report design into logical steps, and answer these questions:

- ❑ What is the data source?
- ❑ How is the data filtered and sorted at the source or the query within the report?
- ❑ What parameters or calculations are applied before the data is parsed and rendered?
- ❑ How is the data grouped and organized?
- ❑ What aggregations are performed on numeric measure fields?
- ❑ How is the grouped and aggregated data visualized in the report interface?

An automated report conversion tool can be useful for migrating a large volume of reports from another product if the source and target layouts are similar. But if the architecture of the reporting tool is so different that the design can't be nearly duplicated, or if you need to change the design to take advantage of more advanced features in Reporting Services, you'd do well to start over. In many cases, converting reports helps you to discover the need to redesign. Again, some of the reports may convert straight across, while others warrant a fresh start — usually with much better results.

Importing Access Reports

Using the Report Designer, you have the ability to import reports from Microsoft Access. Prior to Reporting Services for SQL Server 2000, Access was the only substantial reporting tool in the Microsoft armada of products. Since the early 1990s, Access was the product of choice for creating reporting solutions and still is for many desktop solutions. Its greatest limitation, however, is that it must be installed on the user's desktop and can effectively be used only in a single-user or small-network environment.

If you are already familiar with creating reports in Access, this may be a good starting point to learn report design in Reporting Services. Most basic Access reports will import very nicely. There are some functions and expressions used in Access that are not supported, and Access reports that run program code behind them will likely not work without some adjustments. Most basic report functionality will work. Grouping and sorting features are preserved, as are most expressions and formatting. The use of domain functions and any custom code is not supported. Once you get the basics down, though, I would recommend that you leave Access reports behind and learn to design more advanced reports the Reporting Services way.

Designing for Extensibility

If your goal is to create a reporting solution that will work for users with different needs, there are several things to be considered. The users may need to:

- ❑ **Browser Compatibility** — View reports in Internet Explorer or different web browsers.
- ❑ **Offline Viewing** — Download reports for offline viewing.
- ❑ **Mobile Device Support** — Access reports from a web-enabled hand-held device or cell phone.
- ❑ **Rendering Format Limits and Considerations** — View or save reports in Microsoft Excel to manipulate report data after rendering.

Reporting Services can meet all these needs if you understand the requirements and plan ahead. Let's briefly discuss some of these design considerations.

Browser Compatibility

A solution should be designed to meet the needs of the least capable user or application platform. The optimal design for the Web has always been a moving target. If, when designing reports, you view them only in the latest version of Internet Explorer, you may not be aware of incompatibilities or design issues for other browsers. Creating solutions independent of the client platform for a diverse audience will always be challenging, with a certain degree of unpredictability.

Reporting Services renders to HTML 4.0 by default, which, theoretically, should work in any compatible web browser. However, the interpretation of this standard is subtle, and Microsoft doesn't guarantee that reports will work correctly in any other browser but the current, released version of Internet Explorer. Reports with interactive design elements like drill-down and auto-hide sections, for example, generate client-side JavaScript. This script runs in the user's browser to produce effects and interactive functionality. Theoretically, pages containing many JavaScript functions should run in newer versions of Internet Explorer and other browsers. In a report, scripted features include documentation maps, bookmarks, and show/hide features (used for drill-down reports). On the standard report toolbar, scripted features provide the ability to zoom, search, refresh, export, and request help.

Another variable to consider when using HTML is the font typeface and size. If you make a point to use common fonts, this is not typically an issue. However, the user's configuration isn't always predictable. Font files on the user's computer can be uninstalled or deleted, and default font sizes can be changed in the browser. A popular solution for unpredictable HTML results is to use a proprietary document format typically read in a downloadable viewer. Rendering reports to an Adobe Portable Document Format (PDF) document will ensure that reports are displayed and printed consistently.

Offline Viewing

Reporting Services can render reports in three different forms of HTML, including HTML 4.0 for desktop browsers, HTML 3.2 for mobile devices, and a MIME-encoded HTML called *MHTML* (or *web archive*). MHTML is a more recent standard that encapsulates content that would normally be linked to separate files, typically graphics, into a single document. Using this format simplifies web content rendering for portability, but it isn't supported in all browsers (including Pocket Internet Explorer). Even when using standard HTML format, most report files will be self-contained with the exception of any graphics. If all the content is contained in one file, it will be easier to download and view offline. If your users are consistently using Internet Explorer or a browser you have tested thoroughly, consider rendering reports in MHTML to preserve embedded graphics content. If you don't have that kind of control over the user's environment, PDF document rendering may be the best choice.

Another possibility is to allow the user to download report content into a storage file and then render the content using your own client-side solution. Reports rendered as Comma Separated Values (CSV) can be opened in Microsoft Excel, where the user can format or further manipulate the data. Data saved to an XML file may be imported or read using Excel, Word, or a custom application. The Excel rendering format currently supports Microsoft Excel versions 2002 and 2003 only.

Mobile Device Support

Portable electronic devices are available in different sizes and shapes. This medium could prove to be a very convenient reporting solution for users who need to get information on-the-go. Web-enabled cellular phones generally fit into three categories:

❑ The Windows Mobile, Pocket PC, and Palm OS devices with integrated cellular phones have the advantage of a relatively larger display (240 × 320 pixels) and a more traditional-style web browser.

❑ The new generation of smartphones runs a slightly scaled-down version of the Windows Mobile operating system with a smaller display (176 × 220 pixels) and fewer features, but in a more convenient size.

❑ The standard web-enabled cell phone. It's hard to find a new cell phone that doesn't offer the capability to surf the web. Most of these phones have very small displays, and many will display only text.

The simple fact is that you can develop reporting solutions using Reporting Services for all these devices, making it possible and convenient for users to access information wherever they are.

Of course, screen size is one of the most significant limitations, so reports may simply be scaled down to a smaller page size to fit a smaller screen size. The Pocket PC and smartphone browsers will run client-side JavaScript to support drill-down and other such effects. To support less capable devices, you can design simple text reports rendered in HTML.

Rendering Format Limits and Considerations

A significant design goal for Reporting Services is its ability to render reports into a variety of formats. This offers a great deal of flexibility and opportunity for reports to meet specific business requirements and to be integrated into a variety of business solutions. It's important to understand that each rendering format has certain capabilities and restrictions. I hear from consulting clients on a regular basis who ask when a rendering limitation is going to be "fixed" or enhanced. Although the product team does their best to enhance each rendering extension within reason, we simply have to accept the architectural characteristics of the different viewers and applications used to view reports. My response (often echoed from similar questions posed to the product team) is that each renderer generally uses the capabilities of the related viewer. Here are some examples:

- ❑ PDF- and image-rendered reports don't support drill-down and drill-through features. This is simply not possible.

- ❑ Subreports often don't work well with Excel rendering. Although several enhancements were made to the Excel renderer because of its popularity, you can still expect these reports to behave differently than HTML at times. In HTML rendering, items can be placed at any axis point in the report body. The Excel renderer has to define rows and columns for the resulting worksheet and then output report items to an exact grid. This means that textboxes and other items that are slightly misaligned at design time may end up in the same column in the resulting report.

- ❑ HTML-rendered reports can have pages of differing lengths. HTML is not considered to be a pixel-perfect print format, and, because of the different ways that an HTML browser handles tables, borders, or margins, the report layout may not be ideal for page printing. If you want to print a report, render it to PDF or use the client-side printing capability in the Report Manager.

Summary

Like constructing a house or building, you must first lay a foundation and start with the basic building blocks. In this chapter, you saw some examples and learned to use the essential constructs of common reports. You learned to create a data source and dataset to obtain data from a database. In Chapter 7, you will learn more about consuming data from different data sources and how to filter and manipulate that data as it flows to your reports.

Using the common data range items and report items — namely, the textbox, table, matrix and chart — you can visualize a range of data by aggregating a grouping on meaningful field values. You learned to add totals, fixed sorting, and interactive sorting to a table. You also learned to do some basic formatting to the table and matrix layout.

You used some basic chart styles to visualize reseller product sales data by sales territories and time periods. You've seen how basic column and pie charts are used to display data in a meaningful way.

You learned about report rendering and formatting options and how reports can be read on mobile devices, third-party viewers, and different web browsers. Reporting Services is highly extensible, and reports can be integrated into different types of applications.

This chapter was a starting point for report design. In the following chapters, you will apply these and other techniques to create more advanced and compelling report solutions to solve business problems and to enable users and business leaders to be more effective and to make informed decisions.

7

Designing Data Access

Chapter 6 used the new Report Builder 2.0 to design some simple reports. As of the initial release of SQL Server 2008, Report Builder 2.0 doesn't include the Graphical Query Designer and Report Wizard tools; these features are due to be added in a service pack or subsequent product release. To demonstrate the full report design experience, this chapter uses Business Intelligence Development Studio (BIDS). The differences between the two report designers are minor enough that it really shouldn't make a difference, and you should be able to use either.

A big part of the report design process is often query design. In nearly all cases, your reports are based on a data source of some kind. Therefore, the first order of business when designing a report is to create a connection and define the queries necessary to retrieve the report data. This chapter discusses the essential first steps of report design — how to consume data. Although this is typically simple and straightforward, there are several options to be considered when designing data sources and queries. Although SQL Server Reporting Services is packaged with the SQL Server database product, it may be used with other database products as data sources. This chapter discusses the following topics:

- ❑ Creating stand-alone and shared data sources
- ❑ Designing queries and datasets
- ❑ Grouping and filtering data in a T-SQL query
- ❑ Using parameters to filter data at the database
- ❑ Using parameters to filter data at the Report Server
- ❑ Obtaining data from other data sources

Every report will have at least one data source (with the rare exception of a special-purpose report that doesn't use any data). The simplest of reports will have a single data source to provide data for a single dataset. The data source defines a connection as a string of text stored either in the report definition file or in a separate shared data source file that can be shared among several reports. This connection information may include security credentials. The dataset defines a query expression or a reference to query objects stored in the database. The dataset is also contained within the report definition. Figure 7-1 depicts how data flows to the report. The data source provides the ability to connect to the database, and the dataset contains a query expression that populates the report with data.

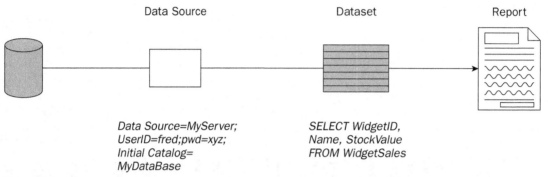

Data Source=MyServer;
UserID=fred;pwd=xyz;
Initial Catalog=
MyDataBase

SELECT WidgetID,
Name, StockValue
FROM WidgetSales

Figure 7-1

More complex reports may require multiple datasets to provide data for different data ranges or items in the report or to feed values to parameter value selection lists. Datasets can be based on query expressions from the same data source, as shown in Figure 7-2:

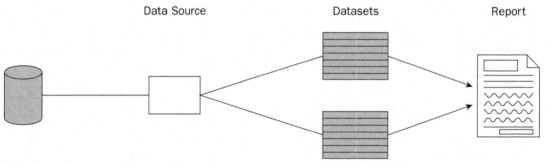

Figure 7-2

Multiple datasets can get their data from multiple data sources. This model would enable a report to have parameter selection values to be obtained from a local database and report data to be obtained from a central data store. In some cases, data regions, subreports, and various report items might obtain data from multiple sources through associated datasets, as shown in Figure 7-3.

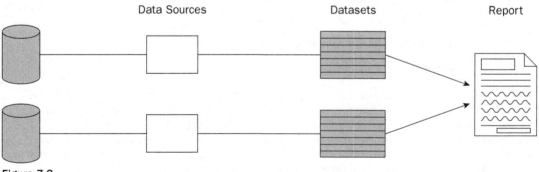

Figure 7-3

As you can see, almost anything is possible in terms of combining data sources and datasets. Data sources can be practically any database product or any data source you can query by means of standard connection libraries or drivers. Reporting Services consumes data using the .NET data providers, which include support for SQL Server, Oracle, and all OLE DB providers. These include almost any database product that supports ODBC access or a capable ISAM driver. Datasets in Reporting Services are always Read Only, so there is no need to specify cursor types or locking options.

Federating Data Sources

It's true that you can combine the data from multiple data sources into a single report, but each data region gets its data from a single dataset. This means that to group data together in a table, matrix, list, or chart, the data must come from a single query fed by one data source. Before you get too excited about this architectural restriction, you need to understand the bigger picture and then plan accordingly. There are a few ways to work with Reporting Services to combine data from more than one data source.

Here's a quick story to explain: I was working with a large consulting client a couple of years ago. Microsoft had subcontracted with Hitachi Consulting to send me out to teach a Reporting Services class and to do a little group mentoring. I was to introduce Reporting Services to a dozen or so of their developers and discuss some of the challenges they were facing with a competing product. They also sent a junior-level consultant with me from Microsoft Consulting Services. The client let me know up front that one of their requirements was that they must be able to combine the data from two separate database platforms into a single report table, and that if we couldn't make Reporting Services do this, they weren't interested in using the product. I thought this might be an opportunity to have some fun with the greenhorn consultant from MCS.

At the start of the class, our client sponsor said something to the effect of, "Before we go any further, let's get to the bottom of this issue . . . product XYZ, which we've been using for report design, allows us to federate multiple data sources into a single query. Can we do this with Reporting Services?" I said, "Well, let's ask the guy from Microsoft!" He squeamishly answered that Reporting Services wasn't designed to do this, and the client was about ready to send us both home. At this point, I spoke up and told them that the SQL Server platform actually handles this elegantly and more efficiently. Because Reporting Services is part of an enterprise-capable data platform, federated queries are possible at the database server level using linked servers and ad hoc distributed queries — and this is far more efficient, secure, and appropriate than bringing result sets to the report server to combine them. To do so using the other method promotes inefficient design. Another method is to use a subreport to combine and coordinate the results from two sources. Just keep in mind that this can be even less efficient than the former method.

Linked Servers and Ad hoc Distributed Queries

There are really two different ways to federate data in SQL Server. One is to create a persistent connection to a remote database server from a designated SQL Server, known as a *linked server*. This is an administrative task performed on the SQL Server using the `sp_addlinkedserver` system stored procedure and managed within the Server Objects area in SQL Server Management Studio. A linked server can be used to connect to any data source or database product using an ODBC driver or OLE DB provider. User credentials for the remote connection are stored in the linked server definition. Once established, a table accessed through the linked server connection can be used as if it were in a local database.

Rather than defining a permanent connection, another option is to use the OPENDATASOURCE or OPENROWSET system functions in a query. These functions enable you to specify remote databases and tables in a query. If the Report Designer has appropriate permissions to access remote objects, tables from different servers can be specified in the query, yet the data is actually combined at the data source hosting the query before being returned to the Report Server. Because these queries can be complex to write and debug, it's often a good idea to create views or stored procedures on the database server to contain the script, rather than to promote the use of ad hoc federated queries in reports. Keep in mind that federating data will inevitably come with some added cost of query performance, increased network traffic, and security compromises.

The need to perform federated data source reporting is often a symptom of a greater business need that should be addressed at the solution level. When it becomes necessary to combine data from multiple sources for reporting and data analysis, this should help define the requirement for a central data warehouse with data fed from different sources at scheduled intervals.

Business Intelligence Reporting

When designing any kind of business solution, it's always a good idea to step back and look at the big picture. Maintaining a solution-level perspective will usually help to ensure that your report design efforts will continue to solve changing business problems. With an intelligent design reporting application, the introduction of future requirements is less likely to render the whole solution obsolete.

One of the most important considerations of a reporting solution is the structure of the data used for reporting. Nearly all business goes through a similar cycle of data evolution. At the beginning, the data structure is simple. Reports are often based on a few simple tables in a single, relational database used to manage day-to-day operations and for simple reporting. As time goes on, multiple data sources are introduced, each housing specialized data to support various business processes. Because business decisions are made based on information from multiple sources, this data must be consolidated. As users and applications compete for access to databases, using transactional data sources may no longer be viable. As a result, data marts and data warehouses may become necessary to simplify the data used in reports. A query used to bring together data from complex data structures can be complicated, slow, and difficult to manage.

Along with the volume and complexity of business data, reporting requirements also expand, making it more and more difficult to squeeze meaningful reporting metrics out of traditional data sources. Relational data bases and T-SQL queries may be used to group, aggregate, and perform calculations, but these queries can be slow and complicated. The next step in the process may be to store data in a multidimensional data structure designed specifically for data analysis. Microsoft SQL Server Analysis Services is an On-Line Analytical Processing (OLAP) storage engine that can significantly improve performance and support for self-service reports and reports with complex calculations.

An exhaustive discussion of BI data sources is beyond the scope of this book, but these are important considerations. Although we will not cover relational data warehouse or OLAP cube design, we will talk about designing reports to use these data structures as sources. In brief, the general choices for report data sources are:

- ❏ Operational, transactional database with data stored in normalized table structures using a relational database product such as SQL Server or Oracle

- ❏ Relational data mart or data warehouse using simplified fact/dimension star schemas

- ❏ Multidimensional OLAP cubes such as SQL Server Analysis Services

- ❏ A non-traditional data source such as an XML web service

We work with a lot of companies, large and small, to architect enterprise reporting solutions. Typically, the best way to build a business reporting solution is to make sure that reports don't use live application databases for their data sources. If you can simplify the way data is stored and optimize a decision-support database used only for reporting, life will be so much simpler. I realize that may be a big undertaking. Very often the person charged with designing reports has been directed to use a specific data source, and it may be completely outside the scope of a person in that role to build a utopian BI solution. However, if you have the tools, the skills, and the time to "do it right," designing a full-fledged BI solution with a relational data mart and OLAP cubes can make the reporting part of the equation much easier and faster (both to design reports and for users to run).

Although there is much to consider, depending on the size and scope of the data and business reporting needs, Figure 7-4 depicts the general layout of a fully evolved, corporate reporting environment. Due to the relative complexity of the data stored in the operational databases illustrated on the left side of the diagram, operational reports are typically static and simple in design, based on unstructured data. Data is organized as it moves through transformation packages and into a data warehouse and OLAP cubes, where the data is structured and simplified. This affords the opportunity to design more complex and useful reports that run quickly and produce reliable results. Reports on the right side of the illustration require less effort to design and debug because of the efficiency of hierarchal data structures.

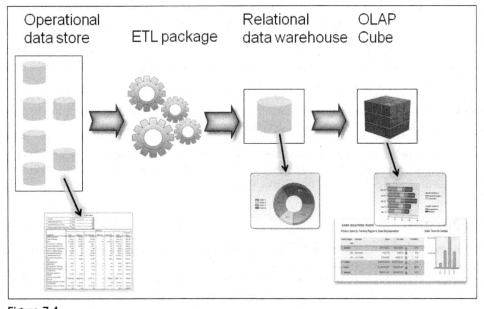

Figure 7-4

The examples in this chapter will use a relational data warehouse. Chapter 9 demonstrates reports using data from an OLAP cube.

Reporting for Relational Data

Now you'll take a closer look at how queries are created and how data is provided for a report. At this point, it's important to understand the basic building blocks for reports. The discussion will begin with some of these fundamentals. You will go through several short walk-through exercises so that you can see and experience how it works.

A query or command statement that produces a set of report data is called a *dataset*. Within the report design tool, this is actually referred to as both a "dataset" and a "dataset." I would argue that the first is more correct than the latter, but it's probably not a point worthy of a street fight or even a simple argument.

By the way, the term *dataset* in Reporting Services has nothing in common with a programming object in the ADO.NET namespace with the same name. Why does the term *dataset* mean two completely different things in different Microsoft technologies? We ran out of new words in the English language a long time ago, so we're now recycling some words and phrases.

Data and Query Basics

Reporting Services is capable of obtaining data from a variety of data sources. Nearly all relational database products are queried using a form of Structured Query Language (SQL), which means that a query created for one database product (say, IBM DB2) may be somewhat portable to a different data source (perhaps Oracle, MySQL, SyBase, or Microsoft SQL Server). Most database products implement a form of SQL conforming to the ANSI SQL standard. Microsoft SQL Server, for example, conforms to the ANSI 92 SQL standard, and other products may conform to other revisions (like ANSI 89 SQL or ANSI 99 SQL). Beyond the most fundamental SQL statements, most dialects of SQL are not completely interchangeable and will require some understanding of their individual idiosyncrasies.

Other specialized database products may use a different query language. Microsoft SQL Server Analysis Services is a data storage and analysis product that uses multidimensional cube structures to organize complex data for business intelligence and decision-support systems.

The main point here is that you can use whatever query language your database product understands. Reporting Services provides a Query Editor designed especially for T-SQL and a generic Editor that will accommodate other query languages or SQL dialects.

Data Sources

A data source contains the connection information for a dataset. Data sources either can be created only for a specific report dataset or can be shared among different reports. Because most reports will get data from a common data source, it often makes sense to create a shared data source. There are several advantages in using shared data sources. Even if you don't have several reports that need to share a central data source, it takes no additional effort to create a shared data source. This may still be advantageous in this case as the data source is managed separately from each report and can be easily updated if necessary. Then, as you add new reports, the shared data source will already be established and deployed to the Report Server.

There are three different ways to create a data source in a BIDS/Visual Studio report project:

❏ From the Add Item template, launched from the Project right-click menu

❏ In the Report Wizard

❏ When defining a dataset

Let's look at each of these options in detail.

Creating a Data Source from the Project 'Add Item' Template

You can add a new shared data source to a project and then use that data source in any report in the project. To do this, in the Solution Explorer, point to Reports, and then right-click on and choose Add ⇨ Add New Item. The options in this dialog include Report Wizard, Report, and Data Source. Selecting the Data Source option creates a shared data source.

Using this technique will present the Shared Data Source Properties dialog. Although the layout of this window is slightly different, the functionality is exactly the same as the Wizard pages described in the following section.

Creating a Data Source in the Report Wizard

The following steps are provided to help get you started with data sources and datasets. In this exercise, you will run the Report Wizard in a BIDS report project and then define the data source and dataset properties for a new report. The exercise will continue in the following sections to help you develop some basic T-SQL query language skills and then to use parameters and filtering in a report design. If any of these topics are not new to you, you should be able to quickly skip ahead to later material that will be more educational for you.

The Report Wizard is launched from a report project in BIDS. From the Solution Explorer, right-click on the Reports folder, and choose Add Report to launch the Report Wizard. The first page in the Wizard will give you the opportunity to select an existing shared data source or create a new data source, as shown in Figure 7-5. Name the data source **AdventureWorksDW2008**. You can name a data source anything you like, but I typically use the actual name of the database for which the data source provides connectivity.

Figure 7-5

For this SQL Server 2008 database, leave the data source Type property as Microsoft SQL Server. Click the Edit button to build a connection string. This opens the Connection Properties dialog, as shown in Figure 7-6.

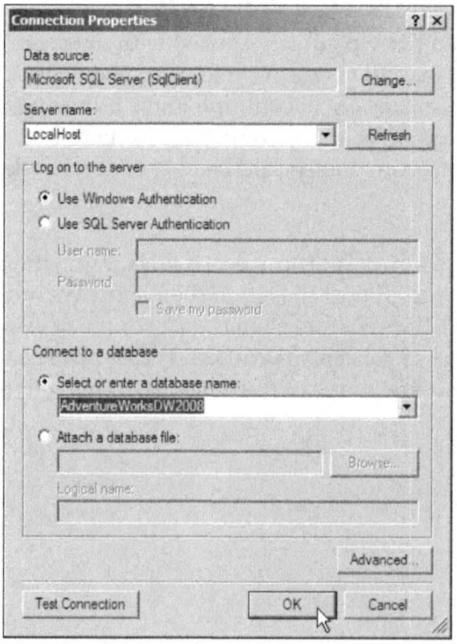

Figure 7-6

Note that this dialog might be a little different if you select a different option in the Type dropdown list. Although many of these options do correspond to standard data providers (and may include .NET native providers, OLE DB data providers, and ODBC drivers), these are actually data processing extensions that were installed with, or added to, the Reporting Services configuration. For example, selecting the SQL Server Analysis Services type will result in a dialog window that is unique to Analysis Services connections.

Whether using the Report Wizard or adding a new data source directly from the Project Add Items dialog or the Data Sources folder in the Solution Explorer, the interface is the same. The only significant difference is whether you click OK to save the data source or Next to move to the next page in the wizard.

> **A word of caution about this dialog. . . . You can either type or select from a list of database servers in the Server name dropdown list. If you choose to use the drop-down option, rather than typing the server name, a process runs that searches all available servers on your network. This can be time-consuming, so if you are on a large corporate network, you might just want to type your database server name. If the database server is a default instance, simply type the server name or address. If it is a named instance, type the server name or address followed by a backslash and the instance name.**

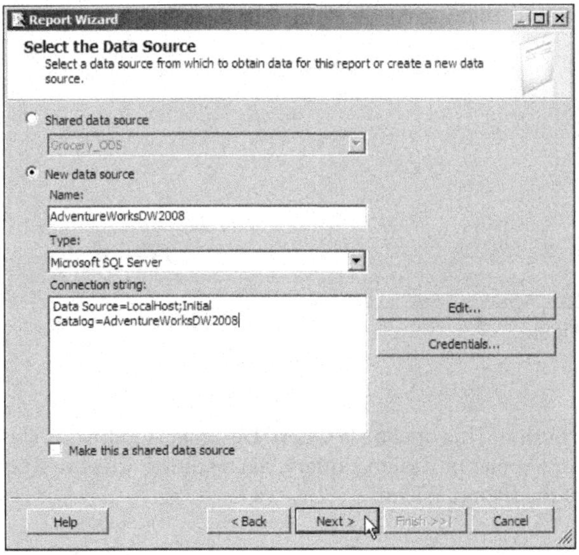

Figure 7-7

If your development database is the default instance on your development computer, you can simply type **LocalHost**, **(local)**, or a period to have the local database server name automatically discovered by the data provider.

185

If you are working with a local development database server installed on the same computer, type **LocalHost**. Otherwise, enter the name of the database server. In the next step, you choose the security authentication method to be used by the database server to check security credentials. SQL Server may be configured to use Integrated Windows Authentication or both SQL Server Security and Integrated Windows Security. In a development environment, integrated security is a simple choice.

Finally, select or type the database name. Click the OK button to close this dialog and enter the new information into the Connection string property, as shown in Figure 7-7.

Click the Next button to move to the page titled *Design the Query*, as shown in Figure 7-8. You can enter a query in one of three ways: typing directly into the Query string box in this page of the Report Wizard, using the generic Query Builder window to enter the query text, or using the Graphical Query Designer to generate the query text.

Figure 7-8

Click the Query Builder button. This opens the Query Designer window, as shown in Figure 7-9. After using the Query Designer to enter or design a query, the resulting script will be placed in the Query string box in this page of the Report Wizard.

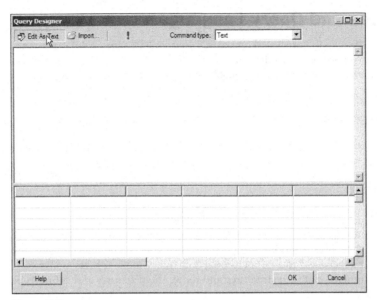

Figure 7-9

This Designer window has two views: the generic Query window and the Graphical Query Builder. You can toggle between these two modes using the "Edit As Text" button on the toolbar in the upper-left corner. You used the graphical builder in the previous chapter, so I'm not going to repeat the same exercise here. This is a useful tool, and I continue to use the Graphical Query Builder, especially when I am less familiar with the source database or I need to throw together a query quickly for prototyping. However, if you're not careful, it can promote poor query design.

With some experience and familiarity with a database, you may choose to just type the query text into the Query string box. We'll come back to this in just a moment. Go ahead and leave the Query Designer open in preparation for the rest of the exercise.

After a query has been entered, you will click OK on the Dataset Properties dialog, which will generate the fields definitions for the dataset, allowing you to design the report.

Creating a Data Source When Defining a Dataset

If you create a new report without using the Report Wizard, data sources are selected or created using the Report Data pane when creating a dataset. When you place the first data range object on the report body, the Data Source Properties dialog is presented, which will lead you through the process of defining a data source and dataset without using the Report Wizard.

Regardless of the method used, a *data source* is simply a connection string saved into the report definition or shared data source file.

Data Sources and Query Languages

The examples in this chapter are based on the SQL Server 2008 sample databases and use the native SQL Server and Analysis Services client data providers. When creating a data source, if you choose any data provider other than SQL Server, queries must be written in the query language appropriate for that product. For most relational database products, this will be a dialect of SQL. For example, Oracle uses a version of SQL called *PL/SQL*, and Microsoft Access uses Access SQL. Some providers require unique types of query expressions or scripting code specifically designed for that data source environment.

When defining a dataset's query expression, the Designer will display one of the two similar query windows. If you are using the SQL Server data provider, the T-SQL Query Designer will be displayed. In the case of another data provider that uses another query language or dialect of SQL, a generic Query window is displayed.

To query cube structures in Analysis Services (which is an OLAP database engine), a specialized expression language called *Multidimensional Expressions* (MDX) is used. Like SQL Server 2005, the current implementation of Reporting Services supports MDX queries. Unlike the Cube Browser in Analysis Services and other specialized multidimensional data query tools, reports are based on data that is flattened to two-dimensional (2D) structures and represented as rows and columns like a SQL query.

If you have not used MDX with OLAP cubes, you might find it interesting to contrast this language with more familiar SQL queries. In this sample MDX query expression for the Adventure Works DW 2008 OLAP database, measures and KPI values (from a key performance indicator, defined in the Adventure Works cube) are returned on the columns axis, and dimension hierarchy members are on the rows axis:

```
SELECT
  {
      [Measures].[Reseller Sales Amount]
    , [Measures].[Reseller Gross Profit Margin]
    , KPIGoal("Channel Revenue")
    , KPIStatus("Channel Revenue")
  } ON Columns,
  (
      [Date].[Calendar].[Calendar Year]
    , [Sales Territory].[Sales Territory].[Region]
  ) ON Rows
FROM [Adventure Works]
;
```

This example is offered merely to pique your interest at this point. You will learn how to design datasets and reports for SQL Server Analysis Services in Chapter 9.

T-SQL Query Design

If you are using SQL Server as the report data source, queries are written using T-SQL. For some reports, writing the query will be a simple matter of using the Graphical Query Designer that you used in the previous chapter to create a basic report. However, most business reports require a little more than just drag-and-drop queries, so some basic T-SQL skills are essential for report design.

> *This section takes you through some of the basics and even demonstrates some intermediate-level grouping and filtering techniques. If you are new to T-SQL and will be using SQL Server 2005 or 2008 for your report data sources, you should pick up a copy of* Beginning T-SQL for Microsoft SQL Server 2005 and 2008.

Serious query design is performed in SQL Server Management Studio. You will use Management Studio to design queries and then paste the text into the Reporting Services Query Designer.

In the following exercise, you will design a series of T-SQL queries, progressively adding features, and then use this for a report dataset. You will use the generic Query Designer in the Reporting Services report design environment and the Query Designer in SQL Server Management Studio. You'll begin where you left off — with a data source that provides a connection to the AdventureWorksDW2008 relational data warehouse.

Leave the Report Designer open, and then open SQL Server Management Studio. When prompted, connect to the relational database engine on your local server, as shown in Figure 7-10.

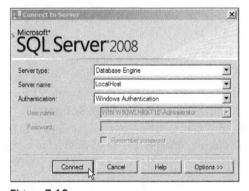

Figure 7-10

Using the Object Explorer on the left side of the window, expand Databases, and then select the AdventureWorksDW2008 database. In the toolbar, click the New Query button (see Figure 7-11).

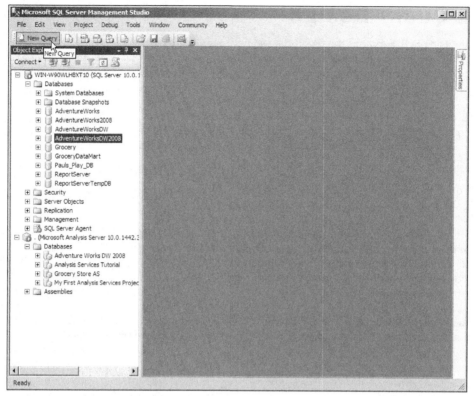

Figure 7-11

Data Warehouse Star Schema

If you haven't worked with a data warehouse star schema before, let's just take a moment to discuss some simple concepts. In a book on the topic of data warehouse design, the following information would occupy one of several chapters (in much greater detail, of course).

The purpose of a database of this type is to simplify data for reporting. Records are organized into two categories of tables. The numeric values that feed summarized or aggregated data point values are called *measures* or *business facts*. These exist in Fact tables (often prefixed with Fact . . .). The Dimension tables (often prefixed by Dim . . .) contain attributes used to organize and describe these business facts. The dimensional attributes can be used to form multilevel hierarchies (e.g., the date dimension is often used to group measure data by the year, quarter, and then month). That's it — the ten-cent tour of data warehouse dimensional design. In summary, for our purposes, the dimension table attribute columns will be used to group, order, and organize records, and the measure columns, from a fact table, are used as aggregated numeric reporting metrics.

A new Query window opens in the Management Studio design pane. The Management Studio Query Designer includes IntelliSense code completion features that help with query design. If you write queries in the right way, the Designer will suggest object names and complete the query script as you type. To take advantage of this useful functionality, write the structure of the query first.

Type the following text into the query pane:

```
SELECT

FROM

ORDER BY

;
```

This is the essential structure for a T-SQL query. Each of these language clauses is followed by a database object name used to return data from the query.

You can use the Object Explorer to see the table and column names that you will use. You can drag these from the tree view into the Query pane, or you can type them. This query will use columns from the DimDate, FactResellerSales, and DimSalesTerritory tables.

The completed FROM clause should match the following added text:

```
SELECT

FROM
   DimDate D INNER JOIN FactResellerSales F ON D.DateKey = F.OrderDateKey
   INNER JOIN DimSalesTerritory ST ON F.SalesTerritoryKey = ST.SalesTerritoryKey

ORDER BY

;
```

Rather than memorizing the database object names and typing the whole thing by hand, however, let the Designer do the work for you.

Begin typing the first table name and . . . magic things happen! Notice that when you type the first few characters, a list of object names appears, and the characters you type are matched against the items in the list. You can also use the keyboard's up and down arrow keys to find an item nearby in the list. As soon as you have the DimDate table selected (Figure 7-12), press the Tab key.

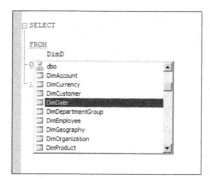

Figure 7-12

Rather than continuing to use the long object names (like DimDate), I've defined object aliases. By preceding the table name *DimDate* with the letter *D*, from now on I simply use the letter *D* to represent this table name.

Now fill in the SELECT clause by listing the columns separated by commas.

The ORDER BY clause is similar but includes only the dimension table columns. The fact table values (OrderQuantity and SalesAmount) will be aggregated in the report, so I don't care about the order of these values in the query result set. Since I want the report to be grouped by the dimension attributes CalendarYear, CalendarQuarter, SalesTerritoryCountry, and SalesTerritoryRegion, sorting records in this order will assist the report design.

The completed query is ready for testing. Verify that your query matches the following text, and then click the Execute button on the Management Studio toolbar.

```
SELECT
   D.CalendarYear, D.CalendarQuarter, ST.SalesTerritoryCountry
   , ST.SalesTerritoryRegion
   , F.OrderQuantity, F.SalesAmount
FROM
   DimDate D INNER JOIN FactResellerSales F ON D.DateKey = F.OrderDateKey
   INNER JOIN DimSalesTerritory ST ON F.SalesTerritoryKey = ST.SalesTerritoryKey
ORDER BY
   D.CalendarYear, D.CalendarQuarter, ST.SalesTerritoryCountry
   , ST.SalesTerritoryRegion
;
```

The query results should look like those in Figure 7-13.

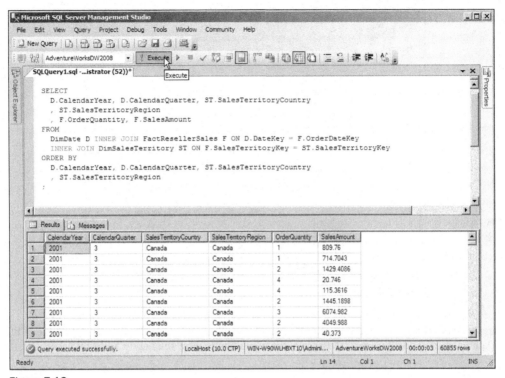

Figure 7-13

Note the record count in the lower-right corner of the Query results pane. I'll come back to this. For now, just note that the query returns 60,855 rows.

> *The following examples will work in either report designer, BIDS or Report Builder 2.0. Keep in mind that there are subtle differences between the two designer interfaces, but the functionality of these tools is very similar.*

Highlight and copy the query text from the Management Studio Query Designer window. Now switch back to the Report Designer, and paste the query text into the Dataset Properties or Query Design window. Click OK to close the Query Design window (if you were using this window), and then click OK to close the Dataset Properties window (see Figure 7-14).

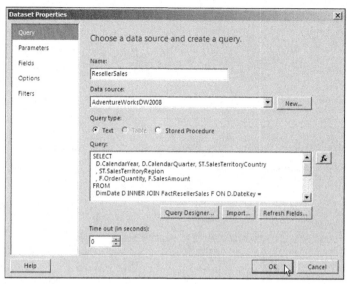

Figure 7-14

Figure 7-15 shows the report design after this dataset has been created. The Report Data pane in BIDS or the Data pane in Report Builder 2.0 displays the available field for the newly added dataset.

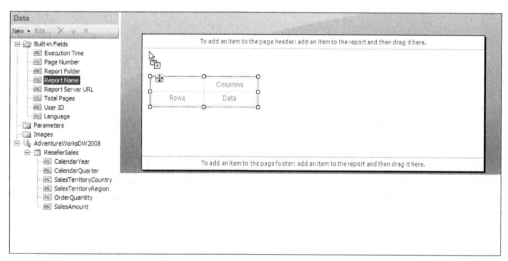

Figure 7-15

To build the report, add a matrix from the Insert menu or toolbox. Move the matrix down the report body to make room for a title.

Drag the Report Name from the Built-in Fields list into the top of the report body.

Drag fields from the dataset into the matrix column and row group header cells. Drag the CalendarYear and CalendarQuarter fields into the column headers. Drag the SalesTerritoryCountry and SalesTerritoryRegion fields into the row headers, to match Figure 7-16.

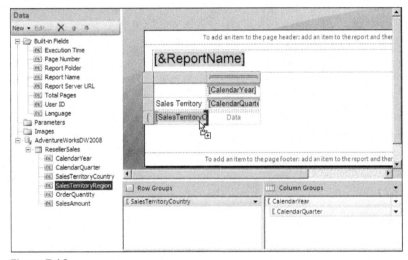

Figure 7-16

Drag the SalesAmount field into the Data cell. Right-click on the cell, and format the number as currency.

Click the Preview button on the ribbon, or choose the Preview tab in the Report Design window to view the report. Remember that you haven't done any formatting, so it should look like Figure 7-17.

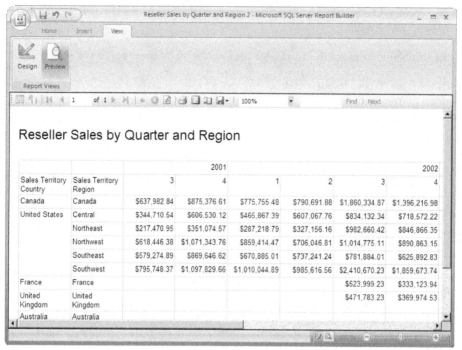

Figure 7-17

With the exception of a little beautification effort, this report design is pretty much done . . .

. . . or is it? Think about it. The query returns more than 60,000 rows of raw data that has aggregated into 10 rows and 12 columns in this matrix report. In a production environment, the results of this query would be streamed across the corporate network from the database server to the Report Server, only to be grouped and summed up into only 120 cells? This is not a particularly efficient solution. When designing a report, always consider the scalability of your design. Imagine if there were 100 times the volume of data — that's 6 million rows. This would be grossly inefficient!

> *For the rest of the query examples, you will be making simple changes to the base query defined above. You can simply edit the dataset with these changes. Of course, you also have the option to make modifications in the Management Studio Query Designer and then copy-and-paste the changes into the report dataset.*

Since the results will be grouped in the report, if you can group the data in the query, you save the report rendering engine from having to do dual duty, and you can send a lot less data over the network. Grouping in the query does add some complexity to the SQL statement, but it reduces this complexity elsewhere.

The grouped version of this query looks like this:

```
SELECT
    D.CalendarYear
  , D.CalendarQuarter
  , ST.SalesTerritoryCountry
  , ST.SalesTerritoryRegion
  , SUM(F.OrderQuantity) AS OrderQuantity
  , SUM(F.SalesAmount) AS SalesAmount
FROM
  DimDate D INNER JOIN FactResellerSales F ON D.DateKey = F.OrderDateKey
  INNER JOIN DimSalesTerritory ST ON F.SalesTerritoryKey = ST.SalesTerritoryKey
GROUP BY
    D.CalendarYear
  , D.CalendarQuarter
  , ST.SalesTerritoryCountry
  , ST.SalesTerritoryRegion
ORDER BY
    D.CalendarYear
  , D.CalendarQuarter
  , ST.SalesTerritoryCountry
  , ST.SalesTerritoryRegion
;
```

Even though the complexity of this query has grown, you'll notice that it's a little easier to read. At some point in the process of adding more and more appendages to a query, try to clean it up and make it easier to read. I can't emphasize how important it is to make sure that your query scripts are well organized and easy for you and others to read. Use tabs, returns, and spaces liberally. By placing delimiting commas at the beginning, rather than the end, of each line, they are not only easier to read but easier to remark out or remove without breaking the query.

This T-SQL language pattern is relatively simple as long as you adhere to some basic rules. Every column in the SELECT list must either be included in the GROUP BY list or must be passed to an aggregate function. In the example, the two measure fields are aggregated using the SUM function. The output from a function doesn't naturally return a column name, so it's common to define an alias using the AS keyword. This example actually defines the column aliases using the original column names, which is perfectly acceptable. You will typically want to set the ORDER BY list to match the GROUP BY list.

This query design is very "copy-and-paste-able." In other words, once you get this working in one query, it's pretty easy to duplicate the pattern in subsequent queries and reports.

Executing this query in the Management Studio Query Designer produces only 96 rows. This means that the result set is less than 1/600th of the size with exactly the same report results! Imagine how much faster this report might run if you had proportionally more data.

Filtering Techniques

When retrieving report data from a data source, it's important to consider the most efficient way to filter report data based on the user's selection criteria. Many databases contain large amounts of data. Therefore, it is always important to retrieve just the right amount of data required for reporting. At times, a report will only be used to view data for a narrow range of values, and at other times, the user may specify different criteria, causing the report to render a varied range of related values.

In the case of a narrow range of possible values, it makes more sense to retrieve only the associated data. However, if users specify different criteria during a session — causing the data source to be re-queried multiple times — it could prove to be slow and an inefficient use of resources.

In Figure 7-18, parameters presented to the data source cause data to be filtered and return only the data for a single rendering of the report. The dataset represents the database server's result set on the client side (the Report Server). As you see in the diagram, this is a small volume of data, because it has already been filtered at the database.

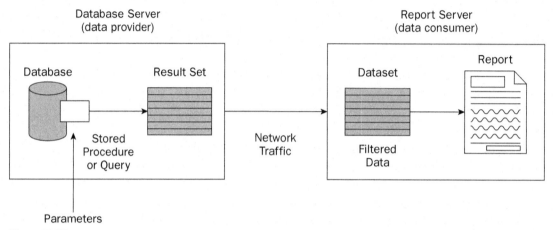

Figure 7-18

By passing selection criteria parameters at the database object level, network traffic can be greatly reduced, and the report is rendered more efficiently. However, if the user will be providing different parameter values to render several views of the same report within a session, the database will be queried repeatedly, perhaps resulting in longer overall wait times, and much of the same data will be moving across the network multiple times. In Figure 7-19, a larger volume of data is returned from the database server since it is unfiltered. Filtering then occurs by using report parameters on the Report Server against the cached set of records on the Report Server.

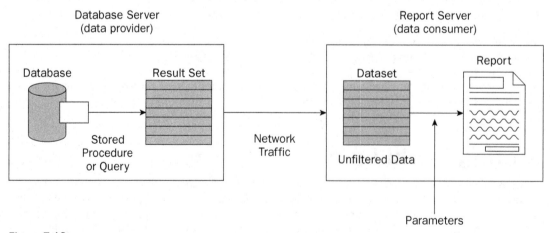

Figure 7-19

If all of the data necessary for each query to be executed in a user's session is obtained in one result set, it will result in a greater volume of network traffic for a single execution. However, it may reduce subsequent report rendering times.

Selection parameters can be applied to data at the report level rather than at the data source. Because all the data is cached (held in memory), reports will render much faster. This technique can reduce the overall network traffic and rendering time. The report can also be configured so that the cached data is saved to disk, usually for a specific period of time. This technique is presented in Chapter 13.

You certainly don't want to retrieve unnecessary data from the data source, so a combination of these two techniques may be the appropriate solution, depending on specific reporting needs. For example, if you are a regional sales manager and you wish to get sales summaries for each of the territories within your region, you may begin your session by retrieving all of the regional sales data for a range of dates. For each territory report, this data is simply filtered down to the territory level. If these were long-running report queries, it might actually be more efficient to retrieve all the sales data for the date range and then filter the sales regions on the Report Server.

Filtering a Query

Filtering records in the query is performed by adding a WHERE clause. Make the following changes to the query:

```
SELECT
    D.CalendarYear
  , D.CalendarQuarter
  , ST.SalesTerritoryCountry
  , ST.SalesTerritoryRegion
  , F.OrderQuantity, F.SalesAmount
FROM
    DimDate D INNER JOIN FactResellerSales F ON D.DateKey = F.OrderDateKey
    INNER JOIN DimSalesTerritory ST ON F.SalesTerritoryKey = ST.SalesTerritoryKey
WHERE
    D.CalendarYear = 2003
ORDER BY
    D.CalendarYear
  , D.CalendarQuarter
  , ST.SalesTerritoryCountry
  , ST.SalesTerritoryRegion
;
```

Before rows are returned from the database server, candidate rows are scanned, and only qualifying rows are returned when the CalendarYear value is 2003. Execute the report, and note that only the 2003 calendar year and related quarters are displayed in the matrix.

Parameter Concepts

Using parameters in report design isn't complicated, but until you have a chance to do some creative things with them in both queries and report expressions, you might not fully appreciate the power of parameters. This section starts by explaining how parameters are defined in simple queries and reports and explains how you might need to use (and define) parameters in more complex reports.

There are two (and possibly three, depending on your query technique) different types of parameters with which you may contend in report design: data-set parameters and report parameters. Dataset parameters can be derived from database objects, such as stored procedures and user-defined functions, or they can be derived from a parameterized query statement. As Figure 7-20 illustrates, there can be three different layers in the design process where you can encounter parameters.

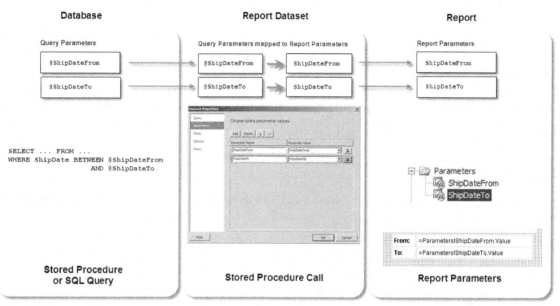

Figure 7-20

Most commonly, report parameters will be derived from parameters defined in an ad hoc query or SQL stored procedure. But you don't have to have a parameterized query to use parameters in a report, as you'll see in a later example.

When using SQL Server as the data source, parameters are defined in the SQL syntax by prefixing the names with a single @ symbol. In a stored procedure, these parameters are defined first and then used in the procedure body much as you would in an ad hoc query. The Report Designer automatically parses the query and generates corresponding report parameters. The third section of Figure 7-20 shows the Report Parameters dialog open with the two derived parameters. If you use the Graphical Query Builder or generic Query Designer to write a T-SQL statement, the Report Designer will resolve data-set parameters and database object parameters and prompt for the parameter values when running the query. Data-set parameters are mapped to report parameters in the Dataset Properties dialog. This dialog is accessible when editing the dataset in the Report Data pane of the Report Designer.

For most basic queries, the Report Designer will populate this dialog and match the parameters for you. But if have created a very complex or unusual data-set query, you may need to match the data-set and report parameters manually. Parameter resolution is performed when you test a query in the Query Designer, click the Refresh Fields button, or close the Dataset Properties dialog.

Let's step out of this exercise for a moment to show a different example. The following query contains two parameters used to specify a range of date values for filtering a Date type field:

```
SELECT
    D.CalendarYear
  , D.CalendarQuarter
  , D.MonthNumberOfYear
  , D.FullDateAlternateKey AS OrderDate
  , ST.SalesTerritoryCountry
  , ST.SalesTerritoryRegion
  , SUM(F.OrderQuantity) AS OrderQuantity
  , SUM(F.SalesAmount) AS SalesAmount
FROM
  DimDate D INNER JOIN FactResellerSales F ON D.DateKey = F.OrderDateKey
  INNER JOIN DimSalesTerritory ST ON F.SalesTerritoryKey = ST.SalesTerritoryKey
WHERE
  D.FullDateAlternateKey BETWEEN @ShipDateFrom AND @ShipDateTo
GROUP BY
  D.CalendarYear
  , D.CalendarQuarter
  , D.MonthNumberOfYear
  , D.FullDateAlternateKey
  , ST.SalesTerritoryCountry
  , ST.SalesTerritoryRegion
ORDER BY
    D.CalendarYear
  , D.CalendarQuarter
  , D.MonthNumberOfYear
  , D.FullDateAlternateKey
  , ST.SalesTerritoryCountry
  , ST.SalesTerritoryRegion
;
```

For each of these two parameters, the Data type has been set to Date/Time in the Report Parameter Properties dialog (see Figure 7-21).

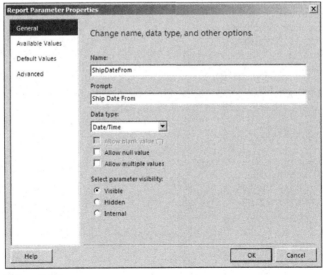

Figure 7-21

When the report is run, the result is that a date picker control is used to select a date (see Figure 7-22). The user clicks the calendar icon next to the textbox to reveal the calendar dropdown; uses the controls to select a year, month, and date; and then clicks the View Report button on the parameter bar.

Figure 7-22

Filtering Data with Query Parameters

Parameters are often used to filter data at the data source. Whether the data is to be filtered within the report or not, filtering at least some of the data within the database is an essential technique for most report solutions. If you have created parameterized stored procedures in SQL Server, you are already familiar with this pattern. The technique applies to stored procedures and query expressions that use very similar syntax. Let's start with a simple ad hoc query expression and then move on to creating a stored procedure.

Query parameters begin with the @ symbol and must conform to the naming convention standards for T-SQL identifiers. The name should not contain spaces or certain punctuation characters and can't begin with a numeral; for simplicity, just use letters. In stored procedures, parameters must be declared before they are used. In an ad hoc query, simply make up parameter names when you need them. In the WHERE part of our example SQL statement, use a parameter to represent a variable valuable, as follows:

```
SELECT
    D.CalendarYear
  , D.CalendarQuarter
  , ST.SalesTerritoryCountry
  , ST.SalesTerritoryRegion
  , F.OrderQuantity
  , F.SalesAmount
FROM
  DimDate D INNER JOIN FactResellerSales F ON D.DateKey = F.OrderDateKey
  INNER JOIN DimSalesTerritory ST ON F.SalesTerritoryKey = ST.SalesTerritoryKey
WHERE
  D.CalendarYear = @Year
ORDER BY
    D.CalendarYear
  , D.CalendarQuarter
  , ST.SalesTerritoryCountry
  , ST.SalesTerritoryRegion
;
```

To test this query, you must execute it in the Report Designer's Query Editor, because Management Studio doesn't know what to do with the parameter. If you execute this query and enter **2003** when prompted for the Year parameter, the original 60,855 rows are reduced to 26,758. Aside from letting the user see only the data he or she wanted, this certainly won't hurt performance.

Now, let's combine filtering with grouping records and see what happens. Add the GROUP BY clause from the earlier example, and then execute this query in the Report Designer Query Editor. Enter **2003** for the Year parameter. Viola! Only 36 rows are returned.

```
SELECT
      D.CalendarYear
    , D.CalendarQuarter
    , ST.SalesTerritoryCountry
    , ST.SalesTerritoryRegion
    , SUM(F.OrderQuantity) AS QtySum
    , SUM(F.SalesAmount) AS AmtSum
FROM
    DimDate D INNER JOIN FactResellerSales F ON D.DateKey = F.OrderDateKey
    INNER JOIN DimSalesTerritory ST ON F.SalesTerritoryKey = ST.SalesTerritoryKey
WHERE
    D.CalendarYear = @Year
GROUP BY
      D.CalendarYear
    , D.CalendarQuarter
    , ST.SalesTerritoryCountry
    , ST.SalesTerritoryRegion
ORDER BY
      D.CalendarYear
    , D.CalendarQuarter
    , ST.SalesTerritoryCountry
    , ST.SalesTerritoryRegion
;
```

Over time, reports tend to grow and expand. Users will inevitably ask for more fields, more totals, and other features. Allowing the requirements to evolve in this manner can make your reports unruly and difficult to support — especially when you have different people involved in this haphazard and incremental style of design. Writing well-designed queries will go a long way in achieving efficient, maintainable reports. Carefully consider whether functionality should be built into the query or the report design. Often, handling business challenges in the query will make the report design much easier.

Creating a Parameter List

When you run this report, you are prompted to type a parameter value into the parameter bar area above the report. Although this works, it's not very convenient. You can provide a list of values for the user to select from by modifying the properties of the Year parameter. You can either create a list of available values by adding them in the Available Value page of the Parameter Properties dialog or use a query to return a list of available values.

To create a query-driven list, first create a new dataset called *YearList* under the same data source as the previous dataset. Enter the following T-SQL statement, and verify that this returns a list of calendar year values:

```
SELECT DISTINCT CalendarYear
FROM DimDate
ORDER BY CalendarYear
```

Figure 7-23 shows the Dataset Properties dialog for this new data-set query.

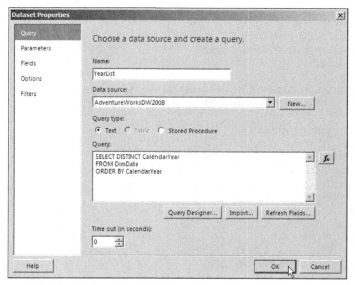

Figure 7-23

To set up the parameter list, right-click on the Year parameter in the Report Data pane, and choose Parameter Properties. Select the Available Values page of the Report Parameter Properties dialog, and select the radio button labeled Get value from a query. Now, just select the new dataset and the CalendarYear field for both the Value field and Label field properties. Verify that this page looks like Figure 7-24, and then click OK.

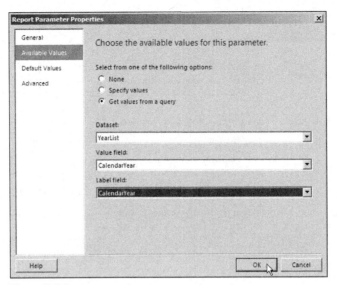

Figure 7-24

You can build a simple table report to view the results of the query. A sample report is provided in the Chapter 7 sample project.

Now, preview the report. Select a year from the dropdown list, and click View report to see the results. You'll see that only sales records from the selected year are included in the results.

Multi-Value Parameters

You can configure parameters so that a user has the option to select a combination of values. This is easy to do using the Report Parameter Properties dialog.

Modify the Year parameter by right-clicking on and selecting Parameter Properties for the Year parameter in the Report Data pane. Check Allow multiple values in the resulting Report Parameter Properties dialog (see Figure 7-25), and click OK.

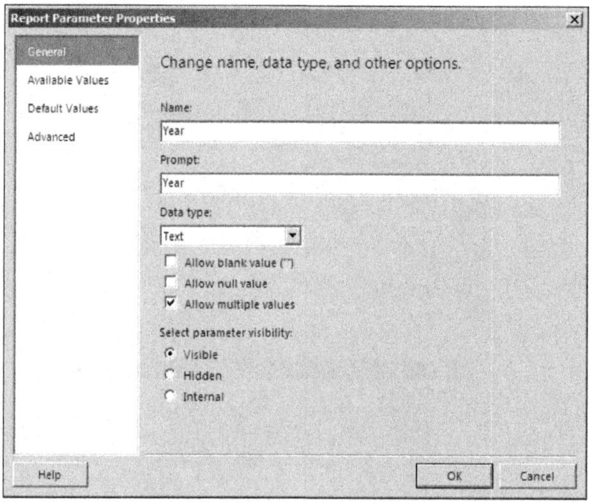

Figure 7-25

Changing this setting changes the behavior of the parameter dropdown list, but it doesn't enable the SQL Server database engine to deal with the changes. A simple modification is required in the query syntax. By making the report parameter multi-valued, this changes it to an array type object. When the report parameter value(s) is mapped to the corresponding query parameter value (which is not an array), the value is converted to a string value containing a comma-separated list. Both T-SQL and MDX contain parsing functions that know how to deal with comma-delimited values. In T-SQL, the IN function will match a field value against items in such a list.

Modify the main data-set query by making the following change in the WHERE clause. Replace the equals sign with the IN function, and place parentheses around the @Year parameter reference.

```
SELECT
    D.CalendarYear
  , D.CalendarQuarter
  , ST.SalesTerritoryCountry
  , ST.SalesTerritoryRegion
  , SUM(F.OrderQuantity) AS QtySum
  , SUM(F.SalesAmount) AS AmtSum
FROM
  DimDate D INNER JOIN FactResellerSales F ON D.DateKey = F.OrderDateKey
  INNER JOIN DimSalesTerritory ST ON F.SalesTerritoryKey = ST.SalesTerritoryKey
WHERE
  D.CalendarYear IN ( @Year )
GROUP BY
    D.CalendarYear
  , D.CalendarQuarter
  , ST.SalesTerritoryCountry
  , ST.SalesTerritoryRegion
ORDER BY
    D.CalendarYear
  , D.CalendarQuarter
  , ST.SalesTerritoryCountry
  , ST.SalesTerritoryRegion
;
```

Now run the query. You should see, as in Figure 7-26, that the Year parameter dropdown list contains items preceded with checkboxes.

Figure 7-26

Select any combination of Year values, and then click the View Report button to test the report. Records should be filtered for the set of years you've selected.

Cascading Parameters

A parameter can depend on another parameter so that the list of available values for a parameter is filtered based on another parameter selection. For example, if you offer users a list of product categories and another list of product subcategories, the subcategory list would only show subcategories for a selected category.

The Report Data pane in Figure 7-27 shows the objects defined in the finished report. As you can see, two parameters are defined for the user to select the product category (named *CatKey* in this example) and the product subcategory (named *SubcatKey*). A data-set query corresponds to each parameter. These are named *CatList* and *SubcatList*, respectively. (I like to give parameters names that are similar to the fields.)

Figure 7-27

The most logical way to define these objects is to work backward through the process from the user's perspective. That is, a user will select a product category to see a filtered list of subcategories. After he or she selects a subcategory, the report will be filtered, based on the subcategory selection. To design this, you would add the subcategory filtering to the main data-set query and then create the filtered subcategory query and corresponding parameter. Finally, you would define the category query and parameter. The following steps you through creating each of these objects and the filtering mechanism in the main data-set query in the proper order:

1. Right-click on the main report dataset, and choose Query. Your dataset may be named **Dataset1**. It's renamed to *ResellerSales* in this example. Note that if you rename a dataset after using it, you must update the DatasetName of any affected data range or report items used in the report.

2. Modify the FROM and WHERE clauses to match the following query script:

```
SELECT
      D.CalendarYear
    , D.CalendarQuarter
    , ST.SalesTerritoryCountry
    , ST.SalesTerritoryRegion
    , SUM(F.OrderQuantity) AS QtySum
    , SUM(F.SalesAmount) AS AmtSum
FROM
   DimDate D INNER JOIN FactResellerSales F ON D.DateKey = F.OrderDateKey
   INNER JOIN DimSalesTerritory ST ON F.SalesTerritoryKey = ST.SalesTerritoryKey
   INNER JOIN DimProduct P ON F.ProductKey = P.ProductKey
WHERE
   D.CalendarYear = @Year AND P.ProductSubcategoryKey = @SubcatKey
GROUP BY
      D.CalendarYear
    , D.CalendarQuarter
    , ST.SalesTerritoryCountry
    , ST.SalesTerritoryRegion
ORDER BY
      D.CalendarYear
    , D.CalendarQuarter
    , ST.SalesTerritoryCountry
    , ST.SalesTerritoryRegion
;
```

3. Now for the subcategory list query. Right-click on the AdventureWorksDW2008 data source, and add a new query named **SubcatList**. Either use the Query Builder or manually enter this query text:

```
SELECT      ProductSubcategoryKey, EnglishProductSubcategoryName
FROM        DimProductSubcategory
WHERE       ProductCategoryKey = @CatKey
ORDER BY    EnglishProductSubcategoryName
```

When you closed the Dataset Properties dialog after making changes to the main dataset, the referenced SubcatKey parameter was automatically generated and added to the list of available parameters.

4. Right-click on the SubcatKey parameter, and select Parameter Properties from the menu. The Report Parameter Properties dialog is displayed (see Figure 7-28).

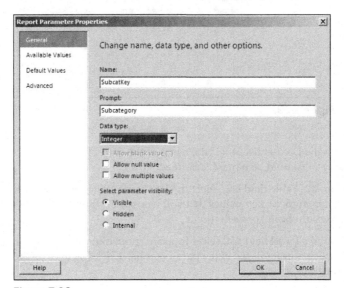

Figure 7-28

5. Change the Prompt to a friendly name for this parameter. Your users don't need to see the cryptic parameter name. Change the Data type to Integer.

6. Choose the Available Values page, and select Get values from a query. Three dropdown lists are displayed, as shown in Figure 7-29.

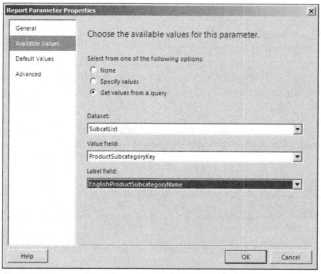

Figure 7-29

6.1. From the Dataset list, select the name of the dataset that returns product subcategory values. It should be named *SubcatList*.

6.2. From the Value field list, select the ProductSubcategoryKey field. This is the field containing numeric key values that will be used for filtering the main query after the user makes a subcategory selection.

6.3. From the Label field list, select EnglishProductSubcategoryName. This is the friendly value the user will see in the parameter list. Click OK to close the Report Parameter Properties dialog.

7. Right-click on the AdventureWorksDW2008 data source, and add a new query named **CatList**. Either use the Query Builder or manually enter the following for the query text. Click OK to close the Dataset Properties dialog.

```
SELECT    ProductCategoryKey, EnglishProductCategoryName
FROM      DimProductCategory
ORDER BY  EnglishProductCategoryName
```

8. In the Report Data pane, right-click on the CatKey parameter, and select Parameter Properties from the menu. The Report Parameter Properties dialog is displayed.

9. Like the main report dataset, when you closed the Dataset Properties dialog after making changes to the SubcatList dataset, the referenced CatKey parameter was automatically generated and added to the list of available parameters.

10. Right-click on the CatKey parameter, and select Parameter Properties from the menu. The Report Parameter Properties dialog is displayed (see Figure 7-30).

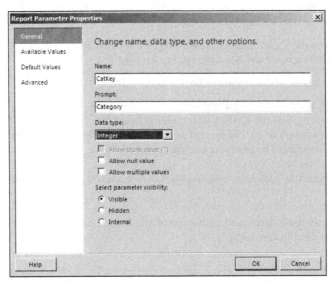

Figure 7-30

11. Change the Prompt to a friendly name for this parameter. Your users don't need to see the cryptic parameter name. Change the Data type to Integer. Choose the Available Values page, and select Get values from a query. Three dropdown lists are displayed, as shown in Figure 7-31.

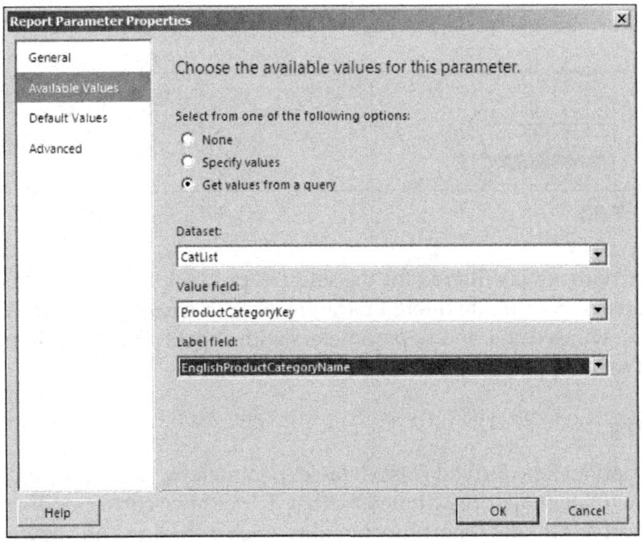

Figure 7-31

11.1. From the Dataset list, select the name of the dataset that returns product subcategory values. It should be named *CatList*.

11.2. From the Value field list, select the ProductCategoryKey field. This is the field containing numeric key values that will be used for filtering the main query after the user makes a category selection.

11.3. From the Label field list, select EnglishProductCategoryName. This is the friendly value the user will see in the parameter list.

12. Click OK to close the Report Parameter Properties dialog.

13. The last thing to do is make sure the parameters are in the right order. Referring back to Figure 7-27, verify that the CatKey parameter is listed before the SubcatKey parameter. You can rearrange parameters using the up and down arrows in the toolbar of this pane. If everything checks out, you should be ready to test the report.

Preview the report. Since the Year parameter was left over from the previous example, make sure it has a valid selection.

The Category parameter list is displayed with a list of all product categories (see Figure 7-32). Note that the Subcategory list is disabled and empty.

Figure 7-32

Make a category selection, and you will see the Subcategory list become available with a list of values filtered by the previous category selection. Select a subcategory, and then click the View Report button (see Figure 7-33).

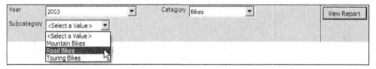

Figure 7-33

The report should run with results filtered for the selected product subcategory. As you can see, multiple parameters may be used to coordinate filtered parameters or to narrow down the results of the report. In Chapters 9 and 10, you will see how to use parameters with expressions to design even more interesting report behaviors and to build very creative solutions.

Report Parameters

In addition to report parameters derived from data-set parameters, you can explicitly add report parameters of your own. These report parameters (that do not have corresponding query parameters) can be added to support additional report functionality, such as hiding and showing report sections, page numbers and dynamic formatting.

The following example demonstrates some simple report parameters used to dynamically set values on the report. Later we'll apply this technique to some more practical report features. This example is intended to demonstrate two very simple report parameters for academic purposes.

1. First, create a new report without using the Wizard. You can use the Start "pearl" button in Report Builder 2.0, or in BIDS, you can select Add and then Add New Item from the Solution Explorer's right-click menu.

2. Select Report from the report item templates in the Add New Item dialog. Do not specify a dataset for the new report.

3. Report parameters are added in the Report Data pane. Right-click Parameters, and add a report parameter named **ReportTitle**.

4. Click OK to save the parameter, and then repeat the process to add a report parameter named **TextColor**. For this parameter, use the Available Value page to add a list of simple color values like Red, Blue, Yellow, and Black. The Value and Label for each of the items should be the same. Click OK to save this parameter.

5. Next, drag and drop each of the two parameters onto the report body. This creates a textbox for each. Click in the second textbox, and insert text before the "@TextColor" reference, as you see in Figure 7-34. You can also change the font size and weight for these textboxes.

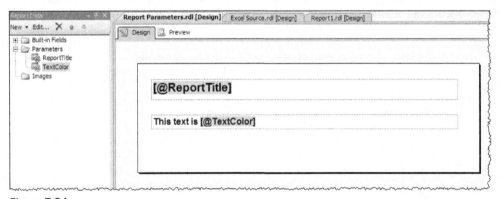

Figure 7-34

I'll be covering the use of expressions thoroughly in Chapter 8. Using an expression to set properties is easy, though. You've actually been doing this just by dragging and dropping fields and parameters into the Report Designer.

6. With the Property Pane visible, click on the second textbox, find the Color property, and then either type or use the Expression Builder to set the property to an expression. Set the Color property for the second textbox to use the following expression:

```
=Parameters!TextColor.Value
```

Now preview the report, and notice what happens. The parameter bar prompts you to enter a report title and to select a color. When you click on the View Report button, the first textbox displays the text entered into the ReportTitle parameter, and the second textbox displays not only the specific color name but the text, as well (see Figure 7-35).

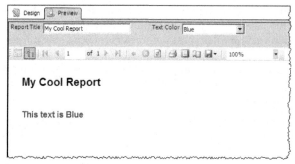

Figure 7-35

Yes, I know this book is printed in black and white, so to clarify, the text in this figure, "This text is Blue" is blue.

As you can "see," this is an effective way to feed values to the report to be used in expressions. Chapter 8 expands this technique to provide filtering and dynamic formatting.

Using Stored Procedures

There are several advantages to using stored procedures rather than verbose T-SQL queries in a report. Complex queries can be stored as reusable database objects. Stored procedures can run more efficiently and provide greater security and control.

The following T-SQL script is used to create a stored procedure in SQL Server Management Studio. Once created, the procedure is simply referenced and executed by name from the report.

```
CREATE PROCEDURE spGet_ResellerSalesByRegion
  @ShipDateFrom Date
 ,@ShipDateTo   Date
AS
SELECT
  D.CalendarYear
  , D.CalendarQuarter
  , D.MonthNumberOfYear
  , D.DateKey
  , ST.SalesTerritoryCountry
  , ST.SalesTerritoryRegion
  , F.OrderQuantity
  , F.SalesAmount
FROM
  DimDate D INNER JOIN FactResellerSales F ON D.DateKey = F.OrderDateKey
  INNER JOIN DimSalesTerritory ST ON F.SalesTerritoryKey = ST.SalesTerritoryKey
WHERE
  D.FullDateAlternateKey BETWEEN @ShipDateFrom AND @ShipDateTo
ORDER BY
  D.CalendarYear
  , D.CalendarQuarter
  , D.MonthNumberOfYear
  , D.DateKey
  , ST.SalesTerritoryCountry
  , ST.SalesTerritoryRegion
;
```

The best way to go about querying a data source will depend highly on your requirements. Refer back to the earlier discussion about filtering techniques where processing parameters (on the database server, the client, or both) affects performance, efficiency, and the flexibility of your reporting solution. Handling parameters on the database server will almost always be more efficient, while processing parameters on the client will give you the flexibility of handling a wider range of records and query options without needing to go back to the database every time you need to render the report.

Using a parameterized stored procedure is typically going to provide the most efficient means for filtering data since it returns only the data matching your criteria. Stored procedures are compiled to native processor instructions on the database server. When any kind of query is processed, SQL Server creates an execution plan, which defines the specific instructions that the server uses to retrieve data. In the case of a stored procedure, the execution plan is prepared the first time it is executed, and then it is cached on the database server. In subsequent executions, results will be returned faster since some of the work has already been done.

Filtering Data with Report Parameters

So far you've only filtered data at the database level. In cases in which users may be using the same report in one sitting to view data for different criteria, it may be more effective to retrieve a larger result set from the data source and then filter the report data on the Report Server.

As you've already seen, parameters defined in a query or stored procedure that serves as a report dataset are pulled into the report as report parameters. You can also define your own parameters and use expressions to filter data at the report level.

Using the report from the previous query filtering exercise, suppose that you want to return records for all subcategory values from the database and then filter by SubcatKey on the Report Server. Why would you want to return more records from the database server than those displayed in the report? This may seem to be inefficient at first, but perhaps not if you consider the bigger picture. If you have a long-running query and you anticipate that a user will run the report multiple times with different parameter values, it may actually be more efficient to get all the data at the beginning of the user's session. Query results can be cached on the server for a user's session or for all users. After it has been deployed to the server, a report can be configured to cache data for a period of time, to the benefit of other users.

The first change to make is to remove the query filter for the SubcatKey parameter. This query will continue to filter results for the product subcategory, using the Year parameter.

You must also add the ProductSubcategoryKey column to the SELECT column list. You didn't have to return this column when you used it for filtering in the query. In order to use this field for data-set filtering, it must now be returned.

```
SELECT
    D.CalendarYear
  , D.CalendarQuarter
  , ST.SalesTerritoryCountry
  , ST.SalesTerritoryRegion
  , P.ProductSubcategoryKey
  , SUM(F.OrderQuantity) AS QtySum
  , SUM(F.SalesAmount) AS AmtSum
FROM
  DimDate D INNER JOIN FactResellerSales F ON D.DateKey = F.OrderDateKey
  INNER JOIN DimSalesTerritory ST ON F.SalesTerritoryKey = ST.SalesTerritoryKey
  INNER JOIN DimProduct P ON F.ProductKey = P.ProductKey
WHERE
  D.CalendarYear IN ( @Year )
GROUP BY
    D.CalendarYear
  , D.CalendarQuarter
  , ST.SalesTerritoryCountry
  , ST.SalesTerritoryRegion
  , P.ProductSubcategoryKey
ORDER BY
    D.CalendarYear
  , D.CalendarQuarter
  , ST.SalesTerritoryCountry
  , ST.SalesTerritoryRegion
  , P.ProductSubcategoryKey
;
```

The SubcatKey parameter remains in the report definition even though it's been removed from the query.

In the Report Data pane, right-click on the main dataset, and then choose Dataset Properties. In the Dataset Properties dialog, select the Filters page. Click the Add button to define a new filter expression for the dataset. Select the ProductSubcategoryKey field in the Expression dropdown list. Next to the Value textbox, click on the Expression button (labeled *fx*), as shown in Figure 7-36.

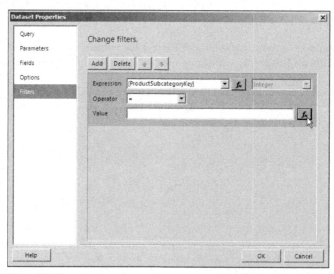

Figure 7-36

216

Clicking on this button on any Dialog window opens the Expression window, allowing you to build an expression using fields, built-in objects, and parameters in the report.

To create an expression that references the SubcatKey parameter value, choose Parameters in the Category list. In the Values list on the right side of the dialog, double-click on the SubcatKey parameter to insert the expression into the Expression box at the top.

You can also type text directly into this window. Verify that your expression looks like Figure 7-37, and then click the OK button to accept these changes.

Figure 7-37

If you've worked with previous versions of Reporting Services, you'll notice that expressions now appear in a different format. The Value box in Figure 7-38 shows a token for the SubcatKey parameter that corresponds to the complete expression you generated in the Expression Editor dialog. Click OK to accept these changes.

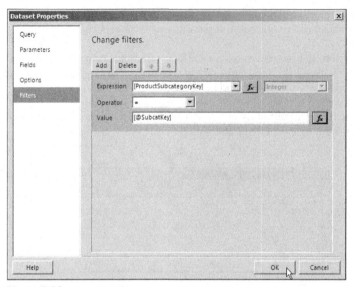

Figure 7-38

This report should behave just like it did before, with one important difference. If you run the report once with a set of parameter values, it will take as long to run and render the report as it has before. However, if you choose a different subcategory value from the parameter dropdown list and then re-run the report, it should run faster than before. This may not be as apparent with a small set of data, but in production, with much larger data volumes, this design change would have a significant impact on performance.

Let's review how data-set filtering works. The Year parameter filters data at the database. The resulting data is cached in memory on the Report Server, where the subcategory filter further limits results.

You could easily extend the design of this report using more complex items, sorting, and grouping. The data-set query could also be replaced with a stored procedure. With these building blocks, you now have the ability to create efficient reports that move the appropriate volume of data across network connections and allow users to use filtering criteria without needing to re-query the entire dataset.

Using Other Data Sources

After using Reporting Services with SQL Server databases and then later with others, I realized that I had become a bit spoiled. It's true that you can use practically any standard database product as a data source for reports; you're not going to have the assistance of the Graphical Query Builder and other automated features of the Report Designer. Nevertheless, Reporting Services can work with the language syntax and features of most databases; you'll just need to do some of the easy stuff yourself. This section showcases a few different products we've used as data sources. One point to keep in mind is that the compatibilities and behaviors will be influenced by a number of factors, including the features and capabilities of the data provider or database driver you are using. Many database product vendors don't develop their own data providers, so the capabilities and behaviors of a data source will vary not only between different versions of a product, but also by the native or third-party provider you have installed.

218

The technique demonstrated a little later in the chapter with an Access query (in the section "Building a Query in a String Expression") is a universal pattern that applies to all database products. I strongly recommend that you take a look at this technique as it will be useful to you at some point, regardless of the data source you use for reporting.

Microsoft Access

Microsoft Access is built on top of the JET Database Engine, with data stored in a single MDB file. This is simple and convenient for small, portable databases. However, Microsoft continues to take steps to replace JET databases with SQL Server and the desktop implementations of SQL. These include the SQL Server 2000 Desktop Database Engine (MSDE) and SQL Server 2005 Express Edition. As a desktop application, Access may also be used as a front-end to SQL databases. If you have the luxury to build a new database solution, it may be best to use one of these newer products in place of older Access databases. But if you have existing solutions based on older Access databases, it will likely be easier to continue to work with them in their present form.

There are two standard data providers that may be used to connect to Access databases. The JET 4.0 .NET OLE DB provider is newer and should be a little more efficient than using the older Access ODBC driver. The fact is that the data provider is rarely going to be a performance bottleneck, so this is probably a moot point. The OLE DB provider is easier to use and doesn't require a separate ODBC Data Source Name (DSN) to be configured. One of the nice features of the new data provider is that it will accept Transact-SQL and translate it into Access-specific syntax. Although Access SQL and Transact-SQL are very close, there are some subtle differences. This feature enables the Report Designer to use the Transact-SQL Graphical Query Builder when a dataset uses a JET data source.

Figure 7-39 shows the Connection Properties dialog used when defining an Access database connection using the JET OLE DB provider.

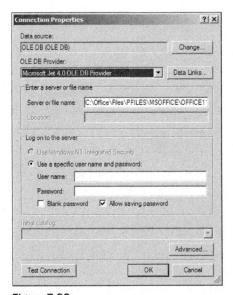

Figure 7-39

Note that the default security credentials used with an unsecured Access database are the Admin user with a blank password. Even if you were to explicitly provide this information and check the Blank password box, the dialog doesn't show these values. This is because the data provider knows to use default credentials when the database hasn't been secured.

The connection string and credentials are shown in Figures 7-40 and 7-41, respectively.

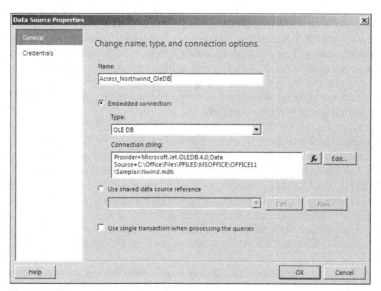

Figure 7-40

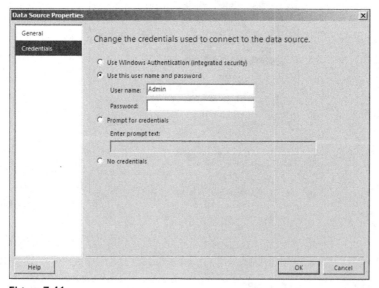

Figure 7-41

Select the Credentials tab to view or modify the user authentication information.

Access has some minor quirks that you should be aware of. Any file-based data source can present a challenge for Reporting Services because the service must have the necessary security access to open the database file. If the MDB file is on the Report Server, this shouldn't be a concern, but if the file is on another network share, it may be. If you get file sharing errors, make sure that Reporting Services runs using a network account that has privileges to open the Access database file and its containing folder.

Parameterized Access queries have always presented a challenge in custom code, outside of simple Access forms applications. The JET database engine has difficulty resolving parameter values passed into queries and may report errors even if the values are passed using the correct data type and format. For example, the following Access query defines and then uses two parameters to filter order records in the Northwind sample database:

```
PARAMETERS [ShipDateFrom] DateTime, [ShipDateTo] DateTime;
SELECT Orders.ShippedDate
  , Orders.OrderID
  , [Order Subtotals].Subtotal
  , Format([ShippedDate],"yyyy") AS [Year]
FROM Orders INNER JOIN [Order Subtotals]
    ON Orders.OrderID = [Order Subtotals].OrderID
WHERE (((Orders.ShippedDate) Is Not Null AND (Orders.ShippedDate)
    BETWEEN [ShipDateFrom] AND [ShipDateTo]));
```

Even when the ShipDateFrom and ShipDateTo query parameters are correctly mapped to corresponding report parameters, the report runs with an error. If you are connecting via the JET OLE DB provider, it reports this error:

```
No value given for one or more required parameters.
```

If the Access ODBC driver is used, the native JET error is reported:

```
Too few parameters. Expected 2.
```

The easiest way I've found to work around the Access query parameterization issue is to build the query string using an expression rather than to rely on this feature. It's not hard to do. The first step is to define the parameters in your report. With the report parameters in place, they can be referenced in the data-set query expression. There is no need to define the parameters or any other properties of the dataset, because this will be handled in the expression.

Building a Query in a String Expression

This technique can be used typically when other options, such as using the Graphical Query Builder and defining query parameters, won't work in the Designer. Any expression may be used to build a text string and can include Visual Basic functions and custom code. The resulting string is simply presented to the database engine through the connection's data provider. No other parsing or processing is performed. The query expression must be entered using the generic Query Designer window for the dataset.

```
="SELECT Orders.ShippedDate, Orders.OrderID, [Order Subtotals].Subtotal,
ShippedDate "
  + "FROM Orders INNER JOIN [Order Subtotals] ON Orders.OrderID = [Order
Subtotals].OrderID "
  +
"WHERE Orders.ShippedDate Is Not Null AND Orders.ShippedDate BETWEEN #" +
Parameters!ShipDateFrom.Value + "# AND #" + Parameters!ShipDateTo.Value + "#"
```

Because this is a Visual Basic expression, double quotes are used to encapsulate literal text. Line breaks cannot be used without terminating and concatenating the string using the + or & characters. Parameter values are concatenated into the query string with appropriate delimiters. The two parameter expressions refer to the parameters I defined in the report.

Note that this is an Access SQL query, rather than T-SQL. Pound sign characters (#) are used to delimit dates, rather than single quotes.

Some variations of this technique can be useful to meet specific needs. Rather than building the entire query string in the data-set designer, you can call a custom Visual Basic function to do the work in programming code. Parameters could be passed to this function that returns the entire query.

An unfortunate side effect of using this expression query technique is that the data-set designer will not allow you to execute the query. If you need to make any changes to the query expression that will update the fields available to the report, you must convert the query back to a SQL expression (by removing the = and ' characters), execute the query, and update the Fields list using the Refresh button. Another option is to manually edit the Fields list.

I recommend that you paste the expression into Notepad, modify the expression in the data-set designer to update the Fields list, and then paste the expression back into the designer. This will save effort and give you an "undo" option if things don't go well.

Microsoft Excel

As a quick-and-easy data source, Excel is a great tool. I am continually amazed by the proliferation of Excel spreadsheets as production enterprise databases used in large business. Even at Microsoft, this practice is commonplace. I think this is largely due to the fact that business data comes from business people, and business people use Excel. I'll leave the data management and consolidation discussion for another time. The fact remains that a lot of important data exists in Excel files, and you can create reports to view this data as you would with any database system.

Figure 7-42 shows an Excel data source example. When connecting to Excel, you use the simple OLE DB connection type and then build a connection string that includes the JET OLE DB provider and the full path to the Excel document file. This currently works with XLS files up to the Office 2003 version.

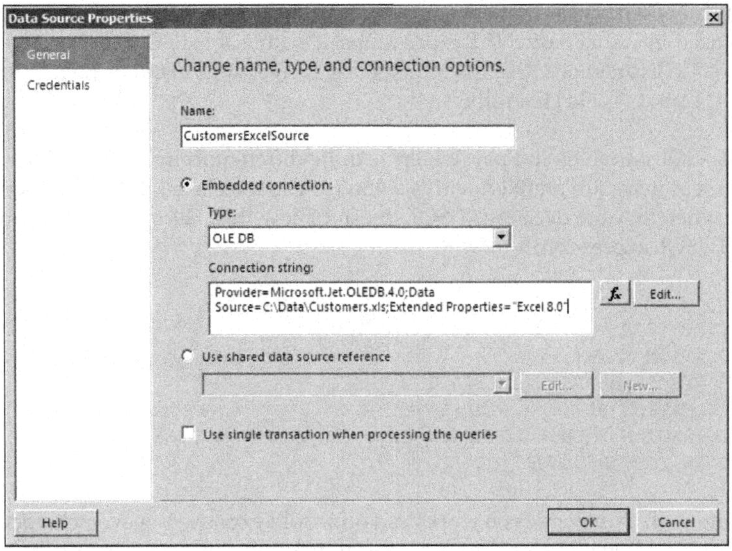

Figure 7-42

The data-set query text uses a simplified version of the SQL query language. The data provider treats a Worksheet object as if it were a table and Worksheet columns like table columns. The Worksheet name is enclosed in square brackets with the name preceded by a dollar sign. The column names are derived from column header text in the first row, and any text containing spaces or other disallowed characters must be enclosed in square brackets, like this:

```
SELECT
    CustomerID
  , CustomerName
  , [Street Address]
  , City
  , State
  , [Zip Code]
  , Phone
FROM [Sheet1$]
```

Oracle P/L SQL

Connecting reports to an Oracle database is quite easy to do. Depending on the version of Oracle and the Oracle client software, you can use the ODBC, Simple OLEDB, or native Oracle Client data providers. The native Oracle Client provider is preferred and is simple to use. When creating a data source, choose the Microsoft OLE DB Provider for Oracle; enter the server name and the user name and password required to log in to the Oracle database server.

Oracle PL/SQL is an ANSI-compliant dialect that is very similar to Transact-SQL in most regards. Newer implementations use the ANSI join syntax rather than the =, *=, and =* syntax in the WHERE clause to denote joins. This style was popular until just a few years ago and is still habitual for many Oracle SQL query designers.

Oracle has a handful of data types that are equivalent to T-SQL types. Since Reporting Services uses the .NET data types used in Visual Basic.NET expressions, it's advisable to explicitly convert field values when they are used in expressions. Use the Visual Basic conversion functions [i.e., `CStr()`, `CDbl()`, `CInt()`, `CDate()`, `CBool()`, etc.] liberally.

The syntax for PL/SQL variables and parameters is quite different from T-SQL. Rather than prefixing them with an @, these items are prefixed with a colon (:). Variables used in PL/SQL script may be assigned a value when they are declared. T-SQL doesn't allow this. Here is a brief example of a parameterized PL/SQL expression:

```
SELECT
      SL.STORE_CODE
     ,SL.LOCATION_NAME
     ,SL.TELEPHONE_NUMBER AS LOCATION_PHONE
FROM STORE_LOCATION SL
   INNER JOIN REGION R ON R.LOCATION_ID = SL.LOCATION_ID
WHERE SL.STORE_CODE = :STORE_CD
```

Testing for equality with a numeric type works as you would expect. However, character type comparisons may be performed using the LIKE operator. String concatenation is performed using double pipe symbol characters, rather than the plus sign used in T-SQL.

```
SELECT
      SL.STORE_CODE
     ,SL.LOCATION_NAME
     ,SL.TELEPHONE_NUMBER AS LOCATION_PHONE
FROM STORE_LOCATION SL
   INNER JOIN REGION R ON R.LOCATION_ID = SL.LOCATION_ID
WHERE SL. LOCATION_NAME LIKE '%' || UPPER(:STORE_NM) || '%'
```

SyBase Adaptive Server

Adaptive Server's query language is most similar to SQL Server because these products share some history. Like SQL Server, SyBase databases can implement stored procedures for modularized, more efficient query processing. Overall, I've found Adaptive Server to be fairly easy to use with Reporting Services, but it may require a little extra effort to prepare SQL queries. Simple queries can be written using the generic Query Designer. Stored procedures are executed using a string expression similar to the following example:

```
="spMonthEndSalesByCust
 '" + Parameters!MonthEndDateMonth.Value, Parameters!monthEndDateYear.Value + "'"
```

There are some known minor data-type incompatibilities with report parameters. In particular, you may find it easier to use string-type parameters for dates rather than the native Date type. If you use date or numeric parameters, you may need to convert them in the query expression. Since SQL queries and stored procedure calls are assembled as a string expression, parameters need not be converted to explicit types. Type conversion will be performed by the database engine.

The Report Server and development computer will need to have the Sybase ASE OLE DB Provider installed and configured correctly. This will enable you to create connections using the Microsoft Simple OLE DB Provider with the installed Sybase client components.

Best Practices

❑ Use shared data sources to reuse the connection information. Data sources are not redeployed to the server by default to preserve server settings. Remove the report and data source file from the Report Server and re-deploy to update connection information and certain report metadata.

❑ When using complex query expressions, keep a copy of the last working query script in a separate query tool window or in Notepad.

❑ When using an expression for a dataset (e.g., ="SELECT..."), if changes are made to the query expression, you may need to remove the string encapsulation characters from the text to run the query. Make a point to execute the query and click on the Refresh toolbar button to update the report fields definition. After the fields metadata has been updated, make any changes you like to the query text.

❑ Filter records in the query or stored procedure to reduce network traffic and reduce Report Server processing overhead. Filter data in the report to reuse the same result set in an improved response time for longer, interactive report sessions.

❑ Plan ahead and filter data consistently in the dataset, report item, or group.

❑ In MDX queries, add and configure parameters before making any manual changes to MDX script. You cannot modify or view the query using the graphical MDX Query Designer after making manual changes. Chapter 9 covers these options in greater detail.

Summary

Defining data sources and datasets to manage data source queries is the starting point for almost any data-driven report. It's essential to understand basic data storage and query architecture to achieve the best design. Data can be filtered within the database server or in the report. Making the correct choice and finding the best combination of these options will improve performance and provide flexibility with the least amount of overhead.

Defining shared data sources in your projects makes it much easier to maintain data connections for all of your reports as a group. Changing the database location or security credentials becomes a much simpler proposition. The datasets for your reports define queries for retrieving data and may be used as the source for the report and repeatable data regions or to provide data values for report parameters.

An ad hoc query expression is stored in the report within the report definition, and a stored procedure is stored in the database. Using stored procedures is an effective means for processing parameters and filtering data before sending it to the report, while using a report filter lets you reuse the data you've already retrieved. A combination of these parameterized filtering techniques may be an optimal solution for more complex reporting needs.

By applying the skills and techniques you've learned in this chapter, you can start designing more powerful and useful reports that consume and visualize the right data in the most appropriate way.

Advanced Report Design

In Chapter 5, you learned about basic report design components and building blocks for simple reports. Chapter 6 showed you how to lay out a report using these report items and data regions. In this chapter, you will learn how to use these same essential components to assemble more complex and useful reports. You can follow along using the sample reports contained in the Chapter 8 project that is included with the book downloads at Wrox.com.

The real power behind Reporting Services is its ability to creatively use data groups and combinations of report items. Calculations and conditional formatting may be added by using simple programming code. Whether you are an application developer or a report designer, this chapter contains important information to help you design reports to meet your users' requirements, and to raise the bar with compelling report features.

The following topics are covered in this chapter:

❑ Advanced data grouping features

❑ Headers and aggregation

❑ Lists and data regions

❑ Links and drill-through reports

❑ Building advanced expressions

❑ Using custom code to extend formatting and apply business logic

❑ Advanced charting features

Previous chapters have used the Report Builder 2.0 Designer and Business Intelligence Development Studio, demonstrating the similarities and subtle differences between these two tools. At this point, you have graduated from the Report Wizard and Graphical Query Designer. This chapter focuses on report design techniques rather than the tools for the demonstrations. I will use the BIDS Designer only. The same techniques and design patterns can be applied with either tool; however, the Report Builder 2.0 Designer is optimized for simple reports. If you are unfamiliar with the BIDS Designer or Visual Studio 2008, please work through Chapters 5 and 6 before you continue. You should be able to add a new report to a project, create or select a shared data source, create a dataset, and add items to the Report Designer by now.

Although you will be exploring more advanced report design techniques, I've made it a point to keep the datasets simple. For most of the examples, you'll simply use a list of products with categories and subcategories. This will help to keep things simple while focusing on report design features rather than the intricacies of the data.

Configuring Headers and Footers

Page headers and footers can be configured so that they are displayed and printed on all pages or omitted from the first and/or last pages. Unlike many other reporting tools, there is no designated report header or footer. This is because the report body will act as a header or footer, depending on where you place data region items. If you were to place a table an inch below the top of the report body, this would give you a report header 1 inch tall. And since there is no set limit to the number of data regions or other items you can add to a report (and you can force page breaks at any location), all of the space above, below, and in-between these items is essentially header and footer space.

You have a lot of flexibility for displaying header and footer content. In additional to the standard report and page headers and footers, data region sections can be repeated on each page, creating additional page header and footer content. Figure 8-1 shows a table report with each of the header and footer areas labeled.

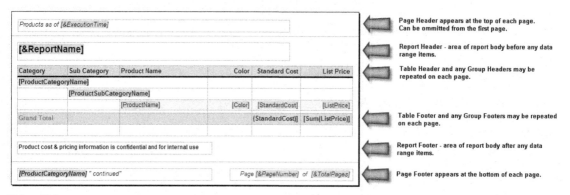

Figure 8-1

To make this report easier to view, I've shortened the page height on this report to 5 inches in order to conserve space. Figure 8-2 shows the first rendered page of this report.

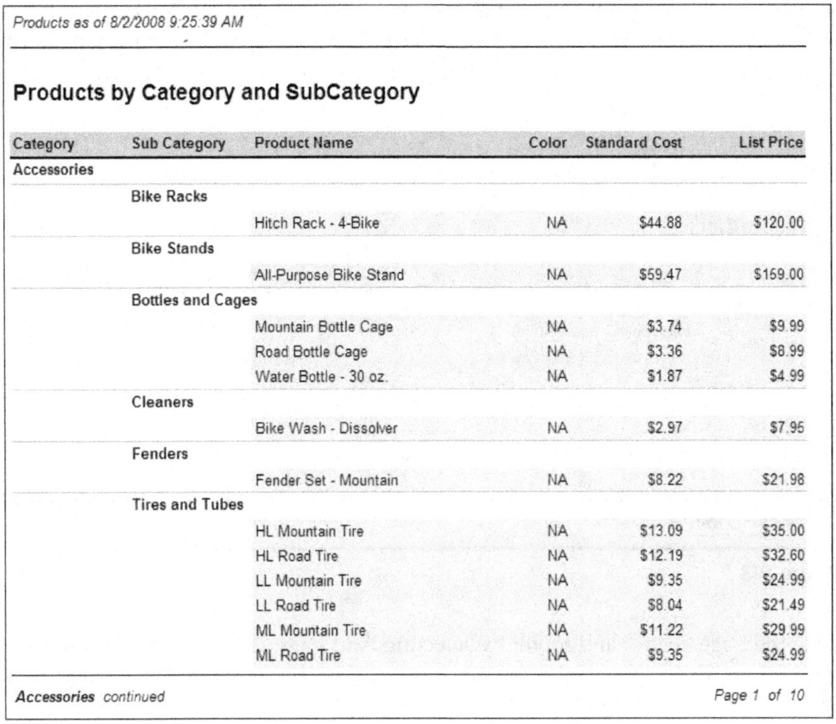
Products as of 8/2/2008 9:25:39 AM

Products by Category and SubCategory

Category	Sub Category	Product Name	Color	Standard Cost	List Price
Accessories					
	Bike Racks				
		Hitch Rack - 4-Bike	NA	$44.88	$120.00
	Bike Stands				
		All-Purpose Bike Stand	NA	$59.47	$169.00
	Bottles and Cages				
		Mountain Bottle Cage	NA	$3.74	$9.99
		Road Bottle Cage	NA	$3.36	$8.99
		Water Bottle - 30 oz.	NA	$1.87	$4.99
	Cleaners				
		Bike Wash - Dissolver	NA	$2.97	$7.95
	Fenders				
		Fender Set - Mountain	NA	$8.22	$21.98
	Tires and Tubes				
		HL Mountain Tire	NA	$13.09	$35.00
		HL Road Tire	NA	$12.19	$32.60
		LL Mountain Tire	NA	$9.35	$24.99
		LL Road Tire	NA	$8.04	$21.49
		ML Mountain Tire	NA	$11.22	$29.99
		ML Road Tire	NA	$9.35	$24.99

***Accessories** continued* Page 1 of 10

Figure 8-2

Note the page header containing the date at the top of this page, the repeated table header, and the table footer showing the continuation of the CategoryName group and then the page footer with the page number and page count.

In earlier versions of Reporting Services, you were restricted from placing fields in the page headers and footers because these areas were added to the final report output after the data was processed and before pagination was applied by the rendering extension. This restriction is no longer in place. As you can see, I am referring to the ProductCategoryName field in the page footer. You also have access to several resources such as global variables, parameters, and report items.

> *If you have prior version experience with Reporting Services, it will be helpful to point out some changes. What were previously called* Globals *are now referred to as* Built-in fields, *which are now accessible from the Report Data pane to the left of the Report Designer pane. The way that expressions are displayed in the Designer has also changed. Behind the scenes, expressions haven't changed, but they appear to be more sentence-like than the literal string concatenation syntax used previously. The mechanics of expressions are explored in greater detail below in this chapter, in the section titled, "Using Expressions and Custom Code."*

Here are the steps used to design this report if you would like to build it from scratch. The report in Design view is shown in Figure 8-3. You can also review the finished report in the Chapter 8 sample project and use the following steps to review the design:

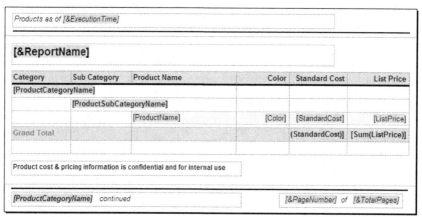

Figure 8-3

1. Enable the page header and footer by selecting Add Page Header and Add Page Footer from the Report menu while the report is open in Design view. Using the report properties, you can optionally leave a page header or footer off the first or last page of the report.

2. Now that the page header and footer are visible in the Report Designer, drag the Report Name built-in field from the Report Data pane into the header area. Drag the Execution Time built-in field to the page header, click in the new textbox, and then add the text Products as of before the ExecutionTime field expression.

3. Add a line and place it immediately below this textbox in the page header. Resize the page header area as needed.

4. After the table in the report body, add a textbox with some static text: **Product cost & pricing information is confidential and for internal use**. This will serve as the report footer and will only be displayed once on the last page, below the table.

5. Add the ProductCategoryName field to the page footer. Place the cursor in this textbox and add the text **continued** after the field reference and a space.

6. Draw a new textbox in the right side of the page footer. Drag and drop the PageNumber built-in field, type a space, the word **of**, a space, and then drag the built-in field TotalPages to the textbox — in that order. Check the results with Figure 8-3.

7. Finally, add a horizontal line below the textbox in the page header, and add another line above the two textboxes in the page footer.

Aggregate Functions and Totals

So far you've seen that if you drop a numeric field into a group or table footer cell, an expression is added applying the SUM() aggregate function. The Designer only assumes that you will want to sum these values, but this function can be replaced with one of several others.

Reporting Services supports several aggregate functions, similar to those supported by the T-SQL query language. Each aggregate function accepts one or two arguments. The first is the field reference or expression to aggregate. The second, optional argument is the name of a dataset, report item, or group name to indicate the scope of the aggregation. If not provided, the scope of the current data region or group is assumed. For example, suppose a table contains two nested groups based on the Category and Subcategory fields. If you were to drag the SalesAmount field into the Subcategory group footer, the SUM(SalesAmount) expression will return the sum of all SalesAmount values within the scope of each distinct Subcategory group range:

Function	Description
AVG()	The average of all non-null values
COUNT()	The count of values
COUNTDISTINCT()	The count of distinct values
COUNTROWS()	The count of all rows
FIRST()	Returns the first value for a range of values
LAST()	Returns the last value for a range of values
MAX()	Returns the greatest value for a range of values
MIN()	Returns the least value for a range of values
STDEV()	Returns the standard deviation
STDEVP()	Returns the population standard deviation
SUM()	Returns a sum of all values
VAR()	Returns the variance of all values
VARP()	Returns the population variance of all values

In addition to the aggregate functions, there are special-purpose functions that behave in a similar way to aggregates but have special features for reports:

Function	Description
LEVEL()	Returns an integer value for the group level within a recursive hierarchy. The group name is required.
ROWNUMBER()	Returns the row number for a group or range.
RUNNINGVALUE()	Returns an accumulative aggregation up to this row.

Examples of aggregate function expressions and recursive levels are found in the following sections for table and matrix report items.

Adding Totals to a Table or Matrix Report

We've had the ability to add totals and subtotals to matrix groups in previous versions of Reporting Services, but this capability has been improved significantly in the latest version. Because the matrix and table data regions are both based on the tablix report item, the technique you'll see here will work the same way for both of these report types.

Before continuing, let's clarify how this feature works. Adding a total to a group adds a new row (for row groups) or column (for column groups) that applies an aggregate function to all the members of *that* group. If you think about this, we're actually adding a total that applies to the *parent* of the group. Think about it using this example: if columns are grouped by Quarter and then by Year, and if you were to add a total to the Quarter column group, the total would be for all of the Quarters adding into the Year. This means that a total applied to the top-most group will always return the grand total for all records in the data region. We've included a report with the samples to help make this point. You can see this report in Design view at the end of this section in Figure 8-9.

Start with the Reseller Sales by Quarter and Region report in the Chapter 8 samples project. The following example adds a column group total to the existing matrix report and then modifies the total to use a different aggregation function from the detail cells. Start by reviewing the basic matrix report shown in Figure 8-4. This simple report uses a dataset with values grouped by Sales Territory Region on rows and two groups: CalendarYear and Calendar Quarter on columns. A total has already been added to the row group.

Reseller Sales by Quarter and Region

Sales Territory Region	2003 1	2	3	4
Canada	$1,008,618.48	$1,349,998.82	$1,744,784.06	$1,547,904.07
Central	$561,693.38	$696,188.72	$943,545.18	$804,164.16
France	$238,772.52	$332,124.68	$957,497.18	$845,409.65
Northeast	$669,685.59	$853,015.70	$750,813.87	$590,422.69
Northwest	$682,808.11	$798,513.43	$1,717,248.82	$1,441,964.69
Southeast	$477,542.79	$594,869.06	$741,877.72	$614,990.33
Southwest	$1,353,316.04	$1,818,365.81	$2,197,165.73	$1,762,924.67
United Kingdom	$273,906.59	$290,827.61	$862,226.63	$733,185.01
Australia			$450,884.41	$396,546.56
Germany			$560,152.50	$638,714.18
Total	$5,266,343.51	$6,733,903.82	$10,926,196.09	$9,276,226.01

Figure 8-4

Adding a total to a group displays total values for all fields in the data area of the matrix. Since this matrix contains only the SalesAmount field, this is the value that will be totaled. Our objective is to define a total for all CalendarYear group values. Since this is the top-level column group, this will essentially be a grand total for all rows. Defining a total for a group at a lower level would create a subtotal break. Totals can be placed before or after group values. For a column group, adding totals after the group inserts a total column to the right of the group. Inserting a total before the group places totals to the left of the group columns.

Now to add a column group total, right-click on the CalendarYear header cell, and choose Add Total ⇨ After (see Figure 8-5).

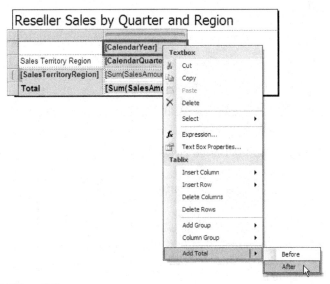

Figure 8-5

Note the new column added to the right of the CalendarYear and the associated cells.

By default, group totals are aggregated like the data cells in the same group, using a sum in this case. Let's apply a different aggregation function at the total level.

Double-click on the data cell in the right-most column for the SalesTerritoryRegion row group. This opens the Placeholder Properties dialog you see in Figure 8-6. The Value property for this textbox was copied from the original data cell, which is [Sum(SalesAmount)]. Modify this expression to use the AVG() function in place of the SUM() function. Verify the syntax with Figure 8-6.

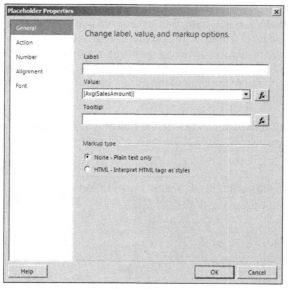

Figure 8-6

Figure 8-7 shows the finished report in Design view.

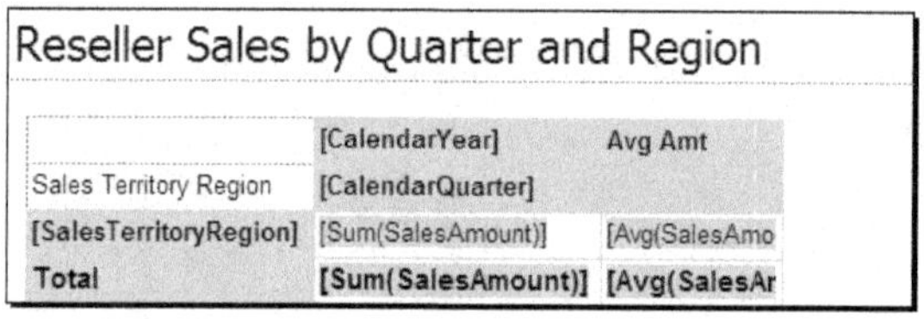

Reseller Sales by Quarter and Region

	[CalendarYear]	Avg Amt
Sales Territory Region	[CalendarQuarter]	
[SalesTerritoryRegion]	[Sum(SalesAmount)]	[Avg(SalesAmo
Total	**[Sum(SalesAmount)]**	**[Avg(SalesAr**

Figure 8-7

Switch to the Preview tab in order to view the report. Note that the right-most column contains the average quarter price for each year (see Figure 8-8).

Reseller Sales by Quarter and Region

Sales Territory Region	2003 1	2	3	4	Avg Amt
Canada	$1,008,618.48	$1,349,998.82	$1,744,784.06	$1,547,904.07	$1,412,826.36
Central	$561,693.38	$696,188.72	$943,545.18	$804,164.16	$751,397.86
France	$238,772.52	$332,124.68	$957,497.18	$845,409.65	$593,451.01
Northeast	$669,685.59	$853,015.70	$750,813.87	$590,422.69	$715,984.46
Northwest	$682,808.11	$798,513.43	$1,717,248.82	$1,441,964.69	$1,160,133.76
Southeast	$477,542.79	$594,869.06	$741,877.72	$614,990.33	$607,319.97
Southwest	$1,353,316.04	$1,818,365.81	$2,197,165.73	$1,762,924.67	$1,782,943.06
United Kingdom	$273,906.59	$290,827.61	$862,226.63	$733,185.01	$540,036.46
Australia			$450,884.41	$396,546.56	$423,715.48
Germany			$560,152.50	$538,714.18	$549,433.34
Total	**$5,266,343.51**	**$6,733,903.82**	**$10,926,196.09**	**$9,276,226.01**	**$894,518.60**

Figure 8-8

We've included a final example to demonstrate a more complex matrix report with row and column totals at a few more levels. This report is included in the sample project for you to analyze on your own. As mentioned, it might be easier to think of a group total as the total of a group's parent. Figure 8-9 demonstrates this point in a report with three groups on rows and three groups on columns. We've made a point to label the two column group total headers appropriately. Note that the total for the Calendar_Year group is labeled the Grand Total. The total placed on the Calendar_Quarter group is titled Calendar_Year Total.

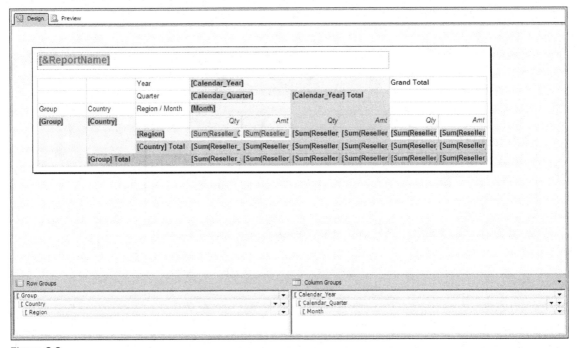

Figure 8-9

Creating Report Templates

When you choose to create a report from the Solution Explorer or File menu in BIDS, the new RDL file is actually copied from a selected template. A *template* is really nothing more than a partially completed report file. You can add your own report templates to the BIDS report project template items folder. The default installation path for this folder is C:\Program Files\Microsoft Visual Studio 9.0\Common7\ IDE\PrivateAssemblies\ProjectItems\ReportProject.

Simply design a report with any settings, items, and formatting you want to use as a starting point for new reports, and save the RDL file to this location.

On a new consulting client project, I will typically create a new report with page headers and footers, built-in fields such as page numbers, standard titles, borders, colors, and background images to match the client's UI standards. I will add the company logo and save a portrait and landscape page orientation version of the report to the templates folder. I typically will not add a dataset or any data-bound data region items to the template.

Figure 8-10 shows a simple example. This report contains a page header and footer with tiled background images and some standard built-in fields and titles. The report header contains our company logo image and a textbox with the formatted report execution date and time. The report page size height and width properties are set for a portrait and landscape version of this file.

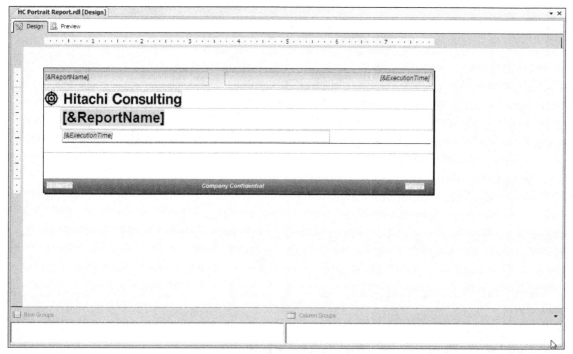

Figure 8-10

To make these templates available for future report design, copy them to the project template items folder (see Figure 8-11).

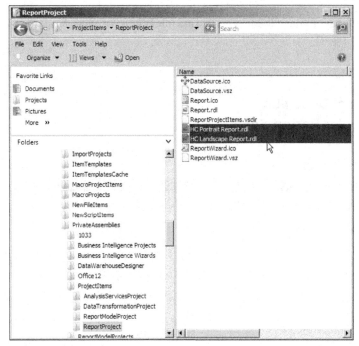

Figure 8-11

Now, right-click on the Reports folder in Solution Explorer and choose Add ⇨ New Item.

The Add New Item dialog opens, showing the new report templates. As Figure 8-12 shows, when you select a template, a new report will be added to the project using the template name followed by an incremental number.

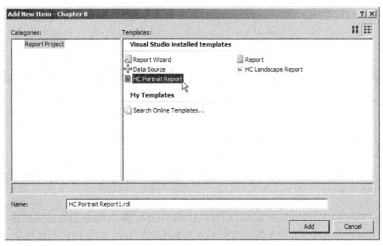

Figure 8-12

Report design goes much faster because a lot of the work has already been done. After adding a dataset and table, all the items contained in the template are integrated with the standard report. Figure 8-13 shows the finished report.

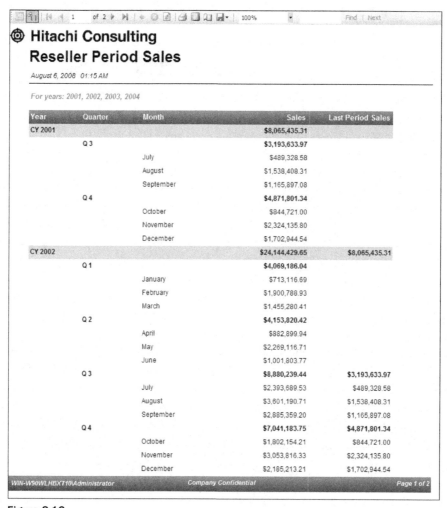

Figure 8-13

Creating Composite Reports

In this section, you will see how to build more capable reporting interfaces by combining data regions and other report items.

As a product like Reporting Services matures, it will inevitably become easier to use. In SQL Server 2008 Reporting Services, we're seeing this principle in action. Compared with prior versions, it's much easier to design a report by simply dragging and dropping objects onto the design surface. In order to design more advanced reports, it's often necessary to work with objects at a lower level and to understand their core architecture, rather than relying so much on the simplified design tools.

Before moving on to start building bigger, better, and more sophisticated reports, let's go back to the basics and take a closer look at a few of the fundamental report design components at a deeper level.

Anatomy of a Textbox

The textbox is one of the most fundamental and most common report items. Generally, all text and data values are displayed using textboxes. The cells of a table and matrix contain individual textboxes. In addition to the text displayed, there are several useful properties used to manage the placement, style, and presentation of data. `Font`, `Color`, `BackGroundColor`, and `BackGroundImage` properties make it possible to dress up your report data with tremendous flexibility.

The `BorderStyle` properties of a textbox are similar to those of other report items (such as a rectangle, list, table, and matrix). Once you have mastered the textbox properties, you should be able to use these other items in much the same way. When using a table, group separation lines are created by setting the border properties for textboxes in header and footer rows (typically by selecting the entire row and setting the textbox properties as a group).

Three property groups are used for borders. In the Properties window, these groups are expanded using the plus sign (+) icon to reveal individual properties. The group summary text can actually be manipulated without expanding the properties, but it's usually easier to work with specific property values. The `BorderColor`, `BorderStyle`, and `BorderWidth` properties each contains a Default value that will apply to individual properties (e.g., Left, Right, Top, and Bottom) that have not otherwise been set. This provides a means to set general properties and then override the exceptions. By default, a textbox has a black BorderColor and a 1 point BorderWidth with the BoderStyle set to None. To add a border to all four sides, simply set the Default BorderStyle to Solid. Beyond this, individual properties may be used to add more creative border effects. Figure 8-14 shows a textbox with a variety of border styles.

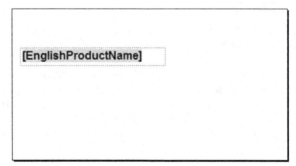

[EnglishProductName]

Figure 8-14

Most report items support padding properties, which are used to offset the placement of text and other related content within the item. Padding is specified in points. A unit of measure from the printing industry, a *PostScript point* is 1/72 of an inch, or approximately 1/28 of a centimeter.

Padding and Indenting

Figure 8-15 depicts the four padding properties, in the Padding group of the Properties pane, applied to all textbox items. The Padding properties provide an offset between textbox borders and the contained text. This can be used to indent text and provide an appropriate balance of white space.

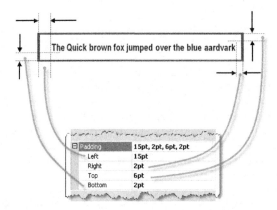

Figure 8-15

Three similar properties were added to the 2008 product version that provide more flexibility for text indentation. Use the HangingIndent, LeftIndent, and RightIndent properties to control paragraph-style text in rich-formatted textboxes. These properties also enable the new Word rendering extension to apply hanging static text indentations.

Embedded Formatting

A new capability, introduced in SQL Server 2008, allows the text in a textbox to be structured and formatted, much like a document or Web page.

To format a range of text, simply highlight the text in the textbox and use the toolbar or Properties window to set properties for the selected text. Figure 8-16 shows a range of highlighted text with the HangingIndent and LeftIndent properties set to 18 points and 12 points, respectively. Note that certain keywords and phrases within the text are also set using bold and italics. Some title text has also been isolated with bold and larger fonts.

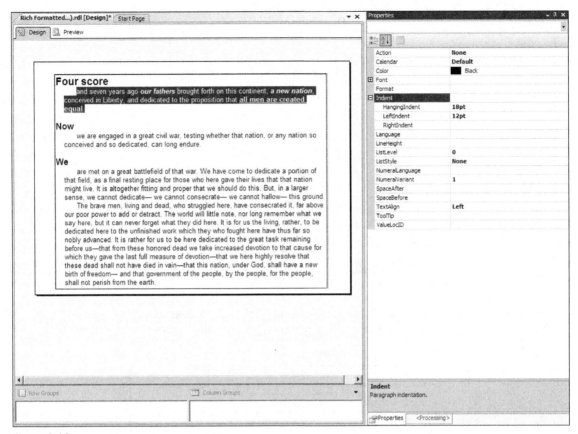

Figure 8-16

Embedded HTML Formatting

Another option is to embed simple HTML tags within text. This provides a great deal of flexibility for using expressions or custom code to return formatted text. The following HTML tags are supported:

Tag	Description
`<A>`	Anchor
	For example:`<HRef="www.somesite.com">Click Here</A>`
`<FONT>`	Sets font attributes for a group of text. Used with the attributes color, face, point size, size, and weight.
	For example: `<FONT color=Blue face="Arial" size=6>Hello</FONT>`
`<H1>`, `<H2>`, `<H3>`, `<H4>`, ...	Headings
`<SPAN>`	Used to set text attributes for a range of text within a paragraph.

(continued)

Tag	Description
`<DIV>`	Used to set text attributes for a block of text.
`<P>`	Paragraph break
` `	Line break
`<LI>`	List new line
`<B>`	Bold
`<I>`	Italic
`<U>`	Underscore
`<S>`	Strikeout
`<OL>`	Ordered list
`<UL>`	Unordered list

Here is an example of a textbox containing embedded HTML tags. The text shown in Figure 8-17 with embedded tags can also be stored in a database table and bound to the textbox using a data-set field.

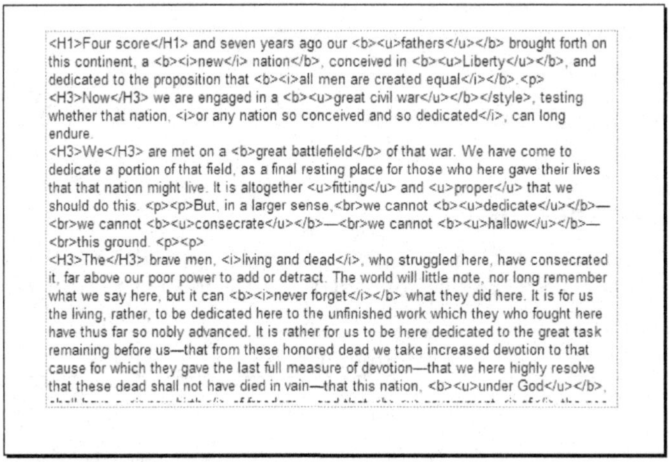

Figure 8-17

When using static text, rather than text fed from a dataset, it is necessary to set one more property — the `MarkupType`. Highlight the text containing the embedded HTML tags, right-click, and choose Text Properties from the menu. In the Text Properties dialog, on the General page, set the Markup type property to the selection shown in Figure 8-18, "HTML - Interpret HTML tags as styles."

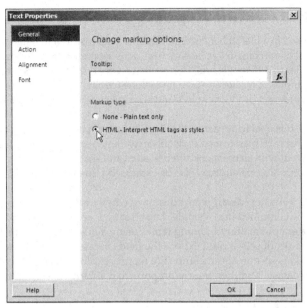

Figure 8-18

The output for the rendered report is shown in Figure 8-19.

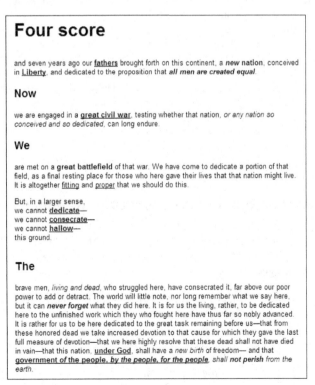

Figure 8-19

Designing Master/Detail Reports

Most data can be expressed in a hierarchal fashion. Whether data is stored in related tables in a relational database, as dimensional hierarchies in a cube structure, or as separate spreadsheets or files, this information can usually be organized into different levels. This is often a very natural way to present information for reporting. Common examples of master/detail data include invoices and line items, customers and orders, regions and sales, categories and products, colors and sizes, and managers and workers.

The best way to organize this data in a master/detail report will depend largely on how your users want to see the data visualized. For each master record, details may be presented in a rigid tabular or spreadsheet-like form or in free-forum layout with elements of different sizes and shapes placed at various locations within a repeating section. And, of course, details may also be expressed visually using charts, icons, and gauges.

The last consideration for master/detail report design is whether the data source for the master records and detail records can be combined into a single data stream. If records exist in different tables in the same database, this is a simple matter of joining tables using a query. If the records can't be combined in a query or view, the two result sets should expose the fields necessary to join them together, and a subreport can be used. This section about composite reports explores techniques for combining data ranges to filter a single dataset and then uses subreports to combine two separate data sources.

Groups and Data-Set Scope

One of the fundamental reasons that composite reports work — and are relatively easy to construct — is the principle of data-set scope. The term *scope* refers to the portion of data from a dataset that is available within a group. When a data region, such as a table, list, or matrix, is rendered, the data is sectioned off into the subranges according to a group definition. Any report items or data region items placed in a grouped area, header, or footer only have visibility to the data currently in scope. This means that if a table, for example, has a group based on the ProductCategory field and another table is placed in the group header, a table will be rendered for each distinct ProductCategory value. Each table instance will "see" a range of detail records filtered by this group value. This can be an incredibly powerful feature as there is no stated limit to the number of items that can be embedded within a group; nor is there a limit to group levels and nested embedded data regions. Now, with that said, we have not found it practical to embed several data regions to create overly complex reports.

In this section, we will apply this principle of group embedded data regions for each of the data region containers. This includes the list, table, and matrix.

Using a List to Combine Report Items and Data Regions

The list item is the simplest of all data regions. Like the table and matrix, a list is an implementation of the tablix report item with certain properties pre-set to provide the list behavior. It contain one cell with no headers or footers, and, instead of a textbox, it contains an embedded rectangle item. This allows other report items to be dragged and dropped anywhere within the list area.

> *We've created a report called* Product Cost and List Price — List. *You can open and review this report in the Chapter 8 project as you learn how it was created.*

One list visually represents one group, and the body of the list is simply repeated for each underlying data row. Using the properties for the list, it is associated with a dataset. After placing a list item on the report, fields dragged from a dataset in the Report Data pane will bind the list to the dataset and create data-bound textboxes. The example in Figure 8-20 shows formatted textboxes used for labels and values and a line used a row separator. The textbox on the right contains an expression to calculate a product's profit margin by subtracting the StandardCost from the ListPrice field values.

Figure 8-20

Like most report items, properties for the list may be set using the standard Properties window or the custom Properties dialog.

We've already defined a dataset for this report. The DataSetName property for the list was set when we dragged a field from this dataset into the list item in the Report Designer. We'll set the Grouping in the next step.

Note that a list contains a details group by default, but this needs to be set up to group on a distinct field value — usually a field with redundant values so that each group will contain multiple detail rows.

Click the dropdown list on the (Details1) Row Groups, and then choose the Group Properties item from the menu (see Figure 8-21).

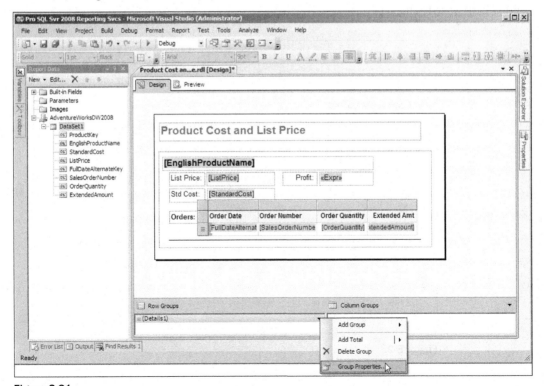

Figure 8-21

In the Group Properties dialog (Figure 8-22), add a group expression and select the EnglishProductName field in the "Group on" row. Click OK to save this setting.

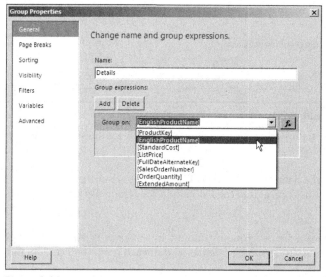

Figure 8-22

Figure 8-23 shows what the report looks like in preview.

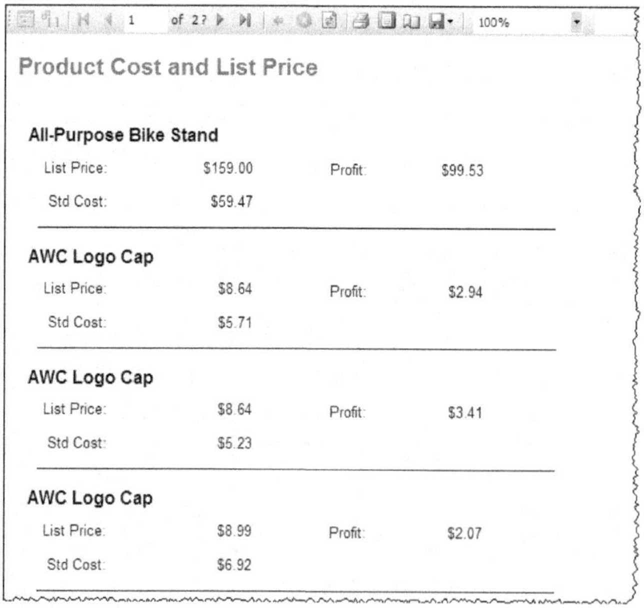

Figure 8-23

For each product, I want to see the related orders. Expand the list height to make some room, and add a table within the list area. Drag appropriate order detail fields to the table. You can see this table and the fields we've added in Figure 8-24.

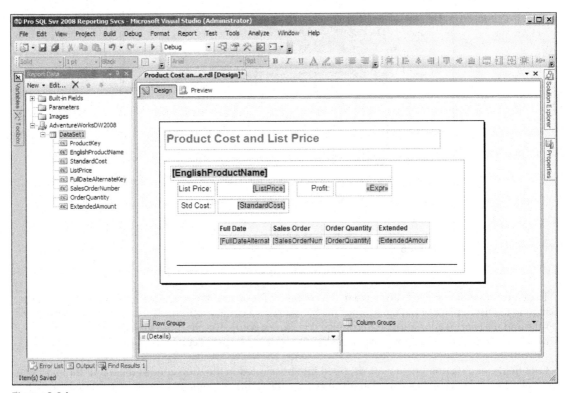

Figure 8-24

A finished copy of the following report in the sample project is named *Product Cost and List Price — Embedded Table*.

When previewed, this report shows order detail in a table below each product detail section, as shown in Figure 8-25.

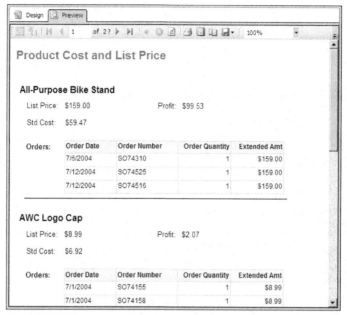

Figure 8-25

To demonstrate how the list can be used as a container for other data range items, we've added a chart item to the list in place of the table. Since the list contains a detail group that returns only one record at a time and the chart is configured to recognize this parent group, the chart has visibility to this level of detail. In other words, each instance of the chart sees only one product record.

Data fields (or data point fields) are dropped into or selected in the drop zone at the top of the chart. If a pie chart has a Series Axis expression (drop zone to the right), multiple pie slices are rendered for each distinct group value. Since this chart has no series value, two fields will result in two slices; one for the StandardCost and another for the ListPrice field value. You'll learn more about configuring the chart below in this chapter.

Figure 8-26 shows the finished sample report, named *Product Cost and List Price — Embedded Chart*.

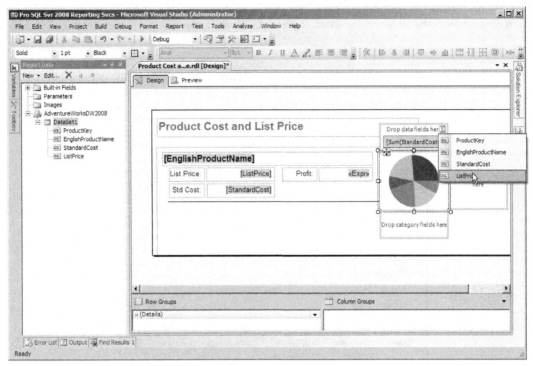

Figure 8-26

Figure 8-27 shows this report in preview. Each row of the report displays a pie chart with the calculated profit as a percentage of the ListPrice field value.

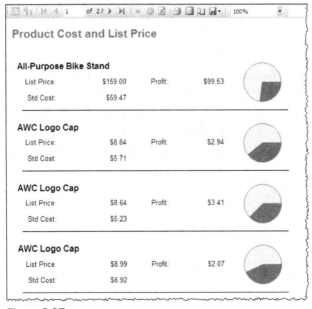

Figure 8-27

Now the best of both worlds: the sample report named *Product Cost and List Price — Embedded Table and Chart* contains both the table and the chart. Figure 8-28 shows it in preview.

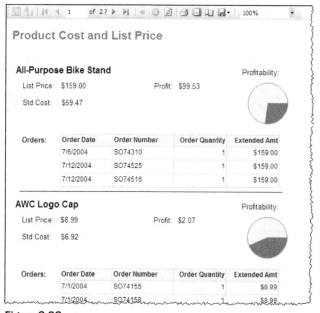

Figure 8-28

The list item works well when repeating graphical items such as images and charts. Although the list offers a great deal of flexibility, it can require quite a lot of detail work if used for complex columnar reports and those with multiple levels of grouping. Consider using a table instead of a list when all the data fits into rows and columns.

The next couple of reports, showing a chart embedded into a table and a matrix, are created using the same basic pattern, so we need not go over the design details. These are included in the Chapter 8 sample project. The report shown in Figure 8-29 is a table report grouped on Fiscal Year and then Fiscal Quarter. You cannot have an embedded object within a details group, so we removed the details group in the Row Groups pane. The chart is dragged into an empty cell. With the details group removed, the SalesAmount and the embedded chart are in the scope of the lowest-level table group (which is the Fiscal Quarter).

Product Category Sales Profile by Year

Thursday, August 07, 2008 1:28 AM

Fiscal Year	Fiscal Quarter	Sales Amount	Category Trend (Sales Qty)
⊟ 2002	1	$8,538.89	
	2	$11,696.48	
	3	$4,945.69	
	4	$11,633.79	
⊟ 2003	1	$44,359.33	

Figure 8-29

As you see, the chart category axis is grouping on the product category field with a single data point based on the sales quantity field. Each instance of the table shows the isolated sales quantities across each product category for a specific fiscal quarter.

A chart can also be placed in a matrix group in the same manner. The Product Category Sales Profile by Year and Region report (shown in Figure 8-30) has a column group defined on the SalesTerritoryGroup field. Because columns are rendered for each distinct group value, the chart is repeated in each column group, and the scope of the chart is for a combination of fiscal quarter and sales territory group.

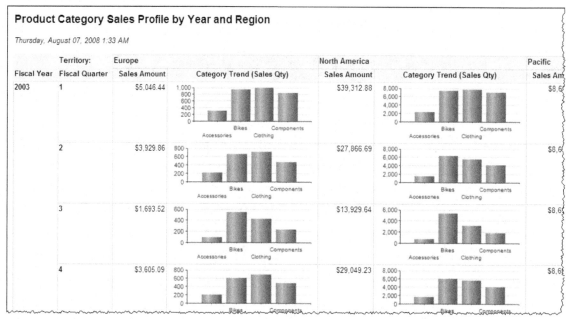

Product Category Sales Profile by Year and Region

Thursday, August 07, 2008 1:33 AM

	Territory:	Europe		North America		Pacific
Fiscal Year	Fiscal Quarter	Sales Amount	Category Trend (Sales Qty)	Sales Amount	Category Trend (Sales Qty)	Sales Am
2003	1	$5,046.44		$39,312.88		$8,6
	2	$3,929.86		$27,866.69		$8,6
	3	$1,693.52		$13,929.64		$8,6
	4	$3,605.09		$29,049.23		$8,6

Figure 8-30

In summary, data region objects (such as charts, tables, and matrices) can be embedded within other data region groups, as long as the data is served up from a single dataset.

Designing Subreports

The concept of a subreport isn't new. In fact, most reporting tools offer this feature, and the Reporting Services implementation of subreports is not much different from tools like Microsoft Access or Crystal Reports. Before getting into the details of subreport design, let's review some basic guidelines.

When I started using Reporting Services to design reports with nested groups and data regions, my first impulse was to use subreports. This seemed like the best approach because I could design simple, modular reports and then put them together. The programming world promotes the notion of reusable objects. However, the downside to this approach is that subreports can create some challenges for the report rendering engine, resulting in formatting issues and poorer performance. In SQL Server 2000 and 2005, subreports didn't render in Excel, and they still can't be used in a page header or footer. Improvements have been made for Excel rendering, but I'm not quite ready to dismiss my bias and recommend the use of subreports in all cases.

The bottom line is that subreports are useful for implementing a variety of design patterns, but they are not the cure-all. If you can design a report by embedding data regions into a list, table, or matrix, you may get better results than if you use a subreport to do the same thing.

A *subreport* is a stand-alone report that is embedded into another report. It can be entirely independent, with its own dataset, or, using parameters, you can link the contents of a subreport to data in the main report.

There are some limitations to the content and formatting that can be rendered within a subreport. For example, a multicolumn report may not be possible within a subreport (depending on the rendering format used). If you plan to use multiple columns in a subreport, test your report with the rendering formats that you plan to use.

There are generally two uses for subreports. The first use is for embedding one instance of a separate report into the body of another report with an unassociated data source. The other scenario involves using the subreport as a custom data region to display repeated master and detail records in the body of the main report. From a design standpoint, this makes perfect sense. Using a subreport allows you to separate two related datasets and perhaps even data sources, linked as you would join tables in a SQL query. It allows you to reuse an existing report so you don't have to redesign functionality you've already created. However, there may be a significant downside. If the master report will consume more than just a few records, this means that the subreport must execute its query and render the content many times. For large volumes of data, this can prove to be a very inefficient solution. Carefully reconsider the use of subreports with large result sets. It may be more efficient to construct one larger report with a more complex query and multiple levels of grouping, rather than assume the cost of executing a query many times. I rarely use subreports in standard reporting scenarios. If I do, the main report is limited to one or a few records.

A subreport can be linked to the main report using a correlated parameter and field reference, so that it can be used like a data region, but this is not essential. A subreport could be used to show aggregated values unrelated to groupings or content in the rest of the report.

Creating a subreport is like creating any other report. You simply create a report and then add it to another report as a subreport. If you intend to use the main report and subreport as a Master/Detail view of related data, the subreport should expose a parameter that can be *linked* to a field in the main report. In the following walk-through, you'll build a simple report that lists products and exposes a subcategory parameter. The main report will list categories and subcategories, and the product list report will then be used as a data region, like a table or list in previous examples.

Federating Data with a Subreport

When the data source for a master data region is different from the data source for detail records, using a subreport can be just the ticket for creating a master/detail report. The following example combines report data from two different data sources.

In the Chapter 8 sample project, you will find two reports named *Product Details* and *Product Orders Subreport*. The Product Details report contains a list whose data source is the data warehouse database: AdventureWorks2008. The Product Orders Subreport contains a table with a data source based on the OLTP database: AdventureWorksDW2008. Records in the DimProduct table, located in the AdventureWorksDW2008 database, can be related using the ProductAlternateKey column. This contains ProductNumber values from the Product table in the AdventureWorks2008 database.

Figure 8-31 shows the Product Orders Subreport in the Designer. This report is simply a table bound to the following query. The data source for this dataset is the AdventureWorks2008 transactional database.

```
SELECT
      Sales.SalesOrderDetail.ProductID
    , Production.Product.ProductNumber
    , Sales.SalesOrderDetail.OrderQty
    , Sales.SalesOrderDetail.LineTotal
    , Sales.SalesOrderHeader.OrderDate
FROM
      Sales.SalesOrderDetail
      INNER JOIN Sales.SalesOrderHeader
      ON Sales.SalesOrderDetail.SalesOrderID = Sales.SalesOrderHeader.SalesOrderID
      INNER JOIN Production.Product ON Sales.SalesOrderDetail.ProductID =
Production.Product.ProductID
WHERE
      Product.ProductNumber = @ProductNumber
ORDER BY Sales.SalesOrderHeader.OrderDate
```

The actual query in the sample report limits records to a small date range to keep the number of records manageable. This isn't relevant to the example, so I've simplified the query script shown here.

Note the ProductNumber parameter, which will be passed from the master report. Each instance of this report will be filtered for a specific product.

The master report is shown in Figure 8-31. This report contains a list data region that is bound to the following query and whose data source is the AdventureWorksDW2008 data warehouse database.

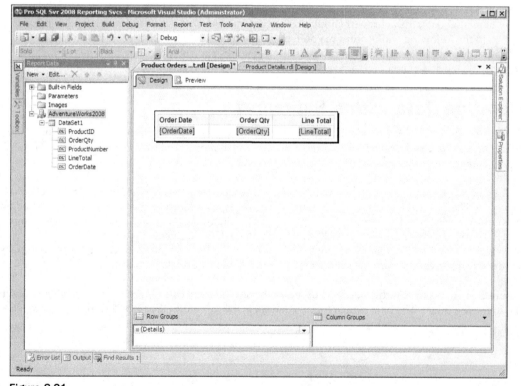

Figure 8-31

```
SELECT
        ProductKey
      , ProductAlternateKey
      , EnglishProductName
      , StandardCost
      , ListPrice
FROM    DimProduct
WHERE   (StandardCost IS NOT NULL) AND (ListPrice IS NOT NULL)
ORDER BY EnglishProductName
```

The WHERE clause criterion is to simplify the example and may be omitted in production.

The details group for the list is set to the EnglishProductName field. This satisfies the requirement that in order for a data range to contain a nested data range object, it must have a group defined. The subreport is created by dragging and dropping the Product Orders Subreport report from the Solution Explorer into the list area.

Note that regardless of the dimensions of a subreport at design time, when dropped into a containing report, it will always appear as a square area that will usually use up more design space than necessary (which will also expand the dimensions of its container). After resizing the subreport, I also had to resize the list to appear as it does in Figure 8-32.

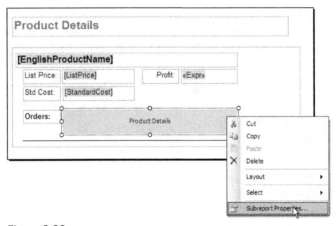

Figure 8-32

Right-click on the subreport, and choose Subreport Properties to set the parameter/field mapping. The Subreport Properties dialog, shown in Figure 8-33, is used to map a field in the container report to a parameter in the subreport.

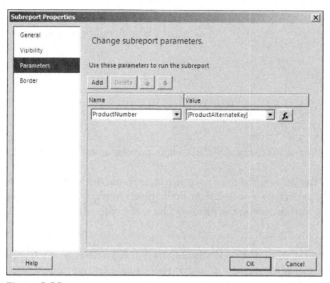

Figure 8-33

Navigate to the Parameters page, and then click Add to define a parameter mapping. Under the Name column, select the ProductID parameter. Under the Value column, select the ProductAlternateKey field. Click OK to save these changes and close the Subreport Properties dialog.

This completes the report design. Using lists and subreports typically makes the design process more ad hoc and artful than when using more rigid tables. Go back and check the size and placement of items so that they fit neatly within the subreport space. This often takes a few iterations of preview and layout to make the appropriate adjustments.

At this point, you should be able to preview the report and see the nested table/subreport, as shown in Figure 8-34.

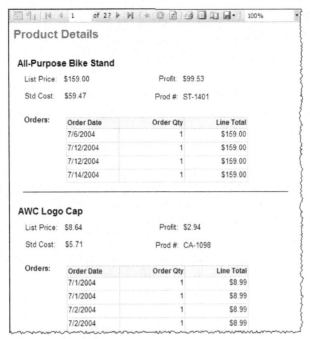

Figure 8-34

Execution and Resource Implications

There is no doubt that subreports enable you to do some things you can't do with any other report design technique. But to give you an appreciation for the ugly side of subreports, let's run a trace using SQL Server Profiler to compare the embedded table report we created above with this subreport. Let's see how many queries run on the server and how individual connections are required. We'll start the Profiler trace and then run the Product Cost and List Price — Embedded Table report.

Figure 8-35 shows the trace results. As you can see, after the initial session start-up, only one query runs. (Each query will have a BatchStarting and BatchCompleted event.)

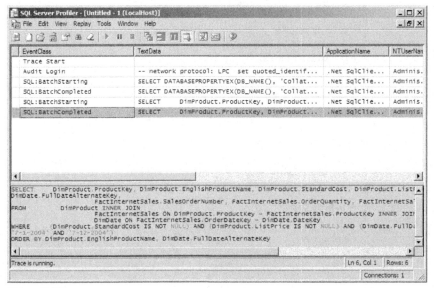

Figure 8-35

Contrast this to the subreport. We'll start a new trace and then run the subreport. The trace results in SQL Server Profiler are shown in Figure 8-36. Note the height of the vertical scroll bar; this is only the last page of a very long set of trace results. The entire trace screen capture would be 12 pages long! To save a tree or two, just imagine what this would look like. Imagine that after this report were put into production for a few years and business expanded, that it was run for a thousand products. Never assume that data volumes will always be small or that users will always make reasonable parameter selections before running a report.

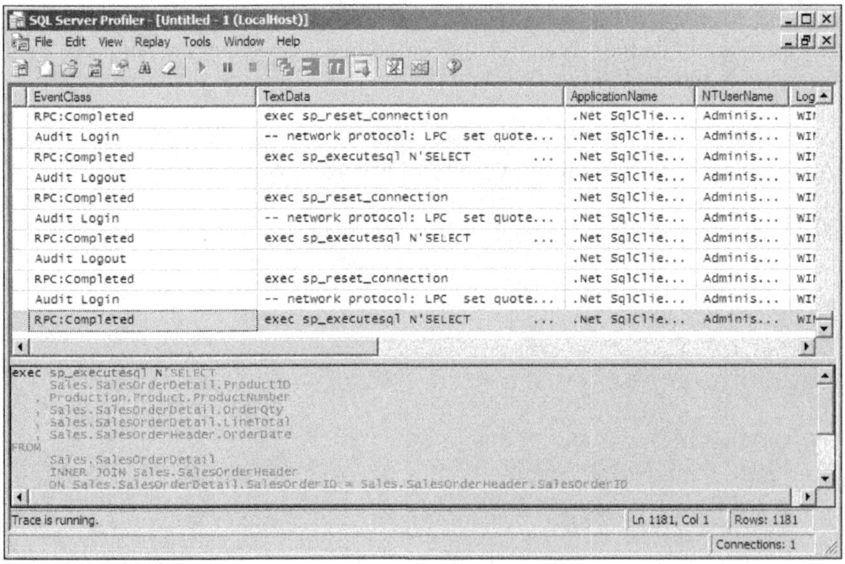

Figure 8-36

The Profiler trace for this report recorded 294 individual query executions (once for the master query, returning products in the AdventureWorksDW2008 database, and then once for each of the corresponding product orders in the AdventureWorks2008 database). For each query, a connection is open, an execution plan is prepared and run, and the connection is reset — 294 times. Although the .NET native SQL Server client and the database engine will optimize this process by recycling connections and query execution plans, the overall result will certainly not be as efficient as a report running on a single query.

In the final analysis, if you must coordinate data in a master/detail fashion, you generally have three options:

- ❑ Stage the data into one physical database.
- ❑ Create a federated view on the server using a linked server or OPENROWSET query.
- ❑ Create a subreport like the one you just examined.

In any case, try to keep the number of master records to a minimum by using a static filter or parameter in the WHERE clause. If the data for the master and detail area of the report can be sourced from a single query and you can't limit the scope of the master records, avoid using a subreport, and use an embedded data range instead.

Navigating Reports

Reports of yesterday were static, designed for print, and could, at best, be previewed on a screen. To find important information, users would simply browse through each page until they found the information they were looking for. Today, you have several options to provide dynamic navigation to important information — in the same report or to content in another report or an external resource.

Creating a Document Map

The *document map* is a simple navigation feature that allows the user to find a group label or item value in the report by using a tree displayed along the left side of the report. It's sort of like a table of contents for report items that can be used to quickly navigate to a specific area of a large report. You typically will want to include only group-level fields in the document map rather than including the detail rows.

The document map is limited to the HTML-, Excel-, and PDF-rendering formats. In Excel and HTML formats, the document map may not survive when saving report files to an older document format, such as Pocket Excel on a Pocket PC device.

The sample report provided in the Chapter 8 project is Products by Category and SubCategory (Doc Map). We've added the CategoryName and SubCategoryName groupings to the document map. In the Group Properties dialog for the Category row group (see Figure 8-37), on the Advanced page, set the Document map property using the dropdown list to the ProductCategoryName field.

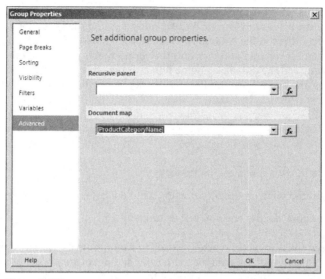

Figure 8-37

Be careful and specify the document map label property only for items that you want to include in the document map. For example, if you specify this property for a grouping (as is done here), don't do the same for a textbox containing the same value. Otherwise, you will see the same value appear twice in the document map.

A report with a document map is illustrated in Figure 8-38. The report name is the top-level item in the document map, followed by the product category and subcategory names.

Products by Category/Subcategory

Category	SubCategory	Product	Product #	Color	Std Cost	List Price
Accessories						
	Bike Racks					
		Hitch Rack - 4-Bike	RA-H123		$44.88	$120.00
	Bike Stands					
		All-Purpose Bike Stand	ST-1401		$59.47	$159.00
	Bottles and Cages					
		Mountain Bottle Cage	BC-M005		$3.74	$9.99
		Road Bottle Cage	BC-R205		$3.36	$8.99
		Water Bottle - 30 oz.	WB-H098		$1.87	$4.99
	Cleaners					
		Bike Wash - Dissolver	CL-9009		$2.97	$7.95
	Fenders					
		Fender Set - Mountain	FE-6654		$8.22	$21.98
	Helmets					
		Sport-100 Helmet, Black	HL-U509	Black	$13.09	$34.99
		Sport-100 Helmet, Blue	HL-U509-B	Blue	$13.09	$34.99
		Sport-100 Helmet, Red	HL-U509-R	Red	$13.09	$34.99
	Hydration Packs					
		Hydration Pack - 70 oz.	HY-1023-70	Silver	$20.57	$54.99

Document map tree:
- Document Map Sample 1
  - Accessories
    - Bike Racks
    - Bike Stands
    - Bottles and Cages
    - Cleaners
    - Fenders
    - Helmets
    - Hydration Packs
    - Lights
    - Locks
    - Panniers
    - Pumps
    - Tires and Tubes
  - Bikes
  - Clothing
  - Components

Figure 8-38

You can show or hide the document map using the left-most icon in the Report Designer's Preview or the Report View Toolbar in the Report Manager or SharePoint Report Viewer web part after the report is deployed to the server.

My experience has been that the drill-down and document map features usually don't work well together since these both provide some duplicate functionality. The document map should be used to navigate to a visible area of the report.

Links and Drill-through Reports

Links and drill-through reports are powerful features that enable a textbox or image to be used as a link to another report by passing parameter values to the target report. The target report can consist of a specific record or multiple records, depending on the parameters passed to the target report. The following example uses the Products by Category report in the Chapter 8 sample project. The Product Name textbox is used to link to a report that will display the details of a single product record. The Product Details report, shown in Figure 8-39, is very simple. It contains only textboxes and an image bound to fields of a dataset based on the Products table. This report accepts a `ProductID` parameter to filter the records and narrow down to the record requested.

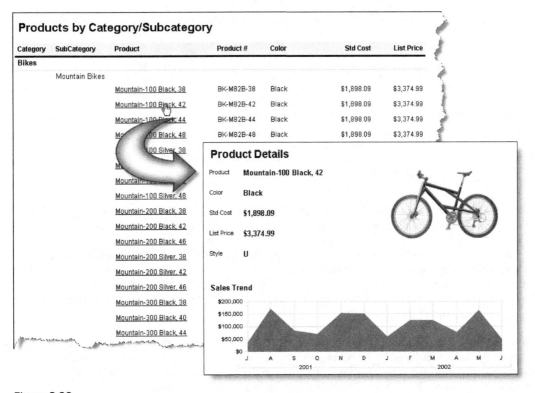

Figure 8-39

Any textbox or image item can be used for intra-report or inter-report navigation, for navigation to external resources like Web pages and documents, and also to send e-mail. All these features are enabled by using navigation properties that can be specified in the Textbox Properties or Image Properties dialog. First, open the Text Box Properties dialog by right-clicking on the textbox and selecting Properties from the menu. In the Text Box Properties dialog, use the Actions page to set the drill-through destination and any parameters you would like to pass.

Figure 8-40 shows the Text Box Properties dialog Action page for the Products by Category — Table with Groupings and Drillthrough report in the Chapter 8 sample project.

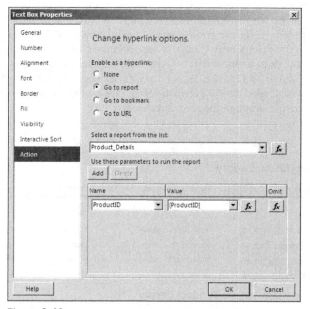

Figure 8-40

Note the navigation target selections under the "Enable as a hyperlink" option list. When you choose "Go to report," the report selection dropdown is enabled, listing all reports in the project. A report selected from this list must be deployed to the same folder on the Report Server as the source report. A drill-through report is typically used to open the report to a filtered record or result set based on the value in this textbox. (Remember that the user clicked this textbox to open the target report.) The typical pattern is to show a user-friendly caption in the textbox (the product name in this case) and then pass a key value to the report parameter to uniquely identify records to filter in the target report. In this case, the ProductID value is passed.

To enable this behavior, add a parameter mapping used when running the target report. All parameters in the target report are listed in the Name column. In the Value column, select a field in the source report to map to the parameter. A new feature is apparent in the right-most column. An expression may be used to specify a condition in which the parameter is not passed to the target report.

By default, drill-through reports are displayed in the same browser window as the source report. There are a few techniques for opening the report in a secondary window, but none are out-of-the-box features.

My favorite technique is to use the "Go to URL" navigation option and open the target report using a URL request. Although this is a little more involved, it provides a great deal of flexibility.

To navigate to a report in a separate web browser window, call a JavaScript function to create a pop-up window using any browser window modifications you like. The function call script, report folder path, report name, and filtering parameters are concatenated together using an expression. Here's an example:

```
="JavaScript:void window.open('http://localhost/reportserver?/Sales Reports/
Product Sales Report&rc:Toolbar=False&ProductID=" & Fields!ProductID.Value &
"', '_blank', 'toolbar=0,scrollbars=0,status=0,location=0,menubar=0,resizable=0,
directories=0,width=600,height=500,left=550,top=550');"
```

Expressions are discussed below, but this short example at least gives you an idea about the kinds of customizations possible with custom code and expressions.

Navigating to a Bookmark

A *bookmark* is a textbox or image in a report that can be used as a navigational link. If you want to allow the user to click an item and navigate to another item, assign a bookmark value to each of the target items. To enable navigation to a bookmark, set the "Go to bookmark" property to the target bookmark.

Using bookmarks to navigate within a report is very easy to do. Each report item has a BookMark property that can be assigned a unique value. After adding bookmarks to any target items, use the "Go to bookmark" selection list to select the target bookmark in the properties for the source item. This allows the user to navigate to items within the same report.

Navigating to a URL

The "Go to URL" option can be used to navigate to practically any report or document content on your Report Server; files, folders, and applications in your Intranet environment; or the World Wide Web. With some creativity, this may be used as a powerful, interactive navigation feature. It can also be set to an expression that uses links stored in a database, custom code, or any other values. It's more accurate to say that any URI (Uniform Resource Identifier) can be used since a Web request is not limited only to a Web page or document. With some creative programming, queries, and expressions, your reports could be designed to navigate to a Web page, document, e-mail address, Web Service request, or a custom web application, directed by data or custom expressions.

A word of caution: Reporting Services does not make any attempt to validate a URL passed in an expression. If a malformed URL is used, the Report Server will return an error, and there is no easy way to trap or prevent this from occurring. The most effective way to handle this issue is to validate the URL string before passing it to the "Go to URL" property.

Reporting on Recursive Relationships

Representing recursive hierarchies has always been a pain for reporting and often a challenge to effectively model in relational database systems. Examples of this type of relationship (usually facilitated through a self-join) can be found in the DimEmployee table of the AdventureWorksDW2008 sample database. Most reporting tools were designed to work with data organized in traditional, multi-table relationships. Fortunately, our friends at Microsoft built recursive support into the reporting engine to deal with this common challenge. A classic example of a recursive relationship (where child records are related to a parent record contained in the same table) is the employee/manager relationship.

The Employee table contains a primary key, EmployeeID, that uniquely identifies each employee record. The ManagerID is a foreign key that depends on the EmployeeID attribute of the same table, and it contains the EmployeeID value for the employee's manager. The only record that won't have a ManagerID would be the president of the company or any such employee who doesn't have a boss.

Representing the hierarchy through a query would be quite difficult. However, defining the dataset for such a report is very simple. You simply expose the primary key, foreign key, employee name, and any other values that you want to include on the report.

To see how this works, perform the following steps:

1. Create a new report and define a dataset using the AdventureWorksDW2008 shared data source. The data-set query is very simple and includes both the primary key and a recursive foreign key. The ParentEmployeeKey for each employee contains the EmployeeKey value for that employee's supervisor or manager.

```
SELECT    EmployeeKey, ParentEmployeeKey, LastName, Title
FROM      DimEmployee
WHERE     Status = 'Current'
```

2. Add a table data region to the report body, and drag the LastName and Title fields to the detail row. For demonstration purposes, we've also dragged the EmployeeKey and ParentEmployeeKey fields.

3. Insert a column to the table titled **Org Level**. (We'll get to this momentarily.)

4. Now, edit the Detail group properties using the dropdown button for this item in the Row Groups pane, as shown in Figure 8-41.

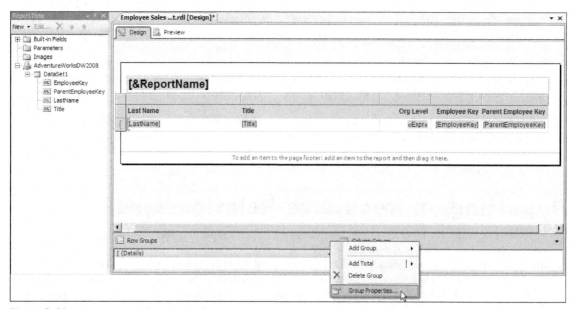

Figure 8-41

This action opens the Group Properties dialog. To define a recursive group, two properties need to be set. First, the group must be based on the unique identifier for the child records. This is typically a key value and must be related to the unique identifier for parent records — usually a parent key column in the table.

5. Use the General page to set the group expression to the EmployeeKey field, as shown in Figure 8-42.

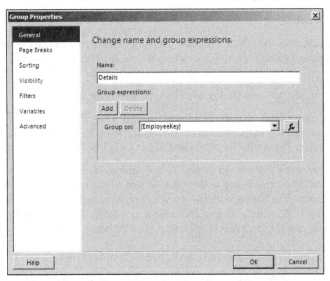

Figure 8-42

6. Move to the Advanced page on this dialog, and set the Recursive parent property to the ParentEmployeeKey field, as shown in Figure 8-43.

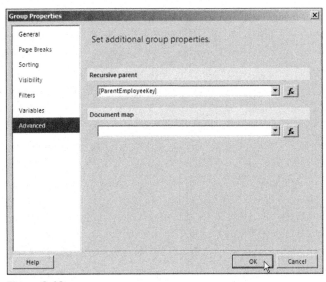

Figure 8-43

7. Go ahead and preview the report. Although the records are actually arranged according to each employee's pecking order in the company, it's not very obvious that this recursive hierarchy report is really working. You need to make a change so that the report lets you visualize the employee hierarchy (who reports to whom).

8. Switch back to Design view and right-click on the detail cell in that new Org Level column. Select Expression from the menu, and type the following in the Expression dialog:

=LEVEL("Details")

This expression calls the LEVEL function, passing in the name of the Details group. This function returns an integer value for a row's position within the recursive hierarchy defined for this group.

9. Click OK on the Expression dialog, and then preview the report again.

This time, you see numbers in the Org Level column. The CEO (the only employee record without a ParentEmployeeKey value) shows up at level 0. This is Ken Sanchez. The employees who report to Mr. Sanchez are listed directly below and are at level 1 within the hierarchy . . . and so on.

You're not done. The report's still not very visually appealing, so let's indent each employee's name according to their level. The easiest way to do this is to use a little math to set the Left Padding property for the LastName textbox. You'll start with the same expression as before. Padding is set using Postscript points. A point is about 1/72 of an inch, and there are about 2.83 millimeters to a point. Since this is such a small unit of measure, we'll indent our employee names 20 points per level.

10. Right-click on the LastName textbox, and choose Textbox Properties.

11. Once in the Textbox Properties dialog, move to the Alignment page. Under the Padding options section, click on the Expression button (labeled *fx*) next to the Left property box.

12. In the Expression dialog, type the following text:

=((LEVEL("Details") * 20) + 2).ToString & "pt"

13. Verify that your design environment looks like Figure 8-44.

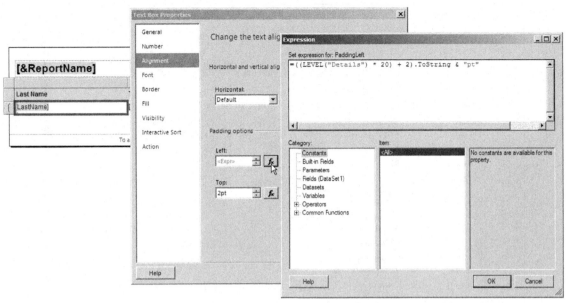

Figure 8-44

14. Click OK on the Expression Editor window, and then click OK to close the Text Box Properties dialog.

As of this printing, the DimEmployee table in the AdventureWorksDW2008 database contains some logic errors that cause this report to return erroneous data. Since this sample data may have been corrected by the time you read this, check your report with Figure 8-44. If you see incorrect results, run the following query in Management Studio to remove these erroneous records from the report results:

```
USE AdventureWorksDW2005
GO
UPDATE DimEmployee SET Status = NULL
WHERE EmployeeKey IN(2,32,49,72,84,158,195,48,73,280,106,109)
```

15. Preview the report, and check it against Figure 8-45. Now you see each employee name indented according to his or her position in the organization. You can verify these results by noting the level value in the Org Level column and the correspondence between the EmployeeKey and ParentEmployeeKey column values.

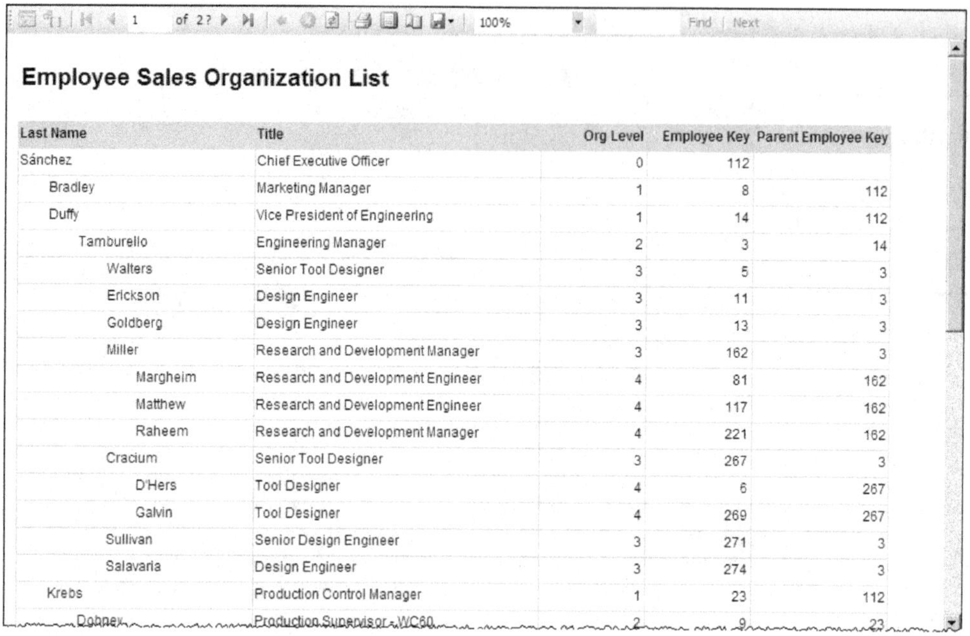

Employee Sales Organization List

Last Name	Title	Org Level	Employee Key	Parent Employee Key
Sánchez	Chief Executive Officer	0	112	
Bradley	Marketing Manager	1	8	112
Duffy	Vice President of Engineering	1	14	112
Tamburello	Engineering Manager	2	3	14
Walters	Senior Tool Designer	3	5	3
Erickson	Design Engineer	3	11	3
Goldberg	Design Engineer	3	13	3
Miller	Research and Development Manager	3	162	3
Margheim	Research and Development Engineer	4	81	162
Matthew	Research and Development Engineer	4	117	162
Raheem	Research and Development Manager	4	221	162
Cracium	Senior Tool Designer	3	267	3
D'Hers	Tool Designer	4	6	267
Galvin	Tool Designer	4	269	267
Sullivan	Senior Design Engineer	3	271	3
Salavaria	Design Engineer	3	274	3
Krebs	Production Control Manager	1	23	112
Dobney	Production Supervisor - WC60	2	9	23

Figure 8-45

After verifying the report, you should remove these extra columns in a production-ready report.

Using Expressions and Custom Code

Perhaps we've put the cart before the horse with regard to expressions. In previous examples, you've typed some expression text without receiving any explanation. This couldn't be avoided because using expressions is central to doing a lot of interesting things in Reporting Services. But we've just gotten started!

Any textbox bound to a data-set field or built-in field actually contains an expression, but in an effort to simplify the design interface, expressions are no longer displayed in the Report Designer. Perhaps this might make life less hectic for entry-level report designers, but the rest of us have to be mindful that what we see in the Designer is not exactly what's going on behind the report design surface.

You'll recall that you can build simple composite expressions in a textbox by dragging items from the Report Data pane into a textbox. For example, if you want to display the page number and total number of report pages in the page footer, insert a textbox into the page footer and do the following:

1. Drag the PageNumber built-in field from the Report Data pane into the textbox.
2. Place the cursor at the end of this text, hit the space bar, type the word **of**, hit the space bar, and then drag the TotalPages built-in field to the end of the text.

This produces an expression that appears like this in the Report Designer:

```
[&PageNumber] of [&TotalPages]
```

After the cursor leaves the textbox, the Report Designer displays the following nondescriptive label in gray:

```
<<Expr>>
```

Now let's get to the bottom of this. What value is really stored in this textbox? Right-click and choose Expression to find out. This opens the Expression Builder dialog to reveal the true identity of the expression. If you've worked with previous versions of Reporting Services, this will look very familiar. That's right — it's the same Visual Basic expression code that Reporting Services has used all along. Nothing has changed except the Report Designer user interface. The expression built by doing the drag-and-drop thing in the Designer is really just a simplified shorthand representation of this VB expression that Reporting Services stores in the RDL file:

```
="Page " & Globals!PageNumber & " of " & Globals!TotalPages
```

There's a little history behind this that may be worth pointing out. You'll recall that Reporting Services was originally designed to be an application developer-centric tool, used by programmers in Microsoft Visual Studio. As time went on and the product matured, the powers-that-be at Microsoft took a good hard look at Reporting Services and realized that the industry was asking for a more information worker-centric reporting tool. Several incremental steps have helped Reporting Services become this dual-identity product that appeals to both programmers and business users. The downside is that, in places, the product can be a bit schizophrenic. In addition to the Designer's drag-and-drop expressions and the Expression Editor's expression syntax differences, the built-in fields in the Report Data pane are referred to as members of the Globals collection within true report expressions. The term *built-in fields* is just a friendly term and not a syntax convention.

Using the Expression Builder

You've already used a few expressions in the basic report design work you've done so far. Any field reference is an expression. In the Group Properties dialog, you used a field expression. In an earlier example (Figure 8-10), we created a report template and used an expression to show the page number and total pages so that it reads Page X of Y when the report is rendered. Expressions are used to create a dynamic value based on a variety of built-in fields, data-set fields, and programming functions. Expressions can be used to set most property values based on a variety of conditions, parameters, field values, and calculations. Let's take a quick look at common methods to build simple expressions. We'll use the same example as before, only this time in the Expression Builder.

To display the page number and page count, right-click on the textbox and in the dropdown list, select Expression, and use the Expression window to create the expression. There are two different ways to enter the expression. One method is to select and paste items from the object tree and member lists. You can either double-click on an item or click Paste to add items to the expression. The other method is to simply type text into the expression text area. This uses the IntelliSense Auto List Members feature to provide dropdown lists for known items and properties.

1. Begin by typing

    ="Page" &

    in the Expression box, and then click the Built-in Fields item on the object tree view. All related members are listed in the adjacent list box.

2. Double-click on the PageNumber item in the list.

3. Place the cursor at the end of the text, and type the text

    & "of" &

    and then select and insert the TotalPages field.

The finished expression should read as follows:

```
="Page " & Globals!PageNumber & " of " & Globals!TotalPages
```

The Expression window (also called the *Expression Builder*) should appear, as shown in Figure 8-46.

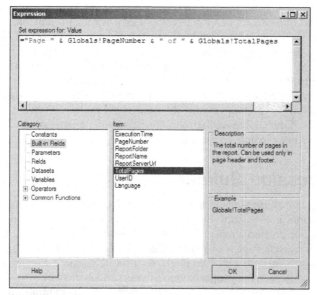

Figure 8-46

The term *globals* (or *built-in Fields*) applies to a set of variables built in to Reporting Services that provide useful information like page numbers. A list of available global variables, fields, and parameters can be found in the Expression Builder.

As mentioned, you'll see this dialog again. In fact, it's something that you will likely use quite a bit. In the Properties window, you can set many property values by using the dropdown list to select the item labeled <*Expression . . .* >. In the custom Properties dialog for each report item, the Expression dialog is invoked using the buttons labeled *fx* adjacent to each property value. In the previous chapter, you learned how parameter values are passed into a query to limit or alter the result set. Parameters may also be used within the report to modify display characteristics by dynamically changing item properties.

Calculated Fields

Custom fields can be added to any report and can include expressions, calculations, and text manipulation. This might be similar in functionality to alias columns in a query or view, but the calculation or expression is performed on the Report Server after data has been retrieved from the database. Calculated field expressions can also use Reporting Services global variables and functions that may not be available in a SQL expression.

Let's start with a report you have already seen and replace a simple expression previously used in a textbox with a calculated field. This is the Product Details report we used in the Subreport section, prior to placing the Product Orders Subreport into the list data region. Figure 8-47 shows a textbox used to calculate the profit margin for each product by subtracting the StandardCost field from the ListPrice. The Expression dialog is shown for this textbox.

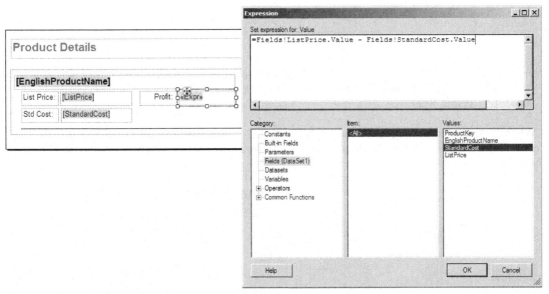

Figure 8-47

Rather than performing the calculation on the textbox, let's add a calculated field to the data-set definition so that this calculation can be reused by other objects in the report.

Use the Report Data pane in the Report Designer to select the dataset that you want to use. Right-click on the dataset, and choose Add Calculated Field (see Figure 8-48).

Figure 8-48

The Dataset Properties dialog opens. In the Fields page, click on the Add button to add a new item to the Fields collection. Type the new field name, and then click the expression button (fx) next to the Field Source box on this new row.

When the Expression dialog opens, simply type or build the same expression as before. Verify the results with Figure 8-49, and then click OK on both of these dialogs to save the newly calculated field to the dataset.

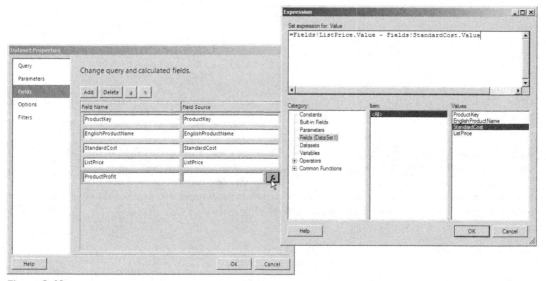

Figure 8-49

Using the calculated field is no different from using any other field derived from the data-set query. Just drag and drop the new field from the Report Data pane to the textbox on the report. Note the ProductProfit field reference in the textbox, as shown in Figure 8-50.

Figure 8-50

You can use the expression button to invoke the Expression Builder to use any functionality available within the design environment in addition to the database fields exposed by the data-set query. These calculations will be performed on the Report Server rather than on the database server.

Conditional Expressions

You've seen some simple examples of using expressions to set item values and properties. Let's take a look at one more example of a conditional expression, and then we'll discuss using program code to handle more complex situations. We're using the Conditional Formatting 1 report in the Chapter 8 sample project. The table in this report returns a list of products with current inventory values. The Product table in the AdventureWorks2008 database contains a ReorderPoint value that informs stock managers when they need to reorder products. If the inventory count falls below this value, you can set the inventory quantity to appear in red next to the name. Using a conditional expression in this manner is similar to using conditional formatting in Excel.

The following example uses a dataset with the SQL expression:

```
SELECT     Product.Name, Product.ReorderPoint
         , ProductInventory.Quantity
FROM       ProductInventory INNER JOIN Product
           ON ProductInventory.ProductID = Product.ProductID
ORDER BY   Product.Name
```

The table bound to this dataset has three columns: Name, ReorderPoint, and Quantity. On the Quantity textbox in the detail row of the table, the Color property is set to an expression containing conditional logic instead of set to a value. You can use the Expression Builder or just type this expression into the Properties window under the Color property:

```
=IIF(Fields!Quantity.Value < Fields!ReorderPoint.Value, "Red", "Black")
```

We've also done the same thing with the Font > FontWeight property so that if the inventory quantity for a product is below the reorder point value, the quantity is displayed in both red and bold text.

Preview the report to check the results; these should be as shown in Figure 8-51.

Product Inventory / Reorder

Name	Reorder Point	Quantity
Adjustable Race	750	408
Adjustable Race	750	324
Adjustable Race	750	353
All-Purpose Bike Stand	3	144
AWC Logo Cap	3	288
BB Ball Bearing	600	585
BB Ball Bearing	600	443
BB Ball Bearing	600	324
Bearing Ball	750	427
Bearing Ball	750	318
Bearing Ball	750	364
Bike Wash - Dissolver	3	36
Blade	600	532
Blade	600	388
Blade	600	441
Cable Lock	3	252
Chain	375	236
Chain	375	192

Figure 8-51

IIF() *Is Your Friend*

Even if you're not a programmer, learning a few simple Visual Basic commands and functions will prove to be very valuable and will likely meet the vast majority of your needs. The most common and useful function you're likely to use in simple expressions is the IIF (Immediate If) function. As you saw in the previous example, the IIF() function takes three arguments. The first is an expression that returns either True or False. If the expression is True, the value passed into the second argument is returned. Otherwise (if the first expression is False), the third argument value is returned. Take another look at the expression used in the previous example:

```
=IIF(Fields!Quantity.Value < Fields!ReorderPoint.Value, "Red", "Black")
```

If the expression `Fields!Quantity.Value < Fields!ReorderPoint.Value` yields a `True` result (where the `Quantity` is less than the `ReorderPoint`), the value `"Red"` is returned. Otherwise the value returned is `"Black"`.

In cases where an expression may return more than two states, `IIF()` functions can be nested to form multiple branches of logic. In this example, three different conditions are tested:

```
=IIF( Fields!Quantity.Value < Fields!ReorderPoint.Value, "Red",
IIF(Fields!ListPrice.Value > 100, "Blue", "Black" ))
```

Let's analyze the logic. If `Quantity` is not less than the `ReorderPoint`, the third `IIF()` function argument is invoked. This contains a second `IIF()` function, which tests the `ListPrice` field value. If the value is greater than `100`, the value `"Blue"` is returned; otherwise, the return value is `"Black"`. According to the definition of this function, the second argument is the `"TruePart"` value, and the third argument is the `"FalsePart"` value. This means that the value in the second position is returned if the expression evaluates to `True`, and the value in the third position is returned if it is `False`.

Beyond the simplest of nested functions, expressions can be difficult to write and to maintain. In addition to decision structures, you can use common functions to format the output, parse strings, and convert data types. Count the opening and closing parentheses to make sure that they match. This is yet another example of where writing this code in a Visual Basic class library or forms project is helpful because of the built-in code-completion and integrated debugging tools. Consider using these other functions in place of nested `IIF()` functions.

The `SWITCH()` function accepts an unlimited number of expression and value pairs. The last argument accepts a value that is returned if none of the expressions resolves to `True`. You can use this in place of the previous nested `IIF()` example:

```
=SWITCH( Fields!Quantity.Value < Fields!ReorderPoint.Value, "Red",
  Fields!ListPrice.Value > 100, "Blue", 1=1, "Black" )
```

A completed version of the sample report containing this modification is named Conditional Formatting 2.

Unlike the `IIF()` function, there is no `FalsePart` value. Each expression and return value are passed as a pair. The first expression in the list that evaluates to `True` causes the function to stop processing and return a value. This is why we included the expression `1=1`. Since this expression will always evaluate to `True`, this becomes the catch-all expression that returns `"Black"` if no other expressions are `True`.

Visual Basic .NET supports many of the old-style VBScript and VB 6.0 functions, as well as newer overload method calls. In short, this means that there may be more than one way to perform the same action.

The following table contains a few other Visual Basic functions that may prove to be useful in basic report expressions:

Function	Description	Example
FORMAT()	Returns a string value formatted using a regular expression format code or pattern. Similar to the Format property but can be concatenated with other string values.	=FORMAT(Fields!TheDate.Value, "mm/d/yy")
MID() LEFT() RIGHT()	Returns a specified number of characters from a specified position [if using MID()] and for a specific length. You can also use the .SUBSTRING() method.	=MID(Fields!TheString.Value, 3, 5) =LEFT(Fields!TheString.Value, 5) = Fields!TheString.Value.SUBSTRING(2, 5)
INSTR()	Returns an integer for the first character position of one string within another string. Often used with MID() or SUBSTRING() to parse strings.	=INSTR(Fields!TheString.Value, ",")
CSTR()	Converts any value to a string type. Consider using the newer TOSTRING() method.	=CSTR(Fields!TheNumber.Value) =Fields!TheNumber.Value.TOSTRING()
CDATE() CINT() CDEC() ...	Type conversion function similar to CSTR (). Used to convert any compatible value to an explicit data type. Consider using the newer CTYPE() function to convert to an explicit type.	=CDATE(Fields!TheString.Value) =CTYPE(Fields!TheString.Value, Date)
ISNOTHING()	Tests an expression for a Null value. May be nested within an IIF() to converts nulls to another value.	=ISNOTHING(Fields!TheDate.Value) =IIF(ISNOTHING(Fields!TheDate.Value), "n/a", Fields!TheDate.Value)
CHOOSE()	Returns one of a list of values based on a provided integer index value (1, 2, 3, etc.).	=CHOOSE(Parameters!FontSize.Value, "8pt", "10pt", "12pt", "14pt")

There are hundreds of Visual Basic functions that can be used in some form, so this list is just a starting point. For additional assistance, view the Online Help index in Visual Studio, under Functions [Visual Basic]. This information is also available in the public MSDN library at msdn.Microsoft.com.

Using Custom Code

When you need to process more complex expressions, it may be difficult to build all the logic into one expression. In such cases, you can write your own function to handle different conditions and call it from a property expression.

There are two different approaches for managing custom code. One is to write a block of code to define functions that are embedded into the report definition. This technique is simple, but the code will be available only to that report. The second technique is to write a custom class library compiled to an external .NET assembly and reference this from any report on your Report Server. This approach has the advantage of sharing a central repository of code, which makes updates to the code easier to manage. The downside of this approach is that the configuration and initial deployment are a bit tedious.

Why Visual Basic?

Before releasing the .NET Framework in 2002, Microsoft offered two significant programming languages with very different capabilities. The C++ language was for very serious programming but required serious programming skills. The Visual Basic language has long been the flagship extension to practically all Microsoft desktop products. VB programming emphasizes simplicity and ease-of-use. Along with the framework, a new language, called C# ("C-sharp") was created to use all of the new .NET capabilities. The Visual Basic language underwent a major overhaul to bring it up to speed with the framework. One of the goals of the .NET platform was to separate the capabilities of the framework from the syntax of the languages. Since the inception of .NET, there has been a long-standing debate over the relative strengths and weaknesses of these two languages. Although there have been numerous articles and white papers comparing VB and C#, even industry experts have been reluctant to make broad statements about one language being superior to another. An unspoken belief among seasoned professionals is that C# is the "more serious" programming language.

At the pre-launch event for SQL Server 7.0 in 1998, Steve Ballmer offered career advice to the many database administrators in attendance. His advice was to learn Visual Basic programming. This seemed like a bold statement to make to the System Admin (rather than the developer) community. Years later, this advice seems apropos given that Windows services — including the file and directory systems, Web Server, and database transformation services — may all be scripted and automated using Visual Basic code.

When Reporting Services was still in beta test phase, I was asked to make a presentation for the .NET Programmers User Group at Microsoft campus. When I announced that Reporting Services supports only Visual Basic embedded code, half the group was nearly transformed into a lynch mob — and I was looking for an exit. Why was VB chosen over C#? Was this an effort to "dummy down" or simplify report programming? Perhaps VB is the "lowest-common denominator" of the languages. At a lunch meeting with members of the Reporting Services product development team, I posed this question. Jason Carlson told me that they chose VB because it's a natural expression language. In most cases, conditional report logic must be processed in one line of code. The C# language, although powerful, tends to require multiple lines, whereas multiple functions can be nested in one line using a VB expression. I have used both languages, but as a long-time VB programmer, I was delighted to learn that VB was clearly a better choice for this job.

Using Custom Code in a Report

A report can contain embedded Visual Basic .NET code that defines a function you can call from property expressions. The Code Editor window is very simple and doesn't include any editing or formatting capabilities. For this reason, you might want to write the code in a separate Visual Studio project to test and debug before you place it into the report. When you are ready to add code, open the Report Properties dialog. You can do this from the Report menu. The other method is from the Report Designer right-click menu. Right-click on the Report Designer outside of the report body, and select Properties. On the Properties window, switch to the Code tab, and write or paste your code in the Custom Code box.

The following example starts with a new report. Here is the code along with the expressions that you will need to create a simple example report on your own. The following Visual Basic function accepts a phone number or Social Security Number (SSN) in a variety of formats and outputs a standard U.S. phone number and properly formatted SSN. The Value argument accepts the value, and the Format argument accepts the values Phone or SSN. You're only going to use it with phone numbers, so you can leave the SSN branch out if you wish.

```
'**************************************************************
'    Returns properly formatted Phone Number or SSN
'    based on Format arg & length of Value arg
'    PT
'**************************************************************
Public Function CustomFormat(Value as String, Format as String) as String
    Select Case Format
    Case "Phone"
        Select Case Value.Length
        Case 7
            Return Value.SubString(0, 3) & "-" & Value.SubString(3, 4)
        Case 10
            Return "(" & Value.SubString(0, 3) & ") " _
                    & Value.SubString(3, 3) _
                    & "-" & Value.SubString(6, 4)
        Case 12
            Return "(" & Value.SubString(0, 3) & ") " _
                    & Value.SubString(4, 3) & "-" & Value.SubString(8, 4)
        Case Else
            Return Value
        End Select
    Case "SSN"
        If Value.Length = 9 Then
            Return Value.SubString(0, 3) & "-" _
                    & Value.SubString(3, 2) & "-" & Value.SubString(5, 4)
        Else
            Return Value
        End If
    Case Else
        Return Value
    End Select
End Function
```

The dataset in this report gets its data from the Vendor and related tables in AdventureWorks2008 and returns three columns: FirstName, LastName, and Phone. The SQL expression used to retrieve this information is as follows:

```
SELECT     Contact.FirstName, Contact.LastName, Contact.Phone
FROM       Vendor
           INNER JOIN VendorContact ON Vendor.VendorID = VendorContact.VendorID
           INNER JOIN Contact ON VendorContact.ContactID = Contact.ContactID
```

These three columns are used in a table bound to the dataset. The Value property of the Phone column uses an expression that calls the custom function preceded by a reference to the Code object:

```
=Code.CustomFormat(Fields!Phone.Value, "Phone")
```

Figure 8-52 shows the report in design layout view. I didn't think you needed to see a preview of the report. It's a list of contacts with a properly formatted phone number. Trust me.

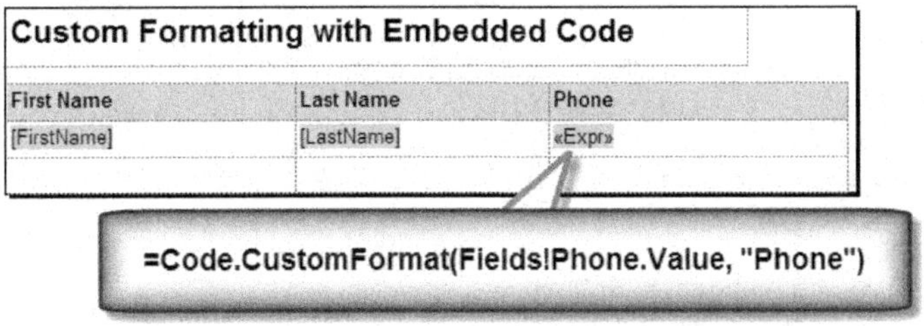

Figure 8-52

Using a Custom Assembly

Rather than embedding code directly into each report, using a custom assembly can be a central repository of reusable code to extend the functionality of multiple reports. In Reporting Services, custom assembly support is enabled by default. However, the code in the assembly will have restricted access to system resources. If you intend for the assembly to interact with the filesystem or perform data access, you will need to modify some configuration settings in order to grant the appropriate level of access to your code. We'll discuss these conditions after a simple walk-through to create an assembly that won't require any special settings.

To begin, create a class module project. You can write this code in any .NET language since it's going to be built into an assembly. The methods you create can be either static or instanced. It's a little easier to use static methods so that you don't have to manage the instancing and life of each object. This simply means that you will declare public functions in your class using the Static keyword in C# or the

Shared keyword in Visual Basic. Using the same code logic as in the previous example, the Visual Basic class code would look like this:

```vb
Public Class Report_Formats
    '*****************************************************************
    '     Returns properly formatted Phone Number or SSN
    '     based on Format arg & length of Value arg
    '     PT
    '*****************************************************************
    Public Shared Function CustomFormat(Value as String _
                                        , Format as String) as String
        Select Case Format
        Case "Phone"
            Select Case Value.Length
            Case 7
                Return Value.SubString(0, 3) & "-" _
                    & Value.SubString(3, 4)
            Case 10
                Return "(" & Value.SubString(0, 3) & ") " _
                    & Value.SubString(3, 3) _
                    & "-" & Value.SubString(6, 4)
            Case 12
                Return "(" & Value.SubString(0, 3) & ") " _
                    & Value.SubString(4, 3) & "-" _ & Value.SubString(8, 4)
            Case Else
                Return Value
            End Select
        Case "SSN"
            If Value.Length = 9 Then
                Return Value.SubString(0, 3) & "-" _
                    & Value.SubString(3, 2) & "-" _ & Value.SubString(5, 4)
            Else
                Return Value
            End If
        Case Else
            Return Value
        End Select
    End Function
End Class
```

After debugging and testing the code, save and build the class library project in Release configuration, and then copy the assembly (DLL) file to the ReportServer\bin folder. The default path to this folder is C:\ProgramFiles\MicrosoftSQLServer\MSRS10.MSSQLSERVER\ReportingServices\ReportServer\bin.

In the Report Properties dialog (this is where you entered the code in the previous topic example), select the References page, and add the reference by browsing to the assembly file. The reference line shows metadata from the assembly, including the version number, as you can see in Figure 8-53.

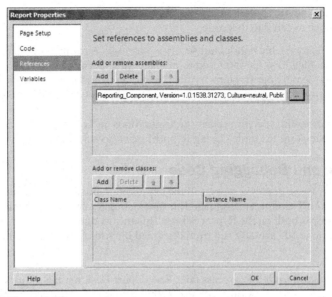

Figure 8-53

To use a custom method in an expression, reference the namespace, class, and method using standard code syntax. The expression for the `CustomFormat` method should look like this:

```
=Reporting_Component.Report_Formats.CustomFormat(Fields!Phone.Value, "Phone")
```

The report should look exactly as it did in the previous example.

Custom Assembly Security

When using a custom assembly deployed to your Report Server, the assembly must run with the appropriate level of security access. This is a common challenge for all server-side .NET applications. A thorough discussion of this topic is beyond the scope of this book. If you are a seasoned developer, these should be familiar topics, and if you are not, you should consult a .NET application developer to assist with the configuration of your custom assemblies.

In short, the steps to deploy and configure an assembly to run on your Report Server are not much different from any other remotely deployed component, and the permissions will depend on the resources used by the assembly. For example, a component that interacts with the local filesystem or consumes features of another component or database connections will require privileges to do so. The following are some of the more common steps to make custom assemblies more accessible:

1. Build the assembly with a strong name. Use the `SN.exe` command-line utility to create a strongly named key pair, and then reference the generated key file within the `AssemblyInfo` class file in the class library project.

2. Register the assembly in the Global Assembly Cache (GAC) on the Report Server. Not only does this elevate the trustworthiness for the assembly, it also provides downward version compatibility control.

3. You can apply the `AllowPartiallyTrustedCallers` assembly attribute to allow the Reporting Services engine to call into this code.

4. You can explicitly enable nondefault security permissions for the assembly using policy configuration files. Two files are used to manage these permissions. The `rssrvpolicy.config` file controls assembly permissions for the development and preview environment. The `rspreviewpolicy.config` file controls permissions on the Report Server.

For additional assistance with specific security considerations and configuration details, use SQL Server 2008 Books Online to look up the topic "Using Reporting Services Security Policy Files."

Errors, Warnings, and Debugging Code

When you preview or try to deploy a report, all the expressions and embedded code in the report are cranked through the .NET Common Language Runtime debugger and native code compiler. If no errors are found, an assembly is built on the Report Server. This means that when reports execute, all the expression and program code actually run from compiled binaries rather than from the Visual Basic source code.

Errors are listed in the task list if this process fails. The Report Designer has a quirk that can be a bit confusing until you get used to it. Along with errors that prevent the code compiling and report deployment, there is another set of information that shows up in this list. Some conditions may cause Reporting Services to be less than ecstatic with your code but not unhappy enough to prevent it from compiling. These are called *warnings*, and they appear on the task list below any errors. The confusing thing is that Visual Studio displays this list only when errors occur. This means that you can build a big, elaborate report that runs perfectly until you make one, small mistake in the code. When you try to preview this report, you might suddenly see 30 issues displayed on the task list. These may include "can't deploy shared datasource..." and "textbox42 has a BackgroundColor set to ... which is invalid." If this happens to you, don't get too excited — this is just the way the Designer works. Those warnings were there all along. Visual Basic just didn't put the list in front of you until you committed a serious infraction. Start at the top of the list, and work down until you see an error description that makes sense. Double-click on this line. In most cases, this will go to the properties for the offending report item, allowing you to make the correction and move on.

When testing reports in the Visual Studio Report Designer, your custom assembly is loaded into memory when it is first invoked and cannot be unloaded until you exit Visual Studio. This means that if you make code changes and re-deploy the assembly, these changes may not be available to the report unless you cycle the Visual Studio application. The best way to work around this is to make a point to deploy your report to your local Report/Web Server and test it using the Report Manager.

Chart Reports

The charting capabilities in SQL Server 2008 Reporting Services have been amped up significantly since the product was released. The fact is that charting was pretty good to begin with, but there's always room for improvement. A chart data region is based on a dataset just like any data region and uses groups, query parameters, and filters in much the same way as a table, list, or matrix.

The original chart capabilities in Reporting Services for SQL Server 2000 were based on the 2003 edition of Dundas Charts from Dundas Software. Microsoft licensed this code, and Dundas went on to add new features while the feature set in Reporting Services remained fairly constant and unchanged through the 2005 version. The 2008 version brings a relatively full-featured adaptation of the current Dundas Charts feature set. The product team has done an impressive job of making chart design behave a lot like the rest of the report design experience.

Because charts are now so capable and feature-laden, you can take them as far as you need to. Subsequently, the effort necessary for chart design may range from very simple to very tedious. Having been down this road many times, I recommend that after you familiarize yourself with charting basics, you approach design with some specific design objectives. Otherwise, you're likely to get lost in the interface.

Why use a chart to present data? After all, isn't a chart simply a graphical representation of a group of numbers? Wouldn't rows and columns of values be just as effective? To fully understand the impact and perhaps the importance of presenting information graphically, it's important to understand the needs and objective of the report reader and how the information will be used.

Analyzing information is usually a process rather than a single event. Regardless of the type of business or industry, users typically approach business information in stages. First, it's important to consider the different roles of users in order to understand their respective stages of information discovery. Some may have a specific task they perform, and the information they use will be focused on that task. Other users may be leaders and decision-makers in various capacities, whose objectives are more broad and complex.

Consider the CEO whose first objective is often to find out whether there are any disasters to address. This executive isn't concerned with specific details or even short-term trends, but in getting a meter reading on the business. After the CEO learns that there are no fires to put out, the next objective is to get a broad view of sales and productivity trends for different areas of the business. Typically, one of the most important questions addressed by effective business reporting solutions is "How Are We Doing?" Depending on the size and type of business, a high-level leader may also be interested in understanding some of the lower-level details regarding operations, production, sales, and other business specifics. Executives typically benefit from dashboard-type reports that provide the high-level status information they use to take periodic business meter readings. Executives also need access to more detailed information to be used for occasional follow-up but will usually get their information from others.

Contrast the perspective of the CEO with that of the operational business leaders: the Sales Manager, Marketing Director, or Production Manager. These people need to have their finger on the pulse of specific business areas. They will be concerned with short- and long-term trends in their respective areas of responsibility. Questions to be answered for operational leaders might be "What products or campaigns are successful and which are not?" or "Who are my top (and bottom) producers?" Unlike the CEO, these individuals must be connected with every aspect of their micro-organization and must be armed with detailed, accurate information so that they can make proactive decisions.

Consider that some users might need to have information spoon-fed to them in a specific format, whereas others might want to explore data — pivoting, sorting, and grouping it themselves.

Chart Types

Some of the more common chart types (like column, bar, line, and area) can be used for different views of the same data. Pie and doughnut charts present a more simplified view and work well with fewer dimensions. Other charts are more specialized and may be appropriate for multi-value data points, range values, and variances.

When a report is viewed, the chart output is rendered to a bitmap and streamed to a PNG-type image. This image is then linked or embedded in the report. There are 12 general chart types available, as described in the following table:

Chart Type	Description
Column	This is a classic vertical bar chart with columns representing values along the Y-axis. Like-valued items along the X-axis are grouped together, and bars representing the same X-axis values in each group have the same colors or patterns. Series values may also be grouped and subgrouped. Columns can have point labels, and the colored bars may be labeled using a legend. Columns may be arranged side-by-side (along the X-axis) or in front of one another (along the Z-axis.) Columns may appear to be extruded from their base using a rectangular or circular (cylindrical) shape.
Bar	This is functionally the same as a column chart turned 90°. It has the advantage of more accurately depicting value comparisons for layouts in which you have more available horizontal space.
Area	Like a column chart with a trend line drawn from one point to the next in the series. This type of chart is appropriate for a series of values that tend to progress over a relatively even plane that describes a "level," "up," or "down" trend. It is not at all appropriate for series values that tend to jump around. The solid shading of the charted area depicts a volume of data values.
Line	Like the area chart, but the area of the charted area isn't filled. This type of chart is useful for comparing multiple series (along the Z-axis) without obscuring trend lines behind a series.
Pie	The classic pie chart is an excellent tool for comparing relative values. Unlike bar, column, line, and area charts, the aggregate value isn't quantified. Users understand pie charts because they put comparative values into a proportional context and can drive quick decision support at a glance. Pie chart views can be exploded to visually separate each slice.
Doughnut	A doughnut is a pie with a hole in the middle. A three-dimensional (3D) doughnut rendering may expose smaller slices more clearly than a pie chart since each slice has four sides rather than three.
Scatter	Plots several points in a range (both X and Y) to show trends and variations in value. The result is more like a cloudy band of points rather than a specific aggregated point or line.
Bubble	This chart is a technique for charting points on three dimensions. Values are plotted using different sized points, or bubbles, on a two-dimensional (2D) grid. The size of the bubble indicates the related value along the Z-axis.

Chart Type	Description
Stock	This chart plots values vertically like a column chart. For each item along the Y-axis series, a vertical line indicates a start and end value for the range. A tick mark in the line can indicate a significant value in that range or an aggregation of the range. This type of chart is useful for showing trading stocks with opening, closing, and purchase values; wholesale, retail, and discount prices and so on.
Shapes	Shape charts like the funnel and pyramid are effectively a single, stacked column chart. These are typically used to model sales and production against goals, and sales opportunity pipelines.
Ranges	Range and Gantt charts are often used to visualize project phases and the progress of stages in a process.
Polar	Polar and radar charts plot points from a central hub at different angles and distances in a radial fashion.

Column Charts

The chart shown in Figure 8-54 is an example of a simple column chart. The X-axis series values are product categories, and the Y-axis values represent annual sales revenue. In this view, the legend at the bottom indicates the X-axis series values. Several visual elements can be modified to alter the color, shading, borders, text, formatting, labeling, and value placement. This figure shows the default property settings.

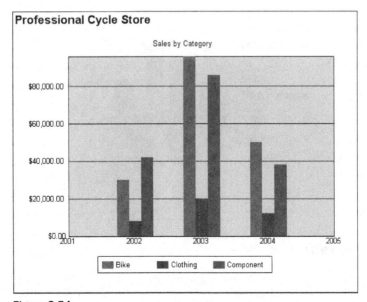

Figure 8-54

Figure 8-55 shows the same chart with 3D modeling.

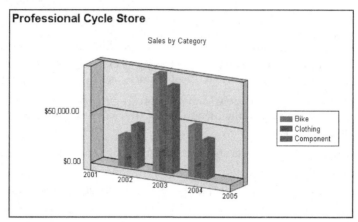

Figure 8-55

You can use 3D modeling to show data in a more interesting presentation, but this can also be distracting and less effective for analysis. Figure 8-56 shows a more extreme 3D view of the same data with perspective. This chart is set up with a fairly extreme 3D and perspective view, just to show you what can be done. This type of view tends to distort the values, and the clustering (stacking the columns along the Z-axis) can hide some columns from view.

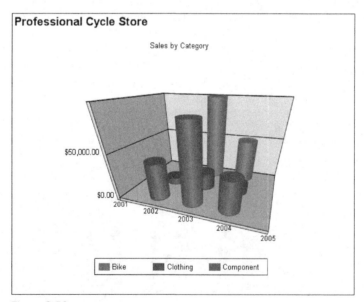

Figure 8-56

You have control over several 3D properties to generate more realistic representation of the chart data. Be careful to maintain the appropriate balance between artistry and accuracy. Notice that it's difficult to quantify and distinguish the difference in height between the front-right column and the right-most column in the back. The degree to which it makes sense to use these features will depend largely on the purpose of the chart. Is it sufficient to demonstrate that one data point is less than or greater than another, or do these points need to be strictly measurable? This type of view can be effective for making an impact, but a flatter view is usually more appropriate to maintain accuracy.

Figure 8-57 is a 3D view with cylindrical columns arranged in a clustered formation. When used correctly and in appropriate moderation, this 3D chart adds a sense of realism while remaining readable.

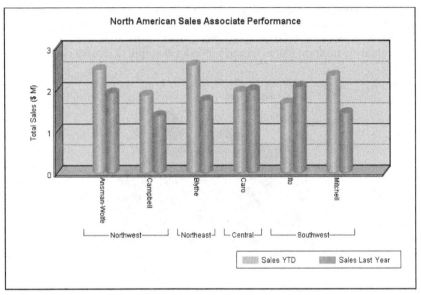

Figure 8-57

Stacked Charts

Column and bar charts can have their bars stacked. This appends the different colored bars (for a like series value) into one bar with multiple colored bands. This may be an appropriate method for showing the accumulation of all values within the series point. The individual values are displayed in a different color as a percentage of the bar. In essence, each bar becomes like a linear pie chart (see Figure 8-58).

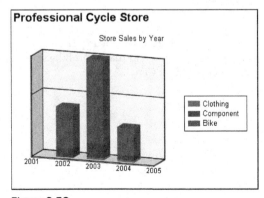

Figure 8-58

To emphasize the proportion of like values rather than the comparative accumulation, the 100 percent stacked view (not pictured) will make all of the bars in the chart the same length rather than depicting the sum of all the values in the bar.

Area and Line Charts

An *area chart* plots the values of each point and then draws a line from point to point to show the progression of values along the series. This is an effective method for analyzing trends and works well when values tend to climb, decline, or remain level in the series. This type of chart is accurate when data exists for all category values on the X-axis. It typically doesn't work well to express a series of values that are not in a relatively uniform plane. Figure 8-59 is an example of an area chart.

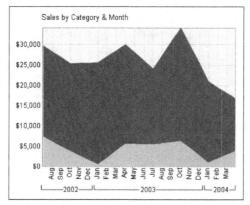

Figure 8-59

A *line chart* is a variation of an area chart using a line or ribbon rather than a solid area. The line chart works better than the area chart for comparing multiple categories for a series of values, as one layer may obscure another in the area view. In the preceding example, the area chart works because values are sorted in a way that larger values are in the background and other points in the foreground are smaller, and the trend increases back to front.

Pie and Doughnut Charts

A pie chart is an excellent tool for comparing proportional values. Display options for a pie chart include exploded and 3D views. The 3D pie chart in Figure 8-60 clearly shows that Touring Bike sales are a small percentage, around 10 percent of total Bike Sales, and that Road Bike sales account for about half of the total sales. I call this piece "Pacman Gets a Root Canal."

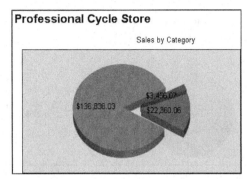

Figure 8-60

A *doughnut chart* is a pie chart with a hole in it. This is a rather profound concept, isn't it? Actually, in cases in which there may be several smaller slices, the doughnut chart can be a little easier to read and provides a little variation on an age-old chart theme. The chart shown in Figure 8-61 is the same as the previous chart without the exploded view and a legend showing the series labels.

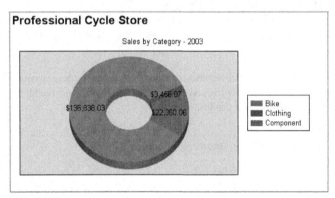

Figure 8-61

Pie charts traditionally are used to show multiple slices representing their data point percentage of the whole. In the usual form, data values grouped on another axis will result in slices automatically generated with the same style settings and contrasting colors from a standard color pallet. There are eight color pallets provided in the Designer. Sometimes data may need to be presented as a percentage value, or you might simply have two values and need to express one as a percentage of the other. This is possible by adding multiple value groups to the chart with each representing a specific slice. In Figure 8-62, only two values are presented. In this example, values in the dataset exist for Bike Sales and Total Sales. Using an expression or a calculation in the query, subtracting Bike Sales from the total provides a value for Other Sales.

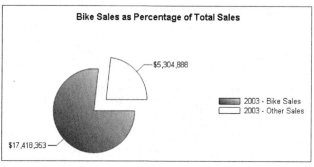

Figure 8-62

I created a specific group for these two values. Another advantage of using this approach is that you can set the color and styles for each slice independently.

Bubble and Stock Charts

Bubble charts are essentially a point plotted in a grid representing three dimensions. The value of the Z-axis is expressed by the size of the bubble. Imagine that the bubble exists in a 3D plane and will appear large if it is closer to you. Actually the "bubble" can be a circle, square, triangle, diamond, or cross shape. This also means that a combination of shapes can be used to represent different data elements in the same chart space.

In Figure 8-63, employees' vacation and sick hours are plotted above their names. The number of vacation hours is represented by the bubble's vertical distance from the 0 baseline, and the number of sick hours is represented by the size of the bubble.

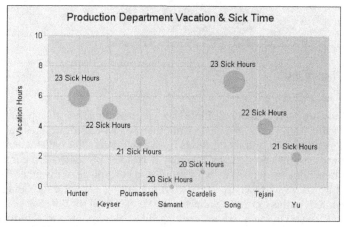

Figure 8-63

The chart shown in Figure 8-64 is a stock chart. For each product, a line is plotted to span a range of values and has a large tick mark to indicate the position of a value within the high/low range. In this example, the beginning (lowest point of the line) of the range is the standard cost of the product. The tick mark represents the last receipt cost, and the high range of the line is the list price.

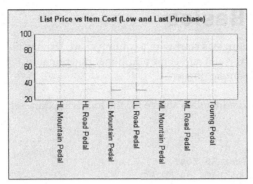

Figure 8-64

The Anatomy of a Chart

There is typically a lot of detail work involved in chart design and many properties to manage. Figure 8-65 shows the major property groups for charts. Although some charts have a few unique properties and some may not support all properties, generally these properties are shared across all chart types.

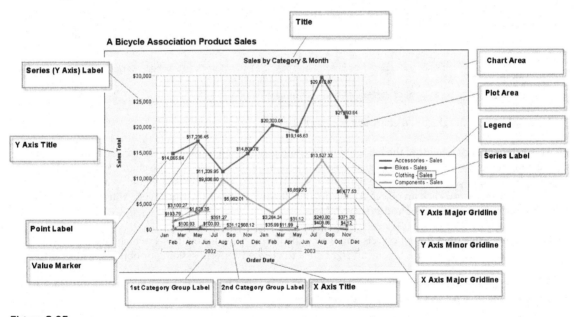

Figure 8-65

The chart is just a container, and the chart area does most of the work.

After placing the chart in the report body, you can drag fields from the Dataset window directly onto the chart design surface. At minimum, a chart should have one aggregated field for the value and one grouped field for the category. The category and series groups represent the X-axis and Y-axis in bar, column, line, area, and point charts.

Chart Design Basics

To get started with chart design, let's start with a column chart, the most basic report type. After designing a single axis report, you'll add some additional functionality. Finished copies of all these reports are in the Chapter 8 sample project.

First, create a new report, and add a data source for the following data-set query. The same query is used in all the chart examples:

```
SELECT
    DimDate.CalendarYear AS Year
  , DimDate.EnglishMonthName AS Month
  , DimSalesTerritory.SalesTerritoryCountry AS Country
  , SUM(FactResellerSales.OrderQuantity) AS Qty
  , SUM(FactResellerSales.TotalProductCost) AS Cost
FROM
    DimSalesTerritory INNER JOIN FactResellerSales
      ON DimSalesTerritory.SalesTerritoryKey = FactResellerSales.SalesTerritoryKey
    INNER JOIN DimDate
      ON FactResellerSales.ShipDateKey = DimDate.DateKey
GROUP BY
    DimDate.CalendarYear, DimDate.EnglishMonthName
  , DimSalesTerritory.SalesTerritoryCountry, DimDate.MonthNumberOfYear
HAVING
    (DimDate.CalendarYear = 2003)
    AND
    DimSalesTerritory.SalesTerritoryCountry IN('Canada', 'United Kingdom', 'France')
ORDER BY
    Year, DimDate.MonthNumberOfYear, Country
```

Next, add a new 3D clustered chart to the report body.

This is where understanding the basic chart anatomy is helpful. The design interface is optimized for working interactively with design-time objects. There are a lot of objects in the chart Designer with clickable hotspots. Until you get the hang of it, selecting the right object is like poking around in the dark. As soon as you click an object, a selection border and handles are displayed. You will also see the object name and type in the Properties window.

For practice, click on different objects and watch the Properties window to see which objects you've found. For any selected object, you can right-click to view a Properties dialog or object-specific options.

If you decide against the 3D effect, this is easy to change. Find the Chart Area object, and right-click to show the menu. Choose Chart Area Properties (see Figure 8-66).

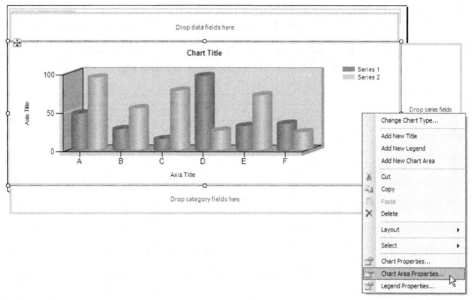

Figure 8-66

Disable the 3D effect using the "Enable 3D" checkbox on the 3D Options page, as shown in Figure 8-67. This keeps the cylinder columns but flattens the chart, which will be more appropriate for the rest of this demonstration.

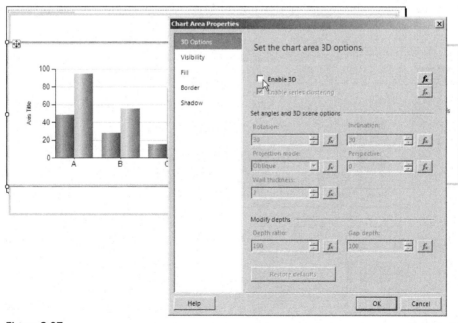

Figure 8-67

Click once on the chart background and then once again to show the axis group drop zones. The Data Axis zone is titled "Drop data fields here." The series and category zones are similarly titled. You can add fields using two different techniques: either drag fields from the Report Data pane data-set field list or hover over the drop zone to display the smart tag field list. Using either technique, add the Qty field to the Data Axis. Figure 8-68 shows this selection in the smart tag field list.

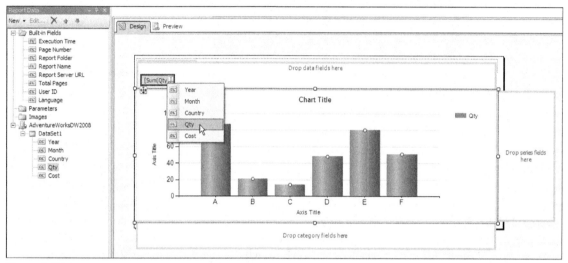

Figure 8-68

Add the Year and Month fields to the category drop zone. You can use either technique, but make sure they appear in the correct order, as shown in Figure 8-69. Adding multiple Category Axis fields causes the values to be displayed in multiple levels with set braces around each group of distinct values. You'll see this for the Year and Month groups when this report is previewed.

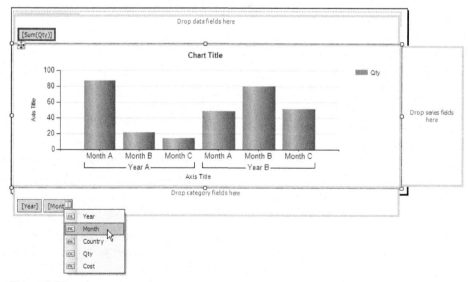

Figure 8-69

Believe it or not, you have created a functional chart. Preview the report to view the data shown in Figure 8-70. It's not pretty (yet), but it works.

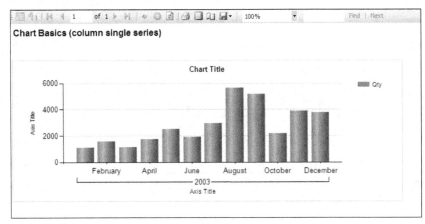

Figure 8-70

For this chart type, adding a field to the Series Axis on the right side of the chart Designer will place multiple columns in each Category Axis group. This type of visualization is appropriate when you can control the data characteristics so that you have a small number of distinct series values. Since this query is limited to three Country values, this will work.

Add the Country field to the Series Axis zone on the right side of the Designer, as in Figure 8-71.

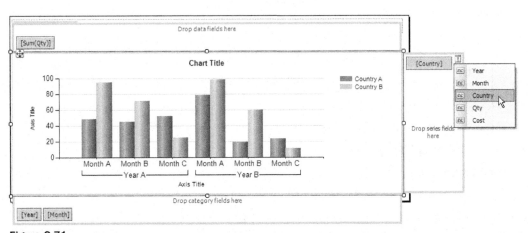

Figure 8-71

A preview of the report, shown in Figure 8-72, has groups of three columns displayed for each month. The default color palette is being used, so each Country corresponds to a color indicated by a color swatch and key label in the legend.

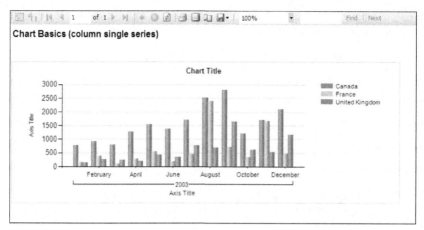

Figure 8-72

The final step for this report is to dress it up with correctly formatted axis labels and titles.

Set the Series Axis format by right-clicking on the number on the left side of the chart. Use the Axis Properties menu selection (see Figure 8-73) to open the Value Axis Properties dialog.

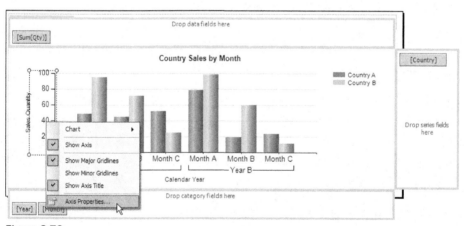

Figure 8-73

Several properties can be set for each axis using a dialog similar to the one shown in Figure 8-74, including label characteristics, major and minor tick marks, scale lines, grids, and various formatting. Use the Number page to format these labels similar to the example given here.

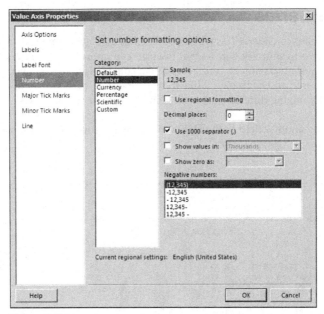

Figure 8-74

The chart title and the series and category two axis title text can be edited in place by simply clicking each title. Label these as appropriate, and then preview the report. The results should be similar to Figure 8-75.

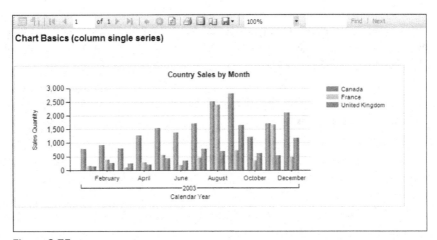

Figure 8-75

This gets you started, but it's certainly not the end of the road. This chart report shows some basic information with only one data point. Next, you'll learn how to add another field to the Data Axis and display these values in a meaningful way for your users.

Adding a Data Series

There are some important considerations when you need to display multiple data fields in a single chart. The purpose of a chart is to simplify data so that the user can immediately understand the scope and meaning of the data presented without confusion. The challenge is that when you add elements, the chart can become cluttered and confusing. I like to bring the state of this chart to that point and then resolve the problem by mixing different axis scales, chart types, and chart areas.

In the Designer, adding another field to the Data Axis is easy. Figure 8-76 shows the addition of the Cost field.

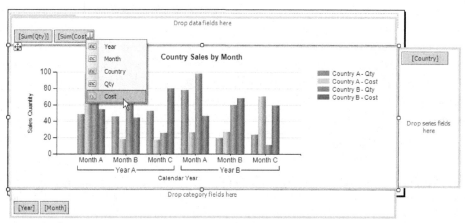

Figure 8-76

Figure 8-77 shows that we have a confusing report interface. We've created a mess by adding these two fields side by side. We have two different fields that have little to do with each other being measured on the same scale. The Series Axis scale is formatted for sales quantities and not for costs.

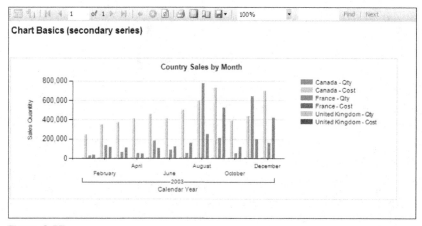

Figure 8-77

We not only have both quantities and costs in each group, but countries are also in the mix. The chart is doing its best to make sense of this by combining the Data Series and Category Series values in the legend labels and assigning a unique color to each combination. This is far too busy. If we are going to add the cost axis to this chart, the Country will have to go. There are other ways to visualize this data across multiple countries, perhaps using a composite layout — but not in this report.

Delete the Country field from the Category Axis area on the right.

Adding a Secondary Axis

Most of the 2D chart types support a primary and a secondary axis. To enable this feature to show a different scale for the Cost field, right-click on the field in the Data Axis area, and choose Series Properties from the menu. Use the Axis and Chart Area page on the Series Properties dialog to change the series axis position to the Secondary Axis (see Figure 8-78).

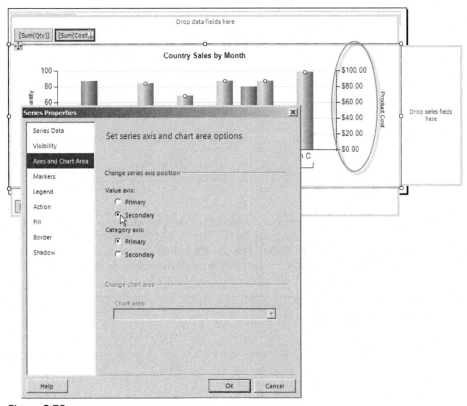

Figure 8-78

The Secondary value axis enables a separate numeric scale on the right side of the chart. This series will be completely independent from the Primary value axis, even though values are plotted in the same chart space.

You can format the secondary axis using the same procedure as above for the primary axis.

By default, the chart-rendering engine applies some smart logic to resize axis labels and will often hide some of the label values if all the values don't fit comfortably in the axis caption area. This will be the case with the Month field labels unless you intervene.

Right-click on the Category Axis, and change these properties. On the Axis Options page of the Category Axis Properties dialog, change the Interval property to the value 1, as shown in Figure 8-79. Click OK to accept this change.

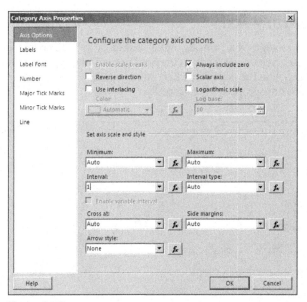

Figure 8-79

I've also set the Number format for currency and added the chart legend. Figure 8-80 shows the previewed report results. Each month has two columns: one for the sum of the Qty field across each month. This value corresponds to the primary axis scale on the left. The second, lighter column for each month is the sum of the Cost field and is measured using the secondary axis scale on the right side of the chart.

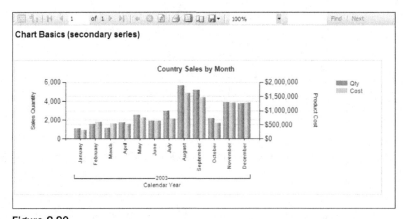

Figure 8-80

There is one more thing you can do to make this chart a little easier to read. Most users will probably struggle with a side-by-side columns metaphor for each month. It's confusing that for a given month, two columns of the same height represent two drastically different values. If the two series were displayed as a different but compatible chart type, it would be easier to make the distinction. This is an easy change to make.

In the Designer, right-click on the Cost field in the Data Axis area, and choose "Change Chart Type" (see Figure 8-81). Choose the "Line with Markers" chart type.

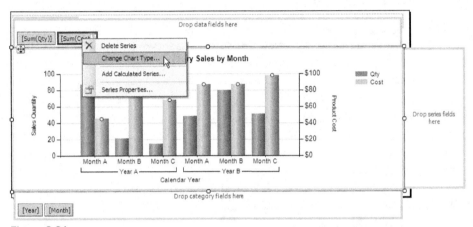

Figure 8-81

That's it! The chart is ready for primetime viewing. Figure 8-82 shows the finished chart, complete with two separate axes and scales. Total sales quantities are plotted using columns on the primary axis scale, displayed on the left. A secondary axis scale is formatted to reflect the total cost for each month. These values are expressed using a line chart, which is visually separate from the column chart values. The chart legend adds clarity, and everything is neatly titled and formatted. It's a beautiful thing.

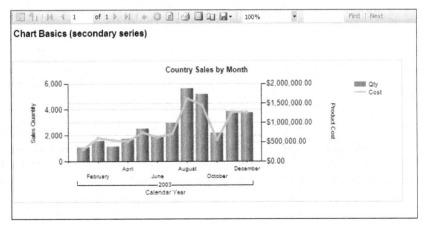

Figure 8-82

Using Multiple Chart Areas

Reporting Services charts now support multiple chart areas. This powerful feature enables you to place multiple charts, of different types and characteristics, in the same chart container. Each of these chart areas is based on the same dataset and can be aligned and correlated with a sibling chart in a variety of different ways. The following is a simple example.

Using the chart report we have been designing, you are going to separate the two data fields into different chart areas, arranged vertically. By aligning the Category Axis, any changes in the data will be consistently reflected in both chart areas.

To make room for the second chart area, increase the height of the chart by stretching it vertically. Right-click on the chart, and choose "Add New Chart Area," as shown in Figure 8-83.

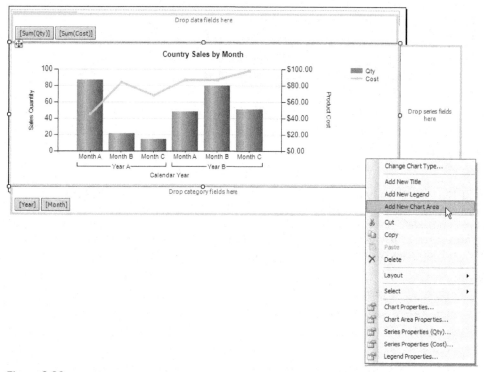

Figure 8-83

The new chart area will appear as only white space until a series axis is assigned to it. Right-click on the Cost field in the data Axis area and choose Series Properties. In the corresponding Series Properties dialog, on the Axes and Chart Area page, use the Change chart area dropdown list to select the new chart area. Verify your settings with Figure 8-84, and then click OK to close the Series Properties dialog.

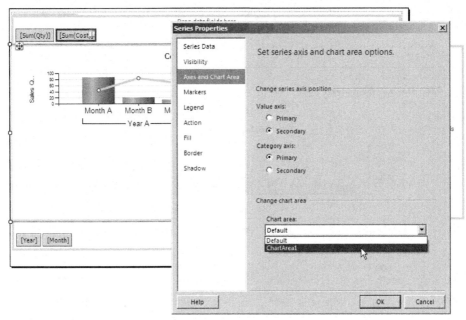

Figure 8-84

To set properties for the chart area, right-click on the chart in the Designer, and choose Chart Area Properties (ChartArea1). The Chart Area Properties dialog is shown in Figure 8-85. On the Alignment page, use the "Align with chart area" dropdown list to choose the Default chart area. Click OK to accept this change and then preview the report.

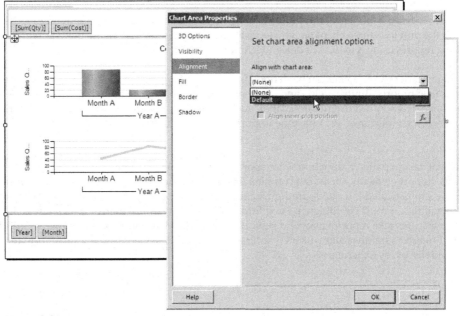

Figure 8-85

Figure 8-86 shows the final report with two aligned chart areas. The first column chart displays sales quantity values, and the second line chart shows total costs.

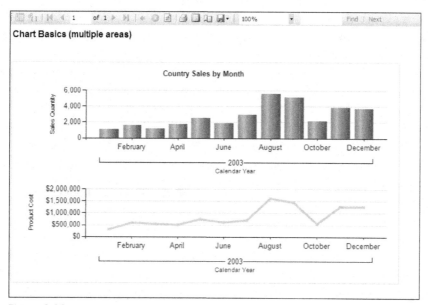

Figure 8-86

Summary

This chapter covered a lot of ground. Building on the basic design concepts and building blocks you learned in the previous three chapters, you were able to raise the bar and create more powerful and compelling reports using a variety of design techniques.

Report page headers and footers can be defined in a report template, where the design can be reused in all of your new reports. Built-in fields and summary information can be added to page headers and footers to display and print useful information such as the report name, execution date and time, page numbers, and the report user — to provide important context information if the report is printed or archived.

The essential design patterns for composite reports include the use of embedded data regions and subreports. Report elements, including complex data regions, can be nested in a list, table, or matrix to create more sophisticated interface paradigms. Subreports can provide this same functionality when a master/detail report must coordinate related information managed in different data sources. Report navigation features take reporting beyond static, passive data browsing. Document maps, drill-down, and drill-through techniques allow users to interact with reports to create a dynamic information analysis and discovery experience.

Expressions and custom programming take report design to new heights by allowing a single report to deliver more functionality, behaving more like a multifunction business application than a traditional report.

The charting capabilities in Reporting Services for SQL Server 2008 are vastly improved and easier to use in many ways. New chart types provide more options to visualize business data to information workers. Advanced charts provide a more flexible means to deliver actionable information through compelling new features that include multi-series charts and chart areas.

Part III

Business Intelligence Reporting

Reporting with Analysis Services

SQL Server 2008 Analysis Services is used to store and aggregate data, specifically to support decision-support systems, ad hoc reporting, and business data analysis. Once designed, cube data is easy to navigate to produce complex, business-relevant results for business leaders and information workers.

This chapter will introduce some of the basic concepts of OLAP and multidimensional storage systems. You will use the Report Designer to create Multidimensional Expressions (MDX) language queries, with and without the MDX Graphical Query Builder. You will learn to build advanced and compelling reports using parameters, pivot tables, and KPI indicators in a table or matrix report.

Finally, you will learn to use cube actions and apply best practices and safety checks to your report solutions that use OLAP data stores.

Why Analysis Services for Reporting?

Every year at the Professional Association for SQL Server (PASS) Community Summit, I take a poll of the Reporting Services session attendees and ask who is using Analysis Services or plans to in the near future. Over the past three years, the number of positive respondents has increased significantly, but the overall percentage is still a significant minority — perhaps 25 percent. Do you need to use SQL Server Analysis Services to manage your data for reporting and analytics? This depends on a few factors.

You'll recall that Chapter 7 discussed data storage options for business reporting data and referred to the diagram in Figure 9-1. In all but the smallest business environment, the data collected and managed by various business processes is stored in different databases and systems. Getting reliable answers to important business questions from these data sources can be challenging at best. Consolidating this data into a central data store is no simple matter, but the value to the business is significant and often critical.

Data is transformed from multiple data sources, staged, validated, and optimized for reporting. The simplified relational data structures are stored in subject area data marts or a central data warehouse. The data organized in a relational data warehouse structure supports faster queries and helps report designers create reports without the unnecessary complexity found in most operational database systems that are primarily designed for transactions.

The fact is that once the necessary effort has been expended to build and populate a data warehouse, taking the next step of creating OLAP cubes on this data is relatively easy.

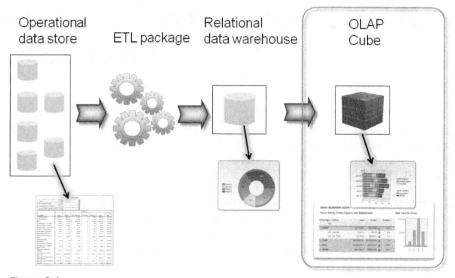

Figure 9-1

Making the leap from the operational data store to a relational data warehouse may be sufficient in a small business with unsophisticated reporting needs. However, even for a medium-scale business environment, there are many advantages to including Analysis Services in the solution. Generally, moving to an OLAP solution enables capabilities in four categories:

❑   Data in a cube is "browseable" without writing sophisticated queries. Information is organized into dimensional hierarchies so that report designers can simply drag and drop to design report datasets.

❑   Information workers can design their own reports without understanding the underlying data structure and with no query-writing skills. Users simply select from predefined measures and hierarchies to create queries and design reports.

❑   Sophisticated calculations are built into the cube using calculated members. Users and report designers can select from calculated members as easily as they can use standard measures and other cube members.

❑ Cube-based queries typically run very fast, even when the cube is derived from very large sets of data. The improved performance is due primarily to preaggregated values stored in optimized, non-relational hierarchies in the OLAP data storage engine.

The bottom line is that building an OLAP cube with Analysis Services is generally easy to do if you have a properly designed relational date warehouse. It's much easier to navigate than a relational database. Cubes enable self-service reporting and effective data exploration. And, sometimes most importantly, cubes can be very fast compared to other data sources and reporting solutions.

If you work for a small company or in an environment with manageable volumes of data, you will likely find significant advantages. Because Analysis Services is already covered under your SQL Server product license, there is little or no cost to build cubes and realize these benefits.

If you work for a large company and work with larger volumes of complex business data, you probably don't need much persuasion to recognize the advantages of using cubes to help solve these challenges. Making the move to OLAP cubes will help you take reporting to the next level while solving performance and query design issues at the same time.

Using Reporting Services with Analysis Services Data

Reporting Services works natively with several Analysis Services capabilities. These include:

❑ Native support for non-additive measures and calculations. Rather than building sophisticated expressions and calculation logic into reports, Reporting Services lets you take advantage of features already built into the Analysis Services cube.

❑ Analysis Services and the MDX query language support custom formatting defined for measures in the cube. Reports may be designed to use this formatting without duplicating this effort in the report design.

❑ Drill-through reports can work for MDX datasets with some basic knowledge of MDX member reference formatting and special field properties present in Reporting Services for MDX reports.

❑ Cube data may be protected through user role-based security. This works with no special report provisions if user credentials are provided to data sources using Windows Authentication.

❑ Summary reports that would normally aggregate a lot of data run much faster with cubes. Take advantage of this capability by designing summary reports and dashboards with drill-through actions to lower-level, detail reports.

Most reports that use Analysis Services as a data source are fairly easy to design for two reasons. The mission of OLAP is to make data easy to use. A properly designed cube simplifies your business data by organizing it into predefined, hierarchal structures with business facts preaggregated and ready to use by dragging and dropping into the MDX Query Designer. The Report Designer is friendly with an MDX-based dataset and will automatically generate parameter lists, cascading parameters, and filtering logic. In many ways, designing a report for OLAP is easier than for a relational database, owing to the simplification applied in the cube and these enhancements to the Report Designer.

Most OLAP reports are usually simple in design, just because of the nature of the cube. With predefined drill-down paths, and multiple multilevel hierarchies, it should be natural to visualize this information in a matrix or multi-axis chart. Business leaders now expect to see data presented in standard formats, using key performance indicators (KPIs) to present business metrics in dashboards and business scorecards with gauges and iconized graphical indicators. In the following exercises, you will see how using an OLAP data source with dimensional hierarchies, measures, KPIs, calculated members, and related cube elements makes business report design simple and manageable.

Multidimensional Expression Language

The MDX query language is part of the OLEDB for OLAP specification from Microsoft. The MDX query language is used in several different OLAP products from different vendors such as IBM Cognos, Hyperion EssBase, Business Objects, and, of course, Microsoft SQL Server Analysis Services. Like SQL, the language varies from product to product, but the concepts and core features are the same — or at least very similar in some categories.

MDX: Simple or Complex?

Most IT professionals who want to learn MDX already know a little or a lot of SQL. They have worked through the process of reporting on transactional databases, migrating to a data warehouse, and building queries on a relational/dimensional model, and now realize the benefits of a truly dimensional storage engine to solve complex business problems. This presents an interesting challenge for most of these people. You see, MDX is a simple query language that sits squarely on the multidimensional foundations of OLAP technologies — all of which exists for the sole purpose of the simplification of business data. So, if OLAP and MDX are so *simple*, why does the industry perceive it to be so difficult to learn? There's a simple answer. MDX is very different from SQL, but on the surface it looks a lot like SQL. This means that anyone making the transition must struggle through a mental paradigm shift — from two-dimensional (2D), row-set-based thinking to multidimensional, axis-based cell-set thinking. Making this mental transition is not so difficult with a little bit of practice, but it's easy to slip back into an SQL mindset if you don't stay in practice. Here's the interesting twist: when you're done working with all these cool, multidimensional concepts, you're going to take the output and pound it back into a 2D result so that you can display it on a screen or print it on a 2D sheet of paper.

I'd love to launch into a discourse on sets, axes, tupples, slicers, subcubes, and other really nifty OLAP concepts, but this isn't the time or place. This is one of those topics that can't be introduced without sufficient background and an exhaustive set of exercises. So, you are not going to learn everything you need to know about MDX in this short section of this book on Reporting Services. My purpose is to provide some exposure to the kinds of things you can do using this powerful query language for OLAP. For most cube report work, you shouldn't need to know more than some basic commands and functions. However, if you plan to do extensive work with MDX, you should pick up *Professional Microsoft SQL Server 2008 Analysis Services with MDX* or take a class on MDX for SQL Server Analysis Services. The language and query techniques haven't changed much between SQL Server 2005 and 2008.

The MDX Builder

When choosing the SQL Server Analysis Services data processing provider as you define a report data source, the MDX Query Designer is automatically invoked for any new datasets. Your first objective will be to work with data-set results from a query generated by the MDX Query Designer. After exploring this feature, you'll write MDX queries without the aid of the builder.

I teach a lot of classes on MDX and Analysis Services reporting and have worked on projects with IT professionals who have substantial MDX experience. I hear criticism about the MDX builder tool and some if its limitations. Rather than just echoing the product documentation, I'd like to comment on this. I suppose that the baseline for building queries is the T-SQL Query Builder tool, which has been in production for at least 12 years. Manual modifications to a T-SQL query are captured by the graphical builder and reformatted for forward compatibility. In contrast, the MDX builder doesn't have this capability. Even the slightest modification to the generated query script will render the graphical builder inoperable.

Here's what I think: The graphical MDX Query Designer generates well-formed, efficient MDX script. If you design all necessary calculated members into the cube, you shouldn't have to make changes to the report queries. If you do need to write advanced MDX queries, then you probably don't need to use the graphical designer anyway. Compared to T-SQL, MDX queries are usually simpler and less verbose because business rules are resolved in the cube rather than in the query. Regardless of what I think, the MDX Query Designer works the way it does, and you're best off to work with it and take advantage of its capabilities when it serves your needs.

Creating a Data Source

Let's start by creating a shared data source for the Adventure Works DW 2008 sample Analysis Services database:

1. In the Solution Explorer for a report project, right-click Shared Data Sources, and choose Add New Data Source. The Shared Data Source Properties dialog opens (see Figure 9-2).

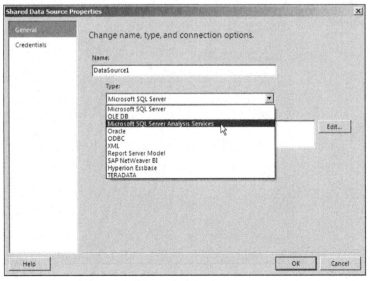

Figure 9-2

2. Select the Microsoft SQL Server Analysis Services data provider from the Type dropdown list.

3. Click on the Edit button to the right of the Connection string box to open the Connection Properties dialog, as shown in Figure 9-3.

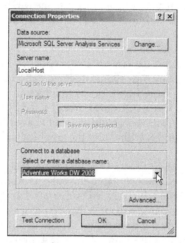

Figure 9-3

4. Type **LocalHost** or the name of your Analysis Services server in the "Server name" box. From the dropdown list in the "Connect to a database" section, select the Adventure Works DW 2008 OLAP database. Click OK to accept these connection settings.

5. Back in the Shared Data Source Properties dialog, change the Name to **AdventureWorksDW2008_AS** (see Figure 9-4). This is to differentiate between a relational data source and this Analysis Services data source for databases that have the same or similar names.

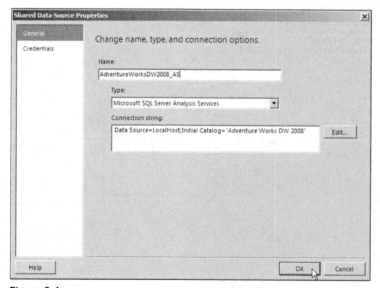

Figure 9-4

You can see that a connection string is generated and placed in the Connection string box. Click OK to save the new shared data source.

You will choose this shared data source for all the examples used in this chapter. Because the data source uses the Analysis Services data provider, the Report Designer will generate MDX queries rather than the T-SQL queries you've seen in previous examples using the SQL Server data provider.

Building the Data-Set Query

Now let's design a report using a key performance indicator (KPI) defined in the Adventure Works cube. A KPI is a standardized set of related members used to report the state of a business metric. In this case, you want to report the current value, goal, and status of Channel Revenue by product category, for a selected calendar year. This section will not step you through every click and keystroke since you already know how to design reports. This section will step through the MDX-specific features and then instruct you to use the report design skills you've acquired in previous exercises. Of course, you're also welcome to open the completed report in the Chapter 9 sample project.

1. To get started, create a new report without using the Report Wizard, and add a table to the report body. When the table is added, a new data source and dataset will be generated. The Data Source Properties dialog opens, as shown in Figure 9-5. Note that this is actually a Wizard dialog and that the Next and Back buttons are used to navigate between pages.

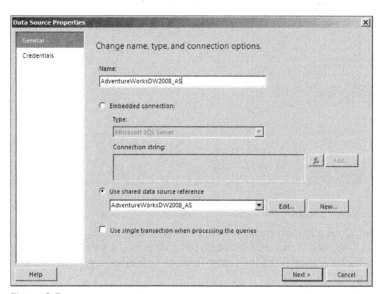

Figure 9-5

2. From the "Use shared data source reference" dropdown list, select the new shared data source you created. Copy (Ctrl+C) the name of the shared data source, and paste (Ctrl+V) it into the Name box at the top of this dialog. Click Next to move to the Query Designer page.

The MDX Query Designer, shown in Figure 9-6, is used to construct the query using simple drag-and-drop. I've labeled this figure to point out the important components of this screen. At first, you will use the cube metadata pane to select cube members and then drag them into the cube member drop area (or data pane). I'll refer back to other components on this figure as we continue to work with this tool.

I tend to work from the inside out, dragging in measures and then the dimension members. This may seem a little backward, but it's a logical approach.

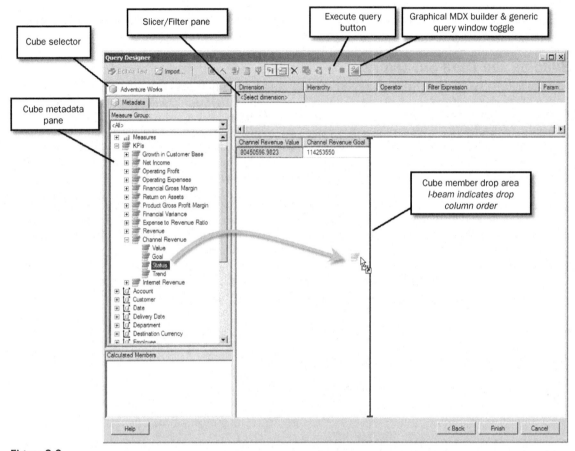

Figure 9-6

3.   Using the "Cube metadata pane," expand the KPIs node and the Channel Revenue KPI. Drag the Value, Goal, and Status members into the data pane. Note that a large, vertical I-beam bar indicates the drop position of the current member. Use this to position these members in the proper order.

The metadata pane enables you to explore and select from any member of the cube structure. Figure 9-7 details various members of the Adventure Works sample cube. In short, measures, calculated members, and KPIs represent numeric values for reporting. All other members are used to group, filter, and provide navigational paths to these values. I've expanded nodes in the metadata pane to demonstrate examples of each of these elements.

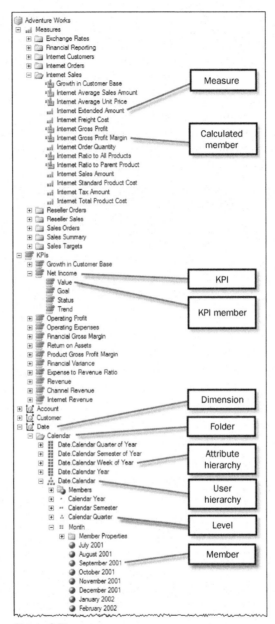

Figure 9-7

All cube attributes are organized into subject-specific dimensions. Dimensions have two types of hierarchies — attribute hierarchies and user hierarchies. An *attribute hierarchy* is simply a flat collection of dimension members derived from a specific data attribute. A *user hierarchy* has multiple levels of attributes organized into a logical drill-down structure. For the most part, you want to use user hierarchies for all drill-down and structured reporting. As a matter of convention, hierarchies consist of levels and members. Members are just the individual attribute values for a level (e.g., Years, Quarters, or Months). Note that attribute hierarchy levels typically have the same name as the hierarchy (e.g., [Date].[CalendarYear].[CalendarYear]), and user hierarchies do not. The user attribute name is typically more explicit (e.g., [Date].[Calendar].[CalendarYear]). Unless specifically hidden in the cube design, the members of every user hierarchy level will correspond to the members of an attribute hierarchy.

4. After dragging the KPI members to the data pane, expand the Product dimension and drag the Product Categories hierarchy to the left-most position in the drop area (also known as the Data pane), as shown in Figure 9-8. The Query Designer parses the hierarchy levels and generates columns for each. The query runs and shows the results grouped by the attribute members, in order of the column placement.

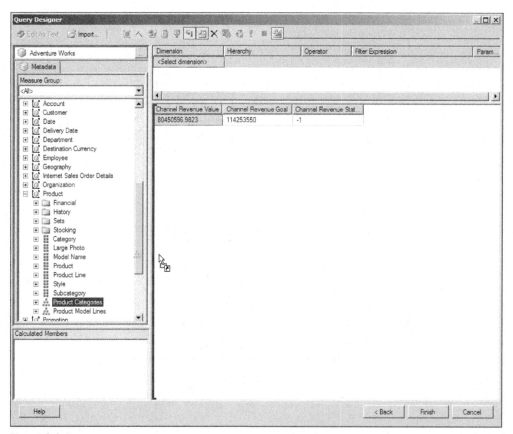

Figure 9-8

Using Parameterized Queries

The query created with the previous steps is complete and usable but returns results for all the cube data. To filter data from a cube, you "slice" the cube to limit the scope of the query to certain members of a hierarchy. This is performed using the filtering pane of the MDX Query Designer. Use the following steps to add a parameterized filter to the query you just created:

1. To filter the results, drag the Calendar Year attribute hierarchy into the Filter pane (see Figure 9-9). This will parse the hierarchy and place elements into the Dimension, Hierarchy, and Operator columns.

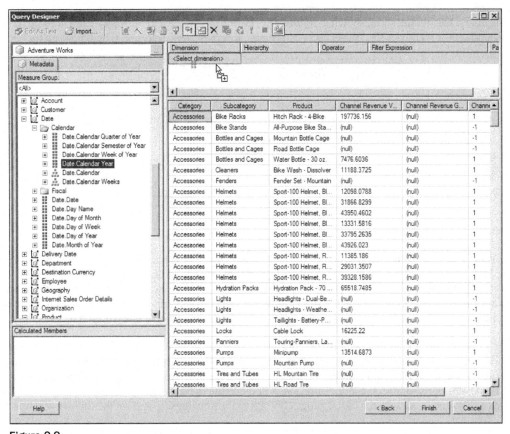

Figure 9-9

2. Use the Filter Expression dropdown window to set the default filter member. Note that every hierarchy has an "All" member, used to include all members of the hierarchy. Check on "All Periods" to set the filter to include all members. This essentially negates the filter unless a different selection is made.

3. Depending on your screen size, the right-most column may not be in view. If not, scroll and adjust the columns to view the Parameter column. Check on this box to generate a related report parameter for this filter.

Slicing the Cube

The concept of a filter is actually contrary to the way OLAP works. We commonly use the term *filter* because most people understand this notion based on their experience with relational database technologies. However, what we've actually defined here is more accurately known as a *slicer*. To limit the results of an OLAP dataset, we aren't going to tell the query engine to scan through individual rows, looking for values that match certain criteria. We're actually telling it to "slice" off a portion of the cube, which is already organized into predefined ranges of grouped and sorted attributes. An important distinction between these two conventions is that slicing doesn't toss out the rest of the cube that doesn't meet the WHERE clause criteria (as a true filter would). It sets the context, or CurrentMember property, for the specified hierarchy. Members of the hierarchy outside this scope are still accessible to functions and operators that may be used in the query. The default slicer, shown in Figure 9-10, is set to use the All member, which will return data for all calendar year members. Of course, users can change this parameter selection when they run the report.

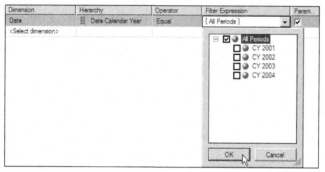

Figure 9-10

The Value and Goal KPIs are typically used to return a measure or calculated value. The Status and Trend members are used to simplify the state of the KPI performance based on some scripted logic and to drive a graphical dashboard indicator of some kind. In the case of Channel Revenue, the Status KPI member returns an integer with one of three values to indicate the state of channel revenue. The value negative 1 (−1) indicates poor performance, 0 is marginal, and 1 indicates acceptable or exceptional performance.

After the query, designing most reports that use Analysis Services is no different from any other. Figure 9-11 shows a table report we've designed for this query. This is the Channel Revenue by Territory report in the Chapter 9 sample project. We've simply defined groups on the sales territory region hierarchy levels and used the fields derived from the Value and Goal KPI members in the detail row of the table. To visualize the Status KPI member, we added a radial gauge (180° N) to the detail group and set the following properties:

Object	Property	Value
RadialScale1	MinimumValue	−2
	MaximumValue	2
RadialRange1	FillColor	Red
	FillGradientType	None
	StartValue	−2
	EndValue	0
	StartWidth	60
	EndWidth	60
	Placement	Cross

Object	Property	Value
RadialRange2	FillColor	Lime
	FillGradientType	None
	StartValue	0
	EndValue	2
	StartWidth	60
	EndWidth	60
	Placement	Cross
RadialPointer1	FillColor	Black
	Value	=Sum(Fields!Channel_Revenue_Status.Value)
	MarkerLength	35

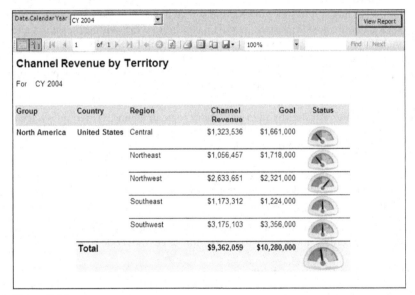

Figure 9-11

After setting up the detail row textboxes and gauge, we added a total to the Country group and copied and pasted the gauge to the same column cell in the total row. The only change for this gauge is that the pointer value must use an AVG function instead of a SUM function. The gauge shows a red and a lime-green range with the pointer pointing to one of three positions, depending on the Status KPI member value.

You are encouraged to explore some of the standard features that were added as a result of using the MDX Query Designer. The parameter dropdown is completely configured and populated with a hidden dataset to provide Calendar Year values. Items on the list below the All member are indented. Had we used a user hierarchy, all the levels would be indented appropriately to indicate their position within the hierarchy. All parameter lists are automatically generated as multi-valued selection lists. This, of course, can be changed in the Report Parameter Properties dialog.

The majority of reports we create with an Analysis Services data source are this simple. Because the calculation and KPI business logic are designed into the cube, no extra work is necessary when reports are designed. With the Report Builder 2.0 Designer, information workers can design reports with very little or no knowledge of cube design or MDX query scripting. Using practically any MDX-based dataset, reports can be designed with a table, matrix, chart, or combinations of the data ranges and other report items, to visualize business information in the most appropriate format.

Modifying the MDX Query

We're now crossing a bridge, and on the other side is an environment that is a little more complex and delicate than the one we just left behind. Reporting Services enables you to do a lot of very interesting things with MDX and OLAP data sources, but the Query Designer was not engineered for advanced MDX. We do a lot of MDX reporting, and we often step into client projects where others have tried to implement complex MDX queries and have failed. Over the past few years, working on these projects, we've discovered what has and hasn't worked, and we've developed techniques for achieving the desired results. One of our most important lessons has been to work with the product and its capabilities. I've had numerous conversations with members of the Reporting Services product team on this topic, and the advice I often receive is "We didn't intend for you to write an MDX query that way, and we don't support that particular technique. You can achieve the same result by doing it this way." I'd like to share some of these techniques with you.

I've not had very good luck adding my own parameter logic to a handwritten query. It can be done, but the Query Designer is very particular about script changes and will intervene at the most inconvenient times. I recommend that you do one of the following:

❑ Use the MDX Query Designer to design the original query with the built-in parameter logic and supporting datasets, and then make modifications to the query logic, leaving the parameter logic alone.

❑ Manually write a simple query with a hard-coded filtering to set up the query metadata, and then replace the entire query with an expression or custom code function.

We will explore both of these options in turn.

Building a Query Using the MDX Designer

Let's start with a copy of the report you just completed. The objective is to define three calculated members, based on the same KPI members you used. These calculated members don't exist in the cube, and let's say that you don't have permission to modify the cube structure to add them to the cube design. In addition to the Value, Goal, and Status members for the Channel Revenue KPI, you also need to see what these values were for the prior year.

1. To get started, open the main data-set query in the report, switch to the generic query view, and then copy the MDX script to the Clipboard.

2. Open SQL Server Management Studio, connect to Analysis Services, and then click on the New Query button on the toolbar to open a new MDX query.

3. Paste the query from the Report Designer in the Query window.

4. Apparently, the Reporting Services MDX Query Designer was created before carriage returns were invented. Add a few to make this query more readable.

5. The nested parameter references won't work in Management Studio, so simplify this query to run without them. The easiest way to do this is to divide the first part of the script, up to the ON ROWS expression, from the rest with a few carriage returns. (This example uses only the first part for testing.) To complete the test query, you just need to add a FROM clause with the cube name and terminate this query with a semicolon.

6. Highlight only the first query, and click on the Execute button on the toolbar. Your screen should look like Figure 9-12.

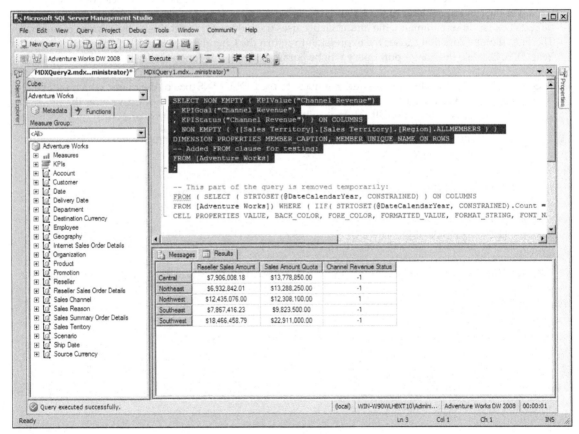

Figure 9-12

7. To add the calculated members to the query, type the following into the Query window before the existing script:

```
WITH
MEMBER Measures.[Last Year Value]
AS ([Date].[Calendar Year].CurrentMember.PREVMEMBER, KPIValue("Channel Revenue"))
, FORMAT_STRING="$#,##0.00"
MEMBER Measures.[Last Year Goal]
AS ([Date].[Calendar Year].CurrentMember.PREVMEMBER, KPIGoal("Channel Revenue"))
, FORMAT_STRING="$#,##0.00"
MEMBER Measures.[Last Year Status]
AS ([Date].[Calendar Year].CurrentMember.PREVMEMBER, KPIStatus("Channel Revenue"))
```

To explain the logic for each of these calculated members, we'll examine the first one. A new member named *Last Year Value* is added to the Measures collection, applying this expression:

```
([Date].[Calendar Year].CurrentMember.PREVMEMBER, KPIValue("Channel Revenue"))
```

This member will return the Channel Revenue KPI Value for the previous Calendar Year, based on whatever the current member of the Calendar Year hierarchy is. If your user selects **2004** for the DateCalendarYear parameter, the WHERE clause uses the parameter to set this as the current member. The PREVMEMBER function causes the expression to return the Channel Revenue KPI Value for Calendar Year 2003. Because the final report query will be parameterized, this functionality is completely dynamic.

8. You want to add these three new members to the COLUMNS axis of the query, which will be interpreted as three new fields in the report. Remove the NON EMPTY directive after the SELECT clause. This ensures that all columns will be returned, even if no data is present.

To add the new calculated members to the query, apply the following changes:

```
WITH
MEMBER Measures.[Last Year Value]
AS ([Date].[Calendar Year].CurrentMember.PREVMEMBER, KPIValue("Channel Revenue"))
, FORMAT_STRING="$#,##0.00"
MEMBER Measures.[Last Year Goal]
AS ([Date].[Calendar Year].CurrentMember.PREVMEMBER, KPIGoal("Channel Revenue"))
, FORMAT_STRING="$#,##0.00"
MEMBER Measures.[Last Year Status]
AS ([Date].[Calendar Year].CurrentMember.PREVMEMBER, KPIStatus("Channel Revenue"))

SELECT { KPIValue("Channel Revenue")
, KPIGoal("Channel Revenue")
, KPIStatus("Channel Revenue")
, [Last Year Value], [Last Year Goal], [Last Year Status]
 } ON COLUMNS
, NON EMPTY { ([Sales Territory].[Sales Territory].[Region].ALLMEMBERS ) }
DIMENSION PROPERTIES MEMBER_CAPTION, MEMBER_UNIQUE_NAME ON ROWS
-- Added FROM clause for testing:
FROM [Adventure Works]
;
```

9. Run the query to verify that it works. You should now see six columns in the results. The reason that the new members don't return a value is that the current member of the Calendar Year has not been set. To do this, add a WHERE clause to slice the cube on Calendar Year 2004.

```
WITH
 MEMBER Measures.[Last Year Value]
 AS ([Date].[Calendar Year].CurrentMember.PREVMEMBER, KPIValue("Channel Revenue"))
 , FORMAT_STRING="$#,##0.00"
 MEMBER Measures.[Last Year Goal]
 AS ([Date].[Calendar Year].CurrentMember.PREVMEMBER, KPIGoal("Channel Revenue"))
 , FORMAT_STRING="$#,##0.00"
 MEMBER Measures.[Last Year Status]
 AS ([Date].[Calendar Year].CurrentMember.PREVMEMBER, KPIStatus("Channel Revenue"))

SELECT { KPIValue("Channel Revenue")
 , KPIGoal("Channel Revenue")
 , KPIStatus("Channel Revenue")
 , [Last Year Value], [Last Year Goal], [Last Year Status]
 } ON COLUMNS
 , NON EMPTY { ([Sales Territory].[Sales Territory].[Region].ALLMEMBERS ) }
DIMENSION PROPERTIES MEMBER_CAPTION, MEMBER_UNIQUE_NAME ON ROWS
-- Added FROM clause for testing:
FROM [Adventure Works]
WHERE [Date].[Calendar Year].&[2004]
;
```

10. Apply this change, check your query with the following script, and then run the query. You should now see the 2003 values for the new calculated members. You can check this by making note of the values, changing the WHERE clause with 2003 rather than 2004, and then running it again.

11. To prepare the query for the report, you need to add all the parameter logic from the original query. Remove the FROM and WHERE lines from the new query, and then merge the two halves back together. Your final query should look like this:

```
WITH
 MEMBER Measures.[Last Year Value]
 AS ([Date].[Calendar Year].CurrentMember.PREVMEMBER, KPIValue("Channel Revenue"))
 , FORMAT_STRING="$#,##0.00"
 MEMBER Measures.[Last Year Goal]
 AS ([Date].[Calendar Year].CurrentMember.PREVMEMBER, KPIGoal("Channel Revenue"))
 , FORMAT_STRING="$#,##0.00"
 MEMBER Measures.[Last Year Status]
 AS ([Date].[Calendar Year].CurrentMember.PREVMEMBER, KPIStatus("Channel Revenue"))

SELECT { KPIValue("Channel Revenue")
 , KPIGoal("Channel Revenue")
 , KPIStatus("Channel Revenue")
 , [Last Year Value], [Last Year Goal], [Last Year Status]
 } ON COLUMNS
 , NON EMPTY { ([Sales Territory].[Sales Territory].[Region].ALLMEMBERS ) }
```

(continued)

(continued)

```
DIMENSION PROPERTIES MEMBER_CAPTION, MEMBER_UNIQUE_NAME ON ROWS
FROM ( SELECT ( STRTOSET(@DateCalendarYear, CONSTRAINED) ) ON COLUMNS
FROM [Adventure Works]) WHERE ( IIF( STRTOSET(@DateCalendarYear,
CONSTRAINED).Count = 1,
STRTOSET(@DateCalendarYear, CONSTRAINED), [Date].[Calendar Year].currentmember ))
CELL PROPERTIES VALUE, BACK_COLOR, FORE_COLOR, FORMATTED_VALUE, FORMAT_STRING,
FONT_NAME, FONT_SIZE, FONT_FLAGS
```

12. Now you're ready to update the query in the report. Copy the query from the Management Studio Query window, and paste it over all of the script in the Report Designer Query window (see Figure 9-13). Click on the Execute button to test the query and refresh the field collection.

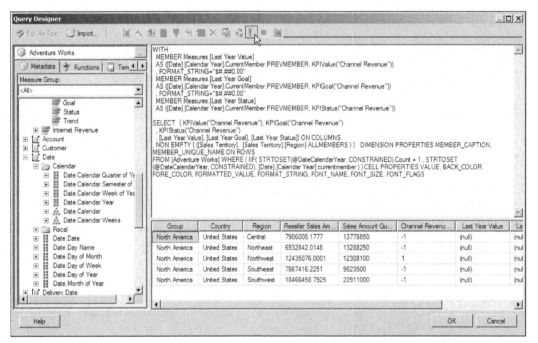

Figure 9-13

The rest of the report design is pretty straightforward. As you can see in Figure 9-14, the three new calculated members are added to the data-set fields collection and can be used to add columns to the table using the same drag-and-drop technique you have used before.

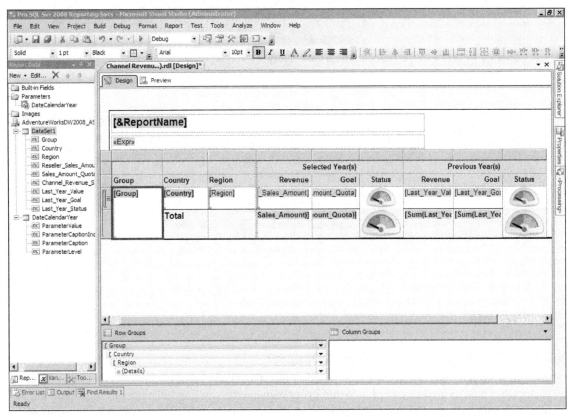

Figure 9-14

The gauges can also be copied and pasted from the original Status column. On the new gauge, click on the pointer, and then use the smart tag to update the field binding to use the Last_Year_Status field.

Figure 9-15 shows this report in preview. A copy of the completed report is also available in the Chapter 9 sample project.

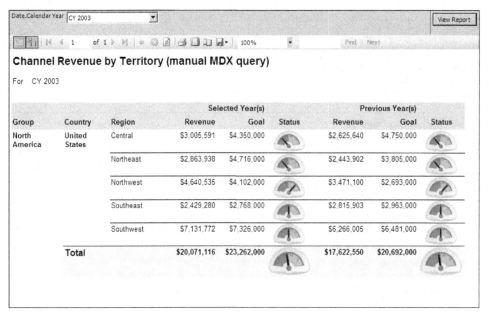

Figure 9-15

Building a Query without Using the MDX Designer

You can write your own queries without the aid of the MDX Query Designer quite easily, but it can get tricky when queries become complex. Writing your own queries can provide more flexibility than the Query Designer affords, but you must start with a simple query to define the query metadata. You can then typically get away with making changes to the column axis members logic, adding function calls and calculated members, that don't otherwise affect the structure of the query metadata.

A simple MDX query can be typed or pasted directly into the Query Designer's generic Query window, and, as long as the query conforms to the Designer's standards, it should work just fine. One of these rules is that all measures must be on the columns axis. Typically, measures belong on the columns axis, which might seem to be a reasonable assumption for most any query, although it is not a restriction in the language itself.

Use the Reseller Sales and Margin report in the Chapter 9 sample project for reference as you walk through the steps to create it.

First, create a new dataset using an Analysis Services data source. Manually adding the following query script is perfectly acceptable to the Query Designer:

```
SELECT
    {[Measures].[Reseller Sales Amount]
  , [Measures].[Reseller Gross Profit Margin]} on Columns
  , ([Product].[Product Categories].Members) On Rows
FROM [Adventure Works]
WHERE [Date].[Fiscal Year].&[2004]
;
```

However, if you want to parameterize the slicer expression on the WHERE clause, the Query Designer won't accommodate an in-line expression to dynamically build the WHERE logic. Here's a simple work-around using an expression to build the query text.

First, to make things interesting, add two report parameters to be used dynamically in the query. Manually add a string-type parameter named Year and a Boolean-type parameter named IncludeEmpty.

The Year parameter's available values will come from a list of Fiscal Year members based on the following MDX query:

```
WITH
   MEMBER Measures.YearUniqueName AS
   [Date].[Fiscal Year].CurrentMember.UniqueName

SELECT
      {Measures.YearUniqueName} ON COLUMNS
   , [Date].[Fiscal Year].Members ON ROWS
FROM [Adventure Works]
;
```

The YearUniqueName calculated member in this query value is then substituted for the Year parameter placeholder in the query. In the sample report, view the Available Values properties for this parameter. Note that the parameter isn't associated with the dataset, because this will be resolved in an expression.

The Boolean-type parameter named IncludeEmpty is used to determine when rows with blank cells in each column should be returned in the query results. In MDX, this feature is enabled by placing the text **NON EMPTY** before the row axis expression.

You can accomplish all this by using an expression to build the query script. Rather than opening the Query Designer from the Dataset Properties dialog, click on the expression button to the right of the Query box (see Figure 9-16).

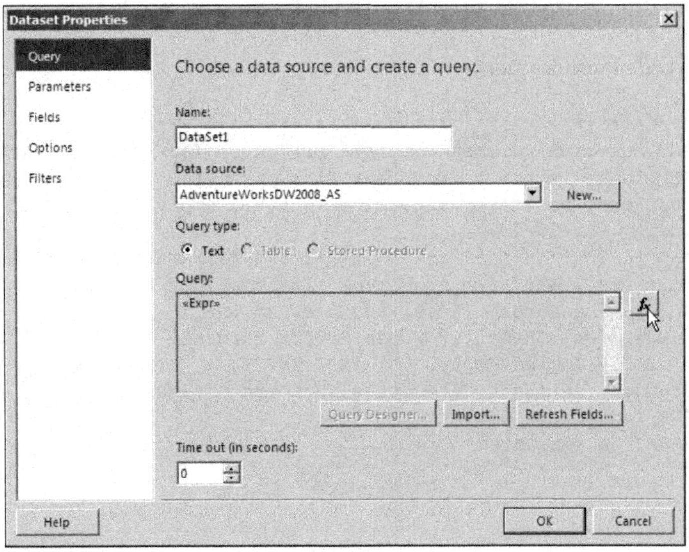

Figure 9-16

In the Expression window, build the following script using VB.NET string concatenation techniques (see Figure 9-17). I've broken this string up into several lines for readability, with the parameter values assembled in line. The same technique can easily be applied to a larger query.

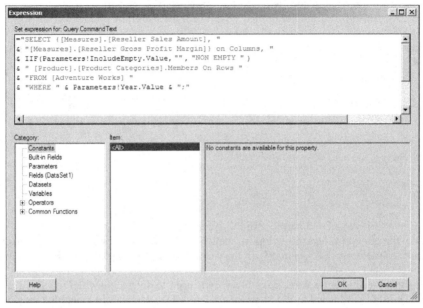

Figure 9-17

This works great for simple string concatenation. But if you need to apply more complex, conditional logic, you can build the query in a VB function embedded in the report and then call the function from an expression. To create the function, open the Report Properties dialog from the Reports menu or right-click on the Report Designer window outside the Body to open this dialog.

Here is the custom code for this report:

```
'***************************************************************************************
'       Custom function returns complete MDX query for DataSet CommandText
'       WHERE clause is built from YearParam parameter
'       IncludeEmpty parameter determines whether empty row are returned.
'       P. Turley - 8-30-08
'***************************************************************************************
Function ReportQuery(YearParam As String, IncludeEmpty As Boolean) As String
  Return  "SELECT {[Measures].[Reseller Sales Amount] " _
        & ", [Measures].[Reseller Gross Profit Margin]} on Columns " _
        & ", " & IIF(IncludeEmpty, "", "NON EMPTY ") _
        & "[Product].[Product Categories].Members On Rows " _
        & "FROM [Adventure Works] " _
        & "WHERE " & YearParam
End Function
```

Similar functions can be compiled to, and referenced from, a central .NET assembly to be shared among multiple reports. This assembly, based on a Visual Studio Class Library project, can be written using C# or any other .NET-compliant programming language. To learn more about referencing an external library, see Chapters 8 and 17.

To modify a report outside the Report Designer, first close the Report Designer for the report you want to modify. Using the Solution Explorer, select the report, and copy and paste it to make a backup copy.

Right-click on the report, and choose View Code. This opens the RDL file without the Report Designer. Use the Find feature (Ctrl+F) to search for the word *DataSet*, and then scroll down to the dataset you need to change. The element tag for a dataset named *DataSet1* will read `<DataSet Name="DataSet1">`.

Find the `CommandText` element, and paste the MDX script or make the change in this tag.

Close and save the RDL file. You can open this report in the Designer to test it, but you shouldn't try to open the Query Designer unless you're prepared to go back and apply these changes again.

Also, before making manual changes in the MDX Query Designer, always copy the current working query to Notepad or Management Studio first. This way, if the Query Designer decides that it doesn't like your changes, you can always revert back to the last working version.

Using Date Parameters

You've probably noticed by now that date values are handled differently in cubes than in typical relational database scenarios. Date values are usually parsed and separated into specific date part members and then organized into hierarchies. This is for convenience and efficiency. When filtering data, rather than contending with real date-type ranges (which are the source of many application logic errors), cubes generally organize data values by year, quarter, month, week, day, and so on. This way, you typically can say "Give me the sales from this month to that month" rather than "Give me the sales records from 5:00:00.000 A.M. on this date through 11:59:59.999 P.M. on another date." See the difference? Because you're not managing transactions in a cube, a measure value can simply belong to a month or week or day, rather than to a specific point in time.

There are many occasions when users will want reports to include data for a range of dates. Even though you typically don't store dates as date/time-type values in the dimensions, you can still accommodate these users with a little bit of creative design.

The Reseller Sales by Territory and Date sample report has a data-set query that slices sales using a range of Date member values. The Date member is not a date/time type but a string including the month, date number, and year. Regardless of the face value of this member, a range of these date members can be used to filter measure values. Your objective is to use two date-type parameters to drive a standard calendar selection interface. The selected dates will be converted to dimension member key values and then passed as parameters to the query. You'll build the report to show the default behavior, and then add support for the date-type parameters.

Figure 9-18 shows the query design. Note the Range option chosen for the filter operator applied to the Date member.

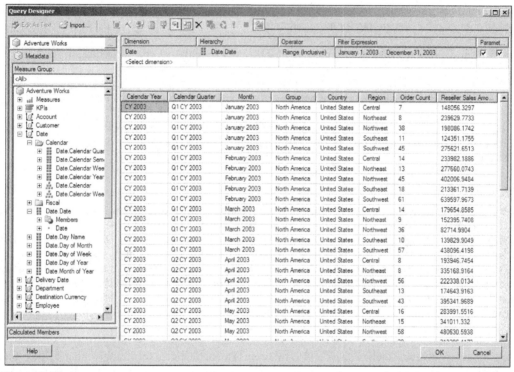

Figure 9-18

There's nothing particularly special about this matrix report. As you can see in Figure 9-19, the parameter list contains one row per date. If you had only 5 years of dates in the cube, each list would have more than 1,800 items to scroll through. This is marginally functional and not the most ideal method to prompt users for date values.

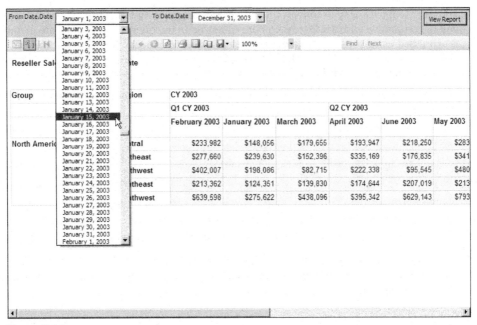

Figure 9-19

Now to work the magic.

1. Start by changing the parameter data type from Text to Date/Time (see Figure 9-20). This will change the parameter prompt to use a calendar dropdown, but the resulting value will be incompatible with the Date member in the query.

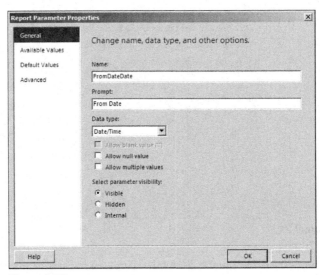

Figure 9-20

You need to have a way to convert the date values returned by the parameter selections into values compatible with the Date member referenced in the query. The actual Date member is expressed using the `UniqueName` property of the Date dimension attribute member. For example, the key value for December 25, 2008 is `[Date].[Date].&[20081225]`. This is easy enough to convert using a VB.NET function you will embed into the report.

2. Open the Report Properties dialog, and enter the following text into the Code window:

```
Function DateParameter(DateValue As Date) As String
    Dim sDateUniqueName As String
    Dim sDateKey As String
    sDateKey = YEAR(DateValue).ToString() _
                    & RIGHT("0" & MONTH(DateValue).ToString, 2) _
                    & RIGHT("0" & DAY(DateValue).ToString(), 2)
    sDateUniqueName = "[Date].[Date].&[" & sDateKey & "]"
    Return sDateUniqueName
End Function
```

This function takes a date value as the input argument `DateValue`, parses it into properly formatted date parts, assembles the date member `UniqueName` reference, and then returns this value from the function.

3. In the DataSet Properties dialog for the main report dataset, the date-type report parameters are mapped to the query parameters through this function. On the Parameters page, as shown in Figure 9-21, click on the Expression button (*fx*) next to the first parameter to open the Expression Builder.

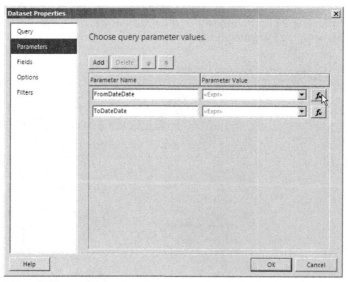

Figure 9-21

Figure 9-22 shows the correct syntax to call the `DateParameter` function, passing in the `FromDateDate` report parameter.

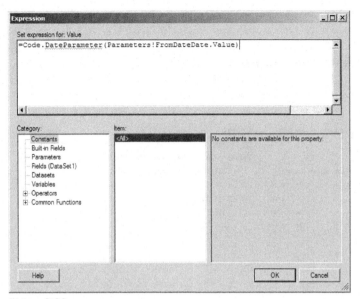

Figure 9-22

4. Click OK to accept the expression.

5. In the DataSet Properties dialog, open the Expression Builder for the second parameter. Repeat this step, and enter the same expression for the `ToDateDate` report parameter.

The report is ready to preview. Figure 9-23 shows the parameter bar after you've made these changes. Calendar controls are now displayed for each parameter, making a date selection much easier.

Figure 9-23

The previewed report, shown in Figure 9-24, reveals that the report runs with these changes. For testing purposes, we've added four textboxes above the table to show the two parameter values. The second row of values displays the output from the `DateParameter` function—the same values you passed into the data-set query.

| From Date | 1/1/2004 | | To Date | 3/31/2004 | | | View Report |

| | | ◄ 1 | of 1 ► ►| | | ⊘ | | 🖨 | | | ▼ | 100% | ▼ | | Find | Next |

Reseller Sales by Territory and Date

1/1/2004 12:00:00 AM   3/31/2004 12:00:00 AM

[Date].[Date].&[20040101]   [Date].[Date].&[20040331]

Group	Country	Region	CY 2004		
			Q1 CY 2004		
			February 2004	January 2004	March 2004
North America	United States	Central	$253,954	$113,950	$256,327
		Northeast	$140,656	$139,988	$194,685
		Northwest	$443,015	$287,292	$434,405
		Southeast	$188,758	$114,993	$196,513
		Southwest	$510,497	$472,202	$457,090

Figure 9-24

Non-Additive Measures

Often, the values you need to see on reports are calculated using more complex logic than simple sums. Measure values can be based on statistical functions, on rolling or weighted averages, or on industry-specific standard calculations. Special logic is often required to calculate common metrics such as inventory counts, profit, and ratios. Regardless, these aren't calculations you should have to repeat in every report. One of the great advantages of using SQL Server Analysis Services is that all the necessary business logic for reporting and analysis can be designed into the cube. This means that once the business rules are sorted out in the cube design, you simply use the measures, calculated members, and KPIs with full confidence that the results will be accurate and reliable.

Let's use a simple example of an average sales amount calculation. You can use your imagination to extend this scenario to other business cases that would apply to your situation. The Adventure Works cube contains a measure named *Reseller Average Sales Amount*. The logic behind this calculation relies on the knowledge of individual transaction sales amounts that are actually not present in the cube. In fact, unless we were to go back to the original data source for these sales records, we couldn't calculate this value ourselves. Fortunately, Analysis Services performs some magic when it processes the cube and aggregates this measure value. It figures out which values must be stored in the cube and which values can be derived at query time. In the case of an average measure, it must store the average at every level of a dimensional hierarchy, because it's not possible to derive an average from a range of average values at a lower level. Although it's interesting to know how Analysis Services performs these aggregations and stores selected values, you can sleep soundly at night knowing that you don't have to worry about it.

Enter Reporting Services. When you drag-and-drop a field onto a report item or data region at a group level above a detail row, the Report Designer always applies the SUM function to a numeric value. It assumes that you want to roll up individual values into a summed total. This is a helpful assumption most of the time but not when your measure fields don't sum, or if you want to do something else with them. What if the measure were a standard deviation or a weighted, rolling average? How would you roll this up into a group footer?

It doesn't matter. This is Analysis Services' job, and you should not have to worry about it. Here's a simple example to illustrate the simple solution. Figure 9-25 shows a basic matrix report, named *AS Avg Sales* in the Chapter 9 sample project. The detail and total value cells were designed by dragging the Sales_Amount_Quota and Reseller_Average_Sales_Amount fields to the detail area of the matrix. We've made a point to expand the column widths so that you can see the expressions. As you see, the Designer applied the SUM function to all four of these cells.

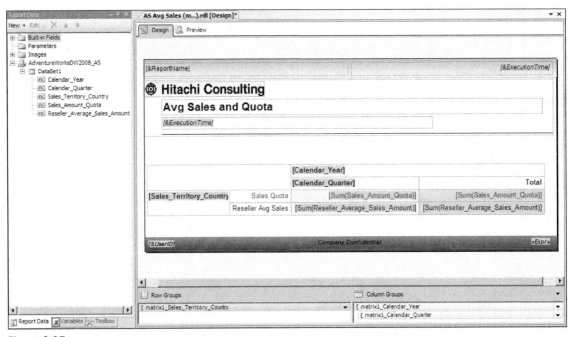

Figure 9-25

Figure 9-26 shows the report in preview. We've called out one example showing that the total for two quarterly sales averages is the sum of these values. This is an inaccurate total. (Read on.)

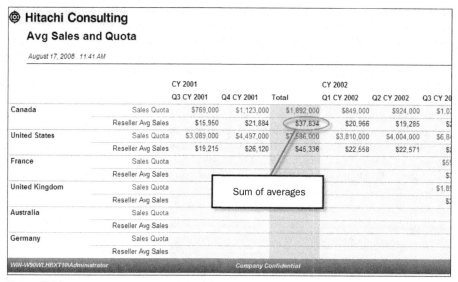

Figure 9-26

Using the Aggregate Function

The solution to this problem is to let Reporting Services know that it should not try to aggregate any values. The measure values for an OLAP query have already been aggregated, and the value at each level represents the appropriate roll-up of subordinate levels. This is done by replacing occurrences of SUM with the AGGREGATE function.

Figure 9-27 shows the report with these changes. We have replaced all of the SUM function references with AGGREGATE by editing each expression.

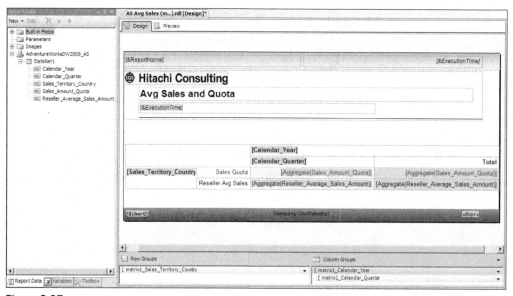

Figure 9-27

Preview the report again to see the results. Note that all the Sales_Amount_Quota total values remain the same, because this is an additive measure and these values were already using the SUM function in the cube. The summed value from the cube (which you see here) and the summed values in the report are the same. However, the Reseller_Average_Sales_Amount totals are different. This is because the calculation returned from the cube in Figure 9-28 is the calculated average rather than the sum of averages you saw in the previous example.

Hitachi Consulting

Avg Sales and Quota

August 17, 2008 11:45 AM

		CY 2001			CY 2002		
		Q3 CY 2001	Q4 CY 2001	Total	Q1 CY 2002	Q2 CY 2002	Q3 CY 20
Canada	Sales Quota	$769,000	$1,123,000	$1,892,000	$849,000	$924,000	$1,0
	Reseller Avg Sales	$15,950	$21,884	$18,917	$20,966	$19,285	$
United States	Sales Quota	$3,089,000	$4,497,000	$7,586,000	$3,810,000	$4,004,000	$6,8
	Reseller Avg Sales	$19,215	$26,120	$22,909	$22,558	$22,571	$
France	Sales Quota						$5
	Reseller Avg Sales						$
United Kingdom	Sales Quota			True average			$1,8
	Reseller Avg Sales						$
Australia	Sales Quota						
	Reseller Avg Sales						
Germany	Sales Quota						
	Reseller Avg Sales						

WIN-W90WLHBXT10\Administrator   *Company Confidential*

Figure 9-28

MDX Properties and Cube Formatting

As you've looked at the MDX queries generated by the MDX Query Designer, you may have noticed several properties references in the MDX script under the headings CELL PROPERTIES, DIMENSION PROPERTIES, and CUBE PROPERTIES. This is evidence of one of the most significant differences between Analysis Services and a relational database product like SQL Server 2008. When you run a T-SQL query for an SQL Server database, the result set contains very little information aside from the column names and values. Sure, there is a little bit of metadata used by the data provider and client components, such as data types, numeric scales, and string lengths. The formatting of the query results is entirely in the hands of whichever client application is consuming the data.

MDX-based queries provide a mechanism for returning a variety of useful information about different objects returned from a query. Within the cube design, every measure can be formatted, and every calculated member can have font, color, and other styling characteristics associated with it. Dynamic expressions defined in the cube are used to modify these properties based on threshold values or any other logic. This way, profit-related measures are displayed in green, and losses are in red and bold text. These properties are returned through the query results as metadata tags associated with each cell and dimension member. The query script can explicitly request that certain properties be returned.

Reporting Services uses these properties by generating corresponding properties for each field object it derives from an MDX query. These field properties are accessible in the Report Designer Expression dialog. When you select a field, the Value property is referenced by default. Just back the cursor up to the period following the field name to see all the available field properties. Figure 9-29 shows an example setting the Color property of the textbox used to display the Sales_Amount_Quota.

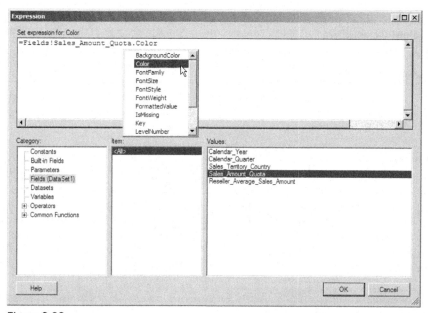

Figure 9-29

Unfortunately, the current version of the Adventure Works DW 2008 sample Analysis Services database doesn't implement any dynamic formatting, so I'm unable to easily demonstrate this feature without using a cube you don't have access to.

Drill-Through Reports

As you know, a drill-through report uses a report action to navigate to a second report when the user clicks on a report item (often a textbox) that contains a reference value of some kind. The typical scenario for drill-through reports is where a high-level summary report lists dimension members in a data region in a table or matrix. Using the example of a table report showing sales summary information for products, if users were to click on a product name, they might expect to see sales details for that product. If a report based on relational tables were used for drill-through, you would expect a key value, such as the ProductID, to be passed from the source report to a parameter in the target report, and used to filter records.

MDX-based reports can play this role as well as any other data source. The difference is in the way that keys and unique identifiers are defined in a cube. Every dimensional attribute does have a key value, but it might not necessarily correspond to a primary key value in a relational data source. Because attributes are organized into hierarchies, the unique value used to describe an attribute preserves the entire hierarchy lineage through a property called the `UniqueName`. This is the value passed to any parameters generated by the MDX Query Designer, and it is considered to be a best practice to use the same technique for drill-through reports. The value of a dimension member is derived from the MDX Name property for a member by default. For a product, this would just be the product name as it appears on the report. The `UniqueName` property value is derived from the `ProductKey` field in the DimProduct table and would look something like this:

```
[Product].[Product].&[470]
```

The example provided in the Chapter 9 sample project consists of a source and target report that you can use as an example of this functionality. The Top 10 Product Internet Sales by Year report contains a table with an action configured for the Product textbox. The Product Sales by Year report has a parameter called *Product* that filters an MDX query bound to a chart. The source report contains an action defined on the Product textbox, which passes a value using the following expression to the target report:

```
=Fields!Product.UniqueName
```

The target report, Product Sales by Year (MDX drill-through target), contains a query parameter named `ProductProduct` that was generated by the MDX Query Designer when this report was designed.

Figure 9-30 shows the Action settings for the source report product textbox. Note the expression used in the Value column of the parameter mapping.

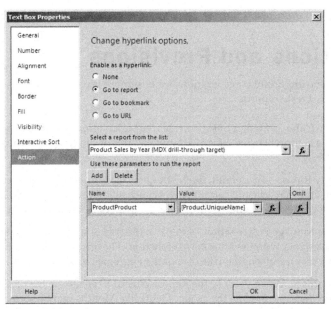

Figure 9-30

Cube Report Actions

Report navigation can also be driven by the cube itself. Cube actions are designed in a cube and exposed as metadata in an MDX query cell-set result. When a compatible cube-browsing client (which includes Excel PivotTables, Office Web Components PivotTable, and Proclarity UI components) displays a query result, hotspots are generated for the related cells. The user can choose a drill-through action for the relevant cell and navigate to a report or other target defined by the cube action.

From a report design perspective, designing a report to receive a report action is exactly the same as designing a drill-through target report. You simply create a parameter to filter the results of a query.

Parameter Safety Precautions

If a drill-through report, URL, or cube report action is exposed to the Internet or an uncontrolled network environment, precautions should be taken to prevent script injection attacks. There are two common safety precautions used when passing parameters to an MDX query. The first is implemented by default in the script generated by the MDX Query Designer. Parameters are passed to the functions STRTOSET or STRTOMEMBER with the CONSTRAINED optional argument flag. This flag instructs the MDX query processing engine to disallow any dynamic script or function calls in the parameter text. The other provision that you can implement yourself is the URLEscapeFragment function. Passing any MDX object reference to this function will MIME-encode any characters that could be used to embed script. The query processor will decode any valid characters on the receiving end after validating the unaltered text. This sample code returns a properly escaped form of a dimension member reference:

```
UrlEscapeFragment(SetTostr({[Dim].[MyHierarchy].CurrentMember}))
```

Best Practices and Provisions

The following are some important considerations for designing reports for Analysis Services. Keep these factors in mind as you create reports:

- ❑ **Leverage the Cube** — Design business rules and calculations into the cube. Report and query design with a comprehensive cube is a simple matter of dragging and dropping members into the Query Designer.

- ❑ **Allow Empty Rows** — By default, the MDX Query Designer eliminates rows that have all empty cells. This may impede certain reports such as charts and matrices. To include all rows, regardless of empty cells, remove the NON EMPTY directive on the rows axis.

- ❑ **Let the Cube Manage Aggregation** — Replace the SUM or FIRST aggregate functions added by the Report Designer with the AGGREGATE function. This instructs Reporting Services to let the Analysis Services query engine take care of the aggregate values.

- ❑ **Sorting Months** — When you use the Report Wizard to create a table or matrix report, groups are sorted on the same field as the group. Fields like Months will be sorted in alphabetical order. Since the members are already sorted correctly in the cube dimension, this is resolved by removing the Sort expression for the group.

❏ **Cascading Parameters** — Auto-built MDX queries create multiple datasets with interdependent parameters. Removing an unneeded parameter can be challenging. Check each hidden data-set query for references to the parameter, and remove those references or delete the dataset and rebuild it without the parameter.

❏ **Use the Query Designer to Create Parameters** — Allow the MDX Query Designer to create parameter and filter logic, and then make modifications to the query after making a backup copy.

❏ **Use Expressions and Custom Code** — As an alternative to using the Query Designer in either graphical or generic mode, assemble the query using an expression or custom function.

Summary

SQL Server 2008 Analysis Services is a powerful tool to store and manage critical business information to support business decisions and analytics. If Analysis Services is used correctly, compelling and useful reports can be created very easily using Reporting Services. Business users shouldn't need to understand the MDX language to design day-to-day reports with Report Builder 2.0, but with some basic MDX knowledge, BI solution developers can create advanced visualizations and powerful business dashboards that would be slow and difficult to design with a relational data source.

The advantages afforded by Analysis Services and the OLAP query engine are numerous. Queries are lightening fast, data is simplified and accessible, and business-specific calculations are managed in a central location. Using Reporting Services to design reports for Analysis Services data can create a fast, secure, and reliable BI solution with uniform results across the business enterprise.

10

Report Solution Patterns and Recipes

This chapter serves as a practical guide to designing reports and building reporting solutions in the real world. It contains a few examples of advanced and creative report designs as recipes to solve specific business problems. This is a high-level guide and not step-by-step instructions. You will use the techniques you've learned in the previous chapters to implement specific functionality. Specifically, this chapter covers the following topics:

❑   Reporting project guidelines, key success factors, and the solution scope

❑   Defining and managing report specifications and the development process phases

❑   Migrating and converting reports from other reporting tools

❑   Working with the strengths and limitations of the Reporting Services architecture

❑   Recipes and models for several advanced reporting features and techniques

In the previous chapters, you've learned what you can do with Reporting Services, and you have been given several options to implement various report functionality. The last edition of this book provided a chapter that offered practical guidance for designing reports based on real-world experience. This chapter takes a different approach to introducing report development patterns by focusing not on what you *can* do but what you *should* do. Over the past three years, I have spent the majority of my professional time building reporting solutions for consulting clients. Collectively, we've developed reporting solutions for a very large software producer, one of the world's largest media and entertainment companies, a global aerospace manufacturer, an international investment bank, utility companies, retail services, food services, telecommunications providers, and government agencies. I've made it a point to build the content for this chapter over time while working on different projects. These and other projects have afforded us challenging opportunities to discover effective patterns for designing a variety of report styles.

We have also had the opportunity to work closely with members of the Reporting Services product team at Microsoft to better understand the long-term goals for Reporting Services' features and capabilities. This has provided insight into the mechanics of the product's components and why they behave as they do. Without fully understanding the design goals in constructing the architecture of this product, it's easy for a report designer to ask questions like, Why does it work that way? . . . Why did that do that? Reporting Services has some limitations that may not make sense to the casual user. I've found that most advanced capabilities that I would like to include in reports can be implemented, but not necessarily using my chosen technique. As I've run up against limitations and have discussed these with the product architects and product managers, the answers are often in the vein of: "That feature wasn't designed to work that way. You can accomplish the same thing by using this other feature or technique." My goal is to share these techniques and capabilities with you.

Unlike the previous chapters on report design, I'm not going to do much hand-holding in this chapter. By now, you should know how to use the features of the Report Designer and how to change properties, create queries, and use all of the report items. For each of the report design techniques that follow, I'll give you enough information to explain the concept and demonstrate the technique, but I won't walk you through the entire process from start to finish. This will save time and avoid redundancy with material covered in the previous chapters.

Reporting Project Requirement Guidelines

Reporting projects are a special breed of software solutions. In the software world, successful projects don't just happen without deliberate efforts to manage evolving requirements and to steer the creative effort. Whether you are a corporate application developer, an independent consultant, or the person who wears all the hats in the department, your project should have a sponsor who defines the requirements and takes delivery of the finished product. We could spend volumes discussing lessons learned about failed and successful projects. In short, the secrets of success nearly all come down to effective communication and the involvement of a customer stakeholder. We've discussed some of these principles and ideas in previous chapters. This section is a concise set of guidelines that you may consider using to help you and your project sponsor to cover the essentials.

Key Success Factors

Reporting projects have a much better chance of being successful when the business requirements are well defined and clearly communicated. In particular:

❑ Report specifications should be documented using a standard format for all reports.

❑ Report specifications are a "living, breathing" document that will evolve as the report goes through its life cycle.

❑ Report layout should be mocked up and included in the specifications, in order to capture the stakeholder's vision.

❑ Report designers must understand the source data. In cases in which the designer isn't familiar with the database design and business data, specific queries or stored procedures should be defined and prepared before report design.

❑ The database schema should be frozen before work begins.

❑ Accurate samples or real data should be available to support the design and testing of all reports.

❑ Report designers should update report specifications to reflect any layout, data, and business rule changes that might have occurred during development, and to include further relevant details to assist in future maintenance.

These may seem like lofty goals. The fact is that often you may not be able to control all of these factors. Experience will help you to know where to draw the line between the situations in which you should work with less-than-ideal conditions and the situations in which you should put your foot down and insist that these conditions be met before you begin work. In any case, be sure to clearly communicate your concerns and the associated risks.

Solution Scope

Reports often have many dependencies on other parts of a solution, and if these pieces aren't in place before reports are designed, this can hold up the report work and waste considerable time and money. Reporting solutions require that the right type of database is in place, that it has been populated with all of the data necessary to build the reports, and that the user and business report requirements are well defined and documented. They also require that at least two environments have been set up to host the reports: a development environment and a production environment. (In more involved scenarios, you might want to introduce a test/QA environment.)

The scope of the solution should be understood before report work begins. Without a clear understanding of all the related components of the solution, the project can easily spin out of control, with more work being started than finished.

Common examples of solution scope challenges include:

❑ Report performance problems prompt database schema changes or the constructing of de-normalized fact tables containing duplicate data.

❑ Realizing that changing transactional data doesn't support reporting scenarios, the database is redesigned while in production.

❑ Database and report features are added as you go and not according to a predefined plan, causing each report to take on different behavior and features.

The process of periodic data extraction to populate the reporting database system is known as ETL (Extract, Transform, and Load). A separate data mart or data warehouse is created to store preaggregated decision-support data. A complex ETL process is created to periodically copy new data into the decision-support database.

When a data warehouse is not available and out of the scope of the report project, you may consider using an operational data store (ODS). An ODS reflects transactional data closer to real time, as opposed to the historical volumes in a data warehouse, but which has gone through some data cleansing and integrity checking for more accurate reports.

Needless to say, if these kinds of issues aren't mitigated and managed, even simple projects may be doomed before they start. Ideally, a report designer should be on the receiving side of business requirements and should participate in helping to clarify the details rather than making up new requirements as the project moves along. In most cases, the report designer should rely on the business analyst/information worker as the subject-matter expert of the data in context, allowing for a separation of concerns and better defined tasks.

Reporting on Existing Data Sources

If you are walking into an environment where the databases already exist, you should carefully review and discuss the long-term viability of the solution with your project sponsor. If this is a small, simple database that isn't likely to grow significantly over its useful life, then you may be in good shape. However, small-database reporting solutions that perform well in test and design scenarios may not fare so well when loaded up with truckloads of data and accessed by many concurrent users.

The system should have a defined capacity and a plan to scale up when you need to support large volumes of data and high workloads.

Reporting on Transactional Sources

In even moderately sized systems, reporting on live data can often be challenging. If user applications are locking data rows and inserting new records while reports run, this creates resource contention and performance issues. Reporting on changing data can also be risky because the report can only capture a single moment in time, while this data continues to change. While using common solutions such as "dirty reads" (uncommitted reads) might address the contention issue, you would still need to identify whether reading uncommitted data is acceptable for your reporting solution.

Decision-support database systems are typically designed to be exclusively Read Only and use data structures much simpler than those used by equivalent transactional databases. This optimizes report performance and keeps the data consistent for a set period of time. Users understand that they aren't looking at the most current data, but they know it should be accurate as of the end of business on the previous day.

One of the challenges when reporting on data in an existing database is that the database may not have been designed with your reporting requirements in mind. Even the simplest reporting requirements can often be difficult to meet without writing very complex queries. This can slow performance and only support a certain amount of data. For small and simple database systems, reporting on the same tables in a transactional database as the rest of the applications may be the easiest choice.

Building an End-to-End Reporting Solution

With Reporting Services, you can create an entire user experience by prompting for input parameters, customizing query operations, interactive filtering, sorting, and using report item actions and navigation features for drilling down (and through) to more details. However, this all assumes that the data sources contain the necessary data in a form that is both accessible and scalable to meet future demands. If this isn't the case, what might have looked like a simple reporting project can take on a whole new dimension. Decision-support systems often involve a separate database that is populated at regular intervals from one or more transactional sources. Typically, scripts run during off hours to copy new data from the main database into a set of simplified tables designed especially for reporting.

Data Marts and Data Warehouses

A *data mart* is a decision-support database used within a department or business unit to serve up report data to meet a set of specific business requirements. It could be as simple as a small set of de-normalized tables in a relational database, or it could be a set of OLAP cubes in a hierarchical database system like Microsoft Analysis Services. Queries for OLAP reporting will be written in a hierarchical expression language, like MDX, rather than the set-based T-SQL language.

Data warehouses and data marts are similar in principle but different in scale. A *data warehouse* is typically a large-scale, enterprise-wide system that meets the reporting needs of many business groups and departments, and will nearly always be deployed as a specialized OLAP system.

An effective ETL process involves not only copying new data from one system to another, but also transforming many rows from many source tables into preaggregated rows of conformed data that describe specific facts. The conformation process means that similar data from disparate systems can be ubiquitously identified, regardless of which system it originated from. In the end, the decision-support data, populated by the ETL process, helps meet reporting business requirements as effectively as possible. Tools such as SQL Server Integration Services (formerly Data Transformation Services, or DTS) are often used to implement ETL.

Sample and Test Data

During report design, it is very important to work with data similar to that of report users. Sample or "mocked-up" data is often meaningless in a business context and doesn't exhibit the same characteristics as the real thing. This data should represent variety and should adhere to the same business rules as real data so that data grouping, sorting, and filtering features can be designed with predictable results. Where possible, production data (or at the very least, production-like data) should be used for report design and testing. Sensitive information can be scrubbed by using search-and-replace iterations and calculations to modify numeric and currency values.

It is usually harder to implement new reporting solutions in parallel with the implementation of a new decision-support system because realistic test data may not be available. In those cases, it is recommended to start the reporting system design and implementation later in the project timeline of the main transactional system implementation. Not only does this allow for business data analysts and information workers to become familiar with the new data model, but it also provides a richer set of test data for testing with the new reports.

In addition to using real data, it's important to work with a manageable set of data so that reports run quickly. Large data volumes can slow report design significantly. To design a bug-free report typically takes several iterations of testing after adding each feature. If it takes several minutes to render a report, this can slow the process by hours and days. When it takes a long time to test a report, I often find myself trying to use this downtime more effectively by working on other tasks. In the end, I find myself starting (more than finishing) multiple things on a slow-running machine. While this is partially mitigated by the .RDL.DATA files created by the Report Designer, in order to cache preview data, if you are dealing with a large dataset to begin with, you still have a delayed response while the report is being rendered. It's tough to keep track of all the loose ends, especially when queries are timing out and reports are crashing with errors.

Report Specifications

Work with your users and project sponsor to design a report specification template that addresses your unique business needs. Some reports may query data from multiple tables, and users may not be familiar enough with the data structures to specify column names and keys for joins. In this case, you may need to involve a database expert to help with these requirements. Other reports may get their data from existing views or stored procedures, making this part of the process a whole lot easier.

You might find that if the project sponsor and users aren't familiar with the data structures, you are left to make assumptions about how the tables should be joined and queried. In these cases, the report specification becomes more of a checklist and a forum to validate assumptions and to answer questions. This also lengthens the development cycle of the report because you have the onus of learning the details of the data model.

Ultimately, the burden must be left to the project sponsor to provide and approve the specific requirements for each report. This, of course, should be performed with the assistance and cooperation of the report designer as you discuss each feature. Remember that the key to success is effective communication. On larger projects or when reporting on more complex databases, you may need to separate the business requirements of the report from the technical specification, perhaps by using two separate documents to gather these requirements. In any case, the key is to involve users and business stakeholders in obtaining buy-off and validating the results.

The following table contains a list of suggested sections for a report specification that should work for most report projects, but can be edited to meet any special requirements.

Report Specification Description	Full report name and description		
Report Category or Group	Reports are often grouped by business function, features, or user audience.		
Priority	1 = High, 2 = Medium, 3 = Low		
Business Problems/ Questions Answered	Describe the business problem and include any details and assumptions made that lead to the report dataset.		
Data Source	Database, tables, stored procedures, cubes, etc.		
Fields	**Schema Field Name**	**Column Title**	**Format**
Table columns and cube dimension member and measures are collectively called *fields* in Reporting Services. List all fields by name with the related report column title and data format.	Actual table column or member name	Report column heading title	Currency, percent, date/time–short/ long, decimal places, etc.

Row Heading(s)	If report format and data are not self-described, some sections of table row headings may require labels.		
Filtering	How is the data filtered — static filters and parameter-based filters? At database server? At report server? List filtered fields and criteria.		
Grouping	How is data grouped — Static, dynamic, or based on parameter field selection? Subgroups? Are groups indented or formatted differently? List groups and field(s) for each group.		
Sorting	How is data sorted — static, parameter-based, sorting within groups, interactive (column header sorting)? List the sort field(s).		
Parameters	**Parameter Name**	**Source**	**Default**
Parameters used for user input or selection may be presented in textboxes, checkboxes, radio buttons, or dropdown lists. May be used to filter, group, sort, show/hide items, rows, columns, etc.	Name and prompt text for parameter (if applicable)	Single value, static list, data-driven list of values	The default value of the parameter
Calculations and Calculated Fields	What calculations are performed in the report? Indicate operational order of precedence and conditions — e.g., if 0 or NULL values; division by zero; negative results; conditional formatting.		
Layout Sample	Include a sample of the report (can be an Excel mockup, or a screenshot).		
Query Details	If including technical details, include SQL or MDX query or explain logic driving any calculations, joins, and aggregations.		
Notes			

Development Phases

As with any software development project, each component or report should progress through a series of design and development phases. These may include prototyping or proof-of-concept, design, testing, and deployment. There are a couple of different ways to keep reports organized: multiple environments or multiple logical folders and/or projects for each phase.

Multiple Reporting Environments

The multiple environment approach involves maintaining multiple reporting environments that reflect the phases of design and development. The most common scenario is to have a development report server, a test/QA server, and, finally, the production environment. This is more involved, requiring a well-defined report promotion and deployment path. It also requires that multiple server environments be set up.

The idea is to keep the report development in the dev/sandbox environment, and as report development is complete, the report can be deployed to the next stage, testing. In the test/QA environment, analysts can verify the report's integrity and validate report data and layout. Once the report has gone through testing and validation, it can be marked ready for production, and go through any formalized promotion processes, such as change control, and so on.

I like to take advantage of the built-in deployment mechanism in Visual Studio for report projects and the support for multiple configurations within one solution. The solution's Properties dialog offers a Configuration Manager from which you can edit and add new configuration options to your solution (see Figure 10-1). You can then create a new configuration for each phase of the project and set different deployment targets for those configurations.

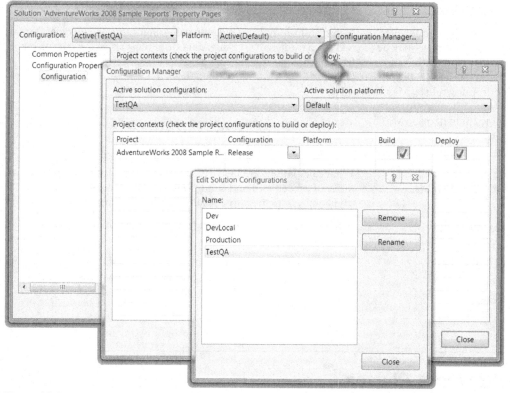

Figure 10-1

With recent advances in hardware virtualization technology, this approach may not be as difficult or expensive — especially if the IT group already supports virtualization for other projects — although it may require a bit more effort up front. When virtualization is not an option, though, the cost of hardware and licensing may quickly shoot down this option.

Multiple Logical Folders and Projects

When following the multiple folder approach, you might find it helpful to create separate projects and folders and then graduate reports from one project to another as they are verified and pass testing criteria.

For each of the Visual Studio projects, within a master solution, create duplicate shared data sources. You can drag and drop reports from one project to another and then remove the previous report using the Solution Explorer. When you right-click on the old report and choose the Remove option, the second Remove option will leave the file in the project folder and simply remove the entry from the project file. Because a new copy is created in the destination project, you should choose the Delete option so that you maintain only one copy of the report definition file.

For each report project, set the `TargetFolder` property of a deployment folder to a name that corresponds to the project name (i.e., *Prototype Phase*, *Design Phase*, *Test Phase*, and *Completed Reports*).

Finally, there is one last thing to remember about what will happen on practically every report project. In the beginning, your sponsor will tell you what reports and features they want and you'll work with them to capture all of the requirements in detail. Things will generally go pretty smoothly until they begin testing and you come up on a deadline. In the eleventh hour, users will start asking for things and your sponsor will request changes.

You'll learn of some minor misunderstandings you may have had about the early requirements, and this will prompt even more changes. Some last-minute changes are inevitable in any project, but when a change is requested, it must be in writing. Whether in hand-written form, in a document, or an e-mail message, keep and save these requests. You should be able to trace every new request back to an earlier requirement or obtain a clear understanding that it is a new requirement. If users request changes, you should have the project sponsor approve them. In the end, managing these changes will go a long way toward ensuring the success of your report project.

Quick and Easy Report Deployment

By combining both of the techniques described above, you can actually achieve a very easy, although less formalized, deployment process. If you maintain separate physical (or virtual) reporting environments, which, in turn, have multiple folders to which reports are deployed, you can configure Visual Studio to push your reports to the correct folders for each environment!

Just set up the Configuration Manager options for your solution, and then use separate projects within the solution that represent each folder within the Report Server. Finally, in the Project properties, set each project's `TargetFolder` to the appropriate destination folder in the report server.

Now you can choose a target environment (Development, Test/QA, Production), right-click on the solution name in Solution Explorer, and choose Deploy. This will send every project's items (reports and shared data sources) to their respective folder on the Report Server. Alternatively, you can "control-click" each report in the Solution Explorer in order to select multiple items, and then right-click on the selection and choose Deploy so that only the report you selected will be deployed to the Report Server.

Migrating and Converting Reports

One of the most common scenarios in large businesses moving to Reporting Services is the desire to migrate or convert reports created using another reporting tool. Many large businesses that have existing applications will have reporting solutions in Crystal Reports, Business Objects, or Access reports. There has been a significant interest in "converting" Crystal Reports to Reporting Services reports. There are several challenges making this difficult to achieve easily.

Recognizing this need, some third-party report migration tools have been developed by companies that offer report migration services. In many cases, these do an effective job of moving Crystal Reports into Reporting Services Report Definition Language (RDL) files. These tools leverage the fact that the Report Definition Language is an open specification format that provides a well-documented set of guidelines for building RDL documents.

There is no single method for fully automating report conversion from Crystal Reports without some manual intervention. One of Reporting Services' greatest strengths is the ability to consolidate similar reports into one, to achieve a more flexible, single report. In many cases, several Crystal Reports or Access reports may be distilled into a handful of SSRS reports to address the same business challenges. There are several features that other reporting applications don't offer when compared with Reporting Services. Moreover, the guidelines and best practices for designing reports with Reporting Services do not always align with those of other tools, and by simply copying a report design from another tool, you will not take advantage of what Reporting Services has to offer. The best practice for report migration is to start, not just with existing reports, but with the user and business requirements, and meet them by effectively using the unique features in Reporting Services. With a large number of existing reports, report conversion can move this process along in large strides.

If you can use existing reports to model design elements, layout and formatting, calculation expressions, query strings, and connection information, this will likely save time and money when compared with starting over from scratch. However, you are almost guaranteed to find better ways to meet your requirements by considering a different approach, consolidating similar reports, and using updated features. The structure of these reports will often be different.

For example, Crystal Reports uses a banding approach for grouped data, wherein the report itself defines data-bound grouped sections. In contrast, a Reporting Services report is simply a blank design canvas upon which report items are used to define data regions for one or more datasets or query result sets. Since grouped data regions may be implemented using a tablix, chart, or gauge report item, depending on the need, there isn't a one-to-one correspondence between these report architectures.

Crystal Reports also relies heavily on formulas and functions for mathematical calculations and conditional formatting, whereas Reporting Services allows designers and developers to use one of three techniques including Visual Basic in-line expressions, code-behind VB functions and snippets, or external .NET assemblies written in your language of choice. This provides a great deal of flexibility to implement custom functionality. Converting all but the simplest expressions from Crystal Reports formulas to Visual Basic expressions would be nearly impossible, especially when the original Crystal Report did not use VB syntax for formulas and calculations.

Finally, one of the most significant challenges for developers who might want to create and distribute a report conversion application is a legal constraint imposed by the proprietary Crystal Reports format (RPT). Programmatically querying the structure of a Crystal Reports report requires components and libraries licensed by Business Objects (owners of the Crystal Reports technology), which prohibits their use for report conversion and distribution with third-party software.

Working with the Strengths and Limitations of the Architecture

Never assume that anything works the way you want it to. Keep in mind that some of the chief goals of this product are to render reports in a variety of presentation formats using server-side components. In doing so, a report rendered to a specific format may not take advantage of all the capabilities offered by that format, a client tool, or markup language. For example, reports rendered to HTML don't offer all of the advanced behavior you might implement in a custom-built web page with cascading style sheets and JavaScript. If you were to design a report in Microsoft Excel, you might design the workbook with formulas used to recalculate the spreadsheet rather than using literal values for summaries and totals. The general approach is that Reporting Services renders using methods to address the commonality of all these formats. There's always room for more features and advanced functionality. Some of these may be added to the product in later versions because this makes sense for mass consumption. Because of the modular architecture of Reporting Services, certain features can be added through custom programming extensions.

OfficeWriter for Reporting Services

An interesting feature that did not make the final cut for Reporting Services 2008 is the OfficeWriter tools, which enable users to design reports completely in Office Word and Excel while using Reporting Services for calculations and data retrieval in the background.

This feature will push the envelope in terms of allowing non-developers, information workers, and analysts to develop Reporting Services reports using a tool they are already familiar with. They never have to leave the Word or Excel environment and can fully leverage their capabilities while building out new reports.

We will definitely be watching for this feature set in a future release or service pack of the product.

I think it's important to define boundaries, not to be critical but to better understand the possibilities and limitations. In software, we're always trying to do something new — something that has never been done before (at least not within a particular environment). To this end, there are some fundamental questions that can help you understand just how you might approach a problem and whether a goal can be achieved within the constraints of your capabilities and resources. When I go into a new consulting opportunity, the first thing that I try to do is to take inventory of the skills necessary to get the job done and then let my client know where we stand: "I can do this . . . I've done that . . . I know someone who can help me with this . . . but I don't know much about that thing, and I don't know if I'm the right person to tackle it. I'll give it a shot, but we may need to consider bringing in another resource." After all, if I'm not honest with my clients, this could just turn out to be a bad experience for everyone, damaging my credibility and the business relationship with the client.

This is the approach I'd like to take in this section. Reporting Services can do some wonderful things, but it's important to understand the boundaries and limitations of certain features. Perhaps the same capability may be possible using another feature, or perhaps you may be barking up the wrong tree entirely. You are not likely to build every conceivable type of report, and over time you will probably create a handful of reports using techniques that you will duplicate repeatedly as you build more reports of the same style. Therefore, not all of these reports may apply to you, but they may give you some ideas about new ways to solve old problems.

It's not easy to find the limits of most products. For some reason, that information isn't listed in the product specifications and documentation — at least not in bold type. I've had very little success going to a large software vendor asking: "Hey, tell me what your product can't do." Wouldn't it be nice when shopping for a car or a house, if the salespeople would just list the comparative shortcomings of their product? I think it would make the process so much easier. For this discussion, that is where I'd like to start. The following table details some of the more recognizable limitations of the Reporting Services architecture. This is by no means intended to be a complete list, nor is it a list of bugs or issues. It's simply a guideline of design constraints to be aware of when taking reports to the next level. I've also provided some common alternatives to implement desired functionality.

Area	Limitation	Alternatives
Data presentation	In the report body or a group section, all fields must be aggregated, even if the dataset only returns one row.	Use an aggregate function even if your query returns one row or all rows for the field return the same value. Typically, you should use the `FIRST()` function for character and date data and the `SUM()` function for numeric data.
Formatting	Conditional formatting expressions can be complicated and difficult to maintain, especially when nesting Boolean logic and when same expression is repeated for multiple report items and fields.	Write a Visual Basic function in the Report Properties ⇨ Code window, and call the function as an expression for each report item — for example, `=Code.MyFunction(Fields!MyField.Value)` In certain cases, you might also be able to leverage the newly introduced Report and Group variables to hold certain values.
	Aggregate functions don't return zero for summaries on "NULL" values. Our users want to see zeros.	Use a Visual Basic function to return a zero in place of a NULL value — for example, `=IIF(IsNothing(SUM(Fields!MyField .Value)), 0, SUM(Fields!MyField.Value))` Or, pass values to a Visual Basic function to convert null, empty string, or no value to a zero or another value — for example, `=Code.NullToZero (Fields!MyField.Value)`

Area	Limitation	Alternatives
Rendering	HTML rendering doesn't support some table design formatting. For example, narrow columns used for spacing and borders are padded with extra space.	This is a characteristic of HTML rendering and is not considered a bug. If reports require more exact tolerances, users should be instructed to use printer-friendly rendering formats like PDF and TIFF.
	Using images in place of borders causes extra vertical and horizontal padding and column misalignment.	Most rendering formats were not designed to use images in place of borders. Images placed in table cells will typically be padded. Report design is a little different from web design, and some of the techniques may not work. Reports should be tested in all common rendering formats when using images borders.
	Reports don't support events like Access does. I want to count pages, rows, groups, and report item values.	Reporting Services 2008 introduces the concept of on-demand processing, and Report and Group Variables. These variables are set once and can be retrieved from within their scope. With the combination of these new variable types and some custom code, you are able to recreate those counts.
Actions	Code variables aren't tracked across multiple "postings" of an interactive report. I need to keep track of values that are modified by code as my user interacts with a report.	You can use report parameters and set the action of the interactive item to "post" to the same report, passing the changed value in the parameter collection.

Report Recipes

In the following section, I've compiled a description of reporting challenges and solutions we've encountered, developing reports for our clients. For each "solution recipe," I provide a brief list of skills, techniques, and resources needed to apply the report feature. This should give you a good idea of how prepared you may be to use the techniques based on your skill set and the level of complexity. Some of these are easy to duplicate, whereas others require more advanced skills, which may include Transact-SQL and Visual Basic programming. These are not intended to be exercises or step-by-step instructions. I have made a point to provide enough information to demonstrate the concepts and techniques. However, to implement these solutions, you will need to apply the skills you learned in the previous chapters.

Multiple Criterion Report Filtering

Report design requirements may call for complex combinations of parameter values used to filter report data. Using Transact-SQL, you should be able to handle practically any advanced filtering criteria and filter the data before it reaches the report server. However, if you need to use report filtering to provide the same kinds of filtering support against data already cached by the dataset query, the Report Designer has some significant limitations in this area. For example, let's say that my report has two parameters for filtering product records: ProductCategory and PriceRange. In this simplified example, the parameter values for both of my parameter lists are the same as the parameter label values.

The ProductCategory parameter list values are shown in the following table:

Parameter Value	Product Category Field Match
Bikes	Bikes
Components	Components
Clothing	Clothing
Accessories	Accessories
All Bike Related	All Bike Related
All	All

And the following table shows the PriceRange parameter list values:

Parameter Value	Price Range Field Match
Less than 50	<50
50 to 99	>=50 AND <100
100 to 499	>=100 AND <500
500 and higher	>=500
All	All prices

Contending with the various combinations of these and other parameter values in the confines of the Report Designer's filtering user interface would be very difficult to do. The most flexible method is to write a separate Visual Basic function to handle the matching logic for each parameter and field combination. This code is called for each row. The function returns a value to be matched with a field in the row. If the values match, the row is returned. The following custom code is added to the report on the Code tab of the Report Properties dialog:

```
Function MatchProductCategory(ParamValue As String, FieldValue As String) As String
    Select Case ParamValue
        Case "Bikes", "Components", "Clothing", "Accessories"
            Return ParamValue
        Case "All Bike Related"
            If FieldValue = "Bikes" Or FieldValue = "Components" Then
                Return FieldValue
            End If
        Case "All"
            Return FieldValue
    End Select
```

```
End Function

Function MatchPriceRange(ParamValue As String, FieldValue As String) As Decimal
    Select Case ParamValue
        Case "Less than 50"
            If FieldValue < 50 Then Return FieldValue
        Case "50 to 100"
            If FieldValue >= 50 And FieldValue < 100 Then Return FieldValue
        Case "100 to 500"
            If FieldValue >= 100 And FieldValue < 500 Then Return FieldValue
        Case "500 and Higher"
            If FieldValue >= 500 Then Return FieldValue
        Case "All"
            Return FieldValue
    End Select
End Function
```

Using the Filters tab on the Dataset Properties dialog, as shown in Figure 10-2, executes each of the functions, matching its return value to the corresponding field.

This technique takes all the complexity out of this simple dialog and puts it where it belongs — in program code. That environment gives you the control needed to contend with practically any set of business rules.

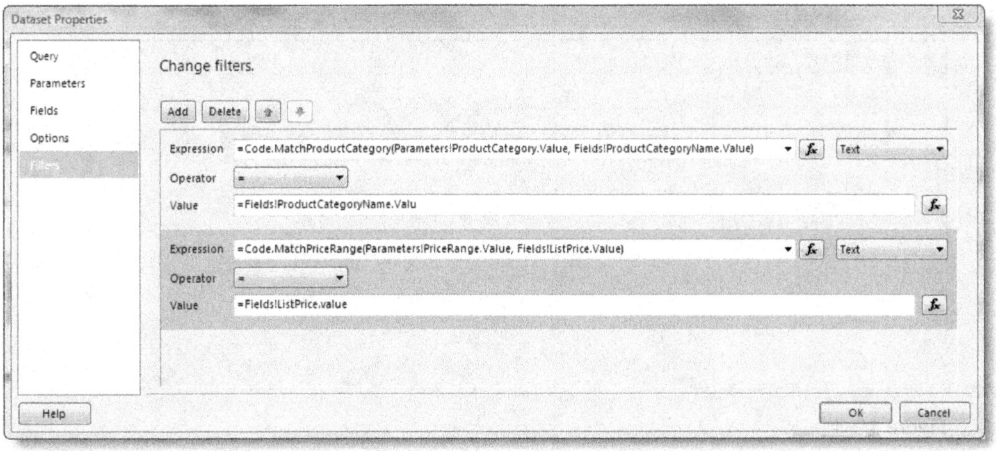

Figure 10-2

Customizing Gauges with External Images

The new gauge report items offer a high level of customization, allowing the report designer to create gauges that satisfy the needs of most business requirements. There are so many properties waiting to be customized, that most of us will ever need to tweak them all.

As discussed in previous chapters, you can customize gauges all the way down to the pointer(s) and dials. An interesting option is to set the BackFrame to a custom image, whether embedded or external. If you prefer that your gauges mimic those of the hot rod dashboard, then you are in for a treat!

You will need:

❑ A good-quality PNG or GIF image at 96 DPI of a custom frame for your gauge.

❑ A gauge item to apply the image back frame.

Begin by embedding a new image into the report definition. You simply need to right-click on the Images item in the Report Data window and select Add Image. Find the file location of your custom gauge frame image, and click OK.

Now, drag and drop a new gauge item from the toolbox onto the report body. Select the Radial Gauge type, as shown in Figure 10-3, and click OK. Click inside the body of the gauge so the actual radial gauge item is selected and not the panel or another child item of the gauge.

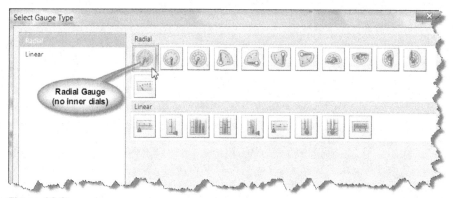

Figure 10-3

In the Properties window for the selected gauge, expand the BackFrame section, and then expand the FrameImage section. Set the Source property to Embedded and the Value property to the name of the custom image you embedded into the report in the first step, as shown in Figure 10-4.

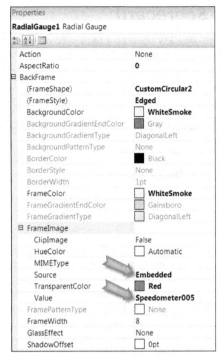

Figure 10-4

Your frame should now display with the new frame image. Figure 10-5 shows a before-and-after shot of the gauge item, in which a custom frame was applied as well as several customizations to the pointer size and color, scale radius and number placement, and so on.

As you can see, you can create very realistic and appealing gauges that are sure to catch the reader's eyes.

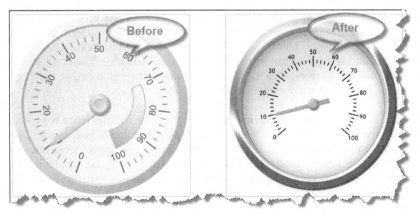

Figure 10-5

Creating a Business Scorecard

This type of reporting scenario has quickly become a mainstay in enterprise business applications. Also known as executive dashboards, business scorecards provide summary level progress and success status information for business leaders.

You will need:

- ❑ A query expression with data-based or calculated target, budget, variance, and actual values.
- ❑ A multigroup table with drill-down features.
- ❑ Small images for use as progress indicators.
- ❑ An expression used to translate KPI and target values to indicator images.

Executive Dashboards

To understand and appreciate the value of this type of reporting interface, you need to walk in the shoes of corporate business leaders. A typical corporate officer deals with a lot of people and a variety of information in a day and often needs to make immediate decisions based on this information. When moving from meeting to meeting, transaction-level details are too granular for most decisions. Business leaders need to know how the business is performing overall and whether there are areas of concern or notable success. I've sat in a lot of meetings with a general manager or director sitting on one side of the table and subject experts on another. The officer begins by saying, "So, how are we doing?" The subject expert gives a lengthy presentation, stepping through PowerPoint slides, charts, graphs, and diagrams that depict trends and variances based on mountains of data. After the presentation, the officer concludes with the question, "So, how are we doing?" Scorecards and dashboards answer this all-important question using succinct summary values and simple graphical, symbolic progress indicators.

Although simplification is a key concept, scorecards go beyond just keeping reports simple. Trends and success indicators should be clear and easy to understand but should provide an avenue to discover more detail and to view related trends and summaries. These objectives are easily achieved using drill-down and drill-through report features.

Targets and KPIs

These are the fundamental concepts behind business scorecards. For any given measurement, a target is simply an objective value. Targets are often data-driven values such as a Budget, Quota, Baseline, or Goal. A KPI, or Key Performance Indicator, is a set of thresholds used to measure actual values with the target. KPIs may define banding indicators to signify a range of variances like poor, acceptable, and exceptional performance. KPI thresholds may be a single point, corresponding to the target, percentage, or fixed increment offsets with any number of indicator bands.

When considering longer-term trends, you may want to recognize the difference between a positive trend using a KPI and whether or not a value represents a successful outcome, as a KSI (key success indicator). For example, sales for a particular product may have been unprofitable since it went on the market. If sales are rising, a KPI would show positive sales growth, whereas a KSI would indicate that the company is still in the red. We might simply define two targets, one to measure short-term progress and the other to measure overall profitability.

Indicators

Indicators are graphical icons, representing the state of an actual value with respect to a KPI band. On the scorecard, corresponding indicator icons might be red, yellow, and green symbols. Indicators are typically common symbolic metaphors such as traffic lights, colored shapes, progress bars, gauges, and directional arrows. Figure 10-6 shows some common indicator graphics embedded in a sample report.

Figure 10-6

Calculating Variance

Variance is the difference between an actual and a target value. If time variances will be used extensively, the queries used to make these calculations can be very intensive. Aggregating and calculating sales totals, for example, for a given month over last month, quarter, or year can require some heavy-duty query processing (even with a modest number of detail rows). Ideally, this type of data should be stored in a data mart or data warehouse with precalculated variance values stored in the database. The AdventureWorksDW database contains some preaggregated summary values, but as you can see, even for this simple report with only year-over-year variances, the query is fairly complex.

```
SELECT
    ThisYearSales.SalesTerritoryRegion
  , ThisYearSales.SalesTerritoryKey
  , ThisYearSales.CalendarYear
  , ThisYearSales.LastName
  , ThisYearSales.FirstName
  , ThisYearSales.EmployeeName
  , SUM(ThisYearSales.ExtendedAmount) AS ExtendedAmountSum
  , SUM(ThisYearSales.SalesAmountQuota) AS SalesAmountQuotaSum
  , SUM(LastYearSales.ExtendedAmountSum) AS ExtendedAmountSumLastYear
FROM (
    SELECT
        DimSalesTerritory.SalesTerritoryRegion
      , DimSalesTerritory.SalesTerritoryKey
      , DimDate.CalendarYear
      , DimEmployee.LastName
      , DimEmployee.FirstName
      , DimEmployee.EmployeeKey
      , DimEmployee.FirstName + ' ' + DimEmployee.LastName AS EmployeeName
      , FactResellerSales.ExtendedAmount
      , FactSalesQuota.SalesAmountQuota
    FROM DimEmployee
        INNER JOIN FactSalesQuota
            ON DimEmployee.EmployeeKey = FactSalesQuota.EmployeeKey
        INNER JOIN DimDate
            ON FactSalesQuota.DateKey = DimDate.DateKey
        INNER JOIN FactResellerSales
            ON DimEmployee.EmployeeKey = FactResellerSales.EmployeeKey
```

(continued)

(continued)

```
                    AND DimDate.DateKey = FactResellerSales.OrderDateKey
                INNER JOIN DimSalesTerritory
                    ON DimSalesTerritory.SalesTerritoryKey =
                                    FactResellerSales.SalesTerritoryKey
            ) AS ThisYearSales
    INNER JOIN
        ( SELECT
                FactResellerSales.EmployeeKey
              , DimDate.CalendarYear
              , DimSalesTerritory.SalesTerritoryKey
              , DimSalesTerritory.SalesTerritoryRegion
              , FactResellerSales.ExtendedAmount AS ExtendedAmountSum
            FROM FactResellerSales
                INNER JOIN DimDate
                ON FactResellerSales.OrderDateKey = DimDate.DateKey
                INNER JOIN DimSalesTerritory
                ON DimSalesTerritory.SalesTerritoryKey =
                                    FactResellerSales.SalesTerritoryKey
            ) AS LastYearSales
        ON LastYearSales.CalendarYear = ThisYearSales.CalendarYear - 1
        AND ThisYearSales.EmployeeKey = LastYearSales.EmployeeKey
        AND ThisYearSales.SalesTerritoryKey = LastYearSales.SalesTerritoryKey
    GROUP BY
      ThisYearSales.SalesTerritoryRegion
      , ThisYearSales.SalesTerritoryKey
      , ThisYearSales.CalendarYear
      , ThisYearSales.LastName
      , ThisYearSales.FirstName
      , ThisYearSales.EmployeeName
    ORDER BY
      ThisYearSales.SalesTerritoryRegion
      , ThisYearSales.CalendarYear
      , ThisYearSales.LastName
      , ThisYearSales.FirstName
```

When running complex queries like this one, you may need to increase the default connection time-out setting on the data source. The default setting is 15 seconds, which may not be sufficient for this query on all hardware. In a production application with data volumes greater than the sample database, I would recommend testing query performance and possibly using an Analysis Services database with cubes and precalculated aggregates. To populate the data warehouse, you will use queries similar to this one and store the results for later retrieval.

Figure 10-7 shows a simple tablix with two groups, in the SalesTerritoryRegion and CalendarYear fields. This tablix is much like several previous examples. The detail row is hidden by default, allowing for drill-down using the SalesTerritoryRegion textbox. Two more images will serve as indicators. These are based on expressions used to change the indicator image.

Territory Region	Employee	Quota	Total Sales	Year Variance	
	Year				
[SalesTerritoryRegion]		[Sum(SalesAmountQuotaSum)]	[Sum(ExtendedAmountSum)]	«Expr»	
	[CalendarYear] [EmployeeName]	[SalesAmountQuotaSum]	[ExtendedAmountSum]	«Expr»	

Figure 10-7

You will notice that the images have a white background even though background colors are used to separate the rows. This is done only to simplify this example. The images are simply added to the cells in the table header. If you want to use transparent images over a colored or shaded background, you will need to add rectangles to the header cells and then place images in the rectangles. This way, you can set the BackgroundColor property for each rectangle and take advantage of the image transparency.

Looking at the columns with text headers, the first column contains the SalesTerritoryRegion field in the first group header and the CalendarYear field in the detail row.

The second column contains the EmployeeName in the detail row.

The third text column is for the SalesAmountQuotaSum field. The header uses the SUM() function to aggregate the details for the sales territory.

The fourth text column contains total sales values, using the ExtendedAmountSum field.

The last column of text boxes, labeled *Year Variance*, calculates the total sales amount annual variance. In the header row, the expression uses the SUM() function. In the detail row, the SUM() function is omitted. Values in this column are formatted as percentages.

```
=1-(Sum(Fields!ExtendedAmountSumLastYear.Value) /
Sum(Fields!ExtendedAmountSum.Value))
```

The expression for the sales first set of indicators (the images column after total sales column) calls a Visual Basic function to apply the KPI threshold banding. Figure 10-8 shows this custom code.

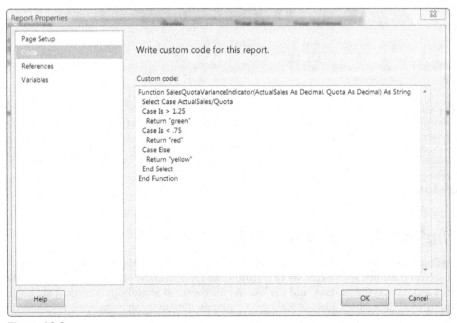

Figure 10-8

Because the image names for the green, yellow, and red indicators contain their respective names, you just need to build the string with these values and return it in the Value property of the image item using the following expression:

```
="indicator_" & Code.SalesQuotaVarianceIndicator(Sum(Fields!ExtendedAmountSum.Value)
   , Sum(Fields!SalesAmountQuotaSum.Value)) & "_16"
```

For variety, I've resolved the second indicator column images using only an in-line expression rather than using a custom function. This is the expression for the header row. The detail row expression is the same but without the SUM() function. As a rule, once I've decided to use custom code, I'll typically continue to use custom functions for all but the simplest expressions so that I can keep business logic in one place.

```
=IIF(Sum(Fields!ExtendedAmountSum.Value) / Sum(Fields!ExtendedAmountSumLastYear
   .Value) < .8, "indicator_yellow_16", nothing)
```

This expression returns the yellow warning icon image when this year's sales amount is less than 80 percent of last year's. Figure 10-9 shows the rendered report with some region sections drilled open.

Territory Region	Employee	Quota	Total Sales	Year Variance
	Year			
⊟ Australia		$34,477,742,000.00	$90,832,802.68 ◇	11.67 %
	2004 Syed Abbas	$5,964,000.00	$838,371.83 ◇	27.61 %
	2004 Lynn Tsoflias	$34,471,778,000.00	$89,994,430.84 ◇	11.52 %
⊞ Canada		$4,553,054,438,000.00	$5,212,015,252.09 ◇	3.13 %
⊞ Central		$667,643,292,000.00	$733,226,632.24 ◇	-24.60 %
⊟ France		$358,964,400,000.00	$296,861,407.18 ◇	-94.95 % △
	2003 Ranjit Varkey Chudukatil	$155,848,050,000.00	$127,732,117.15 ◇	-100.80 % △
	2004 Ranjit Varkey Chudukatil	$203,116,350,000.00	$169,129,290.02 ◇	-90.52 % △
⊟ Germany		$108,753,048,000.00	$256,651,057.98 ◇	11.91 %
	2004 Amy Alberts	$10,440,000.00	$29,159.46 ◇	-383.30 % △
	2004 Rachel Valdez	$108,742,608,000.00	$256,621,898.52 ◇	11.95 %
⊞ Northeast		$952,565,932,000.00	$1,089,906,579.19 ◇	-12.11 %
⊞ Northwest		$315,563,882,000.00	$1,432,052,150.51 ◇	6.20 %
⊞ Southeast		$1,369,038,707,000.00	$1,910,103,414.51 ◇	-54.45 % △
⊞ Southwest		$2,434,130,476,000.00	$3,886,400,104.68 ◇	5.12 %
⊞ United Kingdom		$472,244,884,000.00	$517,339,091.80 ◇	-53.58 % △

Figure 10-9

Reporting on SharePoint 3.0 List Data

The SharePoint platform is Microsoft's technology for enterprise portal and content management. It is a very powerful platform with a rich set of features and tools to allow storage and categorization of documents and data, collaboration, and the like. At the center of SharePoint's content are lists, which are synonymous with data tables. Lists contain data and metadata that can be queried via SharePoint's Web Service layer.

Reporting Services ships with an XML data provider that you can use to connect to an XML Web Service and retrieve data to be consumed by a report. In this section, you will be leveraging this data provider to connect to SharePoint's Web Service endpoint and retrieve list data.

You will need:

❑   An existing, running SharePoint 3.0 instance, with at least one site configured.

❑   Access to the SharePoint Web Service URL.

First, add a new report, or open an existing report in your report project. Then add a new data source (embedded or shared). In the data source's General Properties dialog, choose the XML type for a data connection from the dropdown list.

Next, you need to provide the URL to the SharePoint Web Service that retrieves List data. The URL will be in the format shown in Figure 10-10.

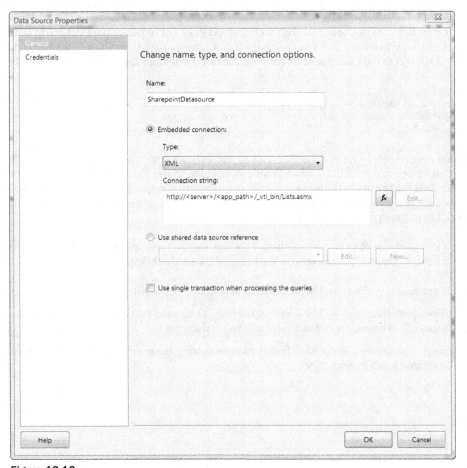

Figure 10-10

The <app_path> is optional and may depend on how your SharePoint site is configured in the web server. For example, if you have a portal configured at the URL http://MyPortal.com, your URL to the web service should be http://MyPortal.com/_vti_bin/Lists.asmx.

Now switch to the Data Source Properties dialog's Credentials page, and choose Windows Authentication (Integrated Security), or, if your SharePoint site is configured for anonymous authentication, choose No Credentials. Those are the two credential options that you will be able to leverage while using SharePoint, and which are supported by the Report Designer.

Now you are ready to create your report dataset that will consume the XML data. Add a new dataset to the report, give it a name, and choose the SharePoint data source created in the previous steps. The SharePoint Lists Web Service endpoint provides several web methods that you can invoke for working with lists, content types, list items, and files. For the purpose of this report, you are concerned only with two of these following web methods:

❏ GetListCollection — Gets the names and GUIDs for all lists in the SharePoint site.

❏ GetListItems — Gets information about items in a list specified by the query parameters

Let's start with GetListCollection. This web method does not require a parameter and is, therefore, a quick and easy way to ensure that you can connect and retrieve data from SharePoint. Enter the following XML text in the Query textbox for your dataset (remember that XML is case-sensitive):

```
<Query>
    <Method Namespace="http://schemas.microsoft.com/sharepoint/soap"
Name="GetListCollection" />
</Query>
```

You should now be able to go into the Query Designer, execute your query, and return data. This will confirm that you have connected to SharePoint successfully. Under the covers, the SharePoint web site is serving up XML fragments in the form of CAML (Collaborative Application Markup Language — an XML-based language used by Windows SharePoint Services to describe/define views and fields in a list). Click OK to finish creating your dataset.

Now, let's look at the GetListItems method. This web method requires a set of parameters to be passed in. Here is a list of required parameters (in the order of the method signature):

❏ listName (string) — The display name or GUID of the list, surrounded by curly braces ({})

❏ viewName (string) — The GUID of the view to be used for the list, surrounded by curly braces ({}). If blank, the default view will be used for the list.

❏ query (XMLNode) — An XML fragment representing the query that determines the records to be returned and in what order

❑ viewFields (XMLNode) — An XML fragment representing the fields that should be determined and in what order

❑ rowLimit (string) — Represents the number of items to be returned by the result set

❑ queryOptions (XMLNode) — An XML fragment representing the different options that can be assigned for the SharePoint Query object

❑ webID (string) — An optional string representing the GUID of the parent web site for the list. We will not be using this parameter for our example

A caveat of reporting on SharePoint lists is that not every list has the same schema definition. This means that you cannot dynamically change the list name parameter value in the report to any list you may have in SharePoint. Reporting Services expects a fixed set of columns in the dataset so that it can map out the fields for the report.

With that in mind, you'll create a new report that queries for a particular list and displays its data. Start by adding a new report to your project. Then, add a new dataset to the report, similar to the one in the previous steps, and give it a name. Enter the following XML fragment in the Query textbox of your dataset (make sure that there is no trailing slash after the web method name in the URL of the SoapAction element):

```
<Query>
    <Method Namespace="http://schemas.microsoft.com/sharepoint/soap/"
Name="GetListItems">
        <Parameters>
            <Parameter Name="listName">
                <DefaultValue>My List Name</DefaultValue>
            </Parameter>
            <Parameter Name="viewName">
                <DefaultValue></DefaultValue>
            </Parameter>
            <Parameter Name="rowLimit">
                <DefaultValue></DefaultValue>
            </Parameter>
        </Parameters>
    </Method>
<SoapAction>http://schemas.microsoft.com/sharepoint/soap/GetListItems</SoapAction>
</Query>
```

Notice that you must specify the DefaultValue element for the listName parameter so that the Report Designer can statically define the fields for the dataset. You also include two other parameter names, viewName and rowLimit, but leave their inner values empty in XML so that Reporting Services can pass report parameters to them.

If you don't specify the Parameters XML Node with a default value for the `listName`, *you may experience SOAP exceptions while running the query. It is best to always explicitly include it instead of only relying on the XML data provider in Reporting Services to "translate" data-set parameters into the method's parameters.*

So, let's set up the parameters for the dataset to match those parameters provided in XML. In the Parameters section of the Dataset Properties dialog, add new parameters, as shown in Figure 10-11.

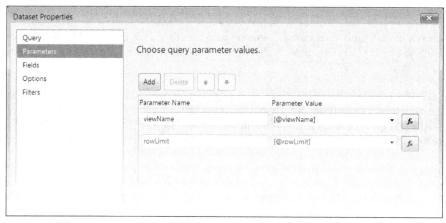

Figure 10-11

When you create the data-set parameters and don't specify parameter values, the Report Designer automatically creates report parameters that match the name of the data-set parameter and then assigns the report parameter values to the data-set parameters. This saves you a few steps and mouse clicks. One last thing before you click OK to finish creating the dataset is to click the Refresh Fields button. This will make the Designer run the query and grab metadata about the result set in order to build the fields that you can use in the report.

Now you are ready to start building your table with report data. Just drag and drop a new table on the report body and then drag a few of the fields from the dataset onto the table details row. When you are done, you should be able to preview the report and get back SharePoint list data, as shown in Figure 10-12.

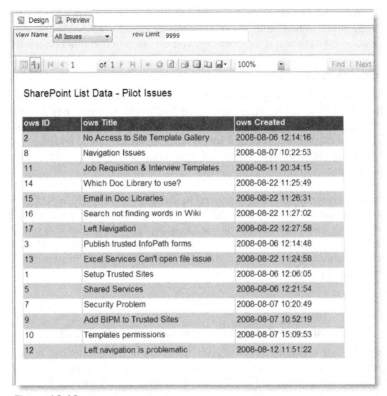

SharePoint List Data - Pilot Issues

ows ID	ows Title	ows Created
2	No Access to Site Template Gallery	2008-08-06 12:14:16
8	Navigation Issues	2008-08-07 10:22:53
11	Job Requisition & Interview Templates	2008-08-11 20:34:15
14	Which Doc Library to use?	2008-08-22 11:25:49
15	Email in Doc Libraries	2008-08-22 11:26:31
16	Search not finding words in Wiki	2008-08-22 11:27:02
17	Left Navigation	2008-08-22 12:27:58
3	Publish trusted InfoPath forms	2008-08-06 12:14:48
13	Excel Services Can't open file issue	2008-08-22 11:24:58
1	Setup Trusted Sites	2008-08-06 12:06:05
5	Shared Services	2008-08-06 12:21:54
7	Security Problem	2008-08-07 10:20:49
9	Add BIPM to Trusted Sites	2008-08-07 10:52:19
10	Templates permissions	2008-08-07 15:09:53
12	Left navigation is problematic	2008-08-12 11:51:22

Figure 10-12

Report Localization

At some point during your endeavors as a report designer/developer, you will run into the issue of
report localization. Localization simply means that you have taken care of using lookup resources for each
supported locale and culture in order to hold any static strings that will be displayed on the report — it
allows you to have language and culture-aware reports. With localization, your reports should strive to
be culture-neutral and language-neutral so that you can truly achieve a good level of globalization.

Reporting Services provides several mechanisms that take care of certain aspects of localization. The
RDL schema provides a Report Language property that can be used to set the appropriate culture and
locale information that will be used to format dates, numbers, and currency. It also provides support for
right-to-left languages such as Hebrew. The ReportViewer control and most of the Report Manager UI
provide localized strings, which means that UI elements surrounding your report RDL will already be
translated and formatted according to the user's current culture settings (defined by browser and OS).
Out of the box, Reporting Services, configured in native mode, supports 10 languages. In SharePoint
Integration Mode, you get an additional 12 (see http://msdn.microsoft.com/library/ms156493
.aspx for more details).

However, you are still required to take a few additional steps in order to provide a fully localized RDL — that is, one that knows how to handle string lookups for the current culture. With the use of .NET Globalization features and a custom code assembly, you can accomplish this very easily.

Multicultural Considerations

There are some considerations to keep in mind when following this approach. You will be using a single report RDL to display text in different languages. For tabular reports, column headers that contain static localized text will need to accommodate the longest string values among the language you plan to support; otherwise, you might encounter odd text wrapping, which can be an issue for glyph- or character-based languages such as Japanese or Chinese, where the different combination of characters implies different meanings.

If your report displays currency amounts, you need to identify whether you will be providing converted currency values. If your data stores only U.S. dollar amounts, you may have to specify in the report the currency that is being used, or you may choose to use an external service that provides currency conversion calculations. In either case, you will want to be extremely careful about how you present this type of information, and also take into consideration any latency incurred from making expensive invocations to external services.

Parameter Prompt Expressions and the RDCE

In early previews of Reporting Services 2008, there was a new feature that allowed the ability to apply expressions to Report parameter prompt text. While this would go hand-in-hand with the ability to fully localize a report and provide seamless culturally neutral reports, the feature was removed in the final release version.

As in previous versions of Reporting Services, the parameter prompt text still can only hold static text, which means that you cannot use the standard parameter toolbar to collect user input for multilanguage reports without forcing all end-users to understand the same language.

To address this shortcoming, developers might be forced to create multiple copies of the same report, each for a different language, which unfortunately defeats the purpose of dynamic string lookups for localization.

A new feature in Reporting Services 2008 named the *Report Definition Customization Extensions* (RDCE) provides hooks into the preprocessing of reports so that the developer can customize the report definition. Using the RDCE, the developer can ultimately address the parameter prompt issue by extending Reporting Services.

This is particularly interesting for report localization because it allows the custom extension to investigate values in parameters and user and locale information, and then provide a customized report definition on the fly that gets executed for that report request. More information is available at the following URL: http://msdn.microsoft.com/library/cc281022.aspx.

Creating the External Resource Lookup with .NET

This section shows how you can leverage .NET Globalization and Resource files to store your static string values for multiple languages, and then how to retrieve those values from within the report body. The .NET project will provide a set of "satellite" assemblies that will contain the culture-specific resources.

You will need:

❏ A .NET class project with different resource files for each supported language, defining the static text you want the report to look up.

❏ A static method that takes a key and returns a value from the current culture's resource file.

❏ An RDL file that defines an external assembly reference.

❏ Textbox expressions within the report body that call the external assembly.

The following example does not get into details of how to write code or create classes using .NET. If you need to implement this solution, you should have a certain level of experience with writing custom code.

In Visual Studio, create a new class library project, in your language of choice, and give it a name. Within your class file, add the following lines of code:

```
using System;
using System.Globalization;
using System.Resources;
using System.Reflection;

namespace Wrox.Localization
{
    public class Localizer
    {
        private ResourceManager rm;
        public string ResourceName { get; set; }

        public Localizer()
        {
            Initialize();
        }

        public Localizer(string resourceName)
        {
            this.ResourceName = resourceName;
            Initialize();
        }

        void Initialize()
        {
            string currentNs = this.GetType().Namespace;
            rm = new ResourceManager(currentNs + "." + this.ResourceName
                , Assembly.GetExecutingAssembly());
```

(continued)

(continued)

```
        }

        public string GetLocalText(string key)
        {
            return rm.GetString(key);
        }

        public string GetLocalText(string key, string culture)
        {
            return rm.GetString(key, new CultureInfo(culture));
        }
    }
}
```

This defines your class with a private member, the `ResourceManager` object that will get values out of the resource files. It also defines a public method, `GetLocalText()`, with two overloads: one that takes a key and another that takes both a key and a culture name. This is important to note, because by allowing a resource name to be set as a class property, you can reuse this class for other reports and won't need to hardcode report-specific details.

Next, you need to add a new resource file to the project for each culture that you need to support. The main resource filename does not include a culture. However, satellite resource filenames for different cultures need to have the culture name appended after the resource name, but before the file extension. The naming syntax is `<Resource Name>.<Culture Name>.resx`.

For example, if the default culture file is `MyResource.resx`, the Chinese (Taiwan) equivalent would be `MyResources.zh-TW.resx`. Figures 10-13 and 10-14 show the contents of the sample resource files for both the default culture (en-US) and the French (fr-FR) culture, respectively. To include new cultures later on, just create new resource files (with Visual Studio or any text editor), and then use the `RESGEN.exe` command-line tool, if not using Visual Studio, or build from the IDE, to compile into satellite assemblies that you can just drop into the report server's BIN folder.

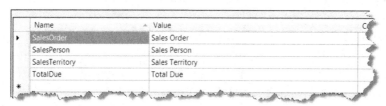

Name	Value	C
SalesOrder	Sales Order	
SalesPerson	Sales Person	
SalesTerritory	Sales Territory	
TotalDue	Total Due	

Figure 10-13

Name	Value	C
SalesOrder	Ordre de Ventes	
SalesPerson	Vendeur	
SalesTerritory	Territoire de Ventes	
TotalDue	Total	

Figure 10-14

Make sure that each of the resource files in the project has the Build Action property set to Embedded Resource. This tells the compiler to build each resource file in its own satellite assembly and place the file in its respective culture folder under the project's BIN folder.

The next step is to deploy the main assembly and the satellite assemblies to Visual Studio's PrivateAssemblies folder, as well as to the report server's BIN folder. The former allows you to execute the report in the preview window of the Report Designer, and the latter is the actual server where the report will be deployed once it has been developed. Figure 10-15 shows all the files and folders that need to be copied over.

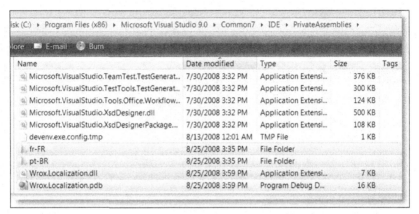

Figure 10-15

You will need to restart Visual Studio in order for the new assemblies to be loaded. Next, open your report in the Designer, and add a reference to the assembly from the Report Properties window, as shown in Figure 10-16.

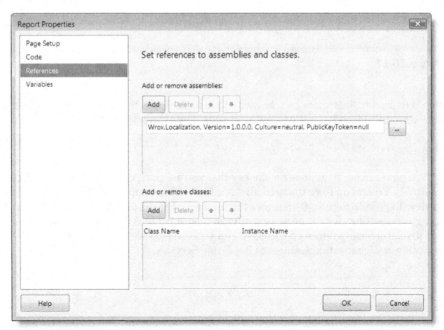

Figure 10-16

Because you used an overloaded constructor to your `Localizer()` class, you cannot use the Class Name/Instance Name options in the References window to create an object instance of your custom class. This would invoke the default constructor. In order to create the object instance, you must override the `OnInit` event of the Report's Code object and place your object instantiation within that event. This technique is described in the SQL Server Books Online.

Also, you must create a public variable in the report scope to which you can assign the newly instantiated `Localizer()` object. Figure 10-17 shows the code snippet required to do just that.

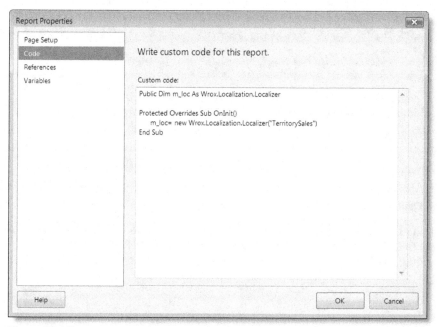

Figure 10-17

The last step is to modify the expression for each of the textboxes in the report that contain static text with a call to your custom code for the localized strings. The expression syntax should look as follows:

```
=Code.m_loc.GetLocalText("SalesTerritory")
```

The string `"SalesTerritory"` represents the key that you are retrieving from the current culture's resource assembly. When you have updated all static text with lookup expressions, you can deploy your report and view the result. Figure 10-18 shows the final result of the report running in Internet Explorer with the Languages settings for the browser configured with fr-FR as the primary culture. You can see that the text strings are being retrieved correctly, and you can also see the rest of the Report Manager UI utilizing the built-in Globalization features of Reporting Services.

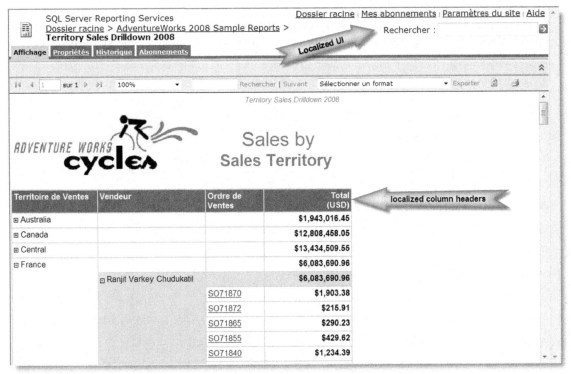

Figure 10-18

Dynamic Grouping

I get called in to consulting client sites often to rebuild a set of existing Crystal or Access reports in Reporting Services. They will typically have several reports for each data entity or table that are grouped, sorted, and filtered a little differently. This solution allows you to consolidate data groups for the same table into one report. The following example consolidates the reports "Product Sales by Territory," "Product Sales by Category," and "Product Sales by Subcategory" into one report with user-selectable field grouping.

You will need:

❑   A tablix presenting a tabular set of grouped values.

❑   A report parameter with a list of fields in the dataset for sorting.

❑   A group expression using the report parameter to resolve the grouping field name.

❑   Heading and summary expressions referring to the dynamic group expression.

377

This works best with simple tabular reports that have one group. The dynamic grouping is based on a single parameter selection that returns the name of a field from the report's main dataset. Figures 10-19 and 10-20 show the settings for the GroupBy parameter. Note that the Value column for the parameter list contains the actual Field names for selected fields in the dataset.

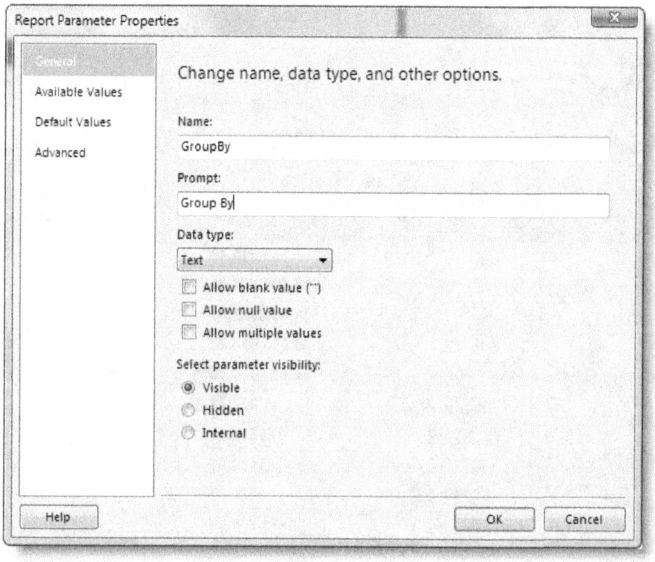

Figure 10-19

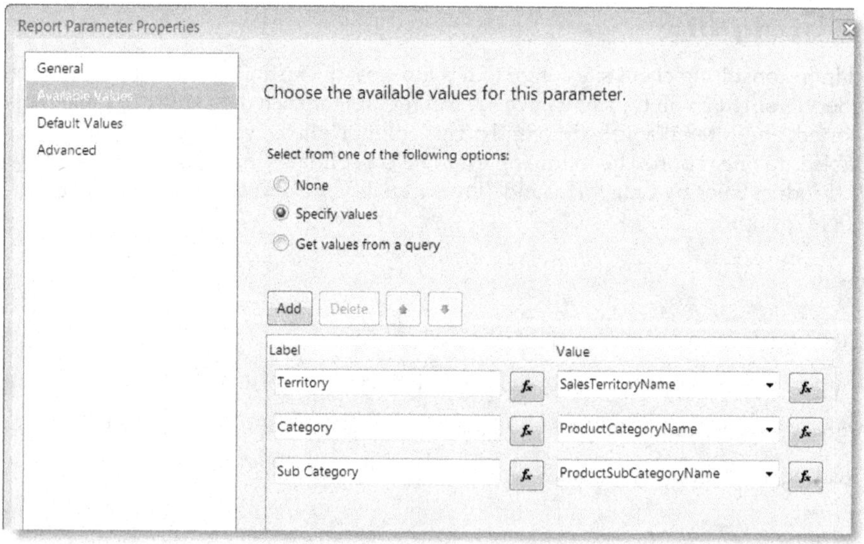

Figure 10-20

A group is defined in the table based on an expression that uses this parameter to resolve the field value. In the report header, you want to show the Field name, and in the group header, you want to show the actual field value. To return the friendly Field name that was displayed in the parameter dropdown list, refer to the Label property of the parameter. The field value is displayed using the compound expression: =Fields(Parameters!GroupBy.Value).Value. The inner reference (Parameters!GroupBy.Value) is resolved first to return the Field name, which is passed to the outer expression (Fields(<field name>).Value) to resolve the field value from the Field name.

Figure 10-21 shows the properties for the Tablix group. The same expression is used to define the group. On the Sorting tab of the Grouping and Sorting Properties dialog, shown in Figure 10-22, the sorting expression is set to match the group expression.

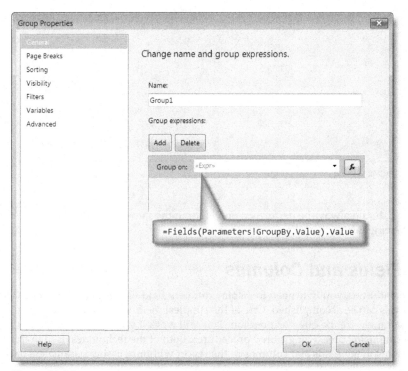

Figure 10-21

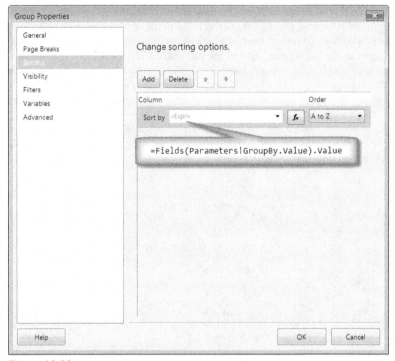

Figure 10-22

Since grouping should always be performed on values in the same sort order, the same expression is used on the Sorting tab.

Dynamic Fields and Columns

Under some conditions, you may need to display different field values in table columns. There are several ways this can be accomplished. One of the simplest methods to change column sources and values is to parameterize the query expression. This will work if you are using ad hoc SQL expressions but not if you are using preexisting stored procedures. Both of the techniques used in this example are more efficient, resolving fields and columns in the report without passing parameters back to the database server.

You will need:

❑   A data-set query, including any source fields you need to consolidate into a dynamic column.

❑   A parameter with a list of values used for field selection.

❑   An expression defined on a calculated field, referencing the parameter list values.

The first step is to include all the source fields in the data-set query. You want to define a calculated field called *Price* that will dynamically be mapped to either of two existing data fields. The Product table contains two price fields, StandardCost and ListPrice, which represent the wholesale and retail product prices.

A report parameter named `PriceSource` is configured with the list values `Wholesale` and `Retail`. These values are used to switch the custom field mapping between these two data fields. Figure 10-23 shows the custom field expression for the custom Price field in the Dataset Properties dialog's Fields page.

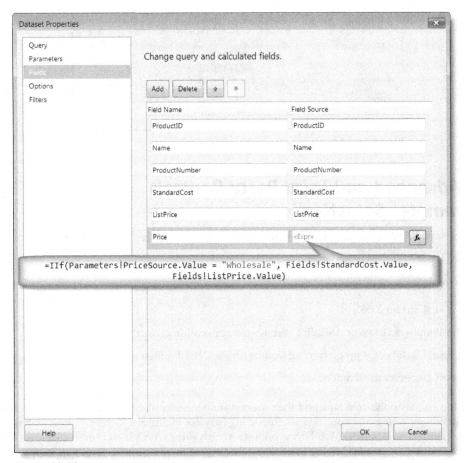

Figure 10-23

Instead of using the `StandardCost` and `ListPrice` fields in the report body, you are using the calculated field `Price`, which reflects the parameter value.

Dynamically Hiding and Showing a Row or Column

This technique is very simple. Using a parameter, a row or column may be dynamically shown or hidden by setting the Hidden property. Instead of the custom field used in the previous example, both of the data fields could have been included in the report. The table columns then could be shown and hidden based on the parameter selection.

This example will hide or show a column based on a parameter selection. I've added a report parameter of type Boolean, named ShowProductNumber. Figure 10-24 shows the expression used to manipulate the Hidden property for the selected column. The expression simply uses Boolean logic to set the column's visibility to a hidden state when the expression evaluates to true.

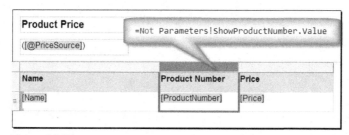

Figure 10-24

Using Advanced and Third-Party Controls for Parameter Selection

From a custom Windows or web application, you can replace the parameter selection interface with your own controls and interface.

You will need:

❑   Visual Studio 2008.

❑   A Windows Forms or ASP.NET Web Forms application project.

❑   Visual Basic or C# programming skills with the .NET Framework.

❑   Any parameterized report.

Depending on the application type and the programming tools available, there are a few different ways to incorporate reporting into applications. Reporting Services includes a ReportViewer control for .NET Windows Forms and ASP.NET Web Forms projects, which ships with Visual Studio 2008. You can also use a Frame or an IFrame HTML tag to encapsulate a report in an ASP.NET project or in practically any other type of web application, and then use the URL Access features of Reporting Services to generate reports.

It is important to point out that the ReportViewer control that ships with Visual Studio 2008 RTM and SP1 is still based on the Reporting Services 2005 processing and rendering engine. Thus, it can only consume 2005-based RDL reports in local mode. However, the ReportViewer control can still connect to a Reporting Services 2008 server in server mode and thereby even render 2008-based RDLs that use features such as RichText. The only limitation of the VS 2008 controls in server mode is that the Windows Forms incarnation of the control specifically cannot visualize all RichText capabilities, but you still get all 2008 features on exporting to formats like Excel, PDF, and the like.

The product team at Microsoft is currently working on updating the ReportViewer *controls to be released likely in early 2009, based on the completely new Reporting Services 2008 processing and rendering engine, and therefore will be able to consume 2008-based RDLs in* local *mode. In addition, the updated version will behave correctly when placed into an ASP.NET AJAX* UpdatePanel. *(Thanks to Robert Bruckner at Microsoft for the insight into the future of the* ReportViewer *control.)*

Using the ReportViewer control, the standard parameter bar can be hidden, and then standard or third-party UI controls may be used to prompt the user for parameter values. There are many advanced controls available for Windows and web application development. Figure 10-25 shows a Windows Forms application that uses controls from the Infragistics NetAdvantage suite. Two MonthView controls are used for the date range selection. A pair of UltraTree controls allows countries to be selected by dragging and dropping flag icons from one list to another.

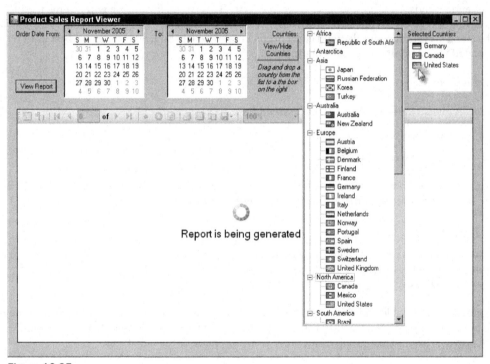

Figure 10-25

The nice thing about using ready-made, custom controls is that you can get a lot of bang for the buck and save yourself programming time. There are several good third-party control offerings from different companies. The example above showcases the Infragistics NetAdvantage suite of UI controls. It's one of the most evolved and comprehensive, containing several dozen very capable and attractive controls that require little programming effort to implement impressive functionality.

The `ReportViewer` control rounds out the Reporting Services features by allowing reports to be tightly integrated into business applications with ease and tremendous flexibility. I encourage you to be creative and use your imagination to develop interesting report wrappers and parameter selection interfaces. Use advanced controls like these to enhance the user's experience and take reporting beyond out-of-the-box features.

Creating Sparklines

Edward Tufte, one of the most recognized experts on the subject of data visualization, presents the idea of *sparklines*. As Tufte describes it in his book *Beautiful Evidence*, sparklines are "small, high-resolution graphics embedded in a context of words, numbers, and images." These are simple, word-sized graphics that are an alternative to large, busy charts used to communicate a simple trend or series of measurements. In order to be meaningful, sometimes charts need to have annotated gridlines, point labels, and legends. However, some charts can effectively serve their purpose without the use of supporting text labels. To illustrate observations like "sales are improving," "a product is profitable," or that a trend is cyclical, a simple trend chart needs little or no labeling. Sparklines are best used when embedded in text or other report formats.

You will need:

❏   A query expression used to return trend data.

❏   A small, simplified chart item.

❏   A table item to display master rows.

Column and line charts are best suited for this type of presentation. The example uses a line chart to show sales trends data from the AdventureWorksDW2008 database.

Sales Trends

This example shows product category sales on each row and sales by year in an associated line chart, plotting sales totals by month. This report's dataset is based on a query that returns aggregated reseller and Internet sales by year and month, and then by product category.

In Figure 10-26, the table and chart are added and set up in separate areas of the report body. They're both bound to the same dataset. After the table is configured, the dataset is added to the table. As in previous examples, a group header row is used in place of the detail row.

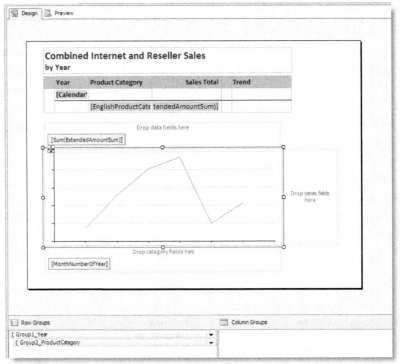

Figure 10-26

The chart is configured with no gridlines or labels at all. Its purpose is to show relative sales trends, not specific values. In a production reporting solution, I might create a separate chart report, similar to the sparkline chart but with more detail. Figure 10-27 shows this report in Design view.

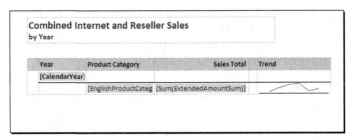

Figure 10-27

Finally, Figure 10-28 shows the finished report. The trend line shows sales totals over the course of the year. Whether data points represented days, weeks, or months, the effect would be the same.

Combined Internet and Reseller Sales
by Year

Year	Product Category	Sales Total	Trend
2001			
	Accessories	$20,239.66	
	Bikes	$10,665,953.45	
	Clothing	$34,467.29	
	Components	$615,474.98	
2002			
	Accessories	$93,796.84	
	Bikes	$26,664,534.04	
	Clothing	$489,820.19	
	Components	$3,611,041.24	
2003			
	Accessories	$594,999.24	
	Bikes	$35,186,943.67	
	Clothing	$1,022,601.53	
	Components	$5,486,723.33	
2004			
	Accessories	$569,710.18	
	Bikes	$22,597,735.69	
	Clothing	$591,688.92	
	Components	$2,091,051.85	

Figure 10-28

Summary

With Reporting Services, you can create just about any type of report design that is required. Advanced solutions often take a bit of creative thought, and you may need to step outside the standard feature set to get there. Given the flexible architecture of this product, many compelling results can be achieved. In summary, this chapter covered the following topics:

❑ We began with a set of simple guidelines for gathering report requirements and managing your user and sponsor's expectations by creating a detailed specification for each report.

❑ The key success factors for reporting projects include a clear understanding of the entire solution scope and where reports fit into the picture. Requirements should be specified before you begin, and requirement changes must be documented and approved.

❑ When you understand the limitations and capabilities of the Reporting Services platform, you will find interesting ways to achieve your reporting goals. You saw several examples of how requirements can be addressed by applying some of the techniques discussed in earlier chapters. You also saw several advanced techniques involving the creative use of the flexible architecture of this very capable product. Most advanced capabilities require the use of some custom programming, and extending most features requires only simple expressions.

❑   Using Windows Forms or ASP.NET Web Forms controls, user input and parameter selection can be enhanced to provide a richer user experience. Through programmatic rendering and image manipulation, reports may be enhanced to include dynamic graphical content, extending capabilities beyond standard reporting features.

❑   By combining the tablix with a chart component in the group details, you are able to deliver compelling, eye-catching sparkline reports that represent trend data in a tabular format.

By now, you should have a few tricks up your sleeve to answer reporting requirements with some nifty features. With your imagination and a little experimentation, you're likely to find the right techniques for your solutions by building on what you've learned here.

Part IV

Enabling End-User Reporting with Report Builder 1.0

Report Models

A report model is a predefined way to access data that has already been set up by an experienced report designer. The model provides end-users with all the data they will need to build the reports that interest them. Without the report model, end-users would have to track down each piece of data in the database system, likely with the help of a Database Administrator (DBA). The correct data is often in disparate tables throughout the database system. The model allows for these end-users to then use this model data and perform ad hoc queries against it. A report model can be built against an SQL Server database, an SQL Server 2005 or later Analysis Services cube, or an Oracle database running version 9.2.0.3 or later. To better understand how report models are built and which features they include, you will do a simple walk-through using the AdventureWorksDW2008 database.

This chapter covers:

❑   Creating Reporting Services report models

❑   Working with report model data sources

❑   Creating report model data source views

❑   Setting report model properties

❑   Deploying report models

❑   Creating report models for Analysis Services

Getting Started

To begin, open up the SQL Server Business Intelligence Development Studio (BIDS). In the Development Studio, you can create various business intelligence projects. Go to File ➪ New ➪ Project, and select the Report Model Project template, as shown in Figure 11-1.

Once you have opened a new report model project, there are three folders within the Solution Explorer:

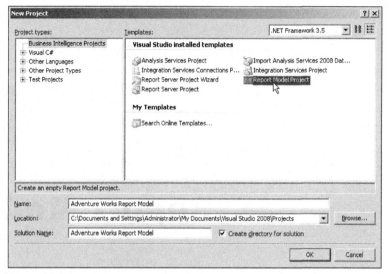

Figure 11-1

- ❑ **Data Sources** — Contains connection information to one or more SQL Server databases.

- ❑ **Data Source Views** — Contains logical representations of SQL Server databases.

- ❑ **Report Models** — Contains models that translate SQL Server structure into user-friendly entities and attributes.

The next sections walk you through each of these three major components: Data Sources, Data Source Views, and Report Models.

Creating the Report Model Data Source

Data sources contain information for connecting to an SQL Server or Oracle database. Data sources can use either the SqlClient Data Provider or the OracleClient Data Provider, as shown in Figure 11-2.

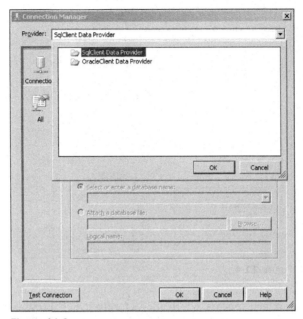

Figure 11-2

To create a new data source, navigate to the Solution Explorer, right-click on the Data Sources folder, and select Add New Data Source, as illustrated in Figure 11-3.

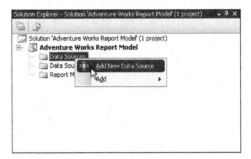

Figure 11-3

When adding a new data source, the Data Source Wizard is initiated. This Wizard will step you through the creation of a database connection. After moving past the Welcome screen, select the New button to open the Connection Manager window, as shown in Figure 11-4.

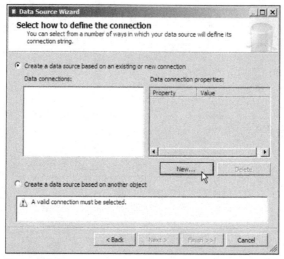

Figure 11-4

The Connection Manager screen appears, which allows for the detailed connection information for the new data source. Fill out the screen to connect to the **AdventureWorksDW2008** database, as shown in Figure 11-5.

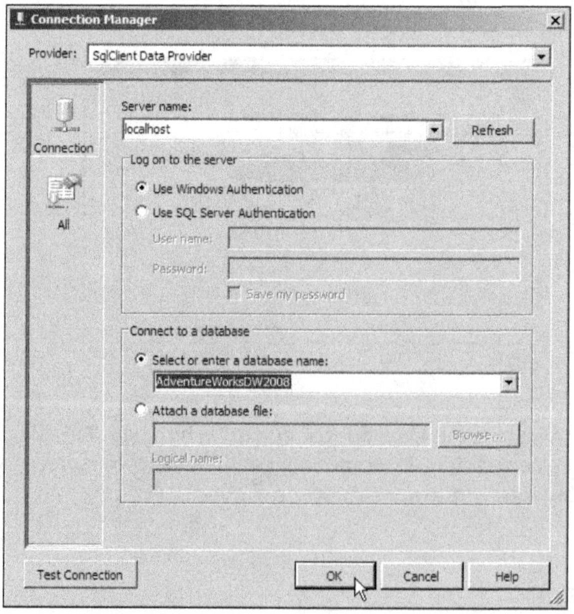

Figure 11-5

Once you have set up the new connection, continue through the Data Source Wizard by clicking Next. The final screen of the Wizard will let you assign a name to your data source. In this scenario, you can leave the default name as "Adventure Works DW2008" and then click Finish, as shown in Figure 11-6.

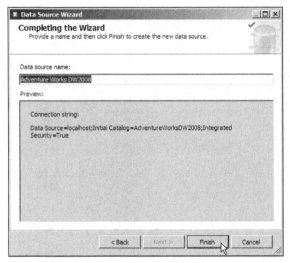

Figure 11-6

The Connection Manager and Data Source Wizard are now common components used throughout projects in the BIDS. Once you have created a data source in Connection Manager, it will be available for use in Analysis Services and Integration Services projects.

Now that the data source has been created, you can move on to creating the Data Source view.

Building a Data Source View

Data Source views represent a logical layer above the database schema. Within a Data Source view, you can create primary keys and foreign key relationships as well as calculated values. Building a well-defined Data Source view is one of the key steps to creating a report model. All report models must be based on information retrieved from the Data Source view. In this section, you look at building the Data Source view, working with productivity features and the code behind a Data Source view.

To create a Data Source view, navigate to the Solution Explorer, right-click the Data Source Views folder, and select Add New Data Source View, as shown in Figure 11-7.

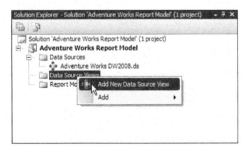

Figure 11-7

The first step to creating a Data Source view is specifying the data source. Only one data source can be defined per Data Source view. Figure 11-8 illustrates selecting the AdventureWorksDW2008 connection created earlier in the chapter.

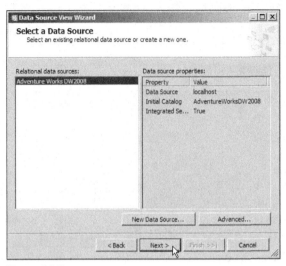

Figure 11-8

After selecting the data source and specifying relationship matching, the Data Source View Wizard enables you to select tables and views defined in the data source. In this example, you select a limited number of tables from the AdventureWorksDW2008 database, although there is no limitation that prevents you from selecting all available tables and views. Select the following tables, as illustrated in Figure 11-9:

❏ DimProduct

❏ DimProductCategory

❏ DimProductSubcategory

❏ DimGeography

❏ DimDate

❏ FactResellerSales

❏ DimReseller

❏ DimSalesTerritory

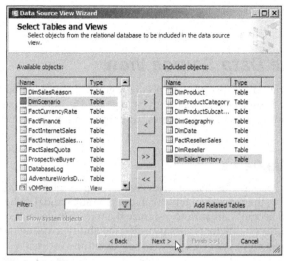

Figure 11-9

Below in this section, you look at creating new diagrams within the Data Source view to help group logical subject areas within a large set of tables.

The final step in the Data Source View Wizard allows you to name the view. In this example, give the view the name **Adventure Works DW2008 DSV**, as illustrated in Figure 11-10, and click Finish to complete the Wizard. A new file named *Adventure Works DW2008DSV.dsv* is now listed in the Data Source Views section.

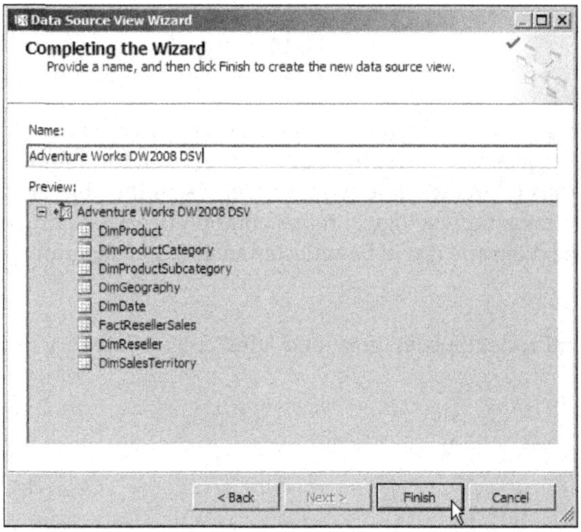

Figure 11-10

In the next sections, you look at working with Data Source views after completing the Data Source View Wizard.

Manipulating the Data Source View

The Data Source View Wizard is a nice starting point for getting your main tables established, but in most situations, the Data Source view will need to be massaged a little. This section describes how to create additional diagrams to organize your views, add new relationships, and work with named queries.

Data Source View Diagrams

The example data source view in this chapter uses only a small number of tables. In a relatively small database application, the number of tables can often be substantial. When dealing with a large number of tables, it often becomes difficult to organize them in a single relational diagram. To help alleviate some of this confusion, Microsoft has included the ability to create multiple relational diagrams within a single Data Source view. Start by opening the AdventureWorks DW2008 DSV.dsv Data Source view created above by double-clicking on it in the Solution Explorer. In the upper-left corner of the Data Source View Designer, you should notice a pane called *Diagram Organizer*, which you will use to create new diagrams. Figure 11-11 illustrates adding a new diagram to the Data Source view created above.

Figure 11-11

After clicking New Diagram, you can rename the diagram to **Products**. Now that you have added a new diagram to the project, you can simply drag tables from the Tables window to include them in the diagram. All the tables listed in the Tables window represent the objects contained within the Data Source view. Diagrams are simply a logical representation to ease editing of the objects. If you make a change to a table in one diagram, it will be reflected in all other diagrams with which the table is associated.

Drag DimProduct, DimProductSubcategory, and DimProductCategory over to the Diagram pane, as shown in Figure 11-12.

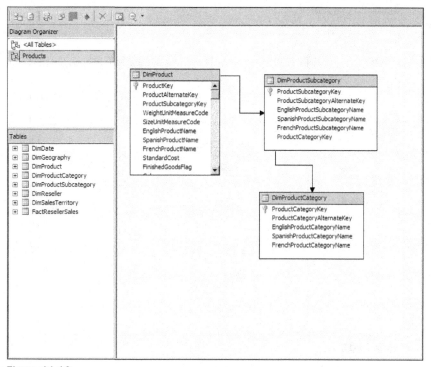

Figure 11-12

Building Data Source View Relationships

In a Data Source view, you can also work with primary key–foreign key relationships within a data source. Creating new primary key–foreign key relationships is often necessary if the underlying database does not already contain the relationships. Since relationships created in the Data Source view are only logical relationships, this will not affect the underlying database.

The FactResellerSales table in the AdventureWorksDW2008 database contains three time-related columns: OrderDateKey, ShipDateKey, and DueDateKey. These columns relate to the DimDate table based on the DateKey column. Open the "<All Tables>" diagram by clicking on it in the Diagram Organizer pane, as illustrated in Figure 11-13.

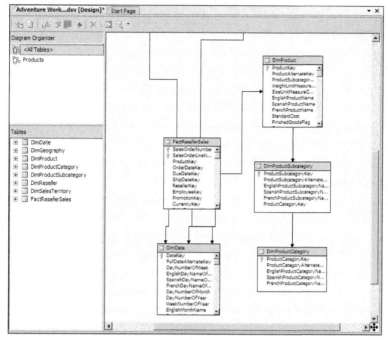

Figure 11-13

In this diagram, you should notice the three relationships from FactResellerSales to DimDate. To examine how the relationship is defined, double-click on the arrows connecting the two tables. In this example, you can click on the left-most arrow connecting to DimDate to view the FactResellerSales. ShipDateKey-to-DimDate.DateKey relationship, as illustrated in Figure 11-14.

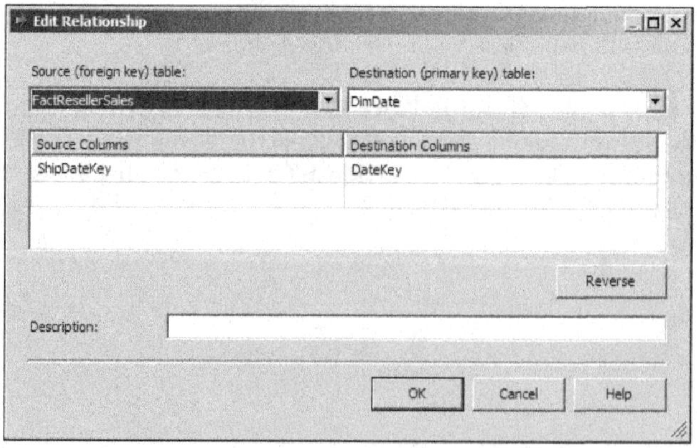

Figure 11-14

Within the Edit Relationship window, you can specify tables and columns used as both the primary and foreign keys. You can also reverse relationships, if they were created incorrectly, and add a meaningful description.

Relationships in the Data Source view are extremely important in a report model. These relationships will later be used to create roles within the report model. A *role* allows a user to navigate from one section of the report model to another and tells the semantic query processor how to retrieve data. Roles are also used to implement a feature of Report Builder 1.0 called *infinite drill-through*. This feature allows the report developer to create a single report, and then Reporting Services will create reports at run time when users click on related items. For example, a user could build a report that contains the sales amount for each of the product categories. Once the report is deployed, a user can click on a product category and see sales information for each of the related subcategories.

Using Named Queries in Data Source Views

Another major feature of the Data Source view is its ability to use named queries. When a table or view is added to a Data Source view, a reference to that table or view is created. If the table or view schema changes, items bound to the schema can break. It is not uncommon in applications to have column names or table names change during the life of the application. Therefore, to alleviate this issue, queries instead of direct references can be created within the Data Source view.

Queries offer flexibility on top of the Data Source view. If a column name changes in the underlying database schema, the query can be updated to reflect this change. Column names can be aliased, and breaking changes can be avoided. It can be considered best practice to change your Data Source view tables to named queries. There is no negative performance impact, so the flexibility you gain is well worth it. Figures 11-15 and 11-16 illustrate replacing the FactResellerSales table with a new named query by right-clicking on the table in the Data Source view.

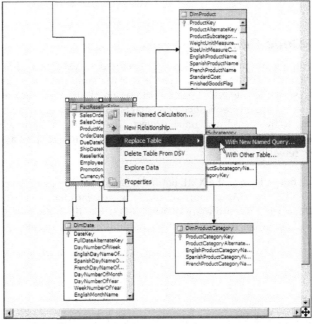

Figure 11-15

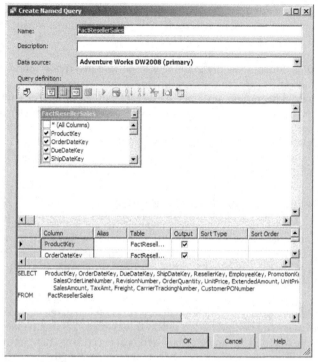

Figure 11-16

Now that you have seen some of the core features around creating a Data Source view, let's look at the XML code generated by the designer.

Data Source View Code Behind

All the source files created in a report model project are stored as XML files. This is important for a couple of reasons. First, the use of XML allows developers to manipulate files easily through programmatic interfaces such as the .NET System.Xml assembly. Second, report model developers can now use standard source control systems such as Visual SourceSafe to store their projects. This offers the advantage of versioning to Business Intelligence projects. If a mistake is made while a file is being updated, users of a source control system can simply revert their changes and avoid costly and sometimes error-prone rework.

In this section, you will take a look at the XML behind a Data Source view. If you have worked with typed datasets in ADO.NET, the XML schema should look very familiar. To view the XML behind a Data Source view, right-click on the AdventureWorksDW2008DSV.dsv file in the Solution Explorer, and click View Code. Figure 11-17 illustrates viewing the XML behind the AdventureWorksDW2008 DSV we created.

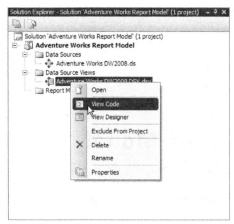

Figure 11-17

The Data Source view XML starts with both an ID tag and a Name tag. The ID tag is the object name given to the Data Source view. When new objects, such as a report model, are associated with the Data Source view, they will reference the value in the ID tag. If the ID values are changed after objects are associated with the Data Source view, those items will be unable to read from it. The Name tag is the friendly name displayed in the Business Intelligence Development Studio interface. This value can be updated as needed without breaking other items. By default, the ID and Name tags will have the same value.

The next major section of the Data Source view is contained within the Annotation tag. Each Annotation tag contains information about how the Data Source view should be displayed within the designer. Annotation tags also contain information related to how initial relationships were established within the Data Source view. Once the Data Source view is created, the Annotations section does not include any information crucial to the function of the view — it is solely for display purposes. Thus, if you delete the entire section, the report model will continue to function; however, you will not have a very pretty designer to work in.

Following the Annotations tag is the DataSourceID tag. This tag represents a reference to the ID tag in one of the project's data sources. Modifying this tag can break the relationship between the two objects.

The next tag in the document is the Schema tag. This tag contains the core definition of the Data Source view. It breaks down into two major areas: elements and relationships.

The section starts with one main element tag. This tag represents the entire Data Source view as a single complex type. Within the main element tag are element tags for each of the individual tables. The table element tags contain the name of the object as well as a query or reference to the underlying table. Within each element tag for a table are element tags for the table's different columns. The column element tags contain the column names, data type, and other defining properties.

After moving through all of the table element tags, you will find a variable list of tags for each unique constraint within the Data Source view. These tags contain information about primary keys defined within the view. Each constraint will have an indication of its type as well as an XPath reference to its related table and column.

The final section of the Data Source view XML contains information about the references defined between the tables in the view. These sections are enclosed in `xs:keyref` tags. Each primary key–foreign key relationship is identified.

Now that you have seen how to create a relational data source connection and Data Source view, let's take a look at generating a report model.

Building the Report Model

In this section, we'll look at the Report Model Wizard and build a simple model based on the AdventureWorksDW2008 database. Once the model is created, you will look at different ways to improve your report model. Finally, you will look at deploying the model for end-users to work with.

Using the Report Model Wizard

You start building a report model by using the Report Model Wizard. The Wizard will step through selecting the relational data source as well as the Data Source view. However, the final step of the Wizard runs the model generation rules. These rules are key to creating a layer that end-users can easily understand.

Let's first take a look at adding a new report model to our project. To add a new report model, right-click on the Report Models folder in the Solution Explorer, and select Add New Report Model (see Figure 11-18).

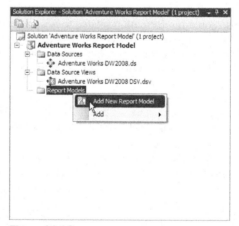

Figure 11-18

Adding a new report model invokes the Report Model Wizard. The first step in the Wizard has you select your Data Source view. Figure 11-19 illustrates selecting the AdventureWorksDW2008 DSV.dsv Data Source view created in this chapter.

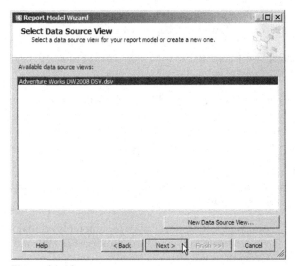

Figure 11-19

The Select Data Source View dialog will display a list of all Data Source views associated with an SQL Server connection. It is possible to add other Data Source views to your report model project. Below in this chapter, creating report models using Analysis Services is discussed.

After selecting a Data Source view, you will see the "Select report model generation rules" dialog. This dialog, which is key to creating the report model, allows you to select all the rules that will be applied to the underlying Data Source view (see Figure 11-20).

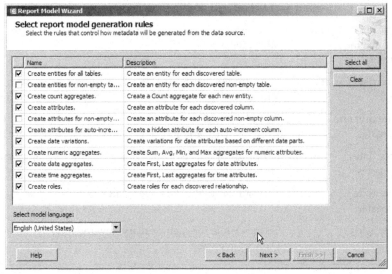

Figure 11-20

The report model is generated by going through two passes of rules defined on the report server. The implementation of the rules can be found at the following location:

```
<install drive>\Program Files\Microsoft SQL Server\MSRS10.MSSQLSERVER\Reporting
Services\ReportServer\ModelGenerationRules.smgl
```

Tables 11-1 and 11-2 show each of the rules and describe how they are implemented against the Data Source view.

Table 11-1: Pass 1

Name	Description
Create entities for all tables.	Builds report model entities for any tables contained in the Data Source view. System tables and the dtproperties table are excluded from the Model Generation Wizard.
Create entities for non-empty tables.	Builds report model entities only for tables that have a row count greater than 0.
Create count aggregates.	For each entity in the report model, a count aggregate is added. If the Data Source view contains a table named *Product*, an entity called *Product* will be created along with an attribute #Product that represents the count of rows within the Product table.
Create attributes.	Creates attributes for each column in a table that is not a foreign key and not an auto-increment column.
Create attributes for non-empty columns.	Creates only attributes for columns that contain data. A query against the data source is required to identify the number of unique values stored in a given column. If that number is greater than 0, the column is included.
Create attributes for auto-increment columns.	If this option is selected, auto-increment columns are also included as attributes of an entity.
Create date variations.	For columns that have a data type of DateTime, additional attributes are added for the day, month, quarter, and year of each date.
Create numeric aggregates.	For columns of type Integer, Float, and Decimal, attributes for Sum, Average, Min, and Max aggregates of the column are added.
Create date aggregates.	For columns of type DateTime, Min, and Max, aggregates of the column are added.
Create time aggregates.	Very similar to the data aggregates, but instead specialized for time.
Create roles.	Creates a role for each primary key–foreign key relationship defined in the Data Source view

Table 11-2: Pass 2

Name	Description
Lookup entities	Once the attributes are created through Pass 1, Pass 2 looks at each attribute to identify if it is eligible to become a lookup. By default, lookups are added to columns that are not aggregated (`DateTime`, `Integer`, `Float`, `Decimal`) and are not auto-increment columns.
Small lists	Lists are created for entities with less than 200 rows.
Medium lists	Lists are created for entities with between 200 and 500 rows.
Large lists	Filter lists are created for entities with greater than 500 rows.
Very large lists	Requires that large entities (greater than 5,000 rows) have mandatory filters.
Set identifying attributes.	*Identifying attributes* are columns that can uniquely identify items in the entity. Identifying attributes are determined based on a combination of non-null requirements, data types, and use as a foreign key.
Set default detail attributes.	*Default detail attributes* are identified as those attributes most likely to further define an entity. Default detail attributes are also defined based on a combination of non-null requirements, data types, and use as a foreign key.
Role name only	Looks at identifying attributes and determines the role name to be used in role definitions.
Numeric/date formatting	Sets the default sort direction to Descending for numeric and date attributes.
Integer/decimal formatting	Sets the default formatting for `Integer` and `Decimal` type attributes to General Number format.
Float formatting	Sets the default formatting for `Float` type attributes to two decimal places.
Date formatting	Sets the default formatting for `DateTime` type attributes to the General Date format.
Discourage grouping.	Discourages grouping of items that have a unique occurrence of greater than 80%.
Dropdown value selection	Creates dropdown selections for attributes that have greater than 0 and less than 200 unique values.
List value selection	Creates list selections for attributes that have greater than 200 and less than 1,000 unique values.

After selecting the generation rules, the Wizard moves to the Update Statistics dialog. This dialog presents two options: "Update model statistics before generating" and "Use current model statistics in the data source view." The statistics this dialog is referring to are not statistics from the underlying database; they are statistics from the Data Source view. These statistics include properties such as the maximum length of a column. The Report Model Designer uses this information to help create the new report model.

Statistics on a report model only need to be updated when the database changes. So, for the first run of the Wizard, it is suggested that you select the "Update model statistics before generating" option. Any further passes through the Wizard can simply use the information then stored in the Data Source view.

Completing the Report Model Wizard requires two steps. The first step is to name the model. In this example, give your report model the name **Adventure Works DW2008 DSV**, as shown in Figure 11-21. The second step is to run the Rules Generation Wizard.

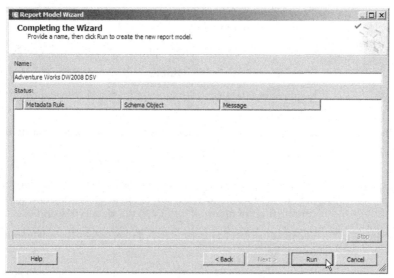

Figure 11-21

To start the Report Model Wizard, click the Run button. Running the Wizard can take a few moments. As the model is generated, you will see an output of all the rules that are applied. You should see all the tables identified in the Data Source view, as well as their corresponding columns. After the run has completed, click the Finish button.

After clicking Finish in the Report Model Wizard, you will see a new file named *AdventureWorks DW2008 DSV.smdl* in the Solution Explorer. The file is also opened in the Designer on the main canvas of Visual Studio. SMDL, which stands for "Semantic Model Definition Language," is the XML schema used to represent a Reporting Services report model. The next section will explore the makeup and editing of the report model.

Working with Reporting Services Report Models

To understand the report model, you will explore the model created in the previous section. In this section, you will add the DimEmployee table to your repost model. The first step to adding the DimEmployee table is to edit the AdventureWorks DW2008 DSV.dsv Data Source view. Open the Data Source view by double-clicking on it in the Solution Explorer. Right-click the design surface and select Add/Remove Tables, as illustrated in Figure 11-22.

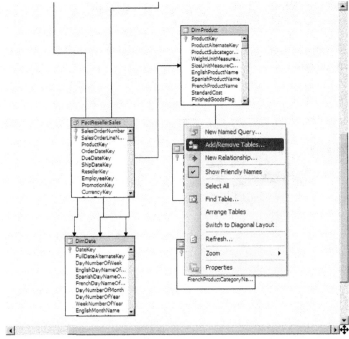

Figure 11-22

In the Add/Remove Tables dialog, select the table DimEmployee and move it to the "Included objects," as illustrated in Figure 11-23.

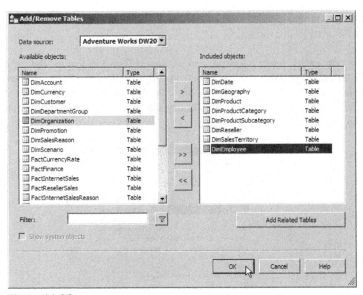

Figure 11-23

Click OK to close the Add/Remove Tables dialog, save and close the Data Source view, and then return to the Adventure Works DW2008 DSV.smdl designer.

To add `DimEmployee` attributes to your report model, right-click on the Model node, and select New ⇨ Entity, as illustrated in Figure 11-24.

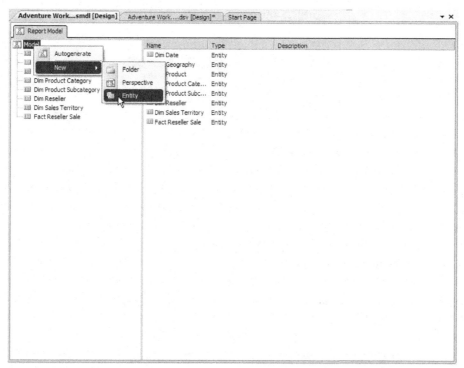

Figure 11-24

Right-click on the new entity, select Rename, and rename it **Dim Employee**. Before you can generate the new Dim Employee entity, you must set its `Binding` property. The `Binding` property tells the report model which table or view in the Data Source view contains the attributes for the entity. Using the Properties window, modify the Dim Employee entity's `Binding` property to use the DimEmployee table, as illustrated in Figure 11-25.

Figure 11-25

Now that you have bound the new entity, you are ready to generate its model. Right-click on the Dim Employee entity, and select Autogenerate, as illustrated in Figure 11-26.

Figure 11-26

You will be prompted with a warning that says "Regenerating an existing model item cannot be reversed." In this case, that is perfectly acceptable because you have not done any modifications to the Dim Employee entity. If this were an existing entity that you had modified, you would not want to auto-generate the model. For this example, select **Yes** from the warning dialog. Click through the Report Model Wizard dialog, using the defaults, and notice that it is the same dialog as illustrated above when you first created the report model. When you are finished running the Wizard, you should have a completed entity like that shown in Figure 11-27.

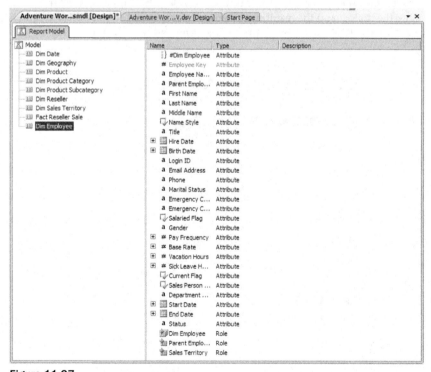

Figure 11-27

The final step in adding the Dim Employee entity is to define its identifying attributes. In this case, `EmployeeKey` will uniquely identify the entity. To set the identifying attributes, navigate to the Properties window of the Dim Employee entity, and click the Builder button (the button with the ellipsis) for the `IdentifyingAttributes` property. This will launch the AttributeReference Collection Editor, as shown in Figure 11-28.

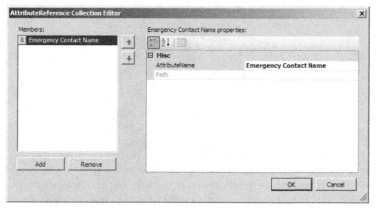

Figure 11-28

To add the EmployeeKey, click the Add button, and select "# Employee Key" from the List Fields. Click OK to close the dialog, and the resulting AttributeReference Collection Editor should appear, as shown in Figure 11-29. Click OK to apply the property setting and save the report model.

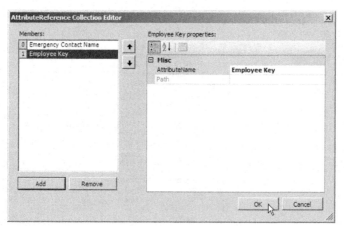

Figure 11-29

Now that you have seen how to create and manipulate a report model, you will look at deploying the model to the report server.

Deploying the Report Model

Report models are deployed to a central report server in much the same way as reports. The smdl file, along with the data source, is published via the Reporting Services Web service. Once the report model is published, it can be used by end-users.

One slight difference between the deployment of models and reports is the number of folders that are created. In reports, you deploy to a single target folder. With report models, you can deploy to both a target Data Source folder and target Model folder. By default, these are simply set to Data Sources and Models, respectively. To change the target folders, right-click on the Report Model project in the Solution Explorer, and select Properties. From there, you will see properties for the different folder locations as well as the Overwrite Data Sources property and Target Server URL.

Once you are ready to deploy the report model to the server, click the Build menu and select Deploy *<project name>*. Deployment of the model consists of two steps: building the model and sending the deploy command.

Building the model consists of checking expression syntax, validating the availability of files, verifying IDs of related objects, and performing other types of validation activities. If the project is verified, the process will continue with the deployment of the package.

To deploy the package, SQL Server Business Intelligence Development Studio invokes the Reporting Services Web service, which contains methods for publishing to the server. When you are deploying a project, you are really deploying the smdl file. This file will be stored in the ReportServer database in the Catalog table. Whenever users make a request for the model, Reporting Services will simply read it back from the database. No file is actually stored on the server's filesystem.

To check that the project has deployed successfully, open Internet Explorer, and connect to the report server URL — for example, `http://localhost/Reports/`. You should see a Data Source folder and a Models folder now created, as shown in Figure 11-30. If you expand the Models folder, you will see your project listed.

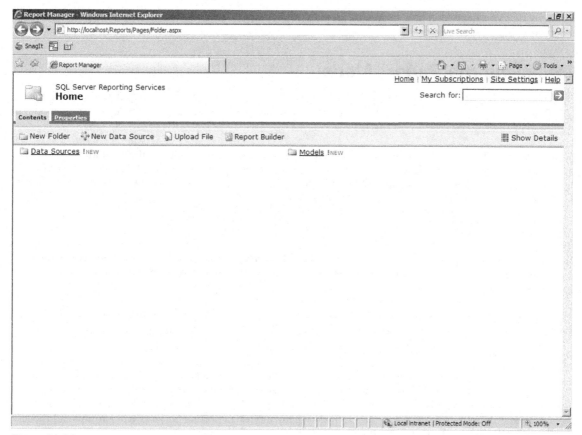

Figure 11-30

Now that the report model has been created and deployed, you can move on to creating reports using the Report Builder 1.0. Chapter 12 walks you through using the Report Builder 1.0 to allow end-user development of reports.

Building Report Models from Analysis Services Databases

The bulk of this chapter discussed building Reporting Services report models using SQL Server. It is also possible, and in my opinion much simpler, to create report models using Analysis Services. Creating a report model from Analysis Services requires the initial creation of an Analysis Services database. Creating Analysis Services databases is outside the scope of this text, so here you will use the AdventureWorks DW2008 Analysis Services sample provided with SQL Server 2008.

To create a report model from an Analysis Services database, you do not need to use the Business Intelligence Development Studio. Most of the work that was done to create a report model from SQL

Server is the same type of work that is done to create an Analysis Services database. Therefore, all you need to do is create a connection to the Analysis Services database in Report Manager and then generate the model from it. The first step is to open the Report Manager in the web browser. The default location is http://localhost/reports.

From Report Manager, click on the New Data Source button to launch the New Data Source entry page. In the New Data Source page, simply give the data source a name and connection string to the Analysis Services database, as illustrated in Figure 11-31. Make sure that you set the appropriate connection string for your database and specify "Windows integrated security" for the "Connect using" setting. Once you have entered the correct settings, click OK to create the data source.

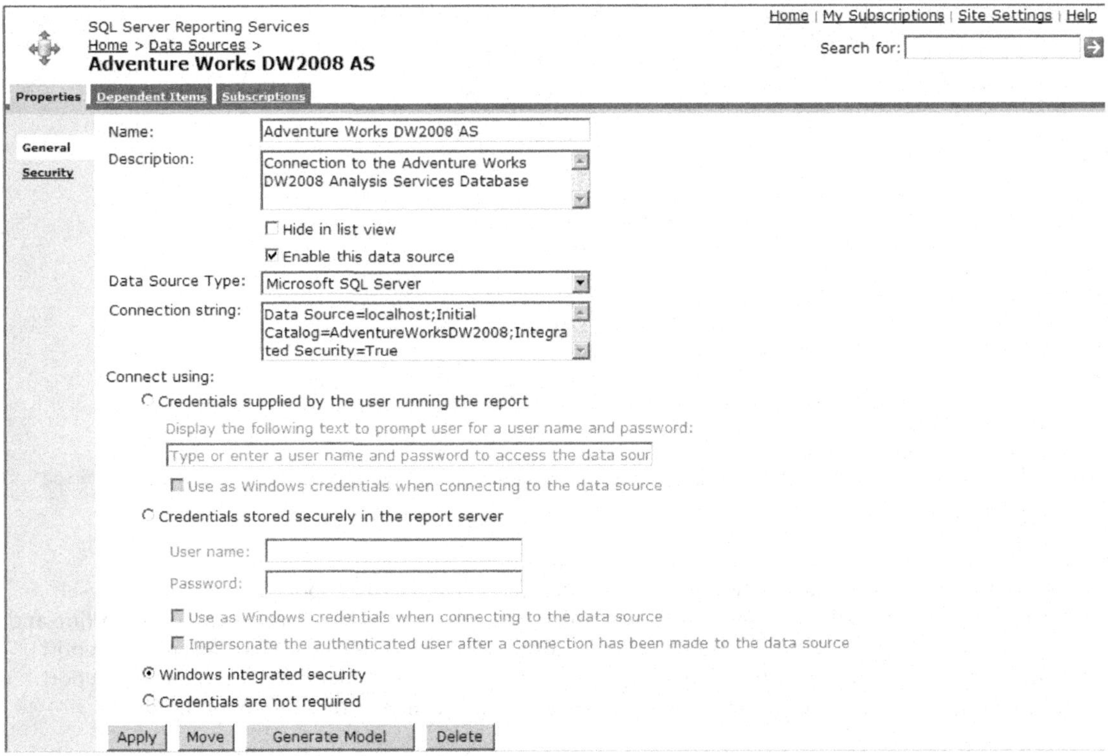

Figure 11-31

The details of the Adventure Works DW2008 data source are shown, as illustrated in Figure 11-31. Scroll to the bottom of the page, and you will see a Generate Model button.

Clicking on the Generate Model button will take you to a new page that allows you to name the Report Model and specify its location. For this example, name the model **Adventure Works DW2008 AS Report Model**, change the location to the Models directory, and click OK, as illustrated in Figure 11-32.

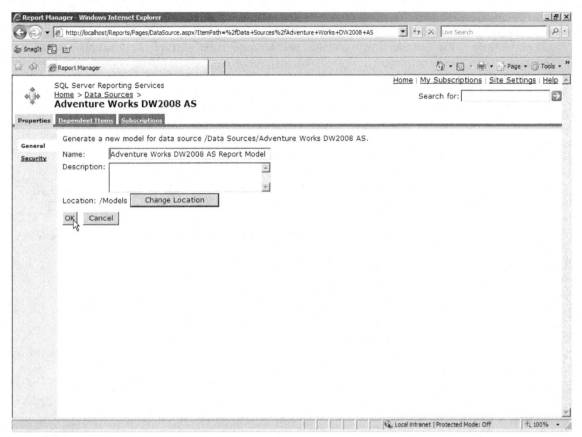

Figure 11-32

Reporting Services uses the Analysis Services definition to generate the report model. The Analysis Services database already contains relationship information as well as information about formatting and aggregates. For this reason, you do not have to go through all of the steps necessary to create a report model from SQL Server. Once the model is created, you can use it just like a SQL Server–based report model. Chapter 12 discusses using the Report Builder 1.0 to create reports from report models.

Summary

This chapter looked at creating Reporting Services report models. You started by creating a data source within your report model project. A data source in a report model project can connect to a SQL database or an Oracle database running version 9.2.0.3 or later. Other databases are not currently supported.

After you created a data source, you looked at adding a Data Source view. The Data Source view is a logical representation of the underlying database. It allows you to add a level of abstraction from your source. You then created named queries to help shield your model from database changes as well as create diagrams to more easily view certain objects.

Once the Data Source view was in place, you could run the Report Model Wizard. The Report Model Wizard runs through several steps, but the key process is generating the model rules. You saw what rules are implemented and how they use the underlying Data Source view to create objects.

After running the Report Model Wizard, you looked at editing the report model. The report model is an XML-based file known as the Semantic Model Definition Language (SMDL). This file is made up of three major components: entities, attributes, and roles. Entities generally represent tables in the Data Source view; attributes generally represent columns; and roles represent relationships between entities.

When the model is completed, you can deploy it to the report server. Deployment consists of two steps: build and deployment. Building the project checks to make sure that the model is syntactically valid. Deploying the project invokes the Reporting Services Web service and publishes the smdl file to the server.

Once the report model is deployed, users can start building reports. After reading this chapter, you should now have an understanding of:

❑ The types of data sources that can be used for report models — SQL Server, SQL Server 2005 Analysis Services or later, and Oracle version 9.2.0.3 or later.

❑ How Data Source views are created and some best practices for using named queries.

❑ How report models are generated and where you can find information about generation rules.

❑ How report models are deployed to the report server.

❑ How report models are created for Analysis Services databases.

In the next chapter, you'll look at the Report Builder 1.0 client and see how it can be used against an existing model.

12

Report Builder 1.0

This chapter looks at using the traditional Report Builder 1.0 application, now termed Report Builder 1.0 by Microsoft, to perform ad hoc reporting. The traditional Report Builder 1.0 application discussed in this chapter has not changed since SQL Server 2005 Reporting Services and is the recommended tool for users who want to continue benefitting from the query design experience as well as the infinite drill capability. As of this writing, Microsoft is working hard on a new version of Report Builder — Report Builder 2.0. Microsoft's plans for the new version of Report Builder 1.0 are discussed later in this chapter.

In March 2004, Microsoft purchased a company called ActiveViews. ActiveViews had a technology that allowed users to build a user-friendly model on top of their data. This model has become the backbone of ad hoc reporting in Reporting Services.

As you move through this chapter, you will be introduced to the Report Builder 1.0 application. Report Builder 1.0 has a traditional Microsoft Office interface for building reports. You will also see how to use different report layouts to fulfill various reporting needs. Once you understand the report layouts, you will move on to formatting and filtering data. The chapter ends with a few administrative items you need to be aware of when deploying this tool to your users.

Report Model Overview

Report models are the key to creating ad hoc reports. They represent the semantic layer on top of your SQL Server Analysis Services data. Report models help users easily identify data elements as well as navigate their relationships.

In Chapter 11, you built a report model using the AdventureWorksDW2008 database. In this chapter, you will leverage that model to create your own ad hoc reports.

If you have not built a report model up to this point, I suggest reviewing the material in the previous chapter and familiarizing yourself with the process. Above and beyond creating reports, building the model is the single most important aspect of doing ad hoc analysis. Without a solid model, users will most likely find creating reports confusing and time-consuming.

Accessing Report Builder 1.0

Ad hoc reporting in Reporting Services uses a Windows smart client application. Smart client applications combine the rich user interface of a Windows application with the ease of deployment found in web applications. To run a smart client application, users navigate to a web server. From the web server, the executable and any dependencies are loaded onto the client machine. The smart client then runs on the user's local machine and can access all the local resources. When an update to the application is available, the smart client application downloads the new bits and is ready to go.

Microsoft decided that to effectively develop ad hoc reports, users would need more functionality than a traditional web application can provide. For this reason, Report Builder 1.0 was introduced using smart client technology.

There are two methods available for accessing Report Builder 1.0. First, you can access Report Builder 1.0 through the following URL:

```
http://servername/reportserver/ReportBuilder/ReportBuilder.application
```

You will need to replace *servername* with the name of your report server and *reportserver* with the name of the report server virtual directory. Using this URL, you could create your own buttons to launch the Report Builder 1.0 application.

The second method for accessing Report Builder 1.0 is through the Report Manager Web interface. When you navigate to Report Manager (`http://servername/reports`), you will see a Report Builder 1.0 button, as illustrated in Figure 12-1. Click on the Report Builder 1.0 button to launch the smart client application.

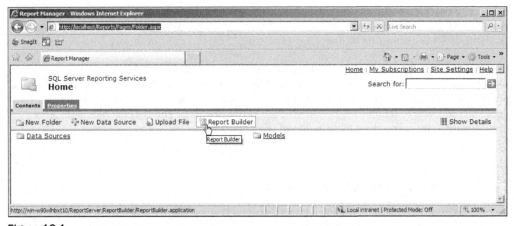

Figure 12-1

When a user clicks on the Report Builder 1.0 button, the smart client application verifies that the required prerequisites to run the application are installed on the local computer. If the prerequisites are not installed, the user is prompted to install them. To run Report Builder 1.0 users will need version 2.0 of the Microsoft .NET Framework installed on the local computer.

In the next section, you'll look at building Reporting Services reports using Report Builder. 1.0

Building Reports

Once you launch Report Builder 1.0, you will be presented with a dialog to select a report model. As was discussed in the previous chapter, report models are the key component for creating ad hoc reports. They represent an easy-to-use representation of your data.

The list of report models presented represents all report models that you have access to on the given report server. You might also notice a +next to some of the report models. You can expand the report model node to view any perspectives associated with the model. *Perspectives* are views of the report model that present a subset of information to the user.

In the previous chapter, you created a small report model from the AdventureWorksDW2008 database. To start designing reports, select the Adventure Works DW2008 AS Report Model data source, which is located in the Getting Started dialog box on the right-hand side of the screen. You will use this model throughout the rest of this chapter. If you have not deployed the report model, please walk through Chapter 11, "Report Models."

Before you build your report, you need to decide which type of layout is appropriate. In the Report Layout window, you are presented with three options:

❑ Table

❑ Matrix

❑ Chart

The following sections describe creating reports with these three layout types.

After you select a report layout in the Getting Started dialog and click OK, the Report Builder 1.0 will present four main windows:

❑ Explorer

❑ Fields

❑ Report Layout

❑ Designer

The Explorer window displays a list of entity collections from the report model. As you select items in the Explorer window, you will notice that the Fields window updates to display all the available attributes for the selected entity. You will use the Explorer and Fields windows to construct your first report. The Report Layout window is where the layout for the report is located. The Designer is where the report will be built. These windows will be discussed in detail as we continue through the chapter.

Table Layout

To understand the table report layout, you will create a simple report that shows Products in the hierarchy (Product Category, Product Subcategory, Product Name) with their associated Sales Amount and Order Quantity. This will build a base around working with related data as well as aggregated values.

To start, select the Adventure Works DW2008 AS Report Model and Table layout from the Getting Started dialog (see Figure 12-2).

Figure 12-2

After selecting the Table layout, you will notice that the Design window displays a base report with one column. You want to start building your report based on the Product Category, Product Subcategory, and Product Name hierarchy. Start at the lowest level of the hierarchy and work your way up. Since *English Product Name* is the lowest level of detail required, you start with that field. Select the Dim Product node from the Explorer window. This will refresh the Field List with all the attributes of Product. Select "English Product Name" from the list, and drag it onto the table in the Design window. Figure 12-3 illustrates adding the Product Name field.

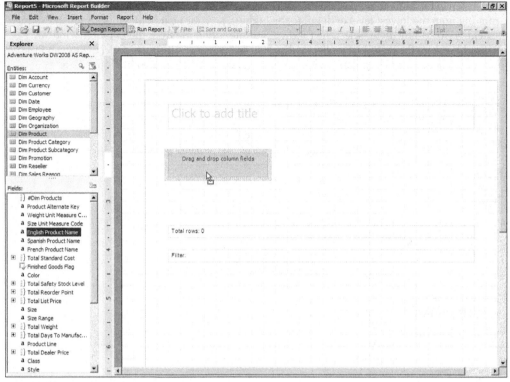

Figure 12-3

Now that English Product Name has been added to the report, you should notice a change in the Explorer window, as shown in Figure 12-4. Selecting the Product Name field told Report Builder 1.0 that you were going to use the Product entity for this report. The change in the Explorer window shows all the related entities to Product. In this model, Product Subcategory, Fact Internet Sales, and Fact Reseller Sales have a direct relationship to product.

Figure 12-4

The next step in building the report is the addition of Product Subcategory and Product Category. You are moving from the lowest level of detail to the highest, so your next field will be English Product Subcategory. To add the field, select the Product Subcategory node from the Explorer window. This should change the Field List to display Product Subcategory attributes. Select "English Product Subcategory Name," and drag it to the left of Product Name, as illustrated in Figure 12-5.

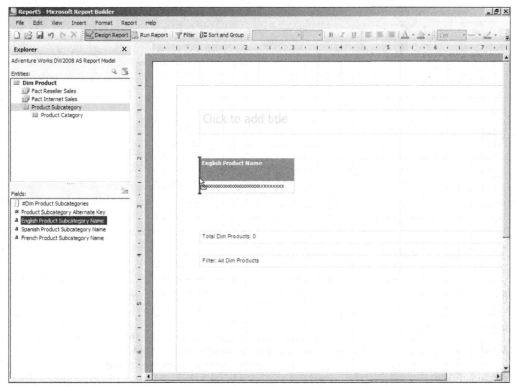

Figure 12-5

To finish the Product hierarchy, click on the Product Category node in the Explorer, and add the English Product Category Name field to the left of Product Subcategory Name. You can also repeat these steps to add Total Sales Amount and Total Order Quantity from the Fact Reseller Sales as Product node. Figure 12-6 illustrates the finished layout.

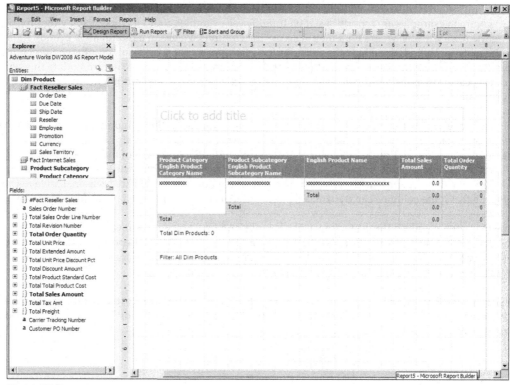

Figure 12-6

Notice that Report Builder 1.0 recognized the hierarchy between Product Name, Product Subcategory, and Product Category. Based on the hierarchy, it created subtotals for each of the levels. You might have noticed that the English Product Name total is unnecessary since it is the lowest level of detail. There are several formatting improvements that you can make. After discussing the different types of layouts, you will come back to formatting your reports. For now, save this report as **Table Layout Product Sales**.

Click on the Save button in the application toolbar to save the report. Clicking on the Save button will present a list of folders located on the report server. Report Builder 1.0 reports are always saved on the report server. Saving reports to the report server requires Publish permissions. Required permissions are covered later in this chapter.

Now that you have created a basic table report, let's look at the next layout option, matrix.

Matrix Layout

The matrix layout is very similar to the table layout. Both deal with a report as rows and columns. However, the matrix report allows you to dynamically change the number of columns based on the data returned. This differs from the static column layout of a table.

The ability to expand a report across columns is sometimes referred to as a *cross-tab* or *pivot table*. A matrix changes its columns based on the data returned. It does not give users the ability to change layout on-the-fly like Microsoft Excel.

That being said, it is a very powerful layout. It will allow you to build very dynamic reports. Some of the most common examples are reports based on time. These examples could include displaying products along the rows with the weeks for a month across the columns. Weeks in a month are a prime candidate for the matrix. Depending on how the calendar for a particular year works out, months can potentially have 4 or 5 weeks. Dynamically expanding your columns in a regular table to accommodate this type of variation can be extremely difficult. With a matrix report, you simply and automatically bring back the appropriate data and the report layouts.

The downside of a matrix report is printing. Anytime you want something to print well, you need to be able to control the page width. Length is less of an issue because data can simply continue on to the next page without losing continuity. However, if the columns fall off to the right of the page, it is often difficult to line items back up again. You can increase a report's width, but when you deal with a matrix report, you will never know with certainty how wide the report will be. For that reason, I always warn my users that if the columns can dynamically grow, there is no guarantee of a beautiful print layout.

Now that you've walked through some of the benefits and trade-offs of the matrix report, let's take a look at creating one. You will again use the Adventure Works DW2008 AS Report Model. In this section, you'll create a report that displays "Total Sales Amount with Product Categories" along your rows and "Year (based on Order Date)" across your columns.

To start, on the Report Builder 1.0 menu, select File ⇨ New. In the Getting Started window, select the Adventure Works DW2008 AS Report Model and the Matrix (cross-tab) Report Layout, as illustrated in Figure 12-7.

Figure 12-7

After you select the Matrix layout, the Design window will load with the Matrix template. The Matrix template is similar to that of the table. However, it is broken down into three distinct areas: Rows, Columns, and Totals.

In this scenario, you want to display Product Categories along your rows. To access the Product Categories, you need to select "Dim Product Category" from the Explorer Window. Once Product Categories is selected, the Field List will include the English Product Category Name attribute. To add it to your report, click "English Product Category Name," and drag it to the report layout section that says "Drag and drop row groups." Figure 12-8 illustrates adding the Product Category Name to the rows.

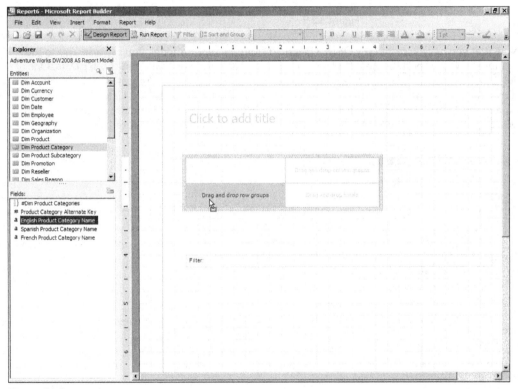

Figure 12-8

The second piece of information you want to display in this report is the Year (based on order date) across your columns. The Order Date field you need is located in the Reseller Sales entity. As the report is now, you cannot see the Reseller Sales entity. This is because Product Category has no direct relationship with Reseller Sales. Product Category is related to Reseller sales through the Product and Product Subcategory entity. Thus, to navigate to Order Date, you will need to select "Dim Product Subcategories" from the Explorer window, then "Dim Products," next "Fact Reseller Sales," and finally "Order Date." Figure 12-9 illustrates the movement through this hierarchy.

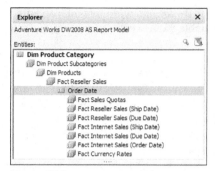

Figure 12-9

Now that you have accessed the Order Date field from the report model, you can add *Year* to the columns of your report. In the Field List, you will see various fields that define Order Date. One of those fields is the Total Calendar Year. This breakdown was defined when the report model was created and allows the user to easily use different date variations in their reports. To add Calendar Year to the report, expand the Total Calendar Year field and then click on "Calendar Year," and drag it to the Report Designer area labeled "Drag and drop column groups," as illustrated in Figure 12-10.

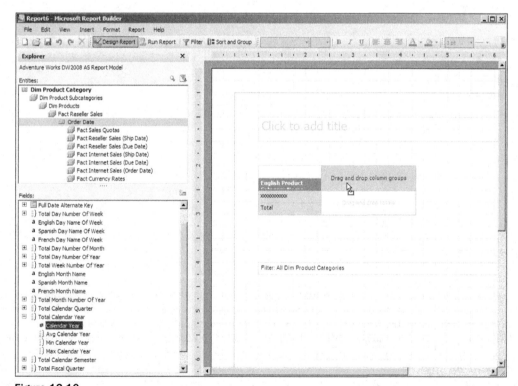

Figure 12-10

The final item you need to add to the report is a data element to total. In this scenario, you are using Total Sales Amount from the Reseller Sales entity. After adding the Calendar Year field to the report, the Explorer displays all the other attributes related to Fact Reseller Sale in the Field List. Select "Total Sales Amount," and drag and drop it on the report area labeled "Drag and drop totals." Once you have added the final field, you should see a report layout similar to the one in Figure 12-11.

Click to add title
Calendar Year (Total Sales
Product Category
0
Total
xxxxxxxxxxx
0.0
0.0
Total
0.0
0.0
Filter: All Fact Reseller Sales

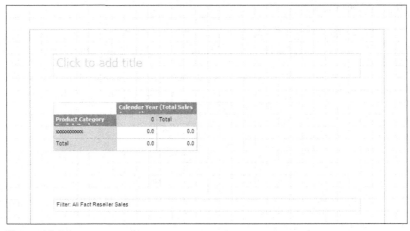

Figure 12-11

To view the results of the report, click the Run Report button from the toolbar. As shown in Figure 12-12, the calendar years are repeated across the columns based on the data returned. You might need to go back to the Designer Report view and widen the columns in order to match the figure exactly. (Formatting a report is discussed below in this chapter.) Finally, click the Save button, and save the report as **Matrix Layout Product Sales**.

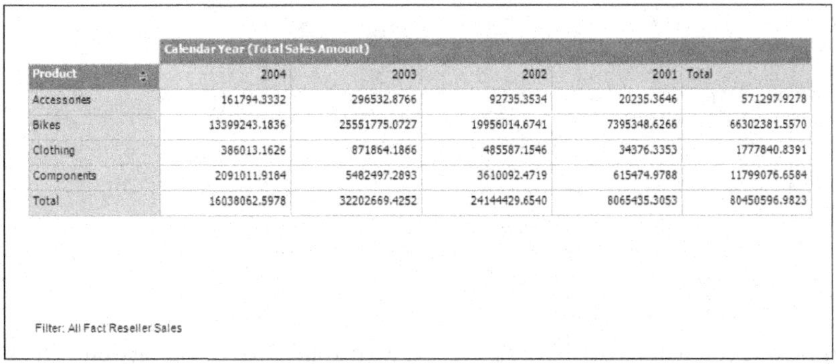

Calendar Year (Total Sales Amount)
Product
2004
2003
2002
2001
Total
Accessories
161794.3332
296532.8766
92735.3534
20235.3646
571297.9278
Bikes
13399243.1836
25551775.0727
19956014.6741
7395348.6266
66302381.5570
Clothing
386013.1626
871864.1866
485587.1546
34376.3353
1777840.8391
Components
2091011.9184
5482497.2893
3610092.4719
615474.9788
11799076.6584
Total
16038062.5978
32202669.4252
24144429.6540
8065435.3053
80450596.9823
Filter: All Fact Reseller Sales

Figure 12-12

Chart Layout

The *Chart layout* enables you to display information in your report graphically. There are a number of different chart types to choose from, including bar charts, line charts, and pie charts. Microsoft recently acquired data-visualization technology from Dundas, which was integrated into SQL Server 2008. In addition, the Dundas technology acquired by Microsoft also brought to the company several graphical components that can be embedded in custom applications.

To start the Chart report, select File ⇨ New from the Report Builder 1.0 menu. In the Getting Started window, select the Adventure Works DW2008 AS Report Model and the Chart report layout (see Figure 12-13).

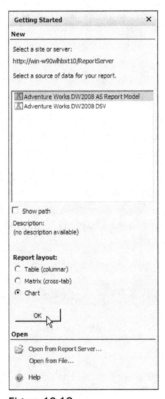

Figure 12-13

For the Chart report, you want to display a pie chart with Total Order Quantity broken down by Sales Territory Region. By default, the Chart type is set to a bar chart. To change the Chart type, right-click on the chart in the designer, and select Chart Type, Pie, Simple Pie, as shown in Figure 12-14.

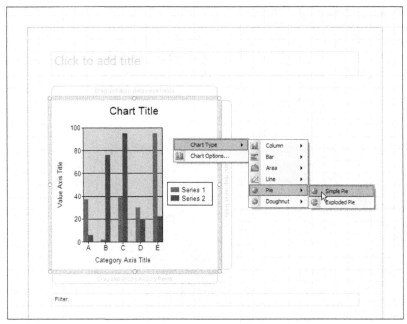

Figure 12-14

Once you have selected the Chart type, the chart in the designer surface exposes the drop areas for data fields. Charts have three different drop areas:

❑ **Data Value Fields** — Data value fields represent the information that will determine how the Chart area is drawn. For bar charts, they will represent the length of the bars. For pie charts, they will represent the size of the pie pieces.

❑ **Series Fields** — Series fields are used to display multiple values side-by-side in the chart.

❑ **Category Fields** — Category fields are used to define the overall grouping of the chart.

In this scenario, you want to display Total Order Quantity by Sales Territory Region. Start by selecting "Fact Reseller Sale" in the Explorer window. From the Field List, select "Total Order Quantity," and drag it to the "Drag and drop data value fields" section in the chart (see Figure 12-15).

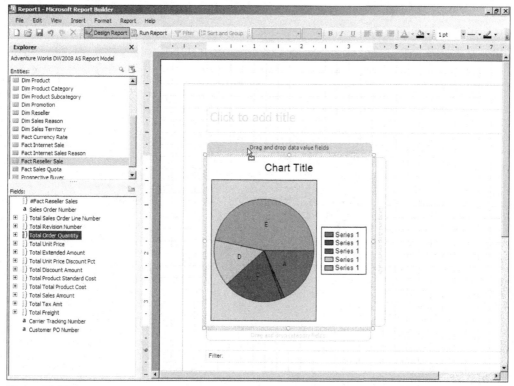

Figure 12-15

Now that you have added Total Order Quantity, you can add your Sales Territory Region. From the Explorer, select "Sales Territory." Drag the Sales Territory Region field from the Field List, and drop it on the "Drag and drop category fields" area of the chart. Figure 12-16 illustrates adding the Sales Territory Region.

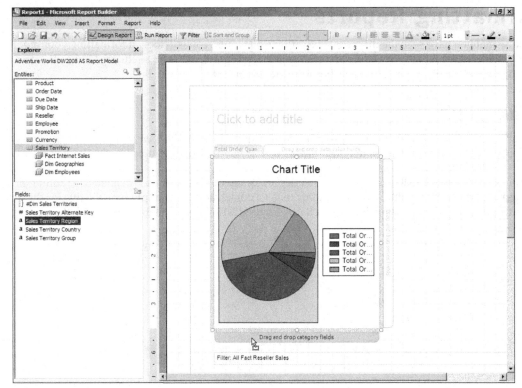

Figure 12-16

Once you have added both fields to the chart, select Run Report from the toolbar. You should now see Order Quantity broken down by Sales Territory Region. Figure 12-17 shows the rendered Chart report. Save this report as **Chart Order Quantity by Sales Territory Region**.

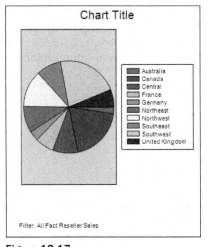

Figure 12-17

Formatting Reports

Now that you have seen the different types of report layouts, you will look at formatting your reports. You will start by looking at adding text elements to the reports, move on to editing field names and widths, and, finally, work with fonts, borders, and alignment.

Adding Text

Let's start by adding a title to the table report created in the previous section. To open the existing report, click on the Open button in the Report Builder 1.0 toolbar, and open the Table Layout Product Sales report.

You should notice a textbox at the top of the Report Designer. This textbox is available for adding titles to your report. To edit the title, click the textbox to get a cursor, and then simply type the title for the report. In this example, you use the title **Product Sales**. Figure 12-18 shows the table report with the new title.

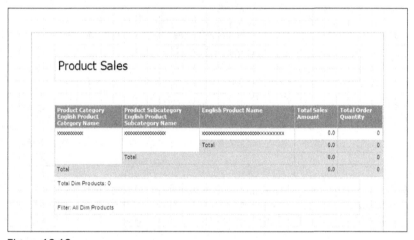

Figure 12-18

Now that your report has a title, go ahead and clean up the formatting for the rest of the table, starting with the column headers. To modify the column headers, simply click on the header to display the cursor, and then type in the new header text. Change your columns to the following:

❑ **Category**

❑ **Subcategory**

❑ **Product Name**

❑ **Sales Amount**

❑ **Order Quantity**

Figure 12-19 illustrates the new column headings.

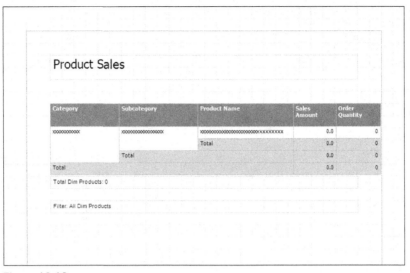

Figure 12-19

Adjusting Column Width and Alignment

Now that your text is displayed correctly, you need to work on the layout of the fields. If you preview the report, you will notice that the Category and Subcategory column widths are larger than necessary to accommodate the text returned from the query. You'll want to reduce those columns to give a little better presentation. To decrease the column width, select the table by clicking on it, and then hover your cursor between the columns. When you move your cursor between the columns, it will change to indicate that you can modify the width. Click between the columns and move the mouse right or left to increase or decrease the width of the columns.

After adjusting the column widths, you might also notice that the alignment of the "Sales Amount" and "Order Quantity" column headers is incorrect. Number fields are right-aligned, and it is good practice to do the same with their respective column headers. In this report, they are left-aligned. To clean this up, highlight the "Sales Amount" and "Order Quantity" cells. To highlight both cells at once, click on "Sales Amount," hold down the Shift key, and click on "Order Quantity." Once you have selected both cells, click the Right Justify button in the toolbar, as illustrated in Figure 12-20.

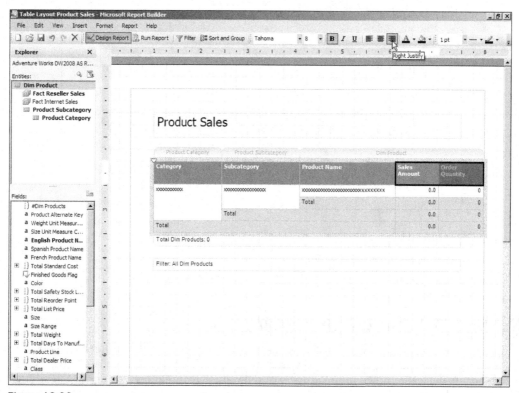

Figure 12-20

Now that you have your numbers formatted correctly and the alignment set, we'll take a look at working with the font and background color.

Modifying Font and Background Color

In your report, there are three levels to the Product hierarchy. To improve the report, you will modify the font for the top-level elements as well as alter the background color for the individual products.

To set the font in your reports, you can simply use the Report Builder 1.0 toolbar. In the sample report, click the Category field textbox directly beneath the "Category" column header, and set the font to 12 point, as shown in Figure 12-21.

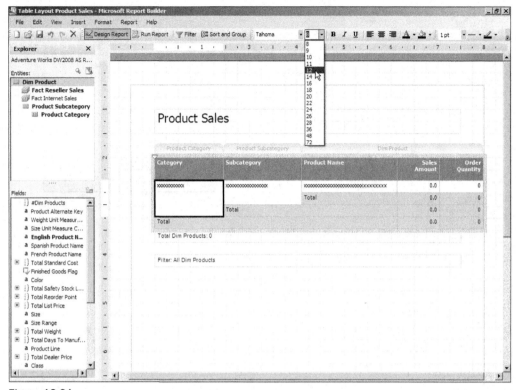

Figure 12-21

You can repeat the same process to set the Subcategory font to 10 point. This should allow you to more easily distinguish the different levels.

The second formatting feature is setting the background color for a set of items. In this scenario, you want to format the Product Name items. You will set the background color to Light Turquoise. To set the background color, select the Product Name, Sales Amount, and Order Quantity detail lines by clicking on the textboxes directly under the column headers and holding down the Shift key. Once you have highlighted the desired cells, use the Fill Color button in the toolbar to select Light Turquoise. Figure 12-22 illustrates setting the background color.

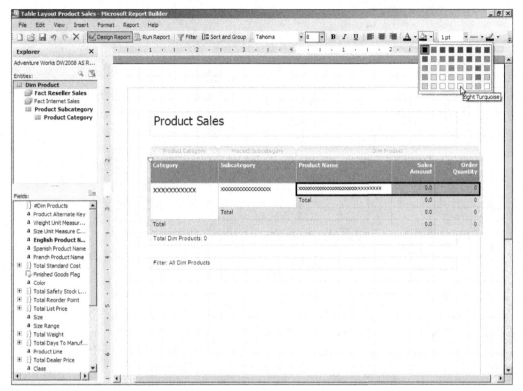

Figure 12-22

There are several formatting features that you can add to your reports. Now that you have given your report a nice look, you need to clean up the data a little. One thing you might have noticed in your report is that some rows come back with no data. There is also no distinct sort order defined in the report. In the next section, you look at how to filter out those empty rows and how to update the sort order.

Filtering and Sorting Reports

Another key set of features for any reporting tool is the ability to filter and sort the data. In this section, you look at removing empty rows from your report, giving users the option to filter the report based on a given time period, and sorting the report alphabetically based on the Product Name.

Filtering Reports

The first thing to do is to remove all the empty data rows. In the Report Builder 1.0 toolbar, you will see a button labeled Filter. Clicking on this button will bring up the Filter Data dialog, as shown in Figure 12-23.

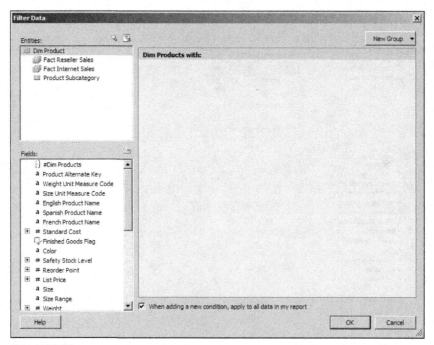

Figure 12-23

There are three main windows within the Filter Data window: Entities, Fields, and the Filter List. The Entities and Fields windows should be familiar from previous sections in this chapter. They contain the data elements and related attributes in the report model. You should notice that your Entities window is already limited to items related to Dim Product, since this is the information contained within your report.

The majority of the filtering functionality will be handled in the Filter List on the right side of the Filter Data dialog. The first item that should be pointed out is the title over the Filter List. In this scenario, it displays the text "Dim Products with." If you click the text, you will be presented with a dropdown list like that shown in Figure 12-24.

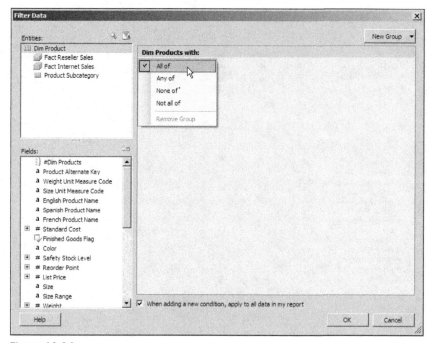

Figure 12-24

The dropdown in Figure 12-24 presents four options:

❏ **All of**   Represents a logical AND condition. All of the expressions in the Filter List must be True to return a result set.

❏ **Any of**   Represents a logical OR condition. If any one of the conditions in the Filter List is True, the data row is returned.

❏ **None of**   Represents a logical exclusive AND condition. If all the conditions are False, the data row is returned.

❏ **Not all of**   Represents a logical exclusive OR condition. If any one of the conditions is True, but not all of them, then the data is returned.

For this scenario, you will use the "All of" option. You will create conditions to test if Sales Amount is not empty and Order Quantity is not empty. If both of those statements are True, you want to return the data row. You will add this filter after examining the other filter types.

An "Any of" report might be something like "Show me all of the sales for people in the United States and Canada." You could add filters to specify "Country" equal to "Canada" or "Country" equal to "United States." "Any of" these two values would be acceptable.

"None of" could be used in a reverse scenario from the previous example. You might want to see sales for people not in the United States or Canada. In that example, you would set filters for "Country" equals "Canada" or "Country" equals "United States." If either of those conditions is True, you would want to remove them from the report.

The last condition, "Not all of," is a little more difficult. Let's say that you want to find customers who purchase only one of a list of products that normally are purchased together. For example, you want to see people who purchase Bikes but not Helmets, or purchase Helmets but not Bikes. In this scenario, you would set filters for "Product" equals "Bikes" or "Product" equals "Helmets" and set the overall condition to "Not all of." Your result set would contain only those people who have purchased one of the products but not both.

Now that you have seen the different conditional statements, you will add the filter for removing empty data rows. There are two elements that you need to test: Sales Amount and Order Quantity. If they are both empty, then you will remove them from the report.

Start by selecting "Fact Reseller Sales" in the Entities window. The Field List now contains the Reseller Sales attributes. Click and drag "Sales Amount" over to the Filter List (large, gray area on the right side of the dialog). You can click the word equals and select "Not." In the textbox to the right of "not equal to," set the value to **0**. You can do the same with "Order Quantity" by dragging it from the Field List to the Filter List.

You should notice that Order Quantity does not have a textbox to enter criteria in. When the report model was generated, it found a small number of unique values for Order Quantity. Because there were a limited number of items, it decided to make it a lookup field. This is probably more appropriate for items like Product, but it does illustrate the point.

To filter out empty Order Quantities, select "equals," and change it to **Is Empty**. Finally, click again on "Is Empty," and select "Not." The resulting filter should look like Figure 12-25.

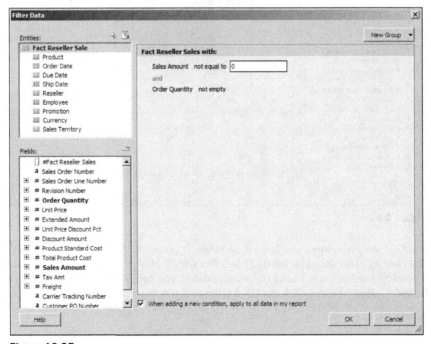

Figure 12-25

441

If you run the report, you should notice that the empty data rows have been removed.

In addition to adding individual filters, you can add groupings. Grouping helps nest logical conditions together. If you click the New Group button in the Filter Data window, you will notice the same four filters outlined above in this section. Within the group, you can then add multiple conditions that are evaluated together.

The second filter you want to add is the ability for the user to select a date range. You will use Order Date in this example. Go back to the report design view, and click on the Filter button. To add the order date, select "Order Date" in the Entities window. You should see a list of attributes related to Order Date. Drag "Full Date Alternate Key" onto the Filter List, and change the condition from "equals" to **On or After**. Since you want a range of dates, you will take Full Date Alternate Key again and drag it into the Filter List, this time changing "equals" to **On or Before**. The final step is to allow the user to select a value. Click either one of the Date filters, and select Prompt from the dropdown. Repeat the same step on the other date. When you have it all set, your Filter List should look like Figure 12-26. Note that you will need to fill in default dates in order for the query to run properly.

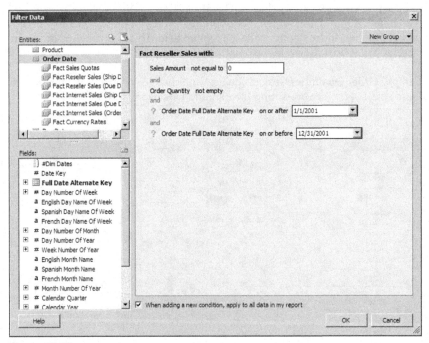

Figure 12-26

For this example, I simply entered in a large date range. If you click the date dropdown list, you will see an item at the bottom of the calendar labeled "Relative Date." Hovering over "Relative Date" exposes a large list of possible time periods. Using the relative dates, you can modify the report to display Product Sales for the last 60 days. You can click the OK button and run the report to see the updated results.

Sorting Reports

The final item to look at in your report is the sort order. It is important in many cases that the user be presented with information that is easily navigable. Right now your report simply shows a list of products in alphabetical order. It might be more useful to show those products with the largest sales amount first.

To add a Sort to your report, first click the Sort and Group button in the Report Builder 1.0 toolbar. When the Sort dialog opens, you should see a listing of all the groups available in a report. In this scenario, you have Product Category, Product Subcategory, and Product.

Within your report, the item that you will be sorting is Product. To sort Products, select Product in the "Select Group" list. For the "Sort by" criteria, you will specify Sales Amount in descending order. Figure 12-27 shows the finished sorting.

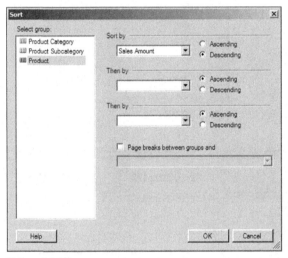

Figure 12-27

You can add multiple sorts for a single item by adding additional values in the Sort dialog. When you run the report, you should notice that within each Product Subcategory, the Products are sorted by Sales Amount in descending order.

You have now seen the core features required to create a report. You've covered the different types of report layouts, adding fields to your reports, formatting numbers, fonts, and backgrounds, and, finally, setting filters and sorting the reports. In the next section, you will look at working with expressions inside reports.

Adding Calculations with Expressions

An advanced feature of Report Builder 1.0 is its ability to add expressions to your reports. Expressions enable you to add custom fields, modify filters, and modify report results. In this section, you look at adding a new custom field to your report. In the process, you will learn about the main areas of the Expression Editor and how they are used.

For this section, you will continue to use the Table Layout Product Sales report. Make sure that the report is open in Design view with the Explorer window and Field List on the left-hand side. Above the Field List is an icon to add new fields. You want to add a field to your report that calculates the Average Price based on Sales Amount divided by Order Quantity. Click on the New Field button, as shown in Figure 12-28, to bring up the Define Formula dialog, as shown in Figure 12-29. Be sure that "Fact Reseller Sale" is selected in the Explorer window.

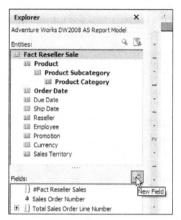

Figure 12-28

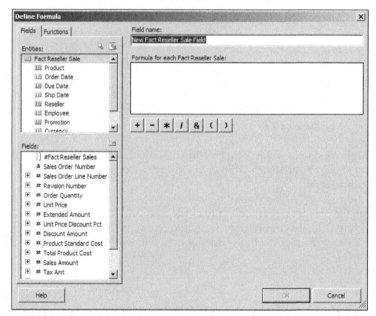

Figure 12-29

The Define Formula dialog has three main sections: Fields, Functions, and the Expression Editor. Fields is the same dialog you have seen throughout Report Builder 1.0. It is broken down into Entities and Fields. The Functions tab presents a list of all available functions within Report Builder 1.0. The functions are grouped by types. Thus, you will find AND, OR, and NOT under the logical folder. As well, you will find AVG, SUM, and COUNT under the aggregate folder. The Expression Editor contains a Field name textbox to define the name of your calculation and the Formula textbox for setting the calculation logic.

To define your expression for Average Price, take the Total Sales Amount (expand the Sales Amount field to see this) divided by the Total Order Quantity (under Order Quantity). It is important that you use the Total and not simply the Sales Amount or Order Quantity. The Total allows you to define your average calculation at different levels without having to rework the formula. Finally, rename the Field name from "New Fact Reseller Sale Field" to **Average Price**. Figure 12-30 shows the completed Average Price calculation.

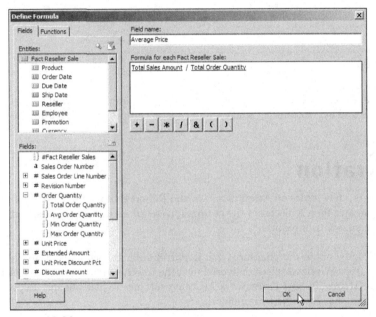

Figure 12-30

Once you have added the formula, you can add it to your report like any other field. Simply click the field in the Field List, and drag it onto the report table. The final layout, including Average Price, should look similar to Figure 12-31.

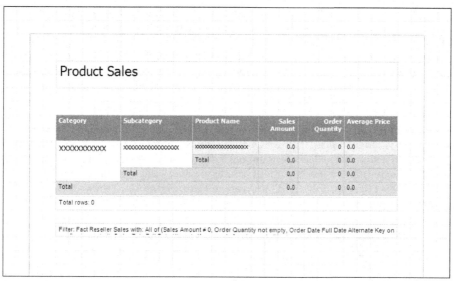

Figure 12-31

Now that you have seen how to create reports with Report Builder 1.0, as well how as to work with formatting, filters and expressions, let's take a look at a few administrative requirements.

Administration

This section covers a few topics on Administration and Report Builder 1.0. First, it looks at the client machine requirements; then it discusses the permissions required to save reports; and finally, it outlines strategies for organizing user reports.

The first thing pointed out in this chapter is that Report Builder 1.0 is not just a simple web application. Report Builder 1.0 is a Windows client delivered over the Internet. To support this functionality, users will have to have Microsoft .NET Framework 2.0. Microsoft has no plans to ship Report Builder 1.0 to support earlier versions of the .NET Framework.

When using Report Builder 1.0, users save reports to the report server. In order to save .rdl files (the structured file created by Report Builder 1.0), a user must have publish permissions. Using Report Manager, you can grant permissions on different folders and set the user role to Publisher. *Publisher* is a default item-level role created when Reporting Services is installed. This role will have sufficient item-level permissions to add and remove reports. However, it also has permissions to create folders, remove models, and to handle a few other tasks that you might not want your users to perform.

If you are concerned about giving users too high a level of permissions, there are two approaches you can use, either independently or together. The first approach is to create your own item-level role. Within the role, you can limit the users' actions to simply managing reports. This will eliminate their ability to move or delete folders, data sources, and other items. If you still want more granular control, you can take advantage of the My Reports feature. This feature can be enabled from either Management Studio or Report Manager. By enabling My Reports, you give the users their own personal folders. They can publish content, add folders, and generally have control over their own small areas in the report server. This feature has been available since Reporting Services 2000; however, there was never a real need for it. With Report Builder 1.0, it has become a much more popular option.

For more information on setting permissions, see Part V, "Administering Reporting Services."

The Future of Report Builder 1.0

As of this writing, Microsoft is working on a new version of Report Builder — Report Builder 2.0 — that will eventually replace the current version of Report Builder 1.0 completely. Report Builder 2.0 will be a completely new application designed to drastically broaden the base of people building custom reports.

In previous versions of SQL Server Reporting Services, users needed to develop full-fledged reports inside a Visual Studio environment. Report Builder 2.0 is planning to change all that by providing a more user-friendly, stand-alone experience. Report Builder 2.0 is being designed from the ground up with the business user in mind and will make use of the Office 2007 Ribbon environment. In fact, Report Builder 2.0 will look and feel just like any other Office 2007 application, such as Word or Excel. In addition to being easy to use, Report Builder 2.0 will have the powerful ability to build reports against report models, relational databases, and OLAP cubes.

In essence, Report Builder 2.0 will have all the report building functionality of the traditional Business Intelligence Development Studio (BIDS) environment. The main difference between Report Builder 2.0 and the BIDS environments will be the target audience. The BIDS environment is targeted at software developers and others who require a full-fledged Integrated Development Environment (IDE) that makes use of software development functionality and techniques such as source control and integration with Team Foundation Server. Report Builder 2.0, on the other hand, will be a stand-alone report-building environment targeting business analysts, managers, and other information workers who need to be able to quickly build data-intensive reports for immediate business knowledge.

Microsoft is designing Report Builder 2.0 and BIDS to use the same report-building code base in order to maintain a parallel report-building experience across both environments. Report Builder 2.0 can be previewed as a separate download.

Summary

In this chapter, you looked at creating ad hoc reports. Ad hoc reports require two major components. First, you need a semantic model that puts your data into a user-friendly form. You saw that Reporting Services 2008 has a report model project that will help you create a user-friendly model. Second, users will need an easy-to-use tool with familiar interfaces. You saw that Report Builder 1.0 provides both a rich user experience and a traditional Microsoft Office–like look and feel.

After reading this chapter, you should have an understanding of:

❑　How to create new reports with Report Builder 1.0

❑　How the different layouts can be used to create interesting reports

❑　How to format report items

❑　How to add filtering and sorting capabilities to your reports

❑　How to add calculations to your reports

❑　Where Report Builder 1.0 is going in the future

Ad hoc reports have been a feature sadly lacking from Reporting Services in the past. It had been our most common reason for implementing competing products. With the introduction of Report Builder 1.0 in SQL Server 2005 Reporting Services, and its continued development into the future, Microsoft has shown that it is committed to building an enterprise-level reporting tool.

Part V

Administering
Reporting Services

Chapter 13: Content Management

Chapter 14: Report Server Administration

13

Content Management

As discussed in Chapter 4, reports are made available through a three-phased process of authoring, management, and delivery. This is referred to as the *reporting life cycle*.

Much of the material in the preceding chapters focused on the authoring phase of the life cycle. This chapter marks the book's transition in focus to the management and delivery phases. The goal of this and many of the subsequent chapters is to show you how to effectively put content you have spent hours, days, or even weeks developing into the hands of your users. All readers, including those primarily focused on report authoring, are encouraged to understand this material.

In this chapter, you explore the management of Reporting Services content. Reporting Services content includes reports, report models, shared data sources, and report resources, as well as the folder structure within which these are maintained. Shared schedules, used by reports for subscriptions, history, and snapshots, are also addressed in this chapter, although these items are maintained at the site level, outside the folder structure.

In Native mode, Reporting Services content management is performed primarily through the Report Manager application. Scripts executed through the RS utility provide an alternative means of performing these tasks.

In SharePoint Integrated mode, content-management activities are performed in a similar manner but through the SharePoint site or through the ReportServer2006 web services endpoint. In this mode, Report Manager and the RS utility are not available.

This chapter focuses on content management in Native mode installations. If you are running in SharePoint Integrated mode, it is important that you understand the concepts explored here and then review the SharePoint-specific aspects addressed in Chapter 16.

This chapter covers:

- ❑ Using Report Manager
- ❑ Content-management activities
- ❑ Item-level security
- ❑ Automating content management

Please note, the examples and screenshots presented in this chapter make use of a Reporting Services site with the Reporting Services samples installed. General instructions on obtaining these are provided in Chapter 3.

Using Report Manager

Report Manager is the primary content-management tool for Reporting Services installations running in Native mode. The application provides an easy-to-use, graphical interface for the navigation of the Reporting Services site. Through Report Manager, various items can be accessed or even altered assuming that you have the appropriate permissions.

For default installations, Report Manager is accessed through the URL `http://servername/reports`. If you are accessing Report Manager from the server on which Reporting Services is installed, you can use `localhost` for the `servername`. Otherwise, provide the IP address or network name for the server. For named instances, use a URL of the form **http://servername/reports_instancename**, with appropriate substitutions for **servername** and **instancename**.

If you are unable to connect to Report Manager using these URLs, verify with your administrator that the application has not been explicitly disabled or that its URL reservation is not configured for an alternate address or non-default port number. If the URL reservation has been altered, you can use Reporting Services Configuration Manager to obtain an alternative URL for Report Manager, as described in the next chapter.

Once you first connect to Report Manager, you are presented with the Contents page of the Home folder (see Figure 13-1). A number of Report Manager's basic features are on display through this page.

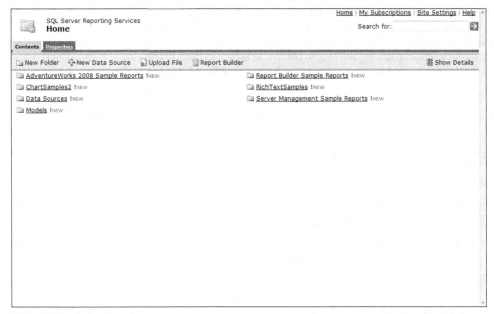

Figure 13-1

At the top of the page is the header. The header provides navigational assistance and access to site-level functionality.

In the far left corner of the header, you see the name of the current item in bold and an icon for the item type. By clicking on the "AdventureWorks 2008 Sample Reports" folder item, in the body of the page, you enter this folder, and the name in bold changes appropriately, as illustrated in Figure 13-2.

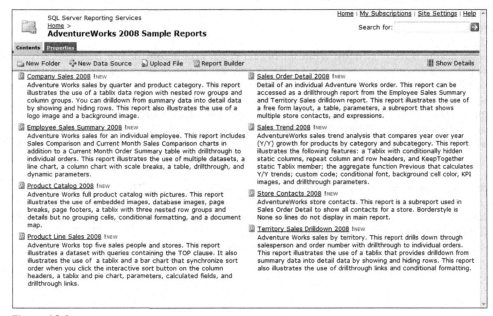

Figure 13-2

Notice in Figure 13-2 that a delimited list has appeared just above the name in bold. This list identifies the current item's path within the folder hierarchy. Each entry in the list is a link to the identified folder. As the AdventureWorks 2008 Sample Reports folder exists just below the Home folder, this list contains just one entry, *Home*. Clicking the Home entry will take you back to the Home folder. The header for the Home folder does not present this delimited list because the Home folder represents the site's root.

On the right-hand side of the header, you will notice a series of links. Which links appear depends on your rights on the system. The following table identifies potentially available links:

Link	Description
Home	This link takes you to the Content page of the Home folder.
My Subscriptions	This link takes you to the My Subscriptions site-level page. This page displays all subscriptions on the site that you own.
Site Settings	This link provides access to the Site Settings pages. From these pages, you can modify general site-level settings, site-level security, and shared schedules.
Help	This link opens a separate browser window displaying the Report Manager Help and Support pages.

Just below these links is a Search box. By entering text in the box and clicking the green button to its right, Report Manager performs a case-insensitive search for items with names and descriptions matching the text you entered. The search, as presented through Report Manager, does not support wildcards or Boolean operators.

> *The Search feature calls the* FindItems *method of the* ReportService2005 *class.* FindItems *supports more complex searches, including the use of Boolean operators and wildcards. In addition,* FindItems *supports the search of a wider range of item properties, not just the name and description properties.*

Below the header is the page body. While the header varies little across the site, the page body varies significantly. As you access various types of items, you will notice type-specific pages presented within the page body. Depending on the type of item engaged, you may be provided access to one or more pages through which you can access various properties of that item. Pages are accessed by first selecting a particular item. That item's default page is presented, with other pages accessible through tabs across the top of the page's body. Tabs provide access to one or more related pages associated with the item. If more than one page is supported within a tab, a list appears on the left-hand side of the page body for accessing these.

Figure 13-3 shows the General Properties page of the AdventureWorks 2008 Sample Reports folder. This page is accessed by selecting the "AdventureWorks 2008 Sample Reports" folder and then clicking its Properties tab. The Properties tab supports a General Properties page and a Security Properties page. The General Properties page is the default for this tab.

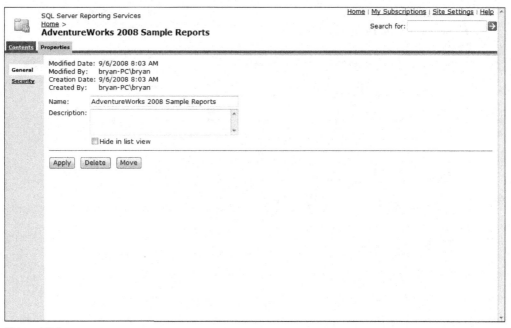

Figure 13-3

Folders support both a Properties tab and a Contents tab. Clicking the Contents tab of the AdventureWorks 2008 Sample Reports folder takes you to the folder's Contents page (refer to Figure 13-2).

The Contents page is the default page of a folder item. Notice that items in this folder are presented in a two-column list. This is referred to the folder Contents page's List view or simply the folder's List view.

Clicking the Show Details button in the gray bar above the list takes you into the folder Contents page's detail view. Notice in Figure 13-4 that the page has been reloaded with content displayed in a tabular format. Also notice more options are available through the gray bar.

> *Notice, too, that the Show Details button now displays the text* Hide Details. *Clicking on the Hide Details button will return you to the Contents page's List view layout.*

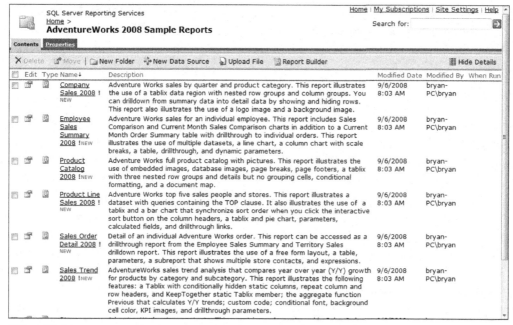

Figure 13-4

The gray bar is used to provide access to various actions throughout the Report Manager application. Notice in the screenshot of Figure 13.4 that the Delete and Move buttons are disabled. Many buttons on the gray bar are disabled until one or more items on the page are selected. Items are selected by clicking the checkbox to their left. Select All functionality is provided by the checkbox in the table heading.

Tables, such as this one, are a frequently used display mechanism in Report Manager. The topmost line of the table identifies Field names, while the lines below represent individual items.

Many tables allow you to sort their contents by clicking individual fields. Not all fields are sortable, but you can easily identify which are by placing your cursor just above a Field name and observing the cursor's icon switch to indicate that a link is present.

Content-Management Activities

Now that you are familiar with Report Manager basics, it's time to take a look at the management of various Reporting Services items through the application. If you skipped over the previous section of this chapter, please review it quickly so that you are familiar with the terminology used here.

In this section of the chapter, you will explore the management of:

❑   Folders

❑   Shared data sources

❑   Report models

- ❏   Reports
- ❏   Report resources
- ❏   Shared schedules

Folders

Most Reporting Services items are housed within a folder hierarchy. This provides a simple, familiar structure for organizing content.

The folder hierarchy is a virtual structure — that is, you will not find it re-created on a Reporting Services server's drives. Instead, the structure exists as a set of self-referencing records in the ReportServer database.

The root of the folder hierarchy is the Home folder. This folder is often denoted by the forward-slash symbol, /. When you first open Report Manager, the Home folder is the folder with which you are first presented.

> *The Home folder is a special folder within Reporting Services. It cannot be moved, modified, or deleted. Other special folders include the My Reports and User Folders folders, which are discussed in Chapter 14 as part of the My Reports feature. Your ability to alter these folders is also limited.*

The default page for the Home folder and every folder in Reporting Services is the Contents page. On the Contents page, items within the folder including any child folders are presented in a double-column list. This is referred to as the folder's *List view* and is illustrated in Figure 13-5.

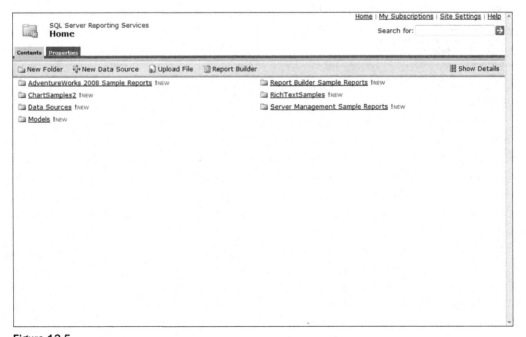

Figure 13-5

In the List view, items are identified by name, an optional description, and an icon denoting the item's type. Types and associated icons are presented in the following table:

Icon	Type
	Folder
	Report
	Linked report
	Report model
	Shared data source
	Resource
	Standard subscriptions
	Data-driven subscriptions

The gray bar at the top of the folder Contents page list presents buttons for creating new folders and shared data sources and uploading items to the folder. You will explore the creation of new shared data sources and upload of items below in this section of this chapter. Of interest now is the New Folder button.

Clicking on the New Folder button takes you to the New Folder page, as shown in Figure 13-6. On this page, you enter a name and a description for your new folder. Selecting the "Hide in list view" option makes the folder hidden in its parent folder's List view.

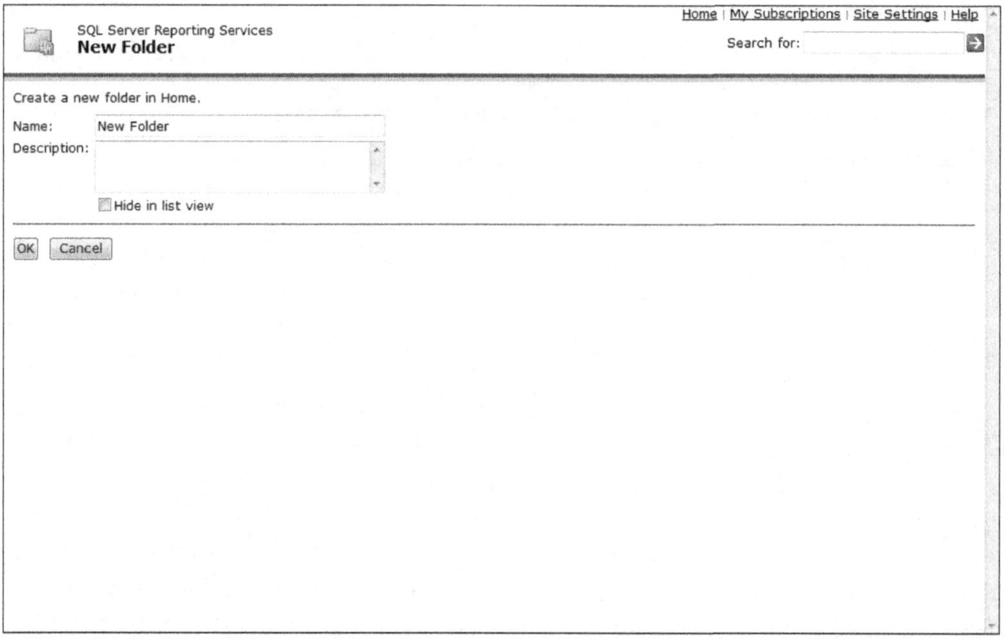

Figure 13-6

Clicking OK submits the request to create the new folder. If a folder or other item with the same name already exists under the parent folder, an error message is presented. If the request is successful, you are taken back to the Contents page of the parent folder from which you originally clicked the New Folder button, as shown in Figure 13-7.

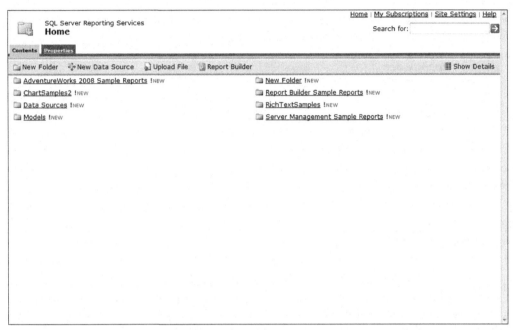

Figure 13-7

If the folder is configured to be hidden in the List view, you will need to switch to the parent folder's Detail view in order to see the new folder. To switch to the Detail view, click on the Show Details button in the gray bar.

To switch back to the List view, click the Hide Details button presented in the Detail view's gray bar.

In Detail view, as shown in Figure 13-8, all the folder's contents are displayed in a tabular format, as discussed in the previous section of this chapter. The table supports Edit, Type, Name, Description, Modified Date, Modified By, and When Run fields, with all but the Edit field being sortable. The default sort is by name, as indicated by the small arrow to the right of the Name field heading.

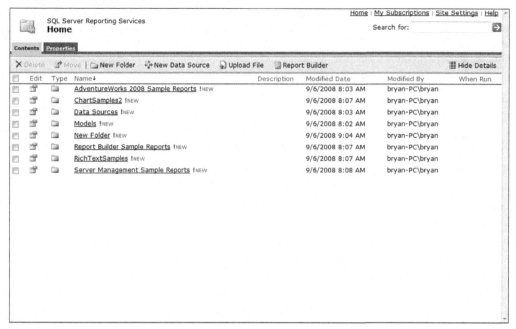

Figure 13-8

Clicking on an individual item's Edit icon takes you to that item's General Properties page. Clicking on an item's Type icon or its name will take you to that item's default page. For reports and reporting resources, the default page is the View page. For folders, the default page is the Contents page in List mode. For all other items, the default page is the General Properties page.

While in the Detail view of a folder's Contents page, selecting the checkbox to the left of one or more items enables the Delete and Move buttons along the gray bar. The Delete button confirms and then drops the items you have selected. The Move button takes you to the Move Items page, which requires you to select where in the site's folder structure the items are to be moved. If you are deleting or moving a folder, the operation will succeed only if you have the required permissions on each item that it contains.

A folder can also be deleted or moved through buttons presented at the bottom of its General Properties page. This page is accessed by clicking the Edit icon to the left of a folder in the Detail view or by selecting the Properties tab of the current folder. It's important to note that this page is not available for the special folders Home, My Reports, and User Folders. Figure 13-9 presents the General Properties page of the AdventureWorks 2008 Sample Reports folder.

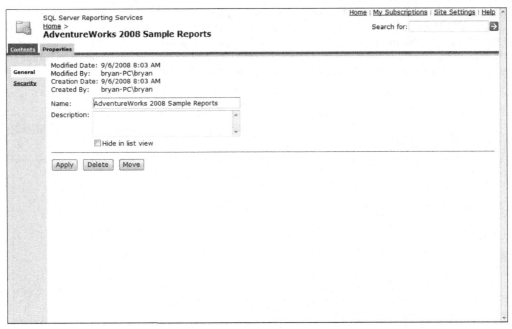

Figure 13-9

So, now that you know how to create, alter, and remove folders, what kind of folder structure should you build for your site? There are a variety of well-reasoned opinions on this subject, providing guidance on naming conventions, standard folder locations, and the balance of the breadth and width of the site's folder hierarchy.

However you ultimately decide to organize your site, our recommendation is that it be driven by a set of guidelines adopted in advance of site construction. In developing those guidelines, it is further recommended you keep the end-user experience at the forefront of your thought process and you consider the maintenance and security implications of your scheme. (Security is discussed below in this chapter.) The guidelines should be reviewed with administrators, report developers, and end-user representatives to not only obtain support but to begin the process of educating those who will be working within this structure.

Shared Data Sources

Shared data sources hold connection information in a secure manner, allowing this information to be centrally administered while being shared among reports and report models throughout the site.

Shared data sources are often created by report authors as part of the report development process in BIDS, as described in Chapter 7. However, Report Manager provides functionality for you to create shared data sources directly within the site. To do this, open Report Manager, and navigate to the folder within which the item will be housed. If you have installed the Reporting Services samples, you will notice a folder called *Data Sources* under the Home folder within which sample shared data sources are stored.

Click on the New Data Source button located on the gray bar of the folder's Contents page. In the resulting New Data Source page, shown in Figure 13-10, enter a name and description for the new item. Set the options that control whether the item is displayed in its parent folder's Contents page List view and/or enabled for use on the site. Then select the registered data extension to be used and enter an appropriate connection string. Which data extension you select determines the syntax of the connection string.

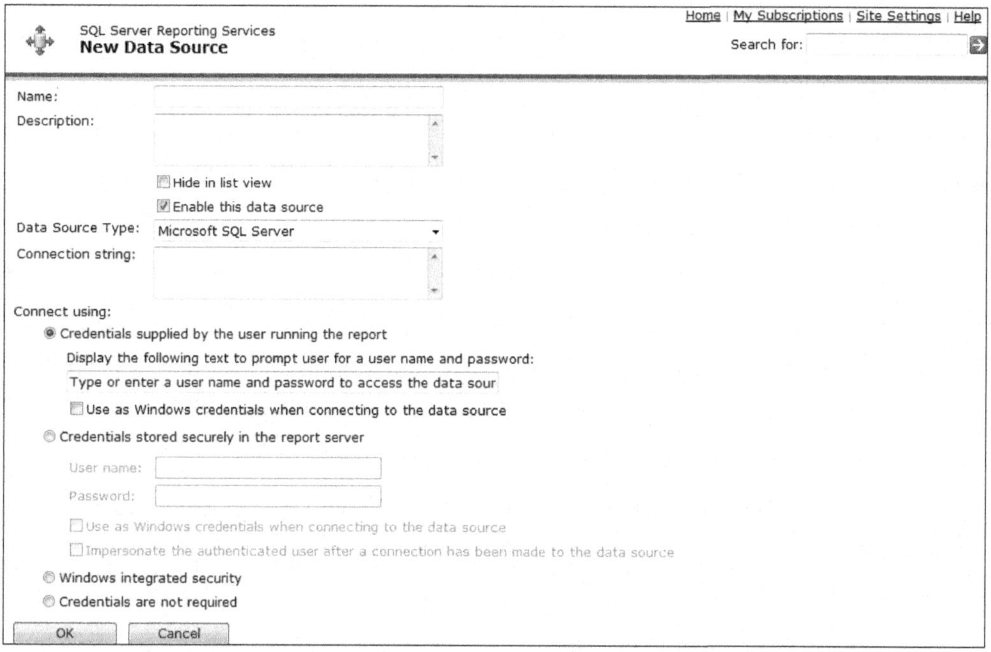

Figure 13-10

It is important to note that Report Manager does not verify the connection string you enter. Unless you have an existing connection string or are very familiar with connection string syntax, you will likely not want to use this feature of Report Manager for creating shared data sources.

Below the connection string, set the security context to be used when establishing the connection. You are provided with the following four basic options, with many of these supporting one or more variations:

❑ **Credentials Supplied by the User Running the Report** — This option allows you to configure a prompt to be presented to the user. The checkbox associated with this option instructs Reporting Services whether to treat these as Windows user credentials.

❑ **Credentials Stored Securely in the Report Server** — This option allows you to enter a username/password combination, which will be encrypted and stored in the primary Reporting Services application database. Again, an option is presented to have Reporting Services treat these as Windows or source-specific credentials. The associated "Impersonate the authenticated user after a connection has been made to the data source" option allows database user impersonation to be employed after the connection has been established. This option provides support for the use of SETUSER functionality within SQL Server.

❑ **Windows Integrated Security** — This option allows the user to be impersonated when making the connection to the external data source. In order for this feature to work, the external data source must be local to the Reporting Services server, or Kerberos must be enabled on the domain. In addition, the Reporting Services server must not have been reconfigured following installation to disable integrated security.

❑ **Credentials Are Not Required** — This option instructs Reporting Services to use the unattended execution account when establishing the connection. This account is not enabled by default and is not recommended for use against most data sources. Whether or not the unattended execution account is enabled, this option is displayed. If you attempt to leverage a data source with this option set and the unattended execution account is not enabled, you will receive an error indicating an invalid data source credential setting. The unattended execution account is covered in more detail in Chapter 14.

Clicking OK creates the data source item and displays it in its folder's Contents page. Clicking on the new shared data source item takes you to its General Properties page, where all the options discussed above can be altered.

In addition, the General Properties page allows the data source to be moved, renamed, or deleted. Moving or renaming a shared data source has no impact on the Reporting Services items referencing it. However, deleting a shared data source will break the reports, report models, and subscriptions dependent on it. To view those items referencing the shared data source prior to deleting it, click the shared data source's Dependent Items and Subscriptions tabs. If the shared data source is deleted, those items listed on these pages will be broken until they are pointed to a new data source.

The shared data source General Properties page also presents a Generate Model button. Use of this button is discussed in the following section.

Report Models

Report models provide the data layer for ad hoc reporting. They record metadata about the structures of an external data source in a manner that makes interaction with these easier for less-technical users. In Reporting Services 2008, report models support SQL Server, Analysis Services, and Oracle (9.2.0.3 or later) data sources. A report model typically is constructed through a Report Model project in BIDS, as described in Chapter 11. Like shared data sources, report models can also be created through Report Manager, although you will have less control over the structure of the model with this approach.

To create a report model within Report Manager, locate a SQL Server, Analysis Services, or Oracle shared data source on the site. In the following screenshots, this is being done using the Adventure Works shared data source within the Data Sources folder created by the Reporting Services samples.

The AdventureWorks2008 database makes use of data types for primary keys that are not supported within report models. Attempting to generate a model with Report Manager using the AdventureWorks2008 shared data source that references the AdventureWorks2008 database will result in an error. For this reason, the model generated in the following screenshots is based on the Adventure Works shared data source that references the Adventure Works 2005 database. This database is available as a sample database for SQL Server 2008 from the CodePlex web site. Its installers are SQL2008.

AdventureWorks_DW_BI_v2005.x86.msi (32-bit), SQL2008.AdventureWorks_DW_BI_v2005.x64
.msi (x64 64-bit), and SQL2008.AdventureWorks_DW_BI_v2005.ia64.msi (IA64 64-bit).

Clicking on a shared data source takes you to its General Properties page. On this page, verify that the
data source makes use of stored credentials or Windows Integrated Security, as shown in Figure 13-11.

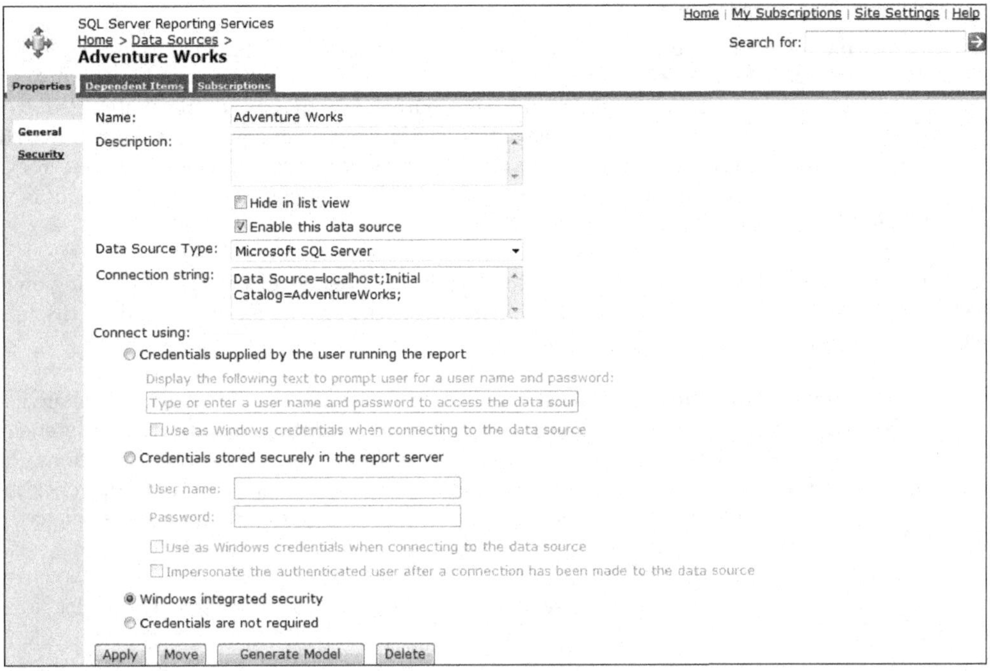

Figure 13-11

Notice the Generate Model button at the bottom of this page. Click on this button to open the New
Model page shown in Figure 13-12. On this page, enter a name and description for your model.

Figure 13-12

The folder within which the new report model will be placed is identified just below the description. If you want to place the model somewhere else on the site, use the Change Location button to set an alternative location.

Clicking OK starts the model generation process. Depending on the data source used, model generation can be an intensive process, taking quite a bit of time to complete. Once completed, you are presented with the new report model's General Properties page, as shown in Figure 13-13.

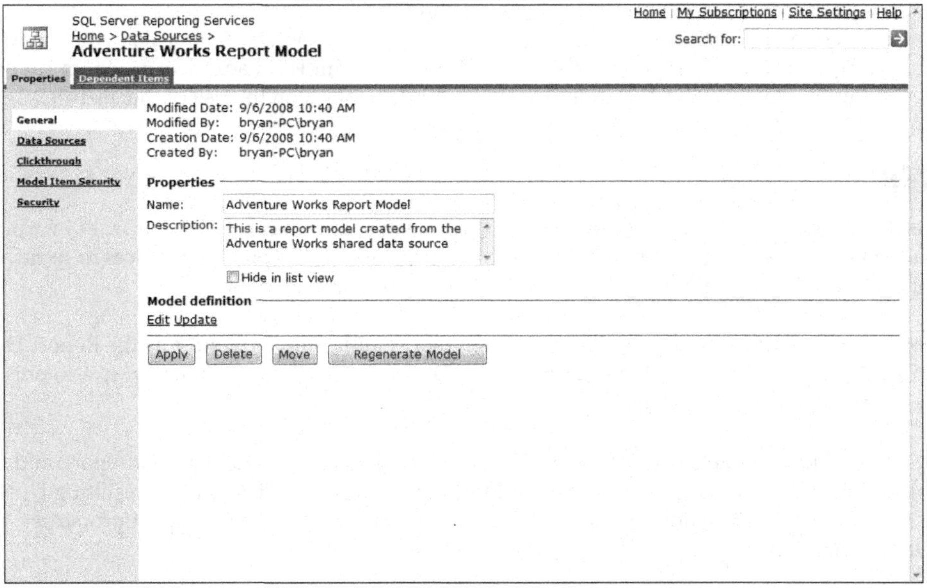

Figure 13-13

From the report model's General Properties page, you can edit its properties and apply basic item management. Before deleting a report model, be sure to review the Dependent Items and Subscriptions pages to identify which Reporting Services items will be affected by this operation.

The model's General Properties page also provides functionality to regenerate the model. You will need to regenerate the model when structural changes have occurred in the external data source that need to be reflected in the model. As with generation, model regeneration can take quite a bit of time to complete.

If a report model is in use when you attempt to regenerate it, an error will occur. To prevent this, access the General Properties page of the shared data source used by the model as shown in Figure 13-11. De-select the "Enable this data source" option, and submit the change. Once model regeneration is completed, re-enable the data source.

The report model's General Properties page also provides access to the model's definition. Clicking the Edit link returns an SMDL file that you can add to a BIDS Report Model project for modification. Any changes made to this definition will need to be deployed from BIDS.

In addition to the General Properties page, Report Manager provides the following Properties pages for the management of report models:

- ❑ The Data Sources Properties page enables you to select the data source used by the report model. As stated above, report models are limited to SQL Server, Analysis Services, and Oracle 9.2.0.3 (or later), and must use stored credentials or Windows Integrated Authentication.

- ❑ The Clickthrough Properties page enables you to replace the pages that Report Builder generates when users click on interactive data elements in reports based on report models. Through this interface, you can specify which custom reports are used when one or multiple elements are engaged.

- ❑ The Model Item Security Properties page enables you to specify a finer level of access to data provided through the report model. By enabling the "Secure individual model items independently for this model" option, you can then select which model elements inherit permissions from their parent items and which will grant Read access to a custom list of groups and users. Books Online provides much more information on the use of this feature.

Reports

Reports present data to end-users in an easy-to-consume manner. They consist of a set of instructions encoded in Report Definition Language (RDL) that is processed by Reporting Services to retrieve data from one or more sources and present this data in various report elements.

Reports are typically created and deployed through report authoring tools such as the Report Designer in BIDS or Report Builder. If you have access to an RDL file, you can deploy a report to a Reporting Services site using Report Manager.

To do this, open the Contents page of the folder within which you wish to place the report, and click on the Upload File button on the gray bar of the folder's Contents page. Through the resulting Upload File page, shown in Figure 13-14, identify the RDL file for the report, set the basic report properties, and then click OK to upload the file.

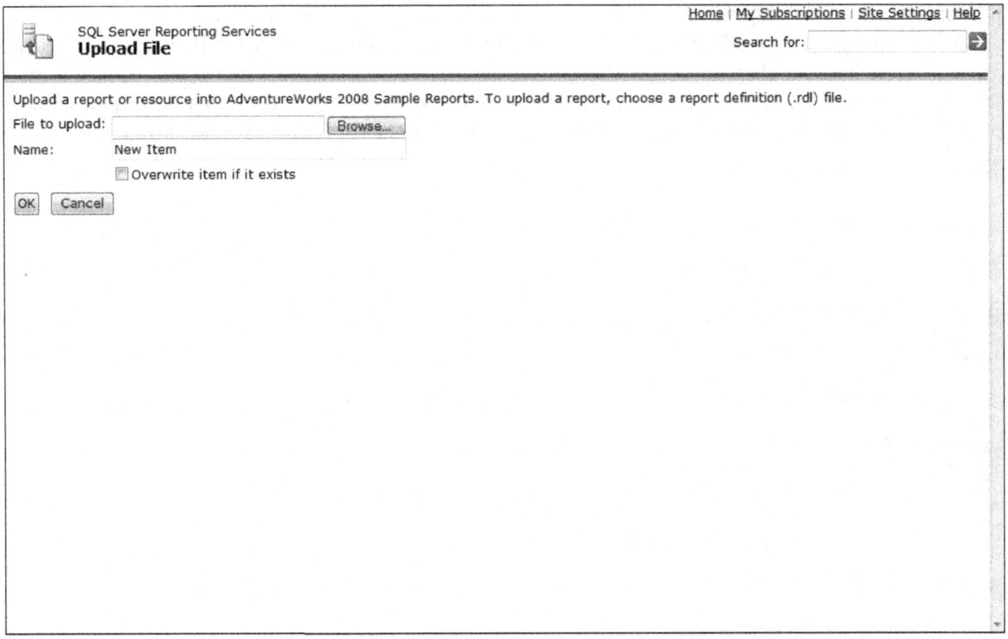

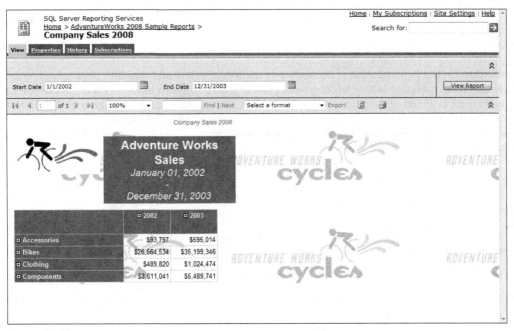

Figure 13-14

Clicking on a report item in Report Manager takes you to its View page. The View page presents an HTML-rendered version of the report (see Figure 13-15). It's a good idea to review your report here after publication to identify any discrepancies between the published report and how it was presented in the Preview mode of your report authoring tool.

Figure 13-15

Clicking on a report's Properties tab takes you to its General Properties page, where you can set the report's basic properties (see Figure 13-16). The Edit link located halfway down the page just below the line labeled "Report Definition" returns the report's RDL file, and the Update link provides another means to upload the RDL file for this report. The Delete and Move buttons do just what you would expect. Deleting a report removes any subscriptions and history for it and orphans any linked reports built off it.

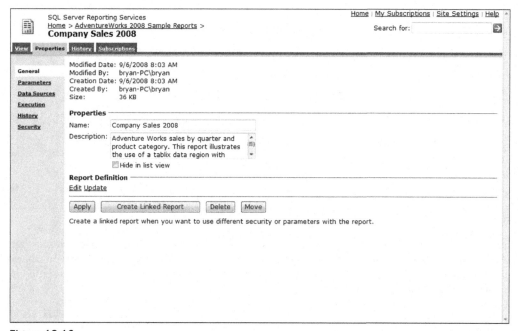

Figure 13-16

The Create Linked Report button at the bottom of the report's General Properties page takes you to the New Linked Report page within which you can create and configure a linked report. You can think of a linked report as a kind of shortcut to a standard report, except that you can configure the linked report's properties differently from those of the report that it references. This includes setting alternative parameter, execution, and security properties. The only thing you cannot configure differently from the base report is the data source to be used.

If a report, linked or otherwise, has parameters, a Parameters properties page is available (see Figure 13-17). On this page, you can set the default value, nullability, visibility, and prompt settings for each report parameter. These settings can be different from those specified during the report authoring phase.

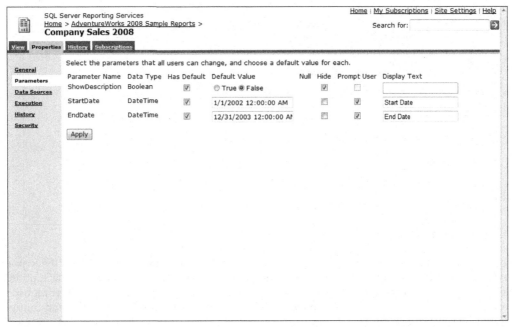

Figure 13-17

If a report makes use of a data source (as most will), the Data Sources properties page is available (see Figure 13-18). On this page, you can configure the report-specific and shared data sources used by a report. You can also swap out report-specific and shared data sources in use by the report. Again, this page is not available for linked reports.

In the sample report displayed below, the data source has been switched from a shared data source to a report-specific data source. This has been done so that modifications to the report's data source, required to support report history, do not affect other sample reports.

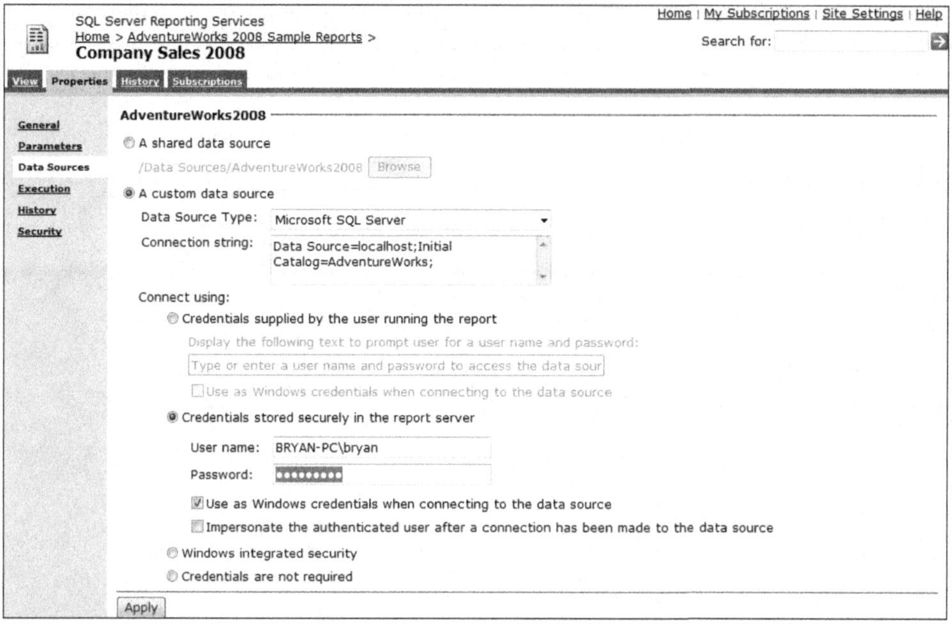

Figure 13-18

The Execution Properties tab, shown in Figure 13-19, is used to configure a report's use of the Reporting Services caching features. By default, the "Always run this report with the most recent data" option is selected. If the "Do not cache temporary copies of this report" suboption is selected, neither report execution caching nor snapshots are employed. (Session caching, discussed in Chapter 4 and configured at the site level, is still in effect.)

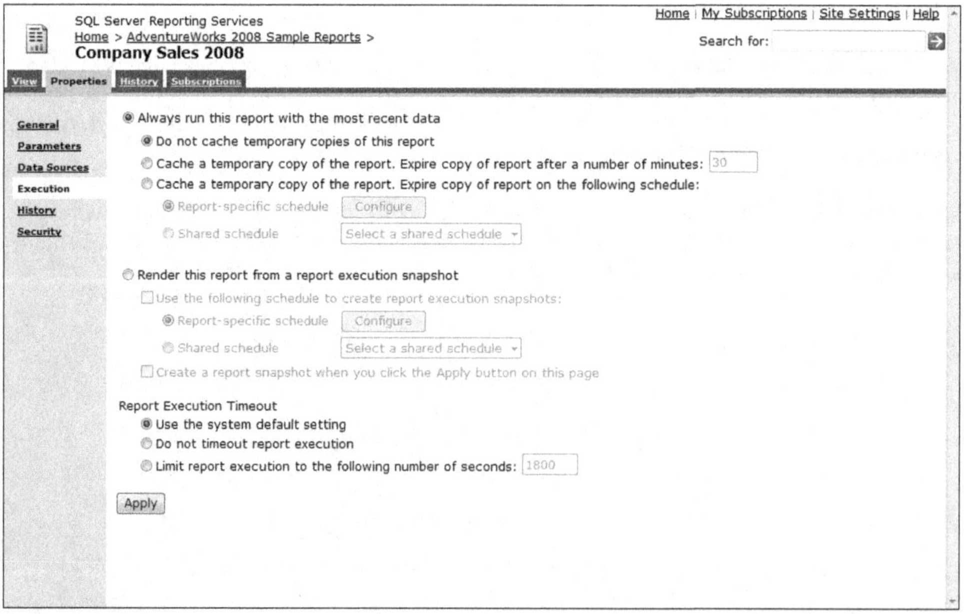

Figure 13-19

Selecting the "Cache a temporary copy of the report" suboptions enables report execution caching. With either of these options set, a copy of the report is cached when the report is run, unless a valid cached copy already exists. That cached copy is held in the ReportServerTempDB database to fulfill subsequent requests until the cache expires. The first of the two "Cache a temporary copy of the report" options instructs Reporting Services to expire the cached copy after a fixed number of minutes. The second option instructs Reporting Services to expire the cached copy at a fixed point in time. The second option allows you to set a report-specific schedule or to use a shared schedule.

The set of suboptions under the "Render this report from a report execution snapshot" option instruct Reporting Services to create and render the report from a snapshot. The snapshot is a scheduled execution of the report. Snapshots eliminate the potentially long run times experienced by the first user of a report once a cached copy has expired. You can specify a report-specific or shared schedule for the timing of the snapshot and can elect to run the snapshot immediately following its configuration. The snapshot will remain valid until the next snapshot is executed.

> *To leverage either report execution caching or snapshots, the report must make use of data sources with cached credentials. The reason behind this is discussed in Chapter 4.*

If a report contains parameters, default values for each of these must be specified for the snapshot. This can limit your ability to make use of snapshots as an execution option. However, the well-thought-out use of dataset filters can allow you to make wider use of a report snapshot. Chapter 7 provides more details on this technique.

The bottom of the Execution Properties page contains settings affecting report execution time-out. The default for a report is to use the system-level setting (which is set to a default value of 1,800 seconds). The "Do not timeout report execution" option specifies that the report will not time out, whereas the "Limit report execution to the following number of seconds" option allows you to specify a report-specific time-out, overriding the system-level setting.

It is generally recommended that you make use of an execution time-out, whether system- or report-specific. The time-out should be sufficient for data to be retrieved and the report to be fully rendered. If you find that you must set long time-outs for your report, consider the use of caching or snapshots as well as the use of subscription features — unless you want your users staring at their screens waiting for the report to render.

Next, the History Properties page is used to configure how report history is maintained within the ReportServer database (see Figure 13-20). The "Allow report history to be created manually" option instructs Reporting Services to allow snapshots to be generated upon demand and cached within report history. (In Report Manager, this is reflected by the presentation of a New Snapshot button in the gray bar on this History page, discussed below.)

> *For a report to support history, its data sources must make use of stored credentials, and all parameters must have been assigned default values. The sample report shown in Figure 13-20 has been modified as described above to meet these criteria.*

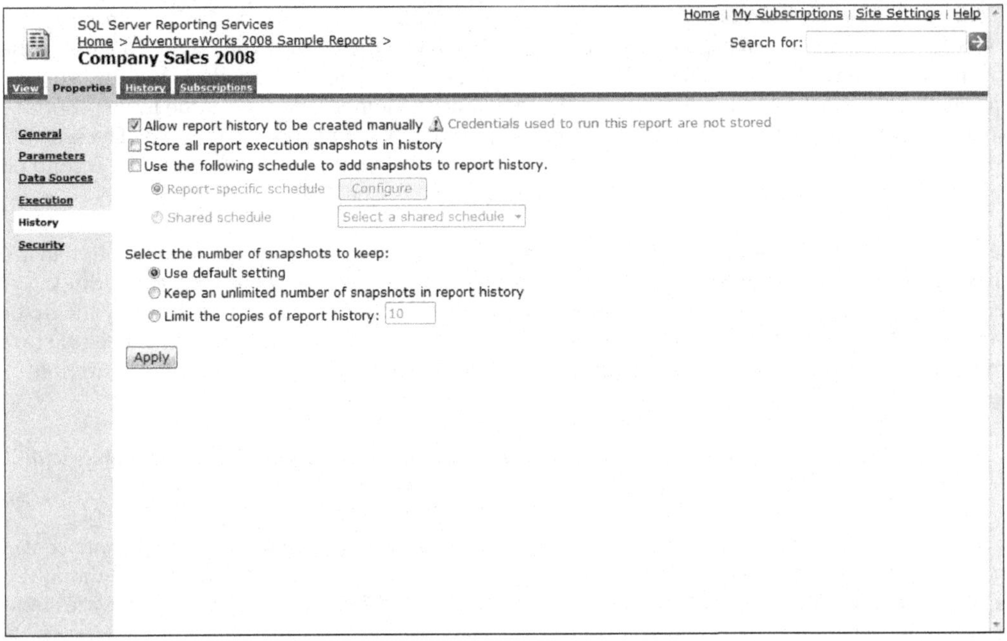

Figure 13-20

The "Store all report execution snapshots in history" option stores all snapshots configured in the Execution Properties page as part of the report history. The "Use the following schedule to add snapshots to report history" option allows you to configure an alternative schedule for recording snapshots to history.

The storage of report history can start to add up within the ReportServer database. The History Properties page provides a set of options to limit the number of historical snapshots maintained for a report. The "Use default setting" option instructs Reporting Services to retain history for this report according to the site-level history setting. This setting has a default value of 10 days. The other two options override the site-level setting with a report-specific value, allowing you to keep history indefinitely or for simply an alternative number of days.

To actually see historical snapshots for a report, navigate to the History page by clicking the report's History tab. Report snapshots stored in history are presented here in a detailed, tabular view, as shown in Figure 13-21.

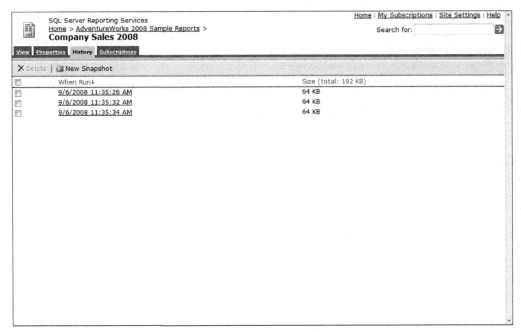

Figure 13-21

If you enabled the "Allow report history to be created manually" option on the History Properties page, you can manually generate a snapshot by clicking the New Snapshot button along the gray bar. Note that in Figure 13-21, manual snapshots have been generated for illustration purposes.

The When Run value associated with each snapshot enables you to see a copy of the report rendered using the selected snapshot. You can remove a snapshot from history by clicking the checkbox to the far left of an item and then clicking on the Delete button in the gray bar above the table.

Clicking the Subscriptions tab opens the report Subscriptions page. On this page, existing subscriptions associated with the report are presented in a sortable table (see Figure 13-22).

In Figure 13-22, two subscriptions are displayed for illustration purposes. These are not automatically created for the Reporting Services samples.

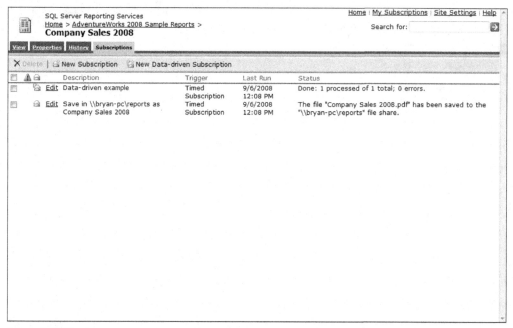

Figure 13-22

Clicking on the New Subscription button allows you to set up a new standard subscription. On the New Subscription page, you specify the subscription delivery mechanism for the report, which then determines what additional information is needed. The settings for both e-mail and file share subscription delivery are identified in the following table:

Delivery Method	Setting	Description
e-mail	To	A semicolon-delimited list of e-mail addresses to which the report will be delivered. These addresses will be listed on the *To* line of the e-mail message.
	Cc	A semicolon-delimited list of e-mail addresses to which the report will be delivered. These addresses will be listed on the *Cc* line of the e-mail message.
	Bcc	A semicolon-delimited list of e-mail addresses to which the report will be delivered. These addresses will not be listed in the e-mail message.
	Reply-To	The e-mail address to which replies should be directed.
	Subject	The subject line of the e-mail message. The default subject line includes two variables that will be replaced with appropriate values at the time of execution.

Delivery Method	Setting	Description
	Include Report	Indicates whether the report should be rendered and included in the e-mail message.
	Render Format	Specifies the format to which the report should be rendered if it is to be included in the e-mail message. If you specify "Web Archive," the report is embedded in the message body. For any other format, the report is included as an attachment.
	Include Link	Indicates whether a link to the report on the Reporting Services site should be included in the e-mail message.
	Priority	Indicates the flag to be used for the message importance.
	Comment	A message to be included in the body of the e-mail message.
Windows File Share	File Name	The name of the file to deliver. You can supply an extension or select the "Add a file extension when a file is created" option to add an extension based on the rendering format selected below.
	Path	The UNC path of the folder to which the file will be delivered.
	Render Format	A rendering format selected from a dropdown list of those available on the site.
	Credentials Used to Access the File Share	The username and password combination used as credentials when accessing the file share specified in the Path setting.
	Overwrite Options	One of three options indicating how to respond to the existence of a file with the name identified in the File Name setting. Options allow the file to be overwritten, the subscription to fail if the file exists, or the file to be written to the share but under a name with a sequential, numeric value appended.

Below the delivery method options are the subscription processing options. These determine whether the subscription is delivered based on a subscription-specific or shared schedule. If the report includes parameters, values for these are entered in the Report Parameter Values section at the bottom of the New Subscription page. Clicking OK creates the new subscription.

Clicking the New Data-Driven Subscription button from the report Subscriptions page opens the Create Data-Driven Subscription Step 1 page, as shown in Figure 13-23, where you give the subscription a name and identify its delivery type. All subscribers of this data-driven subscription will make use of this delivery method.

Figure 13-23

The Step 1 page requires you to specify the data source through which subscription data will be retrieved. You can use a shared data source or elect to create a subscription-specific data source. The data source is then either selected or configured on the Step 2 page. The configuration of a new data source is illustrated in Figure 13-24.

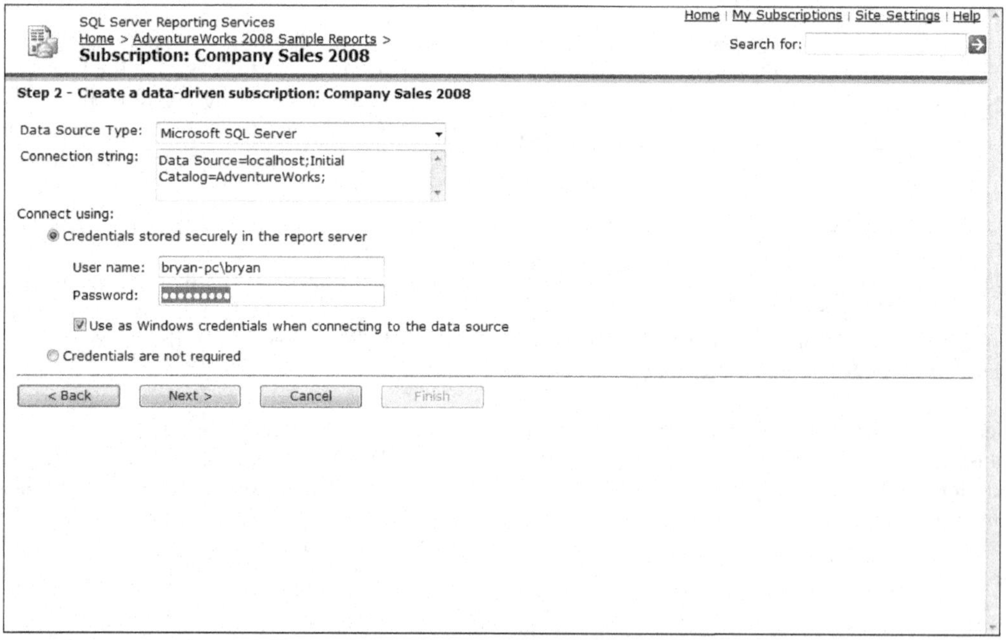

Figure 13-24

On the Step 3 page, shown in Figure 13-25, you enter a query that retrieves the information required by the subscription, along with a time-out. What information is required depends on how you intend to map fields to various options in the next step. A list of delivery method settings and report parameters is provided toward the middle of the page to assist you in developing your query.

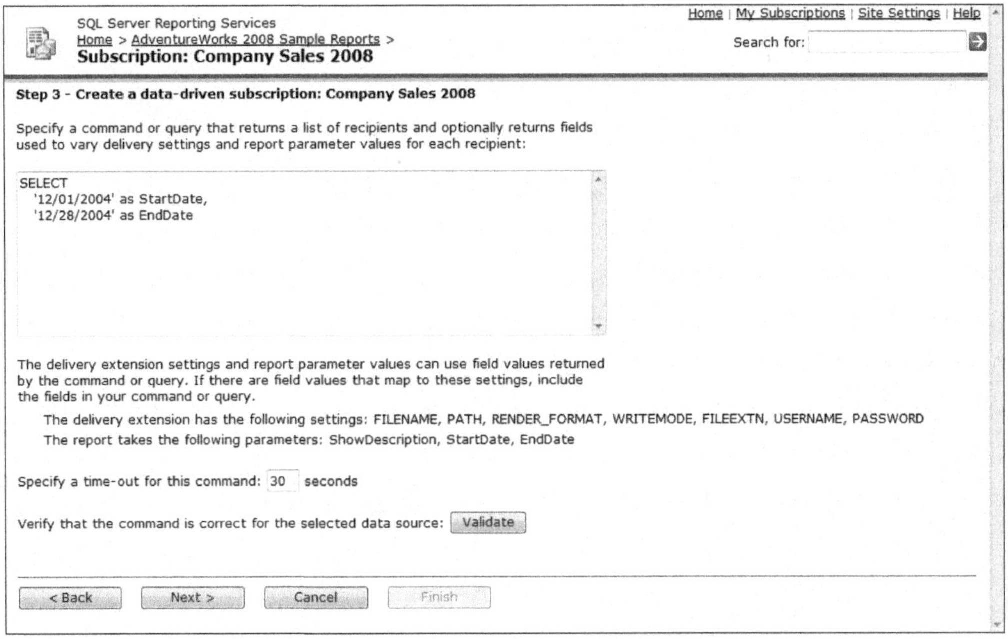

Figure 13-25

In Figure 13-25, a query is configured with hard-coded values for report parameters. Typically, you will create a table in a relational database recording various values used to drive your reports.

Toward the bottom of the Step 3 page, you can specify the query time-out and use the Validate button to test your query against the data source. Clicking on the Next button automatically validates the query before taking you to the Step 4 page.

On the Step 4 page, as shown in Figure 13-26, you map delivery method settings to fields returned by your query. Alternatively, you can map these settings to constants or, in some cases, elect to provide no value.

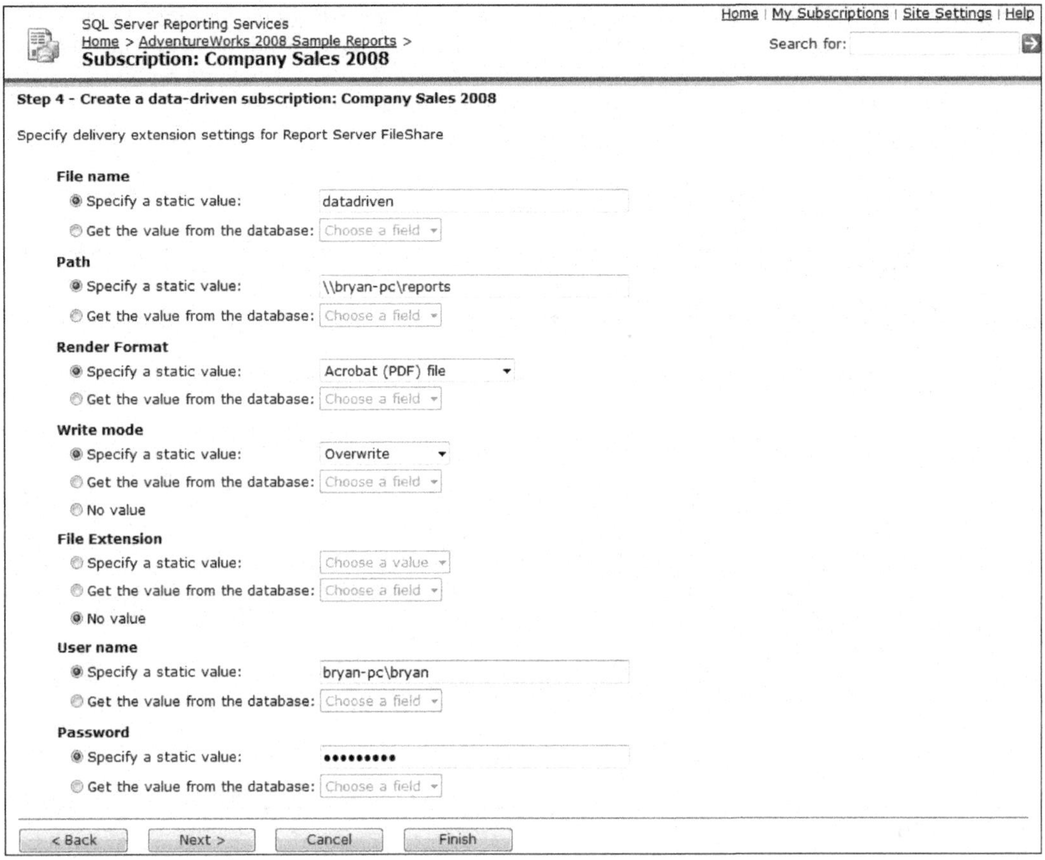

SQL Server Reporting Services
Home > AdventureWorks 2008 Sample Reports >
Subscription: Company Sales 2008

Search for:

Step 4 - Create a data-driven subscription: Company Sales 2008

Specify delivery extension settings for Report Server FileShare

File name
- ⦿ Specify a static value: datadriven
- ○ Get the value from the database: Choose a field ▾

Path
- ⦿ Specify a static value: \\bryan-pc\reports
- ○ Get the value from the database: Choose a field ▾

Render Format
- ⦿ Specify a static value: Acrobat (PDF) file ▾
- ○ Get the value from the database: Choose a field ▾

Write mode
- ⦿ Specify a static value: Overwrite ▾
- ○ Get the value from the database: Choose a field ▾
- ○ No value

File Extension
- ○ Specify a static value: Choose a value ▾
- ○ Get the value from the database: Choose a field ▾
- ⦿ No value

User name
- ⦿ Specify a static value: bryan-pc\bryan
- ○ Get the value from the database: Choose a field ▾

Password
- ⦿ Specify a static value: •••••••••
- ○ Get the value from the database: Choose a field ▾

[< Back]   [Next >]   [Cancel]   [Finish]

Figure 13-26

If the report contains parameters, clicking on the Next button takes you to the Step 5 page, where you map parameters in the report to fields in the query (see Figure 13-27). Again, you can also map a parameter to a constant or elect to provide no value, as appropriate.

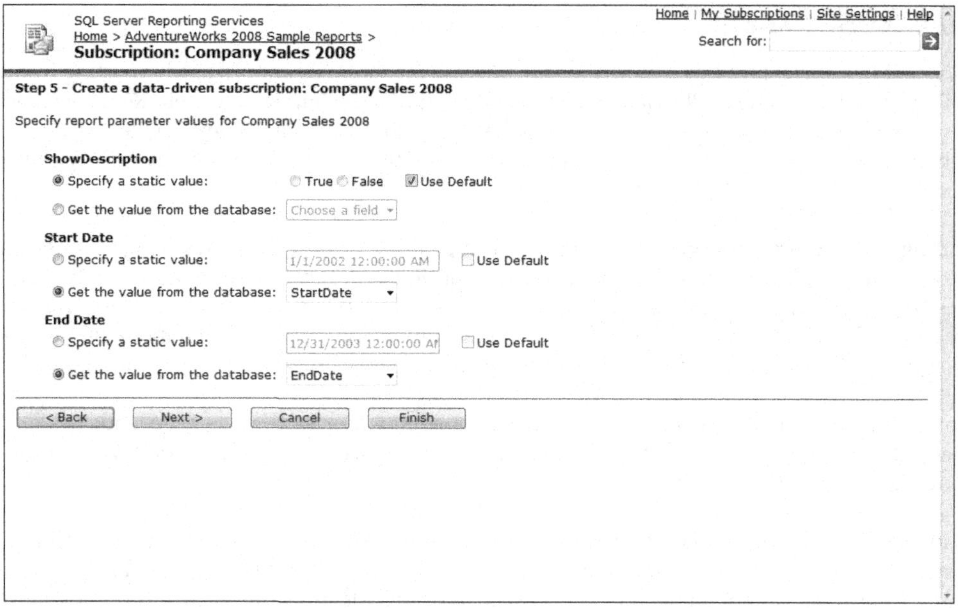

Figure 13-27

Clicking Next takes you to the Step 6 page (see Figure 13-28). Here you identify whether a subscription-specific or shared schedule will be used to control the timing of subscription delivery. You can also elect to have the subscription delivered whenever data for the snapshot associated with the report is updated. If you elect to use a subscription-specific schedule, you will click Next to be taken to the Step 7 page, where this schedule is defined. Otherwise, you will click Finish on the Step 6 page to complete the setup of the data-driven subscription.

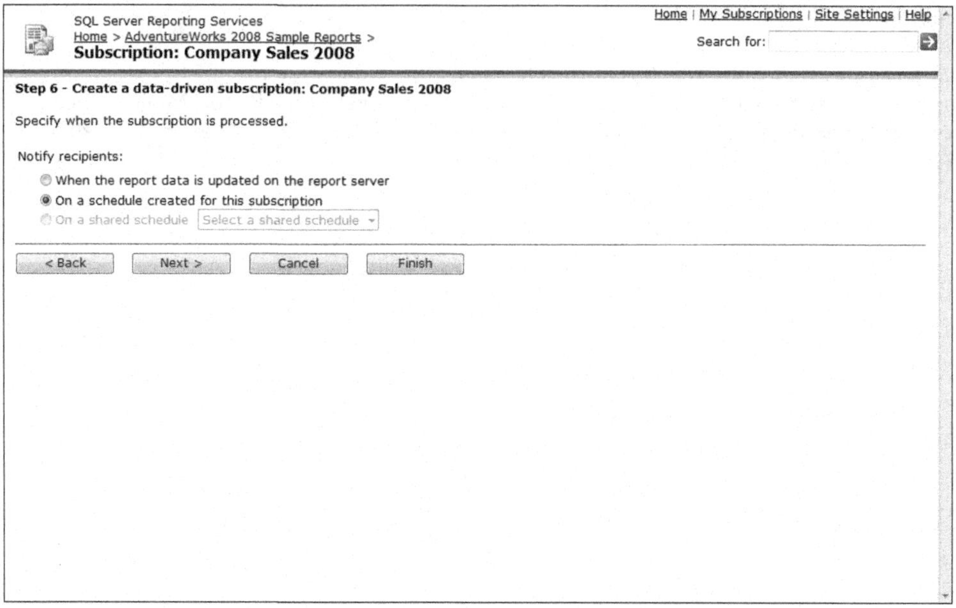

Figure 13-28

Report Resources

Resources are files referenced by a report. Image files are the most commonly used reporting resources, but HTML, XML, XSLT, text, PDF, and Microsoft Office files are often used as well. Reporting Services does not implement any kind of restriction on what kind of resource can be leveraged by a report, so the possibilities are endless. That said, there are practical limitations to what may be used as a reporting resource.

Reporting Services simply serves as a means of storing and returning the binary image of a resource file. The consuming application, whether the Reporting Services report processor or a custom report processing extension, must understand how to consume the resource item for it to be incorporated into the report. Otherwise, your only option is to provide a link to the resource and depend on the report viewing tool, typically a web browser, to handle the binary image for you.

To upload a resource to Reporting Services, open the parent folder's Contents page, and click on the Upload File button. Locate the file to upload, and click OK. Once the file is uploaded, you should see the item displayed within the folder.

Clicking on the item takes you to the resource's View page. If your web browser can render a resource, such as a JPEG or GIF file, the item will be displayed within the body of the Report Manager page. If your web browser cannot render a resource, such as a TIFF file, the browser will prompt you to save the file to your local system.

Clicking a resource's Properties tab provides you access to the resource item's General Properties page. Through this page, you can perform basic maintenance on the item.

Shared Schedules

Shared schedules enable you to define and administer schedules in a centralized manner for use throughout the site.

Shared schedules are managed at the site level, outside the folder structure. To access shared schedules, click on the Site Settings link in the upper-right corner of the Report Manager header. Move to the Schedules page to see a tabular representation of shared schedules on the system (see Figure 13-29).

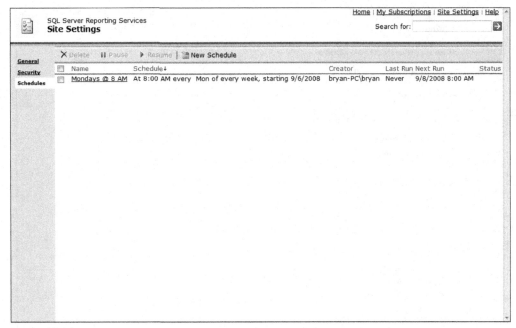

Figure 13-29

Figure 13-29 displays a shared schedule. This schedule has been created for illustration purposes and is not created with the Reporting Services samples.

The table on the Schedule's page presents Name, Schedule (description), Creator, Last Run, Next Run, and Status fields, all of which can be used to sort the table's contents. Selecting one or more items in the table enables the Delete, Pause, and Resume buttons within the gray bar.

Clicking on the New Schedule button in the gray bar on this page takes you to the Scheduling page (see Figure 13-30), where you can enter a name for the schedule and set its frequency of execution. You can also set a date range during which this schedule is executed.

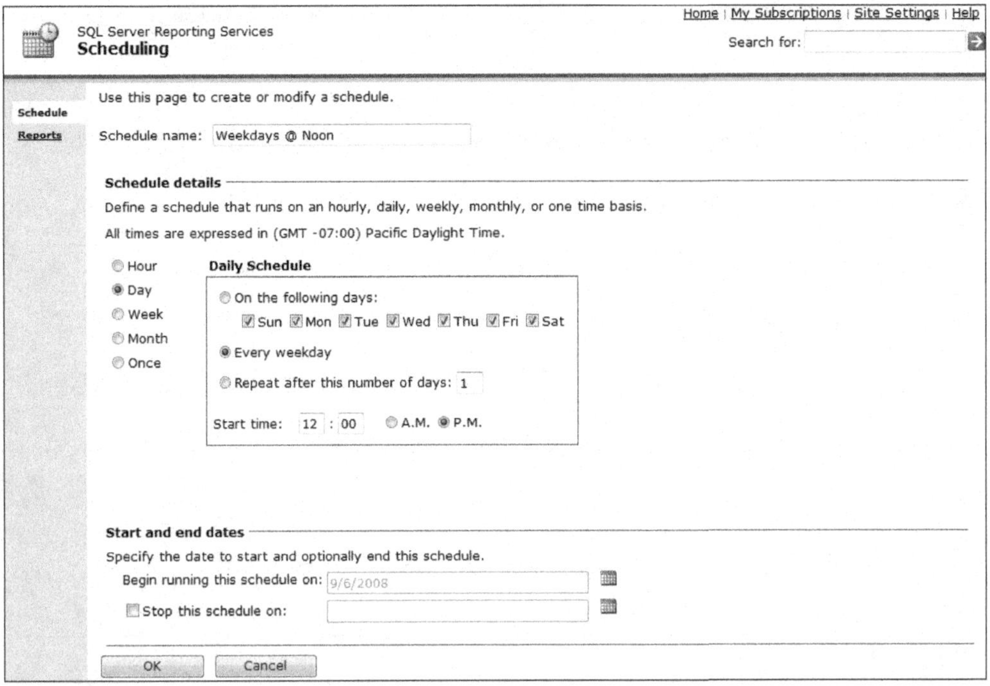

Figure 13-30

Clicking OK submits the request to create the schedule. Behind the scenes, Reporting Services attempts to create a scheduled job through SQL Agent. If the SQL Agent Windows service is not started, you will receive an error message indicating this to be the issue.

Back on the Schedules page, clicking a schedule item's name or schedule value takes you back to the Scheduling page, where you can edit its configuration. Before making changes, it is a good idea to review the schedule's Reports page to identify reports dependent on it.

> You can also create and manage shared schedules through SQL Server Management Studio. Open SQL Server Management Studio, connect to the Reporting Services instance, and locate the Shared Schedules folder under the instance icon. You can right-click on the Shared Schedules folder to create or delete a shared schedule. You can also right-click on an individual schedule to delete it or to access its Properties page. The Properties page provides access to the same properties presented through Report Manager.

Item-Level Security

Whether through Report Manager or any other application, to perform an action against a Reporting Services item, you must have been granted the required permissions. Reporting Services supports a fixed set of permissions associated with each type of item, as identified in the following table:

Item	Permissions
Report	Create Any Subscription Create Link Create Report History Create Subscription Delete Any Subscription Delete Report History Delete Subscription Delete Update Properties Execute Read Policy List Report History Read Any Subscription Read Content Read Data Sources Read Properties Read Report Definition Read Report Definitions Read Security Policies Read Subscription Update Any Subscription Update Data Sources Update Parameters Update Policy Update Report Definition Update Security Policies Update Subscription
Report Model	Delete Update Content Read Content Read Data Sources Read Model Item Authorization Policies Read Properties Update Data Sources Update Model Item Authorization Policies Delete Update Properties
Shared Data Source	Update Properties Delete Update Content Read Properties Read Security Policies Update Security Policies

(continued)

483

Item	Permissions
Reporting Resource	Delete Update Content Read Content Read Properties Read Security Policies Update Properties Update Security Policies
Folder	Create Data Source Create Folder Create Model Create Report Create Resource Delete Update Properties Execute And View List Report History Read Properties Read Security Policies Update Security Policies

Explicitly assigning the right combinations of permissions required to perform an action on the site would be challenging. To simplify things, Reporting Services organizes these permissions into a more condensed set of item-level tasks. These tasks more naturally align with the kinds of activities users need to perform. The table below identifies the task-to-permission mappings.

While important to understand as the underlying mechanism behind item-level security, Reporting Services does not expose these permissions. In addition, Reporting Services does not allow tasks to be created or altered.

Item	Task	Permissions
Folder	Manage data sources.	Create Data Source
	Manage folders.	Create Folder Delete Update Properties Read Properties
	Manage models.	Create Model
	Manage reports.	Create Report
	Manage resources.	Create Resource
	Set security for individual items.	Read Security Policies Update Security Policies
	View folders.	Read Properties Execute and View List Report History

Item	Task	Permissions
Reports	Consume reports.	Read Content Read Report Definitions Read Properties
	Create linked reports.	Create Link Read Properties
	Manage all subscriptions.	Read Properties Read Any Subscription Create Any Subscription Delete Any Subscription Update Any Subscription
	Manage individual subscriptions.	Read Properties Create Subscription Delete Subscription Read Subscription Update Subscription
	Manage individual subscriptions.	Read Properties Create Subscription Delete Subscription Read Subscription Update Subscription
	Manage report history.	Read Properties Create Report History Delete Report History Execute Read Policy Update Policy List Report History
	Manage reports.	Read Properties Delete Update Properties Update Parameters Read Data Sources Update Data Sources Read Report Definition Update Report Definition Execute Read Policy Update Policy
	View reports.	Read Content Read Properties
	Set security for individual items.	Read Security Policies Update Security Policies

(continued)

Item	Task	Permissions
Data sources	Manage data sources.	Update Properties Delete Update Content Read Properties
	Manage data sources.	Update Properties Delete Update Content Read Properties
	View data sources.	Read Content Read Properties
	Set security for individual items.	Read Security Policies Update Security Policies
Models	Manage models.	Read Properties Read Content Delete Update Content Read Data Sources Update Data Sources Read Model Item Authorization Policies Update Model Item Authorization Policies Delete Update Properties
	View models.	Read Properties Read Content Read Data Sources
Resources	Set security for individual items.	Read Security Policies Update Security Policies
	Manage resources.	Update Properties Delete Update Content Read Properties
	View resources.	Read Content Read Properties

Within Reporting Services, tasks are assigned to roles. Reporting Services contains a set of five predefined roles for item-level tasks, as identified in the following table:

Role	Description	Tasks
Browser	Run reports and navigate through the folder structure.	View reports. View resources. View folders. View models. Manage individual subscriptions.
Content Manager	Define a folder structure for storing reports and other items, set security at the item level, and view and manage the items stored by the server.	Consume reports. Create linked reports. Manage all subscriptions. Manage data sources. Manage folders. Manage models. Manage individual subscriptions. Manage report history. Manage reports. Manage resources. Set security policies for items. View data sources. View reports. View models. View resources. View folders.
Report Builder	Build and edit reports in Report Builder.	Consume reports. View reports. View resources. View folders. View models. Manage individual subscriptions.
Publisher	Publish content to a Report Server.	Create linked reports. Manage data sources. Manage folders. Manage reports. Manage models. Manage resources.
My Reports	Build reports for personal use or store reports in a user-owned folder.	Create linked reports. Manage folders. Manage data sources.

To modify the tasks assigned to these roles, open SQL Server Management Studio and connect to the Reporting Services instance. In the Object Explorer pane, expand the Security folder and its Roles subfolder. You will see the Reporting Services item-level roles listed, as shown in Figure 13-31.

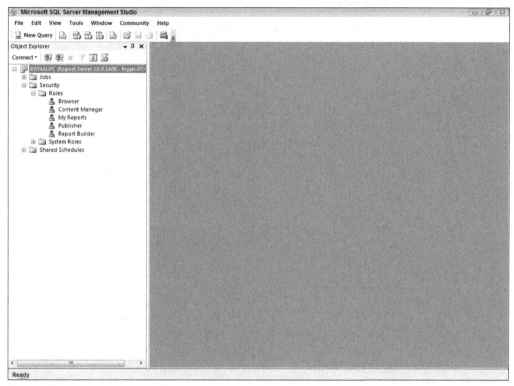

Figure 13-31

Right-click on a role, and select Properties from the Context menu to open its User Role Properties dialog (see Figure 13-32). Here you can change the role's description and tasks assigned to it. Clicking OK saves your changes.

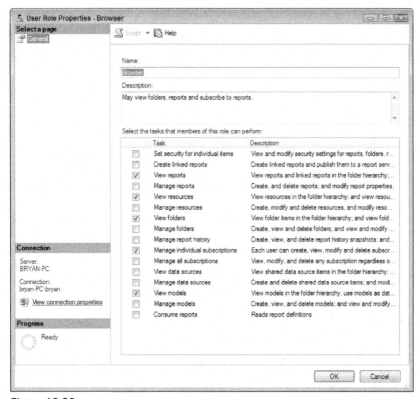

Figure 13-32

Reporting Services also allows new roles to be created. To create a new role, right-click on the Roles subfolder in the SQL Server Management Studio Object Explorer pane, and select New Role from the Context menu. In the resulting New User Role dialog, similar to the User Role Properties dialog pictured in Figure 13-32, provide the name, description, and task assignments for this role. Click OK to create the role.

To drop a role, right-click on the role, and select Delete from the Context menu. You will be asked to confirm this action before the role is dropped. You can drop both custom and predefined Reporting Services roles.

Item-level security is finally implemented in Reporting Services by linking users, roles, and items. In Report Manager, this "linking" is implemented by first navigating to an item and then engaging its Security Properties page. Figure 13-33 shows this page for the Home folder.

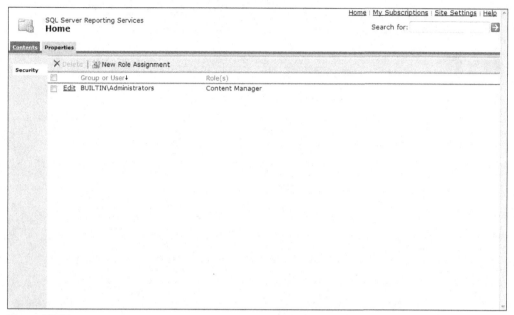

Figure 13-33

Clicking on the New Role Assignment button takes you to the New Role Assignment page, as shown in Figure 13-34. Here, you enter the account name for the user or group to which you wish to assign this access and then select one or more of the roles as appropriate. Clicking OK submits the assignment to Reporting Services.

SQL Server Reporting Services
New Role Assignment

Home | My Subscriptions | Site Settings | Help

Search for:

Use this page to define role-based security for Home.

Group or user name: |

Select one or more roles to assign to the group or user.

Role↓	Description
Browser	May view folders, reports and subscribe to reports.
Content Manager	May manage content in the Report Server. This includes folders, reports and resources.
My Reports	May publish reports and linked reports; manage folders, reports and resources in a users My Reports folder.
Publisher	May publish reports and linked reports to the Report Server.
Report Builder	May view report definitions.

OK   Cancel

Figure 13-34

Creating item-user-role assignments for every item on the site would get old very quickly. So, instead, Reporting Services makes use of inheritance for item-level security. When a user is assigned to one or more roles on a folder, this assignment is inherited by that folder's child items. If these child items include folders, the inheritance cascades down the folder hierarchy.

Inheritance makes administering security much easier, but you might need to break inheritance to set permissions exactly as required. To break inheritance for an item, navigate to that item's Security Properties page in Report Manager. Figure 13-35 shows this for the AdventureWorks 2008 Sample Reports folder located just under the Home folder.

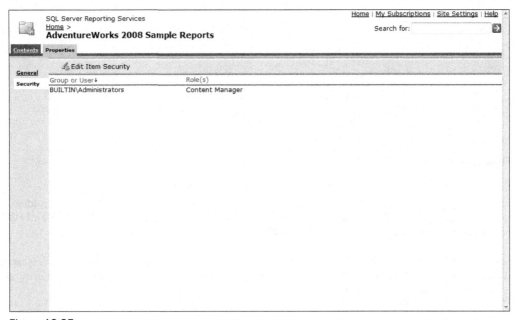

Figure 13-35

Notice that the New Role Assignment button has been replaced by the Edit Item Security button in the gray bar. Clicking on the button triggers a message box asking you to confirm that you wish to break inheritance for this item. Clicking OK on the message box reloads the Security Properties page. You will now notice that the New Role Assignment button is available, as shown in Figure 13-36, allowing you to now create user-role assignments for this item.

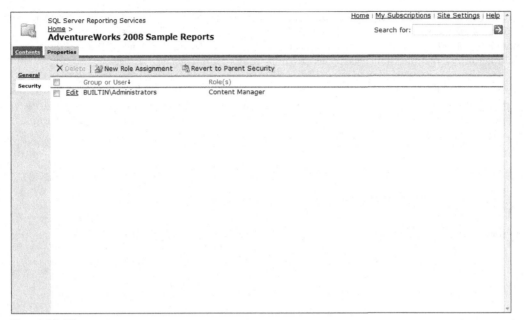

SQL Server Reporting Services
Home >
AdventureWorks 2008 Sample Reports

Home | My Subscriptions | Site Settings | Help

Search for:

Contents **Properties**

General
Security

✕ Delete | 🏷 New Role Assignment   🗂 Revert to Parent Security

	Group or User↓	Role(s)
☐ Edit	BUILTIN\Administrators	Content Manager

Figure 13-36

You will also notice that the user-role assignments that would have been inherited from this folder's parent are preassigned to this item. Selecting the checkbox for any unnecessary assignments and clicking on the Delete button on the gray bar will remove these.

Finally, should you wish to reset this item's security to once again make use of inheritance, click on the Revert to Parent Security button along the gray bar. The item will revert back to inherited security, and any noninherited assignments will be dropped.

Content-Management Automation

Content management consists of many repetitive tasks. Performing these manually can be very time-consuming and risks the introduction of errors. Scripts allow these frequently performed tasks to be automated. If implemented correctly, scripts can produce significant time savings and minimize the risks associated with changes to your environment.

The RS Utility

The RS utility allows scripts to be run against local and remote instances of Reporting Services running in Native mode. The application, rs.exe, is typically located within the <drive>:\Program Files\ Microsoft SQL Server\100\Tools\Binn folder. It is responsible for creating an environment within which a Reporting Services script can be executed.

As part of this responsibility, it handles communications with an instance of the Reporting Services web service. It also handles the declaration and instantiation of variables supplied through the command-line call. These features allow flexible scripts to be developed with relative ease.

The following demonstrates a very simple call to the RS utility. Note the use of the –i parameter to identify the Reporting Services script. The script file is a simple text file with an RSS file extension. Also, note the identification of the web service URL with the –s parameter. In this example, the script is being pointed to the web service presented by the local, default instance of Reporting Services.

```
rs.exe -i "c:\my scripts\my script.rss" -s http://localhost/reportserver
```

In the previous call to the RS utility, the connection to the Reporting Services web service is established using the current user's identity. To specify an alternate identity, a username and password combination can be specified with the –u and –p parameters. In the next example, the connection is being made through the fictional MyDomain\JoeUser account, which has a password p@55w0rd.

```
rs.exe -i "c:\my scripts\my script.rss" -s http://localhost/reportserver-u
MyDomain\JoeUser -p p@55w0rd
```

In Native mode, the Reporting Services web service presents two endpoints, each exposing different classes and functionality:

❑ **ReportService2005** — The ReportService2005 endpoint exposes classes used for content management.

❑ **ReportExecution2005** — The ReportExecution2005 endpoint exposes classes used for report rendering.

In the preceding command-line examples, no endpoint is specified, so RS utility defaults to the ReportService2005 endpoint for content-management functionality. To explicitly identify an endpoint, use the –e parameter with the Mgmt2005 value to indicate that the ReportService2005 endpoint should be used, or the Exec2005 value to indicate that the ReportExecution2005 endpoint should be used. Here is the previous call to the RS utility with the Mgmt2005 endpoint explicitly identified:

```
rs.exe -i "c:\my scripts\my script.rss" -s http://localhost/reportserver-u
MyDomain\JoeUser -p p@55w0rd -e Mgmt2005
```

As mentioned at the start of this section, the RS utility declares and instantiates variables on behalf of your script. Variables are specified using the –v parameter followed by one or more variable–value combinations. Variable–value combinations are separated by an equal sign. Values containing spaces should be wrapped in double quotes. The RS utility will remove the leading and trailing quotation marks when assigning the value to an internal variable. Here is a sample call to the utility with three variables that illustrates these concepts:

```
rs.exe -i "c:\my scripts\my script.rss" -s http://localhost/reportserver-v VarA=1
VarB=apple VarC="keeps the doctor away"
```

The following table shows a complete list of parameters supported by the RS utility:

Parameter	Description
-i	Identifies the script file to execute.
-s	Identifies the URL of the Reporting Services web service.
-u	Supplies the username used to log in to the Reporting Services site.
-p	Supplies the password associated with the username used to log in to the Reporting Services site.
-e	Identifies the Reporting Services web service endpoint to employ: Exec2005 — ReportExecution2005 endpoint Mgmt2005 — ReportService2005 endpoint
-l	Specifies the number of seconds before the connection with Reporting Services times out. The default is 60 seconds. A value of 0 indicates an infinite connection time-out.
-b	Indicates that the script should be executed as a batch.
-v	Provides variables and values to pass to the script.
-t	Instructs the utility to include trace information in error messages.

Reporting Services Scripts

Reporting Services scripts are implemented in VB.NET. Only a few namespaces are supported, making the scripts fairly limited but still powerful enough to handle most content management tasks. Supported namespaces include System, System.Diagnostics, System.IO, System.Web.Services, and System.Xml.

Every script must contain a Sub Main code block. This serves as the script's entry point. However, the Sub Main block does not have to be the first or only code block in the script. This allows you to move code to additional subroutines and functions you declare in the script.

Within the script, the Reporting Services web service is engaged through the rs object. You do not need to declare this object or mess with the details of connecting the object to the web service endpoint specified along the command line. The RS utility handles all those details for you.

The requirement for the script developer is to call the appropriate classes and methods exposed by this endpoint through the rs object. To understand the classes and methods available for each endpoint, refer to documentation available through Books Online.

Variables specified at the command line are automatically declared and initialized for use within the script using the variable name identified at the command line. If you reference a variable that is not explicitly declared within the script or whose name does not match (case-insensitive) the name of a variable declared along the command line, you will receive an undeclared variable error. All variables passed from the command line are passed into the script as strings.

The following code sample is a very simple demonstration script within which the name of the contents of a folder and its subfolders is recursively sent to a text file. The script consists of a single code block, Sub Main. The ReportService2005 endpoint is accessed through the rs object to recursively read the contents of the site starting from a folder identified by the MyFolder variable. The MyFolder variable is passed in from the command line.

```
Sub Main

    'Write the starting folder to the screen
    Console.WriteLine("The starting folder is " + MyFolder)

    'Open the Output File
    Dim OutputFile As New IO.StreamWriter( _
                        "c:\my scripts\contents.txt", False)

    'Obtain an array of Catalog Items
    Dim Contents As CatalogItem() = rs.ListChildren(MyFolder, True)

    'Loop through Array of CatalogItems
    For i As Int32 = 0 To Contents.GetUpperBound(0)

        'Write CatalogItem Type & Path to Output File w/ Pipe Delimiter
        OutputFile.Write(Contents(i).Type.ToString)
        OutputFile.Write("|")
        OutputFile.WriteLine(Contents(i).Path)
    Next

    'Close Output File
    OutputFile.Close()

End Sub
```

This script is saved to a file named *List Contents.RSS* located in the C:\My Scripts folder and is executed against the local Reporting Services instance through the following command-line call:

```
rs.exe -i "c:\my scripts\list contents.rss" -s http://localhost/reportserver-v
MyFolder="/"
```

The "/" value represents the Home folder in the Reporting Services folder hierarchy.

This is a very simple script but demonstrates the basics of Reporting Services script development. Four more scripts, identified in the following table, are available with the Reporting Services samples. These demonstrate a broader range of functionality than the script above but rely on the same basic concepts explored here. If you have installed the Reporting Services samples, you can typically find these scripts within the <drive>:\Program Files\Microsoft SQL Server\100\Samples\Reporting Services\Script Samples folder.

Script File	Description
AddItemSecurity.rss	Demonstrates how to use a script to set item security policies in the Report Server namespace.
CancelRunningJobs.rss	Demonstrates a sample administration script that cancels jobs that are running on a Report Server.
ConfigureSystemProperties.rss	Demonstrates a script that can be used to set system-level, Report Server properties.
PublishSampleReports.rss	Demonstrates a script that publishes the sample reports to a Report Server.

The readme file, located in the same folder, emphasizes that these four scripts are not considered production-ready. A production-ready script will make use of a wide array of variables to improve flexibility and reusability. A production-ready script will also make use of proper error-handling to improve stability and your ability to troubleshoot problems.

These four sample scripts (and the one above) all make use of the ReportService2005 endpoint. This endpoint provides access to content-management functionality, which is what you will most often want to employ with scripts. However, you may occasionally need to render a report through script. The ReportExectution2005 endpoint can be leveraged for this purpose, as demonstrated in the following sample, which renders the Company Sales 2008 sample report to PDF.

```
Sub Main()
    rs.Credentials = _
        System.Net.CredentialCache.DefaultCredentials

    'Get Report Info
    Dim MyExecutionInfo As ExecutionInfo = rs.LoadReport( _
        "/AdventureWorks 2008 Sample Reports/Company Sales 2008", Nothing)

    'Set Parameters
    Dim MyParameters() As ParameterValue = {New ParameterValue(), _
        New ParameterValue(),New ParameterValue()}
    MyParameters(0).Name = "ShowDescription"
    MyParameters(0).Value = "True"
    MyParameters(1).Name = "StartDate"
    MyParameters(1).Value = "1/1/2002 12:00:00 AM"
    MyParameters(2).Name = "EndDate"
    MyParameters(2).Value = "12/31/2003 12:00:00 AM"
    rs.SetExecutionParameters(MyParameters, "en-US")

    'Render Report to Byte Array
    Dim MyReportBytes() As Byte
    MyReportBytes = rs.Render("PDF", Nothing, Nothing, _
        Nothing, Nothing, Nothing, Nothing)

    'Write Bytes to File
```

```
        Dim MyOutputStream As New System.IO.FileStream( _
            "c:\my scripts\test.pdf", FileMode.Create)
        MyOutputStream.Write(MyReportBytes, 0, MyReportBytes.Length)
        MyOutputStream.Close()

    End Sub
```

This script is saved to the Render Report.RSS file in the same folder as before and then called with the following command-line statement:

```
rs.exe -i "c:\my scripts\render report.rss" -s http://localhost/reportserver -e
Exec2005
```

Note that the script presents the ReportExecution2005 endpoint as an object named rs, just as in the previous samples. Regardless of which endpoint is used, the RS utility will expose it through the rs object.

Like the first code sample, this last sample is very basic and requires only limited knowledge of VB.NET and the classes supported by the Reporting Services endpoints. To develop more sophisticated code samples, a tool such as Visual Studio 2008 with automatic syntax checking, IntelliSense, and step-by-step debugging functionality is very helpful (if not essential).

To leverage this tool for script development, launch Visual Studio 2008, and select File ⇨ New ⇨ Project to start a new project. In the New Project dialog, shown in Figure 13-37, select the Visual Basic Windows project type and Console Application project template. Provide a name and location for your project, and click OK. In the screenshots that follow, the project has been named *ConsoleApplication1*.

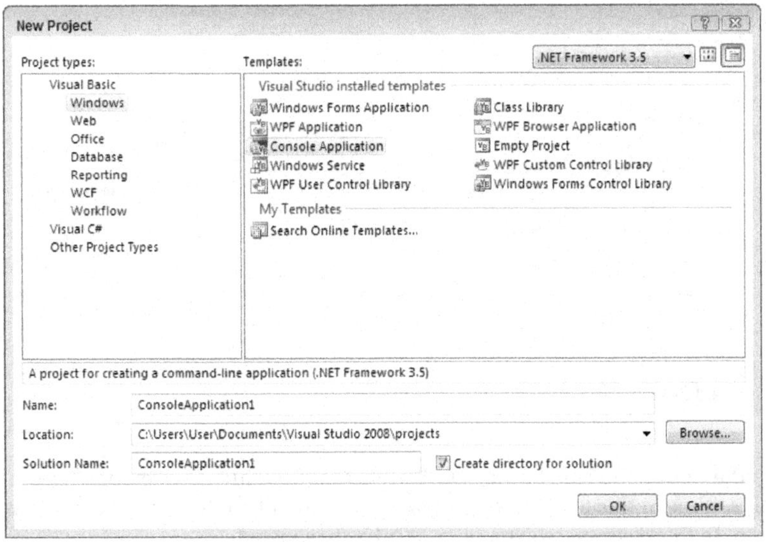

Figure 13-37

The project should open up the Module1.vb code module. From the Project menu, select Add Service Reference. In the resulting dialog, click on the Advanced button to open the Service Reference Settings dialog. Click the Add Web Service button to take you to the Add Web Reference dialog. In the URL textbox, enter the path for the endpoint of interest. Generic paths to the ReportService2005 and ReportExecution2005 endpoints are provided below:

Endpoint	URL
ReportService2005	http://<servername>/ReportServer/ReportService2005.asmx?wsdl
ReportExecution2005	http://<servername>/ReportServer/ReportExecution2005 .asmx?wsdl

Press the Go button to retrieve the web service definition from Reporting Services. If successfully retrieved, the box below the URL should be populated with a list of methods. In Figure 13-38, a reference to the ReportService2005 endpoint of the web service provided by the local, default instance of Reporting Services has been established.

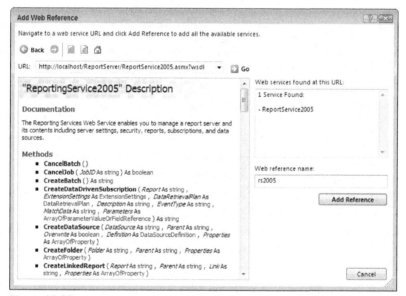

Figure 13-38

Halfway down the right-hand side of the Add Web Reference dialog is a textbox for the name of the web reference. Enter a name in this textbox (other than "rs" to avoid confusion), and click on the Add Reference button. In this example, the name *rs2005* has been used.

Visual Studio should have taken you back to the Module1.vb code module. You now add an `Imports` statement for the web reference just above the module declaration. This will allow you to reference objects from the web service without declaring their direct affiliation. This is the style expected by the RS utility.

You now instantiate an object named *rs* to represent the endpoint within the script. You declare this object at the module level, so place your `Dim` statement just below the line reading `Module Module1`. If you are using the ReportService2005 endpoint, your declaration should read:

```
Dim rs as New ReportingService2005
```

If you are using the ReportExecution2005 endpoint, your declaration should read:

```
Dim rs as New ReportExecutionService
```

Finally, add the following line immediately below `Sub Main()`:

```
rs.Credentials = System.Net.CredentialCache.DefaultCredentials
```

Your code module sample should now look something like the code block below. Remember that in this example, `rs2005` represents a reference to the ReportService2005 endpoint, which is why `rs` has been declared of the type ReportingService2005.

```
Imports MyScriptingProject.rs2005

Module Module1

    Dim rs As New ReportingService2005

    Sub Main()
      rs.Credentials = System.Net.CredentialCache.DefaultCredentials

    End Sub

End Module
```

Next, return to the Project menu, and select the ConsoleApplication1 Properties item. This should be the last item in the menu list. Selecting this should take you to the project Properties page.

If your project is named differently, the name of the menu item will be adjusted appropriately.

On this page, move to the References tab (see Figure 13-39). Alter the selections in the Imported Namespaces list so that only `System`, `System.Diagnostics`, `System.IO`, `System.Web.Services`, and `System.Xml` are selected. Move back to the Module1.vb code module, and save your project.

You now have a project within Visual Studio that provides an environment similar to that available through the RS utility. You can develop and test your script with all the features available through Visual Studio at your fingertips. If you intend to pass variables to your script, you can declare these just above the Dim rs statement. Any script-level variables you need to declare but do not intend to pass from the command line should be declared below the Dim rs statement. This will help keep things simple in the next step.

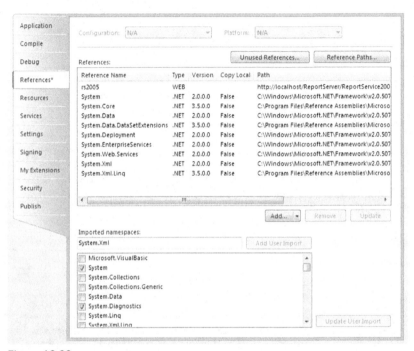

Figure 13-39

Once the code has been properly tested and you are ready to use it with the RS utility, comment out the rs.Credentials statement at the top of the Sub Main block. Then copy all the code just below the Dim rs statement to the end of the module, excluding the End Module statement, to a text file. Save the file in an appropriate location and with an optional RSS file extension. You should now have a working script for use with the RS utility.

The RSScripter

A very common task for content managers is the migration of items from one Reporting Services site to another, often as part of a formal change-control process. This operation is an excellent candidate for automation, so much so that Jasper Smith has developed a utility to auto-generate scripts for this task. RSSScripter is freely available through the SQL DBAs web site at http://www.sqldbatips.com/showarticle.asp?ID=62.

If you decide to download and use this tool, keep in mind that it is not an official Microsoft product and is distributed "as is" and without warranty of any kind.

Summary

In this chapter, you explored various aspects of the management of reports, shared data sources, report models, report resources, and shared schedules. This includes basic content-management activities, item-level security, and automation.

In the next chapter, you will take a look at another important aspect of the management phase of the reporting life cycle: administration.

Report Server Administration

To ensure the integrity and reliability of your Reporting Services environment, it is important that you develop a comprehensive administrative plan for it. This plan should address the following general concerns:

- ❑ Security
- ❑ Backup and recovery
- ❑ Monitoring
- ❑ Configuration

In this chapter, you will explore these topics as they relate to Reporting Services. This will provide you the basic knowledge you will need to then engage users, developers, and IT administrators in the development of a plan tailored to the specific needs of your organization.

Security

Properly securing your Reporting Services environment requires you to find the right balance between risk, availability, and supportability. Following good network, system, and facilities management practices goes a long way toward securing your installation. Specific to Reporting Services, you should consider how to best approach:

- ❑ Account management
- ❑ System-level roles
- ❑ Surface area management

Account Management

Reporting Services must interact with various resources. To access these resources, Reporting Services must present its requests as originating from a specific, valid user. Reporting Services stores credentials, typically username and password combinations, for the following three accounts, each of which is used to handle specific interactions with resources:

❑ The service account

❑ The application database account

❑ The unattended execution account

Whenever possible, it is recommended that you make use of Windows domain user accounts as the source of the credentials for these three application accounts. This allows you to leverage Windows' security infrastructure for credential management.

In addition, it is recommended that you employ accounts dedicated for use in these roles. Reuse of credentials can make longer-term management of these accounts more difficult and can lead to unintended resource access. This can also lead to the accumulation of permissions associated with an account. An account used for one of these roles should have no more permissions than those required for it to successfully complete its operations.

Finally, you should limit the number of trusted individuals with knowledge of these credentials. As individuals move out of roles requiring them to have this knowledge (or move out of the organization altogether), these accounts should be updated to maintain a secure environment. If Windows accounts are used (as is recommended above), inappropriate use can be prevented by prohibiting their use for interactive logins to Windows systems.

The Service Account

During installation, as described in Chapter 3, you are asked to specify the account under which the Reporting Services Windows service operates. This is referred to as the *service account*. Through this account, the Reporting Services Windows service will access various system resources. If your installation runs in SharePoint Integrated mode, this is the account that Reporting Services will also use to access the SharePoint databases.

The Reporting Services service account can be one of three built-in accounts or a Windows user account that you define. Each of these account options is outlined in the following table:

Account	Details
Local System	The Local System account is a built-in account that behaves as a member of the local Administrators group. When accessing resources on the network, it uses the computer's credentials. It is not recommended that you use this for the service account.
Local Service	The Local Service account is a built-in account that behaves as a member of the local Users group. It accesses resources on the network with no credentials.

Account	Details
Network Service	The Network Service account is a built-in account that behaves as a member of the local Users group. When accessing resources on the network, it uses the computer's credentials. It is no longer recommended that you use this for the service account.
User Account	The User Account option allows you to enter the credentials of a local or domain Windows user account. If a local account is used, access to network resources is with no credentials. If a domain account is used, access to network resources is through the domain account. This is the recommended account type for the service account.

The service account requires permissions to specific resources on the system on which the Reporting Services Windows service runs. Instead of granting these rights to the service account itself, the service account obtains these rights through membership in a local group created by the SQL Server set-up application during installation. This group is named SQLServerReportServerUser$*ComputerName*$MSRS10 *.InstanceName,* with MSSQLSERVER used as the instance name for the default instance.

There is no need to directly alter membership to this group when making changes to the service account. Instead, you are strongly recommended to make any changes to the service account using the Service Account page of the Reporting Services Configuration Manager (see Figure 14-1). The tool handles the details of managing membership to this group, updating the Windows service, adjusting encryption keys, altering URL reservations, and granting access to the Reporting Services application databases (if the service account is used as the application database account) — all of which must be performed with a change in the service account.

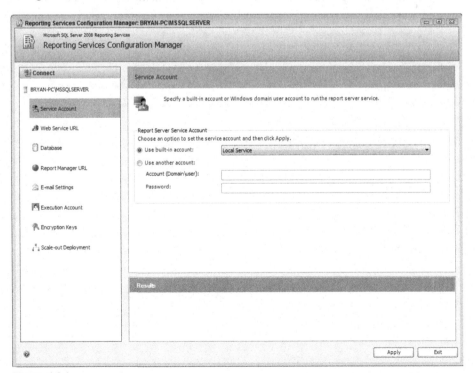

Figure 14-1

Finally, if you are running in SharePoint Integrated mode and you switch the service account, make sure that the account has appropriate access to the SharePoint databases. To do this, open SharePoint Central Administration. In the Reporting Services section, click "Grant database access," and enter the Reporting Services service account information in the resulting dialog. Once this change is saved, it is recommended that you restart the SharePoint Services service to ensure that the appropriate credentials are being used.

The Application Database Account

Reporting Services depends on content stored in its application databases. These databases are hosted by a local or remote instance of SQL Server, as described in Chapter 4. To connect to its databases, Reporting Services must maintain connection string data along with valid credentials for establishing a connection. The credentials are referred to as the *application database account*.

You have three options for the application database account. You can specify a SQL Server authenticated username and password, provide the credentials for a valid Windows user account, or elect to have Reporting Services simply use its service account when establishing the connection.

The SQL Server Authenticated User option requires the SQL Server instance hosting the application databases to support both Windows and SQL Server authentication. By default, SQL Server is configured for Windows (Integrated) authentication only, as SQL Server authentication is considered less secure. It is recommended that you employ the SQL Server Authenticated User option only in special circumstances, such as when Windows user accounts cannot be authenticated.

The application database account is set during installation and can be modified later using the Reporting Services Configuration Manager (see Figure 14-2). If you installed using a default configuration, as described in Chapter 3, the application database account was automatically set to use the service account.

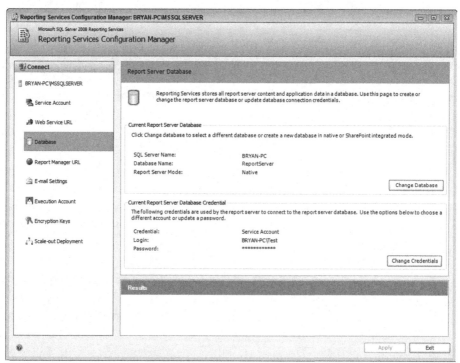

Figure 14-2

If you use the service account or Windows user option, a login will be created within SQL Server mapped to this Windows account. (If you use the SQL Server Authenticated User option, you will need to create a login in advance.) The login is then granted access to the two Reporting Services application databases as well as the master and msdb system databases. Within each database, the account is mapped to a collection of roles that provide it the rights it needs to handle Reporting Services' database operations, including the creation and management of jobs through a SQL Agent. The following table identifies the database roles to which the application database account is mapped:

Database	Roles
Master	public
	RSExecRole
Msdb	public
	RSExecRole
	SQLAgentOperatorRole
	SQLAgentReaderRole
	SQLAgentUserRole
ReportServer	db_owner
	public
	RSExecRole
ReportServerTempDB	db_owner
	public
	RSExecRole

It is important to note that if you change the application database account used by Reporting Services to connect to its application databases, the Reporting Services Configuration Manager does not remove the previous application database account from the SQL Server instance. Instead, a valid login is left within the instance of SQL Server Database Engine, retaining its membership in the database roles identified in the preceding table. If you change the application database account, you should follow up by removing the prior login from these roles or the SQL Server instance altogether.

The Unattended Execution Account

Reports might need to access files on remote servers or data sources that do not require authentication. To access these resources, you can specify that no credentials are required as part of the data source definition. When you do so, you are instructing Reporting Services to use the credentials it has cached for the *unattended execution account* (also known as the *unattended report processing account* or simply the *execution account*) when accessing the resource.

By default, the unattended execution account is disabled and should remain so unless a specific need is recognized that cannot be addressed by other reasonable means. To enable the account and configure its credentials, access the Execution Account page within the Configuration Manager, and provide the required credentials, as shown in Figure 14-3.

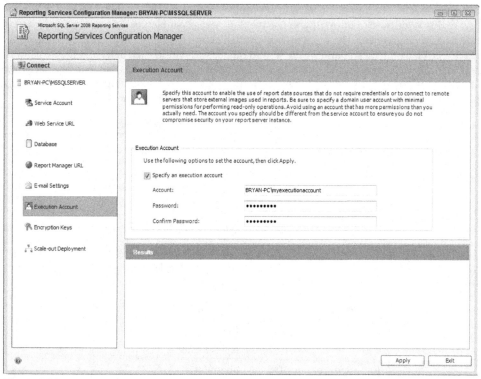

Figure 14-3

System-Level Roles

System-level roles provide members the rights to perform tasks across the Reporting Services site. The following table identifies the tasks that can be granted at the system level:

Task	Description	System Administrator	System User
Execute report definitions.	Start execution from report definition without publishing it to Report Server.	Yes	Yes
Generate events.	Provides an application with the ability to generate events within the Report Server namespace.	No	No
Manage jobs.	View and cancel running jobs.	Yes	No

Task	Description	System Administrator	System User
Manage Report Server properties.	View and modify properties that apply to the Report Server and to items managed by the Report Server.	Yes	No
Manage roles.	Create, view, modify, and delete role definitions.	Yes	No
Manage shared schedules.	Create, view, modify, and delete shared schedules used to run reports or refresh a report.	Yes	No
Manage Report Server security.	View and modify system-wide role assignments.	Yes	No
View Report Server properties.	View properties that apply to the Report Server.	No	Yes
View shared schedules.	View a predefined schedule that has been made available for general use.	No	Yes

Reporting Services comes preconfigured with two system-level roles: System User and System Administrator. The System User role allows users to retrieve information about the site and to execute reports in Report Builder 1.0 that have not yet been published to the site. The System Administrator role allows administrators the rights required to manage the site, including the rights to create additional roles. The specific system-level tasks assigned to these roles are identified in the preceding table.

Additional site-level roles can be created using SQL Server Management Studio, allowing you to permit site-level tasks to be performed by others without granting them System Administrator rights. The process of creating these roles, assigning tasks, and granting membership is nearly identical to the creation of item-level roles, as discussed in Chapter 13, the only difference being that system-level roles are created through the System Roles folder instead of the Roles folder within SQL Server Management Studio (see Figure 14-4).

Figure 14-4

By default, the BUILTIN\Administrators group is assigned to both the System Administrator system-level and Content Manager item-level role within the Home folder. You are encouraged to alter this so that a more appropriate user account or group is assigned these permissions. If you decide to leave the BUILTIN\Administrators group in these roles, carefully consider who is allowed administrative rights on your servers.

Surface Area Management

A feature that is not enabled is not one that can be exploited. This is the general principle behind *surface area management*.

Reporting Services comes with several features disabled. These include the execution account, e-mail delivery, and My Reports. Still other features — such as Report Builder 1.0, Report Manager, the use of Windows Integrated security to access report data sources, and scheduling and delivery functionality — are enabled by default but not necessarily required within your Reporting Services environment. Carefully consider which Reporting Services features are truly required, and disable any not needed. Books Online provides documentation on the disablement for each of these features.

Backup and Recovery

Although redundant hardware solutions offer considerable protection against many types of failure, they do not shield you from every eventuality. Regular backups of the critical components of your Reporting Services environment are required to better ensure its recoverability.

Of course, simply taking backups is not enough. Your backups must be properly managed to ensure their availability following a failure event. This typically involves secured, off-site storage and the development of retention schedules so that you have the option to recover to various points in time.

In addition, those responsible for recovery should have experience with the recovery techniques. They should also be well versed in the procedures for accessing the backup media. It's not a lot of fun to attempt a recovery when you do not know how to locate and use the recovery media.

Finally, you should establish policies regarding how communications and decision making will be handled during a recovery event. You will want to ensure that all those potentially involved understand these policies. This will help minimize confusion during what can be an already stressful situation.

This section of the chapter reviews the backup and recovery of the following critical components of a Reporting Services environment:

- ❑ Application databases
- ❑ Encryption keys
- ❑ Configuration files
- ❑ Other items

Application Databases

Reporting Services makes use of two application databases. The primary database houses content, whereas the secondary database houses cached data. These databases are typically named *ReportServer* and *ReportServerTempDB*, respectively.

> *Although the names of the application databases can vary, the secondary application database must always be named the same as the primary with* TempDB *appended. For example, if the primary application database is named* MyRS, *the secondary database associated with it must be named* MyRSTempDB. *The names of these databases should not be altered once created, and the two databases must always exist within the same SQL Server instance.*

The primary application database, ReportServer, should be backed up on a regular basis and following any significant content changes. This database operates under the Full recovery model, which allows both data and log backups to be performed. If properly managed, the combination of data and log backups allows for point-in-time recovery of the ReportServer database.

The secondary application database, ReportServerTempDB, does not actually require a backup. If you need to recover it, you can create a new database appropriately named within the SQL Server instance housing the ReportServer database. Within this new database, execute the CatalogTempDB.sql script found within the <drive>:\Program Files\Microsoft SQL Server\MSRS10.<instancename>\ Reporting Services\ReportServer folder. The script will re-create the database objects required by Reporting Services. Be sure to run this from within the ReportServerTempDB database you just created.

If you decide to back up the ReportServerTempDB, it is important to note that it operates under the Simple recovery model. This model allows for data backups but not log backups.

Books Online includes a script for the backup and recovery of the ReportServer and ReportServerTempDB databases to another server. This script makes use of the COPY_ONLY *backup option and modifies the recovery model used with ReportServerTempDB. It is important to note that this script is provided in the context of performing a database migration, not a standard backup and recovery operation. Be sure to work with your database administrators to develop a backup and recovery plan that is tailored to the needs of your environment and that you have tested prior to promoting an environment to production status.*

If you recover a backup of ReportServerTempDB, be sure to purge its content following recovery. The following statement can be used to perform this task. Once the database is purged, it is recommended that you restart the Reporting Services service.

```
exec ReportServerTempDB.sys.sp_MSforeachtable
     @command1='truncate table #',
     @replacechar='#'
```

If you need to recover your application databases to another SQL Server instance, it is important to preserve the original names of the databases. If Reporting Services uses a SQL Server–authenticated account to connect to its application databases, you will need to re-create that login in the new SQL Server instance. Following the restore of the databases, you will then need to reassociate the user account in your application databases with the re-created login. The script below demonstrates one technique for performing this task:

```
exec ReportServer.dbo.sp_change_users_login
     @Action = 'Update_One',
     @UserNamePattern = 'MyDbAccount',
     @LoginName = 'MyDbAccount'

exec ReportServerTempDB.dbo.sp_change_users_login
     @Action = 'Update_One',
     @UserNamePattern = 'MyDbAccount',
     @LoginName = 'MyDbAccount'
```

Once the database user and login are properly associated, launch the Reporting Services Configuration Manager against your Reporting Services instance, and locate the Database page, as shown in Figure 14-5.

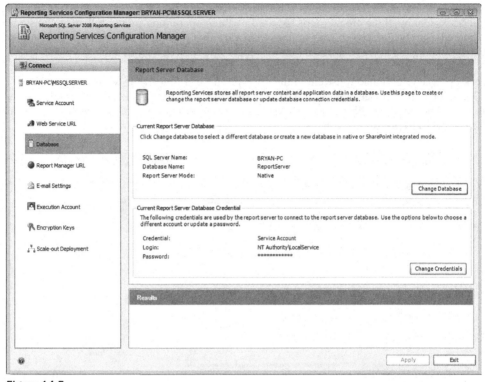

Figure 14-5

From this page, click on the Change Database button, and in the resulting dialog, enter the information required to connect to the primary application database at its new location. Restarting Reporting Services from the Reporting Service Configuration Manager completes the process.

Encryption Keys

Reporting Services protects the sensitive information it stores through encryption based on a *symmetric key* generated during initialization. The symmetric key, per its definition, is used in both encryption and decryption operations. To prevent unauthorized decryption of sensitive data, the symmetric key itself must be protected. This is accomplished by encrypting the symmetric key using an asymmetric key pair generated by the operating system.

Although this protects the symmetric key, also referred to as the *encryption key,* it raises the administrative complexity of the system. Certain operations invalidate the asymmetric key pair. Unless handled properly, these operations will cause Reporting Services to lose its ability to decrypt the symmetric key, leaving its sensitive data inaccessible. These operations include:

❑   Resetting the service account's password

❑   Changing the Reporting Services Windows service account

❑   Changing the name of the server

❑   Changing the name of the Reporting Services instance

If you need to perform these operations, it is critical that you follow the steps outlined in this chapter and in Books Online. If the precise steps required by these operations are not followed, the symmetric key can no longer be decrypted. Your options then are either to recover the key from a backup or to delete it. Deleting the key, as described below, is highly disruptive to your site.

To back up the encryption key, use either the Encryption Keys page of the Reporting Services Configuration Manager (see Figure 14-6) or the rskeymgmt command-line utility with the -e parameter, as illustrated below. With either approach, you will need to provide a name for the backup file along with a password to protect its contents.

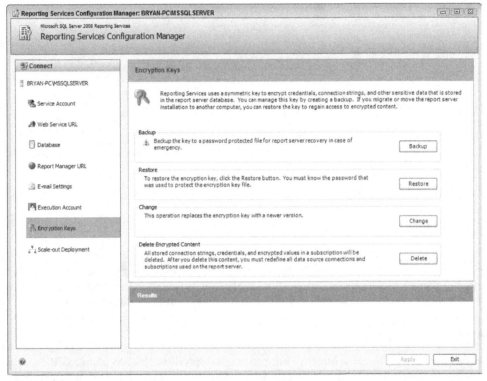

Figure 14-6

```
rskeymgmt.exe -e -i MSSQLSERVER -f c:\backups\rs_20080901.snk -p p@ssw0rd
```

The -i parameter is used to specify the name of the Reporting Services instance on the local system. The default instance is identified with the MSSQLSERVER keyword.

It is recommended that you back up the encryption key when the server is first initialized, the service account is changed, or whenever the key is deleted or re-created. Although it is password-protected, the backup file should be secured to prevent unauthorized access to sensitive information.

If you suspect that the encryption key has been compromised, you can re-create it using the Reporting Services Configuration Manager or the rskeymgmt command-line utility with the -s parameter, as illustrated below. This operation can be time-consuming, so you might want to restrict user access to the Reporting Services instance until finished.

If your Reporting Services instance is part of a scale-out deployment, you will need to reinitialize the other instances in the environment with the newly created key per instructions provided in Books Online.

```
rskeymgmt.exe -s -i MSSQLSERVER
```

To recover the encryption key, use either the Reporting Services Configuration Manager or the rskeymgmt command-line utility with the −a parameter. Both approaches will require you to identify the backup file and supply its password.

```
rskeymgmt.exe -a -i MSSQLSERVER -f c:\backups\rs_20080901.snk -p p@ssw0rd
```

Deletion of the encryption key is considered an operation of last resort. Once completed, you will need to re-create all shared and report-specific connection strings containing it and reactivate all subscriptions. As before, this operation can be performed using the Reporting Services Configuration Manager or the rskeymgmt command-line utility, this time with the −d parameter, as illustrated below:

```
rskeymgmt.exe -d -i MSSQLSERVER
```

If your Reporting Services instance is part of a scale-out deployment, you will need to delete the key on each of the instances in the environment. Please refer to Books Online for instructions for completing this operation.

Configuration Files

Several configuration files affect Reporting Services. To fully recover your installation, you will want backups of these files. Reporting Services itself does not provide a mechanism for this. However, you can use any number of file backup techniques to safeguard these files. The following table identifies the configuration files that you will want to back up and their default locations:

Configuration File	Default Location
ReportingServicesService.exe.config	*<drive>*:\Program Files\Microsoft SQL Server\ MSRS10.*<instancename>*\Reporting Services\ReportServer\Bin
RSReportServer.config	*<drive>*:\Program Files\Microsoft SQL Server\ MSRS10.*<instancename>*\Reporting Services\ReportServer
RSSrvPolicy.config	*<drive>*:\Program Files\Microsoft SQL Server\ MSRS10.*<instancename>*\Reporting Services\ReportServer
RSMgrPolicy.config	*<drive>*:\Program Files\Microsoft SQL Server\ MSRS10.*<instancename>*\Reporting Services\ReportManager
Web.config	*<drive>*:\Program Files\Microsoft SQL Server\ MSRS10.*<instancename>*\Reporting Services\ReportServer
Web.config	*<drive>*:\Program Files\Microsoft SQL Server\ MSRS10.*<instancename>*\Reporting Services\ReportManager
Machine.config	*<drive>*:\Windows\Microsoft.NET\Framework*<version>*\ CONFIG

Other Items

Your backup and recovery plan should consider any custom scripts or components in use by your installation. In addition, you will want to make sure purchased components, installation media, service packs, and hotfixes are available during a recovery event. If you have created a database to house execution log data (discussed below in this chapter), you may want to back this up as well.

Monitoring

Effective monitoring should allow you to quickly identify or even anticipate problems within your environment. Reporting Services provides various features to support this activity. Reporting Services can be used as a tool to present this data to administrators in an easier-to-consume manner.

This section explores the use of:

❑ Setup logs

❑ Windows application event log

❑ Trace logs

❑ Execution log

❑ Performance counters

❑ Server management reports

Set-up Logs

During installation, the set-up application creates a series of text-based log files recording messages and statistics generated as part of the process. By default, these are located in subfolders of the <drive>:\Program Files\Microsoft SQL Server\100\Setup Bootstrap\LOG folder. These subfolders are named using the convention *YYYYMMDD_nnnn*, where *YYYY*, *MM*, and *DD* represent the year, month, and day of the installation. The *nnnn* portion of the name represents an incrementing four-digit number, the highest value of which identifies the most recent installation attempt.

The contents of these folders are a bit overwhelming but worth exploring if you experience errors during an installation attempt. To review the summary status of the most recent installation attempt, simply direct your attention to the Summary.txt file within the <drive>:\Program Files\Microsoft SQL Server\100\Setup Bootstrap\LOG folder.

Windows Application Event Logs

Reporting Services writes critical error, warning, and informational messages to the *Windows application event log*. These messages are identified as originating from the Report Server, Report Manager, and Scheduling and Delivery Processor event sources.

The complete list of Reporting Services event log messages is documented in Books Online. Administrators will want to familiarize themselves with this list and periodically review the Windows Application event log for these and other critical messages. The Windows event logs are viewable using the operating system's Event Viewer applet.

Trace Logs

The *trace logs* are a great source of information about activity taking place within the Reporting Services Windows service. You can locate these files in the <drive>:\Program Files\Microsoft SQL Server\ MSRS10.<instancename>\Reporting Services\LogFiles folder. The logs are by default named *ReportServerService__MM_DD_YYYY_hh_mm_ss*, where *MM, DD, YYYY, hh, mm,* and *ss* represent the month, day, year, hour, minute, and second, respectively, the file was created. Each of these files is viewable using a simple text editor.

By default, Reporting Services is configured to write exceptions, warnings, re-start, and status messages to the trace logs files. Log files are retained for a configurable number of days, and a new log file is created at the top of the day, when the Reporting Services Windows service is started, or when the file reaches a configurable maximum size. The configuration settings affecting the trace logs are found within the RStrace section of the ReportingServicesService.exe.config file typically located within the <drive>:\Program Files\Microsoft SQL Server\MSRS10.<instancename>\Reporting Services\ ReportServer\Bin folder. The RStrace settings are identified in the following table along with their defaults:

Setting	Default	Description
FileName	ReportServerService_	The first part of the filename. A string indicating the date and time the file was created along with a .log extension is appended to this to produce the full filename.
FileSizeLimitMb	32	The maximum size of the trace file in megabytes (MB). A value ≤ 0 is treated as 1.
KeepFilesForDays	14	The number of days to retain a trace file. A value ≤ 0 is treated as 1.
TraceListeners	debugwindow,file	A comma-delimited list of one or more trace log output targets. Valid values within the list include debugwindow, file, and stdout.
TraceFileMode	Unique (default)	A value indicating that each trace file should contain data for a single day. Do not modify this setting.

(continued)

Setting	Default	Description
DefaultTraceSwitch	3	The default trace level for any component identified in the Components setting but for which no trace switch is provided. Values include:
		0 — Disabled 1 — Exceptions and re-starts 2 — Exceptions, re-starts, and warnings 3 — Exceptions, re-starts, warnings, and status messages 4 — Verbose mode
Components	All:3	A comma-delimited list of components and their associated trace levels determining the information to be included in the trace.
		The components represent activities capable of producing trace messages. The valid components are:
		RunningJobs — Report and subscription execution
		SemanticQueryEngine — Report model usage SemanticModelGenerator — Report model generation
		All — Any of the components, except http, not otherwise specified
		http — HTTP requests received by Reporting Services
		The type of message written for each specified component is controlled by a trace level. These levels are:
		0 — Disabled 1 — Exceptions and re-starts 2 — Exceptions, re-starts, and warnings 3 — Exceptions, re-starts, warnings, and status messages 4 — Verbose mode

The http component identified in the table above is new to SQL Server 2008 Reporting Services. It instructs Reporting Services to record HTTP requests to a separate trace log file in the traditional W3C extended log format.

The http component is not covered by the All component. Therefore, the default Components setting of All:3 leaves HTTP logging disabled. To enable HTTP logging, append the http component to the

`Components` list with a trace level of 4. Any other trace level for the `http` component will leave it disabled.

The HTTP trace log files are stored in the same folder as the traditional trace files. Trace configuration settings such as `FileSizeLimitMb` and `KeepFilesForDays` serve double duty, affecting the management of both the traditional and HTTP trace log files.

Two HTTP trace log-specific settings, `HttpTraceFileName` and `HttpTraceSwitches`, are manually added to the ReportingServicesService.exe.config file to override the default HTTP trace log file name and data format, respectively. If the `HttpTraceSwitches` setting is not specified, those fields identified as defaults in the following table are recorded to the HTTP trace logs.

Field	Description	Default
Date	The date of the event	No
Time	The time of the event	No
ActivityID	The activity identifier	Yes
SourceActivityID	The source activity identifier	Yes
ClientIp	The IP address of the client accessing the Report Server	Yes
UserName	The name of the user who accessed the Report Server	No
ServerPort	The port number used for the connection	No
Host	The content of the host header	No
Method	The action or SOAP method called from the client	Yes
UriStem	The resource accessed	Yes
UriQuery	The query used to access the resource	No
ProtocolStatus	The HTTP status code	Yes
BytesSent	The number of bytes sent by the server	No
BytesReceived	The number of bytes received by the server	No
TimeTaken	The time (in milliseconds) from the instant that HTTP.SYS returns request data until the server finishes the last send, excluding network transmission time	No
ProtocolVersion	The protocol version used by the client	No
UserAgent	The browser type used by the client	No
CookieReceived	The content of the cookie received by the server	No
CookieSent	The content of the cookie sent by the server	No
Referrer	The previous site visited by the client	No

The following sample shows the `RSTrace` section of the ReportingServicesService.exe.config file with both traditional and HTTP logging enabled and the `HttpTraceFileName` and `HttpTraceSwitches` settings explicitly configured. Note the `Components` setting with the `http` component specified with a trace level of 4.

```
<RStrace>
    <add name="FileName" value="ReportServerService_" />
    <add name="FileSizeLimitMb" value="32" />
    <add name="KeepFilesForDays" value="14" />
    <add name="Prefix" value="tid, time" />
    <add name="TraceListeners" value="debugwindow, file" />
    <add name="TraceFileMode" value="unique" />
    <add name="HttpTraceFileName" value="RS_HTTP_" />
    <add name="HttpTraceSwitches" value="Date,Time,ActivityID,
        SourceActivityID,ClientIp,UserName,Method,
        UriStem,UriQuery,ProtocolStatus,BytesSent,
        BytesReceived,TimeTaken" />
    <add name="Components" value="runningjobs:3,all:2,http:4" />
</RStrace>
```

It is important that when you modify the configuration file, you make a backup should a problem arise with your changes. Also, please be aware that setting names are case-sensitive although the values do not appear to be.

Execution Logs

Reporting Services stores quite a bit of data about the execution of reports in a collection of tables in the ReportServer database. Collectively, these tables are referred to as the *execution log*.

To make this data accessible, Reporting Services provides a SQL Server Integration Services (SSIS) package named *RSExecutionLog_Update.dtsx* with the Reporting Services samples. The package extracts execution log data from the ReportServer database into a secondary database. If you have installed these samples, you can typically find this package at <drive>:\Program Files\Microsoft SQL Server\ 100\Samples\Reporting Services\Report Samples\Server Management Sample Reports\Execution Log Sample Reports.

The package makes reference to a SQL Server database named *RSExecutionLog*, which you will need to create. After you have created the RSExecutionLog database, you will need to create the table structures it will use to hold your data. The `Createtables.sql` script provided in the same folder as the SSIS package will handle this task for you. When executing this script, be sure that you are using the RSExecutionLog database, as the script itself does not contain a `USE` statement.

Once the database is created, verify that the Connection Managers within the SSIS package are pointed to it. With this done, you are now able to extract data from the ReportServer database to the RSExecutionLog database for review and analysis.

The volume of data associated with the execution logs can get quite large. Reporting Services is configured by default to retain execution log data for 60 days. You can alter this setting through SQL Server Management Studio by connecting to the Reporting Services instance, right-clicking on the instance object, and selecting Properties from the context menu. In the Server Properties dialog, navigate to the Logging page, as shown in Figure 14-7. Here you can change the number of days that the data is retained or disable execution logging altogether.

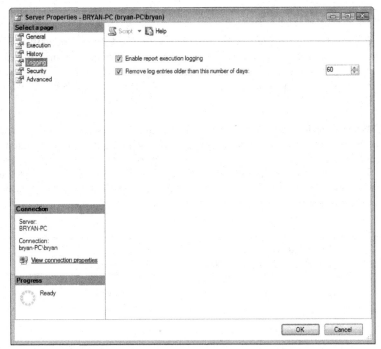

Figure 14-7

The RSExecutionLog database does not have a built-in data clean-up mechanism. The `Cleanup.sql` script provided in the same folder as the SSIS package can be used to purge old data from the RSExecutionLog database. The script uses a hard-coded date of January 1, 2004 as the cut-off point for data expiration. The following code sample shows a section of the `Cleanup.sql` script modified to drop data older than 180 days (about 6 months) from the current date and time.

```
/*
Change this constant for the earliest data
 Everything earlier will be deleted
 */
DECLARE @EarliestTimeStart datetime
/* ORIGINAL CODE
SET @EarliestTimeStart = '2004-01-01 00:00:00'
                         -- ** Always use ODBC cannonical form **
                         -- i.e. yyyy-mm-dd hh:mi:ss(24h)SET
*/
-- NEW CODE
SET @EarliestTimeStart = DATEADD(dd, -180, GETDATE())
```

To consume the execution log data, the Reporting Services samples come with three predefined reports: Execution Status Codes, Report Summary, and Execution Summary. The reports are pretty self-explanatory and can be used as a starting point for the development of a larger array of administrative reports.

Performance Counters

Windows performance counters provide insight into system utilization and stability. Administrators have long used these to monitor the overall health of a system, identify trends that may lead to problems, and verify the effect of changes to various system components. To support this activity, Reporting Services provides three performance objects: MSRS 2008 Web Service, MSRS 2008 Windows Service, and ReportServer Service.

The MSRS 2008 Web Service object presents counters related to report processing, whereas the MSRS 2008 Windows Service object presents counters related to scheduled operations, such as subscription execution and delivery and snapshot execution. The ReportServer Service object presents counters related to HTTP- and memory-related events. Although focused on different subject areas, many of the counters presented by these objects are named and defined identically. The following table lists the counters and the objects with which they are associated.

MSRS 2008 Web Service	MSRS 2008 Windows Service	Report Server Service	Counter	Description
No	Yes	Yes	Active Connections	Number of connections active against server
Yes	Yes	No	Active Sessions	Number of active sessions
No	Yes	Yes	Bytes Received Total	Number of bytes received
No	Yes	Yes	Bytes Received/ Sec	Rate of bytes received per second
No	No	Yes	Bytes Sent Total	Number of bytes sent
No	No	Yes	Bytes Sent/Sec	Rate of bytes sent per second
Yes	Yes	No	Cache Hits/Sec	Number of Report Server cache hits per second
Yes	Yes	No	Cache Hits/Sec (Semantic Models)	Number of times per second that models can be retrieved from the cache
Yes	Yes	No	Cache Misses/Sec	Number of times per second that reports cannot be retrieved from the cache

MSRS 2008 Web Service	MSRS 2008 Windows Service	Report Server Service	Counter	Description
Yes	Yes	No	Cache Misses/Sec (Semantic Models)	Number of times per second that models cannot be retrieved from the cache
No	No	Yes	Errors Total	The total number of errors that occur during the execution of HTTP requests (error codes 400s and 500s)
No	No	Yes	Errors/Sec	Number of errors that occur during the execution of HTTP requests (error codes 400s and 500s) per second
Yes	Yes	No	First Session Requests/Sec	Number of new user sessions that are started per second
No	No	Yes	Logon Attempts Total	Number of logon attempts for RSWindows authentication types
No	No	Yes	Logon Attempts/ Sec	Rate of logon attempts
No	No	Yes	Logon Successes Total	Number of successful logons for RSWindows authentication types
No	No	Yes	Logon Successes/ Sec	Rate of successful logons
Yes	Yes	No	Memory Cache Hits/Sec	Number of times per second that reports can be retrieved from the in-memory cache

(continued)

MSRS 2008 Web Service	MSRS 2008 Windows Service	Report Server Service	Counter	Description
Yes	Yes	No	Memory Cache Miss/Sec	Number of times per second that reports cannot be retrieved from the in-memory cache
No	No	Yes	Memory Pressure State	A number from 1 to 5 indicating the current memory state of the server: (1) no pressure, (2) low pressure, (3) medium pressure, (4) high pressure, (5) exceeded pressure
No	No	Yes	Memory Shrink Amount	Number of bytes the server requested to shrink
No	No	Yes	Memory Shrink Notifications/Sec	Number of shrink notifications the server issued in the last second
Yes	Yes	No	Next Session Requests/Sec	Number of requests per second for reports that are open in an existing session
Yes	Yes	No	Report Requests	Number of active report requests
Yes	Yes	No	Reports Executed/Sec	Number of reports executed per second
No	Yes	Yes	Requests Disconnected	Number of requests that have been disconnected because of a communication failure
No	No	Yes	Requests Executing	Number of requests currently executing

MSRS 2008 Web Service	MSRS 2008 Windows Service	Report Server Service	Counter	Description
No	Yes	Yes	Requests Not Authorized	Number of requests failing with HTTP 401 error code
No	Yes	Yes	Requests Rejected	Total number of requests not executed because of insufficient server resources
No	No	Yes	Requests Total	The total number of requests received by the Report Server service since service startup
Yes	Yes	Yes	Requests/Sec	Number of requests per second
No	Yes	Yes	Tasks Queued	Tasks Queued represents the number of tasks that are waiting for a thread to become available for processing
Yes	Yes	No	Total Cache Hits	Total number of Report Server cache hits
Yes	Yes	No	Total Cache Hits (Semantic Models)	Total number of cache hits made in the model cache
Yes	Yes	No	Total Cache Misses	Total number of cache misses
Yes	Yes	No	Total Cache Misses (Semantic Models)	Total number of cache misses made in the model cache
Yes	Yes	No	Total Memory Cache Hits	Total number of cache hits made in the in-memory cache
Yes	Yes	No	Total Memory Cache Misses	Total number of cache misses made in the in-memory cache

(continued)

MSRS 2008 Web Service	MSRS 2008 Windows Service	Report Server Service	Counter	Description
Yes	Yes	No	Total Processing Failures	Total number of processing failures
Yes	Yes	No	Total Rejected Threads	Total number of rejected threads as a result of thread pressure
Yes	Yes	No	Total Reports Executed	Total number of reports executed
Yes	Yes	No	Total Requests	Total number of requests being processed

Together, these three objects present 72 counters with which you can monitor an installation. It is not advised that you monitor each one of these. Instead, consider using high-level statistics such as Active Sessions, Requests/Sec, Reports Executed/Sec, and First Session Requests/Sec for your day-to-day monitoring. As specific needs arise, you will want to incorporate additional counters until those needs are addressed.

In addition to the Reporting Services performance counters, you might consider monitoring the Reporting Services Windows service from the operating system's perspective. Windows provides a Process performance object through which a number of performance counters are provided. A few of the more commonly monitored counters under this object are listed in the following table:

Counter	Description
% Processor Time	The percentage of elapsed time that all process threads used the processor to execute instructions
Page Faults/sec	The rate at which page faults by the threads executing in this process are occurring
Virtual Bytes	The current size, in bytes, of the virtual address space the process is using

Finally, you will want to keep tabs on a few counters that indicate the overall health of the systems on which Reporting Services resides. Commonly monitored performance counters in this category include those listed in the following table:

Object	Counter	Description
Processor	% Processor Time	This counter is the primary indicator of processor activity and displays the average percentage of busy time observed during the sample interval.
System	Processor Queue Length	Processor Queue Length is the number of threads in the processor queue.
Memory	Pages/sec	The rate at which pages are read from or written to disk to resolve hard page faults. This counter is a primary indicator of the kinds of faults that cause system-wide delays.
Logical Disk	% Free Space	% Free Space is the percentage of total usable space on the selected logical disk drive that was free.
Physical Disk	Avg. Disk Queue Length	Avg. Disk Queue Length is the average number of both Read and Write requests that were queued for the selected disk during the sample interval.
Network Interface	Current Bandwidth	Current Bandwidth is an estimate of the current bandwidth of the network interface in bits per second (BPS). For interfaces that do not vary in bandwidth or for those where no accurate estimation can be made, this value is the nominal bandwidth.
Network Interface	Bytes Total/sec	Bytes Total/sec is the rate at which bytes are sent and received over each network adapter, including framing characters. Network Interface\Bytes Total/sec is a sum of Network Interface\Bytes Received/sec and Network Interface\Bytes Sent/sec.

Server Management Reports

As mentioned above in this chapter, the Reporting Services samples come with three reports for the review of the extracted execution log data. Two other sample reports are provided with the Reporting Services tasks to provide administrators insight into database structures. Collectively, these are known as the *server management reports*.

The server management reports are not intended to address all of your administrative needs. Instead, they illustrate how Reporting Services can be used as a tool supporting its own administration and management. It is not hard to imagine a number of additional administrative reports providing deeper insight into the execution log data. With a little bit of effort, data sources such as the performance counters, trace logs, and the Windows Application event logs can also be integrated and made accessible for reporting.

The possibilities for server management reporting are endless. With some up-front investment to consolidate data sources, you can leverage Reporting Services functionality to reduce the overall administrative burden of your environment.

Configuration

Reporting Services supports several configurable features and options to support the precise needs of your organization. Books Online documents many of these, and still others can be identified with a little exploration. The following sections explore a few of the more frequently configured Reporting Services elements:

❑ Memory management

❑ URL Reservations

❑ E-mail delivery

❑ Rendering extensions

❑ My Reports

Memory Management

The following four settings in the RSReportServer.config configuration file, typically located within the <drive>:\Program Files\Microsoft SQL Server\MSRS10.<instancename>\Reporting Services\ ReportServer folder, determine how Reporting Services manages its memory:

❑ WorkingSetMinimum

❑ WorkingSetMaximum

❑ MemorySafetyMargin

❑ MemoryThreshold

The WorkingSetMinimum and WorkingSetMaximum settings determine the range of memory that Reporting Services may use. By default, these settings are not recorded in the configuration file. Instead, Reporting Services assumes values of 60 percent and 100 percent of the system's physical memory, respectively.

To override these defaults, you can add the settings to the configuration file under the same parent as `MemorySafetyMargin` and `MemoryThreshold`. The values associated with the `WorkingSetMinimum` and `WorkingSetMaximum` settings represent absolute kilobytes of memory. If you are running multiple memory-intensive applications on your Reporting Services server, you should consider implementing these settings to avoid memory contention.

Within the range of memory available to it, Reporting Services implements a state-based memory management model. The `MemorySafetyMargin` setting, defaulted to 80 percent of the `WorkingSetMaximum`, defines the boundary between the low and medium memory pressure states. The `MemoryThreshold` setting, defaulted to 90 percent of the `WorkingSetMaximum`, defines the boundary between the medium and high memory pressure states.

Within each memory pressure state, Reporting Services grants and takes back memory for report requests differently. For systems experiencing consistent loads, operating in the low and medium states is ideal. The default settings for `MemorySafetyMargin` and `MemoryThreshold` favor these states.

For systems experiencing spikes in memory utilization, such as might occur if multiple, large reports are simultaneously processed, the medium and even high memory states may allow for greater concurrency although reports may be rendered a bit more slowly. If this better matches the usage pattern of your system, you might want to lower the `MemorySafetyMargin` and `MemoryThreshold` settings to more quickly move into these memory states.

URL Reservations

If you performed a Files Only installation of Reporting Services, you must configure URL reservations for the Reporting Services Web service and Report Manager. *URL reservations* tell the operating system's HTTP.SYS driver where to direct requests intended for Reporting Services. URL reservations minimally consist of a virtual directory, an IP address, and a TCP port.

Advanced configuration options enable you to associate an SSL certificate with the URL reservation. This is addressed in Books Online.

The virtual directory identifies the application to which communications will be targeted. Report Manager typically uses the `reports` virtual directory, whereas the Web service typically uses the `reportserver` virtual directory.

Named instances typically use the `reports_instancename` and `reportserver_instancename` virtual directories for Report Manager and the Web service, respectively.

The URL reservation's IP address identifies which IP addresses in use by the server the Reporting Services application will be associated with. The URL reservation is typically configured to be associated with all IP addresses in use on the server, but you can configure it to be associated with a specific IP address, including the loopback address, or to work with any IP addresses not explicitly reserved by other applications. This latter option is not recommended in most situations.

Finally, the URL reservation is tied to a TCP port. Typically, HTTP communications take place over TCP port 80. You may have multiple applications on a given server listening on the same TCP port so long as the overall URL reservation is unique on the server. If you specify a TCP port other than 80 (or 433 if you are using HTTPS communications), you will need to include the port number in the URL whenever you communicate with Report Manager or the Web service.

If you are running Reporting Services on 32-bit Windows XP (SP2), TCP ports cannot be shared between URL reservations. Therefore, it is suggested that you use TCP port 8080 on this system for HTTP communications with Reporting Services. For more information on this topic, please see Books Online.

To configure a URL reservation for the Reporting Services Web service, access the Web Service URL page of the Reporting Services Configuration Manager, as shown in Figure 14-8. On this page, enter the virtual directory, IP address, and TCP port for the Web Service's URL reservation. Once changes are applied, you are presented with the Web services URL, which you can click on to test.

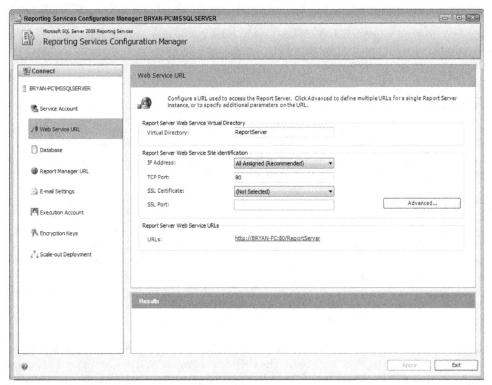

Figure 14-8

To configure a URL reservation for the Report Manager application, access the Report Manager URL page of the Reporting Services Configuration Manager, as shown in Figure 14-9. The Report Manager URL reservation will leverage the IP address and TCP port settings of the Web service's reservation. Enter the Report Manager's virtual directory, apply the changes, and click on the provided URL to test the changes.

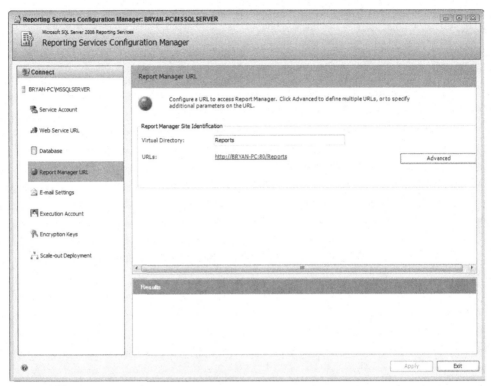

Figure 14-9

This has been a high-level discussion of URL reservations. Advanced options are available that require deeper knowledge of networking concepts. Those familiar with these topics should have no problems understanding the interfaces and configuring Reporting Services appropriately. If you need to configure the Reporting Services URL reservations differently from what is discussed here, it is recommended that you engage your network support staff to explore your options.

E-mail Delivery

E-mail delivery of reports is a powerful feature of Reporting Services for driving report consumption. It also provides opportunities for overuse and abuse and raises the administrative overhead of the environment. Because of this and the potential complexity of its configuration, the feature is disabled by default.

To enable e-mail delivery, you simply configure the e-mail delivery extension. Books Online documents several variations for its configuration, but most systems will make use of what is described as the "minimum configuration."

The *minimal configuration* requires the name or IP address of a remote SMTP server (or gateway) and a valid e-mail account on the SMTP server. This information is entered into the E-mail Settings page of the Reporting Services Configuration Manager, as shown in Figure 14-10, to enable the delivery extension.

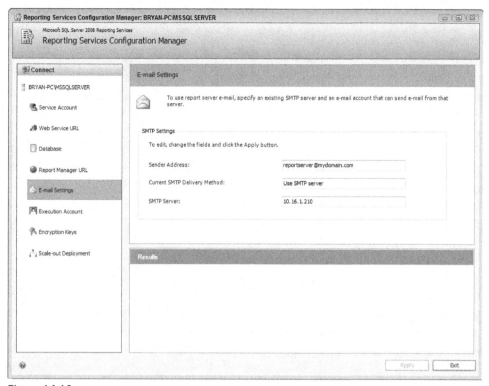

Figure 14-10

Communication with the SMTP server will be through the Reporting Services service account. The service account will require SendAs rights with the SMTP server in order to send e-mail through the configured e-mail account.

If this is not properly set or any other problems prevent Reporting Services from sending e-mail through the SMTP server, error messages will be displayed in the Windows application event log as well as in the status message associated with e-mail-based subscriptions in Report Manager. However, problems with e-mail delivery downstream from the SMTP server will not be reflected in Reporting Services. For this reason, it is recommended that you test your e-mail configuration by setting up a test subscription to a monitored e-mail account and verify end-to-end delivery of the subscription message.

Once configured, users assigned the "Manage individual subscriptions" or "Manage all subscriptions" tasks are presented the option to use e-mail delivery (and any other enabled delivery options) when setting up subscriptions. Reporting Services does not provide a mechanism to secure the e-mail delivery option separately from other delivery mechanisms.

Once enabled, you can disable e-mail delivery by simply removing the settings recorded in the Reporting Services Configuration Manager. Please be aware that although this disables e-mail delivery, subscriptions already configured to use this delivery mechanism will continue to run as is and fail until they are disabled or reconfigured to use another delivery mechanism. For this reason, it is suggested that you disable e-mail delivery in phases.

In the first phase, prevent the creation of new e-mail-based subscriptions by commenting out the appropriate Extension entry within the DeliveryUI section of the RSReportServer.config file. This removes e-mail delivery as an option in Report Manager. The following code sample illustrates this modification:

```
<DeliveryUI>
    <!-- Extension Name="Report Server Email"
Type="Microsoft.ReportingServices.EmailDeliveryProvider.EmailDeliveryProviderControl,
        ReportingServicesEmailDeliveryProvider">
        <Configuration>
          <RSEmailDPConfiguration>
            <DefaultRenderingExtension>MHTML</DefaultRenderingExtension>
          </RSEmailDPConfiguration>
        </Configuration>
    </Extension -->
    <Extension Name="Report Server FileShare"
Type="Microsoft.ReportingServices.FileShareDeliveryProvider.FileShareUIControl,
        ReportingServicesFileShareDeliveryProvider">
              <DefaultDeliveryExtension>True</DefaultDeliveryExtension>
    </Extension>
</DeliveryUI>
```

It is important to note that although this removes e-mail delivery as an option in Report Manager, this does not prevent applications from creating new e-mail-based subscriptions through the Web services interface. If applications make use of this interface to create subscriptions, work with the application owners to disable this feature.

The second phase of disabling e-mail delivery involves reconfiguring any subscriptions making use of e-mail delivery. Work with content owners to determine appropriate alternatives as part of this work. Once migration is completed, you can then safely proceed with disabling e-mail delivery, as described above.

Rendering Extensions

Reporting Services comes preconfigured to render reports to a number of formats. The formats available are determined by the rendering extensions installed on the server and configured in the Render section of the RSReportServer.config file. Below is a sample entry for the Image rendering extension:

```
<Extension Name="IMAGE"
Type="Microsoft.ReportingServices.Rendering.ImageRenderer.ImageRenderer,
    Microsoft.ReportingServices.ImageRendering"/>
```

Each rendering extension entry minimally consists of name and type attributes. These identify the extension within the configuration file. The value associated with the Name attribute serves as a unique identifier for the extension within the configuration file. The Type attribute associates the entry with a particular rendering extension.

The name of the extension displayed to end-users is the rendering extension's default display name, unless an OverrideNames setting is entered into the configuration file. The OverrideNames setting is recorded with the extension, as demonstrated below. In this sample, the default name of the Image rendering extension, *TIFF File*, is overridden with the shortened name of *TIFF*.

```
<Extension Name="IMAGE"
Type="Microsoft.ReportingServices.Rendering.ImageRenderer.ImageRenderer,
    Microsoft.ReportingServices.ImageRendering">
    <OverrideNames>
        <Name Language="en-US">TIFF</Name>
    </OverrideNames>
</Extension>
```

It is important to note that the `Language` attribute associated with the `OverrideNames` setting should match the language settings of the Reporting Services server. If the wrong or no language is specified, the `OverrideNames` entry is ignored, and the rendering extension's default name is used.

As was mentioned in Chapter 4, rendering extensions are capable of supporting various formats. In addition, aspects of how each extension renders to a particular format are configurable. To override the default rendering settings of a particular rendering extension, `DeviceInfo` settings can be added to an extension's entry in the configuration file. In addition, more than one entry for a rendering extension, typically with a different set of `DeviceInfo` settings, can be recorded in the configuration file so long as each extension entry is identified with a unique name attribute.

The following sample illustrates this using the Image rendering extension. In this example, the Image rendering extension is registered twice. In the first entry, the Image rendering extension is configured for its default settings allowing TIFF images to be produced. In the second entry, the Image rendering extension is configured to produce BMP images.

```
<Extension Name="IMAGE"
Type="Microsoft.ReportingServices.Rendering.ImageRenderer.ImageRenderer,
    Microsoft.ReportingServices.ImageRendering"/>
<Extension Name="BMP"
Type="Microsoft.ReportingServices.Rendering.ImageRenderer.ImageRenderer,
    Microsoft.ReportingServices.ImageRendering">
    <OverrideNames>
        <Name Language="en-US">BMP</Name>
    </OverrideNames>
    <Configuration>
        <DeviceInfo>
            <OutputFormat>BMP</OutputFormat>
            <PageHeight>11in</PageHeight>
            <PageWidth>8.5in</PageWidth>
        </DeviceInfo>
    </Configuration>
</Extension>
```

`DeviceInfo` settings are rendering-extension-specific. Books Online documents these settings for each of the default rendering extensions. It is important to note that without configuring device info settings in the RSReportServer.config file, you can still supply device info settings when accessing a report through URL access or Web services calls to control the rendering of the report for a specific request. In addition, URL access is the only mechanism allowing device info settings for the CSV rendering extension to be set resulting in a tab-delimited file.

Finally, the Extension entry for any rendering extensions you do not intend to use should be disabled by commenting it out in the RSReportServer.config file. However, if you simply wish to prevent a file format from being used with a particular subscription delivery option, you should add its name to the `ExcludedRenderFormats` section under the appropriate delivery extension within the RSReportServer .config file. In the following example, the extensions with `Name` attributes set to HTMLOWC, NULL, RGDI, and IMAGE are excluded from use with File Share delivery:

```
<Extensions>
    <Delivery>
        <Extension Name="Report Server FileShare"
Type="Microsoft.ReportingServices.FileShareDeliveryProvider.FileShareProvider,
        ReportingServicesFileShareDeliveryProvider">
            <MaxRetries>3</MaxRetries>
            <SecondsBeforeRetry>900</SecondsBeforeRetry>
            <Configuration>
                <FileShareConfiguration>
                    <ExcludedRenderFormats>
                        <RenderingExtension>HTMLOWC</RenderingExtension>
                        <RenderingExtension>NULL</RenderingExtension>
                        <RenderingExtension>RGDI</RenderingExtension>
                        <RenderingExtension>IMAGE</RenderingExtension>
                    </ExcludedRenderFormats>
                </FileShareConfiguration>
            </Configuration>
        </Extension>
    ...
    </Delivery>

    ...
</Extensions>
```

My Reports

The *My Reports feature* provides users a personal folder in Reporting Services within which they can manage and view their own content. This is a powerful feature for users but one that can get out of hand fast. The critical concern is that users are by default assigned elevated rights within their My Reports folder that allow them to store content on the site with no mechanism to restrict the type or size of that content.

By default, the My Reports feature is disabled. If enabled, a My Reports folder is presented to each user in his or her home directory. The folder is actually a link to a user-specific folder created by Reporting Services within the Users Folders folder. Only System Administrators have direct access to the Users Folders folder.

Within his or her My Reports folder, a user is a member of a pre-set role. By default, this is the My Reports role, which has the following tasks assigned to it:

❑   Create linked reports.

❑   View reports.

❑   Manage reports.

- ❑ View resources.
- ❑ View folders.
- ❑ Manage folders.
- ❑ Manage report history.
- ❑ Manage individual subscriptions.
- ❑ View data resources.
- ❑ Manage data sources.

These tasks, discussed in the previous chapter, provide elevated rights within this space. You might consider removing some of these tasks from the My Reports role or creating an alternative role with lesser privileges and using that as the default role assignment for the My Reports feature.

To enable the My Reports feature, open SQL Server Management Studio, and connect to the Reporting Services instance. Right-click on the instance object, and select Properties to launch the Server Properties dialog. Within the default General page of this dialog, as shown in Figure 14-11, use the checkbox next to the "Enable a My Reports folder for each user" option to toggle this feature on and off. If enabled, you can assign a role to each user within his or her My Reports folder through the dropdown just below the checkbox.

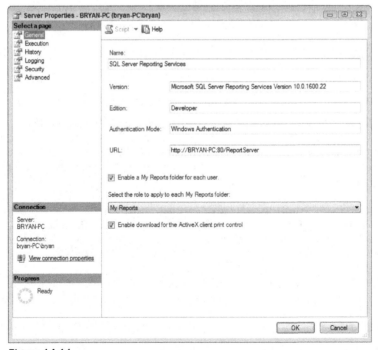

Figure 14-11

If you decide to enable this feature, closely monitor the consumption of space by users, and work with them to understand the feature's appropriate use. If you decide to disable the feature after having made it available, users will no longer be able to access their My Reports folder. However, the content of these folders remains within the system. Any subscriptions and snapshots associated with reports in these folders will continue to run. To properly clean up the My Reports folders, you will need to work with your users to migrate or drop their content.

Summary

In this chapter, you have explored elements of Reporting Services with the goal of developing a comprehensive administrative program. Although there are recommended best practices, there is no one right approach. It is important to understand your options and then work with your users, developers, and administrators to develop a program tailored to your specific needs. Once in place, it then becomes important to follow through on the actions specified and to be on the lookout for threats and changes in needs that may require adjustments to your routines and practices.

Part VI

Reporting Services Integration and Custom Programming

15

Integrating Reports into Custom Applications

Reporting Services was designed to be a flexible reporting technology that can be easily integrated into a variety of scenarios. Many reporting needs will never expand beyond the out-of-the-box functionality provided by Reporting Services. However, if the requirement arises, Reporting Services includes endless opportunities for integration with custom-built applications. The next chapter will explore integrating Reporting Services into a SharePoint environment. However, there are also organizations that maintain a custom corporate reporting portal. In these situations, developers might need a way to display numerous reports in a Web environment. Reporting Services can also be embedded into any of the lines of business applications. Developers might want to use Reporting Services to create invoices or purchase orders directly from their applications. Some organizations may decide that the default Report Manager is not robust enough for their needs. In this situation, a custom reporting management application can be built that completely replaces and expands on the functionality of the out-of-the-box Report Manager.

All these issues can be solved with the features available in Reporting Services. In this chapter, you will take a look at the following three methods of rendering reports from Reporting Services:

❑   Using URLs to access reports

❑   Using the Reporting Services Web service to programmatically render reports

❑   Using the `MicrosoftReportViewer` controls to embed reports

URL access allows you to quickly incorporate Reporting Services reports in applications such as web portals. Programmatic rendering allows for creating custom interfaces. Developers can do anything from implementing their own security architecture around Reporting Services to creating their own parameter interface.

In this chapter, you learn about:

❑ The syntax and structure for accessing Reporting Services through the URL

❑ The reporting items that can be accessed through the URL

❑ The parameter options that can be passed to the URL to control report output

❑ Creating a Windows application that renders reports to the filesystem

❑ Creating a web application that returns rendered reports to the browser

❑ Easily embedding reports in a Windows application using controls

URL Access

Reporting Services' main means for accessing reports is through HTTP requests. These requests can be made through URLs in a web browser or a custom application. By passing parameters in the URL, you can specify the report item, set the output format, and perform various other tasks. In the next few sections, you will look at the features available through URL requests, URL syntax, passing parameters, and setting the output format.

URL Syntax

The basic URL syntax is as follows:

http://server/virtualroot?[/pathinfo]&[prefix:]param=value[&[prefix:]param=value] . . . n]
The parameters in the syntax are as follows:

❑ server — Specifies the instance of Report Server you would like to access. To access your local machine, you can either type the machine name or use the localhost alias.

❑ virtualroot — Specifies the IIS virtual directory you specified during the setup. When installing Reporting Services, you must enter two virtual directories: one for the Report Manager and one for the Reporting Services Web service. By default, the virtual directory you would access is reportserver.

❑ pathinfo — After specifying the server and virtual directory to the Reporting Services Web service, you can pass several parameters to access report objects. The first parameter you pass is pathinfo, which specifies the path to the resource you want to access. To access the root of the Report Server, you can simply place a single forward slash (/).

Once you have listed the path, you can pass various parameters. These parameters will depend on the type of object you are referencing. Reports will have a number of parameters to specify properties such as the rendering format. Each parameter is separated by an ampersand (&) and contains a `name=value` pair for the parameter.

Here is a quick look at retrieving the list of items under the Professional SQL Reporting Services folder:

Note that in the examples throughout this chapter, the text should not contain a carriage return. This was added only for printing.

```
http://localhost/reportserver?%2fProfessional+SQL+Reporting+Services
        &rs:Command=ListChildren
```

Now that you've taken a look at the basic URL syntax, let's see how it is implemented in each of the Reporting Services objects.

Accessing Reporting Services Objects

URL requests are not limited to just reports. You can access various Reporting Services items, including:

❑   Folders

❑   Data sources

❑   Resources

❑   Reports

In this section, you will look at accessing each of the items listed above. You will go through sample URLs and look at items provided in the Adventure Works SQL Server 2008 Sample Databases and Reports.

The Adventure Works SQL Server 2008 Sample Databases and Reports can be downloaded at the following URL: `www.codeplex.com/SqlServerSamples`.

Folders

Accessing folders will be your starting point for looking at URL requests. Let's take a look at the simplest URL request you can make:

```
http://localhost/reports
```

That URL is redirected to the default Home page in Report Manager. With this request, you can see a listing of all reports, data sources, resources, and folders in the root directory of the Report Server, as shown in Figure 15-1. To access another server, simply replace `localhost` with the name of the server.

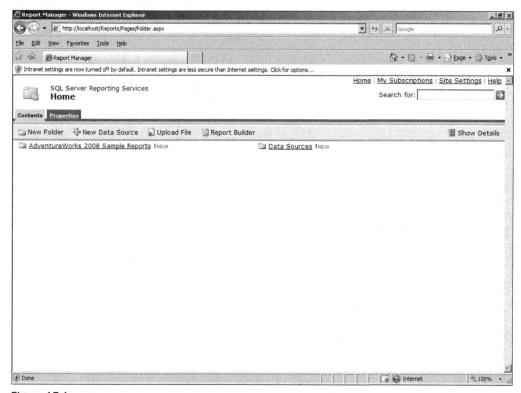

Figure 15-1

To see how other folder URL requests work, simply enter in the URL of the Report Server:

```
http://localhost/reportserver
```

A list of directories hosted by the Report Server is displayed. Clicking on the AdventureWorks 2008 Sample Reports link will give you the following URL, as shown in Figure 15-2:

```
http://localhost/reportserver?%2fAdventureWorks+2008+Sample+Reports
    &rs:Command=ListChildren
```

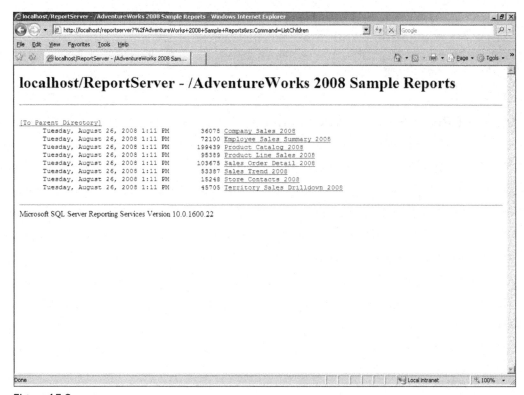

Figure 15-2

This URL contains the following items:

- ❑ **Path to the Report** — %2fAdventureWorks+2008+Sample+Reports

- ❑ **Command to List the Contents of the Directory** — rs:Command=ListChildren

You'll take a closer look at the URL parameters in the "Reporting Services URL Parameters" section below in this chapter.

Data Sources

Through URL requests, you can also view the contents of data sources. Let's take a look at the Data Sources folder. The Data Sources folder can be accessed by either clicking the Data Sources folder from the root folder or entering the following URL:

```
http://localhost/reportserver?%2fData+Sources&rs:Command=ListChildren
```

You'll see the listing of items, as shown in Figure 15-3.

Figure 15-3

If you have deployed the sample reports, you will notice that one of the items listed is AdventureWorks2008. You can tell that this item is a data source by the <ds> tag next to the item name. If you follow the AdventureWorks2008 link, you will be able to view the contents of that data source. Figure 15-4 shows the AdventureWorks2008 data source contents.

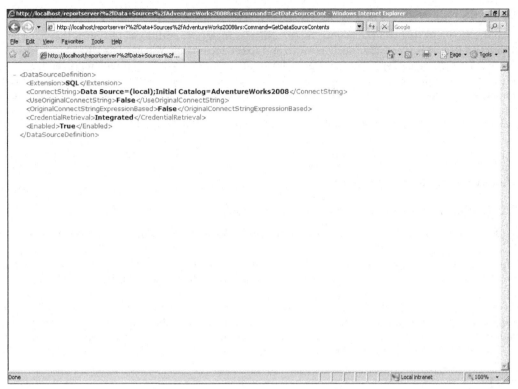

Figure 15-4

Let's take a look at the URL used to view the AdventureWorks2008 data source:

```
http://localhost/reportserver?%2fData+Sources%2fAdventureWorks2008
    &rs:Command=GetDataSourceContents
```

This URL contains the following items:

❑   **Path to the Data Source** — %2fData+Sources%2fAdventureWorks2008

❑   **Command to View the Data Source Content** — rs:Command=GetDataSourceContents

Viewing the data source enables you to quickly see how your data source is configured. Notice that this information is returned in XML format. This allows you to easily work with the data source information. If you have your own reporting application that shares a single connection, you could use this URL to dynamically load this data source information. This information could then be used to make other database connections in your application.

Resources

Resources are items that you use in your reports, such as images or additional resources that have been added to a Report Server folder, such as Word and Excel documents. You can use URLs to access resources stored on the Report Server. Depending on the type of resources you reference, either you will be prompted to open or save a file, such as a Word or Excel document, or the resource will be rendered directly in the browser. The `GetResourceContents` command can be used in the URL to reference the resource. For example, if an image is stored in a directory called *Images*, the URL to the directory and the command `GetResourceContents` can be used to reference that resource, as follows:

```
http://localhost/Reportserver?%2fImages%2fMyImage.jpg&rs:Command=GetResourceContents
```

The URL contains the following contents:

❑   **Path to the Resource** — %2fImages%2fMyImage.jpg

❑   **Command to Retrieve the Resource Content** — `rs:Command=GetResourceContents`

You can use this information in other applications. If you want to reference the image from a web page, you could simply set the `src` attribute of an image tag (`<img>`) to reference the earlier URL.

Resources can also be incredibly handy for storing documents. In your reporting solution, you might want to store readme files to accompany your reports. You can store these documents as resources on the Report Server and then apply different properties to them, such as security. Your application could then point to the resource URL to allow downloading of the document.

Reports

The most important objects you can access through the URL are your reports. This section provides a quick look at the syntax for accessing reports. Below we'll discuss the various parameters you can pass to change things such as report parameters, output formats, and other items.

The basic syntax for accessing a report is very similar to accessing all of your other resources. You should first specify a path to the report and then provide the commands for its output. Let's look at the basic URL for accessing the Company Sales report:

```
http://localhost/ReportServer/Pages/ReportViewer.aspx?%2fAdventureWorks+2008
+Sample+Reports%2fCompany+Sales+2008&rs:Command=Render
```

View the Company Sales report, as shown in Figure 15-5.

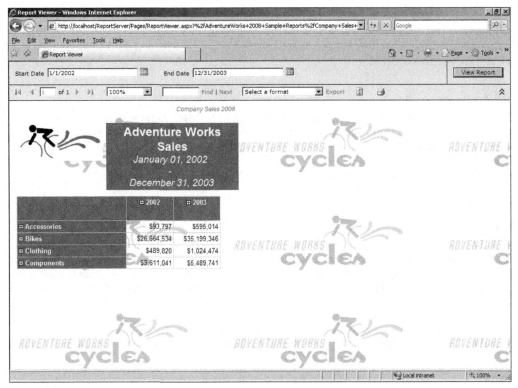

Figure 15-5

The URL contains the following contents:

❏   **Path to the Resource** — %2fAdventureWorks+2008+Sample+Reports%2fCompany+Sales+2008

❏   **Command to Retrieve the Resource Content** — rs:Command=Render

Using URLs is the easiest and most convenient way to embed Reporting Services reports into custom applications. A custom application can simply point to the desired report by either creating a simple hyperlink or by using an HTML rendering object such as the WebBrowser class to render the report within a Windows Forms application. A special Windows Forms control designed for viewing reports will also be covered in the Programmatic Rendering section below in this chapter.

The following section looks at the parameters that can be passed through the URL, including setting report parameters and output format.

Reporting Services URL Parameters

Now that you have seen the basics of obtaining items from your Report Server using URLs, let's take a look at passing some parameters. The next few sections will move through how parameters are passed to Reporting Services and what values for these parameters are available. The majority of the parameter functionality will be focused on report rendering, but some items will also apply to your data source, resources, and folder.

Parameter Prefixes

The first thing you need to take a look at is the different parameter prefixes in Reporting Services. There are five main parameter prefixes in Reporting Services: rs, rc, rv, dsp, and dsu. The following sections look at these prefixes in detail.

rs Prefix

In the earlier examples, you saw the parameter rs:Command. This parameter contains the prefix rs. The rs prefix is used to send commands to the Report Server. The following URL shows an example of the rs prefix being used to call the Command parameter and pass the ListChildren argument to it:

```
http://localhost/reportserver?%2fAdventureWorks+2008+Sample+Reports
    &rs:Command=ListChildren
```

rc Prefix

The second main parameter prefix in Reporting Services is the rc prefix. This prefix is used to interact with the given report output format. For example, if you are outputting your report as HTML, you can control the HTML viewer. You can use this prefix to pass parameters that do things such as hide toolbars or control the initial state of toggle items. The following URL calls the Employee Sales Summary report and turns off the parameter inputs:

```
http://localhost/ReportServer/Pages/ReportViewer.aspx?%2fAdventureWorks+2008
    +Sample+Reports%2fEmployee+Sales+Summary+2008&rs:Command=Render&rc:Parameters=False
```

rv Prefix

The rv prefix is new and is used to pass parameters to reports that are stored in a SharePoint document library. In a SharePoint document library, a SharePoint Report Viewer Web Part is used to display a report, and thus the rv prefix should be used for these reports.

dsu and dsp Prefixes

Parameter prefixes can also be used to send database credentials. Use the dsu prefix to pass the data source username, and use the dsp prefix to pass the data source password. In any Reporting Services report, you could incorporate multiple data sources. So, you need a way to specify which data source the credentials should be passed to. That's where the prefixes come in. The full syntax to use these prefixes is as follows:

```
[dsu | dsp]:datasourcename=value
```

For example, to pass the username *guest* with a password *guestPass* to your AdventureWorks2008 data source, you would use the following URL parameters:

```
&dsu:AdventureWorks2008=guest&dsp:AdventureWorks2008=guestPass
```

Be aware that these credentials will be passed unencrypted over the Internet and will be visible to the end-user. You can encrypt the URL using the Secure Sockets Layer (SSL) on your web server. This will prevent the information from being sent unencrypted but will not prevent the end-user from viewing the credentials that you pass. Make sure that you consider these factors in your reporting solution architecture.

Now that you have seen the different parameter prefixes in Reporting Services, we'll move on to the available parameters that can be used with the rv, rs, and rc prefixes.

Parameters

First, let's take a look at the new SharePoint endpoint parameter that can be used with reports that are hosted in a SharePoint Integrated mode Report Server configuration. The next chapter will go into detail about SharePoint integration, but for now, let's look at the parameters that can be used with the rv prefix. The following table lists the four available values and their uses:

Parameter	Use
Toolbar	The Toolbar parameter is used to modify the toolbar display of the SharePoint Report Viewer Web Part. The default value is Full, but a value of Navigation and None can also be passed to the Web Part. The Full value displays the entire toolbar. The Navigation value displays only the page navigation in the toolbar. And finally, the None value removes the toolbar entirely.
HeaderArea	The HeaderArea parameter is used to modify the header area of the SharePoint Report Viewer Web Part. The default value is Full, but a value of BreadCrumbsOnly and None can also be passed to the Web Part. The Full value displays the complete header. The BreadCrumbsOnly value bread-crumbs in the header. A value of None removes the header from view entirely.
DocMapAreaWidth	The DocMapAreaWidth parameter is used to display the width of the parameter area of the SharePoint Report Viewer Web Part. The value should be a non-negative number and defined in pixels.
AsyncRender	The AsyncRender parameter is used to inform the SharePoint Report Viewer Web Part to either render the report asynchronously or not. The value must be a Boolean value of True or False, with True meaning that the report will render asynchronously. If this parameter is not specified, the default value of True is used.

Now that you have seen the different rv parameters, let's take a look at the rs parameters. The following table lists the four available values and their uses:

Parameter	Use
Command	The Command parameter is used to send instructions to the Report Server about the item being retrieved. Available values return the report item and set session time-out values.
Format	The Format parameter is used when rendering reports. Any rendering formats available on the Report Server can be passed using this parameter.
ParameterLanguage	The ParameterLanguage parameter is used to pass a language in the URL that is different from the language specified in the browser. If this parameter is not specified, then the default is to use the cultural value of the browser.
Snapshot	The Snapshot parameter is used to retrieve historical report snapshots. Once a report has been stored in snapshot history, it is assigned a time/date stamp to uniquely identify that report. Passing this time/date stamp will return the appropriate report.

Now that you have seen the different rs parameters, let's take a look at some of their available values.

Command Parameter

The Command parameter is your main parameter for setting the output of a given report item. It can also be used for resetting a user's session information, which guarantees that a report is not rendered from the session cache. Here is a listing of the possible values that can be passed to the Command parameter:

Value	Use
GetDataSourceContents	The GetDataSourceContents command can be used to return data source information in an XML format. You can use this parameter on shared data sources.
GetResourceContents	This command returns the binary of your Reporting Services resources, such as images, via the URL.
ListChildren	Used in combination with a Reporting Services folder. This lets you view all the items in a given folder.
Render	Allows you to render the report using the URL. Probably the most frequently used command.
ResetSessionTimeout	Can be used to refresh a user's session cache. Because Reporting Services works typically via HTTP, it is crucial for the server to maintain state information about the user. However, if you want to ensure that a report is executed each time the user views a report, this state information needs to be refreshed. Use this parameter to reset the user's session and remove any session cache information.

Format Parameter

The Format parameter is the main parameter for controlling the report output. The available values for this parameter are determined by the different rendering extensions available on your Report Server. The following table shows the output formats available with the default installation of Reporting Services:

Value	Output
Web Formats	
HTML3.2	HTML version 3.2 output. Used for older browsers.
HTML4.0	HTML version 4.0. This format is supported by newer browsers, such as Internet Explorer 4.0 and above.
MHTML	MHTML standard output. This output format is used for sending HTML documents in e-mail. Using this format will embed all resources, such as images, into the MHTML document instead of referencing external URLs.
Print Formats	
IMAGE	The IMAGE format allows you to render your reports to several different graphical device interfaces (GDI) such as BMP, PNG, GIF, or TIFF.
PDF	The Portable Document Format (PDF) can be used for viewing and printing documents.
Data Formats	
WORD	Word output. Users can use this format to output a report into a standard Microsoft Word document format.
EXCEL	Excel output. Users can use this format to further manipulate report data.
CSV	Comma Separated Value (CSV) format. CSV is a standard data format and can be read by a wide variety of applications.
XML	Extensible Markup Language (XML) format. XML has become a standard data format, used by many different applications.
Control Format	
NULL	The NULL provider allows you to execute reports without rendering. This can be very useful when working with reports that have cached instances. You can use the NULL format to execute the report for the first time and then store the cached instance.

When you set the rendering formats via the URL, the report will either be rendered directly in the browser or you will be prompted to save the output file. Let's take a look at rendering the Company Sales 2008 report in PDF format. Enter the following URL using the rs:Format=PDF parameter:

```
http://localhost/ReportServer/Pages/ReportViewer.aspx?%2fAdventureWorks+2008+Sample
    +Reports%2fCompany+Sales+2008&rs:Command=Render&rs:Format=PDF
```

Figure 15-6 shows the output.

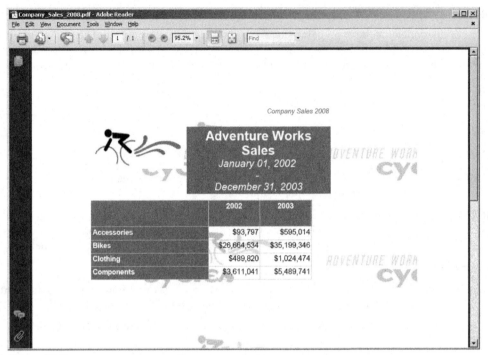

Figure 15-6

Notice that the browser will now prompt you to save the rendered report. This can be easily incorporated into your own custom applications or portals. You can simply give your users a link containing the rs:Format parameter and automatically output the correct format.

Setting Device Information

Now that you have seen the various output formats available in Reporting Services, you need to take a look at the different device information settings for the various formats. The Format parameter enables you to specify the type of format you want, but each format has specific settings that can be useful to you. For example, if you specify the IMAGE format, you get an output in TIFF. What if you wanted a bitmap or JPEG image? Well, to output in a different image format, all you need to do is to just specify device information when passing the URL. Take a look at outputting your Company Sales 2008 report in JPEG format using the following URL (Figure 15-7 shows the output):

```
http://localhost/ReportServer/Pages/ReportViewer.aspx?%2fAdventureWorks+2008
    +Sample+Reports%2fCompany+Sales+2008&rs:Command=Render&rs:Format=IMAGE
    &rc:OutputFormat=JPEG
```

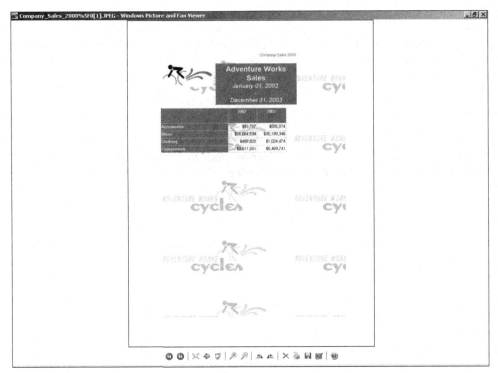

Figure 15-7

Notice that the file type sent back to you is a JPEG image. There are numerous device information settings you can use for each of the rendering extensions. Each device information setting is prefixed using the `rc` prefix. The following syntax can be used for passing device information:

```
http://server/virtualroot?/pathinfo&rs:Format=format&rc:param=value[&rc:param=value...n]
```

Now that you have seen the different output formats and commands you can pass to Reporting Services, let's take a look at passing information to your individual reports.

Passing Report Information through the URL

The previous sections illustrated how a URL can be used to control report rendering. In the next section, you look at how a URL can be used to control report execution. This section starts with an explanation of passing report parameters. These are the parameters that you define while authoring your report. Finally, you'll see how historical snapshots can be rendered using the URL.

Report Parameters

Many of your reports have parameters to control all kinds of behavior. You can use parameters to alter your query, filter datasets and tables, and even change the appearance of your reports. Reporting Services allows you to pass this information directly via a URL request. In the above section, you saw a lot about the parameter prefixes and the available values that can be sent to Reporting Services. With report parameters, you simply need to remove the prefix and directly call the parameter name.

In this example, the Employee Sales Summary 2008 report accepts three parameters: `EmployeeID`, `ReportMonth`, and `ReportYear`. You might want to allow your users to update these parameters through a custom interface you define. When you call the report, you will need to provide the parameter values in the URL, as shown here:

```
http://localhost/ReportServer/Pages/ReportViewer.aspx?%2fAdventureWorks+2008
    +Sample+Reports%2fEmployee+Sales+Summary+2008&rs%3aCommand=Render&EmployeeID=284
    &ReportMonth=12&ReportYear=2003
```

> **Note that the values come from the AdventureWorks2008 database. You can see a list of all of the employees and their IDs by using the following SQL command:**
>
> ```
> SELECT BusinessEntityID, FirstName, LastName
> FROM Person.Person
> ORDER BY LastName ASC
> ```

Let's take a look at calling the report with an `EmployeeID` of 283, which is David Campbell (see Figure 15-8).

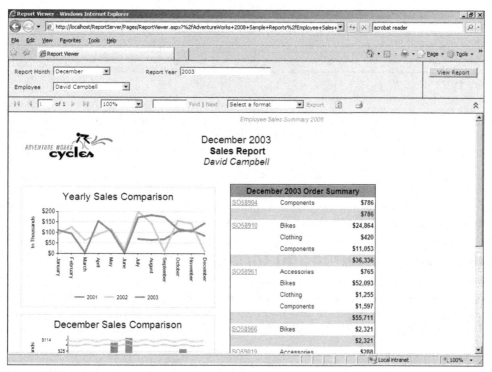

Figure 15-8

Notice that by passing the parameters in your URL, the HTML viewer updates to reflect the values. The parameter name that you use in the URL is defined in the report definition. Since your Report Parameter is called `EmployeeID`, that name is used in your URL.

Now that you have seen how to pass report parameters to the URL, let's look at passing snapshot IDs to render historical execution snapshots.

Rendering Snapshot History

One of the major features of Reporting Services is the ability to create execution snapshots of reports. Say you have a report in which the data updates on a monthly basis. Once the data is updated, it does not change for another month. A perfect example of this would be monthly financial statements. If your data changes only once a month, there is no reason to query your database every time you need a report. Therefore, you can use execution snapshots to store this information after the query has been executed. Going along the same lines as a monthly report, what should happen when your data updates from, say, January to February? You don't want to lose the January snapshot once the February information is available. That is where historical snapshots come into play. When you create the February snapshot, you add January to the snapshot history, and so on for each subsequent month.

Now that you have execution snapshots stored in history, you need some way to access them. Reporting Services gives you a very easy way to do this. As you have already seen, each report has a report path that can be used to render the report. To render a historical snapshot, you simply need to add a parameter for the historical snapshot ID.

The syntax to pass your snapshot ID is as follows:

```
http://server/virtualroot?[/pathinfo]&rs:Snapshot=snapshotid
```

The snapshot ID for your historical snapshot will be the time and date stamp of when the report was added to the history. The time is adjusted to GMT based on the time zone where the historical snapshot was added.

URL Rendering Summary

Through URL rendering, you have seen the various commands that can be passed to Reporting Services that can be used to control the report item display, the format to use, and snapshot information using the rs prefix. Once you have created your commands for the Report Server, you can pass parameters specific to the output format. Using the rc prefix and the device information parameters, you can specify things such as encoding and which items to display in the HTML viewer. After you have specified the report item, you need to know how to output it. You can pass parameters to your report by simply passing the parameter name and value combination.

The next section takes a look at the second part of rendering Reporting Service reports. You can use URLs for simple web applications and web portals, but sometimes you need finer control over report access and rendering. To achieve this, you'll use the Reporting Service Web service to programmatically render your reports.

Programmatic Rendering

There are several ways that reports may be integrated into custom Windows Forms and web applications. These include:

- ❑ Link to a report in web browser window using a URL rendering request.
- ❑ Replace web page content with a report by using SOAP rendering to write binary content to the web Response object.

❑ Use SOAP rendering to write report content to a file.

❑ Embed a report in an area of a web page by setting the source of a frame or `IFrame` tag.

❑ Use the Microsoft `ReportViewer` control in a Windows Forms or Web Forms application.

Rendering using a URL is very handy and easy to implement in many situations, but it does have its limitations. When rendering from the URL, you have to make sure that you use the security infrastructure provided with Reporting Services. For some applications, such as public web sites, you might want to implement your own security. In that case, rendering from the URL will not provide the functionality you need. In this section, you will take a look at rendering reports using the Reporting Services Web service.

You'll connect to the Reporting Services Web service, return a list of available reports, retrieve their parameters, and finally render the report. Let's take a look at three implementations of programmatic rendering. The first implementation is using a Window Forms application to render reports to a file. This will help you to understand the basic principles without a lot of interface work. The second implementation will take you through rendering through an ASP.NET page. You'll see some of the items that need to be considered when working through a web application. Last, you'll read about how the `MicrosoftReportViewer` control can embed reports in a Windows Forms application for viewing.

Common Scenarios

Before you look at the actual programming code for rendering reports, it is important to understand a couple of scenarios in which it is reasonable to do so. There are two scenarios that are commonly experienced while working with clients. They do not represent the only scenarios in which you would write your own rendering code, but do illustrate how and when custom code can be used. Let's look at each of these scenarios.

Custom Security

One of the biggest questions around Reporting Services involves how to use Reporting Services without using the standard security infrastructure. Reporting Services requires you to connect to reports using a Windows identity. In many organizations, this is just not possible. They have mixed environments or nontrusted domains that do not allow for identification to the Report Server. Some clients also have large-scale authentication and authorization infrastructures already implemented.

You can still use Reporting Services in these situations. Using your own security infrastructure involves creating both authentication and authorization code in your environment. After you have determined that a user can access a report, a Windows identity that you define can be used to connect to reports. To hide this security implementation, the Reporting Services Web service can be used. You can render reports directly to a browser or file without passing the original user identity to the Report Server.

Server-Side Parameters

Although URL rendering is by far the easiest way to incorporate Reporting Services in your applications, it does have some limitations. When you send information via a URL, it is very easy for a user to change that URL or see what it is that you pass.

By using the Reporting Services Web service, you can easily hide the details of how you retrieve report information. Parameters are passed through your code instead of the URL. This gives you complete control over how that information is retrieved without exposing it to the users. Let's take a look at your first rendering application.

Rendering through Windows

This section looks at the mechanics of rendering using the Reporting Services Web service. You are going to build a simple Windows application that returns a list of reports from the Report Server. Once you have the list of reports, you'll use the Web service to return a list of report parameters. After entering any report parameters, you'll render the report to a file. These steps will illustrate the main components of rendering through program code.

Building the Application Interface

To start, you need to build your application interface. Let's start by building a simple Windows form. For this example, I've added labels, textboxes, and buttons for basic functionality. Figure 15-9 shows the design view of the form.

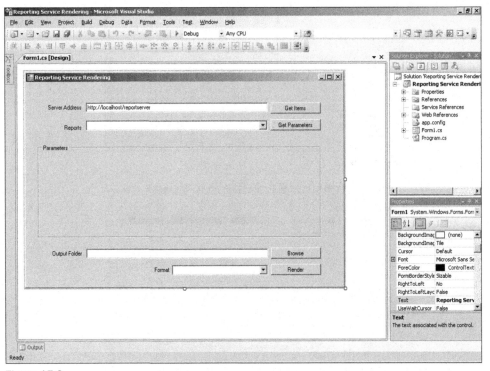

Figure 15-9

This form will allow you to query a given Report Server to return a list of reports. Once it has returned the reports, you can use it to access a list of parameters for the reports. Finally, you'll need to render the report to a given folder location.

Setting up the Web Services

Before you can get into rendering reports, you need to set up a reference to the Reporting Services and Report Execution Web services. Once you have created your web references, you can start to develop the application. The next few figures show you how to create references to the Web services. Start by adding the web references to your project.

Open the Solution Explorer, right-click on the References folder, and then click on the "Add Service Reference" menu item, as shown in Figure 15-10. In the bottom-left corner, click on the Advanced button to open the Service Reference Settings dialog box, as shown in Figure 15-11. Click on the "Add Web Reference" button on the bottom left to open the Add Web Reference dialog.

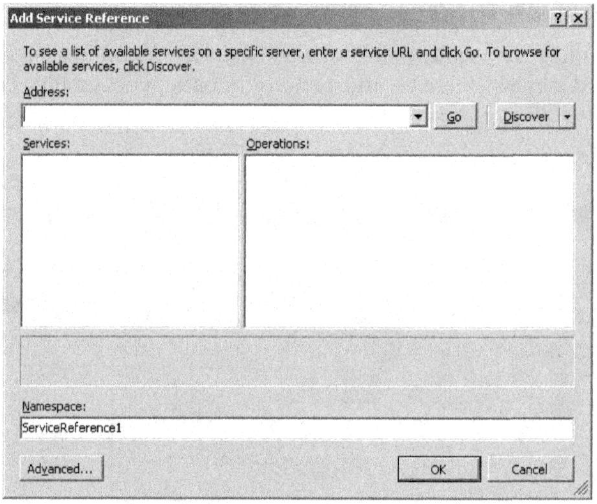

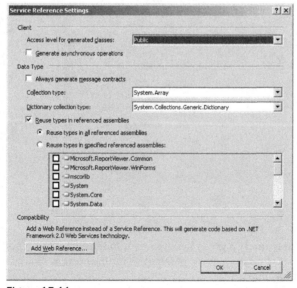

Figure 15-10

Figure 15-11

In the Add Web Reference dialog, enter the location of Web service in the URL dialog. This URL will depend on the Report Server name and the installed location of the Report Server virtual directory. By default, the Report Server virtual directory is located under the root as "/reportserver." For the default virtual directory on a local machine, enter the following URL:

```
http://localhost/reportserver/reportservice2005.asmx
```

If the Report Server is running in SharePoint Integrated mode, the `reportservice2006.asmx` *Web service should be used.*

Once you have entered the URL, hit [Enter] to view a description of the Web service. Enter a name for the new web reference, and click Add Reference. This example uses the name *RSService*. The dialog should look like Figure 15-12 when filled in.

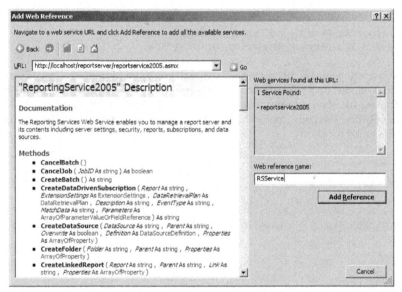

Figure 15-12

Now add the Report Execution Web service by following the same procedure but using a URL similar to the following:

```
http://localhost/reportserver/reportexecution2005.asmx
```

In the example, this service is named *REService*.

Now that you have referenced the Web services, you are ready to start writing your code. The first thing you can do is add a `using` (C#) or `Imports` (VB) statement to your code. The first part of the `using` statement will be the application name followed by the web reference name. In the example, the project is called *Reporting_Service_Rendering* for the C# project and *Reporting_Service_Rendering_VB* for the Visual Basic project.

C#

```
using System;
using System.Collections;
using System.Collections.Generic;
using System.ComponentModel;
using System.Data;
using System.Drawing;
using System.Linq;
using System.Text;
using System.Windows.Forms;
using System.IO;
using System.Web.Services.Protocols;
using Reporting_Service_Rendering.RSService;
using Reporting_Service_Rendering.REService;
```

VB

```
Imports Reporting_Service_Rendering_VB.RSService
Imports Reporting_Service_Rendering_VB.REService
```

After you have added the using or Imports statement, you need to create an instance of the ReportingService2005 and ReportExecutionService objects. These are the main objects that will be used to retrieve a list of reports and their associated parameters and then render the report. At the top of the Windows Forms class code, create the declarations shown in the following sections. The class declaration is included for clarity.

C#

```
public partial class Form1 : Form
{
        private ReportingService2005 _rs = new ReportingService2005();
        private ReportExecutionService _rsExec = new ReportExecutionService();
```

VB

```
Public Class Form1
    Private _rs As New ReportingService2005
    Private _rsExec As New ReportExecutionService
```

Next, you need to set the security credentials that will be used by these objects. In your code, pass the credentials of the currently logged-on user. If you already have your own custom authentication and authorization method in place, you could pass a system identification that you define instead of the current user.

Open the Form Load event in the Windows Form. This is a suitable place for setting the credentials. Inside this event, set the ReportingService2005 and ReportExecutionService object's Credentials property to System.Net.CredentialCache.DefaultCredentials. This will give the Web services the credentials of the currently logged-on user.

C#

```
_rs.Credentials = System.Net.CredentialCache.DefaultCredentials; _rsExec.
Credentials = System.Net.CredentialCache.DefaultCredentials;
```

VB

```
_rs.Credentials = System.Net.CredentialCache.DefaultCredentials _rsExec.Credentials
= System.Net.CredentialCache.DefaultCredentials
```

The final piece you need to add to the Form Load event is the code to populate your dropdown list. This code will add all the format names to the list along with appropriate extensions for each. Begin by creating a small class that helps you populate the dropdown:

C#

```
/*  Helper class for format extensions. */
private class Format
{
    private string _name;
    private string _extension;

    public Format(string name, string extension)
    {
        _name = name;
        _extension = extension;
    }

    public string Name
    {
        get{return _name;}
    }

    public string Extension
    {
        get{return _extension;}
    }
}
```

VB

```
' Helper class for format extensions.
Private Class Format
    Private _name As String
    Private _extension As String

    Public Sub New(ByVal name As String, ByVal extension As String)
        _name = name
        extension = extension
    End Sub

    Public ReadOnly Property Name() As String
```

(continued)

(continued)

```
        Get
            Return _name
        End Get
    End Property

    Public ReadOnly Property Extension() As String
        Get
            Return _extension
        End Get
    End Property
End Class
```

With these classes, you can finish off your Form Load event code. Add the few last lines of code to populate your format combo box:

C#

```csharp
private void Form1_Load(object sender, EventArgs e)
{
    _rs.Credentials = System.Net.CredentialCache.DefaultCredentials;

    //load the format values
    Format[] formats = new Format[8];
    formats[0] = new Format("Excel", ".xls");
    formats[1] = new Format("WORD", ".docx");
    formats[2] = new Format("HTML3.2", ".html");
    formats[3] = new Format("HTML4.0", ".html");
    formats[4] = new Format("XML", ".xml");
    formats[5] = new Format("CSV", ".csv");
    formats[6] = new Format("PDF", ".pdf");
    formats[7] = new Format("IMAGE", ".tif");

    cboFormat.DataSource = formats;
    cboFormat.DisplayMember = "Name";
    cboFormat.ValueMember = "Name";
}
```

VB

```vbnet
Private Sub Form1_Load(ByVal sender As System.Object, _
                       ByVal e As System.EventArgs) Handles MyBase.Load
    _rs.Credentials = System.Net.CredentialCache.DefaultCredentials

    'load the format values
    Dim formats(7) As Format
    formats(0) = New Format("Excel", ".xlsx")
    formats(1) = New Format("Word", ".docx")
    formats(2) = New Format("HTML3.2", ".html")
    formats(3) = New Format("HTML4.0", ".html")
    formats(4) = New Format("XML", ".xml")
    formats(5) = New Format("CSV", ".csv")
```

```
        formats(6) = New Format("PDF", ".pdf")
        formats(7) = New Format("IMAGE", ".tif")

        cboFormat.DataSource = formats
        cboFormat.DisplayMember = "Name"
        cboFormat.ValueMember = "Name"

End Sub
```

You have now created an instance of the ReportingService2005 object, passed the logged-on user's credentials to it, and populated the format dropdown list. The next section looks at connecting to the Report Server and retrieving a list of available reports.

Retrieving Report Information

Now that you have set up the Reporting Services Web service, you need to retrieve your list of reports. To do this, specify the Report Server that you want to query, and then call the ListChildren method of the ReportingService2005 object. ListChildren returns a list of all items, including data sources, resources, and reports. Once you have retrieved the list, you will need to pull out only report items. Finally, you will add the report items to the dropdown.

Let's start by setting the URL to your Report Server. Open the click event of the Get Items button to start your code. Remember that _rs is your reference to the Web service.

C#

```
_rs.Url = txtServer.Text + "/ReportService2005.asmx";
```

VB

```
_rs.Url = txtServer.Text + "/ReportService2005.asmx"
```

The preceding code uses the server location specified in the Server Address textbox concatenated with the reference to the Reporting Services Web service.

Once the URL for the Web service is set, you can get the list of reports. Create an array of CatalogItem objects, and then call the ListChildren method. This method takes two parameters: the folder path on the Report Server and a Boolean value indicating whether to recurse through the directory.

C#

```
CatalogItem[] items;
items = _rs.ListChildren("/", true);
```

VB

```
Dim items() As CatalogItem
items = _rs.ListChildren("/", True)
```

The last step is to loop through the returned list of items and add them to a dropdown list. Similarly to how the formats were loaded, create a class to help data-bind the report items. Let's take a look at the code for this class:

C#

```csharp
private class ReportItem
{
    private string _name;
    private string _path;

    public ReportItem(string name, string path)
    {
        _name = name;
        _path = path;
    }

    public string Name
    {
        get{return _name;}
    }

    public string Path
    {
        get{return _path;}
    }
}
```

VB

```vb
Private Class ReportItem
    Private _name As String
    Private _path As String

    Public Sub New(ByVal name As String, ByVal path As String)
        _name = name
        _path = path
    End Sub

    Public ReadOnly Property Name() As String
        Get
            Return _name
        End Get
    End Property

    Public ReadOnly Property Path() As String
        Get
            Return _path
        End Get
    End Property
End Class
```

Using the `ReportItem` class just created, you can now add the report catalog items to the combo box. The following code is for the `GetItems` button click event, including populating the report dropdown:

C#

```
private void btnGetItems_Click(object sender, EventArgs e)
{
    // Set the path to the report server.
    _rs.Url = txtServer.Text + "/ReportService2005.asmx";

    // Return a list of items from the report server.
    CatalogItem[] items;
    items = _rs.ListChildren("/", true);

    //populate your report combo box
    cboReports.Items.Clear();
    foreach(CatalogItem item in items)
    {
        if(item.Type == ItemTypeEnum.Report)
        {
            cboReports.Items.Add(new ReportItem(item.Name, item.Path));
        }
    }

    cboReports.DisplayMember = "Name";
    cboReports.ValueMember = "Path";

}
```

VB

```
Private Sub btnGetItems_Click(ByVal sender As System.Object, _
                    ByVal e As System.EventArgs) Handles Button1.Click

    'return a list of items from the report server
    _rs.Url = txtServer.Text + "/ReportService2005.asmx"

    'return a list of items from the report server
    Dim items() As CatalogItem
    items = _rs.ListChildren("/", True)

  'populate your report combo box
    cboReports.Items.Clear()
    Dim item As CatalogItem
    For Each item In items
        If item.Type = ItemTypeEnum.Report Then
            cboReports.Items.Add(New ReportItem(item.Name, item.Path))
        End If
    Next item
    cboReports.DisplayMember = "Name"
    cboReports.ValueMember = "Path"

End Sub
```

You will now be able to open your form and return a list of report items. In the next section, you will look at retrieving the parameters for a report.

Retrieving Report Parameters

The next area of programmatic rendering consists of retrieving a list of parameters for your report. This bit of code can be used in various scenarios. The parameter interface that is provided by Reporting Services works well for simple parameters. However, it does not handle many things, like multi-select parameters or more advanced interfaces such as calendar controls. Being able to return a list of parameters allows you to create your own dynamic interface.

In the following example, we will create a simple list of parameters. For each parameter, we will dynamically add a label control and textbox to your form. This example will also include the GetParameters click event to run your code. The first thing you need to do is identify the report that is selected in your report dropdown list.

C#

```
ReportItem reportItem = (ReportItem)cboReports.SelectedItem;
```

VB

```
Dim reportItem As ReportItem = CType(cboReports.SelectedItem, ReportItem)
```

This creates a new ReportItem variable using the selected item of your combo box. The ReportItem class created in the previous section contains a Name and a Path property. You can use this Path property to retrieve your list of parameters.

To return your list of parameters, call the GetReportParameters method of the ReportingService2005 object. This method has two functions. It returns a list of parameters and can validate parameters against the available values defined when creating the report. Let's take a look at the arguments of the GetReportParameters method:

❑ Report — This is the path to the report you want to retrieve.

❑ HistoryID — This is the ID used to identify any historical snapshots of your report.

❑ ForRendering — This Boolean argument can be used to retrieve the parameters that were set when the report was executed. For example, you might create a snapshot of your report or receive it in an e-mail subscription. In both cases, the report is executed before the user views it. By setting the ForRendering property to true, you can retrieve these values and use them in your own custom interface.

❑ ParameterValues — The ParameterValues argument can be used to validate the values assigned to a parameter. This can be useful in guaranteeing that the parameter values you pass to your report match the parameter values accepted by the report.

❑ Credentials — These are the database credentials to use when validating your query-based parameters.

Since you are not working with historical reports or validating values, a number of the properties will not be set. The following code can be used for calling the GetReportParameters method.

C#

```
ReportParameter[] parameters;
parameters = _rs.GetReportParameters(reportItem.Path, null, false, null, null);
```

VB

```
Dim parameters() As ReportParameter
        parameters = _rs.GetReportParameters(reportItem.Path, Nothing, False, _
                          Nothing, Nothing)
```

The last piece of work to do is to create a user interface for your parameters. The ReportParameter objects returned by Reporting Services contain information useful for creating a custom interface. Some of the key properties include the parameter data type, prompt, and valid values. All of these can be used to define your own interface. Finish your code by simply adding a label and textbox to your form for each ReportParameter. Following is the completed GetParameter click event code:

C#

```
private void btnParameters_Click(object sender, EventArgs e)
{
    // Return the list of parameters for the report item.
    ReportItem reportItem = (ReportItem)cboReports.SelectedItem;
    ReportParameter[] parameters;
    parameters = _rs.GetReportParameters(reportItem.Path, null, false, null, null);

    //add the parameters to the parameter list UI
    int left = 10;
    int top = 20;
    foreach (ReportParameter parameter in parameters)
    {
        Label label = new Label();
        TextBox textBox = new TextBox();

        label.Text = parameter.Prompt;
        label.Left = left;
        label.Top = top;

        textBox.Name = parameter.Name;
        // make sure there is a default value
        if ( parameter.DefaultValues != null )
            textBox.Text = parameter.DefaultValues[0];
        textBox.Left = left + 150;
        textBox.Top = top;
        top += 25;

        grpParamInfo.Controls.Add(label);
        grpParamInfo.Controls.Add(textBox);
    }
}
```

VB

```vb
Private Sub btnParameters_Click(ByVal sender As System.Object, ByVal e As _
                    System.EventArgs) Handles Button2.Click

    'return the list of parameters for the report item
    Dim reportItem As ReportItem = CType(cboReports.SelectedItem, ReportItem)

    Dim parameters() As ReportParameter
    parameters = _rs.GetReportParameters(reportItem.Path, Nothing, False, _
                Nothing, Nothing)

'add the parameters to the parameter list UI
    Dim left As Integer = 10
    Dim top As Integer = 20
    Dim parameter As ReportParameter
    For Each parameter In parameters
        Dim label As New Label
        Dim textBox As New TextBox
        label.Text = parameter.Prompt
        label.Left = left
        label.Top = top

        textBox.Name = parameter.Name
        'if there is no value then empty string, otherwise put default value
        If parameter.DefaultValues Is Nothing Then
            textBox.Text = ""
        Else
            textBox.Text = parameter.DefaultValues(0)
        End If
        textBox.Left = left + 150
        textBox.Top = top
        top += 25

        grpParamInfo.Controls.Add(label)
        grpParamInfo.Controls.Add(textBox)
    Next parameter

End Sub
```

Now that you have retrieved your list of reports and built a parameter list, let's take a look at outputting the report to a file.

Rendering a Report to a File on the Filesystem

This section takes a look at rendering a report to a file on the filesystem. Using the ReportExecution2005 web service, you can retrieve a byte array that contains the final report. This byte array can be used in a variety of ways. This example will write the byte array to a file by using the filesystem object. Another example in a later section will write the byte array to the HTTP Response object.

The ReportExecution2005 web service was already set up in the previous sections, so now it can be used to render a report to a file on the filesystem. In the btnRender_Click method, set the URL by concatenating the server text that was entered by the user with the ReportExecution2005.asmx string.

C#

```
_rsExec.Url = txtServer.Text + "/ReportExecution2005.asmx";
```

VB

```
_rsExec.Url = txtServer.Text + "/ReportExecution2005.asmx"
```

Next, you need to set a string argument that will be used for the path of the report.

Before you get into the rendering code, let's take a look at the Render method that is contained within the ReportExecutionService object of the ReportExecution2005 web service. The different parameters are shown in the following table:

Parameter	Data Type	Description
Format	String	Output format of the report
DeviceInfo	String	Information used by a specified rendering format, e.g., specifying the image type (GIF, JPEG) with the IMAGE format
Extension (out)	String	The file extension of the rendered report
Encoding (out)	String	The encoding used for the rendering of the report
MimeType (out)	String	Output returned from Reporting Services containing the MIME type of the underlying report. Useful when rendering a report to the Web. The MIME type can be passed to the Response object to ensure that the browser correctly handles the document returned.
Warnings (out)	Warning Array	Output of any warning returned from Reporting Services during report processing
StreamIDs (out)	String Array	Output of the stream IDs that can be used with the RenderStream method

The Render method returns an array of bytes that represents the rendered report. The array can then be used just as any other byte array, such as writing it to a file on the filesystem or sending it over a TCP connection.

The parameters of the Render method are similar to the values that can be passed using URL rendering.

Now that you have seen the basics around the Render method, let's take a look at the code you need to write for your Render button click event. The first thing you need to do in your code is to retrieve the selected report and output format. Use the Format and ReportItem classes created earlier to retrieve the selected items in your dropdowns.

C#

```
Format format = (Format)cboFormat.SelectedItem;
ReportItem reportItem = (ReportItem)cboReports.SelectedItem;
```

VB

```
Dim format As Format = CType(cboFormat.SelectedItem, Format)
Dim reportItem As ReportItem = CType(cboReports.SelectedItem, ReportItem)
```

You need to retrieve the input parameters specified by the user. Then, you need to create a new function that loops through the textboxes you've created earlier to retrieve their values and return an array of `ParameterValue` objects.

C#

```
private REService.ParameterValue[] REGetParameters()
{
    ArrayList controls = new ArrayList();

    //get the values from the parameter controls
    int len = grpParamInfo.Controls.Count;
    for (int i = 0; i < len; i++)
    {
        if (grpParamInfo.Controls[i] is TextBox)
        {
            controls.Add(grpParamInfo.Controls[i]);
        }
    }

    //add the control information to parameter info objects
    len = controls.Count;
    REService.ParameterValue[] returnValues =
        new REService.ParameterValue[len];

    for (int i = 0; i < len; i++)
    {
        returnValues[i] = new REService.ParameterValue();
        returnValues[i].Name = ((TextBox)controls[i]).Name;
        returnValues[i].Value = ((TextBox)controls[i]).Text;
    }

    return returnValues;
}
```

VB

```
Private Function REGetParameters() As REService.ParameterValue()
    Dim controls As New ArrayList

    'get the values from the parameter controls
    Dim len As Integer = grpParamInfo.Controls.Count
    Dim i As Integer
    For i = 0 To len - 1
        If TypeOf grpParamInfo.Controls(i) Is TextBox Then
            controls.Add(grpParamInfo.Controls(i))
        End If
    Next i

    'add the control information to parameter info objects
    len = controls.Count - 1
    Dim returnValues(len) As REService.ParameterValue
        For i = 0 To len
            returnValues(i) = New PREService.arameterValue
            returnValues(i).Name = CType(controls(i), TextBox).Name
            returnValues(i).Value = CType(controls(i), TextBox).Text
        Next i

    Return returnValues
End Function
```

You can now use the `REGetParameters` function to build an array of input parameters. You can add the following code to your `Render` click event to retrieve the input parameters.

C#

```
REService.ParameterValue[] parameters = REGetParameters();
```

VB

```
Dim parameters As REService.ParameterValue() = REGetParameters()
```

Above in this chapter, we explained how to get the `EmployeeID` *parameter value from the sample database. If you need a quick ID to put in for the Employee parameter, you can use* **284** *for testing.*

Now that you have your list of input parameters, you are almost ready to call the `Render` method. For this, you need to declare variables that will be used for the `HistoryID`, `DeviceInfo`, `Encoding`, `MimeType`, `Extension`, `Warnings`, and `StreamIDs`. Not all of these variables are needed since they are set to `null` and not used; however, they have been declared here to show the syntax of the `Render` method. The final variable you will need for the `Render` method is an array of bytes. This byte array can then be written to the filesystem.

C#

```
byte[] result = null;
string historyID = null;
string devInfo = null;
string encoding;
string mimeType;
string extension;
REService.Warning[] warnings = null;
string[] streamIDs = null;

// Load the report, set the parameters and then render.
_rsExec.LoadReport(pathToReport, historyID);
_rsExec.SetExecutionParameters(parameters, "en-us");
result = _rsExec.Render(outputFormat, devInfo, out extension,
        out encoding, out mimeType, out warnings, out streamIDs);
```

VB

```
Dim result() As Byte
Dim historyID As String
Dim devInfo As String
Dim encoding As String
Dim mimeType As String
Dim extension As String
Dim warnings() As REService.Warning
Dim streamIDs() As String

_rsExec.LoadReport(reportItem.Path, historyID)
_rsExec.SetExecutionParameters(parameters, "en-us")
result = _rsExec.Render(selectedFormat.Name, devInfo, extension, _
        encoding, mimeType, warnings, streamIDs)
```

Finally, you need to take the byte array returned from the Render method and write it to the filesystem. Use the output path specified in the output textbox along with the report name and format file extension to open a file stream. Following is the entire Render button click event along with the final piece of code for writing the file to the filesystem:

C#

```
private void btnRender_Click(object sender, EventArgs e)
{
    // Set the URL by concat with server text.
    _rsExec.Url = txtServer.Text + "/ReportExecution2005.asmx";

    // Grab the path from the selected report and put it in a string.
    ReportItem reportItem = (ReportItem)cboReports.SelectedItem;

    // Grab the format that is selected an dput it in a string.
    Format selectedFormat = (Format)cboFormat.SelectedItem;

    // Prepare report parameter.
```

```
            RService.ParameterValue[] parameters = REGetParameters();

            // Variables used to render the report.
            byte[] result = null;
            string historyID = null;
            string devInfo = null;
            string encoding;
            string mimeType;
            string extension;
            RService.Warning[] warnings = null;
            string[] streamIDs = null;

            // Make sure the parameters have been set first.
            if (parameters.Length != 0)
            {
                // Load the report, set the parameters and then render.
                _rsExec.LoadReport(reportItem.Path, historyID);
                _rsExec.SetExecutionParameters(parameters, "en-us");
                result = _rsExec.Render(selectedFormat.Name, devInfo, out extension,
                        out encoding, out mimeType, out warnings, out streamIDs);

                // Make sure there is an output path then output the file system.
                if (txtOutputFolder.Text != "")
                {
                    string fullOutputPath = txtOutputFolder.Text + "\\"
                            + reportItem.Name + selectedFormat.Extension;
                    FileStream stream = File.Create(fullOutputPath, result.Length);
                    stream.Write(result, 0, result.Length);
                    stream.Close();
                    MessageBox.Show("Report Rendered to File System.");
                }
                else
                {
                    MessageBox.Show("Choose a folder first");
                }
            }
            else
            {
                MessageBox.Show("No parameters, click Get Parameters button"
                        + "first and then set values.");
            }
}
```

VB

```
Private Sub btnRender_Click(ByVal sender As System.Object, ByVal e As System
.EventArgs)
        Handles btnRender.Click

    'return a list of items from the report server
    _rsExec.Url = txtServer.Text + "/ReportExecution2005.asmx"

    'Grab the format that is selected and put it in a string.
```

(continued)

(continued)

```vb
        Dim selectedFormat As Format = CType(cboFormat.SelectedItem, Format)

        'Grab the path from the selected report and put it in a string.
        Dim reportItem As ReportItem = CType(cboReports.SelectedItem, ReportItem)

        'Prepare report parameters.
        Dim parameters As REService.ParameterValue() = REGetParameters()

        'Variables used to render the report.
        Dim result() As Byte
        Dim historyID As String
        Dim devInfo As String
        Dim encoding As String
        Dim mimeType As String
        Dim extension As String
        Dim warnings() As REService.Warning
        Dim streamIDs() As String


    ' Make sure the parameters have been set first
    If ((reportHasParameters = True And parameters.Length <> 0) Or _
        reportHasParameters = False) Then
        _rsExec.LoadReport(reportItem.Path, historyID)
        _rsExec.SetExecutionParameters(parameters, "en-us")
        result = _rsExec.Render(selectedFormat.Name, devInfo, extension, _
                encoding, mimeType, warnings, streamIDs)
        If txtOutputFolder.Text <> "" Then
            Dim fullOutputPath As String = txtOutputFolder.Text + "\" + _
                reportItem.Name + selectedFormat.Extension
            Dim stream As FileStream = File.Create(fullOutputPath, _
                result.Length)
            stream.Write(result, 0, result.Length)
            stream.Close()
            MessageBox.Show("Report Rendered to: " + fullOutputPath)
        End If
    Else
        MessageBox.Show("No parameters, click Get Parameters button first _
                    and then set values.")
    End If
End Sub

Private Sub btnRender_Click(ByVal sender As Object, ByVal e As System.EventArgs) _
                    Handles btnRender.Click

    'get the format and report item from the comboboxes
    Dim format As Format = CType(cboFormat.SelectedItem, Format)
    Dim reportItem As ReportItem = CType(cboReports.SelectedItem, ReportItem)
    'set up variables needed to call render method
    Dim parameters As ParameterValue() = GetParameters()
    Dim encoding As String
    Dim mimeType As String
    Dim parametersUsed() As ParameterValue
    Dim warnings() As Warning
```

```
        Dim streamIds() As String

        'render the report
        Dim data() As Byte
        data = _rs.Render(reportItem.Path, format.Name, Nothing, Nothing, _

            parameters, Nothing, Nothing, encoding, mimeType, _
            parametersUsed, warnings, streamIds)
        'create a file stream to write the output
        Dim fileName As String = txtOutputLocation.Text & "\" & reportItem.Name & _
                            format.Extension

        Dim fs As New System.IO.FileStream(fileName, _
            System.IO.FileMode.OpenOrCreate)

        Dim writer As New System.IO.BinaryWriter(fs)
        writer.Write(data, 0, data.Length)
        writer.Close()
        fs.Close()
        MessageBox.Show(("File written to: " + fileName))
    End Sub
```

Now that you have completed the code for rendering the application, let's try it out. You need to build and run the project. When the form opens, enter your server information in the Server Address textbox and click on the Get Items button, as shown in Figure 15-13.

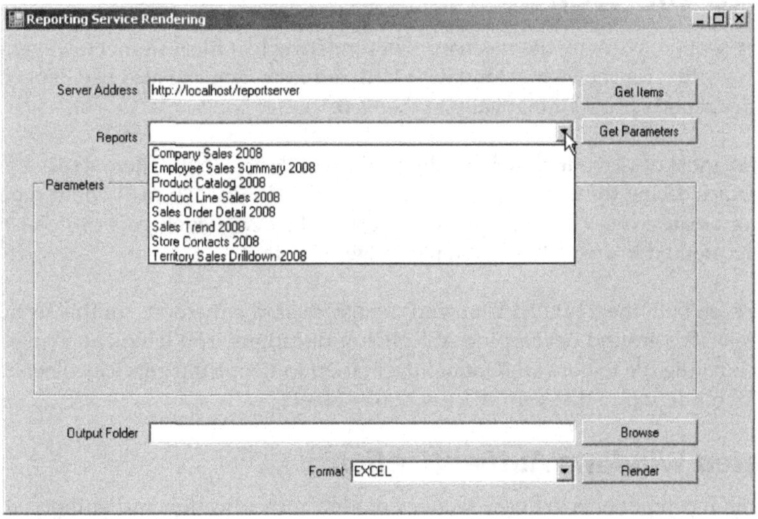

Figure 15-13

Select a report that takes parameters (the example uses the Employee Sales Summary 2008 sample report), click on the Get Parameters button, and then fill in the parameters (the example uses 283 for the Employee ID field). Finally, select an output folder and the rendering format as PDF. After specifying these items, you can click on the Render button to render your report. When the rendering is complete, you will receive a message box letting you know that the file has been written to the specified location, as shown in Figure 15-14. You can now open your saved file in Adobe Acrobat.

577

Figure 15-14

Rendering a Report to the Filesystem Summary

In this section, you learned the basic steps of rendering a report to the filesystem:

❑ Using the ReportingService2005 object's ListChildren method to return a list of reports

❑ Using the ReportingService2005 object's GetReportParameters method to return a list of report parameters

❑ Using the Render method of the ReportExecutionService object to output your report in a given format

These basic steps can be used in numerous applications to render a report. Using these methods, users can create their own custom list of reports and customer report parameter pages, and output the report using the returned byte array. In the next section, you will use some of these same steps to render a report to the Web via the Response object.

Rendering to the Web

In the preceding section, you saw the mechanics of rendering to a filesystem. However, most of today's applications are written for the Web. Along with URL requests, you can also use Reporting Services Web services to render reports programmatically to the Web.

While doing this, most of your steps will be identical to rendering to the filesystem — you simply change the interface. Using the ListChildren method, developers can easily bind reports to an ASP. NET data grid or create a tree view of available reports. Likewise, developers could also use the GetParameters method to create their own parameter interface.

Since you have seen both the ListChilden and GetParameters methods, in this section, you will work more with the specifics around developing ASP.NET applications. You'll look at changes that can be made to the web.config file to pass credential information to Reporting Services. Then you will look at the mechanics of rendering to the ASP.NET Response object.

Using Integrated Windows Authentication

There are two main components to every security model: authentication and authorization. In Reporting Services, you can use Integrated Windows Authentication within an ASP.NET application to authenticate users. Before you start this example, you need to ensure that your application is configured to use Integrated Windows Authentication.

After creating a new ASP.NET web application, you need to open IIS and change some settings of the virtual directory. Make sure that the Anonymous Access has been turned off and Integrated Windows Authentication has been turned on in IIS.

In the sample created for this chapter, the virtual directory used in IIS is the default web site. The pages are called Render.aspx and RenderVB.aspx for the C# and Visual Basic projects, respectively. To set the virtual directories to use Integrated Windows Authentication, you need to check their settings in IIS. Using Integrated Windows Authentication in an ASP.NET web application is the easiest way to take advantage of the security features in Reporting Services. Using this method allows developers to concentrate on other areas of an application without having to build their own authentication mechanism. It also allows for taking full advantage of the Reporting Services role-based security model.

After updating the IIS settings to use Integrated Windows Authentication, you will have to make some modifications to your ASP.NET web application.

Modifying the web.config File

In the web application created for this demonstration, you want to pass the user's security credentials to the Reporting Services Web service. To accomplish this, you have to allow your ASP.NET application to impersonate the currently logged-on user. Setting up impersonation requires adding the following line of code to the web.config file. Place this line after the authentication tag in the file:

```
<identity impersonate="true" />
```

Confirming ASP.NET 2.0

Make sure that in the properties for the web site on the ASP.NET page that ASP 2.0, as shown in Figure 15-5.

Figure 15-15

Confirm that ASP.NET 2.0 is listed as Allowed under the Web Service Extension list, as shown in Figure 15-16. If ASP.NET 2.0 is not listed, you can install it using the following `aspnet_regiis` command:

```
C:\WINDOWS\Microsoft.NET\Framework\v2.0.50727>aspnet_regiis /i
Start installing ASP.NET (2.0.50727).
.......................
Finished installing ASP.NET (2.0.50727).

C:\WINDOWS\Microsoft.NET\Framework\v2.0.50727>
```

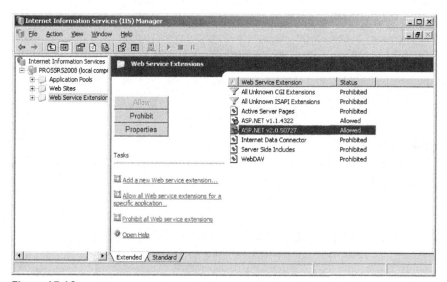

Figure 15-16

Setting up the Report Execution Web Service

The example only needs Rendering functionality, so you will only use the Report Execution Web service. However, you would generally need to also interact with the `reportingservice2005.asmx` web service, as discussed in the previous section.

For this example, we've added a web reference to `http://localhost/reportserver/reportexecution2005.asmx` and named it `REService`.

Rendering to the Response Object

Now that you have set up Integrated Windows Authentication, modified the web.config file, and configured ASP.NET 2.0, you're ready to write some code. In this application, you will have one page that takes in a report path and format from the URL. You'll use this information to call the `Render` method of the Report Execution Web service object and write that information back to the response stream.

This sample will use one ASP.NET page called Render.aspx. Place your code sample in the `Page_Load` event of the page. This would be a logical approach when developing an application around Reporting Services. It allows you to have one point of entry to the Report Server. The page could then be referenced from other areas of an application. For the entry page, you will use a simple Default.aspx page that has the path and format as a textbox and dropdown box. The Default.aspx page will pass the `Format` and `Path` parameters to the Render.aspx page on a button event. Although the input for this example is very simple, a more robust example could be built using the same technique as was shown in the previous section.

Let's add some code to the page's `Page_Load` event to retrieve the report path and format from the HTTP `Request` object:

C#

```
string path = Request.Params["Path"];
string format = Request.Params["Format"];
```

VB

```
Dim path As String = Request.Params("Path")
Dim format As String = Request.Params("Format")
```

Now that you have the report path and format, you can start setting up the `ReportExecutionService` object. This is an instance of the Web Service reference, similar to what you did in the Windows Forms application. As you did with the Windows Forms application, you will create an instance of the `ReportExecutionService` object and then set the credentials to the credentials of the currently logged-on user.

C#

```
//create the ReportExecutionService object
ReportExecutionService _rsExec = new ReportExecutionService();

//set the credentials to be passed to reporting services
_rsExec.Credentials = System.Net.CredentialCache.DefaultCredentials;
```

VB

```
'create the ReportingService object
Dim _rsExec As New ReportExecutionService

'set the credentials to be passed to Reporting Services
_rsExec.Credentials = System.Net.CredentialCache.DefaultCredentials
```

Once the `ReportingService` object has been created and your credentials are set, you can go ahead and render the report. You will create variables to pass any report parameters (none in this example) and capture the reports encoding, MIME type, parameters used, warnings, and stream IDs. The key output parameter, through which you'll render your report, is the MIME type. This parameter will tell the HTTP `Response` object which type of document is being passed back. The following code renders your report to the web application. You should notice that it is identical to the code used in the Windows Forms application.

C#

```
ParameterValue[] parameters = new ParameterValue[0];
string encoding;
string mimeType;
ParameterValue[] parametersUsed;
Warning[] warnings;
string[] streamIds;

//render the report
byte[] data;
data = rs.Render(path, format, null, null, parameters, null, null,
        out encoding, out mimeType, out parametersUsed,
        out warnings, out streamIds);
```

VB

```
Dim parameters As ParameterValue()
Dim result() As Byte
Dim historyID As String
Dim devInfo As String
Dim encoding As String
Dim mimeType As String
Dim extension As String
Dim warnings() As Warning
Dim streamIDs() As String

_rsExec.LoadReport(path, historyID)
_rsExec.SetExecutionParameters(parameters, "en-us")
result = _rsExec.Render(format, devInfo, extension, encoding, mimeType, warnings,
streamIDs)
```

The Render method of the ReportExecutionService object passes back a byte array that can be used in several ways. For the Web, you will write this information directly back to the HTTP Response object. Before you write back the data, however, you need to set some information about the report — namely, a filename. To do this, you use the name of the report followed by an extension that you determine using the value returned in the extension variable.

Now construct the filename using the following code. The code makes use of the information returned from the Render method.

C#

```
string reportName = path.Substring(path.LastIndexOf("/") + 1);
string fileName = reportName + "." + extension;
```

VB

```
Dim reportName As String = path.Substring(path.LastIndexOf("/") + 1)
Dim fileName As String = reportName & "." & extension
```

Finally, you need to put it all together by writing the data and file information back to the Response object. For this, you:

1. Start by clearing out any information that is already in the response buffer.

2. Set the content type of the response equal to the MIME type of your rendered report.

3. Make sure to attach your filename information to the response, if your report is in a format other than HTML.

4. Use the `BinaryWrite` method to write the rendered report byte array directly to the `Response` object.

The following is the completed code for the `Page_Load` event:

C#

```csharp
protected void Page_Load(object sender, EventArgs e)
{
    //get the path and output format from the query string
    string path = Request.Params["Path"];
    string format = Request.Params["Format"];

    ReportExecutionService _rsExec = new ReportExecutionService();

    _rsExec.Url = @"http://localhost/reportserver/ReportExecution2005.asmx";
    _rsExec.Credentials = System.Net.CredentialCache.DefaultCredentials;

    // Prepare report parameter.
    // the GetParameters method could be implemented as was shown in
    // the previous section on rendering to the file system.
    ParameterValue[] parameters = new ParameterValue[0];

    // Variables used to render the report.
    byte[] result = null;
    string historyID = null;
    string devInfo = null;
    string encoding;
    string mimeType;
    string extension;
    REService.Warning[] warnings = null;
    string[] streamIDs = null;

    // Load the report and render it.
    _rsExec.LoadReport(path, historyID);
    _rsExec.SetExecutionParameters(parameters, "en-us");
    result = _rsExec.Render(format, devInfo, out extension, out encoding, _
            out mimeType, out warnings, out streamIDs);

    // Build the report name and path.
    string reportName = path.Substring(path.LastIndexOf("/") + 1);
    string fileName = reportName + "." + extension;

    //write the report back to the Response object
    Response.Clear();
    Response.ContentType = mimeType;
```

(continued)

(continued)

```
    //add the file name to the response if it is not a web browser format.
    if(mimeType!="text/html")
        Response.AddHeader("Content-Disposition", "attachment; filename=" +
                            fileName);

    Response.BinaryWrite(result);
}
```

VB

```
Protected Sub Page_Load(ByVal sender As Object, ByVal e As System.EventArgs)
 Handles Me.Load

    Dim path As String = Request.Params("Path")
    Dim format As String = Request.Params("Format")

    'create the ReportingService object
    Dim _rsExec As New ReportExecutionService

    'set the credentials to be passed to Reporting Services
    _rsExec.Credentials = System.Net.CredentialCache.DefaultCredentials

    'Prepare report parameters.
    Dim parameters(0) As ParameterValue

    'Variables used to render the report.
    Dim result() As Byte
    Dim historyID As String
    Dim devInfo As String
    Dim encoding As String
    Dim mimeType As String
    Dim extension As String
    Dim warnings() As Warning
    Dim streamIDs() As String

    _rsExec.LoadReport(path, historyID)
    _rsExec.SetExecutionParameters(parameters, "en-us")
    result = _rsExec.Render(format, devInfo, extension, encoding, _
            mimeType, warnings, streamIDs)

    Dim reportName As String = path.Substring(path.LastIndexOf("/") + 1)
    Dim fileName As String = reportName & "." & extension

    'write the report back to the Response object
    Response.Clear()
    Response.ContentType = mimeType
    'add the file name to the response if it is not a web browser format.
    If mimeType <> "text/html" Then
        Response.AddHeader("Content-Disposition", "attachment; _
                            filename=" & fileName)
    End If
    Response.BinaryWrite(result)

End Sub
```

This example quickly demonstrates some of the key pieces of code that can be used to render reports to the Web. You first need to set the security context for the application by configuring Integrated Windows Authentication and allowing impersonation from your application. Next, you retrieve a report from Reporting Services by specifying the report path and format. Finally, you use the rendered report data along with its associated MIME type to render the report using the HTTP `Response` object.

Now that the code for your web application is complete, let's take a look at using your Render.aspx page. You can use a simple query string to render your report. A sample query string that renders the Employee List report from the Professional Reporting Services sample reports in HTML 4.0 format is as follows:

```
http://localhost/Render.aspx?Path=%2fAdventureWorks+2008+Sample+Reports
    %2fCompany+Sales+2008&Format=HTML4.0
```

This URL does the following:

❑   It calls the Render.aspx page from your C# project.

❑   It passes in the required parameters: the path (/AdventureWorks 2008 Sample Reports/ Company Sales 2008) and the Format (HTML 4.0).

If you place this URL into Internet Explorer, you'll get the HTML output shown in Figure 15-17.

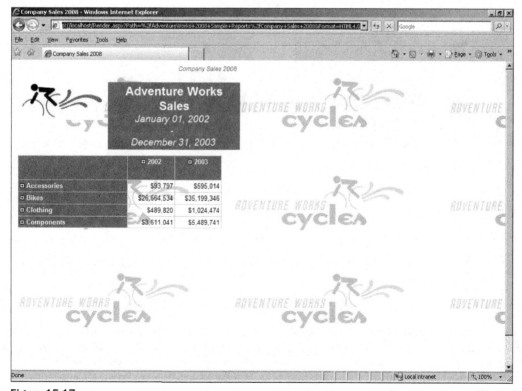

Figure 15-17

Notice that when you enter HTML 4.0 as the output format, the report data is rendered directly in the browser. In your code, the MIME type of your HTTP `Response` is `text/html` in this scenario. When the browser receives the response, it recognizes the MIME type and renders it directly to the browser.

Depending on your security settings, IE 7 will ask if you want to save the .html page or open it. You can click Open to view the report in the browser.

Let's take a quick look at rendering in a format that does not go directly to the browser. Use the following URL to render the same Employee List report but in the EXCEL format:

```
http://localhost/Render.aspx?Path=%2fAdventureWorks+2008+Sample+Reports
     %2fCompany+Sales+2008&Format=EXCEL
```

Figure 15-18 shows the result.

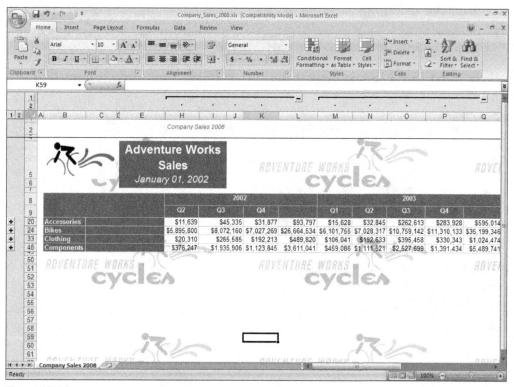

Figure 15-18

Notice this time that when you set the format to EXCEL, you are prompted to save to the filesystem. In this case, the MIME type needs to be set to `application/vnd.ms-excel`. You also need to add header information to the `Response` object that contains the filename Employee_List.xls. The MIME type notifies Internet Explorer that you are sending a file, and the added header gives it the appropriate filename.

In this section, you saw some of the base mechanics around rendering a report using an ASP.NET application. To start, you need to pass the currently logged-on user's credentials. This is accomplished by setting the application virtual directory to use Integrated Windows Authentication and then modifying the web.config file for the application to use impersonation. In the code, you need to call the Report Execution Service Web service to retrieve the report along with content information such as MIME type. Once you have the binary report data, you can write that information directly back to the `Response` object.

Using the `MicrosoftReportViewer` Control

Many improvements have been made in Visual Studio 2008 for working with adding SQL Server 2008 Reporting Services reports to your custom applications. For starters, there is now a Reports Application project listed in the New Project list, as shown in Figure 15-19.

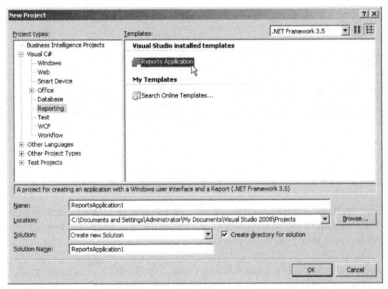

Figure 15-19

When the Reports Application project template is selected, it automatically starts the Report Wizard, as shown in Figure 15-20.

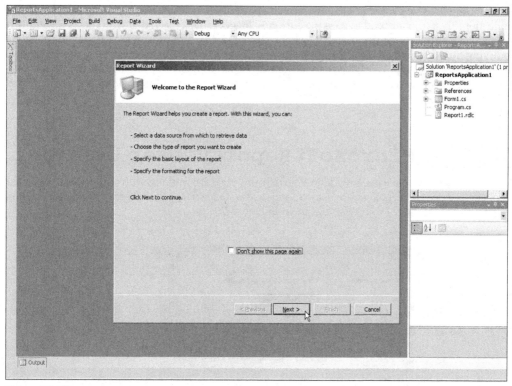

Figure 15-20

The Report Wizard walks you through creating a data source, selecting an existing data source, saving the connection information to the configuration file, choosing the database objects you wish to report on, and then creating a report based on those objects.

The Reports Application project is a great starting point, but the `MicrosoftReportViewer` control can also be added to any custom application. In Visual Studio 2008, the control is automatically made available under a grouping in the toolbox called *Reporting*, as shown in Figure 15-21.

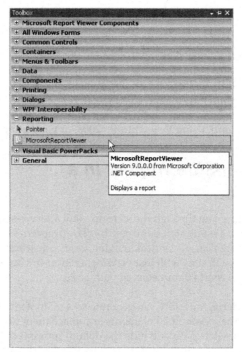

Figure 15-21

The `MicrosoftReportViewer` control is by far the most flexible and, in most cases, the easiest technique for adding a report to your .NET application user interface. Two separate but very similar controls are available — for .NET Windows Forms and ASP.NET Web Forms applications. All the user interface attributes you have seen in the Report Manager and Designer Preview tab can be managed using properties of the control and can be set at design time in the Properties window, or at run time using program code.

The `MicrosoftReportViewer` controls are client-side controls that do not need a SQL Server instance to be used. The only dependency of the controls is the .NET Framework 3.5.

The source data used by the controls can come from any data source, not just SQL Server. The `MicrosoftReportViewer` controls themselves have no knowledge of where the data comes from. Your application brings in the data from whichever source you choose and makes it available to the `MicrosoftReportViewer` controls in the form of ADO.NET DataTables or custom business objects. The `MicrosoftReportViewer` controls don't even know how to connect to databases or execute queries. By requiring the host application to supply the data, you can use the `MicrosoftReportViewer` controls with any data source, including relational, non-relational, and non-database data sources.

Two different report execution scenarios are supported in both types of the `MicrosoftReportViewer` control. The first is where standard, Report Server reports are deployed and executed on the Report Server and then viewed in the control as you would expect. The other is using the `MicrosoftReportViewer` control as a mini-report-hosting engine that allows reports to execute in your application without needing a connection to the Report Server. This requires a version of the report definition file that's been retrofitted for client-side execution. The file is an RDLC file, with C standing for client-side processing.

Both RDL and RDLC formats have the same XML schema, but RDLC files allow some elements to contain empty values. RDLC also ignores the <Query> element of the RDL schema. The <Query> tag will only be included in the XML file if the report began its life as an RDL file and was then converted to an RDLC. RDLC files also contain information that the MicrosoftReportViewer control uses to generate data-binding code. You can create an RDLC report by converting an RDL report into RDLC, using the Report Creation Wizard, using Visual Studio 2008, or generating the RDLC programmatically.

Embedding a Server-Side Report in a Windows Application

The following exercise will take you through the steps to view a server-side report in a Windows Forms application using the MicrosoftReportViewer control. The properties and methods of the Web Forms version of the control are nearly identical, making your code transportable between Windows and Web application projects. You will start with just viewing a report in your custom application and then move on to working with the reports parameters in your code.

As you know, the report rendering interface can generate several toolbar options and parameter prompts. You can either use these default UI elements or replace them with your own. When you start working with the report parameters, you will hide the default prompts and force the user to enter the parameters through your custom application. This provides you with great control over how the user interacts with the report and which parameter values are allowed.

The example uses the Employee Sales Summary report used throughout the chapter. First, you will add a form to your Visual Studio 2008 Windows Application project. Drag and drop the MicrosoftReportViewer control onto the form. Resize and anchor it to meet your needs.

The first thing to notice about the MicrosoftReportViewer control is the dropdown Context menu used to configure the most important aspects of the control. The dropdown allows you to choose a specific report or to choose a report from a Report Server. You can also set the Report Server URL and the report path, as well as kick off the Report Wizard to design a new report and dock the report in the current container. Set the Report Server property to the local report server and then set the report path to the Employee Sales Summary 2008 report, as shown in Figure 15-22.

Figure 15-22

The ReportPath property is the report location in the Report Server hierarchy. In this case, we've selected a report on the local machine to display in the MicrosoftReportViewer control. The location of the Report Server is set using the ReportServerUrl property. The ReportPath and ReportServerUrl properties can also be accessed under the ServerReport grouping in the Properties pane.

Since you're going to use the Report Server for processing, set the `ProcessingMode` property to **Remote**. That will use the Report Server to retrieve source data that will be used in the report. In Remote mode, the `MicrosoftReportViewer` controls display reports that are hosted on a SQL Server 2008 Report Server. The source data for those reports can come from any appropriate data source, not just SQL Server. This behavior is normal report processing behavior.

You are now ready to run the custom application and view the report in a Windows Form, as shown in Figure 15-23.

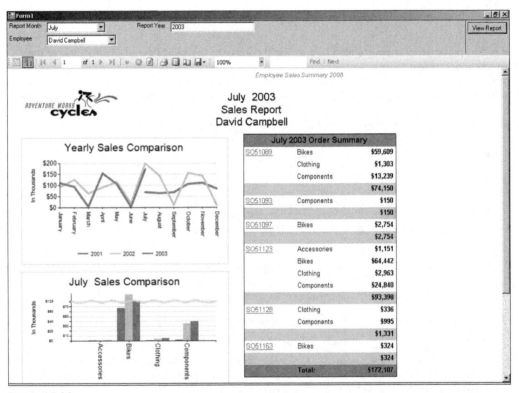

Figure 15-23

You have seen a very simple example of running a report in a custom application; however, you might also want to add functionality to control the parameters that the users see and select.

With everything except the parameters set using the Properties window, the only necessary code sets the parameters and executes the report.

Parameters are managed as an array of `ReportParameter` objects. Since the report has three required parameters, the array is declared with a maximum element index of two to provide three elements. Each of the elements is populated by passing the parameter name and value to each of the three `ReportParameter` constructors.

In order to use the `ReportParameter` object, you need to either add the following `using/imports` statement to your code or instantiate the object using the full `Microsoft.Reporting.WinForms` namespace. Adding the `using/imports` statement provides for much cleaner and easier-to-read code, so add the following statements to your application:

C#

```
using Microsoft.Reporting.WinForms;
```

VB

```
Imports Microsoft.Reporting.WinForms
```

The report parameters are populated by passing the array to the `SetParameters` method of the `ServerReport` object.

Finally, the `MicrosoftReportViewer`'s `RefreshReport` method causes report execution to begin.

The following is the complete code for the button's click event:

C#

```csharp
private void button1_Click(object sender, EventArgs e)
{
    string reportServerURL = @"http://localhost/reportserver";
    string reportPath = @"/AdventureWorks Sample Reports/Employee Sales Summary";
    Employee selectedEmp = (Employee)cboEmployee.SelectedItem;

    ReportParameter[] Param = new ReportParameter[3];
    Param[0] = new ReportParameter("ReportMonth",
                                    cboReportMonth.SelectedItem.ToString());
    Param[1] = new ReportParameter("ReportYear", cboReportYear.SelectedItem
.ToString());
    Param[2] = new ReportParameter("EmpID", selectedEmp.ID);

    reportViewer1.ProcessingMode = ProcessingMode.Remote;
    reportViewer1.ServerReport.ReportServerUrl = new Uri(reportServerURL);
    reportViewer1.ServerReport.ReportPath = reportPath;
    reportViewer1.ServerReport.SetParameters(Param);
    reportViewer1.ShowParameterPrompts = false;
    reportViewer1.ShowPromptAreaButton = false;
    reportViewer1.RefreshReport();
}
```

VB

```vb
Private Sub Button1_Click(ByVal sender As System.Object, ByVal e As _
        System.EventArgs) Handles Button1.Click

    Dim reportServerURL As String = "http://LocalHost/ReportServer"
    Dim reportPath As String = _
```

```
        "/AdventureWorks Sample Reports/Employee Sales Summary"
Dim selectedEmp As Employee = CType(cboEmployee.SelectedItem, Employee)

Dim Param(2) As ReportParameter
Param(0) = New ReportParameter("ReportMonth", _
        cboReportMonth.SelectedItem.ToString())
Param(1) = New ReportParameter("ReportYear", _
        cboReportYear.SelectedItem.ToString())
Param(2) = New ReportParameter("EmpID", selectedEmp.ID)

With Me.ReportViewer1
    .ProcessingMode = ProcessingMode.Remote
    With .ServerReport
        .ReportServerUrl = New Uri(reportServerURL)
        .ReportPath = reportPath
        .SetParameters(Param)
    End With

    .ShowParameterPrompts = False
    .ShowPromptAreaButton = False
    .RefreshReport()
End With

End Sub
```

Figure 15-24 shows the result. The report is displayed in the `MicrosoftReportViewer` control embedded on the form. The standard report parameter bar and prompts are not displayed in the top of the viewer since they were suppressed using the related `MicrosoftReportViewer` properties.

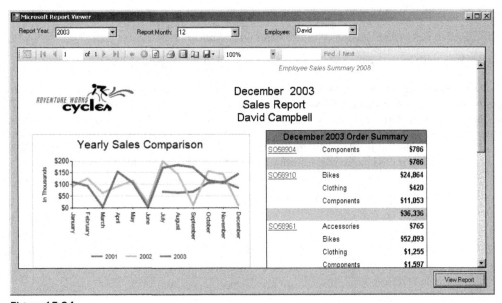

Figure 15-24

The `MicrosoftReportViewer` controls provide an easy-to-implement way of embedding reports in your custom web and Windows applications. Unfortunately, you still have to code the rest of the application in order to provide users with an all-around solution. There's an in-between option, where reports can be made available to users without going through the Report Manager application. That in-between option is SharePoint, which is discussed in Chapter 16.

Summary

In this chapter, we saw three ways to render reports from Reporting Services. The first part of the chapter focused on rendering reports via URL requests. The second part looked at rendering reports programmatically through the Reporting Services Web services. In the last part, you used the `MicrosoftReportViewer` control to easily embed reports in a Windows Forms application.

URL rendering gives you a quick way to add Reporting Services reports to your own applications. You can add Reporting Services reports to custom portals or create your own custom report links in other applications.

Rendering reports directly through an ASP.NET application can be very helpful. It allows developers to create their own interface for items such as parameters. A key point to remember is that Report Manager uses the same Reporting Services Web services that we used in the examples in this chapter. Therefore, anything that you can do from the Report Manager can also be done through your own code. This adds an incredible amount of flexibility for developers of custom applications.

This chapter has shown you how to:

❑   Use simple URL query strings to access reports.

❑   Programmatically work with the Reporting Service and Report Execution Service APIs.

❑   Embed reports into custom Windows and web applications.

❑   Work with the `MicrosoftReportViewer` control in Visual Studio 2008.

Because the Reporting Services APIs are implemented as Web services, you can call them from various types of applications, including .NET Windows applications, ASP.NET web applications, and .NET console applications. You can even use these Web services from Visual Basic 6.0, VBA applications using Microsoft's SOAP library, or essentially any application that can send a properly formatted request to the Report Server. This flexibility allows for the creation of a number of applications, including those that use custom security or pass parameter information stored in other application databases.

16

Integrating Reports with SharePoint

This chapter explores the integration of SQL Server 2008 Reporting Services with the SharePoint technologies. In recent years, SharePoint has become a web portal centerpiece for collaboration and information sharing. As a result, Microsoft has tightly integrated their reporting solution with the SharePoint technologies.

Integration of SQL Server 2008 Reporting Services and SharePoint allows for a user to navigate to their intranet portal and have instant access to company information as well as personalized business reports and key performance indicators (KPIs). The reports can be embedded directly into web portal pages for seamless integration for the user.

SQL Server 2008 Reporting Services can be installed in either Native mode or SharePoint Integrated mode. In Native mode, a user would interact with Reporting Services using two web parts (Report Explorer and Report Viewer). In Integrated mode, SharePoint takes over all the duties of the Report Manager as well as adds SharePoint document management values such as a consistent and user-friendly experience, versioning, security trimming, alerts, enterprise search, and, when properly configured, the meeting of regulatory compliance requirements, to just name a few.

This chapter covers:

❑   A brief overview of the SharePoint technologies, including Windows SharePoint Services, Microsoft Office SharePoint Server, and SharePoint web parts

❑   SharePoint integration with SQL Server Reporting Services in Native mode

❑   SharePoint integration with SQL Server Reporting Services in Integrated mode

❑   SharePoint integration architecture

❑   A comparison between Native and Integrated mode

For the examples in this chapter, it is assumed that you already have a lab environment that consists of MOSS 2007 with Service Pack (SP) 1 installed. If you are using WSS 3.0, the examples should be nearly identical until later in the chapter, where we take advantage of the Report Center template that is part of MOSS Enterprise Edition. It is also assumed that the SharePoint lab environment is installed using the Stand-Alone option on a single Windows Server computer, which will act as both the SharePoint Web front end, application server, and Report Server. Some knowledge of SharePoint is also assumed.

In order to install WSS or MOSS on a Windows Server 2008 computer, you will need to make sure the installation includes SP1. Windows Server 2008 will not allow WSS or MOSS to be installed and then upgraded to SP1 after the installation. A trial version of WSS or MOSS that includes SP1 can be downloaded from the following locations:

WSS 3.0 with SP1 included: `http://technet.microsoft.com/en-us/windowsserver/sharepoint/default.aspx`

MOSS 2007 with SP1 included: `www.microsoft.com/sharepoint/trynow.mspx`

The examples that follow also make use of the sample reports that run against the AdventureWorks2008 database. As of this writing, there is a v2005 schema of the AdventureWorks sample database and a v2008 version of the sample database. Both of these versions are designed to run within SQL Server 2008. There are sample reports that work with the v2005 schema and sample reports that work with the v2008 schema. Microsoft has recently updated and moved the MSI installs of the sample database and reports to the CodePlex site. The most recent versions can be downloaded from the following locations:

Sample Database — `www.codeplex.com/MSFTDBProdSamples`

Sample Reports — `www.codeplex.com/MSFTRSProdSamples`

Links to all SQL Server samples can be accessed by going to the main sample site, at `http://codeplex.com/SqlServerSamples`.

In a real-world situation, several servers would be used to host the SharePoint and SQL Server environments. What I have seen as a standard production enterprise-level implementation is a SharePoint farm that is made up of four Web front-end servers and two application servers, a SQL Server fail-safe cluster, and a dedicated SQL Server Reporting Services server. For simplicity's sake and to make the examples in this chapter easier to follow for the home user, we will put everything on one Windows Server machine.

The SharePoint Technologies

The SharePoint technologies are made up of Windows SharePoint Services (WSS) and Microsoft Office SharePoint Server (MOSS). WSS is a framework built on the .NET framework and is included with Windows Server 2003 and 2008. MOSS, on the other hand, is a finished product built on top of the WSS framework and thus requires its own licensing. Figure 16-1 shows how WSS is built on .NET and ASP .NET, and MOSS is built on WSS.

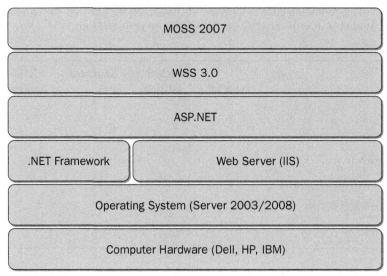

Figure 16-1

SharePoint sites are web-based applications that provide a single point of entry for information across an enterprise. Better yet, sites can be created without any programming. Windows SharePoint sites can be created by anyone with sufficient permissions. The functionality is made available through Windows SharePoint Services. Multiple SharePoint sites can be aggregated into portals through the use of MOSS.

Windows SharePoint Services (WSS)

The Windows SharePoint Services (WSS) framework is included with Windows Server 2003 and 2008 and provides a simple portal solution with minimal overhead. Because WSS is a framework and not a finished solution, further customization is generally required in order to meet the needs of a specific business. The WSS framework is built on the .NET framework and thus provides endless customization options for .NET developers.

Microsoft Office SharePoint Server (MOSS)

Microsoft Office SharePoint Server (MOSS) 2007 is a finished Microsoft product that was built on the WSS framework. Microsoft used the WSS framework to develop a robust, out-of-the-box solution that will fit the needs of many businesses yet is fully customizable. One of the key features that MOSS adds is a template called *Report Center* that is specialized to meet many of the needs of a Business Intelligence solution. The Report Center application template will be explored in greater depth below in this chapter. MOSS requires its own licensing separate from Windows Server. MOSS is released in two versions: Standard Edition and Enterprise Edition.

The information in the following table is from the Microsoft SharePoint web site and lists the functionality provided, out-of-the-box, by the three versions of SharePoint:

Capabilities	WSS 3.0	MOSS 2007 Standard Edition	MOSS 2007 Enterprise Edition
Collaboration	X	X	X
Portals		X	X
Enterprise Search		X	X
Enterprise Content Management		X	X
Business Process and Forms			X
Business Intelligence			X

SharePoint Web Parts

A fundamental SharePoint concept is the *web part*. *Web parts* can be thought of as modular elements containing functionality that is added to the user interface. Typically, web parts display specific information and can be moved around the web page. For example, SharePoint comes with web parts that can display images and list files. They have a consistent format, with a customizable title bar and a web-part dropdown menu available in the upper-right corner.

Traditionally, Reporting Services included two SharePoint web parts — the Report Explorer, for navigating through the Report Server content, and the Report Viewer, for viewing rendered reports. Beginning with the release of Service Pack 2 for SQL Server 2005 Reporting Services, a new way of running Reporting Services with SharePoint was born. The new method installed Reporting Services in a mode called *SharePoint Integrated mode*. This mode has been refined and upgraded with the release of SQL Server 2008 Reporting Services. Integrated mode introduces additional web parts as well as a new way of thinking about managing reports. The Integrated mode will be explored in detail below in this chapter.

Native Mode

In order to interact with Reporting Services in Native mode, you need to install the SQL Server Reporting Services web parts on each server in the SharePoint environment.

Installation

Chapter 3 discussed in detail the installation of SQL Server 2008 Reporting Services in Native mode. The web parts installation file, RSWebParts.cab, was installed on the Reporting Server when Reporting Services was installed. By default, it is located at:

```
C:\Program Files\Microsoft SQL Server\100\Tools\Reporting Services\SharePoint
```

If you are not integrating with a SharePoint environment on the same server where you have installed SQL Server 2008 Reporting Services, you will need to copy this installation file from the Reporting Services computer to the SharePoint computer. Once the file is on the SharePoint server, it will need to be installed. Install the web parts by navigating to the BIN directory of the SharePoint installation and executing the following command from a command prompt:

```
C:\>cd "C:\Program Files\Common Files\Microsoft Shared\web server extensions\12\BIN"

C:\Program Files\Common Files\Microsoft Shared\web server extensions\12\BIN>
stsadm.exe -o addwppack -filename "C:\RSWebParts.cab" -globalinstall

Operation completed successfully.


C:\Program Files\Common Files\Microsoft Shared\web server extensions\12\BIN>
```

Make sure that you are on the computer running SharePoint. In this example, the RSWebParts.cab file has been copied to the root C:\ directory.

After installing the web parts on the SharePoint server, you can use them by adding them to any site in the farm just as you would any other web part, as shown in Figure 16-2.

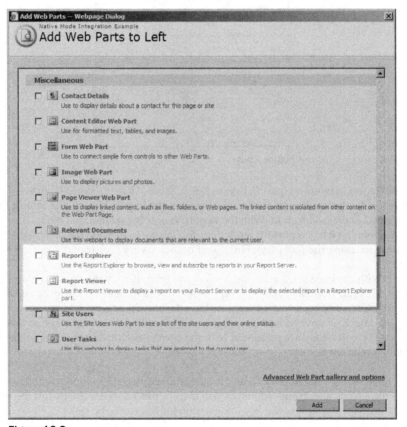

Figure 16-2

Report Viewer

The *Report Viewer* web part is used to display reports in the SharePoint environment. You can interact with reports as you would in Report Manager, using links within the report and DHTML functionality for collapsing report sections. For drill-down reports, the target report displays in the same Report Viewer web part. Drill-through reports, however, are rendered in a new browser window. Depending on the layout of the report and the size of the web part on the page, only a portion of the report may be visible. You'll need to use the scroll bars to view the rest of the report. As with standard web parts, you can change the size of the Report Viewer on the page in the Tool pane. The *Tool pane* is a configuration window that lets you set property values for web parts displayed on the SharePoint page, as shown in Figure 16-3.

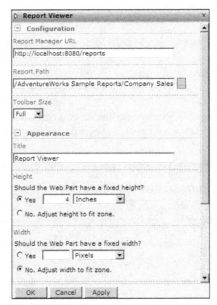

Figure 16-3

You can use the Report Viewer web part in Connected or Stand-Alone mode. In Connected mode, clicking a link in the Report Explorer web part renders the report in the Report Viewer. The Report Explorer web part will be covered in the next section. With the Report Viewer in Stand-Alone mode, it doesn't have the Report Explorer pointing it to a report for rendering. You'll have to provide the path to the report manually. The report path is set using the Tool pane. This might not seem very user-friendly, but it has a purpose.

Once the report path has been set, the Report Viewer can then display the report without user-initiated input or action. This functionality allows for report developers to develop key performance indicator (KPI) dashboard pages. The reports contained in these dashboard pages could run on a schedule and automatically update. Executives could have these dashboards on their Start page so that whenever they open up Internet Explorer, they are presented with the current metrics for their organization without having to interact with the report.

Another use I have seen for the Report Viewer is in manufacturing. Developers will develop a very specific report for a particular group. Monitors will then be placed in key areas, and the workers can simply look up onto the monitor to see key information for their specific tasks.

The Report Viewer web part will show up under the Miscellaneous category when you go to add the web part to a SharePoint page. Simply select the Report Viewer web part to add it to the page.

Once you have added the Report Viewer web part to a page, you can configure it by clicking on the Modify Shared Web Part item under the web part dropdown menu (the small arrow in the upper-right corner of the web part). This will bring up the Tool pane described above (refer to Figure 16-3).

Report parameters are displayed at the top of the web part content area. This parameters section expands to display the report parameters, with the standard Report Manager toolbar below it. Using the toolbar, reports can be exported to an XML file with report data, a comma-separated values (CSV) file, an Acrobat PDF file, a MIME HyperText Markup Language (MHTML) web archive, a Microsoft Excel file, a TIFF image, or to a Microsoft Word document, as shown in Figure 16-4.

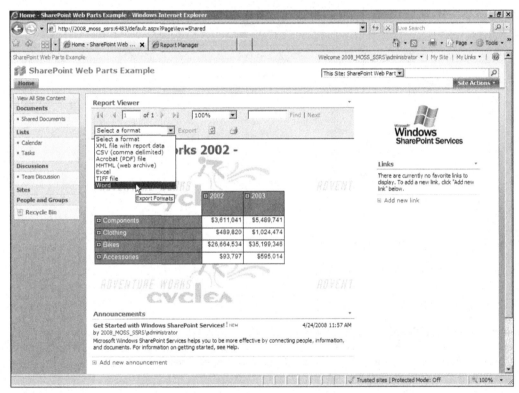

Figure 16-4

Report Explorer

The Report Explorer web part provides a miniature version of the Report Manager web application. The Report Explorer web part allows a user to navigate the content in the Report Server hierarchy. Clicking a report link in the Report Explorer displays the report. There are two ways the report can be displayed: in Linked mode or in Stand-Alone mode. When linked to a Report Viewer web part, the report renders in that web part. When in Stand-Alone mode, the report is rendered in a new browser window. Which mode you choose typically depends on how much screen real estate you have available. Connected mode simply means that data is passed between the two web parts.

Like Report Manager, the Report Explorer web part has a Details view. When in this view, you can create or edit a subscription to a report. If no icons are showing up, you likely have not configured the e-mail settings in the Reporting Services configuration utility. Once e-mail settings are configured, an e-mail icon will show up in the subscriptions column for reports for which you have subscription access.

The Report Explorer web part also provides bread-crumb-trail navigation and columns that can be sorted. In the Report Explorer, however, only folders, reports, and resources are displayed. You don't have access to data sources from the Report Explorer.

Once you have added the Report Explorer web part to a page, you can configure it by clicking on the Modify Shared Web Part item under the Web Part dropdown menu (the small down arrow in the upper-right corner of the web part). Figure 16-5 shows the Configuration window for the Report Explorer.

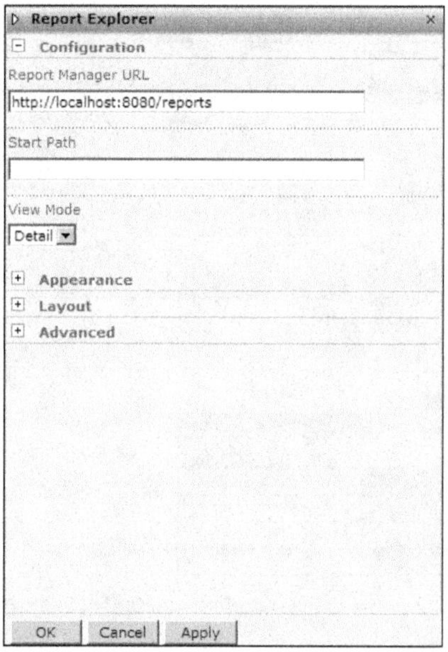

Figure 16-5

You can also launch Report Builder 1.0 from within the Report Explorer web part, as shown in Figure 16-6. The Report Builder 1.0 is a click-once application that is downloaded to your computer from the host computer. The Report Builder 1.0 is covered in detail in Chapter 12.

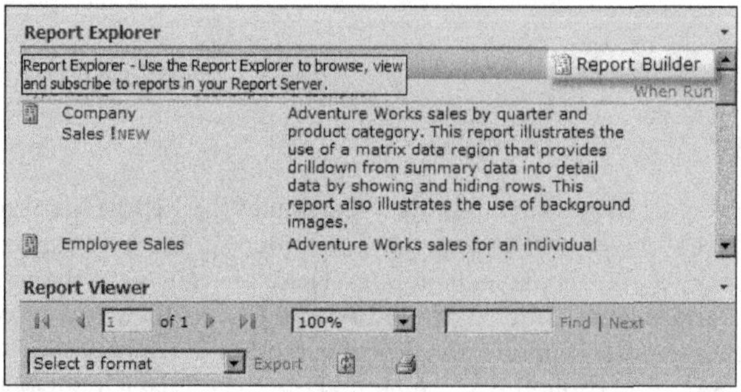

Figure 16-6

Integrated Mode

Configuring Report Services in SharePoint Integrated mode creates a tightly coupled technology that provides for an extremely user-friendly and seamless user experience. In order to achieve Integrated mode in SQL Server 2005 SP2 Reporting Services, the Reporting Services instance had to first be installed in Native mode and then converted to Integrated mode. The installation of SQL Server 2008 Reporting Services has made great improvements in this area. The Installation Wizard now allows for Reporting Services to be installed directly into Integrated mode. The new Reporting Services Configuration utility also provides the functionality to create a new Reporting Services instance in Integrated mode from within the utility itself. We explore this functionality in the following sections.

Installation/Configuration

Chapter 3 walked through a detailed explanation of the Reporting Services installation process. Figure 16-7 shows the Reporting Services Configuration screen of the Installation Wizard that allows for SharePoint Integrated mode to be selected.

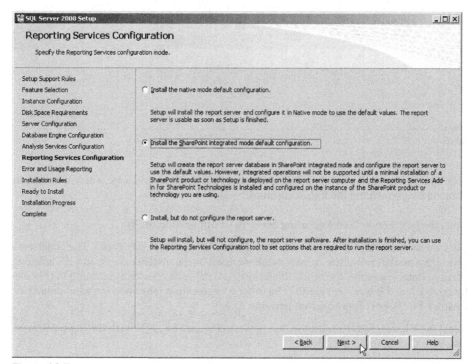

Figure 16-7

The Reporting Services Configuration utility has changed extensively in SQL Server 2008 Reporting Services. In SQL Server 2005 SP2 Reporting Services, there were checkmarks that showed if specific components had been configured. These are gone in SQL Server 2008 Reporting Services, and the entire interface is replaced with a very straightforward Configuration screen, as shown in Figure 16-8.

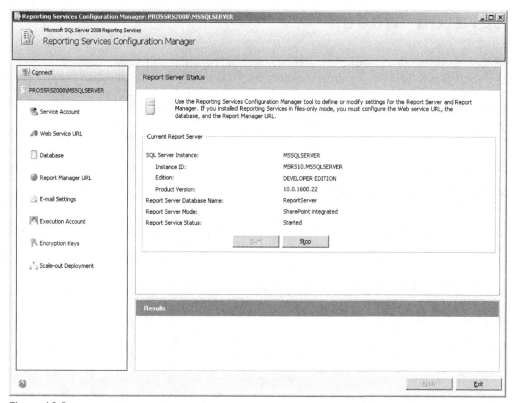

Figure 16-8

If the Reporting Services instance was installed in Native mode, you can create a new database in Integrated mode by performing the following steps:

1. Open the SQL Server 2008 Reporting Services Configuration utility.

2. Click on the Database navigational tab on the left-hand side of the screen. The Database screen gives information about the current database, such as the instance name and ID, edition, version, database name, the mode the reporting database is currently running in (Native or Integrated), and the current status. The other configuration tabs are covered in detail in Chapter 14, "Report Server Administration."

3. Select the Change Database button, as shown in Figure 16-9, to launch the Report Server Database Configuration Wizard.

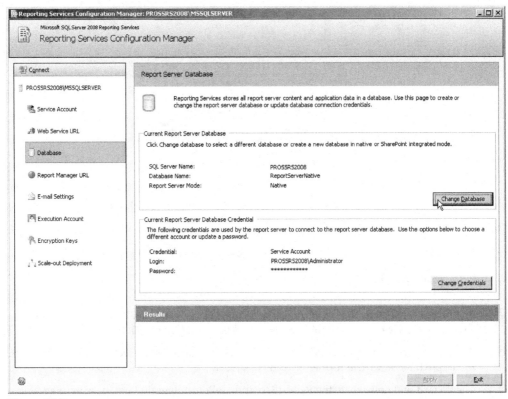

Figure 16-9

4. Select the task to "Create a new report server database" to create a new Reporting Services instance that will be configured in Integrated mode, and then click Next.

5. Type in the name of the database server that will host the Reporting Services instance. If everything is on the same server, this is probably already filled in for you. You can click on the Test Connection button to confirm that you have a successful connection to the database server. Click Next.

6. Type in the name of the Reporting Services database that you want to create in Integrated mode. The default is *ReportServer*; however, we will call this new database **ReportServerSharePointIntegrated**. Make sure to also choose the option of SharePoint Integrated Mode, as shown in Figure 16-10, and then click Next.

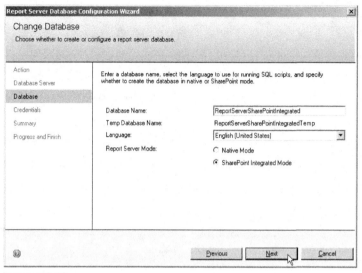

Figure 16-10

7. Specify the credentials that will be used to connect to the database. If everything is on the same server, you can leave the default as *Service Credentials* and then click Next.

8. A summary screen appears, outlining the choices that have been selected while going through the Wizard. Review the information and click Next.

9. The Wizard will now create the ReportServerSharePointIntegrated database in Integrated mode and give a status of each of the processes as it completes. When the entire process has completed, you will be presented with the results screen, as shown in Figure 16-11. Click Finish to exit the Wizard.

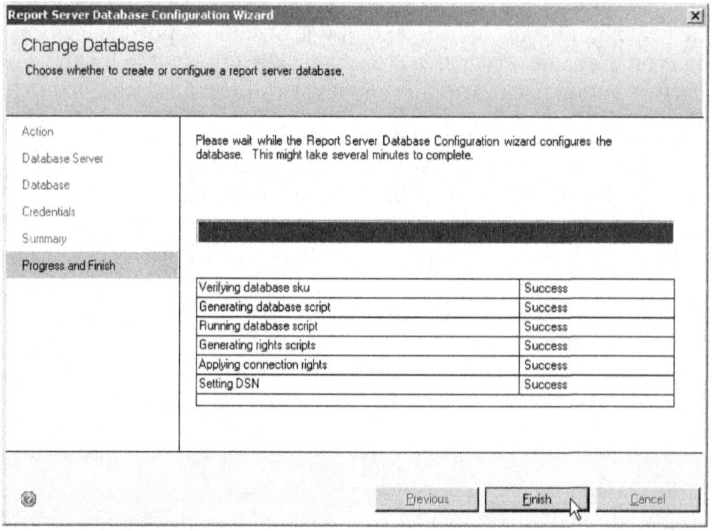

Figure 16-11

The database information from Step 2 is now changed to reflect the new Integrated mode database that was just created.

The next piece to the puzzle of integration is the SQL Server 2008 Reporting Services add-in for SharePoint, which must be installed on all the web front-end servers in the SharePoint farm. In our example, everything is on the same server, so we will install the add-in on this server.

The add-in is a web download and provides the necessary features for tight integration between the Report Server and the SharePoint farm. The SQL Server 2008 Reporting Services add-in for SharePoint provides the following to the SharePoint farm:

- ❑ The Report Viewer web part for viewing Reporting Services reports as well as exporting to other formats. This Report Viewer web part is different from the Report Viewer web part described in the Native mode section. This Report Viewer web part is called *SQL Server Reporting Services Report Viewer* and is designed to interact with reports in SharePoint Integrated mode.

- ❑ A URL proxy endpoint for Reporting Services reports

- ❑ SharePoint application pages for:

  - ❑ Managing reports, data connections, and models

  - ❑ Creating subscriptions and schedules

  - ❑ Security

- ❑ Content types so that SharePoint understands Reporting Services objects

At the time of this writing, you can download the SQL Server 2008 Reporting Services add-in for SharePoint by searching for "Microsoft SQL Server 2008 Feature Pack" using your favorite web search engine. Once at the feature pack download site, look for the rsSharePoint.msi or rsSharePoint_x64.msi file, depending on if you are running a 64-bit processor.

The account used to install the add-in must be a Farm and Site Collection Administrator. When installing using multiple servers, an Active Directory account should be used that is also a member of the local machine's Administrators group on every server that it is being installed on. The add-in needs to be installed on every web front-end server in the farm.

After installing the add-in, you will need to verify that the Reporting Services Integration Feature is turned on for the Central Administration web application. You can do this by opening the Central Administration page and going to Site Actions ⇨ Site Settings. On the Site Settings page, click the link under the Site Collection Administration section called *Site Collection Features*. In the features for the site, activate the Reporting Server Integration Feature, as shown in Figure 16-12. Once the feature is activated, you will have a Reporting Services section in the Applications section of Central Administration, as shown in Figure 16-13.

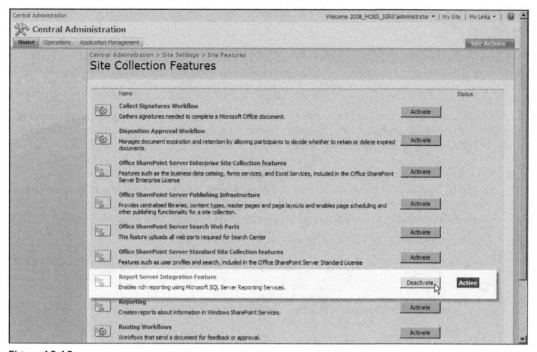

Figure 16-12

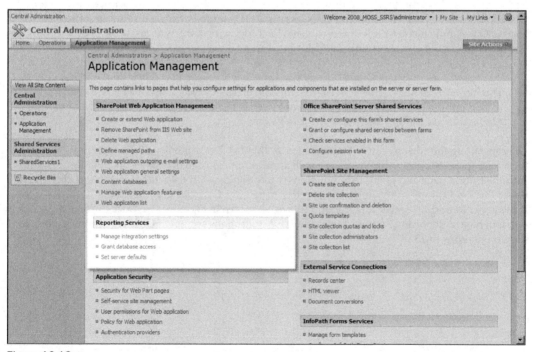

Figure 16-13

Now that the Reporting Services addition has been added to SharePoint, you are ready to configure the farm and tell it what SQL Server 2008 Reporting Service instance it should integrate with.

In the Reporting Services section of the Applications tab in Central Administration, click on the Grant Database Access link. This screen grants the Report Servers' Web and Windows service accounts access to the SharePoint databases. Since the database is running on the same server, just use the defaults and click OK. You will then be prompted for a credential that has access to add the necessary accounts to the database. If you are using a local administrator and everything is on the same box, as in the examples, make sure to use the format *SERVERNAME\administrator*. In this example, the server name is *PROSSRS2008*, so the login would be *PROSSRS2008\administrator* and the password. In a distributed farm environment, you would need to provide credentials that have access to the SharePoint databases and can grant the appropriate access. In most situations, this would be the Farm Administrator account.

The next link down in the Reporting Services section is the Manage Integration Settings link. The Integration Settings page has a Report Server Web Service URL and an Authentication Mode, as shown in Figure 16-14. The Web Service URL should match up with what is configured in the Reporting Services Configuration utility under the Web Service URL navigational tab (see Figure 16-15). This example uses port 8080 since the default MOSS site was using port 80. The Authentication Mode can be either Trusted Account or Integrated Windows Authentication. Since everything is on the same server, we will use Windows Authentication.

The Trusted Account option sends the connection to the Report Server across the network using a predefined trusted account. The trusted account impersonates a SharePoint user on the Report Server. This scenario would be used when using Forms Authentication or when using Integrated Windows Authentication without Active Directory or without kerberos. In these scenarios, the Report Server has no knowledge of the users logging into SharePoint, so a predefined Trusted Account has to be set up so that users will be able to run reports against the Report Server.

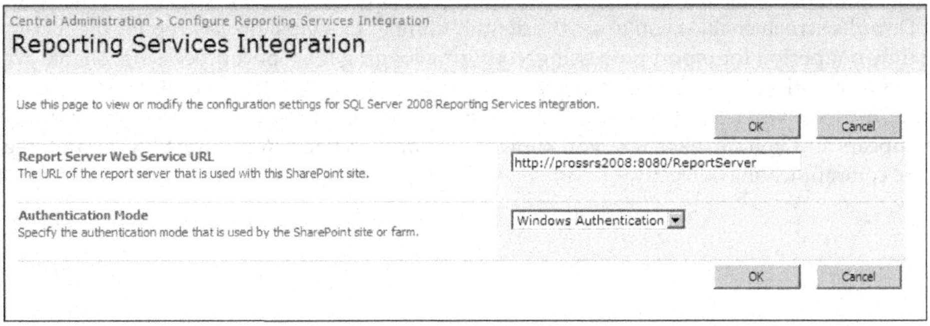

Figure 16-14

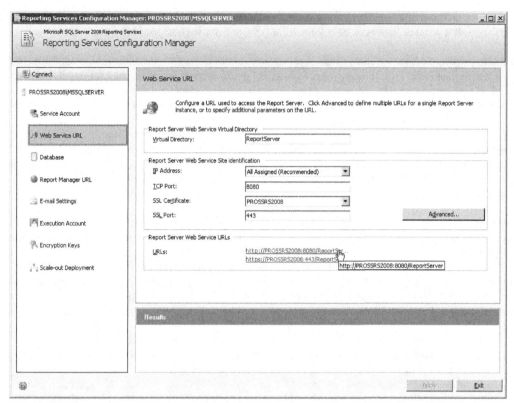

Figure 16-15

The final link in the Reporting Services section in Central Admin is the Set Server Defaults. The Set Server Defaults screen enables you to set the default number of snapshots to keep for the report history, set the time-out period for report processing, configure logging for report processing, enable Windows Integrated Authentication, enable ad hoc reporting, and set a custom Report Builder 1.0 URL, as shown in Figure 16-16. We will keep the defaults but should note an important step. If the Set Server Defaults screen appears and you can click OK, you know that SharePoint and Reporting Services in Integrated mode are communicating correctly.

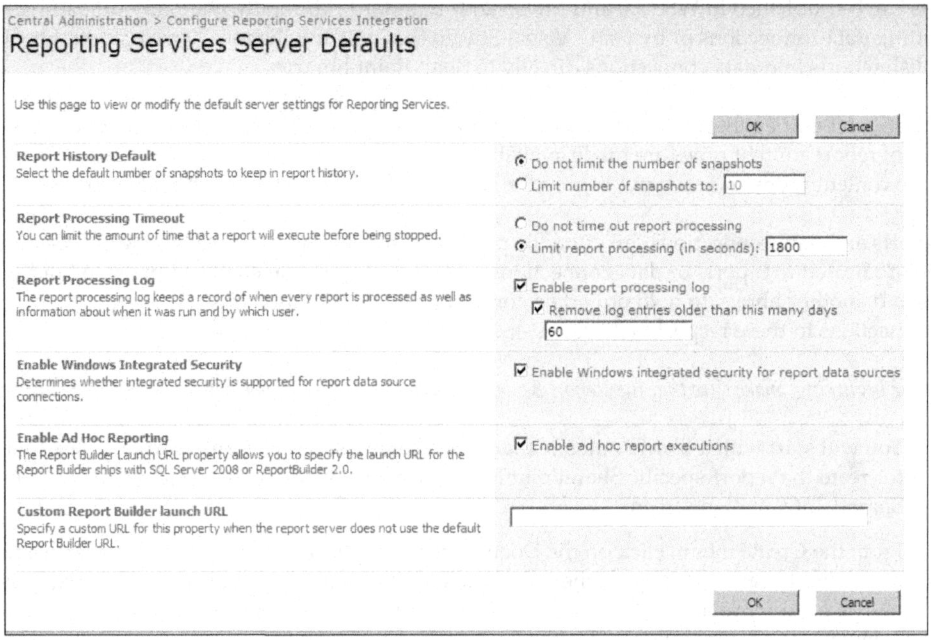

Figure 16-16

In real-world situations, the Set Server Defaults link is often used to troubleshoot communication between SharePoint and the Reporting Services instance. If there is a communication problem, this screen will not load.

At this point, the SharePoint farm is fully integrated with SQL Server 2008 Reporting Services, and you are ready to publish and manage reports.

Publishing Reports

Publishing reports to a SharePoint integrated library can be done in several ways. Since a report is just another document type, like a Word document, it can be uploaded to the report library just like any other document. The same holds true with data connection types.

Once the Reporting Services add-in for SharePoint has been installed on either a WSS 3.0 or MOSS 2007 installation, the farm *knows* about these new content types. You can manually create a Reports and Data Connections library in any site and publish your reports and data connections to these libraries.

WSS 3.0 and MOSS 2007 Standard Edition

Publishing reports in WSS 3.0 and MOSS 2007 Standard Edition is nearly identical. The key difference between these editions is that MOSS 2007 Standard Edition adds additional functionality to the SharePoint environment, such as audiences. It is not until MOSS 2007 Enterprise Edition that major features related to reporting are introduced, namely, the Report Center Enterprise Site template. The Enterprise features are explored below in this chapter.

Reports can be published in WSS 3.0 and MOSS 2007 Standard Edition by manually uploading reports and setting data connections or by using Visual Studio Business Intelligence Development Studio (BIDS) to publish reports and data connections directly to SharePoint libraries.

Once the SharePoint environment has been integrated with SQL Server 2008 Reporting Services, a number of report content types are made available. The following walks through creating libraries that use these content types and then publishing the sample reports from within the BIDS environment.

The reports and data connections can either be published directly to the same library or to separate libraries dedicated to reports or data connections. In this example, you create a library to hold only reports and another library to hold only data connections. You will then publish the sample reports and data connections to these respective libraries.

Before beginning, make sure that the Report Server Integration Feature is activated for the Site Collection.

1. You will start with a SharePoint site that was created using the Blank template. The first step is to create the report-specific SharePoint library. Choose Site Settings ⇨ Create to enter the SharePoint Creation screen.

2. From the Create menu, click on the Document Library link under Libraries to create a new document library. Clicking on the link brings up the form used to create the library. This library will be used for reports, so fill in the name **Reports** and also choose **None** for Document Template, as shown in Figure 16-17.

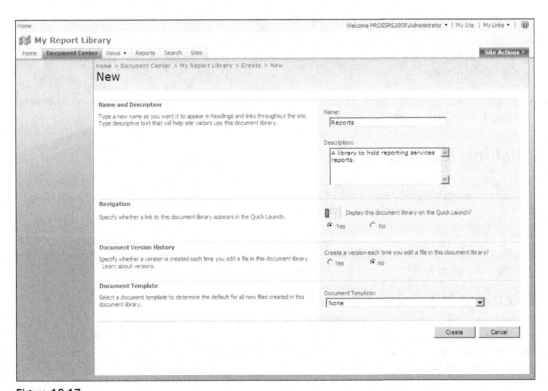

Figure 16-17

3. At this point, you have a document library, but it is not associated with the Reporting Services report content type. To change the content type associated for this library, open the Document Library Settings by choosing Settings ⇨ Document Library Settings from within the newly created document library.

4. By default, the management of content types is turned off in a document library. Click on the Advanced Settings link, and then check Yes for "Allow management of content types" (see Figure 16-18). Click OK to save the setting.

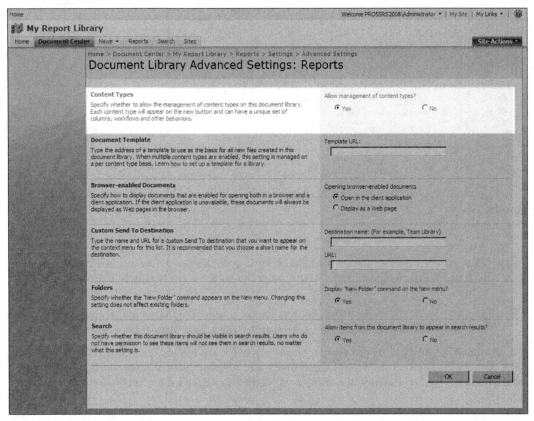

Figure 16-18

5. Now that content type management is allowed, a new section called Content Types appears on the Document Library Settings page. The default content type is Document. Click on this link to open this content type, and then delete it from the library by clicking on the "Delete this content type" link under the Settings section. Click OK to confirm the deletion.

6. Next click on "Add from existing site content types" under the Content Types section in the Library Settings page. Click on the dropdown, and choose "Report Server Content Types" to display the content types that were added with the Reporting Services add-in for SharePoint. There are three content types to choose from: Report Builder 1.0 Report, Report Builder 1.0 Model, and Report Data Source. For this library, you only want to store reports, so add the **Report Builder 1.0 Report** content type, as shown in Figure 16-19, and then click OK.

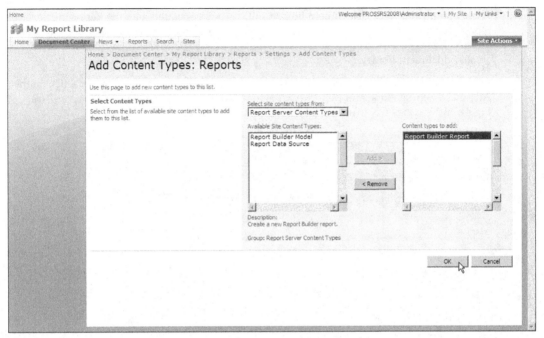

Figure 16-19

7. The Content Types section on the Library Settings page should now include the Report Builder 1.0 Report content type. At this point the library is ready to hold Reporting Services reports.

8. Repeat Steps 1–7 to create a Data Sources library to store the shared data connections. Name the new library **Data Connections**, and choose the content type **Report Data Source**.

You now have one library to hold reports and another library to hold data connections on your blank SharePoint page, as shown in Figure 16-20. You can also have reports and data sources in the same directory, but functionally it is easier to manage reports and data connections in separate libraries.

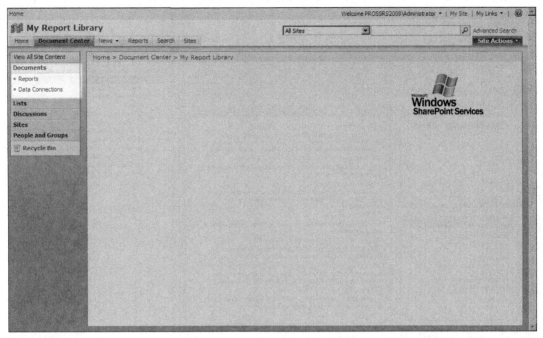

Figure 16-20

Now that you have **Reports** and **Data Connections** libraries to hold the Reporting Services content, you can fire up BIDS and open the sample AdventureWorks project.

The sample project is stored in the following location by default:

```
C:\Program Files\Microsoft SQL Server\100\Samples\Reporting Services\Report
        Samples\AdventureWorks Sample Reports\AdventureWorks 2008 Sample
        Reports.sln
```

Double-click on the solution file to fire up BIDS and load the sample solution, as shown in Figure 16-21. If you do not have BIDS installed, you can go back and install it from the SQL Server 2008 installation media.

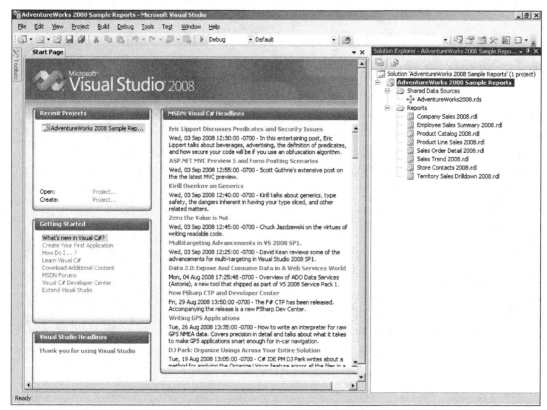

Figure 16-21

Now that the solution is open, you are ready to publish the reports and data connections contained within it to the newly created Reports and Data Connections libraries. Right-click on the AdventureWorks 2008 Sample Reports solution and choose Properties, as shown in Figure 16-22.

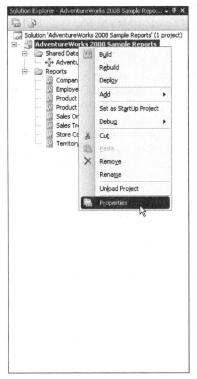

Figure 16-22

The Properties window is displayed with the `TargetDataSourceFolder`, `TargetReportFolder`, and `TargetServerURL` properties. As the name suggests, the `TargetDataSourceFolder` property corresponds to the Data Connections library that you created above, and the `TargetReportFolder` property corresponds to the Reports library. The `TargetServerURL` property is the URL of the blank SharePoint site that contains your libraries. Fill in these fields with values that match your environment. The format is `http://server:port/path/to/SharePointSite/libraryname`. If you are using the default site, you would have something like `http://server/libraryname`. An example of my environment is shown below. Note that I created the blank site as a subsite of the Docs library.

Property Name	Value
`TargetDataSourceFolder`	`http://prossrs2008/Docs/myreports/Data Connections`
`TargetReportFolder`	`http://prossrs2008/Docs/myreports/Reports`
`TargetServerURL`	`http://prossrs2008/Docs/myreports`

Once the settings are correct, click OK to save the settings. Right-click on the AdventureWorks 2008 Sample Reports project in the Solution Explorer, and click Deploy.

You might receive the error "The underlying connection was closed: An unexpected error occurred on a send" as the data connections and reports are attempting to deploy. I received this error depending on the order that I installed the technology stack. The error is a result of the SecureConnectionLevel *for the Report Server being set to 2, which requires SSL encryption.*

To allow the reports to be deployed without requiring SSL encryption, set the SecureConnectionLevel setting to 0 in the rsreportserver.config file located at C:\Program Files\Microsoft SQL Server\ MSRS10.MSSQLSERVER\Reporting Services\ReportServer.

Once the solution has been deployed, you can go back to the Reports folder and see all the reports in the SharePoint library, as shown in Figure 16-23. You can click on a report to view it. The report now has all the content management features that SharePoint has to offer.

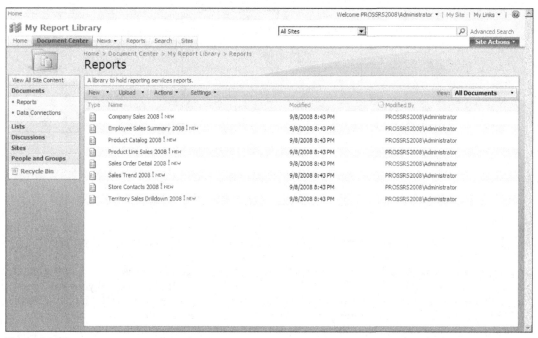

Figure 16-23

If for some reason the report is not displayed when you click on it within the SharePoint Reports library, you will need to check to make sure that it is using the correct data source by clicking the down arrow next to the report to drop down the SharePoint specific menu and choosing Manage Data Sources. Make sure that the connection string in the data source that it is using is correct.

Also, confirm that the AdventureWorks2008 database has been downloaded from the SQL Server samples CodePlex site and installed on the server. The AventureWorks2008 sample database is contained in a file called SQL2008.AdventureWorks_OLTP_DB_v2008.x86.msi. Make sure to include the option to restore the database to the server when installing in order to attach the database to the SQL Server instance.

MOSS 2007 Enterprise Edition

MOSS 2007 Enterprise Edition adds several Reporting Services integration features. In particular, the Report Center Enterprise Site Template is added as well as a Library Type for Reports, a Library Type for Data Connections, and a Content Type called *Report*.

The Report Center site template takes the work out of creating Report and Data Connection libraries manually, as was done in the previous section, by embedding these libraries in the template. Figure 16-24 shows a site created using the Report Center template.

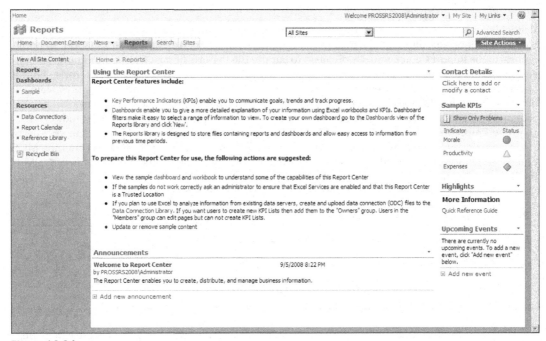

Figure 16-24

In addition to the already created Reports and Data Connections libraries, the Report Center site template also contains a Report Calendar that can be used to track report updates and schedules and can be synchronized with the Microsoft Outlook Calendar.

You can create a Report Center site by selecting the Report Center template from the Enterprise tab when creating a new SharePoint site, as shown in Figure 16-25.

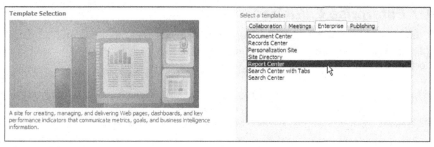

Figure 16-25

Publishing reports to the Report Center is very similar to publishing reports to a WSS 3.0 or MOSS 2007 Standard Edition site, although the manual configuration has been taken out of the equation. To publish reports to the Report Center, you simply need to supply the Reports library, Data Connections library, and site location to the Properties window of the Visual Studio project. When MOSS Enterprise Edition is initially installed, a Report Center site is created in the default site. There is no need to pre-create libraries for these data types, as the Report Center already contains them. These properties can be accessed by right-clicking on the project name in the Solution Explorer section of Visual Studio and choosing Properties. The values take the format of `http://<servername>/<site>/<library>`. My lab environment values are shown in the table below as an example. The name of the server running MOSS Enterprise Edition is *prossrs2008*, the name of the default site that contains the libraries is *Reports*. Within the Reports site, there is a Data Connections library and a Reports Library.

Property Name	Value
`TargetDataSourceFolder`	`http://prossrs2008/Reports/Data Connections`
`TargetReportFolder`	`http://prossrs2008/Reports/ReportsLibrary`
`TargetServerURL`	`http://prossrs2008/Reports`

If you do want to create additional libraries, you can simply create a new library and choose either "Report Library" or "Data Connection Library" on the SharePoint Create page for the Enterprise Edition site.

> *If any of the features are not showing up for a newly created site, make sure that the Office SharePoint Server Enterprise Site Collection Features and the Report Server Integration Feature are activated. These features are generally activated for the default web application when the Reporting Services add-in is installed. If a new web application was created, it will need to be activated in order for the Report Library content type to appear under Library in the Create screen. These features can be activated by going to Site Actions ⇨ Site Setting ⇨ Modify All Site Settings and then navigating to Site Administration ⇨ Site Features.*

SharePoint Site Settings

When Reporting Services is installed in Integrated mode and the Reporting Services add-in is installed on the SharePoint farm, a new section called *Manage Shared Schedules* is created in the SharePoint Site Settings, as shown in Figure 16-26. The new section allows the administrator to manage the shared schedules of the server. In particular, the administrator can add a new shared schedule, delete a schedule, pause a schedule, or run a selected schedule.

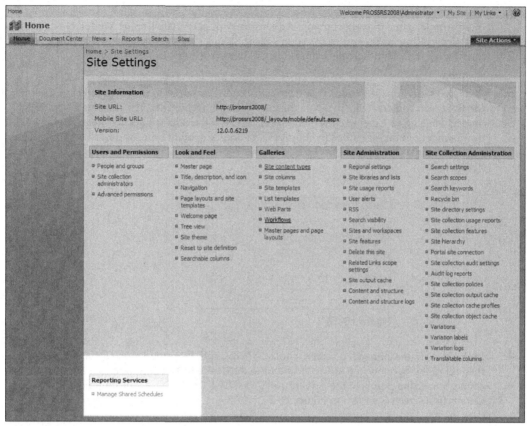

Figure 16-26

Report Models

In Chapter 11, you learned about report models. Report models can be generated from within the SharePoint environment using the following steps:

1. Create a document library that contains the Report Builder 1.0 Model data type. Adding Reporting Services content types to SharePoint document libraries was covered above in this chapter. Once the library contains this content type, select New from the dropdown menu of the library, and choose Report Model, as shown in Figure 16-27.

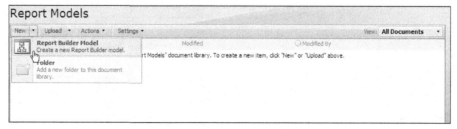

Figure 16-27

2. The Generate Model screen requires a name for the model and also a link to a data source. For this example, name the report model **AdventureWorksDW2008 Report Model**. Next, you need a data connection to the source for your Report Model. Chapter 11 described building report models in detail, so just create a simple model based on a data connection to the AdventureWorksDW2008 database.

3. Before you can browse to your new data connection, you need to cancel out of the Generate Model screen and create it. To create the new data connection, start by creating a document library, or using an existing document library, to hold the data connection item. Make sure that the document library includes the Report Data Source content type, as described above. Create a new item in the document library based on the Report Data Source content type, as shown in Figure 16-28.

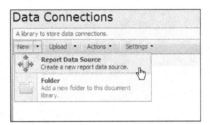

Figure 16-28

4. In the New Data Connection screen, choose Microsoft SQL Server for the Data Source Type, and then fill in the "Connection string" to point to the desired database. In this example, the connection string points to the AdventureWorksDW2008 database. The completed New Data Connection screen is shown in Figure 16-29.

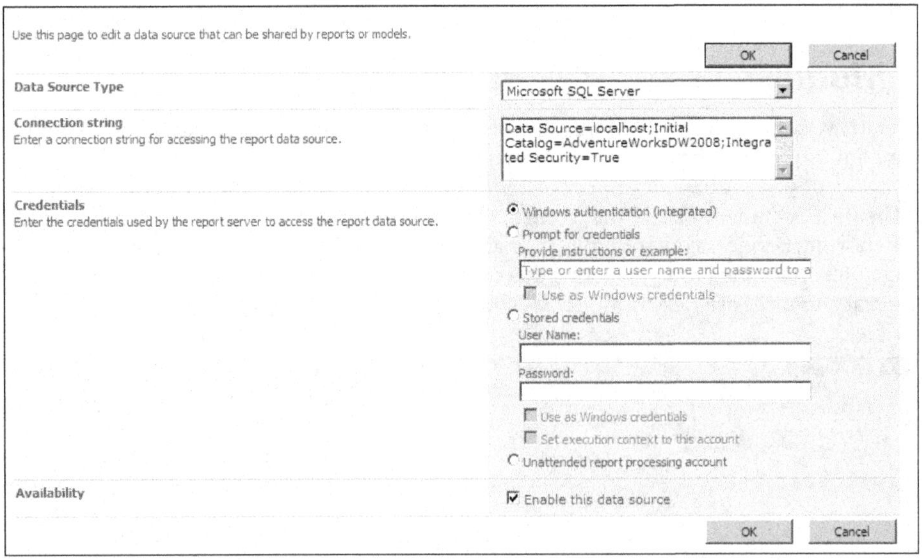

Figure 16-29

5. Now that you have a data connection, you are ready to go back and create a new model. Refer to Steps 1 and 2 above, and then browse to the newly created data connection. The complete configuration should look similar to Figure 16-30.

Home > Reports > Report Models > Generate Model
Generate Model

Use this page to create a Report Builder model. Click the OK button to generate a model. Generating a model may take several minutes.

| | OK | Cancel |

Name *

AdventureWorksDW2008 Report Model   .smdl

Data Source Link *
Select the shared data source (.rsds) file to use for this model.

http://prossrs2008/Reports/Data Connections

| | OK | Cancel |

Figure 16-30

6. Click OK to begin generating the model. When the model has been successfully generated, it will show up as an item in the SharePoint library, as shown in Figure 16-31.

Home > Reports > Report Models
Report Models

| New ▼ | Upload ▼ | Actions ▼ | Settings ▼ | | | View: **All Documents** ▼ |

Type	Name	Modified	◯ Modified By
📄	AdventureWorksDW2008 Report Model ! NEW	9/9/2008 9:43 AM	PROSSRS2008\Administrator

Figure 16-31

A report model can be built from many data sources, including Oracle and SAP, among many others, as shown in the New Data Connection screen in Figure 16-32.

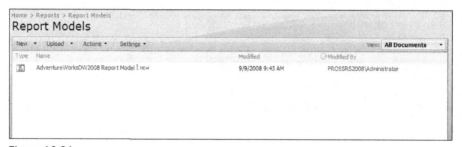

Data Source Type

Microsoft SQL Server ▼

Microsoft SQL Server
OLE DB
Microsoft SQL Server Analysis Services
Oracle
ODBC
XML
SAP NetWeaver BI
Hyperion Essbase

Connection string
Enter a connection string for accessing the report data source.

Credentials
Enter the credentials used by the report server to access the report data source.

◯ Prompt for credentials

Figure 16-32

Report Builder 1.0

In Chapter 12, you learned about Report Builder 1.0. Report Builder can be launched from within the SharePoint environment using one of the following four methods:

❑　From within a library that contains the Report Builder 1.0 Report data type, select New from the dropdown menu of the library, and choose Report Builder Report, as shown in Figure 16-33.

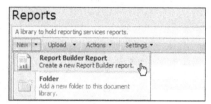

Figure 16-33

❑　From the context menu of a report, choose "Edit in Report Builder," as shown in Figure 16-34.

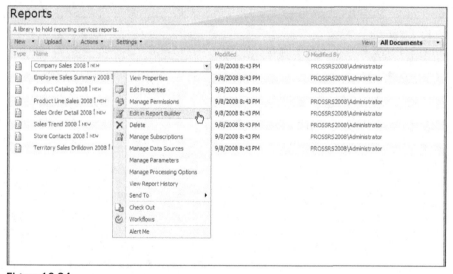

Figure 16-34

❑　From the context menu of a report model, choose "Load in Report Builder," as shown in Figure 16-35.

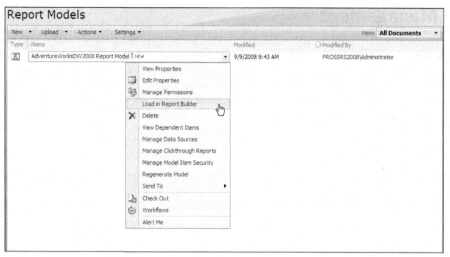

Figure 16-35

❑ After clicking on a report and viewing it in the SharePoint environment, click on the Actions menu, and then click "Open with Report Builder," as shown in Figure 16-36.

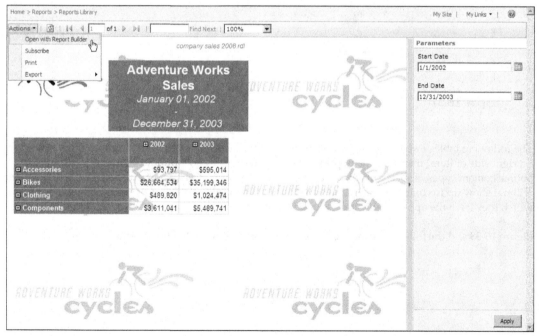

Figure 16-36

Report Management

Chapter 13 described in detail how to manage reports using Report Manager when SQL Server 2008 Reporting Services is installed in Native mode. In Integrated mode, the Report Manager is no longer available. All report management functionality is performed from within the SharePoint environment. Every report has a context menu associated with it for management. The menu can be accessed by hovering over a report until a down arrow appears on the right-hand side of the report name. When this arrow appears, click on it to reveal the context menu for that report, as shown in Figure 16-37.

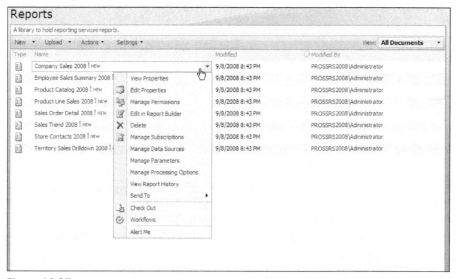

Figure 16-37

The following tables outline the Reporting Services–specific options contained in the context (dropdown on right side of item) menu for the Report Builder 1.0 Report, Report Builder Model, and Report Data Source content types, respectively. If a user does not have access to any particular menu, that menu item will not show up for that user. SharePoint uses security trimming so that users see only the items for which they have the appropriate permissions.

Figure 16-38 and the following table describe the Report Builder 1.0 Report menu items.

Figure 16-38

Item Name	Description
Edit in Report Builder 1.0	Opens the report in Report Builder 1 for editing.
Manage Subscriptions	Opens the subscription management screen that allows for adding a subscription to the report, adding a data-driven subscription to the report, or deleting the report.
Manage Data Sources	Opens the Data Source Management screen that lists the data sources for the report and allows for changing the Content Type and Data Source Link of the data source.
Manage Parameters	Opens a screen that provides management for the parameters contained within the report.
Manage Processing Options	Opens a screen that provides management for processing the report. The screen includes Data Refresh Options, Processing Time-Out Options, History Snapshot Options, and History Snapshot Limits.
View Report History	Displays a history of the report.

Figure 16-39 and the following table describe the Report Builder Model menu items.

Figure 16-39

Item Name	Description
Load in Report Builder 1.0	Loads the model into Report Builder 1.0.
View Dependent Items	Opens a screen that lists the reports that depend on this model.
Manage Data Sources	Opens the Data Source Management screen that lists the data sources for the report and allows for changing the Content Type and Data Source Link of the data source.
Manage Clickthrough Reports	Opens a screen that allows for the management of Clickthrough reports. Clickthrough reports contain detailed information and are accessed by clicking on data items in a main Report Builder 1.0 report.
Manage Model Item Security	Opens a screen that allows for the security management for specific portions of the model.
Regenerate Model	Regenerates the model from the data source.

Figure 16-40 and the following table describe the Report Data Source menu items.

Figure 16-40

Item Name	Description
View Dependent Items	Provides a list of all items that use this data source.
Edit Data Source Definition	Opens a screen that allows for the management of the data source. The screen includes sections for setting the Data Source type, Connection String, Credentials, and Availability of the Data Source. The Data Source Types include the following:
	Microsoft SQL Server
	OLE DB
	Microsoft SQL Server Analysis Services
	Oracle
	ODBC
	XML
	SAP NetWeaver BI
	Hyperion Essbase

SQL Server Reporting Services Report Viewer for Integrated Mode

The previous sections went through publishing and managing reports. Now that the reports are stored, managed, and can be viewed in a SharePoint library, you might still want to present them on a nice dashboard or entry site that users will view instead of navigating to the report library.

The Report Viewer web part can be used in a very similar manner to how it was used when integrated with Reporting Services in Native mode. The SQL Server Reporting Services Report Viewer web part, however, is designed to interact with a Reporting Services instance running in Integrated mode. The web part is listed under the available web parts, as shown in Figure 16-41.

Figure 16-41

The SQL Server Reporting Services Report Viewer web part can be set up to display a single defined report or can receive its report information from a web part based on user interaction. The following example walks through setting up a Reports Library web part that feeds a report to the viewer based on the report selected.

1. The first step is to add the SQL Server Reporting Services Report Viewer web part to the SharePoint page. This example uses the default Report Center page that installs when MOSS is installed. Click Site Actions ⇨ Edit Page to place the page in Edit view.

2. The next step is to add the viewer web part to the left side of the page for viewing the report that the user selects. Click "Add a Web Part to the Top Left Zone," and select the SQL Server Reporting Services Report Viewer Web Part.

3. Now you need a web part from which the user will select the report they wish to view. For this, you can use the Reports Library web part. Click "Add a Web Part to the Right Zone," and select the Reports Library Web Part.

4. Now that both web parts are on the page, you need to configure them. In the top-right corner of the Report Viewer web part, select Edit ⇨ Connections ⇨ Get Report Definition From ⇨ Reports Library, as shown in Figure 16-42.

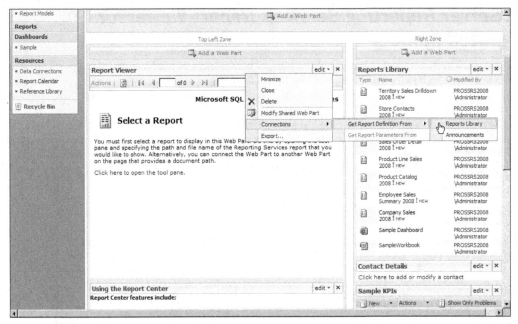

Figure 16-42

5. Finally, click Publish to publish the page back to the content library. Now when a report is selected in the web part on the right side, the report is displayed in the viewer web part on the left side, as shown in Figure 16-43. The size of the web parts and formatting on the screen can, of course, all be formatted to fit with the look and feel of your organization.

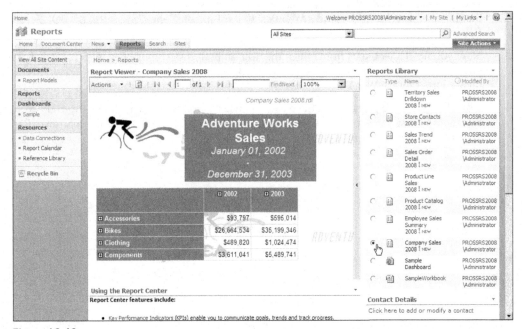

Figure 16-43

Architecture

When SQL Server 2008 Reporting Services is installed in Native mode, it runs in its own completely separate database. It uses an application called *Report Manager* to manage the database and does not share any database elements with the SharePoint environment. In this situation, the SharePoint environment is simply a viewer of the reports. As described previously in the chapter, the Report Viewer web part and the Report Explorer web part are used to view and explore the Report Server. The architecture of Reporting Services in Native mode is covered in Chapter 4.

When Reporting Services is installed in Integrated mode, the integration is achieved through tightly coupled data sharing among the Reporting Services databases and the SharePoint databases. In this configuration, SharePoint becomes the primary mechanism for displaying, managing, and securing not only reports and models but data sources as well.

In the simplest form, everything can be installed on one server. To review from the configuration previously in the chapter, the following components are used in Integrated mode:

- ❑ SharePoint (object model)
- ❑ SQL Server Engine (hosting SharePoint databases)
- ❑ SQL Server Engine (hosting report server databases)
- ❑ SharePoint databases
- ❑ SQL Server Reporting Services databases
- ❑ SQL Server Reporting Services SharePoint add-in

> *When installing SharePoint under the Basic configuration, SQL Server 2005 Compact Edition is used. SharePoint can be installed in an Advanced configuration, in which case the SQL Server 2008 engine can be used to host its content and configuration databases. We suspect that in a future service pack Microsoft will use a SQL Server 2008 engine for the Basic installation of SharePoint.*

In a single server instance, all these components are installed on a single computer. The SQL Server database engine is installed along with SQL Server Reporting Services in Integrated mode, which creates the Reporting Services database. Next, SharePoint (MOSS 2007 or WSS 3.0) is installed, which creates the configuration and content databases. Finally, the SharePoint add-in is installed to provide SharePoint with the Reporting Services features.

In order to distribute some of the features, the next scenario places the database engine on its own server. The database engine continues to host the SharePoint configuration and content databases, as well as the Reporting Services database. In this scenario, the SharePoint instance runs on its own server, and the database engine runs on its own server.

The distribution can continue as the needs of the organization become larger and larger. In a very large organization, there are generally multiple servers that host various pieces of the SharePoint and Reporting Services scenario. A common approach is to distribute SharePoint among application servers and web front-end servers. There is generally a large, fail-safe SQL Server cluster that is used to host the multiple configuration and content databases of the SharePoint farm. There is also a computer that hosts the Reporting Services instance.

Each of these scenarios breaks apart the pieces in order to gain stability and performance. In every scenario, however, the underlying architecture remains the same. The SharePoint database takes control of the Reporting Services objects. The objects are stored in the SharePoint databases but are synced with the Reporting Services database in order to improve report rendering performance.

One of the key benefits of SharePoint is that it provides users with a single access point to store all of their business documents. A SharePoint site could be set up for the executive leadership team that includes all documents they require on a daily basis. With Reporting Services in SharePoint Integrated mode, reports are also stored in these same document libraries and are easily accessed and managed. One of the main benefits of the reports being stored in the SharePoint libraries is that end-users only have to go to their specific SharePoint sites to obtain all their business documents, including their reports. The modern information workers world has become increasingly chaotic, in the digital sense, and Microsoft has achieved great strides in consolidating this chaos into a single point of reference with the SharePoint site.

Native Mode versus Integrated Mode

Determining the best type of integration depends on many variables surrounding the SharePoint farm and level of integration that is desired between the farm and the Reporting Services instance. The content from the following table comes mostly from SQL Server 2008 Books Online (BOL), but it is important enough to include similar content here as well:

	Native Mode	Integrated Mode
Integration	Report Explorer and Report Viewer web parts provide access to the Report Server and the ability to view reports, but all management is done on the Report Server using the standard Report Manager application.	Viewing and managing reports are integrated into the existing web portal environment. A standard SharePoint library is used to store and manage all reports and data connections. The SharePoint server farm becomes the main front-end mechanism for Reporting Services. The actual reporting server becomes a back-end system. A single web part is used to display reports and is easily integrated with other web parts and customized to fit the overall page design. The free Reporting Services SharePoint add-in provides Reporting Services–specific application pages to the SharePoint farm.
Content	Content is stored exclusively on the Report Server.	Content is stored in a SharePoint library on the farm. Content also exists on the Report Server but only for performance reasons. All content is managed through the SharePoint portal.

	Native Mode	Integrated Mode
Security	The Report Server controls all security for content. Management of security is performed through Report Manager.	SharePoint manages and controls all security. Security is integrated with the existing SharePoint farm environment.
Content creation	Content is created using Report Manager or the Reporting Services client tools. Report Builder 1.0 can be launched from Report Manager.	Content is created using the Reporting Services client tools or directly from within a SharePoint site and published to SharePoint libraries. Within a SharePoint site. a user can generate report models, launch Report Builder 1.0, and publish and view the resulting reports.
Requirements	SQL Server 2008	SQL Server 2008
	All versions of SQL Server 2005	SQL Server 2005 SP2
	SQL Server 2000 SP2	
	WSS 3.0 or MOSS 2007	WSS 3.0 or MOSS 2007
	WSS 2.0 or SharePoint Portal Server	
Installation and configuration	Copy web parts from report server to SharePoint servers, install web parts on SharePoint servers, add web parts to SharePoint sites, and configure web parts.	Download and install the SQL Server Reporting Services SharePoint add-in on SharePoint servers, configure Reporting Services, configure SharePoint farm in Central Admin.
Limitations	Must maintain separate security policies. Security in SharePoint is completely separate from security on the Reporting Services server (Report Manager).	Linked reports and the Report Manager application are not supported.
		No support for programmatic batch operations or job management.
	Requires separate Reporting Services tools for managing the reporting environment on the Reporting Services server.	
	Does not include all the content-management features that SharePoint has to offer.	

Although there are some circumstances in which a client has chosen to use Native mode integration, we have increasingly seen most environments take advantage of the tight integration that Integrated mode provides. As an Enterprise Content Management (ECM) system, SharePoint is quickly becoming unmatched with its ease of use and close integration with the Microsoft Office suite. For organizations that are already running a SharePoint environment, there are very few reasons not to take advantage of the SharePoint ECM environment, with all of its features, for reporting needs as well. Users are becoming hyper-connected to the data in their organization, and soon they will just *expect* to see all of their personal KPIs on their intranet Start page.

Summary

SharePoint is a technology that organizations have come to rely on for their intranet, extranet, and Internet web sites. Integrating SQL Server 2008 Reporting Services and the SharePoint technologies is a natural fit and provides a very attractive solution for delivering reports to end-users throughout the organization.

In this chapter, you looked at the following topics:

❑   The SharePoint technologies in general, including Windows SharePoint Services and Microsoft Office SharePoint Server, and SQL Server Engine (hosting SharePoint databases)

❑   A brief introduction to SharePoint web parts

❑   SharePoint integration with SQL Server Reporting Services in Native mode, including the installation and usage of the Report Viewer and Report Explorer web parts

❑   SharePoint integration with SQL Server Reporting Services in Integrated mode, including installation and configuration, publishing reports (WSS, MOSS 2007 Standard, and MOSS 2007 Enterprise), report models, Report Builder 1.0, report management, and the SQL Server Reporting Services Report Viewer for Integrated Mode

❑   The architecture of SQL Server Reporting Services integration with SharePoint

❑   A comparison of Reporting Services integration with SQL Server in Native mode versus in Integrated mode

17

Extending Reporting Services

As you learned in Chapter 2, Reporting Services is a robust and scalable product for enterprise report processing. In addition, Microsoft has created Reporting Services using a modular extensible architecture that gives users the ability to customize, extend, and expand the product to support their enterprise business intelligence (BI) reporting needs. This chapter introduces you to most of the areas within Reporting Services that allow customization and some of the reasons that you may wish to extend the product. The basic requirements for implementing each type of extension are discussed, followed by a detailed example of creating and deploying a data processing extension.

In this chapter, you will learn about the extensibility of Reporting Services and the areas that currently support customization. These include:

❑ Extensibility options

❑ Reasons for extending SQL Server Reporting Services

❑ How to create custom extensions

❑ How to install custom extensions

Reporting Services currently supports extending its behavior in the following areas:

❑ **Data Processing Extensions (DPEs)** — Custom DPEs enable you to access any type of data using a consistent programming model. This option is for you if you cannot access your data using one of the currently supported providers (Analysis Services, Hyperion Essbase, ODBC, OLE DB, Oracle, Report Model, SAP BI NetWeaver, SQL Server, and XML). Microsoft has also released a Feature Pack for SQL Server that provides customized extensions, such as SAP Relational DB and DB2, in addition to the ones built into the product.

❏ **Delivery Extensions** — In Chapter 13, "Content Management," we discussed "subscribing to a report." During this process, one of the required options is the method of delivery. Do you want the report sent to your cell phone in image format, or perhaps delivered to a file share for your perusal at a later date? The ability to extend SSRS with delivery extensions allows you to choose.

Delivery extensions allow you to deliver reports to users or groups of users according to a schedule. E-mail, network file shares, and SharePoint content are the delivery mechanisms currently built into the product. Creating a delivery extension is really a two-part process. You must create the extension itself, as well as a UI tool to manage the extension if you want it to be usable from the SSRS Report Manager. The difficulty in creating a delivery extension is primarily a function of the delivery mechanism.

❏ **Rendering Extensions** — Rendering extensions control the type of document/media that gets created when a report is processed. Theoretically, you could have Reporting Services create any type of media given the ability to extend the product in this area. Microsoft provides the following rendering extensions out of the box:

    ❏ **HTML** — The HTML extension will generate HTML 3.2 for use with older browsers and HTML 4.0 for browsers that support the dynamic HTML standard.

    ❏ **MHTML (Web Archive)** — MHTML is another HTML standard that was created to allow disconnected viewing of HTML documents. All the images in the page are encoded into the document, which increases its size but allows it to be viewed both online and offline.

    ❏ **Excel** — The Excel extension creates Excel-specific MHTML.

    ❏ **Image** — The Image extension allows you to export reports as images in the EMF, GIF, JPEG, PNG, TIFF, and WMF formats.

    ❏ **PDF** — This extension allows the generation of reports in the PDF format.

    ❏ **CSV** — Comma Separated Values emit the data fields separated by commas. The first row of the CSV results contains the Field names for the data.

❏ **Security Extensions** — In its first release, Reporting Services only supported Integrated Windows Security for report access. This was a pretty big problem for some enterprise players. Most companies have heterogeneous networks with multiple operating systems and products. In a perfect world, all our networks, applications, and resources would support some form of "single sign-on," or at least would allow us to build this ourselves. If Microsoft wanted SQL Server to be a key part of an Enterprise Business Intelligence platform, it had to play nice with others. Microsoft fixed this problem in Service Pack 1 for SQL Server 2000 and made it a part of the RTM version in 2005. The release contained fully documented security extension interfaces and an example using ASP.NET Forms–based authentication. You may now implement your custom security model using SSRS.

❏ **Report Processing Extensions (Custom Report Items)** — This extension type came with the 2005 release of Reporting Services, and it allowed us to create custom report items that were processed by the report processing engine. This enables us to extend the RDL standard in order to include functionality not natively supported by the RDL, such as custom maps, horizontal lists, and re-pivotable matrices. Developers can also extend current report items to provide alternative versions that better fit their needs.

❑ **Report definition customization extensions** — This is the latest addition to the list of available extension options supported in the 2008 release. This extension type provides a hook into the pre-processing of the report definition, and enables you to plug in custom code that can modify the report definition stream before it gets processed. This is handy, for example, if you need to modify the layout of the report based on a culture, locale, or user identity that is specified with the report request. Note that you are not guaranteed where or when in the request pipeline the customization will occur, but you are guaranteed that it will always happen before the processing of the report definition takes place. For this extension, a new interface was included and is required to be implemented:

```
IReportDefinitionCustomizationExtension.
```

Extension through Interfaces

Reporting Services uses common interfaces or "extension points" to allow expanding the product in a standard way. Enforcing the requirement that RS extension objects must implement certain interfaces allows Reporting Services to interact with different object types without knowledge of their specific implementation. This is a common object-oriented programming technique used to abstract the design from the implementation.

For an in-depth study of this topic, look at Chapter 3, "Creational Patterns," of Design Patterns: Elements of Reusable Object-Oriented Software, *by Erich Gamma, Ralph Johnson, Richard Helm, John M. Vlissides, and Grady Booch (Addison Wesley, 1994).*

What Is an Interface?

Most C/C++ developers are intimately familiar with *interfaces*. The entire COM programming model is based on them. Visual Basic developers have used them as well, but the VB6 programming environment hides this. Seasoned .NET developers are also familiar with the use of interfaces, as we use them to interact with the FCL (Framework Class Libraries). In fact, Reporting Services itself is exposed to developers through a web service interface. In order to provide complete coverage of extending Reporting Services, a definition and an explanation of interfaces are required.

So what is an interface? An *interface* is a predefined code construct that forms a contract between software components and defines how they communicate. The interface provides an abstraction layer of its entity to the outside.

That sounds great, but what does it mean? It simply means that in order to adhere to the contract defined by an interface, all extension components must contain certain methods, properties, and so on.

In Reporting Services specifically, it means that every single extension component must contain certain methods defined by the IExtension interface. Other interface implementations may be required as well, depending on the type of extension you are trying to create.

Interface Language Differences

There are differences in the way that VB.NET and C# require interface methods to be declared. C# supports "implicit" interface definitions. If the method names and signatures match those of an interface implemented by the class, then the class methods are automatically mapped to their associated interface definitions. We chose System.IDisposable for this example because many of the classes that you will create are required to implement it.

C#

```
public class TestClass : System.IDisposable
{
  //this method is automatically mapped to IDisposable.Dispose
  public void Dispose()
  {
      //write some code to dispose of non-memory resources
  }
}
```

VB.NET requires explicit interface implementation. In order to be mapped correctly, VB.NET requires that you specify that the method is implementing a certain interface. This is done with the Implements keyword, as follows:

VB.NET

```
Public Class TestClass
    Implements IDisposable

    Public Sub Dispose() Implements IDisposable.Dispose
            'write some code to dispose of non-memory resources
    End Sub
End Class
```

Starting with Visual Studio 2005, improved code refactoring features were introduced to the Integrated Development Environment (IDE), making this distinction almost unnecessary. Specifically, Visual Studio 2005 included a new feature we refer to as "Interface AutoComplete." When you indicate that a class should implement a certain interface, Visual Studio can jump in and generate wrapper methods for all the properties, methods, and so on that are required for that interface (see Figure 17-1). This saves a huge amount of typing and is a great productivity enhancement when creating objects designed to "plug in" to an existing framework.

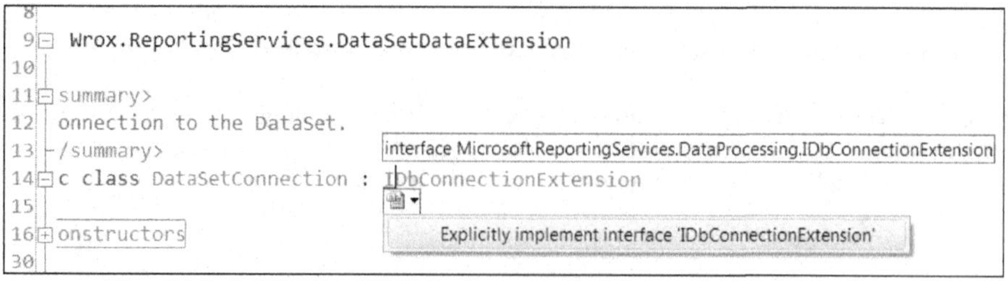

Figure 17-1

Microsoft is also attempting to build "best practices" into Visual Studio. While the two examples shown above are technically correct in that they implement IDisposable, they do not implement the IDisposable design pattern shown in the .NET Framework SDK. When we allow Visual Studio 2005 to do the heavy lifting, it creates a more feature-complete implementation that includes consideration for cascading object chains and explicit release of memory and non-memory resources. Visual Studio would create code similar to the following for IDisposable. We did take liberties with the comments to make it easier to read.

VB.NET

```
Public Class TestDispose
    Implements System.IDisposable

    Private disposed As Boolean = False

    'IDisposable
    Private Overloads Sub Dispose(ByVal disposing As Boolean)
        If Not Me.disposed Then
            If disposing Then
                ' TODO: put code to dispose managed resources
            End If
            ' TODO: put code to free unmanaged resources here
        End If
        Me.disposed = True
    End Sub

    'IDisposable Support
    'Don't change
    Public Overloads Sub Dispose() Implements IDisposable.Dispose
        ' Don't change. Put cleanup code
        ' in Dispose(ByVal disposing As Boolean) above.
        Dispose(True)
        GC.SuppressFinalize(Me)
    End Sub

    ' Don't change
    Protected Overrides Sub Finalize()
        Dispose(False)
        MyBase.Finalize()
    End Sub

End Class
```

C#

```
public class TestDispose : System.IDisposable
{
    private bool disposed = false;

    //IDisposable
    private void Dispose(bool disposing)
    {
        if (! this.disposed)
```

(continued)

(continued)

```
        {
            if (disposing)
            {
                // TODO: put code to dispose managed resources
            }
            // TODO: put code to free unmanaged resources here
        }
        this.disposed = true;
    }

    //IDisposable Support
    //Don't change
    public void IDisposable.Dispose()
    {
        // Don't change. Put cleanup code
        // in Dispose(ByVal disposing As Boolean) above.
        Dispose(true);
        GC.SuppressFinalize(this);
    }

// Don't change
protected void Finalize()
{
        Dispose(false);
        base.Finalize();
    }

}
```

You will be using this Interface AutoComplete feature for the remainder of this chapter. If you are using Visual Studio .NET 2003, we encourage you to upgrade to Visual Studio 2005 or Visual Studio 2008, because extensions for Reporting Services 2008 must be compiled using the .NET Framework version 2.0, which is not available from VS 2003. The generated code for IDisposable is suitable for demonstration purposes, so we won't repeat this code for each object but simply indicate that it is required.

Data Processing Extensions — A Detailed Look

Reporting Services allows you to access data from traditional data sources such as relational databases using the existing .NET data providers. The following providers are supplied as part of the .NET Framework supplied by Microsoft:

- ❏ ODBC
- ❏ OLE DB
- ❏ Oracle
- ❏ SqlClient

DPEs are components that allow you to access data for use within Reporting Services. If that implies a ".NET data provider" to you, then congratulations are in order. These two types of data access objects are very similar and are based on a common set of interface definitions. If you have already built a custom .NET data provider, you may use that provider with Reporting Services with no modification. However, you also can extend your existing provider to provide additional functionality.

To begin, we need to discuss the similarities and differences between a standard .NET data provider and a Reporting Services DPE. Let's start with some architectural information about data providers in general and then dive into the details of creating a custom DPE. The .NET Framework has a data access object model that is very similar to that used in traditional COM-based ADO. The ADO.NET object model is displayed in Figure 17-2.

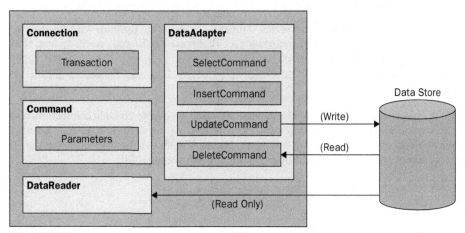

Figure 17-2

Prior to Service Pack 1 of SSRS on SQL Server 2000, Reporting Services data providers were essentially the same as the ADO.NET data providers, except for the fact that Microsoft had implemented wrapper classes around the .NET providers in order for them to meet the Reporting Services extension interface requirements. The Reporting Services requirements were a subset of the data provider requirements. The programming paradigm was the same as well.

With Service Pack 1 came the ability to customize and extend the security model of Reporting Services. This required adding a few things to the object model.

The basic steps for working with a data source are:

1. Make a connection to a data source.

2. Issue a command to manipulate data.

3. Retrieve the results of your query.

These actions map directly to the objects above, although a DataAdapter implementation is not needed because Reporting Services only reads the data.

Table 17-1 summarizes the objects that are normally created in a DPE and provides a description of the object responsibilities.

Table 17-1

Object	Description
Connection	Establishes a connection to a specific data source.
Command	Executes a command against a data source. Exposes a Parameters collection and can execute within the scope of a transaction.
DataReader	Provides access to data using a forward-only, Read Only stream.
DataAdapter	Responsible for retrieving data and for resolving updates with the data source. This object is not required for a DPE because SSRS only needs to read the data in order to create reports.

Each of these objects contains implementation-specific code needed to create a connection, issue commands, or read and update data. Microsoft has enforced a consistent data access mechanism by basing these objects on a set of standard interfaces. Figure 17-3 shows the interfaces that may be implemented when creating a DPE, although not all of them are required.

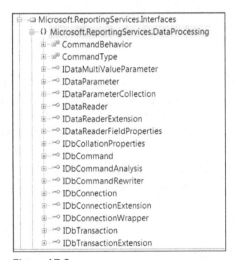

Figure 17-3

You may build a minimalist DataExtension by implementing the required interfaces shown in Table 17-2 and add additional behavior by implementing the optional interfaces as shown in Table 17-3.

Table 17-2

Required Interfaces	Description
IDbConnection	Unique session with a data source
IDbCommand	Represents query command methods to be executed against a data source
IDataParameter	Methods to support passing parameters to a Command object
IDataParameterCollection	Collection of parameters
IDataReader	Methods used to read a forward-only, Read Only data stream
IExtension	Reporting Services–specific interface that supports localization and is implemented by all SSRS extensions

Table 17-3

Optional Interfaces	Description
IDataReaderExtension	Used to provide Resultset-specific aggregation information
IDbCommandAnalysis	Analysis Services–specific extension
IDbConnectionExtension	Unique session with a data source
IDbTransaction	Local transaction (nondistributed)
IDbTransactionExtension	Reporting Services–specific interface that supports localization and is implemented by all SSRS extensions

Creating a Custom Data Processing Extension

Creating a full-blown data provider is no trivial task. The goal of this walk-through is to familiarize you with the .NET data access mechanism, as well as help you create and install a custom Reporting Services DPE. Our implementation is simplified in that it does not support transactions or the use of parameters, and many of the methods are empty unless code is explicitly required. All the images shown were created using the Visual Studio 2008 IDE. The code snippets are given in both C# and VB unless there is a reason to do otherwise.

The Scenario

The first release of Reporting Services (with SQL Server 2000) lacked support for consuming existing ADO.NET DataSet objects. After the release of Service Pack 1, the Books Online documentation contained an example extension that used some of the dataset's intrinsic properties to allow you to query a `DataSet` object and limit the resulting rows based on certain criteria. The only problem was that you were unable to do complex filtering or limit the columns returned by a query.

In SQL Server 2005, Reporting Services gained a new DPE — the XML data extension. This enabled reports to retrieve data from XML content, which could be located in a file, hosted on a web or file server, or, even better, from web services. This new extension provided a XPATH-like syntax for the command text, giving it greater flexibility for searching through data within the XML as well as supporting schemata and namespaces.

Interestingly enough, many companies have data stores that never really talk to each other directly, and remain isolated. These companies usually have requirements to query those data sources and create reports that join all that data together. SSRS 2008 does not provide an explicit mechanism to federate data across multiple servers, besides SQL Server's Linked Server features. If linked servers just are not an option for you, then you are left to come up with a creative solution for the situation.

The XML data extension may be useful in this scenario. You can set up a web service that does the dirty work of joining data from multiple tables in memory using ADO.NET. Then all that SSRS needs to provide to the web method is a collection of command texts to be executed, such as SQL statements or stored procedure names, and the relationship details, such as key columns and types of join. Once the web service has executed the commands and joined the data tables in memory, it returns the XML dataset ready for SSRS to consume.

In our example, we'll provide a similar, but more simplistic extension that will show the fundamental pieces required to implement the Reporting Services Interfaces and consume data from an XML dataset file. The ADO.NET `DataSet` type contains a method that allows it to read in the data from XML and build the internal data table that Reporting Services will consume.

Creating and Setting up the Project

Let's start by creating our project. Launch Visual Studio 2005, and create the project by choosing File ⇨ New Project. Change the name of the Project to *DataSetDataExtension*. Use the Class Library template with the language of your choice. After your project is created, you need to set up your environment to help you work. The Visual Basic IDE tends to hide some things from you, so you are going to make some changes to help our C# brethren follow along. The first thing you want to do is show all your references. The default behavior of VB.NET is to hide them. Choose Project ⇨ Show All Files from the menu. The Explorer tab should now show you all your project references.

Next, you need to add the references to the required Reporting Services DLL file. The `Microsoft.ReportingServices.DataProcessing` namespace is needed to implement the DPE interfaces, and the `Microsoft.ReportingServices.Interfaces` namespace is needed to implement the `IExtension` interface. Both of these namespaces are defined in the same file, `Microsoft.ReportingServices.Interfaces.dll`.

The location of extensions and their dependencies is a subdirectory below the installation directory of SQL Server itself. We will refer to the SQL Server installation path as `<InstallPath>`. The directory for the SSRS extensions DLL that you need is the following:

```
<lt;InstallPath>\MSRS10.MSSQLSERVER\Reporting Services\ReportServer\bin
```

On my machine, this directory is C:\Program Files\Microsoft SQL Server
MSRS10.MSSQLSERVER\Reporting Services\ReportServer\bin.

Choose Project ⇨ Add Reference from the menu. Select the Browse tab, find the appropriate directory, and add the reference. Your Solution Explorer window should now look something like that shown in Figure 17-4.

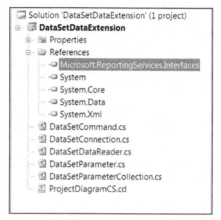

Figure 17-4

The name of the project assembly should be changed to reflect your custom namespace for the project. Choose Project ⇨ Properties from the menu. At this point, you can either choose to fill in the root namespace for your components or put it in your code. The example code contains the namespaces directly. This was another way to avoid IDE problems, as shown in Figure 17-5.

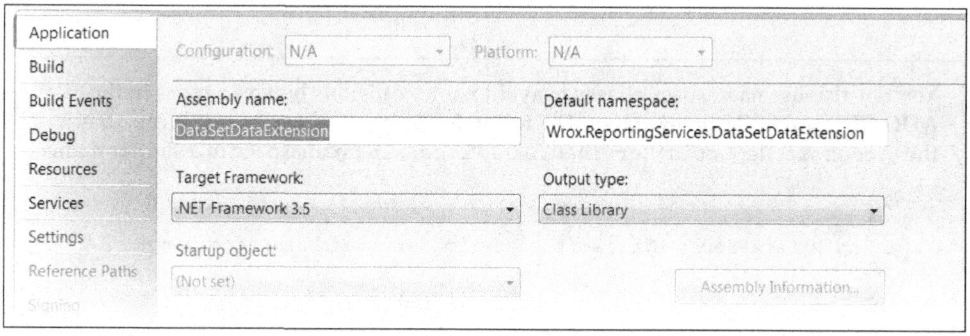

Figure 17-5

Most of the classes created for this project have common requirements. Most of them have empty default constructors, and all of them require the use of some common namespaces. The code below is a skeleton of how each class should look after you create it. Replace the *ClassName* with the name of the class you are working on. This will allow you to concentrate only on the differences between the objects that will be created in your data extension project.

In this example, you will be working with `DataSet` objects that are defined in the `System.Data` namespace. To support the SSRS interface requirements, you should include the `Microsoft.ReportingServices.DataProcessing` namespace at the top of your classes. This is the namespace where the interface `IExtension` is defined. Because the common data interfaces are defined in both ADO.NET and SSRS namespaces, you should fully qualify one of them to avoid name collisions. For the sake of saving keystrokes, we will fully qualify `System.Data` objects types instead of the SSRS one, when we use it. This namespace, however, is not needed in the `DataSetParameter` or `DataSetParameterCollection` classes.

C#

```
using System;
using Microsoft.ReportingServices.DataProcessing;
using System.Data;

namespace Wrox.ReportingServices.DataSetDataExtension
{
    public class DataSetClassName
    {
    }
}
```

VB.NET

```
Imports System
Imports Microsoft.ReportingServices.DataProcessing
Imports System.Data

Namespace Wrox.ReportingServices.DataSetDataExtension
    Public Class DataSetClassName

    End Class
End Namespace
```

> You can also use namespace aliases to avoid name collisions between types in the ADO.NET and SSRS namespaces. The following snippet shows how you can alias the `Microsoft.ReportingServices.DataProcessing` namespace to a shorter name:
>
> ### C#
> ```
> using RSDataProc = Microsoft.ReportingServices.DataProcessing;
> ```
>
> ### VB
> ```
> Imports RSDataProc = Microsoft.ReportingServices.DataProcessing;
> ```

Creating the DataSetConnection Object

The DataSetConnection object is responsible for connecting to the data source and providing a mechanism for accessing both the DPE-specific Transaction and Command objects. These responsibilities are enforced through the IDbConnection interface. The DataSetConnection object is the extension entry point and will be the first object in the extension that will deal with Reporting Services, and, as such, it also is required to implement the IExtension interface, as discussed above.

Because the DataSetConnection object is usually responsible for connecting to an unmanaged resource, it is required to implement IDisposable. The aggregate interface for all these others is IDbConnectionExtension, which is what you will implement. Figure 17-6 shows a diagram created with the Visual Studio class designer. Having the class designer within Visual Studio makes it easier both to implement and understand the relationships between objects in a complex system.

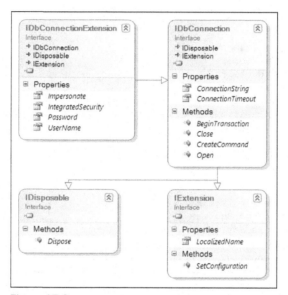

Figure 17-6

To add the DataSetConnection class to the project, choose Project ⇨ Add Class from the menu. Change the name of the class to *DataSetConnection*. Open the file and indicate that the class should implement the IDbConnectionExtension interface, as discussed above. Visual Studio will jump in and create all the wrapper methods for you. Because you will be doing file I/O and using regular expressions to parse your ConnectionString property, you need to add those namespaces to this class.

C#

```
using System;
using System.IO;
using System.Text.RegularExpressions;
using Microsoft.ReportingServices.DataProcessing;
```

VB.NET

```
Imports System
Imports System.IO
Imports System.Text.RegularExpressions
Imports Microsoft.ReportingServices.DataProcessing
```

Variable Declarations

In order to maintain state for your connection object, you need to declare some member variables. The m_connectionString variable will hold the connection string that will be used to connect to the data source. The m_localizedName variable should hold a localized name of the current extension used to list the extension as a data source option in the user interface of tools such as Visual Studio Report Designer or SQL Management Studio. The m_fileName variable will hold the path to the DataSet object persisted (serialized) as XML.

C#

```
private string m_userName;
private string m_password;
private bool m_integrated;
private string m_impersonate;
private string m_connectionString = String.Empty;
private string m_localizedName = "DataSet Data Source";
private string m_fileName;

internal System.Data.DataSet dataSet;
```

VB.NET

```
Private m_impersonate As String
Private m_integrated As Boolean
Private m_password As String
Private m_userName As String
Private m_connectionString As String = String.Empty
Private m_localizedName As String = "DataSet Data Source"
Private m_fileName As String

Friend dataSet As System.Data.DataSet = Nothing
```

Constructors

The DataSetConnection object has an empty default constructor, as well as an overloaded constructor that allows the developer to create the object and initialize the connection string in one line of code.

C#

```
public DataSetConnection(string connectionString)
{
        this.m_connectionString = connectionString;
}
```

VB.NET

```
Public Sub New(ByVal connectionString As String)
    Me.m_connectionString = connectionString
End Sub
```

Implementing IDbConnectionExtension

IDbConnectionExtension adds support for extending the SSRS security model, which is used to authenticate and authorize the connection to the data source. The interface definition is shown below. Notice the unusual use of WriteOnly properties.

C#

```csharp
public interface IDbConnectionExtension : IDbConnection, IDisposable, IExtension
{
    // Properties
    string Impersonate { set; }
    bool IntegratedSecurity {get; set; }

    string Password { set; }
    string UserName { set; }
}
```

VB.NET

```vbnet
Public Interface IDbConnectionExtension
    Implements IDbConnection, IDisposable, IExtension

    ' Properties
    WriteOnly Property Impersonate As String
    Property IntegratedSecurity As Boolean
    WriteOnly Property Password As String
    WriteOnly Property UserName As String
End Interface
```

Impersonate *Property*

Windows supports the idea of impersonation. This is the idea that a process of execution can "assume" the identity of a set of assigned security credentials. The Impersonate property allows the assignment of a string representing the user account whose security context the process should run under.

C#

```csharp
public string Impersonate
{
    set { m_impersonate = value; }
}
```

VB.NET

```
Public WriteOnly Property Impersonate() As String
    Implements IDbConnectionExtension.Impersonate
        Set(ByVal value As String)
            m_impersonate = value
        End Set
End Property
```

IntegratedSecurity *Property*

The IntegratedSecurity property indicates whether or not you want the extension to run using Windows security for both authentication (identifying the user) and authorization (denying/granting a user permission to perform certain actions).

C#

```
public bool IntegratedSecurity
{
    get{ return m_integrated;}
    set {m_integrated = value;}
}
```

VB.NET

```
Public Property IntegratedSecurity() As Boolean
    Implements IDbConnectionExtension.IntegratedSecurity
        Get
            Return m_integrated
        End Get
        Set(ByVal value As Boolean)
            m_integrated = value
        End Set
End Property
```

UserName *and* Password *Properties*

The UserName and Password properties are used during the Reporting Services authentication process. The UserName/Password pair is authenticated against either the Windows credential store or some custom store you provide. Next, a principal object that implements IPrincipal is created and assigned to the current thread of execution. That object contains the user's identity and role membership information and is used to authorize user access to system resources (the data source). Good security practice dictates that this information be available for the shortest time possible — thus the use of Write Only properties.

C#

```
public string Password
{
    set { m_password = value; }
}

public string UserName
{
    set { m_userName = value; }
}
```

VB.NET

```
Public WriteOnly Property Password() As String
  Implements IDbConnectionExtension.Password
        Set(ByVal value As String)
            m_password = value
        End Set
End Property

Public WriteOnly Property UserName() As String
  Implements IDbConnectionExtension.UserName
        Set(ByVal value As String)
            m_userName = value
        End Set
End Property
```

Implementing `IDbConnection`

The `IDbConnection` interface is the standard mechanism that data providers use to control the use of the `DataSetConnection` object. These properties and methods help you make changes to the connection settings, open and close the connection, and associate the connection with a valid transaction. Your connection object does not support transactions because of its Read Only nature and because, in this DPE example, you are working against a filesystem, which is not a resource manager. Below is the definition of the `IDbConnection` interface.

C#

```
public interface IDbConnection : IDisposable, IExtension
{
      IDbTransaction BeginTransaction();
      IDbCommand CreateCommand();
      void Open();
      void Close();
      string ConnectionString { get; set; }
      int ConnectionTimeout { get; }
}
```

VB.NET

```
Public Interface IDbConnection
   Inherits IDisposable, IExtension
     Function BeginTransaction() As IDbTransaction
     Function CreateCommand() As IDbCommand
     Sub Open()
     Sub Close()
     Property ConnectionString() As String
     Property ConnectionTimeout() As Integer
End Interface
```

BeginTransaction *Method*

The `BeginTransaction` method is primarily responsible for initiating a new transaction and returning a reference to a valid, implementation-specific `Transaction` object. The filesystem, which is our data store, does not support transactions, but this method is required by the interface. You need to ensure that the developer who will use your object in code is aware of that fact. This is done by throwing a `NotSupportedException`.

C#

```
public IDbTransaction BeginTransaction()
{
    // this example does not support transactions
    throw new NotSupportedException("Transactions not supported");
}
```

VB.NET

```
Public Function BeginTransaction() As IDbTransaction _
    Implements IDbConnection.BeginTransaction
        ' example does not support transactions
        Throw New NotSupportedException("Transactions not supported")
End Function
```

CreateCommand *Method*

The `CreateCommand` function is responsible for creating and returning a reference to a valid implementation-specific `Command` object. The method uses an overloaded constructor of your custom `Command` object in order to pass that object a reference to the current connection.

C#

```
public IDbCommand CreateCommand()
{
    // Return a new instance of the implementation-specific command object
    return new DataSetCommand(this);
}
```

VB.NET

```
Public Function CreateCommand() As IDbCommand _
    Implements IDbConnection.CreateCommand
        ' Return a new instance of the implementation specific command object
        Return New DataSetCommand(Me)
End Function
```

Open *Method*

In a full data provider implementation, the `Open` method is used to make a data source–specific connection. This sample implementation will use the `Open` method to create an instance of a generic dataset object from ADO.NET and fill it from the XML file provided in our `ConnectionString` property.

C#

```csharp
public void Open()
{
      this.dataSet = new System.Data.DataSet();
      this.dataSet.ReadXml(this.m_fileName);
}
```

VB.NET

```vbnet
Public Sub Open() Implements IDbConnection.Open
      Me.dataSet = New System.Data.DataSet
      Me.dataSet.ReadXml(Me.m_fileName)
End Sub
```

Close *Method*

The Close method is used to close your data source–specific connection. You are going to use the Close method to release the DataSet object that you have in memory.

C#

```csharp
public void Close()
{
      this.dataSet = null;
}
```

VB.NET

```vbnet
Public Sub Close() Implements IDbConnection.Close
      Me.dataSet = Nothing
End Sub
```

ConnectionString *Property*

The ConnectionString property allows you to set the connection string through code. The property uses a private variable to store the current connection string, which is used to provide the information needed to connect to the data source. Most developers are familiar with this property because of its frequent use in both traditional ADO and ADO.NET. In this DPE example, the ConnectionString property is used to indicate the XML dataset file that you are going to parse for data. The user of your DPE should input the path to the file they wish to parse into the connection string textbox of the Report Designer's Dataset dialog or the shared data source's Properties page. You will be storing the connection string value in the private member variable m_connectionString.

C#

```csharp
public string ConnectionString
{
      get {return m_connectionString;}
      set {m_connectionString = value;}
}
```

VB.NET

```
Public Property ConnectionString() As String _
    Implements IDbConnection.ConnectionString
        Get
            Return m_connectionString
        End Get
        Set(ByVal Value As String)
            m_connectionString = Value
        End Set
End Property
```

You want to enforce that the value passed into the `ConnectionString` property meets your criteria for supplying the information needed to connect to the data source. You want to enforce that the string is in the format:

```
FileName=c:\FileName.xml
```

The easiest way to validate the string format is to use regular expressions. You need to modify the `Set` accessor to reflect this change. First, you are going to execute the static/shared `Match` method of the `Regex` class.

You are passing in an expression that basically says "Parse the connection string and make matches on character arrays that are preceded by `FileName=` and are not composed of beginning-of-line characters or semicolons."

All that is left is to test to see if the filename is valid, and, if so, assign it to your private filename variable. Your code should resemble that below:

C#

```
set
{
        this.m_connectionString = value;

        Match m = Regex.Match(value, "FileName=([^;]+)", RegexOptions.IgnoreCase);
        if (!m.Success)
        {
            string msg = "\"FileName=<filename>\" must be present in the connection " +
                    "string and point to a valid DataSet xml file";
            throw (new ArgumentException(msg, "ConnectionString"));
        }

        string filename = m.Groups[1].Captures[0].ToString();
        if (!File.Exists(filename))
        {
            string msg = "Incorrect file name, or file does not exist";
            throw (new ArgumentException(msg, "ConnectionString"));
        }

        this.m_fileName = filename;
}
```

VB.NET

```
Set(ByVal Value As String)
    Me.m_connectionString = Value

    Dim m As Match = Regex.Match(Value, "FileName=([^;]+)", _
            RegexOptions.IgnoreCase)
    If Not m.Success Then
        Dim msg As String = "'FileName=<filename>' must be present string " & _
                    "and point to a valid DataSet xml file"
        Throw (New ArgumentException(msg, "ConnectionString"))
    End If
    If Not File.Exists(m.Groups(1).Captures(0).ToString) Then
        Throw (New ArgumentException("Incorrect FileName", "ConnectionString"))
    End If
    Me.m_fileName = m.Groups(1).Captures(0).ToString
End Set
```

ConnectionTimeout *Property*

The ConnectionTimeout property allows you to set the time-out property of the connection. This is used to control how long the interval for connecting to the source should be before an error is thrown. Your example class does not actually use this value, but it is implemented for consistency and because of interface requirements. Returning a value of 0 indicates that there is an infinite time-out period.

C#

```
public int ConnectionTimeout
{
    get
    {
        // Returns the connection time-out value.
        // Zero indicates an indefinite time-out period.
        return 0;
    }
}
```

VB.NET

```
Public ReadOnly Property ConnectionTimeout() As Integer _
        Implements IDbConnection.ConnectionTimeout
    Get        ' Returns the connection time-out value.
               ' Zero indicates an indefinite time-out period.
        Return 0
    End Get
End Property
```

Creating the DataSetParameter *Class*

The DataSetParameter class is not needed until the command class is created, but because of that dependency you do need to create it. The parameter object is used to send parameters to the command object that can be used in executing commands against the data source. Despite the fact that this class is not used to perform any work, the interface requirements of the command class force you to create it. This class also has interface requirements; it is required to support the IDataParameter interface defined in the Reporting Services DPE assembly.

To add the DataSetParameter class to the project, choose Project ➪ Add Class from the menu, and change the name to *DataSetParameter*.

Declarations

The following declarations are used internally to hold both the value and the name of the parameter. The name is stored in a string variable called m_parameterName. Because the value variable might contain any type of value, the m_parameterValue is declared as an Object type.

C#

```
String m_parameterName = string.Empty;
Object m_parameterValue;
```

VB.NET

```
Dim m_parameterName As String
Dim m_parameterValue As Object
```

Implementing IDataParameter

The IDataParameter interface enforces that your custom parameter class allow a programmer to get and set the name and value of the current parameter.

C#

```
public interface IDataParameter
    {
        string ParameterName { get; set; }
        object Value { get; set; }
    }
```

VB.NET

```
Public Interface IDataParameter
    Property ParameterName() As String
    Property Value() As Object
End Interface
```

Modify the class code to force the DataSetParameter class to implement IDataParameter using the Interface AutoComplete technique discussed at the beginning of the chapter. Your code should resemble the following. The wrappers for all of your interface methods should have been created automatically and surrounded by region tags. Below is what your parameter class definition should look like.

C#

```
namespace Wrox.ReportingServices.DataSetDataExtension
{
    public class DataSetDataParameter : IDataParameter
    {
```

VB.NET

```
Namespace Wrox.ReportingServices.DataSetExtension
    Public Class DataSetParameter

        Implements IDataParameter
```

ParameterName *Property*

The ParameterName property is used to store the name of the parameter in a string variable called m_parameterName. This field is typically used to map to parameters in stored procedures but is unused in this implementation.

C#

```csharp
public string ParameterName
    {
        get { return m_parameterName; }
        set { m_parameterName = value; }
    }
```

VB.NET

```vbnet
Public Property ParameterName() As String _
        Implements IDataParameter.ParameterName
        Get
            Return m_parameterName
        End Get
        Set(ByVal Value As String)
            m_parameterName = value
        End Set
End Property
```

Value *Property*

The Value property is similar to the name created above in that it is not actually used in this example. The value is stored in an object variable called m_value.

C#

```csharp
public object Value
    {
        get { return m_value; }
        set { m_value = value; }
    }
```

VB.NET

```vbnet
Public Property Value() As Object _
        Implements IDataParameter.Value
        Get
            Return m_value
        End Get
        Set(ByVal Value As Object)
            m_value = Value
        End Set
End Property
```

Creating the `DataSetParameterCollection` Class

The `DataSetParameterCollection` class is simply a collection of parameter objects. Although you could have created a custom collection class that implements all the required methods, an easier route exists. The `IDataParameterCollection` interface is basically a subset of the `IList<T>` interface that is used to define other generic collections in the .NET Framework. By using an object already available, you reduce the required coding effort considerably. In our example, `T` will be the type `IDataParameter`, which will be implemented by our custom `DataSetParameter` class.

To add the `DataSetParameterCollection` class to the project, choose Project ⇨ Add Class from the menu. Change the name of the class to *DataSetParameterCollection*.

There is no need to create custom constructors or member variables for use in your collection class. This is because you can use the internal variables and constructors that exist inside the `List<T>` base class that this class inherits from. The properties that you create will be mapped directly to properties and methods that exist in the `List<T>` class.

Namespaces

The `DataSetParameterCollection` class uses the standard namespaces discussed above. There is an additional namespace that is needed because of the use of `List<T>`. You must add the `System.Collections.Generic` namespace and a private variable for our internal collection.

C#

```
using System;
using Microsoft.ReportingServices.DataProcessing;
using System.Collections.Generic;
```

VB.NET

```
Imports System
Imports Microsoft.ReportingServices.DataProcessing

Imports System.Collections.Generic
```

Implementing `IDataParameterCollection`

We have created the `DataSetParameterCollection` class by using an object wrapper around an `IList<T>` generic collection. Generics are a feature available in .NET 2.0 and later versions, so our example will not compile or run within earlier versions of the .NET Framework run time. The `IDataParameterCollection` interface defines a custom `Add` method as well as provides methods to access the members of this collection through the `IEnumerable` interface. The `List<T>` base class implements this interface. Your class will use the internal `List<IDataParameter>` class properties and methods to service its needs.

C#

```
public interface IDataParameterCollection : IEnumerable
{
    int Add(IDataParameter parameter);
}
```

VB.NET

```
Public Interface IDataParameterCollection
    Inherits IEnumerable
    Function Add(ByVal parameter As IDataParameter) As Integer
End Interface
```

The modified code in C# is:

```
namespace Wrox.ReportingServices.DataSetDataExtension
{

    public class DataSetDataParameterCollection : IDataParameterCollection
    {

        List<IDataParameter> paramList;
```

The modified code in VB.NET is:

```
Namespace Wrox.ReportingServices.DataSetDataExtension

    Public Class DataSetDataParameterCollection

        Implements IDataParameterCollection

        Private paramList As List(Of IDataParameter)
```

Since most of the functionality of the DataSetDataParameterCollection class exists through the paramList reference, all that needs to be done is to create the wrapper Add method required by the IDataParameter interface. This method is used by the internal collection to add parameters to an instance of the collection object.

C#

```
public int Add(IDataParameter parameter)
{
    paramList.Add(parameter);
    return paramList.IndexOf(parameter);
}
```

VB.NET

```
Public Overloads Function Add(ByVal parameter As IDataParameter) As Integer _
        Implements IDataParameterCollection.Add

        paramList.Add(parameter)
        Return paramList.IndexOf(parameter)

End Function
```

Creating the `DataSetCommand` Class

The `command` object is responsible for sending commands to the data source. This is enforced by making the object implement the `IDbCommand` interface, which supplies a standard mechanism for passing in commands to be executed against the data source as well as parameters that might be needed in the process of executing these commands. It also defines a property that allows the developer to associate the command with a `Transaction` object. Your implementation is simplified in that it does not support transactions or parameters.

In your implementation, this class is where the majority of the work is done. You need to process the command text to know what data the user wants. You must validate that this text conforms to your requirements, and then you need to create the internal data reference that will supply the data for the data reader object to process. You are going to be using some of the built-in behaviors of the `System.Data.DataSet` class to satisfy your needs.

To add the `DataSetCommand` class to the project, choose Project ⇨ Add Class from the menu. Change the name of the class to *DataSetCommand*. Use the Interface AutoComplete feature to have Visual Studio create the wrappers for the methods that you will implement. Most of the functionality that exists in this extension will live in this class.

Variable Declarations

As most of our work is done in this class, it makes sense that most of our code is also in it. First, you need to create variables to hold your property data. This class is actually going to be a wrapper around some of the built-in `DataSet` functionality, so you will need reference variables for the data-set objects as well as other variables used for text parsing and the like. In order not to be repetitive, we'll discuss the variables in more depth where they are used.

C#

```
//member variables
 int m_commandTimeOut = 0;
 string m_commandText = string.Empty;
 DataSetConnection m_connection;
 DataSetParameterCollection m_parameters;

//dataset variables
 string tableName = string.Empty;
 System.Data.DataSet dataSet = null;
 internal System.Data.DataView dataView = null;

//regex variables
 MatchCollection kwc = null;
 Match fieldMatch = null;

//regex used for getting keywords
 Regex keywordSplit = new Regex(@"(Select|From|Where| Order[ \s] +By)",
     RegexOptions.IgnoreCase | RegexOptions.Multiline
     | RegexOptions.IgnorePatternWhitespace | RegexOptions.Compiled);

// regex used for spliting out fields
 Regex fieldSplit = new Regex(@"([^ ,\s]+)",
```

```
        RegexOptions.IgnoreCase | RegexOptions.Multiline
        | RegexOptions.Compiled | RegexOptions.IgnorePatternWhitespace);

//internal constants
 const int SELECT_POSITION = 0;
 const int FROM_POSITION = 1;
 const string TEMPTABLE_NAME = "TempTable";

//these variables can change
 int keyWordCount = 0;
 int wherePosition = 2;
 int orderPosition = 3;

 bool filtering = false;
 bool sorting = false;
 bool useDefaultTable = false;
```

VB.NET

```
'property variables
Private m_cmdTimeOut As Integer = 0
Private m_commandText As String = String.Empty
Private m_connection As DataSetConnection
Private m_parameters As DataSetParameterCollection = Nothing

'dataset variables
Private tableName As String = String.Empty
Private dataSet As FCLData.DataSet
Friend dataView As FCLData.DataView

'regex variables
Private kwc As MatchCollection
Private fieldMatch As Match
Private tableMatch As Match
Private keywordSplit As Regex = New Regex("(Select|From|Where| Order[ \s] +By)",_
        RegexOptions.IgnoreCase Or RegexOptions.Multiline Or _
        RegexOptions.IgnorePatternWhitespace Or RegexOptions.Compiled)
Private fieldSplit As Regex = New Regex("([^ ,\s]+)", RegexOptions.IgnoreCase Or _
        RegexOptions.Multiline Or RegexOptions.Compiled Or _
        RegexOptions.IgnorePatternWhitespace)

'Constants
Private tempTableName As String = "TempTable"
Private selectPosition As Integer = 0
Private fromPosition As Integer = 1
Private wherePosition As Integer = 2
Private orderPosition As Integer = 3

'internal variables

 Private keyWordCount As Integer = 0
 Private filtering As Boolean = False
 Private sorting As Boolean = False
 Private useDefaultTable As Boolean = False
```

Constructors

You want the users of your processing extension to be forced to create the `Command` object either through the `CreateCommand` method of the `IDbConnection` interface or by passing in a valid `DataSetConnection` object as a parameter. The purpose of this is to ensure that you have access to the underlying `DataSet` object created and parsed in the connection process. This can be done by deleting or not providing an empty default constructor. This prevents the developer from creating the `DataSetCommand` object without the correct initialization. In the constructor, you want to get a reference to the `DataSet` that you opened from the filesystem in your connection object.

C#

```csharp
internal DataSetCommand(DataSetConnection conn)
{
        this.m_connection = conn;
        this.dataSet = this.m_connection.dataSet;
        this.m_parameters = new DataSetParameterCollection();
}
```

VB.NET

```vbnet
Friend Sub New(ByVal conn As DataSetConnection)

        Me.m_connection = conn
        Me.dataSet = Me.m_connection.dataSet
        Me.m_parameters = New DataSetParameterCollection
End Sub
```

Implementing `IDbCommand`

The required interface for all `Command` objects is called `IDbCommand`. It consists of methods that allow the developer to pass commands and parameters to the `Command` object. The most interesting method in our implementation is the `CommandText` method, where you will parse the command string provided by the user and return the appropriate data.

C#

```csharp
public interface IDbCommand : IDisposable
{
        void Cancel();
        IDataReader ExecuteReader(CommandBehavior behavior);
        string CommandText { get; set; }
        int CommandTimeout { get; set; }
        CommandType CommandType { get; set; }
        IDataParameter CreateParameter();
        IDataParameterCollection Parameters { get; }
        IDbTransaction Transaction { get; set; }
}
```

VB.NET

```
Public Interface IDbCommand
    Inherits IDisposable
      Sub Cancel()
      Function ExecuteReader(ByVal behavior As CommandBehavior) As IDataReader
      Property CommandText() As String
      Property CommandTimeout() As Integer
      Property CommandType() As CommandType
      Function CreateParameter() As IDataParameter
      Property Parameters() As IDataParameterCollection
      Property Transaction() As IDbTransaction
End Interface
```

Now that you have created the method wrappers and created all the variables that you need to work, you can begin implementing your IDbCommand methods.

Cancel *Method*

The Cancel method is typically used to cancel a method that has been queued. Most implementations of data providers are multithreaded and support the issue of multiple commands against the data store. You have only created this method to support the IDbCommand interface requirements and should inform the developer of your lack of support by throwing a NotSupportedException.

C#

```
public void Cancel()
{
    // not supported
    throw new NotSupportedException();
}
```

VB.NET

```
Public Sub Cancel() _
      Implements IDbCommand.Cancel
      'not supported
       Throw New NotSupportedException
End Sub
```

ExecuteReader *Method*

The ExecuteReader method returns an extension-specific reader object to the caller so that it can loop through and read the data. The DataSetCommand object creates an instance of your custom reader object by executing this method. A reference to your custom data reader is then returned. Your implementation actually builds a temporary table with a schema built based on the query issued by the user. You don't want to fill this temporary table unless the user actually requests the data, so you are checking to see if it is a schema-only command. You are also checking to see if the users indicated that they want all the fields available from the data source. If that is the case, you use a view of the default DataTable, which already contains all the data.

C#

```csharp
public IDataReader ExecuteReader (CommandBehavior behavior)
{
    if(!(behavior == CommandBehavior.SchemaOnly) && !useDefaultTable)
    {
        FillView();
    }
    return (IDataReader) new DataSetDataReader(this);
}
```

VB.NET

```vbnet
Public Function ExecuteReader(ByVal behavior As CommandBehavior) As IDataReader _
    Implements IDbCommand.ExecuteReader
    If Not (behavior = CommandBehavior.SchemaOnly) AndAlso Not useDefaultTable Then
        FillView()
    End If
    Return CType(New DataSetDataReader(Me), IDataReader)
End Function
```

CommandText *Property*

Reporting Services does not manually create a separate Command object. It uses the CreateCommand method of the IDBConnection interface to return an implementation-specific Command object. We will be using the CommandText property to help us build the data schema that we will return, as well as filling our data source for use of Reporting Services. This method has been broken down into methods reflecting the actual work being done and to facilitate this discussion. Notice the ValidateCommandText method. This method is the entry point for your text-parsing and table-building process.

C#

```csharp
public string CommandText
{
    get
    {
        return this.m_commandText;
    }
    set
    {
        ValidateCommandText(value);
        this.m_commandText = value;
    }
}
```

VB.NET

```vbnet
Public Property CommandText() As String Implements IDbCommand.CommandText
    Get
        Return (Me.m_commandText)
    End Get
    Set(ByVal value As String)
        ValidateCommandText(value)
        Me.m_commandText = value
    End Set
End Property
```

The `ValidateCommandText` method is used to parse the command text to ensure that it meets the requirements for the extension. The first step is to apply the `keywordSplit` regular expression that was defined in the member variable section. The regular expression is `(Select|From|Where| Order[ \s] +By)`, which could be translated into English as: "Match the keywords *Select*, *From*, *Where*, and *Order*, where each is followed by the word *By*, but allow spaces and non-visible characters between them." After you have parsed the statement, you can make some basic assumptions based on the number of matches. At a minimum, you require that the user tell you the Field names and the table name that he or she wants to pull the information from. This means that you must have a `Select` keyword, followed by a Field List, and a `From` keyword, followed by a table name, and thus the minimum keyword count is 2. If you have a keyword count greater than 2, you know that the user has either given you a filtering criteria such as `Where userID = 3` or a sort criteria such as `Order by lastname ASC`. You can find out which by checking the value in the third position. If that value is a `Where` clause, then you can assume that the user wants filtering. If it is not, assume that sorting is the order of the day. If the count is 4, you know that both filtering and sorting are needed.

C#

```csharp
private void ValidateCommandText(string cmdText)
{
    kwc = keywordSplit.Matches(cmdText);
    keyWordCount = kwc.Count;
    switch (keyWordCount)
    {
        case 4:
            sorting = true;
            filtering = true;
            break;
        case 3:
            if (kwc[keyWordCount - 1].ToString().ToUpper() == "WHERE")
                filtering = true;
            else
            {
                sorting = true;
                orderPosition = 2;
            }
            break;
        case 2:
            break;
        default:
            string msg = "Command Text should start with 'select <fields> " +
                         "from <tablename>'";
            throw new ArgumentException(msg);
    }

    ValidateTableName(cmdText);
    ValidateFieldNames(cmdText);

    if (filtering)
```

(continued)

(continued)

```
        {
            ValidateFiltering(cmdText);
        }

        if (sorting)
        {
            ValidateSorting(cmdText);
        }
}
```

VB.NET

```
Private Sub ValidateCommandText(ByVal cmdText As String)
        kwc = keywordSplit.Matches(cmdText)
        keyWordCount = kwc.Count
        Select Case keyWordCount
                Case 4
                        sorting = True
                        filtering = True
                        ' break
                Case 3
                        If kwc(keyWordCount - 1).ToString.ToUpper = "WHERE" Then
                                filtering = True
                        Else
                                sorting = True
                        End If
                Case Else
                        Dim msg As String = "Command Text should start with 'select " & _
                                            "<fields> from <tablename>'"
                        Throw (New ArgumentException(msg))
        End Select
        ValidateTableName(cmdText)
        ValidateFieldNames(cmdText)

        If filtering Then
                ValidateFiltering(cmdText)
        End If

        If sorting Then
                ValidateSorting(cmdText)
        End If
End Sub
```

The next step in the process is validating that the table name and the Field names provided by the user are valid. You have created methods specifically for this purpose. Shown below is the `ValidateTableName` method. In the member declaration section, constant values were created, indicating the assumed positions of the keywords within the command text. The table name must immediately follow the `From` keyword. You then use the position of that keyword to locate the table name. Next, you check to see if your internal `DataSet` contains this table. If so, the table name is valid; otherwise, it is invalid.

C#

```
private void ValidateTableName(string cmdText)
{
    //Get tablename
    //get 1st match starting at end of from
    fieldMatch = fieldSplit.Match(cmdText,
                    (kwc[fromPosition].Index) + kwc[fromPosition].Length + 1);
    if(fieldMatch.Success)
    {
        if(this.dataSet.Tables.Contains(fieldMatch.Value))
        {
            this.tableName = fieldMatch.Value;
        }
        else
        {
            throw new ArgumentException("Invalid Table Name");
        }
    }
}
```

VB.NET

```
Private Sub ValidateTableName(ByVal cmdText As String)
    fieldMatch = fieldSplit.Match(cmdText, _
            (kwc(fromPosition).Index) + kwc(fromPosition).Length + 1)
    If fieldMatch.Success Then
        If Me.dataSet.Tables.Contains(fieldMatch.Value) Then
            Me.tableName = fieldMatch.Value
        Else
            Throw New ArgumentException("Invalid Table Name")
        End If
    End If
End Sub
```

The next step is to validate the Field names. You also want users to be able to use the * character to indicate that they want all the fields without having to list them individually. This is standard SQL syntax. You need to parse all the text between the Select statement and the From statement. This is done using the constant values created above to signify character position and a regular expression to pull out exactly what you are interested in.

The fieldSplit regular expression looks like ([^ ,\s]+), which, in English, reads: "Match all character groups that do not contain spaces, commas, and non-visible white space and have spaces at the end." If the first field is an asterisk, you know that the user wants all fields. This means that you do not have to build a temporary table to reflect the schema and that you can use the table she requested in the From portion of the text. If the first field is not an asterisk, you must build a temporary table reflecting the schema of the data that you will return. To avoid problems with a user changing the fields, and the temp table previously existing, you will simply test for its existence each time and remove it if you must.

Next, you check to see whether the Field names exist in your main table by testing to see whether the column names exist. If they do, the column is valid, and you add a column with this name to your new temp table. You continue to do this as long as the Field names are valid. If an invalid field is submitted, you throw an exception to make the user aware of her mistake.

C#

```csharp
public void ValidateFieldNames(string cmdText)
{
    //get fieldnames
    //get first match starting at the last character of the Select
    // with a length from that position to the from
    fieldMatch = fieldSplit.Match(cmdText,
        (kwc[SELECT_POSITION].Index + kwc[SELECT_POSITION].Length + 1),
        (kwc[FROM_POSITION].Index - (kwc[SELECT_POSITION].Index +
            kwc[SELECT_POSITION].Length + 1)));

    if (fieldMatch.Value == "*")  // all fields, use default view
    {
        this.dataView = this.dataSet.Tables[this.tableName].DefaultView;
        this.useDefaultTable = true;
    }
    else   //custom fields : must build table/view
    {
        //don't use default table
        this.useDefaultTable = false;

        //remove table if exists - add new
        if (this.dataSet.Tables.Contains(TEMPTABLE_NAME))
        {
            this.dataSet.Tables.Remove(TEMPTABLE_NAME);
        }

        System.Data.DataTable table = new System.Data.DataTable(TEMPTABLE_NAME);

        //loop through column matches
        while (fieldMatch.Success)
        {
            if (this.dataSet.Tables[this.tableName]
                        .Columns.Contains(fieldMatch.Value))
            {
                System.Data.DataColumn col = this.dataSet.Tables[this.tableName]
                        .Columns[fieldMatch.Value];
                table.Columns.Add(
                        new System.Data.DataColumn(col.ColumnName, col.DataType));
                fieldMatch = fieldMatch.NextMatch();
            }
            else
            {
                throw new ArgumentException("Invalid column name");
            }
        }

        //add temptable to internal dataset and set view to tempView;
        this.dataSet.Tables.Add(table);
        this.dataView = new System.Data.DataView(table);
    }
}
```

VB.NET

```
Private Sub ValidateFieldNames(ByVal cmdText As String)
    fieldMatch = fieldSplit.Match(cmdText, _
(kwc(selectPosition).Index + kwc(selectPosition).Length + 1), _
(kwc(fromPosition).Index -  kwc(selectPosition).Index + _kwc(selectPosition)
.Length + 1)))

    If fieldMatch.Value = "*" Then
        Me.dataView = Me.dataSet.Tables(Me.tableName).DefaultView
        Me.useDefaultTable = True
    Else
        Me.useDefaultTable = False
        If Me.dataSet.Tables.Contains(Me.tempTableName) Then
            Me.dataSet.Tables.Remove(Me.tempTableName)
        End If
        Dim table As DataTable = New DataTable(Me.tempTableName)
        While fieldMatch.Success
            If Me.dataSet.Tables(Me.tableName).Columns _
                                        .Contains(fieldMatch.Value) Then
                Dim col As DataColumn = dataSet.Tables(tableName) _
                                        .Columns(fieldMatch.Value)
                table.Columns.Add(New DataColumn(col.ColumnName, col.DataType))
                fieldMatch = fieldMatch.NextMatch
            Else
                Throw New ArgumentException("Invalid column name")
            End If
        End While
        Me.dataSet.Tables.Add(table)
        Me.dataView = New System.Data.DataView(table)
    End If
End Sub
```

Assuming that the table name is valid and all of the requested fields are valid, you will use the temp table you have built to satisfy data access requirements. The only thing left to do is add the new table to the existing dataset.

You have now validated all the parts of your query except the filtering and sorting criteria. In the CommandText method, you test whether filtering and sorting are enabled based on your keyword count. If they are enabled, you execute a method that uses the internal behavior of the DataSet class to do the work. In the ValidateFiltering() method, you need to parse out the text based on the keyword count. You either need to grab all of the text after the Where clause, or if an order clause exists, you need to stop there.

C#

```
public void ValidateFiltering(string cmdText)
 {
    if(filtering)
    {
        StringBuilder sbFilterText = new StringBuilder();
        int startPos =0;
        int length =0;

        startPos = kwc[wherePosition].Index + kwc[wherePosition].Length + 1;
```

(continued)

(continued)

```
            if(keyWordCount == 3)   //no "order by" - Search from Where till  end
            {
                length = cmdText.Length-startPos;
            }
            else // "order by" exists -  search from where  position to "order by"
            {
                length =  kwc[orderPosition].Index - startPos;
            }

            sbFilterText.Append(cmdText.Substring(startPos,length));
            this.dataView.RowFilter = sbFilterText.ToString();
        }
    }
```

VB.NET

```
Private Sub ValidateFiltering(ByVal cmdText As String)
    If filtering Then
        Dim sbFilterText As StringBuilder = New StringBuilder
        Dim startPos As Integer = 0
        Dim length As Integer = 0
        startPos = (kwc(wherePosition).Index + kwc(wherePosition).Length + 1)
        If keyWordCount = 3 Then
            length = cmdText.Length - startPos
        Else
            length = kwc(orderPosition).Index - startPos
        End If
        sbFilterText.Append(cmdText.Substring(startPos, length))
        Me.dataView.RowFilter = sbFilterText.ToString
    End If
End Sub
```

After you parse the text, you will use the `DataView.RowFilter` property to filter out results. Simply apply the string that you have extracted to the `RowFilter`, and the `DataView` class takes care of the rest. The same technique is applied to get ordering.

C#

```
public void ValidateSorting(string cmdText)
{
        if(sorting)
        {
            StringBuilder sbFilterText = new StringBuilder();
            int startPos =0;
            int length =0;

            //start from end of 'Order by' clause
            startPos = kwc[orderPosition].Index + kwc[orderPosition].Length + 1;
            length =  cmdText.Length - startPos;

            sbFilterText.Append(cmdText.Substring(startPos,length));
            this.dataView.Sort = sbFilterText.ToString();
        }
}
```

VB.NET

```
Private Sub ValidateSorting(ByVal cmdText As String)
    If sorting Then
        Dim sbFilterText As StringBuilder = New StringBuilder
        Dim startPos As Integer = 0
        Dim length As Integer = 0
        startPos = (kwc(orderPosition).Index + kwc(orderPosition).Length + 1)
        length = cmdText.Length - startPos
        sbFilterText.Append(cmdText.Substring(startPos, length))
        Me.dataView.Sort = sbFilterText.ToString
    End If
End Sub
```

CommandTimeout *Property*

The CommandTimeout property is used to specify how long the Command object should wait for the results of an executed command before throwing an exception. You are not actually using this value, but it must be implemented because of interface requirements. Just return a zero value to indicate that time-outs are not supported.

C#

```
public int CommandTimeout
{
    // Implemented the Property for consistency but it is not used.
    get   { return 0; }

}
```

VB.NET

```
Public Property CommandTimeout() As Integer _
        Implements IDbCommand.CommandTimeout
        Get
            Return 0
        End Get
        Set(ByVal Value As Integer)

        End Set
End Property
```

CommandType *Property*

Most DPEs allow the developer to pass in a command as text, or they can pass in a fully initialized Command object for the Execute reader method to examine and use. The DataSetCommand class accepts only text; any other type will cause your component to throw a NotSupported exception.

C#

```csharp
public CommandType CommandType
{
    // supports only a text commandType
    get { return CommandType.Text; }
    set { if (value != CommandType.Text) throw new NotSupportedException(); }
}
```

VB.NET

```vbnet
Public Property CommandType() As CommandType _
        Implements IDbCommand.CommandType
            Get
                Return CommandType.Text
            End Get
            Set(ByVal Value As CommandType)
                If Value <> CommandType.Text Then
                    Throw New NotSupportedException
                End If
            End Set
        End Property
```

CreateParameter *Method*

The CreateParameter method returns an extension-specific parameter to the Command object. The method must be supported because of the interface requirements, although it is not actually used. The DataSetParameter object is a simple class that implements another interface called IDataParameter, which allows it to be returned as an object of the interface type.

C#

```csharp
public IDataParameter CreateParameter()
{
    //return DataSetDataParameter
    return new DataSetDataParameter();
}
```

VB.NET

```vbnet
Public Function CreateParameter() As IDataParameter _
        Implements IDbCommand.CreateParameter
            Return New DataSetDataParameter
End Function
```

Parameters *Property*

The Parameters property returns a collection that implements the IDataParameterCollection interface. Your custom collection class is the DataSetParameterCollection and satisfies these requirements. The Parameters property allows the developer to index into the Parameters collection to set or get the parameter values.

C#

```
public IDataParameterCollection Parameters
{
    get
    {
        return this.m_parameters;
    }
}
```

VB.NET

```
Public ReadOnly Property Parameters() As IDataParameterCollection _
    Implements IDbCommand.Parameters
        Get
            Return Me.m_parameters
        End Get
End Property
```

Creating the `DataReader` Object

The data reader in our implementation does nothing more than read properties of our internal `DataView`. The behavior of the data reader is enforced by the `IDataReader` interface, which supplies methods to indicate the number, names, and types of the fields that will be read. It also allows the object to actually access the data.

To add the `DataSetDataReader` class to the project, choose Project ⇨ Add Class from the menu. Change the name of the class to `DataSetDataReader`. After adding the class, add the custom namespace, and edit the class definition.

Declarations

The members of the `DataSetDataReader` hold all the information that you will use to build the properties supported by the `DataSetDataReader` class. The `currentRow` variable is used to store the value of the current row as the data is being read from your data file. The `dataView` variable holds a reference to the current view of data from the `DataSetCommand` that is passed in via the constructor. And, finally, the `dataSetCommand` variable will hold a reference to the command that is passed in via the constructor.

C#

```
System.Data.DataView dataView;
DataSetCommand dataSetCommand = null;
int currentRow = -1;
```

VB.NET

```
Private dataView As System.Data.DataView = Nothing
Private dataSetCommand As dataSetCommand = Nothing
Private currentRow As Integer = -1
```

Implementing IDataReader

The IDataReader interface enforces consistency in working with data. It provides properties and methods that allow you to examine the data and its types as well as the Read method that will actually do the dirty work.

C#

```
public interface IDataReader : IDisposable
{
    Type GetFieldType(int fieldIndex);
    string GetName(int fieldIndex);
    int GetOrdinal(string fieldName);
    object GetValue(int fieldIndex);
    bool Read();
    int FieldCount { get; }
}
```

VB.NET

```
Public Interface IDataReader
    Inherits IDisposable
    Function GetFieldType(ByVal fieldIndex As Integer) As Type
    Function GetName(ByVal fieldIndex As Integer) As String
    Function GetOrdinal(ByVal fieldName As String) As Integer
    Function GetValue(ByVal fieldIndex As Integer) As Object
    Function Read() As Boolean
    Property FieldCount() As Integer
End Interface
```

You need to modify your class definition to force the custom DataSetDataReader class to support (implement) the interface requirements.

C#

```
namespace Wrox.ReportingServices.DataSetDataExtension
{

    public class DataSetDataReader : IDataReader
    {
```

VB.NET

```
Namespace Wrox.ReportingServices.DataSetDataExtension
    Public Class DataSetDataReader

        Implements IDataReader
```

GetFieldType *Method*

The GetFieldType method returns the type of data at a particular position within the stream that is being read. This data is used to allow the developer to store the data being read in the correct data type upon retrieval from the data reader.

C#

```
public Type GetFieldType (int fieldIndex)
{
        Return this.dataView.Table.Columns[fieldIndex].DataType;
}
```

VB.NET

```
Public Function GetFieldType(ByVal fieldIndex As Integer) As Type _
    Implements IDataReader.GetFieldType
        Return Me.dataView.Table.Columns(fieldIndex).DataType
End Function
```

GetName *Method*

The GetName method allows the developer to retrieve a data field from the DataReader object by passing in the name of the field to be read.

C#

```
public string GetName(int fieldIndex)
{
        return this.dataView.Table.Columns[fieldIndex].ColumnName;
}
```

VB.NET

```
Public Function GetName(ByVal fieldIndex As Integer) As String _
    Implements IDataReader.GetName
        Return Me.dataView.Table.Columns(fieldIndex).ColumnName
End Function
```

GetOrdinal *Method*

The GetOrdinal method allows the developer to index the data based on its position within the DataReader stream.

C#

```csharp
public int GetOrdinal(string fieldName)
{
        return this.dataView.Table.Columns[fieldName].Ordinal;
}
```

VB.NET

```vbnet
Public Function GetOrdinal(ByVal fieldName As String) As Integer _
    Implements IDataReader.GetOrdinal
        Return Me.dataView.Table.Columns(fieldName).Ordinal
End Function
```

GetValue *Method*

The GetValue method retrieves the actual value from the data stream. All of these methods are typically used together. The developer pulls the type information from the stream, creates variables of the correct type to hold this data, and gets the values of the data using the GetValue function.

C#

```csharp
public object GetValue(int fieldIndex)
{
        return this.dataView[this.currentRow][fieldIndex];
}
```

VB.NET

```vbnet
Public Function GetValue(ByVal fieldIndex As Integer) As Object _
    Implements IDataReader.GetValue
        Return Me.dataView(Me.currentRow)(fieldIndex)
End Function
```

Read *Method*

The Read method is the workhorse of the DataSetDataReader class. The function loops through the current DataView. If a line is successfully read, this is indicated to the user of your extension by incrementing the row count variable currentRow and by returning a Boolean value. As long as true is returned, data is successfully read. False is returned when the internal view hits the end of the result set.

C#

```csharp
public bool Read()
{
        System.Threading.Interlocked.Increment(this.currentRow);
        if (this.currentRow >= this.dataView.Count)
        {
                return false;
        }
        return true;
}
```

VB.NET

```
Public Function Read() As Boolean Implements IDataReader.Read
    System.Threading.Interlocked.Increment(Me.currentRow)
    If Me.currentRow >= Me.dataView.Count Then
        Return False
    End If
    Return True
End Function
```

FieldCount *Property*

The FieldCount property returns the number of fields or columns available in each row of data that the Read method returns.

C#

```csharp
public int FieldCount
{
    // Return the count of the number of columns,
    get { return this.dataView.Table.Columns.Count; }
}
```

VB.NET

```
Public ReadOnly Property FieldCount() As Integer Implements IDataReader.FieldCount
    Get
        Return Me.dataView.Table.Columns.Count
    End Get
End Property
```

Installing the DataSetDataProcessing *Extension*

After creating your custom DPE, you must install it to enable access. The installation process is two steps:

1. Install and configure the extension.

2. Configure extension security.

This particular extension is used both by the Reporting Server and the Report Designer itself, which requires us to install it in two locations. It must be installed on the report server and the workstation used to design the reports (using BIDS/Visual Studio).

Server Installation

Reporting Services has a standard location where extensions should be installed. This location is a subdirectory below the installation directory of SQL Server itself. We refer to the SQL Server installation path as *InstallPath*. On my machine, this directory is C:\Program Files\Microsoft SQL Server\.

Depending on the different SQL Server products you have installed on the machine, the subdirectories under InstallPath may vary. The naming convention for the Reporting Services subdirectory is MSRS10. MSSQLSERVER, where *MSRS10* represents the product and version name (Microsoft Reporting Services v.10).

The directory that you will install the extension into is the bin directory of the report server: InstallPath\ MSRS10.MSSQLSERVER\Reporting Services\ReportServer\bin. Copy your custom DPE assembly into this directory. The extension is now in the correct location, but you need to inform the Report Server of its presence. This is done by editing the configuration file that Reporting Services uses for its settings. This file is called RSReportServer.config and is located in the parent directory. Open this file and look for the <Data> section. Within this section, you should see entries similar to the following:

```
<Data>
    <Permissions>
        <PermissionSet class="System.Security.NamedPermissionSet" version="1"
                    Unrestricted="true" Name="FullTrust"
                    Description="Allows full access to all resources"/>
    </Permissions>
    <Extension Name="SQL"
        Type="Microsoft.ReportingServices.DataExtensions.SqlConnectionWrapper,
            Microsoft.ReportingServices.DataExtensions"/>
    <Extension Name="OLEDB"
        Type="Microsoft.ReportingServices.DataExtensions.OleDbConnectionWrapper,
            Microsoft.ReportingServices.DataExtensions"/>
    <Extension Name="ORACLE"
        Type="Microsoft.ReportingServices.DataExtensions.OracleClient
         ConnectionWrapper,Microsoft.ReportingServices.DataExtensions"/>
    <Extension Name="ODBC"
        Type="Microsoft.ReportingServices.DataExtensions.OdbcConnection
            Wrapper,Microsoft.ReportingServices.DataExtensions"/>

    <Extension Name="DATASET"
  Type="Wrox.ReportingServices.DataSetDataExtension.DataSetConnection
  ,Wrox.ReportingServices.DataSetDataExtension"/>
    </Data>
```

Add the DataSet entry that you see in the highlighted code snippet. The Name tag is the unique name you want users to see when they select your extension. The Type element contains the entry point class for your extension (the first object created and the one that is required to implement the IExtension interface), followed by the fully qualified name of your extension.

Save the file. Reporting Services will now recognize your extension, but you must change the Code Access Security (CAS) policy to give the extension the permissions that it needs to do its job. CAS is a constraint security model used by the .NET framework to restrict which system resources and operations that code can access and perform, regardless of the caller.

Server Security Configuration

The security policy file is located in the same directory as the server configuration file. Simply locate the file called *rssrvpolicy.config*. This file contains the security policy information for SSRS, and an entry should be made that looks similar to the following (replace "<INSTALLPATH>" with the appropriate installation path of the SQL Server Reporting Services instance on the server):

```
</CodeGroup>
```

```
<CodeGroup  class="UnionCodeGroup"
  version="1"
  PermissionSetName="FullTrust"
  Name="WroxSRS" Description="Code group for Wrox DataSet data processing extension">
    <IMembershipCondition class="UrlMembershipCondition"
      version="1"

Url="<INSTALLPATH>\Reporting Services\ReportServer\bin\ DataSetDataExtension.dll" />
</CodeGroup>
```

This CodeGroup policy specifies that we grant FullTrust to our assembly to execute its code. As a best practice, though, you should only grant the permission set required by your code to execute appropriately, thus reducing the possible attack surface.

WorkStation Installation

The next task is installing the extension on your development machine so that you can use it in the Report Designer within BIDS/Visual Studio. The process for installing the extension into the Report Designer is much the same as that for the server, with the exception of the filenames and locations. This is also done by copying the file to a specific directory of your development machine and making an entry in the configuration file so that the designer is aware of the extension.

Copy your extension to the C:\Program Files\Microsoft Visual Studio 9.0\Common7\IDE\ PrivateAssemblies directory. All of the files needed for workstation configuration are located here. The configuration file of the designer is called RSReportDesigner.config. Insert the same information that you inserted at the server-side extension at the end of the <Data> section in this file.

```
<Data
<Extension Name="ODBC"
Type="Microsoft.ReportingServices.DataExtensions.OdbcConnection
        Wrapper, Microsoft.ReportingServices.DataExtensions"/>
```

```
<Extension Name="DATASET"
  Type="Wrox.ReportingServices.DataSetDataExtension.DataSetConnection,
          Wrox.ReportingServices.DataSetDataExtension"/>
</Data>
```

There is one additional requirement in this file. You must also tell Visual Studio what designer to use with your extension. We chose not to implement a custom designer class but to use the Generic Query Designer provided by Microsoft instead. Your query is based on SQL, so this works well. Make an entry in the `<Designer>` section that immediately follows the `<Data>` section.

```
<Extension Name="DATASET"
    Type="Microsoft.ReportingServices.QueryDesigners.GenericQueryDesigner,
            Microsoft.ReportingServices.QueryDesigners" />
```

WorkStation Security Configuration

The next step is to set up the security policy so the extension will run in the designer correctly. The required file is called rspreviewpolicy.config. Add an entry resembling the following into this file (replace "<installPath>" with your actual installation path of Visual Studio):

```
<CodeGroup class="UnionCodeGroup" version="1"
    PermissionSetName="FullTrust"
    Name="WroxSRS"
    Description="Code group for my DataSet data processing extension">
      <IMembershipCondition class="UrlMembershipCondition"
          version="1"
          Url="<installPath>\Common7\IDE\PrivateAssemblies\DataSetDataExtension.dll" />
</CodeGroup>
```

Testing the `DataSetDataExtension`

In order to test the `DataSetDataExtension` extension, a report that uses the custom extension must be created. You must also create a `DataSet` file to contain your data or use the one provided in the sample code. The code is generic enough that you can use it against any serialized dataset. The file included in the example is just a `SELECT * FROM DimCustomer` run against the AdventureWorksDW2008 database and persisted from a dataset object.

Add a new project to your existing solution. Create the project by choosing File ⇨ Add Project ⇨ New Project. If the development environment is set up correctly, you will see the Business Intelligence template folder. Choose the Report Server Project template. Change the name of the project to `TestReport`, and click OK. This will launch the Report Designer with a blank report. Click the link on the Designer canvas to add a new data source and dataset for the report. The Data Source Properties page will appear. Leave the default data source name, and click on the Type dropdown box. Your new `DataSetDataExtension` should now be available as *DATASET*. Using a `FileName` attribute, enter the physical path to your serialized dataset into the Connection String textbox. When you are done, the result should resemble Figure 17-7.

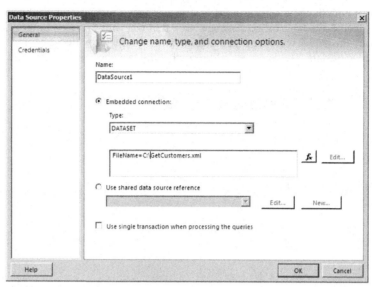

Figure 17-7

Next, you need to indicate the credentials that you wish to use. Click on the Credentials menu on the left side of the Data Source Properties page, which will cause the Credentials window to be displayed. Instruct the data source to "Use Windows Authentication (integrated security)" by selecting the radio button (see Figure 17-8).

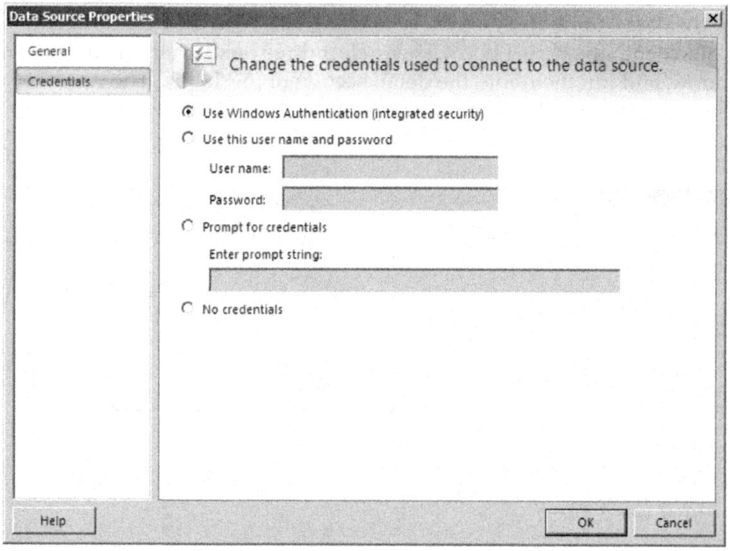

Figure 17-8

After you have set both the type and connection strings, you are ready to set up the basic data query. The dataset we used included a table called DimCustomer that we want to query. Enter SELECT * FROM DimCustomer into the Query window if you are using the sample provided, or some statement that works on your specific data. The query should resemble the text shown in Figure 17-9.

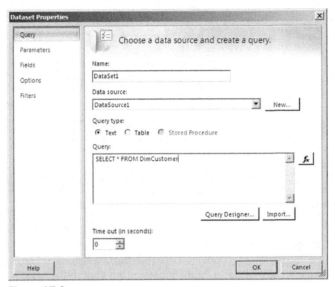

Figure 17-9

Finish setting up the data source and dataset by clicking OK. Now you can drag and drop a new Table item from the toolbox onto the report body. Then select three fields from the dataset, represented in the Report Data window, and put them into the detail section of the Tablix. The resulting report is shown in Figure 17-10.

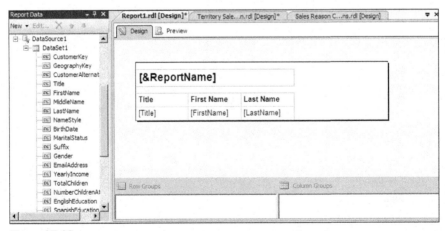

Figure 17-10

Next, you need to see if our extension actually returns data. Click on the Preview tab. The resulting data should resemble Figure 17-11.

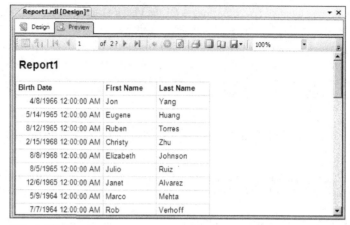

Figure 17-11

Now you know that your extension works. You can experiment with the field-limiting/filtering and field-sorting functionality by right-clicking on the Dataset name in the Report Data window, and selecting the Edit Query menu item. This brings up the Query Designer, where you can enter more advanced queries and test the results (see Figure 17-12).

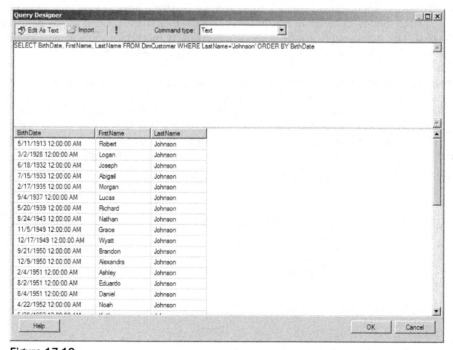

Figure 17-12

Another option for testing the custom data extension is to open a new instance of Visual Studio and load up the extension project. Add a breakpoint on a line of code that you would like to step into, and then select "Attach to process" from the Debug menu.

In the Attach to Process window, select the process for the Visual Studio instance that has the Report Designer open to the test report consuming the data extension.

Finally, click the Attach button, and Visual Studio will attach the project code to the Report Designer. To step into the breakpoint, just preview the report in the Report Designer, and as soon as Reporting Services hits the line of code with the breakpoint, you will be taken to the code view and be able to use all the debugging features of the Visual Studio IDE.

Summary

In this chapter, you learned about the extensibility of Reporting Services and the areas that currently support customization. Specifically, you learned:

❑   Which extensibility options are available

❑   Reasons for extending SQL Server Reporting Services

❑   How to create custom data provider extensions

❑   How to install custom extensions

Along with the extensibility options available in SQL Server Reporting Services, you also learned about some of the business opportunities created. Microsoft has created a flexible, powerful reporting solution that allows you to modify its behavior by implementing the interfaces required by the particular extension type. This functionality is sure to create a third-party market for tools, as well as allow enterprise developers to create custom solutions for the unique needs of their businesses.

Also discussed were the data access methods used by the .NET Framework and specifically how to create a custom DPE to work with non-relational data. The example is very simple and does not stand alone as an application — although it could be easily extended to provide additional functionality such as support for parameters. The primary purpose of the example is to familiarize you with the requirements for creating and installing an extension. This type of extension was chosen because it is used on the server for report processing and on the developer machine for report creation.

RDL Object Model

The Report Definition Language (RDL) is a schema-defined XML specification for how a report file should be structured. In order for Reporting Services to interact with the structure of a report, it needs to understand the RDL schema so that it knows which elements represent which pieces of functionality within the report. Although a simple parsing of the XML document, using the XML Document Object Model (DOM) and an XML querying language such as XPath, would technically enable you to extract this information, it would make for very lengthy and cumbersome code to maintain.

Instead, Reporting Services provides a representation of the RDL schema in an object-oriented fashion. What that means is that the RDL schema in Reporting Services was modeled using objects and properties, all available from a public library, which can be used to examine and manipulate the RDL document. This piece of functionality is called the *RDL Object Model*.

In previous versions of Reporting Services, the object model was not released as a public library and was only available internally to Reporting Services. This meant that a developer had to generate his or her own custom object model based on the RDL schema provided.

You might be asking, "When would I need to use the RDL Object Model?" If you have requirements to generate RDL files on-the-fly or to change any properties of report items, programmatically, this is a great way to do so. It allows for a very flexible platform that could enable your application's users to design simple reports and save them, to be later deployed into a Report Server.

The new object model library also provides methods to upgrade RDLs from previous versions to the current 2008 version, as well as from 2000 to 2005 versions.

Now that we've defined the RDL Object Model, let's see it in action.

Editing Report RDL Files

To get started, you need to add a reference to your Visual Studio project to include the `Microsoft` `.ReportingServices.RdlObjectModel.dll` assembly. This assembly can be found under the install path of Reporting Services (normally at C:\Program Files\Microsoft SQL Server\MSRS10 .MSSQLSERVER\Reporting Services\ReportServer\bin). This assembly contains all the required classes to create and manipulate report definitions.

The namespace `Microsoft.ReportingServices.RdlObjectModel` contains a public `Report` class, which represents an in-memory report definition file. You may choose to create a new `Report` instance or load one from an existing RDL file. In order to load from a file, you will use the following lines of code. To de-serialize an RDL file, you must provide a file path to the `RdlSerializer` class's `Deserialize()` method. The `RdlSerializer` class also contains a `Serialize()` method, which, as the name suggests, will perform the reverse operation and "write" the contents of the `Report` object to a file.

VB

```
Private rdl As Microsoft.ReportingServices.RdlObjectModel.Report

Private Sub LoadReport(ByVal filepath As String)
    Using stream As FileStream = File.OpenRead(filepath)
        Try
            Dim serializer As New
Microsoft.ReportingServices.RdlObjectModel.Serialization.RdlSerializer

            rdl = serializer.Deserialize(stream)
            Console.WriteLine("Report Loaded")

        Catch ex As System.Xml.XmlException
            Console.WriteLine("The file is not in the 2008 RDL schema")

        End Try
    End Using
End Sub
```

C#

```
private Microsoft.ReportingServices.RdlObjectModel.Report rdl;

private void LoadReport(string filepath)
{
    using (FileStream stream = File.OpenRead(filepath))
    {
        var serializer = new
Microsoft.ReportingServices.RdlObjectModel.Serialization.RdlSerializer();
        try
        {
            rdl = serializer.Deserialize(stream);
            Console.WriteLine("Report Loaded");
        }
        catch (System.Xml.XmlException)
        {
```

```
                    Console.WriteLine("The file is not in the 2008 RDL Schema");
            }
        }
    }
```

As with many .NET objects, the `Report` object contains nested types and collections that represent other types defined within the `Microsoft.ReportingServices.RdlObjectModel` assembly. For example, an RDL report contains a `Page` definition, as well as a `Body` definition. Each of these definitions is represented by a type in the model. If you continue to "drill" into the Object Model, you will notice that the `Body` type contains a nested collection of report items, defined as `IList<ReportItem>`. This generic collection of `ReportItem` gives you access to each item defined within the body of the report, such as a tablix, chart, or textbox.

The code sample provided for this Appendix shows how to use Windows Forms controls' ability to do rich binding using a `BindingSource` bound to a `Report` object. It makes it very simple to bind textboxes and other Forms controls to the object's properties and members, and it also takes care of string formats for things such as units of measure.

Once the report object is created and instantiated or loaded, you can start manipulating its properties and content. In the following lines, you will see how you can easily modify the report's author, language, and description, and then save the report to a file. If you're using rich binding as mentioned in the previous paragraph, the following lines of code are handled by the data-binding capabilities of the controls and the `BindingSource` class, so the developer does not have to do the plumbing required to get or set the values of these properties.

VB

```vb
Private Sub ModifyReport()

    rdl.Description = "This description was modified with the Rdl Ojbect model"
    rdl.Author = "Thiago Silva"
    rdl.Language = New ReportExpression("en-US")

    Me.WriteReportToFile("C:\RdlObjecModel\New Report.rdl")

End Sub

Private Sub WriteReportToFile(ByVal filepath As String)
    If String.IsNullOrEmpty(filepath) Then

        Console.WriteLine("Path Not Specified )
        Return

    End If

    Using fs As New System.IO.FileStream(filepath, FileMode.Create)
        Dim serializer As New Microsoft.ReportingServices.RdlObjectModel.RdlSerializer
        serializer.Serialize(inStream, rdl)

        Console.WriteLine("Report saved")
    End Using
End Sub
```

C#

```csharp
private void ModifyReport()
{
    rdl.Description = "This description was modified with the Rdl Ojbect model";
    rdl.Author = "Thiago Silva";
    rdl.Language = new ReportExpression("en-US");

    this.WriteReportToFile(@"C:\RdlObjecModel\New Report.rdl");
}

private void WriteReportToFile(string filepath)
{
    if (string.IsNullOrEmpty(filepath))
    {
        Console.WriteLine("Path Not Specified);
        return;
    }

    using (FileStream fs = new System.IO.FileStream(filepath, FileMode.Create))
    {
        var serializer = new Microsoft.ReportingServices.RdlObjectModel
.RdlSerializer();
        serializer.Serialize(inStream, rdl);

        Console.WriteLine("Report saved");
    }
}
```

Upgrading a Report from Previous RDL Versions Programmatically

In addition to allowing a developer to manipulate the Report object, the RdlObjectModel assembly provides methods for performing conversions from previous RDL schemas to a later one. This is similar to the "Report Upgrade" functionality provided by Visual Studio (or Business Intelligence Development Studio — BIDS), when opening a RDL file still defined with the previous version of the RDL schema.

Unlike the Visual Studio report upgrading feature, though, the developer has the power to write a routine that upgrades several files by iterating within a folder location, without having to manually open each RDL file in Visual Studio to trigger the upgrade. If you have a project with tens or even hundreds of report RDL files, this would be a great way to quickly convert your reports to a later version of the RDL schema.

There are two "upgrader" classes in the assembly: one for upgrading from the 2003 to the 2005 schema, and another class for upgrading from 2005 to the current (i.e., 2008) schema. Both have overloaded methods that accept either a Stream or an XmlReader. The upgrader methods for the 2008 schema actually return the output stream, while the 2005 upgrader methods use a referenced stream parameter and have a void signature.

VB

```vb
Private Sub DoUpgrade(ByVal path As String, ByVal newPath As String)
    Using (Stream fs = File.OpenRead(path))

        Using rdlStream As Stream =
Microsoft.ReportingServices.ReportProcessing.RDLUpgrader.UpgradeToCurrent(fs)
            Me.SaveReportToNewFile(rdlStream, newPath)
        End Using
    End Using
End Sub

Private Sub SaveReportToNewFile(ByVal inStream As Stream, ByVal filepath As String)

    Using output As Stream = New FileStream(filepath, FileMode.Create)
        Dim buffer(32 * 1024) As Byte

        Dim read As Integer

        While (read = inStream.Read(buffer, 0, buffer.Length)) > 0
            output.Write(buffer, 0, read)
        End While
    End Using
End Sub
```

C#

```csharp
private void DoUpgrade(string path, string newPath)
{
    using (Stream fs = File.OpenRead(path))
    {
        using (Stream rdlStream =
Microsoft.ReportingServices.ReportProcessing.RDLUpgrader.UpgradeToCurrent(fs))
        {
            this.SaveReportToNewFile(rdlStream, newPath);
        }
    }
}

private void SaveReportToNewFile(Stream inStream, string filepath)
{
    using (Stream output = new FileStream(filepath, FileMode.Create))
    {
        byte[] buffer = new byte[32 * 1024];

        int read;
        while ((read = inStream.Read(buffer, 0, buffer.Length)) > 0)
        {
            output.Write(buffer, 0, read);
        }
    }
}
```

The preceding code sample shows how to upgrade an RDL file by opening a file stream and passing it to the new `RdlUpgrader.UpgradeToCurrent()` method. The method returns a new `Stream` object containing the 2008 RDL, which you then write to file.

The classes for upgrading from the 2003 to 2005 RDL schema can be found in the namespace `Microsoft.ReportingServices.RdlObjectModel2005.Upgrade`.

Currently, the classes and methods within the RDL Object Model library are not documented in the SQL Server Books Online, as they have not been "officially blessed" as public. So, the best way to drill into the assembly and investigate its public types and members is by using an IL disassembler tool such as Lutz Roeder's .NET Reflector (http://www.aisto.com/roeder/dotnet). Figure A-1 illustrates Reflector disassembling the RDL Object Model assembly, and detailing the `Report` class and its public properties and constructors.

Figure A-1

Summary

The public RDL Object Model can be a powerful tool to enable application developers to build and generate RDL files programmatically, as well as to edit and update existing reports. It allows for great flexibility when dealing with the Report Definition Language and provides an official, strongly typed schema from which to generate report files using any flavor of .NET languages.

T-SQL Command Syntax Reference

SQL Server 2008 recognizes up to four parts of object names. Depending on the context of an expression, some parts may or may not be necessary when referencing an object. When a script runs on a different server or when you are using a different database, related object names may be required. Note that both SQL Server 2005 and SQL Server 2008 recognize the schema name in the third position, whereas SQL Server 2000 and earlier versions recognized the object owner name in the third position. The following table summarizes valid syntax for referencing database objects:

Object Reference	Use and Context
`object`	Used in the context of the local database, on the same server. Object is part of the dbo schema and there are no duplicate object names.
`schema.object`	Used in the context of the local database, on the same server. Duplicate object names that have schema names (and subsequently, different owners) are permitted. Also uses a standard convention for clarity.
`database..object`	Used in the context of the same or different database on the same server. If you haven't specified the owner or schema, assumes the dbo schema.
`database.schema.object`	A three-part name fully describes an object on the same server, in the same or different database.
`server.database .schema.object`	A four-part name is valid in the context of a remote server or the local server, in the local or a different database, and for any schema.

(continued)

Object Reference	Use and Context
`server.database.. object`	The database owner or schema in the third position can be omitted to use the default dbo schema.
`server..schema.object`	The database name can be omitted to use the default database on that server. This is not a typical practice.
`server...object`	Omitting the database and owner or schema name causes the default database and the default dbo schema to be used. This is valid syntax but not a typical practice.

T-SQL Commands, Clauses, and Predicates

Following are the core components of the T-SQL language. New commands for SQL Server 2008 are explicitly called out in this section.

WITH

Introduced in SQL Server 2005, this method is used to define an alias for the result set returned by a SELECT expression.

```
WITH MyCTE
AS
( SELECT * FROM Product WHERE ListPrice < 1000 )
```

Optionally, column aliases can be defined in parentheses following the Common Table Expression (CTE) name:

```
WITH MyCTE ( ID, ProdNumber, ProdName, Price )
AS
( SELECT
    ProductID
  , ProductNumber
  , Name
  , ListPrice
  FROM Product WHERE ListPrice < 1000
)
```

SELECT

❑   To return all columns from a table or view:

```
SELECT * FROM table_name
```

❑ To return specific columns from a table or view:

```
SELECT Column1, Column2, Column3 FROM table_name
```

❑ Column alias techniques:

```
SELECT Column1 AS Col1, Column2 AS Col2 FROM table_name
SELECT Column1 Col1, Column2 Col2 FROM table_name
SELECT Col1 = Column1, Col2 = Column2 FROM table_name
```

❑ To return literal values:

```
SELECT 'Some literal value'
SELECT 'Some value' AS Col1, 123 AS Col2
```

❑ To return an expression value:

```
SELECT (1 + 2) * 3
```

❑ To return the result of a function call:

```
SELECT CONVERT( varchar(20), GETDATE(), 101 )
```

SELECT TOP

❑ To return a fixed number of rows:

```
SELECT TOP 10 * FROM table_name ORDER BY Column1
SELECT TOP 10 Column1, Column2 FROM table_name ORDER BY Column2
```

❑ To return a fixed number of rows with the ties for last position:

```
SELECT TOP 10 WITH TIES Column1, Column2 FROM table_name ORDER BY Column2
```

❑ To return a percentage of all available rows:

```
SELECT TOP 25 PERCENT * FROM table_name ORDER BY Column2
SELECT TOP 25 PERCENT Column1, Column2 FROM table_name ORDER BY Column2
```

❑ To substitute a variable or expression for a top values number:

```
DECLARE @TopNumber Int
SET @TopNumber = 15
SELECT TOP @ TopNumber * FROM table_name ORDER BY Column2
```

❑ To return top values based on an expression:

```
SELECT TOP (SELECT a_column_value FROM some_table) * FROM another_table
```

SELECT INTO

To create and populate a table from a result set:

```
SELECT Column1, Column2 INTO
new_table_name FROM existing_table_or_view_name
```

FROM

❑ Single table query:

```
SELECT * FROM table_name
```

❑ Multi-table join query:

```
SELECT *
FROM table1.key_column INNER JOIN table2 ON table1.key_column = table2.key_column
```

❑ Derived table:

```
SELECT DerTbl.Column1, DerTbl.Column2
FROM
    ( SELECT Column1, Column2 FROM some_table ... ) AS DerTbl
```

WHERE

❑ Exact match:

```
SELECT ... FROM ...
WHERE Column1 = 'A literal value'
```

❑ Not NULL:

```
SELECT ... FROM ...
WHERE Column1 IS NOT NULL
```

❑ Any trailing characters:

```
SELECT ... FROM ...
WHERE Column1 LIKE 'ABC%'
```

❑ Any leading characters:

```
SELECT ... FROM ...
WHERE Column1 LIKE '%XYZ'
```

❑ Any leading or trailing characters:

```
SELECT ... FROM ...
WHERE Column1 LIKE '%MNOP%'
```

❑   Placeholder wildcard:

```
SELECT ... FROM ...
WHERE Column1 LIKE '_BC_EF'
```

❑   Criteria using parentheses to designate order:

```
SELECT ... FROM ...
WHERE
    (Column1 LIKE 'ABC%' AND Column2 LIKE '%XYZ')
    OR
    Column3 = '123'
```

GROUP BY

All non-aggregated columns in the SELECT list must be included in the GROUP BY list:

```
SELECT COUNT(Column1), Column2, Column3
FROM ... WHERE ...
GROUP BY Column2, Column3
```

❑   Designating order:

```
SELECT COUNT(Column1), Column2, Column3
FROM ... WHERE ...
GROUP BY Column2, Column3
ORDER BY Column2 DESC, Column3 ASC
```

WITH ROLLUP

❑   Legacy method to implement a rollup subtotal break:

Note that ROLLUP and CUBE operators cause SQL Server to return a non-two-dimensional result set that is not supported by many APIs and client interfaces.

```
SELECT Column1, Column2, SUM(Column3)
FROM table_name
GROUP BY Column1, Column2
WITH ROLLUP
```

This syntax is still supported in SQL Server 2008, but the new BY ROLLUP syntax is preferred.

BY ROLLUP

This is a new syntax introduced in SQL Server 2008 for implementing a rollup subtotal break:

```
SELECT Column1, Column2, SUM(Column3)
FROM table_name
GROUP BY ROLLUP(Column1, Column2)
```

WITH CUBE

❑ Legacy method to implement a cube subtotal break:

```
SELECT Column1, Column2, SUM(Column3)
FROM table_name
GROUP BY Column1, Column2
WITH CUBE
```

This syntax is still supported in SQL Server 2008, but the new BY CUBE syntax is preferred.

BY CUBE

This is a new syntax introduced in SQL Server 2008 for implementing a cube subtotal break:

```
SELECT Column1, Column2, SUM(Column3)
FROM table_name
GROUP BY CUBE(Column1, Column2)
```

HAVING

❑ To filter results based on values available after the aggregations and groupings are performed:

```
SELECT COUNT(Column1), Column2, Column3
FROM ... WHERE ...
GROUP BY Column2, Column3
HAVING COUNT(Column1) > 5
```

UNION

❑ To combine multiple results with the same column count:

```
SELECT Column1, Column2 FROM table1_name
UNION
SELECT Column1, Column2 FROM table2_name
```

❑ To combine literal values and query results:

```
SELECT -1 AS Column1, 'A literal value' AS Column2
UNION
SELECT Column1, Column2 FROM table1_name
```

❑ To include non-distinct selection (UNION performs SELECT DISTINCT by default):

```
SELECT Column1, Column2 FROM table1_name
UNION ALL
SELECT Column1, Column2 FROM table2_name
```

EXCEPT *and* INTERSECT

❏   To select the differences (EXCEPT) or common values (INTERSECT) between two queries:

```
SELECT * FROM TableA EXCEPT SELECT * FROM TableB
SELECT * FROM TableA INTERSECT SELECT * FROM TableB
```

ORDER BY

❏   To order a result set by one or more column values:

```
SELECT * FROM table_name ORDER BY Column1
SELECT * FROM table_name ORDER BY Column1 DESC, Column2 ASC
```

The default order is ascending. If ordering by more than one column, each column can have a different order.

COMPUTE *and* COMPUTE BY *Clauses*

❏   To generate totals that are appended to the end of an aggregate query result set:

```
SELECT Column1, Column2, Column3
FROM table_name
ORDER BY Column1, Column2
COMPUTE SUM(Column3)
```

The COMPUTE and COMPUTE BY clauses are not very useful in applications because the aggregated results are not in relational form and cannot be used in a dataset.

As of SQL Server 2008, the CUBE and ROLLUP operators are appended to the COMPUTE BY clause (see CUBE and ROLLUP).

FOR *Clause*

The FOR clause is used with either the XML or BROWSE option in a SELECT statement. However, the BROWSE and XML options are completely unrelated. FOR XML specifies that the result set is returned in XML format. FOR BROWSE is used when accessing data through the DB-Library so that rows can be browsed and updated one row at a time in an optimistic locking environment. There are several requirements when using the FOR BROWSE option. For more information, consult SQL Server Books Online, under the topic "Browse Mode."

```
SELECT * FROM table_name FOR XML {XML Option}
SELECT * FROM table_name FOR BROWSE
```

OPTION *Clause*

The OPTION clause is used in a SELECT statement to provide a query hint that will override the query optimizer and specify an index or specific join mechanism to be used along with other hint options.

CASE

❏ To evaluate one or more expressions and return one or more specified values based on the evaluated expression:

```
SELECT expression = CASE Column
WHEN value THEN resultant_value
WHEN value2 THEN resultant_value2
...
ELSE alternate_value
END
FROM table
SELECT value =
        CASE
        WHEN column IS NULL THEN value
        WHEN column {expression true} THEN different_value
        WHEN column {expression true} and price {expression true} THEN other_value
        ELSE different_value
        END,
        column2
FROM table
```

INSERT

❏ To add a new row to a table:

```
INSERT table (column list)
VALUES
(column values)
INSERT table
SELECT columns FROM source expression
INSERT table
EXEC stored_procedure
```

The following is new, multi-table INSERT syntax introduced in SQL Server 2008:

```
INSERT table (column list)
VALUES
(column values),
(column values),
(column values)
```

Note that column values are comma-separated and must appear in the same order as in the column list or in the same order as they are defined in the table.

UPDATE

❏   To update selected columns in a table:

```
UPDATE table SET column1 = expression1, column2 = expression2
WHERE filter_expression
```

❏   To update a table based on the contents of another table:

```
UPDATE table SET column1 = expression
FROM table INNER JOIN table2
ON table.column = table2.column
WHERE table.column = table2.column
```

DELETE

❏   To delete selected rows from a table:

```
DELETE table
WHERE filter_expression
```

❏   To delete rows from a table based on the contents of a different table:

```
DELETE table
FROM table INNER JOIN table2
ON table.column = table2.column
WHERE column = filter_expression
```

DECLARE @local_variable

This creates a named object that temporarily holds a value with the data type defined in the declaration statement. Local variables have scope only within the calling batch or stored procedure. The value of a local variable can be set with either a SET or SELECT operation. SELECT is more efficient than SET and has the advantage of populating multiple variables in a single operation, but the SELECT operation cannot be confined with any data retrieval operation.

```
DECLARE @local_variable AS int
SET @local_variable = integer_expression
DECLARE @local_variable1 AS int, @local_variable2 AS varchar(55)
SELECT @local_variable1 = integer_column_expression, @local_variable2 = character_
column_expression FROM table
```

SET

The SET operator has many functions, from setting the value of a variable to setting a database or connection property. The SET operator is divided into the categories listed in the following table:

Category	Alters the Current Session Settings for
Date and time	Handling date and time data
Locking	Handling SQL Server locking
Miscellaneous	Miscellaneous SQL Server functionality
Query execution	Query execution and processing
SQL-92 settings	Using the SQL-92 default settings
Statistics	Displaying statistics information
Transactions	Handling SQL Server transactions

LIKE

LIKE is a pattern-matching operator for comparing strings or partial strings.

❑ To compare a string value where the compared string is anywhere in the string:

```
SELECT * FROM table WHERE column1 LIKE '%string%'
```

❑ To compare a string value where the compared string is at the beginning of the string:

```
SELECT * FROM table WHERE column1 LIKE 'string%'
```

❑ To compare a string value where the compared string is at the end of the string:

```
SELECT * FROM table WHERE column1 LIKE '%string'
```

❑ To compare a string value where a specific character or character range is in the string:

```
SELECT * FROM table WHERE column1 LIKE '[a-c]'
SELECT * FROM table WHERE column1 LIKE '[B-H]olden'
```

❑ To compare a string value where a specific character or character range is not in the string:

```
SELECT * FROM table WHERE column1 LIKE '[M^c]%' -Begins with M but not Mc
```

ALTER TABLE

❑   To alter the structure of a table by adding or removing table objects such as columns, constraints, and partitions, or by enabling and disabling triggers:

```
ALTER TABLE table_name ADD new_column int NULL;
ALTER TABLE table_name ADD CONSTRAINT new_check CHECK (check expression) ;
ALTER TABLE table_name DROP COLUMN existing_column;
ALTER TABLE table_name ENABLE TRIGGER trigger_name;
ALTER TABLE table_name DISABLE TRIGGER trigger_name;
```

PIVOT *Operator*

❑   To cause a normalized columnar set to be transformed and restructured with repeating column values according to a predefined column list specification:

```
SELECT Column3, [Col2_List_Val1], [Col2_List_Val2], [Col2_List_Val3]... FROM
  (
    SELECT
        Column1  -- Value to aggregate as measure value in pivot cells
      , Column2  -- Value for column headers as column list
      , Column3  -- Value for row headers
    FROM source_table_name
  )   AS Source
PIVOT
  (
    Sum(Column1) FOR MeasureValue
      IN ([Col2_List_Val1], [Col2_List_Val2], [Col2_List_Val3]...)
  )   AS pvt
```

UNPIVOT *Operator*

❑   To cause a pivoted result set to be transformed into a normalized, columnar table structure:

```
SELECT
 Column3, Column2, Column1  -- columns same as pivot source above
FROM
 (
    SELECT
     Column1
    , [Col2_List_Val1], [Col2_List_Val2], [Col2_List_Val3]... FROM
    FROM pivot_source_table_name
 ) AS pvt
UNPIVOT
 (
    Column1 FOR MeasuresValue
      IN ([Col2_List_Val1], [Col2_List_Val2], [Col2_List_Val3]...)
 )
 AS unpvt
```

CREATE DATABASE

❏   To create a database and all associated files:

```
CREATE DATABASE new_database
ON (
   NAME = 'logical_name',
   FILENAME = 'physical_file_location',
   SIZE = initial_size_in_MB,
   MAXSIZE = max_size_in_MB, --If no MAXSIZE specified unlimited growth is assumed
   FILEGROWTH = percentage_OR_space_in_MB)
LOG ON
( NAME = 'logical_log_name',
   FILENAME = 'physical_file_location',
   SIZE = initial_size_in_MB,
   MAXSIZE = max_size_in_MB, --If no MAXSIZE specified unlimited growth is assumed
   FILEGROWTH = percentage_OR_space_in_MB)
COLLATE database_collation
```

CREATE DEFAULT

❏   To create a database-wide default value that can then be bound to columns in any table to provide a default value:

```
CREATE DEFAULT default_name AS default_value
--bind the default to a table column
sp_bindefault default_name, 'table.column'
```

CREATE PROCEDURE

❏   To create a new stored procedure:

```
CREATE PROCEDURE proc_name @variable variable_data_type ...n
AS
...procedure code
```

or

```
CREATE PROC proc_name @variable variable_data_type ...n
AS
...procedure code
```

CREATE RULE

❏   To create a database-wide rule, much like a check constraint, that can then be bound to individual columns in tables throughout the database:

```
CREATE RULE rule_name AS rule_expression
--bind the rule to a table column
sp_bindrule rule_name, 'table.column'
```

CREATE TABLE

❑   To create a new table:

```
CREATE TABLE table_name (
Column1 data_type nullability column_option,
Column2 data_type nullability column_option,
Column3 data_type nullability column_option,
--Column_option = Collation, IDENTITY, KEY...
```

❑   To create a new, partitioned table:

```
CREATE TABLE partitioned_table_name (Column1 int, Column2 char(10))
Column1 data_type nullability column_option,
Column2 data_type nullability column_option,
Column3 data_type nullability column_option
ON partition_scheme_name (column)
```

CREATE TRIGGER

❑   To create a new trigger on a table that fires *after* a DML event:

```
CREATE TRIGGER trigger_name
ON table_name FOR dml_action -INSERT, UPDATE or DELETE
AS
...trigger_code
```

❑   To create a new trigger on a table that fires *instead of* a DML event:

```
CREATE TRIGGER trigger_name
ON view_or_table_name INSTEAD OF dml_action -INSERT, UPDATE or DELETE
AS
...trigger_code
```

CREATE VIEW

❑   To create a new view:

```
CREATE VIEW view_name
AS
...Select Statement
```

CREATE SCHEMA

❑   To create a new database schema with the option of specifying a non-dbo owner with the AUTHORIZATION clause:

```
CREATE SCHEMA schema_name AUTHORIZATION user_name
```

CREATE PARTITION FUNCTION

❑   To create a partition function to use when physically partitioning tables and indexes:

```
CREATE PARTITION FUNCTION partition_function_name ( input_parameter_type )
AS RANGE LEFT --or RIGHT
FOR VALUES (value1, value2, value3, ...n)
```

CREATE PARTITION SCHEME

❑   To create a partition scheme to use when physically partitioning tables and indexes:

```
CREATE PARTITION SCHEME partition_scheme_name
AS PARTITION partition_function_name
TO (filegroup1, filegroup2, filegroup3, ...n)
```

Script Comment Conventions

❑   In-line comment:

```
SELECT ProductID, Name AS ProductName    -- Comment text
```

❑   Single-line comment:

```
/* Comment text */
```

or

```
-- Comment text
```

❑   Comment block:

```
/******************************************************
    spProductUpdateByCategory
    Created by Paul Turley, 5-21-08
    nospam@sqlreportservices.com
    Updates product price info for a category
    Revisions:
    3-24-09 - Fixed bug that formatted C:
              drive if wrong type was passed in.
******************************************************/
```

Reserved Words

Chapter 13 gave some recommendations and guidance about the naming of objects in SQL Server. One of the recommendations was that reserved words should not be used as names of objects. Reserved words typically are easy to see in SQL Server Management Studio, which changes the color of reserved words to blue. If the object names are delimited with double quotes or square brackets, which they often are if you are using a graphical tool to create queries, then they may not show up as being color-coded.

The following keywords have significant meaning within T-SQL and should be avoided in object names and expressions. If any of these words must be used in a SQL expression, they must be contained within square brackets [ ].

ADD	CONTAINS	ELSE
ALL	CONTAINSTABLE	END
ALTER	CONTINUE	ERRLVL
AND	CONVERT	ESCAPE
ANY	CREATE	EXCEPT
AS	CROSS	EXEC
ASC	CURRENT	EXECUTE
AUTHORIZATION	CURRENT_DATE	EXISTS
BACKUP	CURRENT_TIME	EXIT
BEGIN	CURRENT_TIMESTAMP	FETCH
BETWEEN	CURRENT_USER	FILE
BREAK	CURSOR	FILLFACTOR
BROWSE	DATABASE	FOR
BULK	DBCC	FOREIGN
BY	DEALLOCATE	FREETEXT
CASCADE	DECLARE	FREETEXTTABLE
CASE	DEFAULT	FROM
CHECK	DELETE	FULL
CHECKPOINT	DENY	FUNCTION
CLOSE	DESC	GOTO
CLUSTERED	DISK	GRANT
COALESCE	DISTINCT	GROUP
COLLATE	DISTRIBUTED	HAVING
COLUMN	DOUBLE	HOLDLOCK
COMMIT	DROP	IDENTITY
COMPUTE	DUMMY	IDENTITY_INSERT
CONSTRAINT	DUMP	IDENTITYCOL

(continued)

IF	ORDER	SETUSER
IN	OUTER	SHUTDOWN
INDEX	OVER	SOME
INNER	PERCENT	STATISTICS
INSERT	PIVOT	SYSTEM_USER
INTERSECT	PLAN	TABLE
INTO	PRECISION	TEXTSIZE
IS	PRIMARY	THEN
JOIN	PRINT	TO
KEY	PROC	TOP
KILL	PROCEDURE	TRAN
LEFT	PUBLIC	TRANSACTION
LIKE	RAISERROR	TRIGGER
LINENO	READ	TRUNCATE
LOAD	READTEXT	TSEQUAL
NATIONAL	RECONFIGURE	UNION
NOCHECK	REFERENCES	UNIQUE
NONCLUSTERED	REPLICATION	UNPIVOT
NOT	RESTORE	UPDATE
NULL	RESTRICT	UPDATETEXT
NULLIF	RETURN	USE
OF	REVOKE	USER
OFF	RIGHT	VALUES
OFFSETS	ROLLBACK	VARYING
ON	ROWCOUNT	VIEW
OPEN	ROWGUIDCOL	WAITFOR
OPENDATASOURCE	RULE	WHEN
OPENQUERY	SAVE	WHERE
OPENROWSET	SCHEMA	WHILE
OPENXML	SELECT	WITH
OPTION	SESSION_USER	WRITETEXT
OR	SET	

ODBC Reserved Words

Although the ODBC keywords in the following table are not strictly prohibited, as a best practice to prevent driver inconsistencies they should be avoided:

ABSOLUTE	CHAR	DATE
ACTION	CHAR_LENGTH	DAY
ADA	CHARACTER	DEALLOCATE
ADD	CHARACTER_LENGTH	DEC
ALL	CHECK	DECIMAL
ALLOCATE	CLOSE	DECLARE
ALTER	COALESCE	DEFAULT
AND	COLLATE	DEFERRABLE
ANY	COLLATION	DEFERRED
ARE	COLUMN	DELETE
AS	COMMIT	DESC
ASC	CONNECT	DESCRIBE
ASSERTION	CONNECTION	DESCRIPTOR
AT	CONSTRAINT	DIAGNOSTICS
AUTHORIZATION	CONSTRAINTS	DISCONNECT
AVG	CONTINUE	DISTINCT
BEGIN	CONVERT	DOMAIN
BETWEEN	CORRESPONDING	DOUBLE
BIT	COUNT	DROP
BIT_LENGTH	CREATE	ELSE
BOTH	CROSS	END
BY	CURRENT	END-EXEC
CASCADE	CURRENT_DATE	ESCAPE
CASCADED	CURRENT_TIME	EXCEPT
CASE	CURRENT_TIMESTAMP	EXCEPTION
CAST	CURRENT_USER	EXEC
CATALOG	CURSOR	EXECUTE

(continued)

EXISTS	INNER	NATIONAL
EXTERNAL	INPUT	NATURAL
EXTRACT	INSENSITIVE	NCHAR
FALSE	INSERT	NEXT
FETCH	INT	NO
FIRST	INTEGER	NONE
FLOAT	INTERSECT	NOT
FOR	INTERVAL	NULL
FOREIGN	INTO	NULLIF
FORTRAN	IS	NUMERIC
FOUND	ISOLATION	OCTET_LENGTH
FROM	JOIN	OF
FULL	KEY	ON
GET	LANGUAGE	ONLY
GLOBAL	LAST	OPEN
GO	LEADING	OPTION
GOTO	LEFT	OR
GRANT	LEVEL	ORDER
GROUP	LIKE	OUTER
HAVING	LOCAL	OUTPUT
HOUR	LOWER	OVERLAPS
IDENTITY	MATCH	PAD
IMMEDIATE	MAX	PARTIAL
IN	MIN	PASCAL
INCLUDE	MINUTE	POSITION
INDEX	MODULE	PRECISION
INDICATOR	MONTH	PREPARE
INITIALLY	NAMES	PRESERVE

PRIMARY	SOME	TRIM
PRIOR	SPACE	TRUE
PRIVILEGES	SQL	UNION
PROCEDURE	SQLCA	UNIQUE
PUBLIC	SQLCODE	UNKNOWN
READ	SQLERROR	UPDATE
REAL	SQLSTATE	UPPER
REFERENCES	SQLWARNING	USAGE
RELATIVE	SUBSTRING	USER
RESTRICT	SUM	USING
REVOKE	SYSTEM_USER	VALUE
RIGHT	TABLE	VALUES
ROLLBACK	TEMPORARY	VARCHAR
ROWS	THEN	VARYING
SCHEMA	TIME	VIEW
SCROLL	TIMESTAMP	WHEN
SECOND	TIMEZONE_HOUR	WHENEVER
SECTION	TIMEZONE_MINUTE	WHERE
SELECT	TO	WITH
SESSION	TRAILING	WORK
SESSION_USER	TRANSACTION	WRITE
SET	TRANSLATE	YEAR
SIZE	TRANSLATION	ZONE
SMALLINT		

Future Reserved Words

The following table contains keywords that may be reserved in future editions of SQL Server:

ABSOLUTE	COMPLETION	DOMAIN
ACTION	CONNECT	DYNAMIC
ADMIN	CONNECTION	EACH
AFTER	CONSTRAINTS	END-EXEC
AGGREGATE	CONSTRUCTOR	EQUALS
ALIAS	CORRESPONDING	EVERY
ALLOCATE	CUBE	EXCEPTION
ARE	CURRENT_PATH	EXTERNAL
ARRAY	CURRENT_ROLE	FALSE
ASSERTION	CYCLE	FIRST
AT	DATA	FLOAT
BEFORE	DATE	FOUND
BINARY	DAY	FREE
BIT	DEC	GENERAL
BLOB	DECIMAL	GET
BOOLEAN	DEFERRABLE	GLOBAL
BOTH	DEFERRED	GO
BREADTH	DEPTH	GROUPING
CALL	DEREF	HOST
CASCADED	DESCRIBE	HOUR
CAST	DESCRIPTOR	IGNORE
CATALOG	DESTROY	IMMEDIATE
CHAR	DESTRUCTOR	INDICATOR
CHARACTER	DETERMINISTIC	INITIALIZE
CLASS	DICTIONARY	INITIALLY
CLOB	DIAGNOSTICS	INOUT
COLLATION	DISCONNECT	INPUT

INT	NEXT	RESULT
INTEGER	NO	RETURNS
INTERVAL	NONE	ROLE
ISOLATION	NUMERIC	ROLLUP
ITERATE	OBJECT	ROUTINE
LANGUAGE	OLD	ROW
LARGE	ONLY	ROWS
LAST	OPERATION	SAVEPOINT
LATERAL	ORDINALITY	SCROLL
LEADING	OUT	SCOPE
LESS	OUTPUT	SEARCH
LEVEL	PAD	SECOND
LIMIT	PARAMETER	SECTION
LOCAL	PARAMETERS	SEQUENCE
LOCALTIME	PARTIAL	SESSION
LOCALTIMESTAMP	PATH	SETS
LOCATOR	POSTFIX	SIZE
MAP	PREFIX	SMALLINT
MATCH	PREORDER	SPACE
MINUTE	PREPARE	SPECIFIC
MODIFIES	PRESERVE	SPECIFICTYPE
MODIFY	PRIOR	SQL
MODULE	PRIVILEGES	SQLEXCEPTION
MONTH	READS	SQLSTATE
NAMES	REAL	SQLWARNING
NATURAL	RECURSIVE	START
NCHAR	REF	STATE
NCLOB	REFERENCING	STATEMENT
NEW	RELATIVE	STATIC

(continued)

STRUCTURE	TRANSLATION	VARCHAR
TEMPORARY	TREAT	VARIABLE
TERMINATE	TRUE	WHENEVER
THAN	UNDER	WITHOUT
TIME	UNKNOWN	WORK
TIMESTAMP	UNNEST	WRITE
TIMEZONE_HOUR	USAGE	YEAR
TIMEZONE_MINUTE	USING	ZONE
TRAILING	VALUE	

C

T-SQL System Variables and Functions

Variables and functions are often used interchangeably. SQL Server Books Online documents some variables as though they were functions. However, it's important to note that *variables* are used in expressions to obtain a value, whereas *functions* process specific business logic and may return a value. Many functions accept input arguments.

This Appendix, specific for SQL Server 2008, is not meant to be a comprehensive reference, but to provide a convenient guide to many functions and variables. For complete details and samples of usage, consult Books Online.

System Global Variables

The system-supplied global variables are organized into the following categories:

- ❑ Configuration
- ❑ Cursor
- ❑ System
- ❑ System Statistics

Configuration

Variable	Return Type	Description
@@DATEFIRST	tinyint	The system setting for the first day of the week: 1 = Monday 2 = Tuesday 3 = Wednesday 4 = Thursday 5 = Friday 6 = Saturday 7 = Sunday The U.S. default is 7.
@@DBTS	varbinary	The last assigned unique TimeStamp value
@@LANGID	smallint	The current language ID for the server: 0 = US English 1 = German 2 = French . . . and so on.
@@LANGUAGE	nvarchar	The current language string for the server. Returns the language name in the native language form (us_english, Deutsch, Français, Dansk, Español, Italiano, etc.).
@@LOCK_TIMEOUT	int	Lock time-out setting for the current session in milliseconds (ms)
@@MAX_CONNECTIONS	int	The maximum concurrent connections setting for the server
@@MAX_PRECISION	tinyint	The maximum precision setting for decimal and numeric types. The default is 38 significant digits (total to the left and right of the decimal point).
@@MICROSOFTVERSION	int	An internal tracking number used by product development and support groups at Microsoft
@@NESTLEVEL	int	The current number of nested stored procedure or trigger calls. This may be used to limit cascading and/or recursive calls prior to reaching the system limit of 32 recursive calls.

Variable	Return Type	Description
@@OPTIONS	int	The set of query-processing options for the current user session. Multiple options are combined mathematically using bitwise addition (i.e., If SELECT @@OPTIONS & (512 + 8192) > 0 ...). Any combination of option values can be added to determine whether all these options are enabled. Option values: 1 = DISABLE_DEF_CNST_CHK 2 = IMPLICIT_TRANSACTIONS 4 = CURSOR_CLOSE_ON_COMMIT 8 = ANSI_WARNINGS 16 = ANSI_PADDING 32 = ANSI_NULLS 64 = ARITHABORT 128 = ARITHIGNORE 256 = QUOTED_IDENTIFIER 512 = NOCOUNT 1024 = ANSI_NULL_DFLT_ON 2048 = ANSI_NULL_DFLT_OFF 4096 = CONCAT_NULL_YIELDS_NULL 8192 = NUMERIC_ROUNDABORT 16384 = XACT_ABORT
@@REMSERVER	nvarchar	Name of the remote server if executing remote procedures
@@SERVERNAME	nvarchar	Name of the current server
@@SERVICENAME	nvarchar	Name of the Windows service for the current SQL Server instance
@@SPID	int	The process/session ID assigned to the current user's connection
@@TEXTSIZE	int	The current value of the TEXTSIZE option for a query returning data from a text, ntext, or image type. The default setting is 4,096 (4 KB).
@@VERSION	nvarchar	A text string with detailed information about the current version of SQL Server. This includes the major version, build number, service pack, and copyright information.

Cursor

Variable	Return Type	Description
@@CURSOR_ROWS	int	The row count for the currently open cursor. Used for explicit cursor processing following an OPEN command. If an asynchronous cursor is opened, the row count will not be known, and this variable returns -1.
@@FETCH_STATUS	int	Used as a flag to indicate whether the open cursor has navigated past the last row (EOF).
		Status values include: 0 = Normal fetch operation -1 = Fetch past last row or unsuccessful -2 = Fetched row has been removed.

System

Variable	Return Type	Description
@@ERROR	int	Value of the most recent error within the current user session. Error numbers (from the sysmessages table) are used to determine the status of an error condition.
@@IDENTITY	numeric	Value of the most recently generated identity value. This is typically the result of an identity column insert.
@@ROWCOUNT	int	Number of rows affected by, or returned by, the last operation
@@TRANCOUNT	int	Number of currently active transactions. Used to determine the number of nested transactions. The maximum number of nested transactions is 11.

System Statistical

Variable	Return Type	Description
@@CONNECTIONS	int	The total connects that have been opened or attempted since the SQL Server service was last started
@@CPU_BUSY	int	The total time in milliseconds that the server has not been idle since the SQL Server service was last started
@@IDLE	int	The total time in milliseconds that the server has been idle since the SQL Server service was last started

Variable	Return Type	Description
@@IO_BUSY	int	The total time in milliseconds that the server has performed physical disk I/O operations since the SQL Server service was last started
@@PACK_RECEIVED	int	The total number of network packets received by the server since the SQL Server service was last started
@@PACK_SENT	int	The total number of network packets sent by the server since the SQL Server service was last started
@@PACKET_ERRORS	int	The total number of network packet errors that have occurred since the SQL Server service was last started
@@TIMETICKS	int	The number of milliseconds per CPU tick. Each tick takes 1/32 of a second.
@@TOTAL_ERRORS	int	The total number of disk Read/Write errors that have occurred, while performing physical disk I/O, since the SQL Server service was last started
@@TOTAL_READ	int	The total number of physical disk reads that have occurred since the SQL Server service was last started
@@TOTAL_WRITE	int	The total number of physical disk writes that have occurred since the SQL Server service was last started

System Functions

The system functions are organized into the following categories:

- ❑ Aggregation
- ❑ Checksum
- ❑ Conversion
- ❑ Cursor
- ❑ Date and Time
- ❑ Image/text
- ❑ Mathematical
- ❑ Metadata
- ❑ Ranking
- ❑ Security
- ❑ System
- ❑ System Statistics

Aggregation

Function	Return Type	Description
AVG()	(numeric — depends on input)	Calculates the arithmetic average for a range of column values. Internally, this function counts rows and calculates the sum for all non-null values in the column and then divides the sum by the count. Returns the same numeric data type as the column.
COUNT()	int	Counts all non-null values for a column. The row count is returned using COUNT(*) regardless of null values.
COUNT_BIG()	bigint	Same as COUNT() but returns a bigint type rather than an int type.
GROUPING()	int	Used in conjunction with ROLLUP and CUBE operations in a GROUP BY query. This function returns 0 to indicate that it is on a detail row and 1 to indicate a summary row.
MAX()	(numeric or date — depends on input)	Returns the largest value in a range of column values.
MIN()	(numeric or date — depends on input)	Returns the smallest value in a range of column values.
STDEV()	float	Calculates the standard deviation for a range of non-null column values.
STDEVP()	float	Calculates the standard deviation over a population for a range of non-null column values.
SUM()	(numeric — depends on input)	Calculates the arithmetic sum for a range of non-null column values. If all values are NULL, returns NULL.
VAR()	float	Calculates the statistical variance for a range of non-null column values. If all values are NULL, returns NULL.
VARP()	float	Calculates the statistical variance over a population for a range of non-null column values. If all values are NULL, returns NULL.

Checksum

Function	Return Type	Description
CHECKSUM()	int	Calculates a checksum value for a row or range of column values. This function accepts a single column name, a comma-delimited list of columns, or * to use the entire row. Accepts columns of all types except text, ntext, image, cursor, and sql_variant. The returned value itself is meaningless but will consistently yield the same result for a column or row unless a value changes. String comparisons are case-insensitive.
BINARY_CHECKSUM()	int	Calculates a checksum value for a row or range of column values. This function accepts a single column name, a comma-delimited list of columns, or * to use the entire row. Accepts columns of all types except text, ntext, image, cursor, and sql_variant. The returned value itself is meaningless but will consistently yield the same result for a column or row unless a value changes. String comparisons are case-sensitive.
CHECKSUM_AGG()	int	Calculates a single checksum value for a range of int type column values. When applied to the result of the CHECKSUM() or BINARY_CHECKSUM() functions, returns a scalar (single value) checksum value for the entire range of values. Can be used to detect value changes over a table or range of column values.

Conversion

Function	Return Type	Description
CAST()	Returns a specified type	Converts a value to a specified data type. CAST(*the_value* AS *the_type*)
CONVERT()	Returns a specified type	Converts (and optionally formats) a value to a specified data type. Formatting can be applied to numeric and date types. CONVERT(*the_type, the_value*) or CONVERT(*the_type, the_value, format_number*)

Cryptographic

Function	Return Type	Description
AsymKey_ID()	int	Returns the ID of an asymmetric key.
Cert_ID	int	Returns the ID of a certificate.
CertProperty()	sql_variant	Returns the value of a specified certificate property.
DecryptByAsmKey()	varbinary	Decrypts data with an asymmetric key.
DecryptByCert()	varbinary	Decrypts data with the private key of a certificate.
DecryptByKey()	varbinary	Decrypts data by using a symmetric key.
DecryptByKeyAutoCert()	varbinary	Decrypts by using a symmetric key that is automatically decrypted with a certificate.
DecryptByPassPrase()	varbinary	Decrypts data that was encrypted with a passphrase.
EncryptByAsmKey()	varbinary	Encrypts data with an asymmetric key.
EncryptByCert()	varbinary	Encrypts data with the public key of a certificate.
EncryptByKey()	varbinary	Encrypts a string of text using a unique identifier key.
EncryptByPassPhrase()	varbinary	Encrypts a string of text using a passphrase.
Key_GUID()	uniqueidentifier	Returns the global unique identifier of a named encryption key.
Key_ID()	int	Returns the integer ID of a named symmetric key.
SignByAsymKey()	varbinary	Applies a digital signature generated by an asymmetrical key to a block of plaintext.
SignByCert()	varbinary	Applies a digital signature generated by a certificate key to a block of plaintext.
VerifySignedByAsmKey()	int	Verifies that text signed by an asymmetrical key has not been altered.
VerifySignedByCert()	int	Verifies that text signed by a certificate has not been altered.

Cursor

Function	Return Type	Description
CURSOR_STATUS()	smallint	Returns the status of a previously opened cursor. 1 = Open and populated 0 = Contains no records −1 = Closed −2 = No cursor or deallocated −3 = Doesn't exist

Date and Time

Function	Return Type	Description
CURRENT_TIMESTAMP()	datetime	Returns the current date and time and is synonymous with the GETDATE() function. It exists for ANSI-SQL compliance.
DATEADD()	datetime or smalldatetime (depending on input type)	Returns a date value (datetime or smalldatetime) from a date value added by *X* number of date interval units. Units may be Year, Quarter, Month, DayOfYear, Day, Hour, Minute, Second, or Millisecond.
DATEDIFF()	int	Returns an integer representing the difference between two date values (datetime or smalldatetime) in specified date interval units. Units may be Year, Quarter, Month, DayOfYear, Day, Hour, Minute, Second, or Millisecond.
DATENAME()	nvarchar	Similar to DATEPART(). Returns a character string representing the specified datepart for a date value. The datepart parameter is the same as the DATEDIFF() interval and includes Year, Quarter, Month, DayOfYear, Day, Hour, Minute, Second, or Millisecond.

(continued)

Function	Return Type	Description
DATEPART()	int	Similar to DATENAME(). However, it returns the integer value representing the specified datepart for a date value. The datepart parameter is the same as the DATEDIFF() interval and includes Year, Quarter, Month, DayOfYear, Day, Hour, Minute, Second, or Millisecond.
DAY()	int	Returns the day date part for a date as an integer.
GETDATE()	datetime	Returns the current date and time value.
GETUTCDATE()	datetime	Returns the current date and time value, for the Universal Time Zone (UTC), based on the server's time zone settings. UTC is the same as Greenwich Mean Time (GMT).
ISDATE()	int	Returns a flag to indicate whether a specified value is, or is capable of being converted to, a date value.
MONTH()	int	Returns the month part for a date as an integer.
SWITCHOFFSET	datetimeoffset (Date)	Returns and/or modifies the UTC offset for a time zone.
SYSDATETIME	datetime	Returns the current database system time stamp.
SYSDATETIMEOFFSET	datetimeoffset (Date)	Returns the current database time offset.
SYSUTCDATETIME	datetime2	Returns the current database system UTC time stamp.
TODATETIMEOFFSET	datetimeoffset	Modifies the time zone offset for a date and time.
YEAR()	int	Returns the year part for a date as an integer.

Image/Text

Function	Return Type	Description
PATINDEX()	bigint or int (depending on input type)	Returns the character index (first position) for a character string pattern occurring within another character string. Similar to CHARINDEX() but supports wildcards. Returns bigint for varchar(max) and nvarchar(max) type strings; otherwise, returns int.
TEXTPTR()	varbinary	Returns a varbinary text pointer handle to be used with the READTEXT(), WRITETEXT(), and UPDATETEXT() functions. Used for performing special operations on text, ntext, and image type column data.
TEXTVALID()	int	Verifies a varbinary text pointer value, obtained from the TEXTPTR() function.

Error Handling

Function	Return Type	Description
ERROR_LINE	int	Returns the line number of the last error when called in a CATCH block.
ERROR_MESSAGE	nvarchar	Returns the full error text for the last error when called in a CATCH block.
ERROR_NUMBER	int	Returns the system- or user-defined error number for the last error when called in a CATCH block.
ERROR_PROCEDURE	nvarchar	Returns the name of the stored procedure or function that raised the last error when called in a CATCH block.
ERROR_SEVERITY	int	Returns the system- or user-defined severity value for the last error when called in a CATCH block.
ERROR_STATE	int	Returns the state number for the last error when called in a CATCH block.
XACT_STATE()	smallint	Tests the commitability of the current transaction within a CATCH block. Returns –1 if the transaction is uncommittable.

Appendix C: T-SQL System Variables and Functions

Mathematical

Function	Return Type	Description
ABS()	(numeric — same type as input)	Returns the absolute value for a numeric value.
ACOS()	float	Computes the arccosine (an angle) in radians.
ASIN()	float	Computes the arcsine (an angle) in radians.
ATAN()	float	Computes the arctangent (an angle) in radians.
ATN2()	float	Computes the arctangent of two values in radians.
CEILING()	(numeric — same type as input)	Returns the smallest integer value that is greater than or equal to a number.
COS()	float	Computes the cosine of an angle in radians.
COT()	float	Computes the cotangent of an angle in radians.
DEGREES()	(numeric — same type as input)	Converts an angle from radians to degrees.
EXP()	float	Returns the natural logarithm raised to a specified exponent. The result is in exponential form.
FLOOR()	(numeric — same type as input)	Returns the largest integer value that is less than or equal to a number.
LOG()	float	Calculates the natural logarithm of a number using base-2 (binary) numbering.
LOG10()	float	Calculates the natural logarithm of a number using base-10 numbering.
PI()	float	Returns the value for PI.
POWER()	float	Raises a value to a specified exponent as FLOAT(*the_value, the_exponent*).
RADIANS()	(numeric — same type as input)	Converts an angle from degrees to radians.
RAND()	float	Returns a fractional number based on a randomizing algorithm. Accepts an optional seed value.
ROUND()	(numeric — same type as input)	Rounds a fractional value to a specified precision.
SIGN()	float	Returns -1 or 1 depending on whether a single argument value is negative or positive.
SIN()	float	Computes the sine of an angle in radians.
SQRT()	float	Returns the square root of a value.
SQUARE()	float	Returns the square (n^2) of a value.
TAN()	float	Computes the tangent of an angle in radians.

Metadata

Function	Return Type	Description
ASSEMBLYPROPERTY()	sql_variant	Returns descriptive information about a specified assembly property.
COL_LENGTH()	int	Returns the length of a column from the column name.
COL_NAME()	sysname (nvarchar)	Returns the name of a column from the object ID.
COLUMNPROPERTY()	int	Returns a flag to indicate the state of a column property.
DATABASEPROPERTY()	int	This function is maintained for backward compatibility with older SWL Server versions. Returns a flag to indicate the state of a database property.
DATABASEPROPERTYEX()	sqlvariant	Returns a numeric flag or string to indicate the state of a database property.
DB_ID()	smallint	Returns the database ID from the database name.
DB_NAME()	nvarchar	Returns the database name from the database ID.
FILE_ID()	smallint	Returns the file ID from the filename.
FILEGROUP_ID()	int	Returns the ID for a file group name.
FILEGROUP_NAME()	nvarchar(128)	Returns the file group name for a file group ID.
FILEGROUPPROPERTY()	int	Returns a specified file group property value for a file group name and property name.
FILEPROPERTY()	int	Returns a specified file property value for a filename and property name.
FILE_NAME()	nvarchar	Returns the filename from the file ID.
fn_listextendedproperty()	table	Returns a table object populated with extended property names and their settings.
FULLTEXTCATALOGPROPERTY()	int	Returns a flag to indicate the state of a full-text catalog property.
FULLTEXTSERVICEPROPERTY()	int	Returns a flag to indicate the state of a full-text service property.
INDEX_COL()	nvarchar	Returns the name of a column contained in a specified index, by table, index, and column ID.

(continued)

Function	Return Type	Description
INDEXKEY_PROPERTY()	int	Returns a flag to indicate the state of an index key property.
INDEXPROPERTY()	int	Returns a flag indicating the state of an index property.
OBJECT_ID()	int	Returns an object ID from the object name.
OBJECT_NAME()	nchar	Returns an object name from the object ID.
OBJECTPROPERTY()	int	Returns property information from several different types of objects. It is advisable to use a function designed to query specific object types, if possible. Returns a flag indicating the state of an object property.
OBJECTPROPERTYEX()	sql_variant	Similar to OBJECTPROPERTY() but returns descriptive property values.
SCHEMA_ID()	int	Returns the schema ID for a schema name.
SCHEMA_NAME()	sysname (nvarchar)	Returns the schema name for a schema ID.
SQL_VARIANT_PROPERTY()	sql_variant	Returns the base data type and other information about a sql_variant value.
TYPE_ID()	int	Returns the ID for a specified data type name.
TYPE_NAME()	sysname	Returns the data type name of a specified type ID.
TYPEPROPERTY()	int	Returns information about data type properties.

Ranking

Function	Return Type	Description
DENSE_RANK()	bigint	Returns a running incremental value based on an ORDER BY clause passed into the function. Doesn't preserve the ordinal position of the row in the list if there are ties.
NTILE(n)	bigint	Returns an evenly distributed ranking value, dividing the result into a finite number of ranked groups.
RANK()	bigint	Returns a running incremental value based on an ORDER BY clause passed into the function. Preserves the ordinal position of the row in the list with duplicate values for ties followed by subsequent skips.
ROW_NUMBER()	bigint	Returns a running incremental value based on an ORDER BY clause passed into the function.

Rowset

Function	Return Type	Description
CONTAINSTABLE()	table	Returns a table object that can be used in a join operation. Each row in this table contains a Key column value, which is the primary key value for qualifying rows of the queried table. This key value is useful for joining the resulting table object back to the physical table to obtain column values. Two arguments are passed: the name of the indexed table and a search string containing words to be matched.
FREETEXTTABLE()	table	Similar to CONTAINSTABLE(), but the search condition can match inexact phrasing rather than exact words.
OPENDATASOURCE()	table	Used to open an ad hoc connection to a remote OLE DB data source and return a table reference to a database object. Arguments include the name of a registered OLE DB provider, a connection string and the four-part name of a database object.
OPENQUERY()	table	Used to reference an existing linked server and return the results of a query. Arguments include the name of the linked server and a query string.
OPENROWSET()	table	Used to connect to a remote OLE DB data source and return the results of a query. Arguments include the name of a registered OLE DB provider, a connection string, and a query string.
OPENXML()	table	Transforms an XML document string into a rowset table. The table structure conforms to the standard "edge" table format. The sp_xml_preparedocument system stored procedure must be called first to obtain a document handle ID, which is then passed to this function, along with the document text.

Security

Function	Return Type	Description
fn_trace_geteventinfo()	table	Returns a table type populated with event information for a specified trace ID.
fn_trace_getfilterinfo()	table	Returns a table type populated with information about filters applied to a trace, for a specified trace ID.
fn_trace_getinfo()	table	Returns a table type populated with trace information for a specified trace ID.

(continued)

Function	Return Type	Description
fn_trace_gettable()	table	Returns a table type populated with file information for a specified trace ID.
HAS_DBACCESS()	int	Returns a flag indicating whether the current user has access to a specified database.
IS_MEMBER()	int	Returns a flag indicating whether the current user is a member of a Windows group or SQL Server role.
IS_SRVROLEMEMBER()	int	Returns a flag indicating whether the current user is a member of a database server role.
ORIGINAL_LOGIN()	sysname (varchar)	Returns the first user or login name for the first system login in the current session context.
SUSER_SID()	varbinary	Returns the security ID for a specified username.
SUSER_SNAME()	nvarchar	Returns the username for a specified security ID.
USER_ID()	int	Returns a username for a specified user ID.
fn_trace_geteventinfo()	table	Returns a table type populated with event information for a specified trace ID.

String Manipulation

Function	Return Type	Description
ASCII()	int	Returns the numeric ASCII character value for a standard character.
CHAR()	char	Returns the ASCII character for a numeric ASCII character value.
CHARINDEX()	int	Similar to PATINDEX(), returns the index (character position) of the first occurrence of a character string within another character string.
DIFFERENCE()	int	Returns the numeric difference between two character strings based on the consensus Soundex values.
LEFT()	varchar or nvarchar	Returns the left-most X characters from a character string.
LEN()	int	Returns the length of a character string.
LOWER()	varchar or nvarchar	Converts a character string to all lowercase characters.
LTRIM()	varchar or nvarchar	Removes leading spaces from the left side of a character string.

Function	Return Type	Description
NCHAR()	nchar	Like the CHAR() function, returns the Unicode character for a numeric character value.
PATINDEX()	int or bigint	Returns the index (first character position) for the first occurrence of characters matching a specified pattern within another character string. Wildcard characters may be used.
QUOTENAME()	nvarchar	Returns a character string with square brackets around the input value. Used with SQL Server object names so they can be passed into an expression.
REPLACE()	varchar or nvarchar	Returns a character string with all occurrences of one character or substring replaced with another character or substring.
REPLICATE()	varchar or nvarchar	Returns a character string consisting of a specified number of repeated characters.
REVERSE()	varchar or nvarchar	Returns a character string with all characters in reverse order.
RIGHT()	varchar or nvarchar	Returns a specific number of characters from the rightmost side of a character string.
RTRIM()	varchar or nvarchar	Removes trailing spaces from the right side of a character string.
SOUNDEX()	varchar	Returns a four-character alphanumeric string representing the approximate phonetic value of a word, based on the U.S. Census Soundex algorithm.
SPACE()	char	Returns a character string consisting of a specified number of spaces.
STR()	char	Returns a character string value that represents a converted numeric data type. Three arguments include the value, the overall length, and the number of decimal positions.
STUFF()	(character or binary types — depending on input)	Returns a character string with one string placed into another string at a given position and for a specified length.
SUBSTRING()	(character or binary types — depending on input)	Returns a portion of a character string from a specified position and for a specified length.
UNICODE()	int	Returns the numeric Unicode character value for a specified character.
UPPER()	varchar or nvarchar	Converts a character string to all uppercase characters.

System

Function	Return Type	Description
APP_NAME()	nvarchar	Each session is associated with an application name, passed to the database server by explicit program code or by the driver or data provider.
COALESCE()	(same type as input)	Returns the first non-null value from a comma-delimited list of expressions.
COLLATIONPROPERTY()	sql_variant	Returns the value of a specific property for a specified collation. Properties include CodePage, LCID, and ComparisonStyle.
COLUMNS_UPDATED	varbinary	Used only within an Insert or Update trigger. Returns a bitmap of modified column flags for the current table. Bytes are left-to-right with the bits in each byte ordered right-to-left, representing the state (0 = unmodified, 1 = modified) of each column.
CURRENT_USER()	sysname (varchar)	Returns the name of the current user and is synonymous with the USER_NAME() function.
DATALENGTH()	int	Returns the number of bytes used to store or handle a value. For ANSI string types, this will return the same value as the LEN() function, but for other data types, the value may be different.
fn_Get_SQL()	table	Returns a table type populated with the full text of a query based on a process handle. This value is stored in the sysprocesses table referencing an SPID. This function was introduced with SQL Server 2000 SP3.
fn_HelpCollations()	table	Returns a table type populated with a list of collations supported by the current version of SQL Server.
fn_ServerSharedDrives()	table	Returns a table type populated with a list of drives shared by the server.
fn_VirtualFileStats()	table	Returns a table type populated with I/O statistics for database files, including log files.
FORMATMESSAGE()	nvarchar	Returns an error message from the sysmessages table for a specified message number and comma-delimited list of parameters.
GETANSINULL()	int	Returns the nullability setting for the database, according to the ANSI_NULL_DFLT_ON and ANSI_NULL_DFLT_OFF database settings.

Function	Return Type	Description
HOST_ID()	char	Returns the workstation ID for the current session.
HOST_NAME()	nchar	Returns the workstation name for the current session.
IDENT_CURRENT()	sql_variant	Returns the last identity value generated for a specified table regardless of the session and scope.
IDENT_INCR()	numeric	Returns the increment value specified in the creation of the last identity column.
IDENT_SEED()	numeric	Returns the seed value specified in the creation of the last identity column.
IDENTITY()	(same as input)	Used in a SELECT ... INTO statement to insert an explicitly generated identity value into a column.
ISNULL()	(same as input)	Determines whether a specified value is null and then returns a provided replacement value.
ISNUMERIC()	int	Returns a flag to indicate whether a specified value is, or is capable of being converted to, a numeric value.
NEWID()	uniqueidentifier	Returns a newly generated uniqueidentifier type value. This is a 128-bit integer, globally unique value, usually expressed as an alphanumeric hexadecimal representation (such as 89DE6247-C2E2-42DB-8CE8-A787E505D7EA). This type is often used for primary key values in replicated and semiconnected systems.
NULLIF()	(same as input)	Returns a NULL value when two specified arguments have equivalent values.
PARSENAME()	nchar	Returns a specific part of a four-part object name.
ROWCOUNT_BIG()	bigint	Like the @@ROWCOUNT variable, returns the number of rows either returned by or modified by the last statement. Returns a bigint type.
SCOPE_IDENTITY()	sql_variant	Like the @@IDENTITY variable, returns the last Identity value generated but is limited to the current session and scope (stored procedure, batch, or module).

(continued)

Function	Return Type	Description
SERVERPROPERTY()	sql_variant	Returns a flag indicating the state of a server property. Properties include Collation, Edition, Engine Edition, InstanceName, IsClustered, IsFullTextInstalled, IsIntegratedSecurityOnly, IsSingleUser, IsSyncWithBackup, LicenseType, MachineName, NumLicenses, ProcessID, ProductLevel, ProductVersion, and ServerName.
SESSION_USER	nchar	Returns the current username. The function is called without parentheses.
SESSIONPROPERTY()	sql_variant	Returns a flag indicating the state of a session property. Properties include ANSI_NULLS, ANSI_PADDING, ANSI_WARNINGS, ARITHABORT, CONCAT_NULL_YIELDS_NULL, NUMERIC_ROUNDABORT, and QUOTED_IDENTIFIER.
STATS_DATE()	datetime	Returns the date that statistics for a specified index were last updated.
SYSTEM_USER	nvarchar	Returns the current username. The function is called without parentheses.
USER_NAME()	nvarchar	Returns the username for a specified user ID.

System Statistical

Function	Return Type	Description
sys.dm_io_virtual_file_stats()	table	Returns a table type populated with I/O statistics for database files, including log files.
sys.dm_db_index_operational_stats()	table	Returns current I/O, locking, latching, and access method activity for each table or index in the database.
sys.dm_db_index_physical_stats()	table	Returns size and fragmentation information for the data and indexes of a specified table or view.
sys.dm_db_index_usage_stats()	rowset	Returns counts of different types of index operations and the time each type of operation was last performed.
sys.dm_db_missing_index_columns()	table	Returns information about database table columns that are missing an index.

MDX Reference

This Appendix provides information on those aspects of the SQL Server 2008 implementation of the Multidimensional Expressions (MDX) language relevant to Reporting Services authors. The material provided here is intended to provide a quick reference and not to be fully instructional. Nor is it intended to provide an overview of SQL Server Analysis Services. For a complete reference on these topics, please refer to *Professional Microsoft SQL Server 2008 Analysis Services with MDX* (Wrox).

Object Identifiers

All objects within Analysis Services — cubes, cube dimensions, attributes hierarchies, user-hierarchies, hierarchy levels, members, and so on — are referenced through an object identifier. An *object identifier* is a value containing between 1 and 100 characters. The first character of the object identifier must be a letter or an underscore. Subsequent characters can be letters, decimal numbers, or underscores. Object identifiers cannot contain spaces or special characters and cannot be a reserved keyword, as identified in the next section of this Appendix. Identifiers adhering to these rules are known as *regular identifiers*.

An object identifier violating one or more of these rules is known as a *delimited identifier*. A delimited identifier must be encapsulated by square brackets — known as the object's delimiters — in order for the identifier to be correctly interpreted. Although required for delimited identifiers, square brackets can also be used with regular identifiers.

Reserved Keywords

The following table provides a complete listing of reserved keywords within SQL Server 2008 Analysis Services MDX:

ABSOLUTE	CALCULATIONPASSVALUE	DESC
ACTIONPARAMETERSET	CALCULATIONS	DESCENDANTS
ADDCALCULATEDMEMBERS	CALL	DESCRIPTION
AFTER	CELL	DIMENSION
AGGREGATE	CELLFORMULASETLIST	DIMENSIONS
ALL	CHAPTERS	DISTINCT
ALLMEMBERS	CHILDREN	DISTINCTCOUNT
ANCESTOR	CLEAR	DRILLDOWNLEVEL
ANCESTORS	CLOSINGPERIOD	DRILLDOWNLEVELBOTTOM
AND	COALESCEEMPTY	DRILLDOWNLEVELTOP
AS	COLUMN	DRILLDOWNMEMBER
ASC	COLUMNS	DRILLDOWNMEMBERBOTTOM
ASCENDANTS	CORRELATION	DRILLDOWNMEMBERTOP
AVERAGE	COUNT	DRILLUPLEVEL
AXIS	COUSIN	DRILLUPMEMBER
BASC	COVARIANCE	DROP
BDESC	COVARIANCEN	EMPTY
BEFORE	CREATE	END
BEFORE_AND_AFTER	CREATEPROPERTYSET	ERROR
BOTTOMCOUNT	CREATEVIRTUALDIMENSION	EXCEPT
BOTTOMPERCENT	CROSSJOIN	EXCLUDEEMPTY
BOTTOMSUM	CUBE	EXTRACT
BY	CURRENT	FALSE
CACHE	CURRENTCUBE	FILTER
CALCULATE	CURRENTMEMBER	FIRSTCHILD
CALCULATION	DEFAULTMEMBER	FIRSTSIBLING
CALCULATIONCURRENTPASS	DEFAULT_MEMBER	FOR

FREEZE	LINKMEMBER	PARENT
FROM	LINREGINTERCEPT	PASS
GENERATE	LINREGPOINT	PERIODSTODATE
GLOBAL	LINREGR2	POST
GROUP	LINREGSLOPE	PREDICT
GROUPING	LINREGVARIANCE	PREVMEMBER
HEAD	LOOKUPCUBE	PROPERTIES
HIDDEN	MAX	PROPERTY
HIERARCHIZE	MEASURE	QTD
HIERARCHY	MEDIAN	RANK
IGNORE	MEMBER	RECURSIVE
IIF	MEMBERS	RELATIVE
INCLUDEEMPTY	MEMBERTOSTR	ROLLUPCHILDREN
INDEX	MIN	ROOT
INTERSECT	MTD	ROWS
IS	NAME	SCOPE
ISANCESTOR	NAMETOSET	SECTIONS
ISEMPTY	NEST	SELECT
ISGENERATION	NEXTMEMBER	SELF
ISLEAF	NON	SELF_AND_AFTER
ISSIBLING	NONEMPTYCROSSJOIN	SELF_AND_BEFORE
ITEM	NOT_RELATED_TO_FACTS	SELF_BEFORE_AFTER
LAG	NO_ALLOCATION	SESSION
LASTCHILD	NO_PROPERTIES	SET
LASTPERIODS	NULL	SETTOARRAY
LASTSIBLING	ON	SETTOSTR
LEAD	OPENINGPERIOD	SORT
LEAVES	OR	STDDEV
LEVEL	PAGES	STDDEVP
LEVELS	PARALLELPERIOD	STDEV

(continued)

STDEVP	TOPSUM	VALIDMEASURE
STORAGE	TOTALS	VALUE
STRIPCALCULATEDMEMBERS	TREE	VAR
STRTOMEMBER	TRUE	VARIANCE
STRTOSET	TUPLETOSTR	VARIANCEP
STRTOTUPLE	TYPE	VARP
STRTOVAL	UNION	VISUAL
STRTOVALUE	UNIQUE	VISUALTOTALS
SUBSET	UNIQUENAME	WHERE
SUM	UPDATE	WITH
TAIL	USE	WTD
THIS	USERNAME	XOR
TOGGLEDRILLSTATE	USE_EQUAL_ALLOCATION	YTD
TOPCOUNT	USE_WEIGHTED_ALLOCATION	
TOPPERCENT	USE_WEIGHTED_INCREMENT	

Member References

A *member* is a value within a hierarchy. A member is partially referenced by the dimension, hierarchy, and level to which it belongs. Each of these components must adhere to the rules for object identifiers, as described above. Each part of the reference is separated from the others by a period.

The member's key or name value serves as the final part of the member reference. Member names and keys must adhere to the rules for object identifiers. Member keys may be multi-part with each part preceded by the ampersand (&) character.

The following are a few examples of member references in the forms described. Note the use of square brackets for both regular and delimited identifiers. This is done to standardize the form of the reference.

```
[Date].[Calendar].[Month].[January 2004]
[Date].[Calendar].[Month].&[2004].&[01]
```

Alternatively, you can reference a member according to its lineage within a hierarchy. In this form, a member reference is provided for a member on a higher level in a hierarchy. To this reference are appended the period-delimited keys or names of descendants forming the lineage of the initial member reference to the member of interest. The final name or key is the member of interest.

The following presents the members in the previous example in this form. Note that the `[Date].[Calendar]` hierarchy consists of an `(All)` level followed by `[Calendar Year]`, `[Calendar Semester]`, `[Calendar Quarter].[Month]` levels. (The hierarchy contains a `[Date]` level below this, but that is not of interest in these examples.)

```
[Date].[Calendar].[Calendar Year].[CY 2004].[H1 CY 2004].[Q1 CY 2004].[January 2004]
[Date].[Calendar].[Calendar Year].&[2004].&[2004]&[1].&[2004]&[1].&[2004]&[1]
```

If unambiguous, the `[Dimension].[Hierarchy].[Level]` part of a member reference can be abbreviated to any one of the following forms:

```
[Dimension].[Hierarchy]
[Dimension].[Level]
[Hierarchy].[Level]
[Dimension]
```

The entire `[Dimension].[Hierarchy].[Level]` part of the reference can also be omitted. The following examples illustrate these abbreviated forms:

```
[Date].[Calendar].[January 2004]
[Date].[Month].[January 2004]
[Date].[January 2004]
[Month].[January 2004]
[January 2004]
```

Care should be taken when using abbreviated member references. If a reference could represent more than one member within a cube, Analysis Services returns the first one encountered. Although data is returned, you might not receive the data expected.

Sets

Sets represent zero, one, or more members from an attribute or user hierarchy. Sets may be defined through the use of MDX functions, the assembly of members in a comma-delimited list, or a named set.

Within MDX statements, sets are encapsulated by curly braces. The curly braces are optional if the set is not defined as a comma-delimited list of more than one member reference.

The following are examples of valid single-member sets. These sets are equivalent to each other.

```
{[Date].[Calendar].[Month].[January 2004]}
[Date].[Calendar].[Month].[January 2004]
```

The following are examples of valid multi-member sets. The last two of these make use of the `Children` MDX function. All three sets are equivalent to each other.

```
{[Date].[Calendar].[Month].[January 2004], [Date].[Calendar].[Month].[February
2004], [Date].[Calendar].[Month].[March 2004]}
{[Date].[Calendar].[Q1 CY 2004].Children}
[Date].[Calendar].[Q1 CY 2004].Children
```

Sets may be combined to form multi-part sets through a cross-join operation. This is done by first defining basic sets and then combining these sets using the CrossJoin MDX function. You can use the asterisk character (*) as a shorthand notation for the CrossJoin function. The following illustrates the construction of identical multi-part sets using these cross-join methods:

```
CrossJoin({[Date].[Calendar].[Q1 CY 2004].Children},
{[Product].[Categories].[Categories].Members})
{[Date].[Calendar].[Q1 CY 2004].Children} *
{[Product].[Categories].[Categories].Members}
```

Multi-part sets can also be constructed through a delimited list of tuples, as illustrated in the following example:

```
{([Date].[Calendar].[Month].[January 2004],[Product].[Category].[Bikes]),
([Date].[Calendar].[Month].[February 2004],[Product].[Category].[Components]),
([Date].[Calendar].[Month].[March 2004],[Product].[Category].[Accessories])}
```

Tuples

All points within a cube are identified by a coordinate value. The full coordinate value for any point identifies a member from each attribute hierarchy within the cube. This coordinate is known as the *full tuple* (or *complete tuple*) for that point. Partial tuples specify a member value for one or more attributes within the coordinate system. Any attributes not explicitly identified within a partial tuple are supplied by Analysis Services using the following rules:

❑   If the implicitly referenced dimension has a default member, the default member is added to the tuple.

❑   If the implicitly referenced dimension has no default member, the (All) member of the default hierarchy is used.

❑   If the implicitly referenced dimension has no default member, and the default hierarchy has no (All) member, the first member of the top-most level of the default hierarchy is used.

Tuples are encapsulated by parentheses. Parentheses are optional if only a single member reference is used. The following are valid tuple references:

```
([Date].[Calendar].[Month].[January 2004])
[Date].[Calendar].[Month].[January 2004]
([Date].[Calendar].[Month].[January 2004], [Date].[Date].[Date].[January 1, 2004])
([Date].[Calendar].[Month].[January 2004], [Date].[Date].[Date].[January 1, 2004],
[Product].[Category].[Category].[Bikes])
```

The SELECT Statement

The MDX SELECT statement is used to retrieve data from a cube. The statement specifies sets of members along a number of axes. The intersection of members along these axes, coupled with members identified in the statement's optional WHERE clause, form a collection of tuples that identify points within a specified cube or subcube as described in the FROM clause. The values associated with these points, referred to as *cells*, are returned as a *cellset*. Although variations from what is described here exist, this is the basic form of the MDX SELECT statement. The following example illustrates this form:

```
SELECT
    {[Measures].[Sales Amount], [Measures].[Tax Amount]} ON COLUMNS,
    {[Date].[Calendar].[Q1 CY 2004].Children} ON ROWS
FROM [Adventure Works]
WHERE ([Product].[Category].[Category].[Bikes])
```

In addition to the axis definitions and WHERE and FROM clauses, the MDX SELECT statement supports a WITH clause that can be used to specify query-scoped calculated members and named sets. Reporting Services also provides support for parameters within the MDX SELECT statement, although these are not formally part of the statement.

Axis Definitions

The MDX SELECT statement supports the identification of between 0 and 128 axes. Each axis is identified by the formal name of AXIS(*n*), where *n* is the numeric identifier of the axis, the first of which is 0. The axis name can be shortened to be just the number of the axis, and no axis can be skipped. The first five axes, the most frequently used, also support aliases, as identified in the following table:

Formal Name	Shortened Name	Alias
AXIS(0)	0	COLUMNS
AXIS(1)	1	ROWS
AXIS(2)	2	PAGES
AXIS(3)	3	SECTIONS
AXIS(4)	4	CHAPTERS

Along each axis, a set is defined. The set may be singular or composed of multiple sets cross-joined to form a multi-part set. The set may also be the empty set specified by an open and then close curly brace, {}. No hierarchy may be used to supply members in sets along more than one axis.

Within the context of Reporting Services, the MDX SELECT statement defining the cells set to be returned to the report supports up to two axes. Typically, the COLUMNS axis is used to specify members of the Measures dimension, and cross-joined sets are not supported on this axis. These constraints are due to Reporting Services' limitations in converting cell sets into the data table structure it uses internally.

The WHERE Clause

The MDX SELECT statement supports an optional WHERE clause. The WHERE clause, also known as the *slicer*, is used to specify members not otherwise specified within the axis definitions. The members specified in the WHERE clause are incorporated into all tuples defining the cellset to be returned by the SELECT statement.

The WHERE clause typically consists of a single, partial tuple. The members identified within this tuple are from hierarchies not specified along the axis definitions.

Alternatively, the WHERE clause can be composed of a singular or multi-part set. The members of the various hierarchies are aggregated so that the WHERE clause continues to function as a tuple. This is not a common use of the WHERE clause.

The FROM Clause

The FROM clause defines the context within which the query is resolved. The context can be defined as a cube or as a nested MDX SELECT statement, also known as a *query-scoped subcube*, which limits the cube space within which a query is resolved.

The following rules govern the affect of query-scoped subcubes on cube space:

- ❏ If you include the (All) member of a hierarchy, you include every member of that hierarchy.
- ❏ If you include any member, you include that member's ascendants and descendants.
- ❏ If you include every member from a level, you include all members from the hierarchy. Members from other hierarchies will be excluded if those members do not exist with members from the level (e.g., an unbalanced hierarchy such as a city that does not contain customers).
- ❏ A subcube will always contain every (All) member from the cube.

The WITH Clause

The WITH clause is used within an MDX SELECT statement to define query-scoped calculated members and named sets. The WITH clause allows for the construction of one or more calculated members or named sets within a given query, and calculated members and named sets may reference each other. The order of the declaration of calculated members and named sets within a query is unimportant.

A calculated member is an expression providing instruction for the derivation of a member within a hierarchy. The basic form of a named member is as follows:

```
WITH MEMBER [Dimension].[Hierarchy].[Level].[Member] as
    <expression>
```

where *<expression>* is a valid MDX expression resolving to a single member or value. The expression defining the calculated member can be followed by a comma and the FORMAT keyword. The FORMAT keyword can be assigned one of the following named formats:

- ❏ Currency
- ❏ Percent
- ❏ Short Date
- ❏ Short Time
- ❏ Standard

Alternatively, the FORMAT keyword can be assigned an expression identifying a format. See the Analysis Services Books Online article "FORMAT_STRING Contents" for a complete listing of the rules for defining these expressions.

A named set is an expression evaluating to a set of members, stored or calculated. The basic form of a named set is as follows:

```
WITH SET [Set] as
    <expression>
```

where <expression> is a valid MDX expression resolving to a single- or multi-part set.

When more than one calculated member or named set is defined for a query, the WITH keyword precedes the first calculated member or named set only.

The following example illustrates a SELECT statement using the WITH clause:

```
WITH
    MEMBER [Measures].[Tax Percent] as
        ([Measures].[Tax Amount])/([Measures].[Sales Amount])
        ,FORMAT="Percent"
    SET [Periods Of Interest] as
        {[Date].[Calendar].[Q1 CY 2004].Children}
SELECT
    {
        [Measures].[Sales Amount],
        [Measures].[Tax Amount],
        [Measures].[Tax Percent]
    } ON COLUMNS,
    {[Periods of Interest]} ON ROWS
FROM [Adventure Works]
WHERE ([Product].[Category].[Category].[Bikes])
```

Parameters

The MDX SELECT statement provides support for parameters. However, Reporting Services is not capable of exploiting this syntax. Instead, it provides an alternate, substitution-based mechanism for incorporating parameters.

Reporting Services parameters within MDX SELECT statements are identified by variables preceded by the "at" character (@). At execution, the Reporting Services variable is replaced with a string representing the variable's value. This string is encapsulated by double quotes and is therefore interpreted as a string by Analysis Services. To convert the string value to a member, tuple, or set reference, the SELECT statement uses the STRTOMEMBER, STRTOTUPLE, or STRTOSET MDX function, respectively.

Reporting Services uses the CONSTRAINED keyword with each of these function calls. The CONTSTRAINED keyword prohibits the use of MDX functions within the string being evaluated. This is used to prevent injection attacks.

The following illustrates an MDX statement generated by Reporting Services containing a parameter:

```
SELECT
    NON EMPTY {[Measures].[Reseller Sales Amount]} ON COLUMNS
FROM (
        SELECT (STRTOSET(@DateCalendarYear, CONSTRAINED)) ON COLUMNS
        FROM [Adventure Works]
        )
WHERE (
    IIF(
        STRTOSET(@DateCalendarYear, CONSTRAINED).Count = 1,
        STRTOSET(@DateCalendarYear, CONSTRAINED),
        [Date].[Calendar Year].currentmember
        )
    )
CELL PROPERTIES VALUE, BACK_COLOR, FORE_COLOR, FORMATTED_VALUE,
    FORMAT_STRING, FONT_NAME, FONT_SIZE, FONT_FLAGS
```

MDX Functions and Keywords

The following tables provide information on the MDX functions and keywords available for use with Analysis Services through Reporting Services queries. Each table represents a particular category of function or keyword.

Keywords

Keyword	Description
EXISTING	Forces a specified set to be evaluated within the current context. By default, sets are evaluated within the context of the cube that contains the members of the set. The EXISTING keyword forces a specified set to be evaluated within the current context instead.
NON EMPTY	Eliminates any members along the axis for whom only empty cells are returned.

KPI Functions

Function	Syntax	Description
KPICURRENTTIMEMEMBER	KPICURRENTTIMEMEMBER («String Expression»)	Returns the current time member of the specified Key Performance Indicator (KPI).
KPIGOAL	KPIGOAL(«String Expression»)	Returns the member that calculates the value for the goal portion of the specified KPI.
KPISTATUS	KPISTATUS(«String Expression»)	Returns a normalized value that represents the status portion of the specified KPI.
KPITREND	KPITREND(«String Expression»)	Returns the normalized value that represents the trend portion of the specified KPI.
KPIVALUE	KPIVALUE(«String Expression»)	Returns the member that calculates the value of the specified KPI.
KPIWEIGHT	KPIWEIGHT(«String Expression»)	Returns the weight of the specified KPI.

Metadata Functions

Function	Syntax	Description
AXIS	AXIS(«Numeric Expression»)	Returns the set of tuples on a specified axis.
COUNT	«Tuple».COUNT	Returns the number of dimensions in a tuple.
DIMENSIONS.COUNT	DIMENSIONS.COUNT	Returns the number of hierarchies in a cube, including the [Measures].[Measures] hierarchy.
HIERARCHY	«Level».HIERARCHY	Returns the hierarchy that contains a specified member or level.
HIERARCHY	«Member».HIERARCHY	Returns the hierarchy that contains a specified member or level.
LEVEL	«Member».LEVEL	Returns the level of a member.

(continued)

Function	Syntax	Description
LEVELS	«Hierarchy».LEVELS(«Numeric Expression»)	Returns the level whose position in a dimension or hierarchy is specified by a numeric expression or whose name is specified by a string expression.
LEVELS.COUNT	«Hierarchy».LEVELS.COUNT	Returns the number of levels in a hierarchy.
NAME	«Member».NAME	Returns the name of a dimension, hierarchy, level, or member.
NAME	«Hierarchy».NAME	Returns the name of a dimension, hierarchy, level, or member.
NAME	«Level».NAME(Level)	Returns the name of a dimension, hierarchy, level, or member.
ORDINAL	«Level».ORDINAL	Returns the zero-based ordinal value associated with a level.
UNIQUENAME	«Hierarchy».UNIQUENAME	Returns the unique name of a specified dimension, hierarchy, level, or member.
UNIQUENAME	«Member».UNIQUENAME	Returns the unique name of a specified dimension, hierarchy, level, or member.
UNIQUENAME	«Level».UNIQUENAME	Returns the unique name of a specified dimension, hierarchy, level, or member.

Navigation Functions

Function	Syntax	Description
ANCESTOR	ANCESTOR(«Member», «Level»)	Returns the ancestor of a member at a specified level or distance.
ANCESTOR	ANCESTOR(«Member», «Distance»)	Returns the ancestor of a member at a specified level or distance.
ANCESTORS	ANCESTORS(«Member», «Distance»)	Returns a set of all ancestors of a member at a specified level or distance.
ANCESTORS	ANCESTORS(«Member», «Level»)	Returns a set of all ancestors of a member at a specified level or distance.
ASCENDANTS	ASCENDANTS(«Member»)	Returns the set of the ascendants of a specified member, including the member itself.
CHILDREN	«Member».CHILDREN	Returns the children of a specified member.
COUSIN	COUSIN(«Member1», «Member2»)	Returns the child member with the same relative position under a parent member as the specified child member.
CURRENT	«Set».CURRENT	Returns the current tuple from a set during iteration.
CURRENTMEMBER	«Hierarchy».CURRENTMEMBER	Returns the current member along a specified dimension or hierarchy during iteration.
CURRENTORDINAL	«Set».CURRENTORDINAL	Returns the current iteration number within a set during iteration.
DATAMEMBER	«Member».DATAMEMBER	Returns the system-generated data member that is associated with a nonleaf member of a dimension.
DEFAULTMEMBER	«Hierarchy».DEFAULTMEMBER	Returns the default member of a dimension or hierarchy.
FIRSTCHILD	«Member».FIRSTCHILD	Returns the first child of a member.
FIRSTSIBLING	«Member».FIRSTSIBLING	Returns the first child of the parent of a member.
ISANCESTOR	ISANCESTOR(«Member1», «Member2»)	Returns whether a specified member is an ancestor of another specified member.
ISGENERATOR	ISGENERATION(«Member», «Numeric Expression»)	Returns whether a specified member is in a specified generation.

(continued)

Function	Syntax	Description
ISLEAF	ISLEAF(«Member»)	Returns whether a specified member is a leaf member.
ISSIBLING	ISSIBLING(«Member1», «Member2»)	Returns whether a specified member is a sibling of another specified member.
LAG	«Member».LAG(«Numeric Expression»)	Returns the member that is a specified number of positions before a specified member along the member's dimension.
LASTCHILD	«Member».LASTCHILD	Returns the last child of a specified member.
LASTSIBLING	«Member».LASTSIBLING	Returns the last child of the parent of a specified member.
LEAD	«Member».LEAD(«Numeric Expression»)	Returns the member that is a specified number of positions following a specified member along the member's dimension.
LINKMEMBER	LINKMEMBER(«Member», «Hierarchy»)	Returns the member equivalent to a specified member in a specified hierarchy.
LOOKUPCUBE	LOOKUPCUBE(«Cube Name», «Numeric Expression»)	Returns the value of an MDX expression evaluated over another specified cube in the same database.
NEXTMEMBER	«Member».NEXTMEMBER	Returns the next member in the level that contains a specified member.
PARENT	«Member».PARENT	Returns the parent of a member.
PREVMEMBER	«Member».PREVMEMBER	Returns the previous member in the level that contains a specified member.
PROPERTIES	«Member».PROPERTIES(«String Expression»[, TYPED])	Returns a string, or a strongly typed value, that contains a member property value.
SIBLINGS	«Member».SIBLINGS	Returns the siblings of a specified member, including the member itself.
UNKNOWNMEMBER	UNKNOWNMEMBER	Returns the unknown member associated with a level or member.

Other Functions

Function	Syntax	Description
CALCULATIONCURRENTPASS	CALCULATIONCURRENTPASS	Returns the current calculation pass of a cube for the specified query context.
CALCULATIONPASSVALUE	CALCULATIONPASSVALUE(«Numeric Expression», «Pass Value»[[, «Access Flag»], ALL])	Returns the value of an MDX expression evaluated over the specified calculation pass of a cube.
CUSTOMDATA	CUSTOMDATA	Returns the value of the CustomData property.
ITEM	«Tuple».ITEM(«Numeric Expression»)	Returns a member from a specified tuple.
ITEM	«Set».ITEM(«String Expression»[, «String Expression»...] | «Index»)	Returns a tuple from a set.
PREDICT	PREDICT(«Mining Model Name», «Numeric Expression»)	Returns a value of a numeric expression evaluated over a data mining model.
SETTOARRAY	SETTOARRAY(«Set»[, «Set»...][, «Numeric Expression»])	Converts one or more sets to an array for use in a user-defined function.

Set Functions

Function	Syntax	Description
ADDCALCULATEDMEMBERS	ADDCALCULATEDMEMBERS («Set»)	Returns a set generated by adding calculated members to a specified set.
ALLMEMBERS	«Level».ALLMEMBERS	Returns a set that contains all members, including calculated members, of the specified dimension, hierarchy, or level.
ALLMEMBERS	«Hierarchy».ALLMEMBERS	Returns a set that contains all members, including calculated members, of the specified dimension, hierarchy, or level.
BOTTOMNCOUNT	BOTTOMCOUNT(«Set», «Count»[, «Numeric Expression»])	Sorts a set in ascending order, and returns the specified number of tuples with the lowest values.
BOTTOMPERCENT	BOTTOMPERCENT(«Set», «Percentage», «Numeric Expression»)	Sorts a set in ascending order, and returns a set of tuples with the lowest values whose cumulative total is equal to or less than a specified percentage.
BOTTOMSUM	BOTTOMSUM(«Set», «Value», «Numeric Expression»)	Sorts a set in ascending order, and returns a set of tuples with the lowest values whose total is equal to or less than a specified value.
CROSSJOIN	CROSSJOIN(«Set1», «Set2»)	Returns the cross-product of one or more sets.
DESCENDANTS	DESCENDANTS(«Member»[, «Level»[, «Desc_flags»]])	Returns the set of descendants of a member at a specified level or distance, optionally including or excluding descendants in other levels.
DESCENDANTS	DESCENDANTS(«Member», «Distance»[, «Desc_flags»])	Returns the set of descendants of a member at a specified level or distance, optionally including or excluding descendants in other levels.
DISTINCT	DISTINCT(«Set»)	Returns a set, removing duplicate tuples from a specified set.
EXCEPT	EXCEPT(«Set1», «Set2»[, ALL])	Finds the difference between two sets, optionally retaining duplicates.

Function	Syntax	Description
EXISTING	EXISTING	Forces a specified set to be evaluated within the current context. By default, sets are evaluated within the context of the cube that contains the members of the set. The EXISTING keyword forces a specified set to be evaluated within the current context instead.
EXISTS	EXISTS(«Set1», «Set2»)	Returns the set of members of one set that exist with one or more tuples of one or more other sets.
EXTRACT	EXTRACT(«Set», «Dimension»[, «Dimension»...])	Returns a set of tuples from extracted dimension elements.
FILTER	FILTER(«Set», «Search Condition»)	Returns the set that results from filtering a specified set based on a search condition.
GENERATE	GENERATE(«Set1», «Set2»[, ALL])	Applies a set to each member of another set and then joins the resulting sets by union. Alternatively, this function returns a concatenated string created by evaluating a string expression over a set.
HEAD	HEAD(«Set»[, «Numeric Expression»])	Returns the first specified number of elements in a set, while retaining duplicates.
HIERARCHIZE	HIERARCHIZE(«Set»[, POST])	Orders the members of a set in a hierarchy.
INTERSECT	INTERSECT(«Set1», «Set2»[, ALL])	Returns the intersection of two input sets, optionally retaining duplicates.
MEASUREGROUPMEASURES	MEASUREGROUPMEASURES(«String Expression»)	Returns a set of measures that belongs to the specified measure group.
MEMBERS	«Hierarchy».MEMBERS	Returns a member specified by a string expression.
MEMBERS	«Level».MEMBERS	Returns a member specified by a string expression.

(continued)

Function	Syntax	Description
NONEMPTY	NONEMPTY(«Set1», «Set2»)	Returns the set of tuples that are not empty from a specified set, based on the cross-product of the specified set with a second set.
NONEMPTYCROSSJOIN	NONEMPTYCROSSJOIN(«Set 1», «Set2»[, «Set3»...][, «Crossjoin Count»])	Returns the cross-product of one or more sets as a set, excluding empty tuples and tuples without associated fact table data.
ORDER	ORDER(«Set», {«String Expression» | «Numeric Expression»}[, ASC | DESC | BASC | BDESC])	Arranges members of a specified set, optionally preserving or breaking the hierarchy.
STRIPCALCULATEDMEMBERS	STRIPCALCULATEDMEMBERS(«Set»)	Returns a set generated by removing calculated members from a specified set.
SUBSET	SUBSET(«Set», «Start»[, «Count»])	Returns a subset of tuples from a specified set.
TAIL	TAIL(«Set»[, «Count»])	Returns a subset from the end of a set.
TOPCOUNT	TOPCOUNT(«Set», «Count»[, «Numeric Expression»])	Sorts a set in descending order and returns the specified number of elements with the highest values.
TOPPERCENT	TOPPERCENT(«Set», «Percentage», «Numeric Expression»)	Sorts a set in descending order and returns a set of tuples with the highest values whose cumulative total is equal to or less than a specified percentage.
TOPSUM	TOPSUM(«Set», «Value», «Numeric Expression»)	Sorts a set and returns the top-most elements whose cumulative total is at least a specified value.
UNION	UNION(«Set1», «Set2»[, ALL])	Returns the union of two sets, optionally retaining duplicates.
UNORDER	UNORDER(«Set»)	Removes any enforced ordering from a specified set.

Statistical Functions

Function	Syntax	Description
AGGREGATE	AGGREGATE(«Set»[, «Numeric Expression»])	Returns a scalar value calculated by aggregating either measures or an optionally specified numeric expression over the tuples of a specified set.
AVG	AVG(«Set»[, «Numeric Expression»])	Returns the average value of measures or the average value of an optional numeric expression, evaluated over a specified set.
COALESCEEMPTY	COALESCEEMPTY(«Numeric Expression»[, «Numeric Expression»...])	Coalesces an empty cell value to a number or string and returns the coalesced value.
CORRELATION	CORRELATION(«Set», «Numeric Expression»[, «Numeric Expression»])	Returns the correlation coefficient of two series evaluated over a set.
COUNT	«Set».COUNT	Returns the number of cells in a set.
COUNT	COUNT(«Set»[, EXCLUDEEMPTY | INCLUDEEMPTY])	Returns the number of cells in a set. The Count(Set) function includes or excludes empty cells, depending on the syntax used. If the standard syntax is used, empty cells can be excluded or included by using the EXCLUDEEMPTY or INCLUDEEMPTY flags, respectively. If the alternate syntax is used, the function always includes empty cells.
COVARIANCE	COVARIANCE(«Set», «Numeric Expression»[, «Numeric Expression»])	Returns the population covariance of two series evaluated over a set, using the biased population formula.
COVARIANCEN	COVARIANCEN(«Set», «Numeric Expression»[, «Numeric Expression»])	Returns the sample covariance of two series evaluated over a set, using the unbiased population formula.
DISTINCTCOUNT	DISTINCTCOUNT(«Set»)	Returns the number of distinct, nonempty tuples in a set.
LINREGINTERCEPT	LINREGINTERCEPT(«Set», «Numeric Expression»[, «Numeric Expression»])	Calculates the linear regression of a set and returns the value of the intercept in the regression line, $y = ax + b$.
LINREGPOINT	LINREGPOINT(«Numeric Expression», «Set», «Numeric Expression»[, «Numeric Expression»])	Calculates the linear regression of a set and returns the value of y in the regression line, $y = ax + b$.

(continued)

Function	Syntax	Description
LINREGR2	LINREGR2(«Set», «Numeric Expression»[, «Numeric Expression»])	Calculates the linear regression of a set and returns the coefficient of determination, R2.
LINREGSLOPE	LINREGSLOPE(«Set», «Numeric Expression»[, «Numeric Expression»])	Calculates the linear regression of a set, and returns the value of the slope in the regression line, $y = ax + b$.
LINREGVARIANCE	LINREGVARIANCE(«Set», «Numeric Expression»[, «Numeric Expression»])	Calculates the linear regression of a set, and returns the variance associated with the regression line, $y = ax + b$.
MAX	MAX(«Set»[, «Numeric Expression»])	Returns the maximum value of a numeric expression that is evaluated over a set.
MEDIAN	MEDIAN(«Set»[, «Numeric Expression»])	Returns the median value of a numeric expression that is evaluated over a set.
MIN	MIN(«Set»[, «Numeric Expression»])	Returns the minimum value of a numeric expression that is evaluated over a set.
RANK	RANK(«Tuple», «Set»)	Returns the one-based rank of a specified tuple in a specified set.
ROLLUPCHILDREN	ROLLUPCHILDREN(«Member», «String Expression»)	Returns a value generated by rolling up the values of the children of a specified member using the specified unary operator.
STDDEV	STDDEV(«Set»[, «Numeric Expression»])	Alias for STDEV
STDDEVP	STDDEVP(«Set»[, «Numeric Expression»])	Alias for STDEVP
STDEV	STDEVP(«Set»[, «Numeric Expression»])	Returns the sample standard deviation of a numeric expression evaluated over a set, using the unbiased population formula.
STDEVP	STDEVP(«Set»[, «Numeric Expression»])	Returns the population standard deviation of a numeric expression evaluated over a set, using the biased population formula.
SUM	SUM(«Set»[, «Numeric Expression»])	Returns the sum of a numeric expression evaluated over a set.
VAR	VAR(«Set»[, «Numeric Expression»])	Returns the sample variance of a numeric expression evaluated over a set, using the unbiased population formula.
VARIANCE	VARIANCE(«Set»[, «Numeric Expression»])	Alias for VAR

Function	Syntax	Description
VARIANCEP	VARIANCEP(«Set»[, «Numeric Expression»])	Alias for VARP
VARP	VARP(«Set»[, «Numeric Expression»])	Returns the population variance of a numeric expression evaluated over a set, using the biased population formula.
VISUALTOTALS	VISUALTOTALS(«Set», «Pattern»)	Returns a set generated by dynamically totaling child members in a specified set, optionally using a pattern for the name of the parent member in the resulting cellset.

String Functions

Function	Syntax	Description
GENERATE	GENERATE(«Set», «String Expression»[, «Delimiter»])	Applies a set to each member of another set and then joins the resulting sets by union. Alternatively, this function returns a concatenated string created by evaluating a string expression over a set.
MEMBERTOSTR	MEMBERTOSTR(«Member»)	Returns an MDX-formatted string that corresponds to a specified member.
NAMETOSET	NAMETOSET(«Member Name»)	Returns a set that contains the member specified by an MDX-formatted string.
SETTOSTR	SETTOSTR(«Set»)	Returns the set specified by an MDX-formatted string.
STRTOMEMBER	STRTOMEMBER(«String Expression»)	Returns the member specified by an MDX-formatted string.
STRTOSET	STRTOSET(«String Expression»)	Returns the set specified by an MDX-formatted string.
STRTOTUPLE	STRTOTUPLE(«String Expression»)	Returns the tuple specified by an MDX-formatted string.
STRTOVALUE	STRTOVALUE(«String Expression»)	Returns the value specified by an MDX-formatted string.
TUPLETOSTR	TUPLETOSTR(«Tuple»)	Returns an MDX-formatted string that corresponds to specified tuple.

Time Functions

Function	Syntax	Description
CLOSINGPERIOD	CLOSINGPERIOD([«Level»[, «Member»]])	Returns the last sibling among the descendants of a member at a specified level.
LASTPERIODS	LASTPERIODS(«Index»[, «Member»])	Returns a set of members up to and including a specified member.
MTD	MTD([«Member»])	Returns a set of sibling members from the same level as a given member, starting with the first sibling and ending with the given member, as constrained by the Year level in the Time dimension.
OPENINGPERIOD	OPENINGPERIOD([«Level»[, «Member»]])	Returns the first sibling among the descendants of a specified level, optionally at a specified member.
PARALLELPERIOD	PARALLELPERIOD([«Level»[, «Numeric Expression»[, «Member»]]])	Returns a member from a prior period in the same relative position as a specified member.
PERIODSTODATE	PERIODSTODATE([«Level»[, «Member»]])	Returns a set of sibling members from the same level as a given member, starting with the first sibling and ending with the given member, as constrained by a specified level in the Time dimension.
QTD	QTD([«Member»])	Returns a set of sibling members from the same level as a given member, starting with the first sibling and ending with the given member, as constrained by the Quarter level in the Time dimension.
WTD	WTD([«Member»])	Returns a set of sibling members from the same level as a given member, starting with the first sibling and ending with the given member, as constrained by the Week level in the Time dimension.
YTD	YTD([«Member»])	Returns a set of sibling members from the same level as a given member, starting with the first sibling and ending with the given member, as constrained by the Year level in the Time dimension.

UI Functions

Function	Syntax	Description
DRILLDOWNLEVEL	DRILLDOWNLEVEL(«Set»[, «Level»])	Drills down the members of a set to one level below the lowest level represented in the set, or to one level below an optionally specified level of a member represented in the set.
DRILLDOWNLEVEL	DRILLDOWNLEVEL(«Set»[, , «Index»])	Drills down the members of a set to one level below the lowest level represented in the set, or to one level below an optionally specified level of a member represented in the set.
DRILLDOWNLEVELBOTTOM	DRILLDOWNLEVELBOTTOM («Set», «Count»[, [«Level»][, «Numeric Expression»]])	Drills down the bottom-most members of a set, at a specified level, to one level below.
DRILLDOWNLEVELTOP	DRILLDOWNLEVELTOP(«Set», «Count»[, [«Level»][, «Numeric Expression»]])	Drills down the top-most members of a set, at a specified level, to one level below.
DRILLDOWNMEMBER	DRILLDOWNMEMBER(«Set1», «Set2»[, RECURSIVE])	Drills down the members in a specified set that are present in a second specified set. Alternatively, the function drills down on a set of tuples.
DRILLDOWNMEMBERBOTTOM	DRILLDOWNMEMBERBOTTOM («Set1», «Set2», «Count»[, [«Numeric Expression»] [, RECURSIVE]])	Drills down the members in a specified set that are present in a second specified set, limiting the result set to a specified number of members. Alternatively, this function also drills down on a set of tuples.
DRILLDOWNMEMBERTOP	DRILLDOWNMEMBERTOP («Set1», «Set2», «Count»[, [«Numeric Expression»] [, RECURSIVE]])	Drills down the members in a specified set that are present in a second specified set, limiting the result set to a specified number of members. Alternatively, this function drills down on a set of tuples.
DRILLUPLEVEL	DRILLUPLEVEL(«Set»[, «Level»])	Drills up the members of a set that are below a specified level.
DRILLUPMEMBER	DRILLUPMEMBER(«Set1», «Set2»)	Drills up the members in a specified set that are present in a second specified set.
TOGGLEDRILLSTATE	TOGGLEDRILLSTATE(«Set1», «Set2»[, RECURSIVE])	Toggles the drill state of members.

Value Functions

Function	Syntax	Description
IIF	IIF(«Logical Expression», «object», «object»)	Returns one of two values determined by a logical test.
IS	IS	Performs a logical comparison on two object expressions.
ISEMPTY	ISEMPTY(«Value Expression»)	Returns whether the evaluated expression is the empty cell value.
MEMBERVALUE	«Member».MEMBERVALUE	Returns the value of a member.
VALIDMEASURE	VALIDMEASURE(«Tuple»)	Returns a valid measure in a virtual cube by forcing inapplicable dimensions to their top level.
VALUE	«Tuple».VALUE	Returns the value of a measure.

Index